PRIVACY AS PROPERTY

This innovative work offers a new perspective on the established tort of misuse of private information, contending that English law has evolved a sophisticated mechanism for the protection of privacy and the protection of the economic value in private information.

Although information generally is not property, private information now appears to be recognised by English law as a form of property, giving the owner of the information the usual property rights of exclusion, exploitation and transfer.

Balancing philosophical discussion of the fundamentals with a detailed analysis of the practical difficulties of 'propertising' information, the book suggests that English law has evolved a powerful tool for the protection of privacy in this data-driven world.

Privacy as Property

Marcus Smith

•HART•
OXFORD • LONDON • NEW YORK • NEW DELHI • SYDNEY

HART PUBLISHING

Bloomsbury Publishing Plc

Kemp House, Chawley Park, Cumnor Hill, Oxford, OX2 9PH, UK

1385 Broadway, New York, NY 10018, USA

Bloomsbury Publishing Ireland Limited, 29 Earlsfort Terrace, Dublin 2, D02 AY28, Ireland

HART PUBLISHING, the Hart/Stag logo, BLOOMSBURY and the Diana logo are trademarks of Bloomsbury Publishing Plc

First published in Great Britain 2026

A catalogue record for this book is available from the British Library.

A catalogue record for this book is available from the Library of Congress.

ISBN: HB: 978-1-50998-738-2
ePDF: 978-1-50998-740-5
ePub: 978-1-50998-739-9

Typeset by Compuscript Ltd, Shannon

For product safety related questions contact productsafety@bloomsbury.com

To find out more about our authors and books visit www.hartpublishing.co.uk. Here you will find extracts, author information, details of forthcoming events and the option to sign up for our newsletters.

Preface

THIS MONOGRAPH WAS borne out of work done in preparation for the fourth edition of *Smith on the Law of Assignment*. I was revisiting the vexed question of whether 'information' is property, a question on which English law speaks with a forked tongue. I came to the conclusion that whilst 'information' *generally* was not property, 'private information' *was*. To reach that conclusion, it was necessary to define and understand two difficult concepts – what is 'information', and what is 'private'.

By this time, what had been intended as a short insertion into an established work on intangible property had morphed into something different in terms of subject matter, as well as ballooning in both length and significance. I discovered that I was writing a book that examined privacy and which advanced the thesis that private information is a form of intangible property.

I am extremely grateful to Hart Publishing – and particularly Sinead Moloney at Hart – for taking up and enthusiastically backing what was (at the time of acceptance) a singularly unformed proposal. Hart's unstinting enthusiasm for the project has been enormously encouraging.

The thesis of this book is that, without really appreciating it, English law has, in the tort against the misuse of private information, evolved a sophisticated and powerful tool for the protection of our private information. It has done so by rendering our private information our *property*, not to be used without our consent. That English law has achieved this unconsciously is a tribute to the evolutionary development of law through the common law.

To be sure, none of the concepts considered in this book are straightforward. 'Information', 'privacy' and 'consent' are all difficult concepts on their own, and only more so in combination. I have sought to make the discussion as accessible as possible – this is not a book just for lawyers – but without over-simplifying that which is intractable. I hope that I have at least made it interesting.

Privacy matters. It matters because control over our private information is fundamental to controlling how we present our Selves to the world. Privacy is concerned with our identity and the world's perception of that identify. Privacy is an essential, if negative, aspect of freedom of expression: it enables us to control, to a degree defined by law, how our identity is projected into the world by preventing others from using our private information without our consent. Whereas 'freedom of expression' is generally taken to refer to the positive right to say what we wish, privacy is no less important, even though it is a right to prevent or control the use of information relating to us. Privacy is not about the protection of secrets or confidential information: it is about controlling what others can do with data that concerns us.

This book might have been easier to write had it been co-authored. There are many points which, somewhat schizophrenically, I have had to debate with myself. But as Michael Lewis points out in his excellent book *The Undoing Project*, which describes the collaboration between Kahneman and Tversky, collaborations as fruitful as that between Kahneman/Tversky are not only astonishingly rare, but also rarely end well. As it is, I am greatly indebted to John Summers, Sinéad Agnew and David Kershaw for a number of helpful conversations on the subject of private information. Maria Skrzypiec was the most excellent of copy-editors, and (through her tactful deletion of my layered sub-, sub-sub and sub-sub-sub-paragraphs) has rendered this work much more readable than it otherwise would be.

Privacy has attracted the interest of not just lawyers, but economists and concerned technologists. The assistance that the work of economists and technologists has rendered to me in reading around the subject has been immense. Economists have very much influenced my understanding of private information as property (although I do not think anyone has articulated the law as I have done here). Technologists have provided ample, and worrying, illustrations of how technology threatens our privacy whilst enhancing our lives in so many other respects. These works are referenced in the bibliography, and I am hugely grateful for the immense efforts of those who have gone before, and on whose work I have built.

All errors and infelicities are my own. I should apologise to Wales for not regularly referring to the law of 'England and Wales', but the interests of brevity won out.

The cover picture is by an artist whose work I grew to know and love when I was a student in Munich: Marianne von Werefkin (1860–1938). Her painting, *The Red Tree* (1910), conveys, at least to me, the sort of protection the law of private information ought to confer on us all.

MAS
12/xii 2025

Brief Contents

Detailed Contents

Table of Cases

Table of Legislation

Bibliography

Aplin, T; Bently, L; Johnson, P; and Malynicz, S (eds). *Gurry on Breach of Confidence*. Oxford University Press, 2nd edn (2012) .... [2.2], [2.3], [2.5], [2.6], [2.7], [4.28], [4.72], [4.77], [10.14]

Arenson, K. *Rejection of the Fruit of the Poisonous Tree Doctrine in Australia: A Retreat from Progressivism*. (2011) 13 UNDALR 17 .... [8.22]

Baron, D. *You Can't Always Say What You Want*. Cambridge University Press, 1st edn (2023) .... [12.22]

Beale (edn). *Chitty on Contracts*. Sweet and Maxwell, 35th edn (2021) .... [11.43]

Bean, D, Burns, A and Headley, F. *Bean on Injunctions*. Sweet and Maxwell, 15th edn (2025) .... [10.59], [10.65], [10.67]

Bennett, H. *Principles of the Law of Agency*. Hart, 1st edn (2013) .... [9.27]

Bennett, D (ed). *Munkman on Employer's Liability*. LexisNexis, 17th edn (2019) .... [9.70]

Bently, L, Sherman, B, Gangjee, D and Johnson, P. *Intellectual Property Law*. Oxford University Press, 6th edn (2022) .... [4.91], [4.93], [4.97], [6.151]

Bernasek, A and Mongan, D. *All You Can Pay: How Companies Use Our Data to Empty Our Wallets*. Nation Books, 1st edn (2015) .... [1.9], [6.141]

Birkinshaw, P. *Freedom of Information*. Cambridge University Press, 4th edn (2010) .... [3.8], [3.18]

Bonadio, E and Sganga, C (eds). *NFTs, Creativity and the Law: Within and Beyond Copyright*, Routledge, 1st edn (2024) .... [3.2]

Brescia, R. *The Private is Political*. New York University Press, 1st edn (2025) .... [3.13]

Bridge, S, Cooke, E and Dixon, M (eds). *Megarry & Wade: The Law of Real Property*. Sweet & Maxwell, 9th edn (2019) .... [6.120]

Briggs, A. *Private International Law in English Courts*. Oxford University Press, 1st edn (2014) .... [10.132]

Burrows, A. *Remedies for Torts, Breaches of Contract, and Equitable Wrongs*. Oxford University Press, 4th edn (2019) .... [10.32], [10.46]

Bury, JB. *A History of Freedom of Thought*. Williams and Norgate, 1st edn (1913) .... [3.39], [3.43]

Campbell, D (ed). *Terrell on the Law of Patents*. Sweet and Maxwell, 20th edn (2024) .... [10.53]

Card, R. *Card and English on Police Law*. Oxford University Press, 16th edn (2022) .... [8.68]

Chiodo, S. *Private Law and Mass Claims: Regulating in the Place of the State*. Osgoode Studies Legal Research Paper No 5287879 .... [10.122]

Chun, W. *Discriminating Data*. The MIT Press, 1st edn (2021) .... [12.20]

Clayton, R and Tomlinson, H. *Civil Actions Against the Police*. Sweet & Maxwell, 1st edn (1992) .... [8.56], [8.108]

Clayton, R and Tomlinson, H. *The Law of Human Rights*. Oxford University Press, 2nd edn (2009) .... [4.32], [4.144], [4.150], [4.156], [8.55], [8.57], [8.108], [8.132], [8.133]

Coase, R. *The Firm, the Market and the Law*. University of Chicago Press, 1st (paperback) edn (1990) .... [5.32]

Cofone, I. *The Privacy Fallacy*. Cambridge University Press, 1st edn (2024) .... [6.102]

Cole, D. *Pollution and Property*. Cambridge University Press, 1st edn (2002) .... [5.21], [5.23]

Contreras, J. *Intellectual Property Licensing and Transactions: Theory and Practice*. Cambridge University Press, 1st edn (2022) .... [11.11], [11.32]

Cooke, E. *The Hidden World of the Legal Aid Lawyer*. Bristol University Press, 1st edn (2025) .... [10.124]

Coppel, P. *Information Rights*, Volume 1, Hart. 5th edn (2020) .... [4.176], [4.177], [4.178], [4.179], [4.195], [4.196], [8.39], [10.156]

Criado Perez, C. *Invisible Women: Exposing Data Bias in a World Designed for Men*. Chatto & Windus, 1st edn (2019) .... [12.20]

Dahlman, C. *The Open Field System and Beyond*. Cambridge University Press, 1st edn (1980) .... [5.23]

Danov, M. *Private International Law and Competition Litigation in a Global Context*. Hart, 1st edn (2023) .... [10.146], [10.147]

Davies, D. *The Unaccountability Machine*, Profile Bools, 1st edn (2024) .... [3.16]

Davies, G, Caddick, N and Harbottle, G (eds). *Copinger and Skone James on Copyright*, Volume 1, Sweet & Maxwell, 17th edn (2016) .... [4.16], [4.18], [4.19], [4.20], [4.74]

De Soto, H. *The Mystery of Capital*. Black Swan, 1st edn (2001) .... [5.52]

Dicey, A. *An Introduction to the Study of the Law of the Constitution*, MacMillan & Co, 8th edn (1923) .... [4.33]

Dickinson, A. *The Rome II Regulation.* Oxford University Press, 1st edn (2008) .... [10.153], [10.154]
Douglas, S. *Liability for Wrongful Interference with Chattels.* Hart, 1st edn (2011) .... [10.12]
Edelman, J (edn). *McGregor on Damages.* Sweet and Maxwell / Thomson Reuters, 22nd edn (2024) .... [10.33], [10.36], [10.41], [10.43], [10.49], [10.51], [10.85], [10.112]
Eubanks, V. *Automating Inequality" How High Tech Tools Profile, Police and Punish the Poor.* Picador, 1st edn (2019) .... [12.20]
Fairfield, J. *Owned: Property, Privacy and the New Digital Serfdom.* Cambridge University Press, 1st edn (2017) .... [1.9], [1.11], [1.12], [1.13], [1.14], [1.15], [1.49], [1.53], [1.66], [3.66], [3.73], [3.74], [3.75], [3.76], [5.52], [5.68], [6.4], [6.141], [6.169]
Fitzgerald, D. *The City of Today is a Dying Thing.* Faber & Faber, 1st edn (2024) .... [12.31]
Fordham, M. *Judicial Review Handbook.* Hart, 7th edn (2020) .... [6.107], [6.117]
Fried, C. *An Anatomy of Values: Problems of Personal and Social Choice.* Harvard University Press, 1st edn (1970) .... [1.23], [1.24], [1.57]
Friedman, M. *Price Theory.* Routledge, 1st (reprinted) edn (2017) .... [3.16]
Garton Ash, T. *The File.* Harper Collins, 1st edn (1997) .... [4.199]
Gassler, M. *Information Exchange Between Competitors in EU Competition Law.* Wolters Kluwer, 1st edn (2021) .... [3.16]
Gee, S. *Commercial Injunctions.* Sweet and Maxwell, 7th edn (2021) .... [10.67]
Giannoulopoulos, D. *Improperly Obtained Evidence in Anglo-American and Continental Law.* Hart, 1st (paperback) edn 2020 .... [8.22]
Gray, A. *Vicarious Liability: Critique and Reform.* Hart, 1st edn (2018) .... [9.12], [9.13], [9.14], [9.15], [9.16], [9.19], [9.23], [9.25], [9.39], [9.70]
Gray, K. *Property in Thin Air.* [1991] CLJ 252 .... [1.60]
Green, S and Randall, J. *The Tort of Conversion.* Hart, 1st edn (2009) .... [10.11]
Guest, A. *Oxford Essays in Jurisprudence.* Oxford university Press, 1st edn (1961) .... [1.33], [1.56]

Hanlon, W. *The Laissez-Faire Experiment*. Princeton University Press, 1st edn (2024) ....[8.10]

Harbottle, G, Caddick, N and Suthersanen, U (eds). *Copinger and Skone James on Copyright*, Volume 1, Sweet & Maxwell, 19th edn (2025)... [4.74], [7.33], [7.34]

Harbottle, G, Caddick, N and Suthersanen, U (eds). *Copinger and Skone James on Copyright*, Volume 2, Sweet & Maxwell, 19th edn (2025)... [6.57], [10.54]

Hardin, G. *The Tragedy of the Commons*. (1968) 162 Science 1243 ....[5.21]

Hare, C. *Tragedy At Law*, Faber and Faber, 1st edn (1942) ....[10.41]

Hare, I, Donnelly, C and Bell J (eds). *De Smith's Judicial Review*. Sweet & Maxwell – Thomson Reuters, 9th edn (2023) .... [8.7]

Hart, H. *The Concept of Law*. Oxford University Press, 1st edn (1961) ....[9.108]

Hawke, N. *Corporate Liability*. Sweet & Maxwell, 1st edn (2000) .... [9.9], [9.10], [9.50]

Heuston, R. *Essays in Constitutional Law*. Stevens, 2nd edn (1964)... [4.36], [4.39], [4.40]

Hill, K. *Your Face Belongs to Us: The Secretive Startup Dismantling Your Privacy*. Simon & Schuster, 1st edn (2023)...[8.147], [12.20]

Kalpokas, I and Kalpokiene, J. *Deepfakes: A Realistic Assessment of Potentials, Risks and Policy Regulation*. Springer, 1st edn (2022) ....[6.44]

Keynes, JM. *The General Theory of Employment Interest and Money*. MacMillan, 1st edn (1936)...[5.28]

Kulick, A. *Corporate Human Rights?* (2021) 32 European Journal of International Law 537.. [6.92], [6.95]

Kuner, C, Bygrave L, Docksey, C and Drechsler, L. *The E General Data Protection Regulation (GDPR): A Commentary*. Oxford University Press, 1st edn (2020) ....[4.193]

Lambert, P. *The Right to be Forgotten*. Bloomsbury Professional, 2nd edn (2022).. [8.37], [8.38]

Lim, E and Morgan, P (eds). *Private Law and Artificial Intelligence*. Cambridge University Press, 1st edn (2024)....................[9.110]

Liu, C. *Hold Up The Sky*. Head of Zeus, 1st edn (2020) ....[12.10]

MacDonald Eggers, P and Picken, S. *Good Faith and Insurance Contracts*. Informa Law, 4th edn (2018) ....[9.53]

Malek, H (ed). *Phipson on Evidence*. Sweet & Maxwell, 20th edn (2022)... [8.23], [8.25]

Marwick, A. *The Private is Political: Networked Privacy and Social Media*. Yale University Press, 1st edn (2023).............................. [1.9]

McKay, S. *Covert Policing*. Oxford University Press. 2nd edn (2015) ....[8.113], [8.147]

Meade, J. *The Theory of Economic Externalities*. AW Sijthoff, 1st edn (1973) .... [5.7]

Mellifont, K. *Fruit of the Poisonous Tree: Evidence Derivedn from Illegally or Improperly Obtained Evidence*. The Federation Press, 1st edn (2010) .... [8.20]

Mezei, P. *Copyright Exhaustion: Law and Policy in the United States and the European Union*. Cambridge University Press, 1st edn (2018) .... [6.152]

Micklethwaite J and Wooldridge, A. *The Company: A Short History of a Revolutionary Idea*. Phoenix, 1st (paperback) edn (2005) .... [6.90]

Micklitz, H-W and Vettori, G (eds). *The Future of the Person*. Hart, 1st edn (2025) .... [9.110]

Milo D. *Defamation and Freedom of Speech*. Oxford University Press, 1st edn (2008) .... [6.35]

Monbiot, G and Hutchison, P. *The Invisible Doctrine: The Secret History of Neoliberalism*. Allen Lane, 1st edn (2024) .... [5.54]

Monti, A and Wacks, R. *Protecting Personal Information*. Hart, 1st (paperback) edn (2020) .... [1.9], [1.24], [4.151], [4.199], [6.20], [6.22], [7.90], [7.91]

Moor, L. *Communication and Economic Life*. Polity Press 1st edn (2022) .... [5.73]

Moreham, N and Speker, A (eds). *The Law of Privacy and the Media*. Oxford University Press, 4th edn (2024) .... [10.75], [10.79], [10.83]

Morgan J. *Privacy, Confidence and Horizontal Effect: "Hello" Trouble*. (2003) 62 CLJ 444 .... [4.147]

Morgan, J. *Questioning the "True Effect" of the Human Rights Act*. (2002) 22 LS 259 .... [4.147]

Mulheron, R. *Class Actions and Government*. Cambridge University Press, 1st edn (2020) .... [10.122]

Munkman, J. *Damages for Personal Injuries and Death*. Butterworths, 4th edn (1970) .... [10.33], [10.41]

Newton-Smith, W. *The Structure of Time*. Routlednge, 1st edn (1980) .... [3.78]

Nicholas, B. *An Introduction to Roman Law*. Oxford University Press, 1st edn (1962) .... [10.11]

North, D and Thomas, R. *The Rise of the Western World*. Cambridge University Press, 1st edn (1973) .... [5.56]

Ostrom, E. *Governing the Commons: The Evolution of Institutions for Collective Action*. Cambridge University Press, 1st edn (1990) .... [5.22]

Palmer, N. *Palmer on Bailment*. Sweet & Maxwell, 3rd edn (2009)........ [7.53], [7.55], [7.56], [7.57], [7.58]

Parkes, R and Busuttil, G (eds). *Gatley on Libel and Slander*. Sweet & Maxwell, 13th edn (2022)........ [6.35], [6.38], [6.39], [6.41], [6.45], [6.52], [6.118], [6.122], [10.139]

Pinto, A and Evans, M. *Corporate Criminal Liability*. Sweet & Maxwell, 4th edn (2021) .... [9.9]

Posner, R. *The Economics of Private Law: The Collected Economic Essays of Richard A Posner, Volume 2*. Edward Elgar, 1st edn (2001) .... [5.33], [5.34]

Posner, R. *Economic Analysis of Law*. Wolters Kluwer, 9th edn (2014)........ [5.2]

Powell, R. *The Law of Agency*. Pitman, 2nd edn (1961) ....[9.65]

Quill, E and Friel, R (eds). *Damages and Compensation Culture: Comparative Perspectives*. Hart, 1st (paperback) edn (2019)........[10.45]

Radin, M. *Boilerplate: the Fine Print, Vanishing Rights, and the Rule of Law*. Oxford University Press, 1st edn (2013) .... [5.87], [7.80]

Raz, J. *The Authority of Law: Essays on Law and Morality*. Oxford University Press, 1st (paperback) edn (1985) ....[6.15]

Richardson, M. *The Right to Privacy*. Cambridge University Press, 1st edn (2017) .... [1.23], [4.23], [4.41]

Robertson, G. *Lawfare: How Russians, the Rich and the Government Try to Prevent Free Speech and How to Stop Them*. TLS Books, 1st edn (2023)........[11.19]

Robertson, A and Neyers, J. *Private Law and the State*. Hart, 1st edn (2024) ....[10.122]

Roth, A. *Who Gets What and Why? The Hidden World of Matching and Market Design*. William Collins, 1st edn (2015)........ [5.15], [5.30]

Schulhofer, S. *More Essential Than Ever*. Oxford University Press, 1st edn (1980)........[4.162], [4.163], [4.164], [4.165], [4.167], [4.168], [4.169], [4.170], [4.171], [6.147], [6.148], [6.149], [8.99], [8.152]

Sherman, B. *Intangible Intangibles: Patent Law's engagement with Dematerialised Subject Matter*. Cambridge University Press, 1st edn (2024)........[1.59]

Sinnreich, A and Gilbert J. *The Secret Life of Data*. The MIT Press, 1st edn (2024)........ [1.17], [1.61], [3.8], [3.30], [6.25], [12.20]

Smith, M and Leslie, N. *The Law of Assignment*. Oxford University Press, 3rd edn (2018)........ [3.5]

Smith, M, Mulheron R, Leslie, N and Hughes, G. *The Law of Assignment*. Oxford University Press, 4th edn (2026) .... [1.28], [1.35], [1.36], [1.46], [1.49], [1.53], [3.45], [3.70], [4.17], [5.44], [6.4], [6.120], [10.19], [10.122], [10.151], [10.152], [11.4], [11.6], [11.8], [11.10], [11.22]

Spaulding, S. *How We Understand Others*. Routledge, 1st (paperback) edn (2020) .... [6.25]

Stone, A and Schauer, F. *The Oxford Handbook of Freedom of Speech*. Oxford University Press, 1st edn (2021) .... [3.8], [3.13], [3.14], [3.18]

Sturge, G. *Sum of Us: A History of Data in the UK*. The Bridge Street Press, 1st edn (2025) .... [8.97]

Supperstone, M and Goudie, J. *Judicial Review*. Butterworths, 2nd edn (1997) .... [8.101]

Susskind, J. *The Digital Republic*. Bloomsbury, 1st edn (2022) .... [1.9]

Tapper, C. *Computer Law*. Longman, 2nd edn (1982) .... [1.67]

Taylor, A. *English History 1914-1945*. Oxford University Press, 1st edn (1965) .... [8.10]

Tettenborn, A (edn). *Clerk & Lindsell on Torts*. Sweet & Maxwell, 24th edn (2023) .... [5.35], [5.36], [5.37], [5.38], [9.17], [9.21], [10.52]

Torremans, P. *Intellectual Property and Private International Law*. Oxford University Press, 3rd edn (2024) .... [10.135], [10.136], [10.138]

Townshend, J. *A Treatise on the Wrongs Calledn Slander and Libel*. Baker, Voerhis & Co, 3rd edn (1877) .... [6.35]

Véliz, C. *Privacy is Power: Why and How You Should Take Back Control of Your Data*. Bantam Press, 1st edn (2020) .... [1.9], [4.40]

Véliz, C. *The Ethics of Privacy and Surveillance*. Oxford University Press, 1st edn (2024) .... [1.23], [1.24], [1.61], [3.8], [3.25], [4.174], [6.25], [6.35], [12.10]

Ward R and Blundell, D. *National Security: Law, Procednure and Practice*. Oxford University Press, 2nd edn (2024) .... [8.16], [8.75], [8.76], [8.77], [8.78], [8.79], [8.80], [8.82], [8.83], [8.86], [8.87], [8.88], [8.89], [8.90], [8.91], [8.95], [8.114], [8.150]

Warren, S and Brandeis, L. *The Right to Privacy*. (1890) 4 Harvard Law Review 193...................................... [1.1], [1.63], [2.8], [4.2], [4.3], [4.4], [4.6], [4.13], [4.26], [4.27], [6.34], [7.69], [7.111], [8.156]
Watts, P and Reynolds, F. *Bowstead and Reynolds on Agency*. Sweet and Maxwell, 23rd edn (2024) ....[9.63]
Whelan, P. *Parental Liability in EU Competition Law*. Oxford University Press, 1st edn (2023) ....[9.37]
Williams, E. *Capitalism & Slavery*. Andre Deutsch. 1st edn (1964) .... [5.56], [5.57], [5.58]
Wood-Marsden 1998. *Renaissance Self-Portraiture: The Visual Construction of Identity and the Social Status of the Artist*. Yale University Press. 1st edn (1998) ....[6.22]
Zander, M. *Zander on PACE: The Police and Criminal Evidence Act 1984*. Sweet & Maxwell, 9th edn (2023) .... [8.28], [8.30], [8.31], [8.32], [8.72]
Zuboff, S. *The Age of Surveillance Capitalism: The Fight for a Human Future at the New Frontier of Power*. Profile Books, 1st edn (2019) .... [1.9], [1.19], [4.140], [5.62], [5.63], [5.65], [5.66], [5.67], [5.85], [5.86], [5.88], [6.21]

1

Introduction

In which: the reasons why our privacy is increasingly threatened are explored; the role of technology in creating this threat stated; the thesis of this monograph set out and its structure explained; and a preliminary definition of 'private information' is attempted.

I. Why this Book Matters

A. The beginning – Warren and Brandeis

[1.1] In 1890, Warren and Brandeis published a ground-breaking article on the law of privacy.[1] They saw, rightly, that developments in technology and in the social uses of that technology were invading privacy in new ways, thereby degrading protections over our private lives that people had, until then, taken for granted. The technology of which they spoke – photography, telegraph, print media – is very dated. Technology and the social uses of that technology have developed exponentially since their time. The law of privacy – or, at least, our understanding of the law of privacy – has not kept up. It is debateable whether English law, as presently understood, is robust enough to deal with even the developments described as cutting edge in 1890, still less with the exponential developments we face today.

[1.2] The thesis advanced in this monograph is that the English law of privacy *has* kept up with these developments, but that this not been recognised by the practitioners, academics and judges involved in this area of the law.

B. Three phases of threats to privacy

[1.3] The threats to our privacy can be described in three phases. The first phase is where A's privacy can only be directly and physically be invaded by C, such as where C is invited into A's home or, more extremely, trespasses into A's home, either because C has not been invited to enter at all or because C has exceeded the permission to enter granted by A. In all these cases, C may see, hear

[1] S Warren and L Brandeis, 'The Right to Privacy' (1890) 4 Harvard Law Review 193.

and/or experience things that A wishes to have confined to a limited circle of the world, perhaps limited only to C, perhaps not even including C (as where there is a trespass). Many of the older cases deal with this kind of invasion of privacy. The language used to describe these affronts to private life rightly draw upon the language of trespass, of an invasion of the private life. In this 'pre-technology' phase, the links between privacy and trespass (whether to the person or land) are close.

[1.4] The next phase – that which alarmed, and was described by, Warren and Brandeis – involves the ability to record a person's private life, whether by image or in words, and to circulate that record to many people across the world. A key difference between the first and second phases – emphasised by Warren and Brandeis – is mass circulation. In the first phase, the worst that C could do was to publicise or spread, essentially by word of mouth, aspects of A's private life. The element of mass circulation was absent. In the second phase, although the physicality is still present, the record of A's private life can be distributed far more widely through the use of nineteenth and twentieth century technology.

[1.5] There is a second difference, arising out of mass circulation, which is even more important. The link between privacy and A's home or personal territory is broken. In the first phase, an invasion of privacy was really a bilateral act, where C infringes A's rights. If, in the first phase, A ventured into a public space, and C were to tell another, 'I saw A walking their dog on Hampstead Heath, doing handstands and reciting poetry', it is unlikely that A would or could have any grounds for complaint. C's actions would, in this case, be regarded as a natural consequence of venturing into public spaces and it might very well be said that where A ventures into a public space, they are acquiescing, if not consenting, to the potential for this sort of attention.

[1.6] Matters are different if C, a complete stranger to A, photographed or filmed A in the same public place, and sold the images (and sound) to be published across the world. Here, the notion of A's consent or acquiescence becomes much less plausible, particularly if C can capture images and sounds of A at a distance. Recording (particularly at a distance) and mass distribution, the hallmarks of the second phase, mean that the law of privacy has a role even where A ventures into public spaces.

[1.7] The point can most clearly be seen in portraiture. Before the advent of photography, personal images were painted or drawn, generally with the cooperation of the subject, and usually with the subject paying for the privilege. Photography renders the unconsented capture of an image or other information possible, and the press enables mass circulation of that image or other information. The difference between the first and second phases is stark, but not so stark as the difference between the second and the third phase, which starts with the rise of mass information processing by machine. Let's take the 'birthday' of the Internet, January 1983.[2]

[1.8] The third phase exists where there is not just mass publication of private information on an ever-grander scale – the Internet, social media, etc – but where private information is used in ways that do not involve publication of the information. Thus, data giants use information that we willingly provide (or apparently willingly provide) to enable third parties to target advertisements for their products more effectively; or to determine whether our need for a product is such that a higher price can be charged (so-called dynamic pricing). Similarly, the state will use our private information to promote law and order; protect national security; and for a whole variety of other uses.

[1.9] Whereas phase two is characterised by *mass publication* (which characteristic endures), phase three is characterised by the existence of factors, having nothing to do with publication, that render our data of interest to persons like C, whether C is a private or a public (state) actor. It is an error to speak of publication as the only possible misuse of our private information. Misuse *may* involve publication: but publication is just one form of misuse. This book will refer to the *use* (and *misuse*) of information relating to our *private* selves.[3] This wide use – and misuse – of our data for reasons other than mass publication is one of the hallmarks of phase three. Another hallmark is that whereas mass publication is *overt* (and it could hardly be covert), many of the other uses of our data occur in the hidden processing of that data and are *covert* and very difficult to detect.

Example

All of us will have received targeted advertisements, where an ad is targeted at our specific interests using a combination of other data sources and inferred connections – our browsing history, purchase data, app usage, location data and social connections – to predict interests and deliver relevant ads. How comfortable are we with this use of our data? Is it a point of concern that we do

[2] This was when the ARPANET officially transitioned to the TCP/IP protocol, enabling different networks to communicate seamlessly. This date shows that the phases describe trends and overlap.

[3] For cogent descriptions of the extent these invasions, see A Bernasek and D Mongan, *All You Can Pay: How Companies Use Our Data to Empty Our Wallets* (Nation Books, 2015); J Fairfield, *Owned: Property, Privacy and the New Digital Serfdom* (Cambridge University Press, 2017); S Zuboff, *The Age of Surveillance Capitalism: The Fight for a Human Future at the New Frontier of Power* (Profile Books, 2019); A Monti and R Wacks, *Protecting Personal Information* (Hart Publishing, 2020) 1 and Ch 4; C Véliz, *Privacy is Power: Why and How You Should Take Back Control of Your Data* (Bantam Press, 2020) Ch 1; J Susskind, *The Digital Republic* (Bloomsbury, 2022) Ch 4; A Marwick, *The Private is Political: Networked Privacy and Social Media* (Yale University Press, 2023).

not know *what data* is being used? Sometimes, the suspicion Is advanced that household conversations are actively listened to by 'smart' TVs, speakers and the like. The evidence that this is occurring is elusive, for the technology is both proprietary and complex. That is the point: we no longer have control over our personal data.

[1.10] It is pointless to try to give a *current* description of these encroachments into our privacy, for one thing is certain: the state of technology does not stand still. The following can be noted as characteristics of the third phase: (i) disconnected use of information technology; (ii) the Internet of Things; (iii) surveillance in public spaces; (iv) data aggregation. These are discussed in turn.

i. Disconnected use of information technology

[1.11] Simply using devices – even if they are not part of the Internet of Things – creates important data about ourselves. Although the point is a general one, Fairfield (writing in 2017) makes the point that in connection with mobile computing, the data we render up to third parties is considerable.

Example[4]

Mobile computing means mobile signalling of identity. Mobile devices identify us through a wide range of unique tags: media access control (MAC) addresses, universally unique IDs (UUIDs), even static IP addresses. Verizon assigned a unique identifier to all outgoing data requests made by a user, so that anyone who knew the identifier could track the user's web browsing whenever the user went online, without the user's knowledge or even ability to do anything to stop it other than use a virtual private network (VPN). Although Verizon claimed that it gave 'customers choices about how [it] use[d] their data', the Federal Communications Commission found that the company failed to disclose the practice for nearly two whole years after it was first implemented. Verizon's move was like putting a virtual radio tag on all its users' movements, making sure they could be tracked in the Internet wilderness. Another tracking method is called app fingerprinting. App makers can often identify a person uniquely by the combination of applications they have already installed. Think about it – how many people have the exact app combination that you have downloaded on their phones? Quite possibly, just you. Similarly, through a process called browser fingerprinting, a person's online browser can be tracked. Here's an example of the headers that my browser is currently broadcasting:

user-agent:Mozilla/5.0 (Windows NT 10.0; WOW64; rv:45.0) Gecko/20100101 Firefox/45.0

[4] Fairfield (n 3) 60–61.

accept:text/html,application/xhtml+xml,application/xml;q=0.9,*/*;q=0.8

accept-language:en-US,en;q=0.5

accept-encoding:gzip,deflate,br

dnt:1

connection:keep-alive

One real irony is that since I have set my 'do not track' flag in my browser – you can see that in the line 'dnt:1' – I am now more identifiable, since I'm now 'that guy who always sets his do-not-track-flag' in addition to all the other browser characteristics I transmit to each website.

Here is another instance mentioned by Fairfield.

Example[5]

Consider the new Microsoft Windows 10 operating system. It gathers information directly from users' desktops: everything from their keystrokes to their websites visited, and turns that information over to Microsoft. Microsoft sells that information to advertisers – who use it to get a better price out of you – and may also hand the information off to the government without requiring a warrant. Cortana, the digital assistant program that comes with Windows 10, will 'get to know you', which both trains the program to better serve you and permits it to be a better salesperson on behalf of paying advertisers.

ii. The internet of things

[1.12] As technology becomes cheaper and smaller, so it can be embedded in smaller and cheaper devices. We live in a world where many of our devices communicate with one another and convey that information to others. Speaking of the sensors that monitor our activities, Fairfield says:[6]

> Internet of Things scholar Scott Pepper notes that '[s]ome estimate by 2025 over one trillion sensor-based devices will be connected to the Internet or each other.' We wear sensors. Smartwatches, smart glasses, virtual reality headsets, and a vast array of fitness and health trackers record our environment and intimate details. We carry them: smartphones have compasses, cameras, accelerometers, and microphones. We drive them. Cars are increasingly rolling sensor platforms, with the vast majority now containing Event Data Recorders (devices that record driving data in the event of a crash) or more sophisticated and longer-term GPS recorders. And wherever we go, sensors are already there waiting for us, in street corner cameras, pressure-sensitive streets, and smart power grids that can tell us with 96 per cent accuracy what movies we watch.

[5] ibid 123. Again, writing in 2017: the technology may be old, but the force of the point remains fresh.

[6] ibid 55.

[1.13] The use of such data can be dramatic:

Example[7]

In testimony delivered to the Nevada legislature, T Candice Smith recalled driving down crowded Interstate 15 in Las Vagas when her car was turned off by her auto lender. As Smith later told the New York Times, 'The worst thing ever to happen to someone is to be driving on a freeway, the car is going, like, super fast, and your car just instantly powers down.' Smith's lender was one of a number of subprime auto lenders who use 'starter interrupt devices' to remotely disable cars if their customers, many of whom struggle financially, miss a payment. One woman observed that she had to schedule her life and driving around her payments. 'It's like they control my life', she noted. She held up the small device that connected her car to the Internet. 'This thing rules my life'.

Subprime loans have been a cash cow ever since their cousins, subprime mortgages, became more heavily regulated. Lenders figure that because borrowers need cars to keep their jobs, they will do almost anything to make their car payment.

iii. Surveillance in public spaces

[1.14] In an extrapolation from data derived from our *own* appliances (where it can be said that we have some agency in refusing to use devices[8]), we are increasingly tracked in public spaces, where there is no effective choice:[9]

> In the coming years, sensors will mushroom across and throughout infrastructure: smart homes, smart workplaces, and smart cities. Mobile and infrastructural components work together. Consider the sensors in Nomi's Listen technology. Those sensors were installed in supermarkets and stores, embedded into the environment. They were waiting for consumers to walk in the door with their phones. Smart roads interact with smart cars. Cell towers interact with smartphones. In the not-so-distant future, a smart refrigerator might order groceries to be delivered by drone …

iv. Data aggregation

[1.15] Given the amount of data that is available, aggregation of data can bring enormous rewards. Aggregation can occur in two different ways. First, individual data points, differently collected, but all relating to A, may be aggregated in order to understand more about A:[10]

> By implication, the increased number, sensitivity, and reach and range of sensors drastically increase the conclusions data researchers can draw. Two sensors can help

[7] ibid 49–50.

[8] The extent to which we have agency is something to be debated: if an invasion of privacy is necessary for the device to work, that is one thing. But if an invasion of privacy is unnecessarily attached to a device which would work without such invasion, then why should we be put in the position of having to refuse to use a useful device just to preserve our privacy? The agency we have in such cases is limited.

[9] Fairfield (n 2) 62.

[10] ibid 6.

algorithms make three conclusions. Devices can record different parts of our life and algorithms meld the results together to get even more information than each data set would have alone. This relies on two components: first, the increase of data caused by sensor proliferation; and, second, the depth of inference made possible by big data data-mining and algorithmic inferences.

[1.16] Second, individual data points, relating to a group of individuals (A_1, A_2, A_3 … A_n), can be aggregated so as to understand the operation of the group and so, statistically, the behaviour of individuals within the group.

[1.17] Both forms of data aggregation will likely be used in combination. Sinnreich and Gilbert make the disconcerting point that '[t]here is no limit to the amount and variety of data – and, ultimately, knowledge – that may be produced from an object, event, or interaction, given enough time, distance, and computational power'.[11]

Example[12]

Sinnreich and Gilbert describe the mass harvesting of data uncovered by Edward Snowden. They note that '[a]fter these secret programs were revealed, the US government claimed that they posed no threat to everyday Americans' privacy or security, in part because they weren't capturing or analysing the contents of the emails or calls themselves'. The harvesting was of metadata or data about data. As Sinnreich and Gilbert describe, the data harvested could not be described in these terms:[13]

'… civil liberties advocates and privacy researchers began to document the ways in which the kinds of information the NSA collected amounted to more than merely the sum of their data points. Computer scientists from Stanford University reproduced the NSA's methodology in miniature, collecting supposedly anonymised smartphone metadata from 823 participants and doing their best to analyse the quarter of a million phone calls and 1.2 million text messages those participants sent and received over the course of a few months.

Their findings were unequivocal. First, despite the NSA's claims, it was trivial for someone with enough processing power and coding skill to deanonymise telephone numbers, connecting them and their metadata to real human beings and businesses. Second, it was relatively easy to locate those people and businesses in the physical world, even without additional information such as GPS records. Third, it was pretty clear what kinds of relationships existed between the people in the dataset; for instance, married couples stuck out from the rest of the participants like a sore thumb because of their unique communication patterns. Finally, it was very easy to infer sensitive information about deanonymised users – including their health status, religion, drug use, and whether they owned weapons or were seeking an abortion – based on the other phone numbers they interacted with.'

[11] A Sinnreich and J Gilbert, *The Secret Life of Data* (MIT Press, 2024) xii.
[12] ibid 5–7.
[13] ibid.

The point is that aggregated data is *not* anonymous, but can provide very specific, *individuated* data.[14]

[1.18] The third phase has all the attributes of the second phase (whose hallmarks were the easy capture of images/information combined mass publication/distribution), plus a number of additional features that give rise to concern:

(1) These incursions into our privacy often occur with our ostensible or apparent consent. We know – or ought to know – that the reason social media or social networks are offered for no price (or no *monetary* price, for there is no such thing as a free lunch) is because of the data that subscribers to such social media incidentally provide. The capture of such data is regulated in the terms and conditions buried somewhere in the standard form contracts of the providers of these social networks.
(2) We may very well not know how our data (which may or may not be private information: that is one of the key areas to be traversed in this monograph) is being used. Consent may (at least formally) have been given to the *general* use of such data. But such consent is meaningless: it is most unlikely that any sensible individual would agree to permit their data to be used for any and all purposes. Consent to the general use of data is no consent at all. But the precise use to which data is going to be put will rarely be specified, will rarely be evident and is not specifically consented to at all. Often, that is because our data is aggregated with that of many other individuals, such that an individual's data is merged with millions of other data points. It may be that this fact of aggregation renders such exploitation of data harmless or justifiable: but we have seen that aggregated data is capable of being disaggregated and individuated.[15]
(3) More dangerously, our private data may be harvested *covertly*. Given the complexity of the technology, there is a difficult borderline between overt data collection and covert data collection. What can be said is that just as there are many cases where we may have a hazy idea that data is being gathered, there will be as many cases where we have no idea at all what information is being captured at any given moment.

[14] ibid 58–59, which references the work of Sweeney and Samarati, who in 1998 showed that 'using a list of 55,000 voters from an unnamed city, 97 per cent of the supposedly anonymous entries could be linked to specific individuals just by cross-referencing the zip codes and birthdays of the voters with information in other publicly available databases'. Bear in mind that this is research in 1998: since then, both publicly available data and computing power have increased greatly, and the threat to our privacy is correspondingly greater. The same source (at 32–33) makes the valuable point that we better understand ancient history (eg analysis of pottery shards) through application of ever better technology. Similarly, crimes that would be impossible to solve in the past can now be solved with the help of DNA databases.

[15] See para [1.17].

(4) It might be said that even if the use of our data in aggregated ways is, indeed, harmless, there is nevertheless an economic imbalance in terms of where the rewards for the exploitation of such data fall. Of course, aggregating data and putting it into a form where is can be exploited is a matter beyond the individual. An individual only has their data, and lacks the expertise to manipulate vast quantities of data in any event. But it still must be asked whether each provider of an individual data point is properly being rewarded for providing a drop of individually useless data in the stream of hugely valuable aggregated data.[16]

[1.19] The dangers of this third phase are the subject-matter of Zuboff's book *The Age of Surveillance Capitalism*.[17] She coined the term 'surveillance capitalism' to describe those cases where profit is made out of the aggregation and manipulation of our data, so as to predict and even manipulate our conduct – in particular our commercial conduct – so as to generate a profit.[18] Surveillance capitalism is only possible because our information is undervalued so as to enable excess profits to be made by others. Our information is undervalued because our privacy is not regarded as our own property and is insufficiently protected. Referring to Zuboff again:

> Surveillance capitalism operates through unprecedented asymmetries in knowledge and the power that accrues to knowledge. Surveillance capitalists know everything about us, whereas their operations are designed to be unknowable to us. They accumulate vast domains of new knowledge from us, but not for us. They predict our futures for the sake of others' gain, not ours. As long as surveillance capitalism and its behavioral futures markets are allowed to thrive, ownership of the new means of behaviorial modification eclipses ownership of the means of production as the fountainhead of capitalist wealth and power in the twenty-first century.

[1.20] The notion of private information as property is a concept that it is difficult to get our minds around. That is because the nature of information is so elusive. Tangible property – my table, your car – is in itself complex; intangible property (a debt, for example, and some forms of information, like patents and copyright) much more so. This chapter will seek to unpack the relevant concepts, and provide a structure for the rest of the book.

[16] This was the substance of the complaint in *Gormsen v Meta Platforms Inc* [2023] CAT 10 and [2024] CAT 11.

[17] See n 2.

[18] Zuboff (n 2) 8–12, and in particular at 8: 'Surveillance capitalism unilaterally claims human experience as a free raw material for translation into behavioral data. Although some of these data are applied to product or service improvement, the rest are declared as proprietary *behavioral surplus*, fed into advanced manufacturing processes known as "machine intelligence", and fabricated into *prediction products* that anticipate what you will do now, soon, and later. Finally, these prediction products are traded in a new kind of marketplace for behavioral predictions that I call *behavioral futures markets*. Surveillance capitalists have grown immensely wealthy from these trading operations, for many companies are eager to lay bets on our future behavior.'

[1.21] Because our private information is being used in ways both invasive and new, the law of privacy matters now more than it ever has done in the past. This is reflected in the explosion of writing in this area, and a corresponding increase in the interest shown in the areas of law which (to date) have been relied upon most to ensure that our privacy is to some extent respected. First among these are the law of data protection and the law of human rights (specifically Article 8 of the European Convention on Human Rights (ECHR), which protects a person's private and family life). But competition law and the recent protections in the United Kingdom's Digital Markets, Competition and Consumers Act 2024 also play a role.

II. The Thesis Advanced

[1.22] This monograph cannot avoid touching upon areas of law like the ECHR and data protection, but they do not constitute the focus. The thesis advanced in this book is that whilst both the law of data protection and the law of human rights play an important role in protecting privacy, their role is secondary to the property vesting in each of us over our own private information. Where those property rights are infringed, a private action vests in the individual whose property has been invaded, giving them the ability to protect their *own* privacy. It will be suggested this right of action – the action against the misuse of private information, referred to as the 'Action' for short – whilst fully developed in English law, is misunderstood and as a result under-utilised in the protection of our private information. The purpose of this book is to explain the nature of the Action and to describe how it constitutes (if properly deployed) a powerful means of ensuring that our private information is used by third parties in accordance with our will and in line with the proportionate protection of our privacy.

[1.23] There is no such thing as an original idea. The origins of the right to privacy are very firmly rooted in property law.[19] If we go back to the three phases of threats to privacy described above, during the first phase[20] the threats to our privacy were dealt with by the law of property, notably trespass. Such land-based protections become less and less effective, as society progressed out of the first phase and into the second and third phrases.[21] Seeing private information *as property* goes some way to restoring the balance; and references to the idea in the literature can certainly be seen. The notion that private information

[19] See, generally, M Richardson, *The Right to Privacy* (Cambridge University Press, 2017); and C Véliz, *The Ethics of Privacy and Surveillance* (Oxford University Press, 2024) 50. See further Ch 4.

[20] See para [1.3].

[21] See paras [1.4]–[1.7] (the second phase) and [1.8]–[1.19] (the third phase).

is property only begins to make sense when the concepts of 'privacy', and so 'private information', are defined. These are considered in the following chapters, but (as a taster) consider this insight by Fried:[22]

> ... it is necessary to sharpen the intuitive concept of privacy. As a first approximation, privacy seems to be related to secrecy, to limiting the knowledge of others about oneself. This notion must be refined. It is not true, for instance, that the less that it known about us, the more privacy we have. Privacy is not simply an absence of information about us in the minds of others; rather, it is the control we have over information about ourselves.
>
> ...
>
> Privacy, thus, is control over knowledge about oneself. But it is not simply control over the quantity of information abroad; there are modulations in the quality of the knowledge as well. We may not mind that a person knows a general fact about us, and yet feel our privacy invaded if he knows the details. For instance, a casual acquaintance may comfortably know that I am sick, but it would violate my privacy if he knew the nature of the illness. Or a good friend may know what particular illness I am suffering from, but it would violate my privacy if he were actually to witness my suffering from some symptoms which he must know is associated with the disease.
>
> Privacy in its dimension of control over information is an aspect of personal liberty.

[1.24] The moment one talks about *control* over something, property law comes into the frame: property is all about control, *preventing* others from using your property or *licensing* it to others on terms. As Fried says, the 'person who enjoys privacy is able to grant or deny access to others ... Privacy is thus control over knowledge about oneself'.[23] Once this point has been grasped, the property analysis becomes much more intuitive, although the definitional problems of what 'private information' is remain.[24]

[1.25] Property law at one and the same time enables an owner's *enjoyment* of their own property as well as enabling the owner to *exploit* their property. Thus, a landowner may choose to enjoy their property uninterfered with, by

[22] C Fried, *An Anatomy of Values: Problems of Personal and Social Choice* (Harvard University Press, 1970) 140–41.

[23] ibid 140–41.

[24] Some commentators (eg Monti and Wacks (n 3) 9–10) suggest that a satisfactory definition is impossible. If this is so, then a property analysis will fail, because it is a necessary condition of ownership that the thing owned can be defined. How else can an owner exclude a third party from 'their' property, if the thing owned cannot be identified? The thesis of this book is that a definition of private information is possible. Véliz (n 20) 79–80 essays a definition that begins to recognise that private information arises out of a *perception* of one person by another: 'On my account, someone accesses your personal information the moment she knows about that personal data. In other words, it is not enough for the information to be *accessible* to her for you to lose privacy'. It will be the contention in this book that *information is perception*.

excluding everyone else. On the other hand, the landowner may exploit their property, most obviously by selling it and getting money in return. More subtly, without relinquishing ownership, the owner may accept payment from a third party and permit that third party to use their land, as where a landowner permits a fair or a sporting activity on their property. The economic significance of property rights, in ensuring distribution and use of resource, cannot really be overstated. It is the engine of the market economy.

III. What is 'Private Information'?

[1.26] 'Private information' involves a combination of two concepts – privacy and information – each intractable; and in combination only more so. Large parts of this book are devoted to defining: first, the concept of *information*; and, second, the concept of *privacy*. The two concepts in combination – *private information* – constitute, it will be suggested, a form of property that is *already* recognised and protected by English law.

[1.27] The owner of private information can act to *protect* that information (that is, prevent or control its circulation by excluding others, so as to enjoy it themselves) or *monetise* it (that is, by permitting its use on terms, including as to payment). These powers of protection, exclusion and exploitation are the hallmarks of ownership of property. They are exercisable (as property rights tend to be) against 'all the world'. What does this mean?

IV. Rights *in personam* and Rights *in rem*

[1.28] Fundamental to the thesis being advanced is the distinction between an *obligation* and a *property right*.[25] It will be suggested that this distinction has been lost sight of when considering privacy and the nature of private information.

[1.29] The distinction will crop up again and again (hopefully without too much repetition) in this book. Where A enters into an agreement with B, whereby B promises to do something for A, there is a personal obligation on B to perform; and a correlative personal right exercisable by A against B, whereby A can oblige B in some way to perform their obligation. The obligation is personal as between A and B. The relationship between A and B can be said to be *bilateral*.

[25] See M Smith et al, *Smith on The Law of Assignment*, 4th edn (Oxford University Press, 2026) Ch 2.

[1.30] Third parties to the transaction – call them C – are not affected by the legal act (here, the contract) that characterises the relationship between A and B. Because it is *personal* or *bilateral*, the relationship between A and B is (to use the Roman law label) *in personam*. A's right and B's obligation[26] can each appropriately be characterised as *in personam*.

[1.31] *In personam* obligations do not only arise out of contract. Where C runs A over in their car, A has a claim in tort (or delict) against C which, although it does not arise out of contract, is also an *in personam* right subsisting as between A and C.

[1.32] A property right – a right *in rem* as the Romans would call it – is defined by reference to a *thing*, which may be tangible (a piece of land, a table) or intangible (copyright, a patented invention). A's rights in their property are exercisable against *anyone* who infringes those rights. There is no bilateral limit as to the persons against whom A may claim. The potential defendant to A's claim is not B (the person with whom a bilateral relationship exists), but third party C (where there is no existing bilateral relationship).

[1.33] Before questions of infringement can sensibly be considered, it must first be understood what A's rights over their property actually are. *Ownership* – as it will be referred to in this book[27] – is not a single, monolithic, concept, but a bundle of rights vesting in the owner of property.[28] A owns a thing. It is an incursion by a third party into A's rights over that thing (an infringement) that triggers A's rights as owner enabling them to protect or vindicate their control over their property. The existence of an *infringement* is important.

[1.34] Absent an infringement of their property rights, the most that can be said is that A has a *contingent* right to claim against all the world – which we will refer to as O. The contingency, a necessary condition for the bringing of a claim, is an *infringement* of A's rights by an individual falling within the

[26] 'Right' and 'obligation' describe the same thing: only the viewpoint differs. What is A's right is B's obligation.

[27] Property lawyers will say that English law does not really have a concept of 'ownership', but rather a system of rights based around the concept of possession. That is fair enough, but the purists' point is unhelpful. In the first place, possession sits very ill when trying to define an 'owner's' rights in intangible property, which cannot be possessed. Furthermore, 'ownership' is not being used as a single, monolithic concept like the Roman *dominium* but as a bundle of rights which, when viewed in the round and held by a single person – A – appropriately equate to *ownership* and allow us properly to call A an *owner*.

[28] See Honoré's essay 'Ownership' in A Guest, *Oxford Essays in Jurisprudence* (Oxford University Press, 1961) Ch 5. In his essay, Honoré sought to enumerate the various rights that might comprise the highest possible interest in a thing, the 'bundle' of rights in a thing or in property that represents the highest level of interest that can be. This was an interest that Honoré termed 'ownership'.

universe O. O is simply a descriptor of the universe of persons against whom a claim by A might *hypothetically* be brought were the contingency of infringement to be satisfied.[29]

[1.35] A's rights as owner only translate into a cause of action or claim against another where the contingency of infringement is *in fact* satisfied. Where A's rights have been infringed[30] by C (C being a member of the universe O), then A may bring a claim against C.

[1.36] Rights *in rem* thus ditch the bilateral requirement that is a key feature of personal rights. A's property rights are good against 'all the world', O: but can only be advanced against a particular defendant C where that defendant has infringed A's rights in regard to A's property. A's rights are rights *in rem* – they are defined by reference to a *thing*, an object of property – but in concrete terms A will only have a claim against another where that other has infringed (or, in terms of *quia timet* injunctions, threatens to infringe[31]) A's property rights. It is, for this reason if no other, easy to confuse A's assertion of a right that is *in personam* with A's assertion of a right that is *in rem*,[32] for in each case there will be an individual named as defendant to the proceedings. The proceedings will always be a battle between people, A *versus* B or A *versus* C.

V. The 'Players' Involved: A *Dramatis Personae*

[1.37] The person whose private information is infringed or is threatened to be infringed will have enormous interest, in many cases, in pressing their claim. This person – the claimant (as plaintiffs are now called in English law) whose private information is threatened – is referred to in this book as A. A is one of several alphabetical designators that are used to describe people throughout the book. The labels A, B, C and O have already been used. But it is important to state exactly the meaning of the labels attaching to the persons involved. A is

[29] There can be threatened infringements, which can be remediated by way of *quia timet* injunctions. These are considered separately in this book, which will generally refer to *actual* infringements rather than *threatened future* infringements. The aim is to keep things simple, and *quia timet* cases (see n 31 below for a definition) represent an additional layer of complexity, best addressed separately.

[30] Or arguably infringed. A cause of action is no more than an assertion of a claim to a certain standard, which is then adjudicated upon by a court: Smith et al (n 25) Ch 4.

[31] *Quia timet* means 'because he fears'. *Quia timet* injunctions can be obtained against a defendant who threatens to infringe a right. Such injunctions constitute an anticipatory court order preventing the defendant from doing that act. This means that the claimant avoids suffering an invasion of their rights at all.

[32] As with all things, the distinction is never completely clear cut. Personal obligations can be transferred or 'assigned' and so elements of property creep in. The point is most clearly made in Smith et al (n 25) Chs 1 and 34.

the person whose private information is in issue. A is the *owner* of their private information, whatever that may mean.

[1.38] One matter that will be considered in the chapters that follow is whether the class of A is limited to what lawyers call a 'natural' person, or whether A can *also* be a 'legal' person. A quick preview of the conclusions – albeit not the reasoning behind them – is appropriate here:

(1) A 'natural' person is lawyer-speak for a *human being*. Human beings have the greatest interest in protecting their privacy, for privacy is a very human need. *Obviously* the label A includes human beings or natural persons.
(2) The laws of many nations, and certainly the laws of England, invest some entities (not all) with *legal personality*. That is to say, even though these entities (companies, corporations, etc) do not physically exist as people, being intangible things of the law, they can, as 'legal' persons, enter contracts, own property, even employ human beings (ie natural persons). Most people are employed by a company or corporation, a legal person.
(3) As incorporeal 'persons', a corporation or company can have no sense of privacy. Again, that is obvious if one is postulating an entity that cannot think or say or do anything except through human agency. It might, therefore, be said that no legal person should be able to bring an action for the misuse of private information. But that does not follow if (as is the thesis in this book) private information is property, because we know companies and corporations can own property.
(4) Counterintuitive though it is, the conclusion in this book is that a legal person can own private information and can therefore sue to protect it. Accordingly, person A embraces both natural and legal persons.

[1.39] Having defined A, the next question is who can A claim against? Remember that the thesis of this book is that A has a right *in rem* against 'all the world'. But A cannot sue 'all the world', only those persons who arguably:[33] (i) *actually* infringe A's property rights; or (ii) threaten to do so (*quia timet* relief). 'All the world' is referred to as O (picked because the circle embraces everything within it). O is a universe of persons against whom A can *contingently* bring a claim, the contingency being that *someone* in the universe O either threatens to infringe or actually infringes A's rights. So A will never claim against O,[34] only

[33] Why the tricky lawyer's word 'arguably'? That is because, in a society governed by the rule of law, the mere fact that A asserts a right, does not mean that C is automatically liable. C may dispute A's claim, and we have courts of law to resolve such disputes. Until such resolution, A is doing no more than *asserting* a claim that may (or may not) be established. English law maintains a certain degree of 'quality control' in regard to A's claim, based on notions of 'arguability'. In order to take a claim to trial, A does not have to show they are right, but they *do* have to demonstrate a reasonably arguable claim. Questions of practice and procedure are considered in Ch 9.

[34] It is possible – albeit exceptional – to have claims that are *contra mundum*, against all the world. As with all general propositions, there are exceptions, and so 'never' is a bit of an overstatement.

against one or more members of the class O. That person or those persons are referred to as C.[35] Where there are several Cs, the designations C_1, C_2, C_3 etc will be used, but only where it is necessary to distinguish between defendants. (That approach will also be used where there are multiple other actors in the same position, eg claimants A_1, A_2, A_3 etc.)

[1.40] The same question as arose in relation to A,[36] also arises in relation to C: can C be a natural as well as a legal person? The thesis advanced in this book is that C can *only* be a natural person, and *not* a legal person. The response to this from any sensible reader is likely to be one of outrage or incomprehension. Can A not sue Google or Meta or Apple or Microsoft? How can corporations or companies possibly get a free pass to invade A's privacy without A having a remedy against them? The answer is that they do not get a free pass, but that the manner in which liability is attributed to a company or a corporation is sufficiently complex to warrant a chapter of its own (Chapter 8), after the nature of the Action in the 'simpler' cases has been articulated. But the bottom-line, for present purposes, is that C – and so the members of O – are *only* natural persons. There is not a legal person among them. Such legal persons are referred to throughout this book as 'undertakings'.

[1.41] The *undertaking* is a helpful EU concept, which is adopted in this book, though used in a slightly different sense to that propounded in EU law. In Case C-41/90, *Höfner and Elser v Macroton GmbH*,[37] the Court of Justice of the European Union (CJEU) stated that 'the concept of an undertaking encompasses every entity engaged in an economic activity regardless of the legal status of the entity and the way in which it is financed'. The undertaking thus references economic activity without regard to legal structure or personality. Strictly speaking, C (acting on their own) could be an undertaking, and to that extent this book uses a narrower definition so as to *exclude* C acting on their own from the definition of undertaking, which serves to describe the more complex structures where C is part of indertaking U. The nature of undertaking U is not particularly material and is intended to embrace organisations with and without separate legal personality, so as to include companies, corporations, firms, partnerships, government departments and other state institutions, etc.

[35] O refers to universe of parties against whom A could advance a claim if certain contingencies were met. Typically, it will be suggested, such contingencies will be met if O misuses A's private information. In other words, A's rights against O are contingent on an (arguable) infringement by O of A's rights as owner. At that point, O becomes C, an actual defendant, distinguishing themselves from the rest of O by virtue of their allegedly infringing act. Thus, it is right to say that A has rights over property that hold good against the world – all of O – but wrong to say that a cause of action vests in A against O. For a cause of action to vest, there must be an arguable infringement or threatened infringement by a specific person or persons.

[36] See para [1.38].

[37] EU:C:1991:161 at [21].

The relationship between C and U is referenced as C(U), which indicates that the actor C is part of undertaking U.

[1.42] It might be asked why the alphabetical labels jump from A to C, missing out B? That is because C refers to a *third party* who infringes A's privacy. The magic of property rights and claims *in rem* is that persons with whom A has no connection other than the property that A owns and C interferes with can nevertheless be the defendant in a claim brought by A. In short, there is no bilateral relationship between A and C that causes C to stand out from the crowd described as O. The only thing that causes C to stand out is their infringement or threatened infringement of A's rights. Again, it is worth expanding upon this, in order to define B, the person(s) with whom A has a bilateral relationship:

(1) B is a person with whom A has some kind of bilateral relationship, usually contractual, which affects the substance of A's privacy rights as against B, either to make them stronger or weaker.
(2) If A were to consent to B using A's private information (ie to license B to use A's property), and B used that property (the information) in the manner intended by their agreement, A clearly cannot bring a claim against B alleging an infringement of their (A's) privacy.
(3) Conversely, if B were to promise A that they (B) would keep and protect A's information, and disclose it to nobody, and B breached that promise, then A would have a claim against B because of the promise and not because of any *in rem* claim.
(4) The point of the label B is to differentiate those cases where there is something (and usually it will be a contractual thing) that renders B particularly liable or particularly not liable to A. Broadly speaking, A's claim against B will be *in personam*, and A's claim against C will be *in rem*, but that correlation is not absolute. In the running down case considered at paragraph [1.31], there is no pre-existing relationship between A and C. C is best described as a third-party, and yet A's claim is *in personam*.[38] Similarly, there will be cases where there are contractual relations between A and C, even purporting to deal with A's private information, where an *in rem* claim can nevertheless be maintained by A. In other words, the bilateral aspect of the relationship does not inevitably have an effect on A's *in rem* claims.

[38] The difference between the running down case and the privacy infringement case is that whereas the former involves no infringement of a property right, the latter does. However, there are many instances in the tort of negligence where A's property is being protected (from eg negligent damage by C) where it is a stretch to say that C is infringing A's property rights. It is not part of this book to conclusively draw the line between rights *in rem* and rights *in personam*, partly because of space, but mainly because labels should not drive analysis, but analysis should drive labels. The *in rem*/*in personam* distinction is a useful one for purposes of explanation, but seeking to define the line in absolute terms obfuscates rather than clarifies.

(5) Thus, B and C both identify defendants in cases where there has been an arguable infringement of A's rights and as a result A has a cause of action against B or C. The purpose of the distinction between the two defendant types – B and C – is not so much to differentiate between *in personam* claims and obligations and *in rem* claims and obligations (although that distinction will generally hold good) but to identify those cases where a bilateral relationship A ←→ B affects what would otherwise be a vanilla *in rem* claim A ←→ C. This becomes significant when (in Chapter 11) the manner in which A can exploit their property is considered. Such exploitation will almost inevitably involve some form of bilateral dealing between A and B.

[**1.43**] The distinction between *in rem* and *in personam* claims is being emphasised because English law has to date placed insufficient emphasis on the property aspects of private information. Although not particularly evident in the discussion in the cases, privacy claims *appear* to be seen by the English courts through the prism of *in personam* claims rather than *in rem* claims. It is hard to give evidence to support this assertion for two reasons: (i) because this is an unspoken and unarticulated mind-set; and (ii) because A's *in personam* and *in rem* claims will be against specific defendants[39] with the result that the distinction between *in rem* and *in personam* will by no means be obvious from the way in which A's claim has been framed or 'pleaded' by their lawyer.

[**1.44**] For these reasons, the existence of an *in rem* claim vesting in the owner of private information does not receive the emphasis that it should. This book represents a pushback against the apparent but unspoken assumption that information is protected by *in personam* rights alone. This book advances the thesis that English law holds private information to be *property* and that private information vesting in A can be protected by A by way of an action *in rem* that is good against all the world. In other words, *without perceiving anything other than the private information itself*, a third party C can be enjoined (ie injuncted, told not to do something, etc) from using A's private information or will be obliged to pay damages to A if that information is in fact misused. This is a true property right, similar to ownership of land (where the owner can exclude *anyone*) or to a patent (where the owner can prevent *anyone* from using their invention).

VI. A Name for A's Cause of Action

[**1.45**] The cause of action by which A's rights over their private information are vindicated is known as the action against misuse of private information.

[39] See the discussion at paras [1.36] and [1.39].

This is a bit of a mouthful, and (as noted in paragraph [1.22]) it will generally be referred to as the Action in this book. The Action evolved out of the action for breach of confidence, which we will come to in Chapter 2, if only briefly. But the Action has now been recognised as a separate cause of action, albeit one related to the action for breach of confidence. An important role was played by the Human Rights Act 1998 in encouraging, even forcing, the common law to develop in this direction. Significantly, the action for breach of confidence is an *in personam* claim dependent[40] upon an ex ante relationship between A and B (eg a contract or a relationship of trust and confidence), whereas the Action requires no such ex ante relationship and is (it is suggested) properly characterised as a claim by A against C.[41]

VII. What is Property?

A. A starting point

[1.46] Private information, this book asserts, is *property*. What, then, is property?[42] The essential elements that need to be satisfied in order for something to be capable of constituting property are not unrelated to those needed to transfer property.[43] The question is whether those elements can be satisfied in the case of private information. The essential elements that have to be satisfied in order for something to constitute property are twofold:

(1) *Identifiability of subject-matter.* The subject-matter must be capable of unique and precise identification. It must be possible to say 'This thing belongs to A' without there being any undue ambiguity or uncertainty.
(2) *Identifiability of the (first) owner.* It must be possible to say, again without any undue ambiguity or uncertainty, who owns the property in question. Where property is transferred, it will be necessary to differentiate between the first owner and the subsequent owner(s).

These two elements enable the law to facilitate the owner in the assertion of their rights to exclude, exploit and transfer. Where these elements are not present, a property law analysis is either very difficult or else impossible.

[40] Albeit in an increasingly attenuated form.

[41] This book uses the terms 'ex ante' and 'ex post' as a convenient shorthand to describe (in the case of ex ante) circumstances or matters pertaining before a given event and (in the case of ex post) circumstances or matters pertaining *after* a given event.

[42] For a detailed analysis, particularly of intangible property, see Smith et al (n 25) Ch 2.

[43] The requirements are not dissimilar to the requirements for an effective assignment of a chose in action (see Smith et al (n 25) Ch 10); nor to those for the creation of a trust (see ibid (n 25) Ch 11). The requirements for transfer of choses are more extensive, because of the element of transfer, which is not presently under consideration here, but which will arise in Ch 11.

[1.47] A big difference between tangible and most intangible property concerns replicability. The fact that (most[44]) intangible property can be replicated is often deployed by opponents of a property-based analysis of information. It is said that information cannot be property because it cannot be *transferred*, but only *copied* or *replicated*. There is nothing in this point. A work that is subject to copyright – this book, for example – can only be copied by the owner of the copyright. Anyone else copying the work infringes the owner's rights. If the owner A transfers the copyright to B, then although the owner remains physically capable of copying the work, the owner ceases to have the right to do so. Replicability is thus not a barrier to recognising something intangible as property.

[1.48] The fact that property can be transferred implies a *first owner*, the person who can effect the first transfer of the property. That person has to be identifiable in order: (i) to make meaningful the process of transfer (someone has to have the right, and that person must be capable of identification); and (ii) to test whether any subsequent owner is in fact the owner of the property they are laying claim to. All subsequent owners, if they are to assert the rights of an owner, need to show a 'chain of title' back to the first owner.[45]

[1.49] A judge in the United States gave the following definition of 'property':[46]

> Property is a broad concept that includes 'every intangible benefit and prerogative susceptible of possession or disposition.' We apply a three-part test to determine whether a property right exists: 'First, there must be an interest capable of precise definition; second, it must be capable of exclusive possession and control; and third, the putative owner must have established a legitimate claim to exclusivity.'

This definition contains the two elements listed in paragraph [1.46] (identifiability of subject-matter and identifiability of owner), but also a third (namely that the property be capable of exclusive possession and control). Although it is impossible to gainsay the importance of possession and control, these elements are *not* intrinsic to the definition of property. Intangible property – and it is suggested that private information belongs to this class of property – is incapable of possession and not really capable of control without a significant

[44] Debts and rights under a contract cannot be replicated. On the other hand, copyright material and information clearly can be.

[45] As already noted, unadjudicated claims turn on allegation or arguability. A court, adjudicating upon A's claim, must have a reliable, objective, test for ascertaining whether A has a claim against C. Various factors will have to be tested for. One will be whether A actually has the right to bring the claim – whether A is in fact the owner.

[46] Fairfield (n 3) 134, citing Kozinski J in *Kremen v Cohen*, 337 F3d 1024, 1030.

supporting legal framework.[47] If one thinks about intellectual property rights – patents, copyright, etc[48] – there is nothing to possess or to control and the reason they constitute property is because society, for reasons of policy, has *decided* to make property and property rights 'out of thin air'. So, even though a patented invention or a copyrighted work cannot be possessed, third parties infringing the owner's rights can be prevented from doing so or be made to pay damages for their infringement. Long answer short: 'exclusive possession and control' is not an *inherent* attribute of property, but a characteristic *conferred* by operation of law.

[1.50] Put another way, the two attributes of property that have been identified – (i) identifiability of subject-matter; and (ii) identifiability of owner – must and can only be answered through an exploration of a third aspect, namely the nature of the property under consideration, in this case 'private information'. Before coming to the specifics of 'private information', however, a few more general points will be made in regard to the two essential elements identified above.

B. Identifiability of subject matter

[1.51] In *OBG Ltd v Allan*,[49] Lady Hale noted that the 'essential feature of property is that it has an existence independent of a particular person: it can be bought and sold, given and received, bequeathed and inherited, pledged or seized to secure debts, acquired (in the olden days) by a husband on marrying its owner'. This independence manifests itself in two ways: first, ownership of the thing can be transferred; second, the owner of the thing (whoever that person presently may be) may enforce the rights of ownership against any person (O) infringing the owner's rights (C).

[1.52] It is obviously critical to any property regime that the property in issue can be identified. Requiring property to be identifiable without 'any undue ambiguity or uncertainty' can rightly be criticised as itself a vague criterion. The fact is, however, that there are often difficulties in understanding the precise ambit of property owned by a person, which is why the test for property is *not* that it is intrinsically identifiable (although that is the ideal) but that it

[47] See, generally, Smith et al (n 25) and in particular Chs 1, 2 and 34. The point is that with tangible property, self-help is possible: the owner can resist others taking possession; and can use self-help to recover possession that has been lost. Intangible property is incapable of possession, and so the owner can only assert their rights, if they are challenged, in law.

[48] These and other areas of law cognate to private information are considered in Ch 4.

[49] [2007] UKHL 21 at [309].

is *capable* of identification, ultimately (when push-comes-to-shove) through a court process.[50] The question, therefore, is *not* whether it be obvious to anyone that a certain piece of private information belonged to A. Rather, the question is whether, in a disputed case, it is possible for a court satisfactorily (by which is meant objectively, after a proportionate court process) to resolve a property dispute about private information between A and C.

[1.53] Delineation (or the ability to delineate) is important and is regularly encountered in property law (eg accession).[51] Fairfield gives the example of a handful of sand in a sandpit versus a brick amongst a pile of bricks:[52]

> Imagine you owned a 'handful of sand' out of an entire sandbox. It would be hard to determine where your property rights began or ended. But if you owned one brick out of a stack of bricks, you would know your rights with much more certainty. The hard delineation of the physical form makes the determination of rights much easier.

We will see this when we come grapple with the meaning of 'private information'. Its intangibility gives it a will-o'-the-wisp quality that makes analysis intractable.

C. Identifiability of the first owner

[1.54] The 'first owner' is the person at the beginning of any chain of title. The difficulties of *transferring* information have been touched upon and will be reverted to, but this does not remove the importance of being able – with the requisite degree of certainty – to identify A, the original owner of the private information. Property can be transferred: A may dispose of their private information to a transferee. The transferee's rights as owner depend on a chain of title. If the transferee's rights are challenged, then the transferee must be able to say 'I got this property from A, and A was the first owner'.

[1.55] Co-ownership of property is possible, and property might be owned jointly by A_1, A_2 and A_3 as first owners. But this does not alter the fundamental importance of being able to identify a person or persons who can assert against the world the rights of an owner.

[50] This is why 'arguable' infringements rather than 'actual' infringements need on occasion to be differentiated.

[51] See, generally, Smith et al (n 25) Ch 24, where the extinction of property rights is considered in detail. *Accessio*, or 'accession' in English, refers to the case where an owner's property is so incorporated into another's property as to lose its identity and to end the owner's proprietary claims over what was formerly their property.

[52] Fairfield (n 3) 146–47.

D. The essential rights of an owner

[1.56] Having identified the essential attributes of property, it is helpful at this stage briefly to enumerate the essential rights of an owner. As Honoré makes clear, there is no single, immutable, list of the rights of an owner. Property rights consist of a 'bundle' of rights which, viewed collectively, constitute the typical rights of an owner.[53] Property rights are characterised by: (1) the right to exclude; (2) the right to enjoy; and (3) the right to transfer. Thus:

(1) *The right to exclude.* A can exclude all the world from the enjoyment of their property, without necessarily doing anything with the property in question. This right might also be termed the right of 'quiet enjoyment', but it makes more sense to see the world through the prism of contested rights. Thus, as part of their 'quiet enjoyment', A can exclude O from their property.
(2) *A can exploit their property.* This is a form of 'enjoyment' where A renders to C (as one of the universe of O) limited rights to make use of their property. Inevitably, there will have to be a bilateral arrangement between A and C to define C's rights over A's property. Once that arrangement is concluded and effective, C changes label and is properly called B. B's rights in regard to the property will be limited because A remains the owner – this is not a case of *transfer*. The typical way of exploiting intangible property is by way of the licence, whereby an owner A gives permission to another B to use their property without relinquishing ownership.
(3) *The right to transfer or to alienate.* A can divest themselves of ownership, transfer that right to B. A thus ceases to be the owner, and ownership succeeds to B.

VIII. There is No Inevitable Answer to the Questions Being Posed: The Role of Policy

[1.57] Information generally has *not* been regarded as property under English law. It will not be asserted in this book that *all* information is property, only that a sub-set – 'private information' – is property. Some support for this is derived from the conversations had by lay persons and politicians, who – in a digital era of 'big data', where firms are able to generate large profits through the capture and processing of individuals' personal data – often speak of private information in terms of someone's property. Intuitively, it is suggested, we *do* see our private information as something we own and control.[54] The law should (and,

[53] See Honoré (n 28).

[54] This intuition is soundly based once one has understood what 'privacy' and 'private information' actually are: see Fried's analysis at para [1.23].

as contended here, does) reflect this by respecting these rights and giving us the power (the right) to vindicate them.

[1.58] With this non-legal conversation very much in mind, it is important to stress that there is nothing intrinsic in property. Property is a human construct; it is a label. It exists where the law says it exists. Some things naturally lend themselves to a property analysis: land and chattels, for example. This is because they are physical, tangible, things. A table is a thing to be possessed and owned, and the rights of an owner (to exclude, to enjoy and to transfer) can quite naturally be transposed onto or inferred from the physical thing. But the rights over the hypothetical table are nevertheless intangible. All property rights (whether they relate to tangible property or not) are creations of law. It is thus perfectly possible to say that a chattel is incapable of ownership. Under English law, a swan cannot be owned, nor can a cadaver, nor can a human being. But there is no *intrinsic* reason why this should be the case.

[1.59] Conversely, there are some things to which ownership rights do not (in our minds) naturally attach. Generally, this is where the subject matter is intangible. It is, conceptually speaking, very hard to speak of (inevitably) intangible rights over intangible property. Yet such property exists, carved out of thin air. There is no inevitable reason why a person's invention should be property – yet inventions are property (the patent).[55] Air – actually a tangible – tends *not* to be regarded as property because it is not scarce and not easily reduced to a state of possession. Yet, in certain contexts, even air is propertised (eg diving cylinders). The right to emit pollutants is another recent example of a permission carved out of a prohibition and propertised such that the permission becomes transferable and capable of enjoyment by the owner. The database right – considered further below[56] – is another example.

[1.60] The difficulties in the conception of 'property' are well illustrated by Professor Gray's description of the facts in the well-known case *Victoria Park Racing and Recreation Grounds Co Ltd v Taylor*:[57]

> … the plaintiff company in Victoria Park Racing owned a racecourse on which it frequently held what Rich J was to describe as 'competitions in the comparative

[55] The point is well put in the opening words of B Sherman, *Intangible Intangibles: Patent Law's Engagement with Dematerialised Subject Matter* (Cambridge University Press, 2024) 1: 'Questions about the nature of the intangible have never been far from the surface in intellectual property law. Whether when deciding how something that you cannot touch, hear or see is to be identified, demarcated and bounded, or how these incorporeal immaterial things are to be traced as they move between formats, languages and objects, the law has constantly struggled to give property status to intangibles'.

[56] See Ch 4 below.

[57] (1937) 58 CLR 479. Gray discusses the case in his seminal article, K Gray, 'Property in Thin Air' (1991) *Cambridge Law Journal* 252, 264–66.

> merits of racehorses'. The ground was enclosed by a fence and the plaintiff charged members of the public for admission. One of the defendants, Taylor, owned a cottage opposite the racecourse and on his own land he erected a raised wooden platform. From this vantage point he commanded a view of the entire racecourse including, significantly, the boards and semaphores by means of which starting prices were displayed. He was also clearly within earshot of other information announced to members of the racegoing public within the ground. Taylor then arranged with another of the defendants, the Commonwealth Broadcasting Corporation, that a commentator should, from a position on Taylor's platform, broadcast live radio reports on the races to listeners in the Sydney area. The instant popularity of these transmissions stimulated an illicit off-course betting industry in Sydney, and there was unchallenged evidence that punters who would otherwise have attended the race meetings in person now preferred to follow those proceedings from the comfort of their own homes or, even better, from their local hostelry. The plaintiff, perturbed by the catastrophic loss of business, sued for an injunction on the footing of nuisance and breach of copyright. (It was common ground that the mere construction and use of the raised platform constitutes no breach of building or zoning regulations or of the betting and gaming legislation or indeed of the regulations governing broadcasting.)

The plaintiff's claim failed. The High Court of Australia decided – by a majority – that the facts disclosed no cause of action against the defendants. The minority contended that the acts disclosed a claim in nuisance, but it is extremely difficult to understand how these facts can be shoehorned into a nuisance claim. If anything, this is an information case, and the question is whether Taylor was misusing the plaintiff's private information. The facts of the *Victoria Park* case are helpful discussion points for considering the true ambit of A's rights over their private information.

[1.61] Two matters are critical to understanding and resolving cases like the *Victoria Park* case:

(1) *An understanding of what information is.* The nature of information is considered in detail in Chapter 3, but an indication of direction of travel is desirable at this point. There is a tendency to equate stored information with information. Carlyle did so in his famous quotation that '[a]ll that mankind has done, thought, gained or been is lying as in magic preservation in the pages of books'. The manner in which information is stored – and here Carlyle was talking about books as the means of storage, but he could just as well have spoken of DVD-ROMS, hard drives or cloud storage – does not shed light on the nature of information. As Véliz noted,[58] a loss of privacy only occurs when information about A is *(mis)used* by another, C. Misuse can only occur where C has put themselves in a position to *use* A's private information. It is not enough for the information to be

[58] See n 20 and the quotation from Véliz at n 25.

accessible to C: C must *in fact* have accessed it. To access the information, C must perceive it. To revert to the example of the book, the unopened book contains the means to information, not the information itself. It is only when C opens the book and reads and understands what it says there that there is *information* in the mind of C that C can (mis)use. Just as beauty is in the eye of the holder, information is in the mind of the recipient. Our focus on how information is *imparted* (whether in a book or by way of performance, like a lecture or a horse race[59]) misleads us as to the true nature of information, which is the *perception of the recipient*. The law of private information is, at its most fundamental level, concerned with the *control* of the *uses* of private information by C. It is *perception* that enables the use of information.[60]

(2) *A will to protect private information*. In addition to understanding what is being contolled, there must be a will to control. The answer to cases like *Victoria Park Racing* turns not only on an understanding of what is at issue, but also on the willingness of a legal system to afford legal protection to certain classes of claimant in certain types of case. This is a matter, in the first instance, for the legislature. But, in this country, with its common law tradition, the law can evolve in an incremental way, through judge-made law. Judges of course cannot legislate, but they can and must decide the cases before them: (i) in accordance with legislative provision; and (ii) consistently with the decided case law. In the case of private information, through a combination of the Human Rights Act 1998 and the common law, we have reached a point where private information *is* property. It this analysis which gives this book its title: *Privacy As Property*.

IX. Structure of the Book

[**1.62**] This book comprises twelve chapters, including this one. Chapters 3, 6, 7 and 8 consider the essential elements of the Action. Chapter 3 explores what information is; Chapter 6 considers what attributes *private* information has so as to differentiate it from other information; Chapters 7 and 8 consider what

[59] As will be described, this book adopts a very wide definition of information, going well beyond fact and opinion, extending to *anything that can be perceived*. See further Ch 3.

[60] Sinnreich and Gilbert (n 11) xiii draw similar distinctions, using different language: 'Throughout this book we will use the terms *data*, *information*, and *knowledge* a great many times. We do not treat these terms interchangeable, and we use them very deliberately. *Data* refers to discrete, quantitative values extracted from larger, more complex, phenomena. *Information* refers to those mathematical values put into context and thereby given a social meaning. *Knowledge* refers to actionable inferences made from information by interested parties such as governments, marketers, or researchers. This flow from data to information to knowledge is, in our current society, an industrialized process, and many of the technologies and businesses we discuss are part of that pipeline.' In this book, the terms data and information are *not* used as defined by Sinnreich and Gilbert. But their definition of 'knowledge' is within touching distance of the meaning given to 'information' here.

constitutes use and what constitutes misuse of private information, the former considering misuse by private persons (non-state actors) and the latter considering misuse by organs of the state (state actors) like the police, the intelligence services, the tax authorities and the Driver and Vehicle Licensing Authority (DVLA). Thus, the three elements of the Action – (i) (mis)use of (ii) private (iii) information – are covered.

[1.63] Chapter 2 describes how the Action emerged out of the action restraining breach of confidence, with the assistance of the Human Rights Act 1998, which 'brought home' the rights articulated in the ECHR. Chapter 4 considers the rationale and underpinning of privacy law, drawing on: (i) the seminal article by Warren and Brandeis;[61] (ii) cognate areas of law like copyright and trespass; (iii) human rights and data protection law; and (iv) the protection accorded to privacy in the United States. Chapter 5 considers the same terrain from the economic perspective, setting out the economic justification for a proprietary regime regarding private information.

[1.64] Chapter 9 considers undertakings and the law of privacy. It is probably the most intractable chapter in the book, but also one of the most important. As will be seen, information is defined in Chapter 3 as the *perception* of something private about A. In other words, in contrast to all tangible property and some intangible property, A's property exists in the mind of another (a person within the universe of O, referred to as O(C)[62]) without A necessarily being conscious of this at all. For example, O(C) may covertly spy on A. Obviously, A will have no knowledge of this. From this covert spying, O(C) derives a *perception* of A that is private to A. This, it will be contended, is *private information*. The consequence of defining information about A as O(C)'s *perception* of A is that only a human being (a natural person) can infringe A's privacy, apparently leaving Google and Meta and all other corporates free to do what they will without fear of action from A.[63] That is not the law, but until Chapter 8 the discussion will focus on O, C and O(C) as consisting only of natural persons (aka human beings). The liability of undertakings (U) is left to Chapter 8, when the other aspects of A's Action have sufficiently been unpacked and understood.

[1.65] Chapter 10 focuses on aspects of practice and procedure – what A must show to bring a claim, and how a defendant may best defend themselves. Chapter 10 also considers the question of remedies, should A's claim prove to be effective. Any lawyer seeking to frame a claim on behalf of A, or defend against

[61] See n 1.
[62] This particular label – a combination of O and C – will be described in due course. It is not a very pretty label, but it is needed.
[63] This is the problem adverted to in para [1.40].

A's claim, would be well advised to start with Chapter 10: as and when necessary (and this is frequently so) this chapter refers back to the analysis in previous chapters. However, like the rest of this book, an attempt has been made to make this chapter accessible to (and, hopefully, even interesting to) the lay reader. For this reason, although Chapter 10 might have been an extremely long chapter if it aimed to resolve every practitioner question, an effort has been made to focus on the critical points of process, leaving the really technical stuff to other books. This is a monograph, not a treatise.

[1.66] Chapter 11 deals with another intractable question, the question of *exploitation* of private information. How can A monetise their rights? By what means can A avoid – through the deployment, by others, of widely drafted permissions – effectively giving away their private information by signing up to the standard form contract or licence in a software agreement on a mobile phone or computer? Or when subscribing to Facebook or X? Or when using an Internet search engine like Google? This is – in terms of how our privacy is taken away from us – perhaps the most important part of the book. Fairfield refers to the use of contractual licences to 'trump' property rights as the new 'digital serfdom', and he has a point. One of the important themes in this book is that English law at least has given us an escape from 'digital serfdom'. Fairfield's articulation of the problem – although based on a description of United States law – resonates in this jurisdiction:[64]

> Perhaps, like me, you read Joseph Heller's *Catch-22* in high school. In this book about impossible choices during World War II, a pilot could be excused from flying combat missions if he were mentally unfit, but any pilot who did not want to fly was by definition mentally fit. It's a double-bind: colloquially, 'damned if you do, damned if you don't'. That's where the owners of smart and digital property are now. Copyright law and anti-hacking law – the RAM copy doctrine[65] and section 1201 of the Digital Millenium Copyright Act among them – play a large part in this double-bind, but the ties that bind them are contract law. To use our property, we have to sign contracts that give up key rights and ownership interests.
>
> Here's how it works: you have to sign a stack of contracts just to activate a device. When you bring your new device home from the store and power it up for the first time, you are presented with a bunch of screens that ask you to agree to various terms and conditions. We don't read those terms and conditions. Nobody does and nobody could. But you have to agree to them. If you don't you are a copyright infringer. Remember, per the RAM copy doctrine, you made a copy of copyrighted material when you turned your device on – you loaded copyrighted material from storage into active memory. And if you made that copy without a licence – if you don't click 'I Agree' to the terms and conditions of the rightholder – then you've infringed copyright. More practically, if you don't agree, your device will turn into an expensive paperweight.

[64] Fairfield (n 3) 43–44.
[65] See ibid 28–30.

> So you hit 'I Agree' to avoid being a copyright infringer and to actually use your device. Why did you agree to? The contracts are different, but they have quite a few things in common. First, they state that you do not own the software that came with your device and that makes it run. You just licence it. The Copyright Act gives owners certain rights, including the right to make a copy of a computer program in order to use the machine. But when you click 'I Agree', you give up those ownership rights. As soon as you agree that you do not own what you have just bought, you open the door to all kinds of other controls by the manufacturer …

[**1.67**] Fairfield was writing relatively recently, in 2017. But to go back to the dawn of the third phase identified above at paragraph [1.9], Tapper, writing in 1982, is prescient:[66]

> The conventional analysis comprises five propositions. The first of these maintains that intrusions upon personal privacy are greater now than they have ever been before, and that they are increasing at an increasing rate. Secondly it is held that at least part of the blame for this deterioration must be ascribed to the development of modern technology, and especially to the application of computers to data processing which permits virtually instantaneous access to enormous quantities of information. The third proposition is that much of this information is inaccurate, goes unchecked, and worst of all is regarded by its users as being so far above suspicion as to be accepted as conclusive and unalterable evidence of whatever it asserts or suggests. Fourthly, it is feared that this information is available to anyone who wishes whether their access is authorised or unauthorised, open or clandestine, legal or illegal. And finally it is felt that what legal remedies there are have been left so far behind by the speed of technological change as to have become quite incapable of protecting the subject of the information.

One objective of this book is to suggest that Tapper's last proposition, whilst understandable, is unduly pessimistic. As stated, Chapter 11 is critical to an understanding of how our private information is (or is not) protected.

[**1.68**] Finally, Chapter 12 seeks to draw together the threads, and asks where we are going, as a society, in terms of information rights and privacy. As a society, we are very much in the third phase of information use, but (as ever) innovation races ahead of understanding and legal analysis. It was ever thus: the law is reactive to new developments. Although there are times when efforts are made to restrain innovation through the law, this tends simply to drive innovation elsewhere. Law should be reactive. But that reaction – at least in this jurisdiction – has been slow and not necessarily understanding of the true issues and problems and opportunities that we face. These issues, problems and opportunities both, are the subject of Chapter 12.

[66] C Tapper, *Computer Law*, 2nd edn (Longman, 1982) 118–19.

2

The New Cause of Action of Misuse of Private Information

In which: the origin of the action of misuse of private information (the 'Action', for short) is explored; the relationship between the Action and breach of confidence is considered; and the elements of the Action stated.

I. Transition from Breach of Confidence to Misuse of Private Information

[2.1] It is necessary to begin with a cause of action somewhat unrelated to the protection of private information, namely the action for breach of confidence. From that has sprung, aided by the law of human rights, a new and altogether distinct cause of action protecting private information. It is the characterisation and nature of this new cause of action – which (at least for the moment) subsists in addition to and not in substitution of the action for breach of confidence – with which this book is concerned.[1]

II. The Elements of the Original Cause of Action

[2.2] The action for breach of confidence originally protected confidential information and not privacy. As *Gurry* notes, 'the action for breach of confidence enables any person who has an interest in information that is confidential to prevent others who have received, or acquired, the information with notice of its confidential quality from using or disclosing the information'.[2]

[1] As will be seen, it is perfectly possible for the action for breach of confidence to be subsumed into the action against misuse of private information. Whether that occurs very much depends on how far and how widely the new tort is used.

[2] T Aplin et al, *Gurry on Breach of Confidence*, 2nd edn (Oxford University Press, 2012) [1.01].

The cause of action classically requires three elements to be established by the claimant:[3]

(1) that the information is confidential;
(2) that the defendant is under an obligation to the claimant not to use or disclose the information;[4]
(3) that the defendant has used or disclosed, or proposes to use or disclose, the information in breach of the obligation.

[2.3] Because an obligation of confidence may arise independently of contract, the remedy of damages where a defendant has used or disclosed confidential information is not uncontroversially available to a claimant.[5] Partly because damages are not necessarily the best remedy, and partly because damages might not be available, the primary remedy for breach of confidence was seen as the injunction.[6]

[2.4] The last element to be raised is a defence: it may be open to a defendant to justify disclosure – for example, it may be said that disclosure is in the public interest.

III. Juridical Basis

[2.5] Damages is an uncertain remedy for breach of confidence because of the uncertain juridical basis of the cause of action. If – which will not be the case every time – the cause of action were founded on contract, then the scope of the action would be greatly limited, as a contract between A and B would be required in every case. But the question of the availability of damages as a remedy would be easy to answer. The primary remedy for breach of contract is damages. As it is, the position is far less certain:[7]

> The jurisdictional basis of the action for breach of confidence has been a source of lingering uncertainty and controversy. Contract, equity, and property have at different times each provided the basis on which the courts have granted relief and, in some cases, a mixture of these has been relied on. This situation has been regarded as unsatisfactory and as evidence of conceptual confusion on the part of the courts.

[3] These are helpfully set out in summary in *Gurry* (n 2) [1.02].

[4] Although the words 'to the claimant' are not normally stressed, they are important: unless the claimant can show an obligation owed to them, an otherwise perfectly good claim will fail for lack of standing.

[5] See *Gurry* (n 2) Ch 19 and in particular [19.01]–[19.02] and [19.41]–[19.42] as regards claims for compensation under the Human Rights Act 1998.

[6] ibid Ch 18 and in particular [18.01].

[7] ibid [4.01].

[2.6] The juridical bases for the action have variously been described as contract, equity, property and tort.[8] This book is not particularly concerned with the precise characterisation of *this* cause of action, but it is of interest that – without there being a clear statement that information is property – the cause of action of breach of confidence has, at times, been said to have a basis in property law.[9] *Gurry* notes that '[t]he status of the property basis must … be regarded as highly uncertain'.[10] That is surely right so far as 'information' generally is concerned, for information is not generally regarded as property.[11] What is now clear is that the cause of action is classified, as a matter of English law, as a tortious one.[12] That renders damages the default remedy, with the injunction available in an appropriate case.

IV. Redefinition: The Case Law

[2.7] It has long been recognised that the cause of action of breach of confidence has been undergoing 'a process of redefinition'.[13] There has been a shift in the centre of gravity of the cause of action causing it to protect informational privacy rather than confidential information.

[2.8] Although, as recently as 1991, English law did not recognise a right to privacy as such,[14] through the intervention of the Human Rights Act 1998 the position at common law has significantly moved on.[15] The action of breach of

[8] ibid Ch 4.

[9] ibid [4.74]–[4.108].

[10] ibid [4.108].

[11] In this book, a somewhat equivocal approach is taken towards confidential information. The action for breach of confidence continues to exist in English law, but has now been supplemented by the Action. There is a good argument for saying that 'private information' that is protected by the Action *includes* confidential information protected by breach of confidence. If this overlap exists, then breach of confidence's days are numbered, and the tort (as it is now recognised to be) will be subsumed into the Action. But it is too early at the moment to say that this has happened. At present, there are two distinct causes of action, which have a close relationship and almost certainly overlap.

[12] See eg *Campbell v MGM Ltd* [2004] UKHL 22; *Vidal-Hall v Google Inc* [2015] EWCA Civ 311.

[13] To quote from *Gurry* (n 2) [1.03].

[14] *Kaye v Robertson* [1991] FSR 62.

[15] Essentially, privacy was previously a value that was protected by ways other than the Action. In *Wainright v Home Office* [2003] UKHL 53 at [31], Lord Hoffmann suggested that this was a good thing: 'There seems to me a very great difference between identifying privacy as a value which underlies the existence of a rule of law (and may point the direction in which the law should develop) and privacy as a principle of law in itself. The English common law is familiar with the notion of underlying values – principles only in the broadest sense – which direct its development. A famous example is … freedom of speech [as an] … underlying value … But no one has suggested that freedom of speech is in itself a legal principle which is capable of sufficient definition to enable one to deduce specific rules to be applied in concrete cases. That is not the way the common law works.' Although Lord Hoffmann's point that values inform rights is well made, the suggestion that the common law does not align values with rights so that one directly informs the other is to be deprecated. The Action is an example where values and rights align.

confidence has evolved so that it no longer merely protects 'confidential' information arising out of a 'relationship of confidence' but protects privacy even where no relationship of confidence exists or where the information could not (under the 'old' law) be characterised as confidential.[16]

[2.9] In *A v B plc*,[17] it was recognised that '[s]ince the coming into force of the [Human Rights Act] there has been an increase in the number of actions in which injunctions are being sought to protect the claimants from the publication of articles in newspapers on the grounds that the articles contain confidential information concerning the claimants, the publication of which, it is alleged, would infringe their privacy'.[18] Lord Woolf CJ recognised the effect of the Human Rights Act 1998 on established common law causes of action:[19]

> The applications for interim injunctions have now to be considered in the context of Articles 8 and 10 of the European Convention on Human Rights. These articles have provided new parameters within which the court will decide, in an action for breach of confidence, whether a person is entitled to have his privacy protected by the court or whether the restriction of freedom of expression which such protection involves cannot be justified. The court's approach to the issues which the applications raise has been modified because, under section 6 of the [Human Rights Act], the court, as a public authority, is required not to act 'in a way which is incompatible with a Convention right'. The court is able to achieve this by absorbing the rights which Articles 8 and 10 protect into the long-established action for breach of confidence. This involves giving a new strength and breadth to the action so that it accommodates the requirements of those articles.

[2.10] In effect, Article 8 of the ECHR 'operates so as to extend the areas in which an action for breach of confidence can provide protections for privacy'.[20] A duty of confidence will arise whenever the party subject to that duty is in a situation where he either knows or ought to know that the other person can reasonably expect his privacy to be protected'.[21]

[2.11] In *Campbell v MGN*,[22] Lord Nicholls noted that whilst this jurisdiction did not have any 'over-arching, all embracing, cause of action for invasion

[16] S Warren and L Brandeis, 'The Right to Privacy' (1890) 4 *Harvard Law Review* 193 at 193 refer to: 'Political, social, and economic changes entail the recognition of new rights, and the common law, in its eternal youth, grows to meet the demands of society'. There is an excellent summary of how the law has developed in regard to the protection of the individual at 193–95. In this case, the common law required a kick-start from the Human Rights Act 1998, but the development of the law is nonetheless one for which the common law can take the credit.

[17] *A v B plc* [2002] EWCA Civ 337.

[18] ibid [3].

[19] ibid [4].

[20] ibid [6].

[21] ibid [11(ix)].

[22] *Campbell v MGN* [2004] UKHL 22.

of privacy',[23] protection of 'various aspects of privacy is a fast developing area of the law, here and in some other common law jurisdictions'.[24] Lord Nicholls recognised that the English law cause of action for breach of confidence had moved far from its roots:[25]

> The breach of confidence label harks back to the time when the cause of action was based on improper use of information disclosed by one person to another in confidence. To attract protection the information had to be of a confidential nature. But the gist of the cause of action was that information of this character had been disclosed by one person to another in circumstances 'importing an obligation of confidence' even though no contract of non-disclosure existed …

[2.12] The law now imposed a duty of confidence 'whenever a person receives information he knows or ought to know is fairly and reasonably to be regarded as confidential'.[26] As Lord Nicholls recognised, this formulation is 'awkward': the reference to confidentiality 'is not altogether comfortable'.[27] He said:[28]

> Information about an individual's private life would not, in ordinary usage, be called 'confidential'. The more natural description today is that such information is private. The essence of the tort is better encapsulated now as misuse of private information.

[2.13] Lord Nicholls endorsed the approach of Lord Woolf CJ in *A v B plc*,[29] as did Lady Hale.[30] Lady Hale saw the parameters of the tort as defined by the balancing of rights under Article 8 and Article 10 of the ECHR.[31] She framed the threshold of the tort as follows:[32]

> It should be emphasised that the 'reasonable expectation of privacy' is a threshold test which brings the balancing exercise into play. It is not the end of the story. Once the information is identified as 'private' in this way, the court must balance the claimant's interest in keeping the information private against the countervailing interest of the recipient in publishing it. Very often, it can be expected that the countervailing rights of the recipient will prevail.

[2.14] As will be described, the Action does not involve 'balancing' in the way Lady Hale says. Such weighing of factors is more common in the public law

[23] ibid [11].
[24] ibid [11].
[25] ibid [13]. It had 'changed its nature': [14].
[26] ibid [14].
[27] ibid [14]. This is a point that is returned to below. The language of confidentiality does not capture the extent to which English law now protects privacy. Private information is not necessarily confidential information and vice versa.
[28] ibid [14].
[29] ibid [17].
[30] ibid [132].
[31] ibid [132] and [134].
[32] ibid [137].

area, where the law of human rights is most active. The thesis in this book is that A's ability to protect their private information is a *right* capable of being enforced without 'balancing' other values, but where the extent of that right, or its ambit, is circumscribed by the existence of countervailing rights and interests. This may be no more than a re-framing of Lady Hale's 'balancing' exercise, but it is an important re-framing because it moves the law on from the apparently rather subjective approach that Lady Hale appears to be advocating, to a rights-based approach, where the owners of private information have an asset that they can protect or exploit or transfer as they choose. The question ceases to be one of 'balancing' and becomes one of articulating the extent or ambit of A's property rights.

[2.15] In *Vidal-Hall v Google Inc*,[33] the Court of Appeal had to consider whether the cause of action for 'misuse of private information' was a tort for private international law jurisdictional purposes. The Court of Appeal noted that this was the first case where the question of classification actually mattered, in terms of making a difference to outcome.[34] An appropriately detailed consideration of the law was therefore undertaken, including in particular whether breach of confidence and privacy constituted two distinct causes of action. The Court stated:[35]

> Actions for breach of confidence and actions for misuse of private information rest on different legal foundations. As Lord Nicholls said, they protect different interests: secret or confidential information on the one hand and privacy on the other. In the *Campbell* case, [2004] 2 AC 457, [51], Lord Hoffmann described the 'shift in the centre of gravity' when the action for breach of confidence was used as a remedy for the unjustified publication of personal information. In those circumstances, he said, the focus was not on the duty of good faith applicable to confidential personal information and trade secrets alike, but the protection of human autonomy and dignity – the right to control the dissemination of information about one's private life and the right to the esteem and respect of other people.

[2.16] The Court concluded that the Action – an offspring of breach of confidence, now fully-grown and independent – was a tort:[36]

> Against this background, we cannot find any satisfactory or principled answer to the question why misuse of private information should not be categorised as a tort for the purposes of service out of the jurisdiction. Misuse of private information is a civil wrong without any equitable characteristics. We do not need to attempt to define a

[33] *Vidal-Hall v Google Inc* [2015] EWCA Civ 311.

[34] ibid [17].

[35] ibid [25].

[36] ibid [43]. For the lay reader, the law of obligations is to be differentiated from the law of property. The law of obligations has three subject-matter areas: (i) contract; (ii) tort; and (iii) restitution. Confusingly, most property rights are protected by causes of action that are classed as torts: see further Ch 9, Section I on 'proprietary torts'.

tort here. But if one puts aside the circumstances of its 'birth', there is nothing in the nature of the claim itself to suggest that the more natural classification of it as a tort is wrong.

[2.17] The significance of the move away from the need to show a pre-existing relationship of confidence – such that a claim can be brought by a claimant against a defendant where there is no such pre-existing relationship – is enormous. A pre-existing relationship, even if it is not contractual, implies a bilateral relationship between A and B with all the hallmarks of *in personam* rights and obligations. By contrast, a claim that can be brought without such a pre-existing requirement is suggestive of a move away from the *in personam* towards the *in rem*.[37]

V. A Restatement of the Present Legal Position

[2.18] There is a great deal about this 'new' Action that will have to be explored in the chapters that follow, most notably the meaning of 'information' and the meaning of 'private'. Before moving on to these difficult questions, the following preliminary points can be stated:

- It is now misleading to refer to the cause of action of breach of confidence when considering questions of privacy or private information. Although the cause of action of breach of confidence remains (and remains important for the protection of confidential information), that cause of action is only of historical interest when considering the 'new' cause of action of misuse of private information (ie the Action). The relationship between breach of confidence and the Action is a difficult one, because the law is still evolving. There is a great deal to be said for breach of confidence to be subsumed into the Action, and that may happen – but it has not happened yet.
- The Action is a tort. It is a 'proprietary tort',[38] existing to protect A's property interests in their private information. It is a cause of action conferred on the owner of a particular sort of property: private information.
- The Action thus centres on the protection of privacy, protecting of a person's 'reasonable expectation of privacy'. The ambit of the Action is the subject matter of this book and is explored in the following chapters.

[37] It is important not to overstate matters: the point is suggestive only, because exactly the same point (the absence of a pre-existing relationship) can be made as regards a personal injury claim. Even here, however, there needs to be a 'duty of care' which creates some kind of inchoate relationship between defendant and claimant.

[38] See Ch 10, Section II for a discussion of this.

3

The Nature of Information

In which: the nature of 'information' is considered, and the contention advanced that information is best defined by reference to the person who perceives it, and that information is in fact perception in the mind of C. The implications of this thesis are unpacked, and the distinction between (i) perception, (ii) use and (iii) misuse stressed.

I. An Equivocal Categorisation in English Law

[3.1] Whether information can be regarded as property has most often been considered in the context of confidential information which, as has been seen, is protected by the action against the abuse of confidential information.[1] The status of information as property under English law is entirely equivocal. In the 'Spycatcher' case, *Attorney-General v Guardian Newspapers Ltd*,[2] Lord Goff stated:

> I have … deliberately avoided the fundamental question whether, contract apart, the duty lies simply 'in the notion of an obligation of conscience arising from the circumstances in or through which the information was communicated or obtained' … or whether confidential information may also be regarded as property …
>
> The question is difficult for two reasons. The first is because of the large body of conflicting case law. The second is because of the inherent flexibility of the notion of property in English law. As such, the legal status of confidential information returns us to a more fundamental question: what are the limits of the English concept of property?

[3.2] This is not a helpful way of considering the question. *Of course* property is a flexible concept, as the discussions regarding recently evolving forms of property like non-fungible tokens demonstrate.[3] It helps no-one to assert the

[1] Described in Ch 2.

[2] [1990] 1 AC 109, 281.

[3] Tokens are by definition fungible, and so the notion of a 'non-fungible token' (NFTs) is a contradiction. The point about NFTs is that something that is not scarce (eg a digital image, that can be replicated at practically no marginal cost) is rendered scarce and individuated and is given (as a result) particular status as property. E Bonadio and C Sganga (eds), *NFTs, Creativity and the Law: Within and Beyond Copyright* (Routledge, 2024) at 3–4 explain this as follows: 'Let's try to

platitude that the notion of property in English law is 'inherently flexible'. It is necessary to examine the subject matter that may or may not be property; consider the policy questions that arise; and decide, having regard to the nature of the subject matter, the law already determined and these policy questions, what the status of that subject matter is.

II. Information as Property?

A. The scope of inquiry

[3.3] The equivocal classification of information in English law has already been noted. In these paragraphs, some very general points are made regarding information as property, as a foundation on which to build further:

- Neither confidential information nor information generally is property in the legal sense. This is not only a statement of what appears to be the position under English law. It is also a reflection of the fact that neither information nor confidential information appear to have the necessary attributes to render them property. In other words, even if a legislator were to seek to enact a law rendering information or confidential information property, that would be an outcome that would be extremely hard to achieve on a technical level.
- By contrast, it is suggested that private information has the necessary attributes for 'reification' (to render a thing, as a matter of law, property). It is

answer this question looking at a well-known example in postmodern art: imagine that you are presented with the two pictures in Figure 1.1. One is Walker Evan's *Alabama Tenant Farmer Wife*, 1936; the other, Sherrie Levine's famous appropriation, *After Walker Evans: 4*, 1981. Now, without the signature(s) you won't be able to know which one is the original and which one is the copy, that is, they will be fungible, interchangeable. In fact, the two pictures could be copies of Evan's work, or of Levine's. What makes them unique, both, is their signatures – as, you might argue, the digital signature of an NFT. So, we are back to square one. Now, the signature "Walker Evan, Alabama Tenant Farmer Wife, 1936" is just an alphanumeric sequence. Granted, in the blockchain a digital signature is truly unique, in that nobody can reproduce it …, unlike Evan's signature, that can be easily forged; yet the point is that the value doesn't lie in the sequence of characters as such but rather in the artistic and exchange value assigned by the art world to such signature. In fact, the photographs will come with their corresponding certificates proving ownership and provenance. This should not be so strange: there are billions of footballs, yet one signed by Messi will have more value than any other football. It is the signature what makes that particular ball valuable, but only if authenticated. Pablo Picasso used to pay even the most trivial goods and services by cheque, knowing that the cheque, as a traceable container of his signature, will be more valuable than the amount on it.' Ultimately, the driver of the value of non-fungibility is the value attached to that differentiator by the demand of buyers. A football signed by Messi will be more valuable than an unsigned ball; a football signed by me will probably damage the value. A tin of baked beans will have their value augmented by a Messi signature, but if I sign it, its value will probably not diminish, because people do not care about the can. The point is that the law will attach consequences to non-fungibility that *matters* and will attach no consequences to non-fungibility that does *not* matter, preferring to treat the latter as a fungible product, recognising that fungibility is rarely absolute.

also suggested that, under English law as it stands, private information *is* property.

[3.4] These are controversial propositions. The status of private information as property is the subject of this book; and is explored over the coming chapters. It is helpful at this stage to consider why information generally, and confidential information in particular, do not constitute property in law. That is the topic of the next few paragraphs.

B. Is confidential information property?

[3.5] The attributes of confidential information render it unsuitable to be properly classified as property. That is for a number of reasons:[4]

- Confidential information is almost by definition ephemeral, whereas property is enduring. Confidentiality can be lost, and it would be odd if a property right in confidential information could endure beyond the existence of the confidentiality itself. Equally, it would be odd if something ceased to be property because it had ceased to be confidential.
- Confidentiality tends to depend upon an individual relationship between the provider of the information (the confidor) and the recipient of the information (the confidee), which implies an *in personam* obligation owed by B to A, not an *in rem* obligation owed contingently by O to A.
- Where a third party receives the confidential information, it does not axiomatically follow that that this party is subject to an obligation of confidence. Although obligations of confidence can bind third parties, that is the exception and not the rule: another indicator that confidential information per se is not property because it is clearly not protected by an *in rem* proprietary tort.[5]

In short, confidential information is – given its nature – best not regarded as property.

C. Information generally?

[3.6] Information generally cannot be property. Logically, this must follow from the conclusion just expressed with regard to confidential information. If confidential information is not property, then it must follow that information generally, which includes the class known as 'confidential information', cannot

[4] See M Smith and N Leslie, *The Law of Assignment*, 3rd edn (Oxford University Press, 2018) [7.111].

[5] See further para [2.6] and Ch 10, Section II.

in and of itself be property. That does not mean that other, specific, subsets of 'information' cannot be property, even if the subset known as 'confidential information' is not.

[3.7] Given the breadth of matters embraced by the notion 'information', it would be extraordinary if all information could be classed as someone's property. That, indeed, is the problem: 'information' is so ill-defined a concept that it is not possible to understand how a property right in favour of A could be carved out of something so hazy and fluid. The problem is that there is no understanding of what 'information' actually is. From this it follows that until a working definition of 'information' is articulated, it is difficult to reach any view on how *categories* of information (like 'private' information) are to be defined and then treated.

III. The Definition of 'Information'

A. The importance of information

[3.8] Given its centrality, it is surprising that whilst the *importance* of information is stressed in many works, information itself is rarely *defined*.[6] Dictionary definitions describe information as *fact* and/or as *perception of fact*. Does an unread book contain 'information'? Or does the content of the book only become information when received into the mind of the reader? It is not going to be suggested here that the first of these definitions ('information as *fact*') is wrong. But the second is no less valid ('information as *perception of fact*'), and this book very much nails its colours to the *perception* mast.

[3.9] We speak of something as being a 'closed book'. That is a nice way of capturing information as the relationship between an objective circumstance, the content of the book, and the reader's *perception* of that content. Suppose Reader 1 (a native reader) reads and completely understands the content of a book, whereas Reader 2 (reading in a language foreign to them) has a different and defective understanding, whilst Reader 3 (unable to read in this language at all) can only perceive the quality of the book's binding and print, without understanding more. The book is the same in the case of each reader. But the information vesting in the minds of Readers 1, 2 and 3 is different, and is subjective to them. Hence, information as perception.

[6] This is even where information is being treated in some detail: see eg P Birkinshaw, *Freedom of Information*, 4th edn (Cambridge University Press, 2010) 8–10; A Stone and F Schauer, *The Oxford Handbook of Freedom of Speech* (Oxford University Press, 2021). There are exceptions: see C Véliz, *The Ethics of Privacy and Surveillance* (Oxford University Press, 2024) (quoted in Ch 1, n 25); and A Sinnreich and J Gilbert, *The Secret Life of Data* (MIT Press, 2024) (quoted in Ch 1 n 65).

[3.10] We will be coming back to the terms 'information', 'perception' and 'use' repeatedly in this book. Much of what is said throughout this work repre sents a process of refinement arising out of an attempt to understand precisely how 'information as property' works.

[3.11] The importance of information is something of a recurrent theme of this book. It is appropriate to articulate some of the reasons why information matters, in order to assist in grappling with that which is being defined.

i. Informing freedom of expression

[3.12] Freedom of expression is a human right articulated in Article 10 of the ECHR:[7]

> (1) Everyone has the right of freedom of expression. This right shall include freedom to hold opinions and *to receive and impart information without interference by public authority and regardless of frontiers*. This article shall not prevent States from requiring the licensing of broadcasting, television or cinema enterprises.
> (2) The exercise of these freedoms, since it carries with it duties and responsibilities, may be subject to such formalities, conditions, restrictions or penalties as are prescribed by law and are necessary in a democratic society, in the interests of national security, territorial integrity or public safety, for the prevention of disorder or crime, for the protection of health or morals, for the protection of the reputation or rights of others, for preventing the disclosure of information received in confidence, or for maintaining the authority nd impartiality of the judiciary.

[3.13] Without information, freedom of expression is an empty, even a vacuous, notion. It might be said that much of art and literature can or could be expressed without using information. But it certainly cannot be said that art and literature operate in a vacuum, in isolation from information. The need is even greater when other forms of expression (eg the political; the academic) are considered. The point is often made – most explicitly in the context of political discourse[8] but the point holds good generally – that there is a nexus between information and freedom of expression:[9]

> The importance of the informing function of freedom of expression to contemporary democracy is underscored by Article 10 ECHR, which provides that freedom of expression shall include freedom 'to receive and impart information without interference by public authority'. This crucial democratic free speech function can usefully be divided into three categories: (1) expression that informs the electorate so that people can 'vote wise decisions'; (2) expression that informs speakers so that they

[7] Emphasis added.
[8] R Brescia, *The Private is Political* (New York University Press, 2025).
[9] Stone and Schauer (n 6) 90–92, quoting from 90.

can knowledgably participate in public discourse; and (3) expression that informs representatives of the views of the electorate.

ii. Buttressing transparency and accountability

[3.14] It has been said that:[10]

> Freedom of speech has been recognised as 'a necessary condition for the realisation of the principles of transparency and accountability that are, in turn, essential for the promotion and protection of human rights'. For example, the need to protect whistle-blowers has been recognised. The ECtHR has long confirmed that 'the signalling by an employee in the public sector of illegal conduct or wrong-doing in the workplace should, in certain circumstances, enjoy protection …'

[3.15] Information is necessary to report wrongdoing and irregularity, and constraints on this ability to use information serve to limit the effectiveness of transparency and accountability regimes. Provided the term 'whistleblower' is understood to refer not just to employees in the public sector, but to all persons acting bona fide in reporting material matters to the relevant public authority, then the importance of information in buttressing transparency and accountability can be readily understood.

iii. Facilitating the operation of markets

[3.16] Information is of fundamental importance to the operation of markets, both in terms of information that *should* be communicated and information that should *not* be communicated. The distinction between providing and withholding information is the most fundamental issue underlying cartel infringements: under what circumstances can competitors properly and lawfully share information?[11] Information also plays a key role in enabling markets to function efficiently, in particular in terms of deriving a proper price.[12] Whilst price is itself an important information source (and so may be kept confidential),[13] information apart from price more generally serves to lubricate markets and make them better functioning, as well as actually informing price.[14] Market data bleeds into advertising. Advertising is also a form of

[10] Stone and Schauer (n 6) 200.

[11] M Gassler, *Information Exchange between Competitors in EU Competition Law* (Wolters Kluwer, 2021).

[12] A 'proper' price quite fundamentally depends upon the proper control of information. That is why 'insider dealing' is so damaging – it enables a market participant illegitimately to exploit an informational advantage. The problem is that some forms of informational advantage are legitimate.

[13] As to the function of price as a form of information, see M Friedman, *Price Theory* (Routledge, 2017) 9–10.

[14] Stone and Schauer (n 6) 128–30. See also Stone and Schauer (n 6) Ch 24, on free speech and commercial advertising. One of the key aspects of commercial advertising is informing the demand side of a market.

information, whereby buyers and sellers are connected and, more insidiously, buyers are encouraged to spend money to acquire products.[15]

iv. Encouraging innovation

[3.17] Information is central to innovation. As Newton famously said to Hooke in 1675, '... if I have seen further, it is by standing on the shoulders of giants ...': it is the inherited wisdom – information – that facilitates progress, both by securing its publication and by protecting it from publication. Thus, in the well-known 'patent bargain',[16] an inventor publishes the details of their invention, obtaining thereby a limited monopoly over the invention. Equally, where a commercial undertaking seeks to keep trade secrets secret, the law will (within limits) assist.[17]

v. National security and the interests of the state

[3.18] National security and public/state interest are relevant to information in two ways:

(1) Often national security and the public interest involve the *withholding* of *important* information from the rest of the world, including how that information is used. This aspect does not give rise to particular privacy questions because such matters tend to be protected by specific legislation and not the general law of privacy.
(2) On the other hand, the state will often *compel* the production of information from citizens or private individuals. Where that information consists of the private information of others, there is a tension between the interests of the state and the interests of the individual.[18] Again, there will usually be a statutory right to obtain the information, but the law of privacy is engaged where that right is abused – in other words, where information that may be demanded for one purpose, is used for another (which is the essence of *misuse*).

[15] Advertising is a hugely significant economic matter, largely unrecognised by economic theory. See D Davies, *The Unaccountability Machine* (Profile Bools, 2024) 159–60: 'These features of modelling strategy generate detectable blind spots. The concentration on single-value maximisation, for example, is one of the reasons why there is no particularly useful theory of advertising. Advertising is a big industry, and an important activity of firms, and yet economics not only has hardly anything to say about it, it has no real explanation of why it exists at all. Advertising and marketing, despite their obvious importance to businesses in the real world, produce and use a different kind of information from the price and quantity signals which the model can handle.'

[16] See, for example, *Optis Cellular Technologies LLC v Apple Retail UK Ltd* [2023] EWHC 1095 (Ch), [4]–[5].

[17] Through the tort of the protection of confidential information and the Action.

[18] See Stone and Schauer (n 6) 209–211; Birkinshaw (n 6) Ch 2.

vi. Public order, public decency, reputation, etc

[3.19] As Article 10 of the ECHR makes clear, freedom of speech and so potentially the communication and receipt of information may be limited for the protection of morals, or reputation or the rights of others, and there are well-known public order/terrorism offences which limit the ability to communicate information.

[3.20] It will be clear from the foregoing paragraphs that the term 'information' is being used in both of the two ways articulated in paragraphs [3.8]–[3.9]. First, it can refer to substantive content – the book; second, it can refer to the perception of someone receiving the information, whatever its nature or content – the reader of the book. It is in the latter sense that the term 'information' is generally used in this book. The next paragraphs attempt to consider the various definitional possibilities and implications that arise out of this approach (eg information as objective fact; information as communication; information as perception).

B. Information as communication

[3.21] The moment information is defined by reference to some *qualitative* standard, control over information is ceded to whoever defines that standard, which will almost inevitably be some organ of the state.[19] Suppose information were defined by reference to some standard of accuracy or truth: it would follow from this that inaccurate or untruthful material would *not* be information and so would not benefit (or, at least, not benefit fully) from the protections conferred, for example, by Article 10 of the ECHR. Defining information in qualitative terms is, viewed from the standpoint of individual liberty, a fool's game that should be eschewed. The moment it is said that inaccurate or deceitful information is subject to a different form of regulation or control than accurate and truthful information, control is ceded to the entities of the state that define that which is (in)accurate and that which is (un)truthful, which will generally be the courts applying whatever the law in that area might be.[20]

[3.22] If information is to be defined by reference to non-qualitative standards, it follows that there is no point in seeking to parse or classify information by reference to standards of either objective or subjective truth.[21]

[19] Doubtless a combination of the executive, legislative and judicial functions.

[20] This is why 'subject matter' specific definitions of information are dangerous.

[21] Just to be clear what is meant by this: *subjective* truth is something X wrongly believes to be true or accurate. *Objective* truth is something that is true and accurate, whatever X may believe. A fundamental question is whether *anything* can be said to be objectively true. Fortunately, this intractable

This reference to 'truth' leads to a further question: is information to be limited to factual questions? Is information *fact*? That would render opinion something different to, and distinguishable from, information. This is an untenable distinction:

- It is a distinction that is impossible to draw. Suppose X says, 'My garden is 100 metres long' or 'That aircraft is an Airbus A380'. Are these statements of fact or statements of opinion? They are both: X is expressing their opinion on a question of fact. The garden may not be 100 metres long, even if X believes that to be the case; and the aircraft may look like an Airbus, but be a Boeing. In short, factual statements often have a significant loading of opinion, when the factual statement is unpacked. That is probably true of *all* factual statements.
- Some expressions of opinion appear to be 'pure' opinion, but are nevertheless articulating facts. If X says 'Modern art is tripe' or 'The *Mona Lisa* is the finest painting in The Louvre' then there is, in both of these statements, a subjectivity best described as non-factual or opinion, but nevertheless there will be a factual hinterland, from which the opinion extrapolates.[22]
- In one sense, *whatever* X says will be a statement of fact, if only a factual statement of what is, or may be, on X's mind.[23]

[3.23] The discussion of what information *is* suggests that information can be defined *as communication*, as where X communicates to Y, irrespective of what the subject matter might be. That is consistent with the implied definition of information in Article 10(1) of the ECHR, which refers to *receiving* and *imparting* information. Although not actually a definition of information, and in any event not intended as exhaustive, the sense of information as communication, where X imparts and Y receives information, appears to fall within the core meaning of information. The point that is being pressed is that *all* communication between X and Y, however engaged or disengaged with fact, is information. If X tells Y a secret fact, that is as much 'information' as if X were simply to say a breezy 'hello' to Y. The 'hello' conveys nothing by way of fact but can nevertheless tell Y a great deal. Y might, based upon the breezy 'hello', tell Z that X was in a good mood that morning.

question does not arise for consideration, because information is being defined by reference to non-qualitative terms.

[22] The second statement of X is mixed fact and opinion. The presence of the *Mona Lisa* in The Louvre is better classified as fact. But even the assertion that 'Modern art is tripe' is saying *something* factual about the characteristics of modern art. These instances underline the difficulty of differentiating between fact and opinion.

[23] X could be telling an untruth about their state of mind: but whilst that means that the statement is not of X's own perception, it does generate a perception in Y which, even if inaccurate, does not render it any less 'information'.

[3.24] It is therefore suggested, as a starting point to defining information, that *all communication* imparted by X and received by Y is 'information', irrespective of its content. The question is whether this is a sufficiently full and comprehensive definition of information. It will be suggested that it is not.[24] But it is a good starting point.

C. Information as perception

[3.25] There is no reason why information received or, better, perceived[25] by Y needs to have been imparted or otherwise communicated by X or indeed any human actor. The implied definition[26] in Article 10 of the ECHR of information as communication is dangerously narrow. Certainly information can be received by Y through the imparting of information by X to Y. But that is just one, narrow, aspect of the definition. Overemphasis on communication suggests that there is no information in play where X tries to communicate with Y, but fails to do so, as where Y fails to hear X or to understand X's meaning.[27] It is suggested that if information is regarded not as something *communicated* by X, but as something *perceived* by Y, matters become very much clearer.[28]

[3.26] There are many ways in which Y can receive information *other than* through the agency of X or any other human being. Einstein was not told by any person of the theory of relativity and that $E = mc^2$, but his perception of this fact (if it *is* a fact) surely cannot deprive it of the quality of information. This would still have been the case if Einstein had never communicated his theory to anyone else.

[3.27] Y can easily glean a great deal of information from the use of their own senses, without any intervention from any other human being. Where Y perceives water to be salty or a sunset to be beautiful, that is information: (i) even if Y does not convey these impressions to Z; and (ii) notwithstanding the fact that there has been no communication or involvement at all by an imparter of information like X.

[24] Dictionaries tend to define information in this (narrow) way. For example, the *Shorter Oxford English Dictionary* (1990 edn, selected more or less at random) defines information as 'something told; knowledge': see under 'information'.

[25] *Perceived* is the better term, because *received* implies some form of communication, whereas perception is Y's alone, howsoever it is derived.

[26] See para [3.12], where Art of the 10 ECHR is set out. The reference to 'receiving and imparting information' clearly *implies* communication, hence the suggestion that it is unsatisfactorily narrowly framed.

[27] The latter instance is particularly dangerous, because it brings us back to some sort of qualitative assessment of that which X is seeking to communicate to Y.

[28] See Véliz (n 6) 95–96, which consider the relationship between privacy and perception.

[3.28] If Y's perception of the water's saltiness or the sunset's beauty is information, then the following propositions follow:

- Information does not have to be communicated by one person to another in order for it to amount to information. In short, Y can hold information, even if that information has not been communicated to Y but arises out of the use of Y's senses and intellect.
- Information does not have to be used by Y in order to be information. Einstein's understanding of relativity and Y's appreciation of the beauty of sunset do not have to be communicated onwards by them in order for this material to constitute information.
- Information is neither subject matter constrained[29] nor qualitative.[30] But it must *convey* something to Y. Suppose Y opens a book in a language foreign to Y. Y may have all kinds of perceptions about the book – how lovely the binding is, and how strange the script – but the one thing Y will not perceive is the information actually contained in the book. On the other hand, Y_1, fluent in the language in which the book is written, will have perceptions based upon what the book teaches, and will have very different perceptions from Y. The same is true of a musical score: a non-musician will get much less out of the score than a musician, whose perception will be completely different.

On this basis, information is best defined as 'the perception of something within the mind of a human being'. Or, even more simply, as 'perception'.

[3.29] In this way, we lose the definitional shackles of: (i) a need for communication between X and Y; and (ii) a need for communication by Y to Z. The former is simply one way in which Y can perceive something: Y can equally well perceive matters through their own senses without communication from X, by interaction that does not involve communication from X. Similarly, communication of information from Y to Z involves the *use* of information but is not relevant to the definition *of* information. *Use* of information is an important parameter in the Action we are seeking to understand, which centres on the *misuse* of *private* information. But before 'use', 'misuse' and 'private' can be understood, 'information' itself needs to be defined.

[3.30] Taking the definition of information as *the perception of something within the mind of a human being*, it follows that the same event or circumstance – when perceived by multiple human actors – can generate multiple pieces of information in the mind of each such actor, and that these perceptions may not necessarily be the same. Indeed, it would be extraordinary if they

[29] Ie information can relate to anything.
[30] Ie information does not have to be objectively true.

were. Were Y and Z both to be the recipients of X's 'hello', Y might perceive X as cheery while Z might consider X to be morose. There is no need to work out which of these two perceptions is the 'better' or the 'more correct' for the purposes of understanding what is information. The answer is that *both* perceptions are equally information. When 60,000 Arsenal fans see their side concede a goal, there will be 60,000 different perceptions of that event,[31] all of them information. It also follows that perception cannot be incorrect, assuming Y is being honest about their perception. Y can certainly be *mistaken* in their perception, but that does not alter the fact that this is Y's perception.[32] When we come to consider the interplay between the Action (which constrains Y's ability to use their perception) and the law of defamation (which limits Y's ability to say defamatory false things about another), the problem of how to treat a misperception (that is, a perception in Y that is wrong) looms large.

IV. Definitional Consequences

A. The implications summarised

[3.31] To recap: information is that which is perceived by human beings directly through their senses or reasoned (directly or indirectly) from such inputs. Such information is stored or retained in human memory. Information can be entirely internal to the human being and does not depend for its existence on any form of external manifestation (eg communication) in order to *become* or *be* information. It is both necessary and sufficient for information to exist in the mind of the individual human being.[33]

[3.32] With this insight, we can revert to the relationship between claimant A, the holder of a (contingent) right not to have their private information misused, and O, the universe of persons against whom (assuming the

[31] Eg 'the goalscorer was off-side'; 'the goalkeeper could have done more to save the goal'; 'the strike by the goalscorer was amazing'.

[32] Sinnreich and Gilbert (n 6) 23–25 make the point that Galton, the father of both statistical thinking *and* eugenics, was right about the former and wrong about the latter. Yet both sets of perceptions were, at the time, hugely influential. Only the passage of time has rendered the errors in Galton's thinking plain.

[33] To draw from Steinbeck in *East of Eden*: 'Our species is the only creative species, and it has only one creative instrument, the individual mind and spirit of a man. Nothing was ever created by two men. There are no good collaborations, whether in music, in art, in poetry, in mathematics, in philosophy. Once the miracle of creation has taken place, the group can build and extend it, but the group never invents anything. The preciousness lies in the lonely mind of a man.'

contingencies for bringing an Action are satisfied) A might bring a claim. A number of points can be made. These are listed here and then expanded upon below:

(1) It is clear that the members of the universe O can only be human beings ('natural' persons) and *cannot* be 'legal' persons.
(2) The Action controls misuse of information, not perception.
(3) It is necessary to introduce a new character in our *dramatis personae*: O(C).

B. Universe O comprises natural persons only

[3.33] This point has already been made at paragraph [1.40], but without an explanation as to why it is true. Now that 'information' has been defined as perception, it is obvious that 'legal' persons cannot – without more – be defendants to A's claim, because 'legal' persons cannot *perceive*. Perception is a uniquely human attribute and if information is perception, then it follows that a human being is required to perceive it. It follows that the universe of people belonging to O can *only* be human beings (ie natural persons).

[3.34] That does not mean that legal persons get a 'free pass' to abuse our private information. That is the other point made at paragraph [1.40]. Legal persons *are* exposed to a claim by A, but the *manner* in which they are exposed to liability is a complexity considered separately in Chapter 9. The analysis of the Action is best undertaken considering the rights and obligations between natural persons *first*. In other words, we are beginning with the easier case, before layering on complexity.

C. The action controls misuse of information not perception

i. *Freedom of thought: Perceiving information without using it*

[3.35] One implication of the thesis advanced in this book is that A has rights over C's *perceptions*. That is significantly invasive. It is correspondingly important to appreciate the distinction between A having rights and those rights having been infringed by C.

[3.36] Take the case of trespass over land. A owns the land and C, not trespassing, gazes wistfully over A's property and wishes they could go for a walk over it. A cannot sue C for trespass. But A's rights exist nonetheless. They become *capable of vindication* the moment C infringes (by walking over the land) or threatens to infringe (by showing an immediate determination to enter

A's land).[34] The same is true of the distinction drawn in this book between *perception* and *use*. C may very well perceive A's private information, but that involves no infringement of A's rights as owner. Even where C *uses* that perception it is not *necessarily* the case that C is infringing, for the Action differentiates between use and misuse. C is only liable to A for the *misuse* of A's private information.

[3.37] It is very important that C's freedom of perception be protected. Article 9 of the ECHR provides:

> (1) Everyone has the right to freedom of thought, conscience and religion; this right includes the right to change his religion or belief and freedom, either alone or in community with others and in public or private to manifest his religion or belief, in worship, teaching, practice and observance.
> (2) Freedom to manifest one's religion or beliefs shall be subject only to such limitations as are prescribed by law and are necessary in a democratic society in the interests of public safety, for the protection of public order, health or morals, or for the protections of the rights and freedoms of others.

Article 9(1) contains an *absolute* protection of freedom of thought, conscience and religion. The *manifestation* of thought, religion or belief is also protected, though that protection is not absolute, but qualified. That is clear from Article 9(2).

[3.38] Article 9 of the ECHR thus reflects a fundamental distinction that is drawn in this monograph, namely the distinction between the *perception* of information on the one hand and its *use* on the other. The Action that A can bring against C is triggered *not* by C's perception of A's private information, but by C's misuse of A's private information. The concepts of *misuse* and what constitutes *private* information both still need to be unpacked,[35] but the fact that the Action does not constrain perception is a point that can be made without having to understand the concepts of *misuse* and what constitutes *private* information.

[3.39] There is an obvious and critical distinction to be drawn between information vesting *unused* in the mind of C and C's *use* of that information. This distinction is clearly made by Bury:[36]

> It is a common saying that thought is free. A man can never be hindered from thinking whatever he chooses so long as he conceals what he thinks. The working of his

[34] Rights can exist without being capable of vindication, but the converse does not hold true. A right capable of vindication must exist.

[35] The nature of *private* information is considered in Ch 6; the nature of *misuse* is considered in Ch 7.

[36] JB Bury, *A History of Freedom of Thought* (Williams and Norgate, 1913) 7–8.

> mind is limited only by the bounds of his experience and the power of his imagination. But this natural liberty of private thinking is of little value. It is unsatisfactory and even painful to the thinker himself, if he is not permitted to communicate his thoughts to others, and it is obviously of no value to his neighbours. Moreover, it is extremely difficult to hide thoughts that have any power over the mind …

[3.40] Perception of information ought to be free of legal control. Failure to respect C's freedom of thought involves inventing a form of Orwellian thought-crime, with A as the representative of the ubiquitous Thought Police.[37] We often speak of the importance of freedom of expression, but that right is actually highly qualified in the United Kingdom at least.[38] We say less about freedom of thought, but the protection conferred by Article 9(1) of the ECHR is important and deserves emphasis. There is no way that the law, at least in a Western democracy, should or (without enormous and indefensible incursions into civil liberties) could police C's perception or freedom of thought, even if that perception related to the most intimate and private information concerning A. A must simply live with the fact that C knows something about them that A would rather they did not know. The law will not[39] permit any person – A or otherwise – to control C's perception. That would an unwarrantable intrusion into C's freedom of thought.

ii. The distinction between perception and use

[3.41] The protection of A's privacy by way of the Action in no sense involves A being able to control what is in C's mind. To focus on freedom of thought is to ask the wrong question and to focus on the wrong zone of interest. What matters for the purposes of the Action is *not* what goes on in the mind of C, but the extent to which the information held in C's mind is *used* by C.

[3.42] Drawing this distinction between *perception* and *use* is not particularly unusual. It arises in copyright every time a work (say by A) is viewed by C. There is no control over C's perceptions of A's work, whether it be a play or musical performance, a book or a picture. There *is* control over C's use of their perception: copying of an original work is not permitted without A's consent. It is at the point of use that C becomes exposed to a copyright infringement claim by A. Viewed in this light, there is nothing particularly heterodox in A having potential rights over information in the mind of C, provided that A's rights as owner extend only to C's use or exploitation of that information.

[37] Drawing on the dystopian world portrayed by George Orwell in *1984*.

[38] Permissibly so, given the terms of Art 9(2) ECHR.

[39] What is here being expressed is a norm, and the words 'should not' are perhaps more appropriate than the words 'will not', save that the words used are appropriately emphatic to the point being made. The extent to which our society has in the past and does in the present respect freedom of thought is a matter beyond the scope of this book.

iii. Opposing values: Freedom of expression and all that

[3.43] There is, as Bury notes, an inevitable nexus between freedom of thought and freedom of speech: '... freedom of thought, in any valuable sense, includes freedom of speech ...'.[40] The question becomes the extent to which A can, through the Action, police C's freedom of expression by inhibiting C's use of information which C *already has*. It is at the point of *use* that A's ownership and consequent control over A's private information impacts upon C.

[3.44] The impact of A's privacy rights on opposing valuable rights vesting in C is obvious. The 'balancing' of different rights was referred to at paragraphs [3.35]–[3.40]. Clearly, there is a tension between A's rights over their private information and C's rights of freedom of expression, protected by Articles 9 and 10 of the ECHR. But freedom of expression is not the only right that stands in tension with A's rights of privacy, whether these rights arise under Article 8 ECHR or the law of property. Private information is used in many different ways: the developing threats to our privacy were described in paragraph [1.3] ff as comprising three phases. One way in which our privacy is invaded is by having our private information published without our consent. But that is not the only way in which our private information is used, although it is the most overt. Other invasions of our privacy – Zuboff's 'surveillance capitalism'[41] – are hidden from sight and take place covertly. They are nonetheless subject to A's rights as the owner of their private information, but it must be stressed that A's rights are not unlimited. No owner has unlimited rights in respect of their property, whether that property is tangible or intangible. A landowner is constrained by the law of nuisance in the uses to which they can put their land, and the owner of a car is limited by all kinds of rules (civil and criminal) in the manner in which they can drive their car.

[3.45] This chapter is concerned with the definition of information; the limits of A's rights by way of the Action are addressed elsewhere. Nevertheless, it is appropriate to isolate some important limits to the Action that will be addressed more fully in due course:

- *The Action is limited to enabling A to protect their private information.* There are two limits here: (i) the information must be private; and (ii) it must belong to A. A cannot bring an action against C if they cannot arguably[42]

[40] Bury (n 36) 8.

[41] See paras [1.8]–[1.19].

[42] A right of action is just that – a right to bring a claim, which is then adjudicated upon at trial. A right of action is asserted in a particular way (in this jurisdiction by claim form followed by all sorts of other process) and – unless killed off at an interlocutory stage before trial or compromised – the claimant will have their day in court, where the claim may succeed or fail. The point is that a right of action (intangible property in its own right) is no more than an arguable assertion of the necessary facts and matters constituting a claim so as to enable a court to adjudicate upon it. See M Smith et al, *Smith on the Law of Assignment*, 4th edn (Oxford University Press, 2026) Ch 4 and in particular [4.22]–[4.23].

assert that the information: (a) is in nature private; and (b) belongs to A. It cannot be the case that A has rights in regard to *all* of C's perceptions. The Action only serves to protect A to the extent that A has a legitimate interest to protect.

- *The Action is limited to controlling misuse.* The Action does not control C's perception. The Action controls C's *misuse* (or *threatened* misuse) of A's private information. Not all uses by C of A's private information constitute misuses. Some uses are legitimate. In those cases of legitimate use, A's claim against C will fail. There is a very important line to be drawn between *use* and *misuse*.

D. A new character: O(C)

[3.46] The players involved in the Action were described at paragraphs [1.37]–[1.44]. They comprise A, B, C and O (as well as undertaking U, who will feature in Chapter 8). O is the universe of natural persons against whom A can theoretically bring an action. Most of the people within the universe of O will have no perception of A at all. Such persons cannot use, still less, misuse, A's private information, whatever that may be and whatever that may mean. One of the contingencies that *must* be satisfied before A can bring even an arguable claim against C is that C *perceives* A's private information. However, perception of A's private information is a *necessary* but not a *sufficient* requirement for an arguable claim on the part of A: in order to bring an arguable claim, A must assert against C an arguable case of *misuse* of A's private information.

[3.47] It is helpful to refer to those persons within O having a perception of A as O(C), this describing a single human being C, within the universe of O, who has a perception of A's private information but who has not used that perception. O(C) is not someone against whom A can even arguably bring a claim. O(C) merely *perceives* A's private information, and does not *use* it, still less *misuse* it. It is only when *misuse* arguably occurs, that person O(C) crosses the line to become C, a person who can properly be a defendant to A's claim.[43]

[3.48] Although A's rights are *in rem* and so against all the world O, the need for perception of A's personal information by O(C) constitutes an important limiting factor, differentiating O(C) from the rest of O, but also making clear that O(C) cannot properly be named a defendant C in an action brought by A without the additional element of (mis)use.

[43] The words 'properly be a defendant' are deliberate: it is not being suggested that an allegation of misuse will inevitably succeed – merely that A will likely be able to maintain their claim through to trial, without having that claim struck out as too weak before trial.

V. Can Private Information be Property?

A. The question identified

[3.49] This chapter began by identifying the equivocal status of information in English law. The reason for this equivocal status is because the concept of 'information' has not been defined. If you do not know what 'information' is, it is impossible to attribute any kind of status to it. Having defined *information*, but having left the questions of the meaning of *private* information and its *misuse* for the present unarticulated,[44] it must now be asked whether we have done enough to answer the question of whether private information is property.

[3.50] The question 'What is property?' was asked in Chapter 1. It was asserted that the position that English law has reached is that private information *is* property.[45] Having defined information as perception, and specifically private information as O(C)'s perception of A, which perception relates to something that is private to A, the time has come to justify and defend the assertion that private information is property.

[3.51] That defence could be along the lines that there is now enough case law surrounding the Action to demonstrate that the common law has evolved a form of claim (the Action) that operates *in rem*. There are now many cases where A has successfully maintained an action for the misuse of their private information against a party where no bilateral relationship exists between the defendant and A. The facts underlying these decisions involve no bilateral relationship between claimant A and defendant B so as to justify the label *in personam*. These cases look like *in rem* cases and the nature of the Action as a form of proprietary tort (considered in greater detail later on in this book[46]) appears to be well-established, even if not clearly recognised.

[3.52] The proposition could also be defended on the basis that recognising private information as property is a necessary step in order to have an effective regime protecting A's privacy interests. That defence is made in Chapters 4 and 5. Chapter 4 is a widely ranging chapter, which considers the underpinnings and rationale for a proprietary remedy. Amongst other things, this chapter considers the other ways in which privacy is protected – notably by Article 8 of the ECHR and data protection legislation – and notes that these protections, whilst valuable, are not enough to protect A's legitimate privacy and property interests. In other words, the Action does not duplicate remedies that exist elsewhere in the

[44] See Chs 6 and 7.
[45] At para [1.44].
[46] See Ch 10, Section II.

law, but fills what would otherwise be a significant gap in the law. There is thus an important legal policy justification for the existence of an *in rem* remedy. Chapter 5 considers the matter from an economic standpoint, and articulates the economic justifications for an *in rem* remedy.

[3.53] Important though these points are in justifying the assertion made in paragraph [3.50], it is nevertheless necessary to articulate the intellectual justification for holding that private information is property. Unless private information has the elements necessary to constitute property, then it cannot *be* property no matter how desirable that outcome might be in terms of policy. The question we are concerned with is whether private information is *capable* of constituting property, bearing in mind that although the concept of 'information' has been defined, the definition of 'private' remains at large.

[3.54] Two essential elements that property must have were stated at paragraph [1.46]. These are: (i) identifiability of subject matter; and (ii) identifiability of owner. The following paragraphs consider whether private information can meet these minimum requirements for property. At paragraph [1.56] the essential rights of an owner were described as comprising: (i) the right to exclude; (ii) the right to exploit; and (iii) the right to transfer. The extent to which A can plausibly assert these rights in relation to private information is relevant to the question of whether private information *is* property. This question is also considered in the following paragraphs.

B. Identifiability of subject matter

i. The importance of the qualifier 'private'

[3.55] The subject matter of A's rights must be capable of unique and precise identification. If property is incapable of identification, it simply cannot be property. That is why *information* cannot be property, and why the qualification *private* matters so much. The subset of information that is private information meets the requirement of identifiability because private information: (i) must relate to a specific person, here identified as A; and (ii) must have the quality of being private to A.

[3.56] This considerably narrows down the perceptions of O(C) that may be the subject of an Action. The information, to qualify, must be both *personal* to A and *private* to A. These are distinct attributes. It is perfectly possible for information:

- To be private information, but not personal to A. In other words, the information may be someone else's (not A's) private information.
- To be personal to A, but not private, whether to A or to anybody else.

Obviously, there is a link between these two characteristics, but they are distinct qualities.

ii. The problem of unknowing constraint and unknowing infringement

[**3.57**] One of the hallmarks of property is that the owner can exclude third parties from their property.[47] It is not necessary for the third party to *know* that they are infringing an owner's rights in order for them to be at the wrong end of an infringement claim. But the prospect of unknowing infringement – that O(C) might *unwittingly* or *unintentionally* infringe – is certainly a contra-indicator of proprietary status. Property rights tend to be so structured that a reasonable person can, if they want to respect the owner's rights, do so. In other words, it is possible to avoid infringing or at least to minimise the risk of infringing.

[**3.58**] This is an aspect of identifiability. If it were the case that the person potentially subject to A's rights, O(C), might not know of A's rights (or be able to find out about them exercising a degree of effort), and might (even exercising reasonable care) innocently infringe, then that would be a sign that private information is not property.

[**3.59**] Intangible property in particular is exposed to this risk. Where property is tangible, right-minded people know that if a thing (a car, a watch, a house) is not theirs, then: (i) it is likely to be someone else's; and (ii) those rights of ownership (whosever rights they are) ought to be respected. Nothing more is required. Because intangible property lacks physicality, the law needs to build in safeguards to enable an owner's rights to be respected. Thus, patents are registered, and the register is searchable. Whilst it is perfectly possible to infringe a patent unknowingly, infringement being a matter of strict liability,[48] a person concerned that they may be using someone else's invention can protect themselves by a patent search. Copyright, as its name implies, requires the defendant to have copied an original work. If, by remarkable coincidence, a defendant creates by original effort something that is a sufficiently similar copy of someone else's original work, then there is no copyright infringement.[49]

[47] See para [1.56].

[48] In other words, a defendant will be liable as an infringer, even though the infringement was innocent and done without knowledge.

[49] See *Molavi v Gilbert* [2023] EWHC 646 (Ch). The infinite monkey theory states that a monkey hitting keys independently and at random on a keyboard for an infinite amount of time will type any given text, including the complete works of William Shakespeare. In such a case, copyright will not be infringed.

[3.60] The nature of private information is considered in detail in Chapter 6. In order to be private information, a reasonable person, standing in the position of O(C), must know, or on reasonable inquiry ought to know, that their perception is both personal to and private to *someone*. The definition of 'private information' is being anticipated somewhat, but this is the answer to the problem of innocent infringement. It is not necessary for O(C) to know the identity of A, but O(C) does need to be in a position where they are able to avoid infringing *someone's* private information. It is not necessary to know who the owner is in order to respect rights of ownership even of particular persons.

C. Identifiability of the first owner

i. First owners, transfers of ownership and chains of title

[3.61] The importance of the owner of the property being identifiable was noted at paragraph [1.56(2)]. Unless the owner is objectively identifiable, the law cannot determine whether the person asserting ownership over property actually has the right to do so. Because ownership is transferable, any person other than the first owner must prove their title by reference to a transfer or series of transfers beginning with a transfer from the first owner.

[3.62] The question of transfer of private information is considered briefly below, and in detail in Chapter 11. Here we are concerned with the identifiability of the first owner. The heavy lifting in this regard is done, once again, by the qualification 'private'. Thus, when A brings a claim against C, A will have to show not only that the information in question is *private*, but also that it is *personal* to them.

ii. The unconscious or unknowing owner

[3.63] It is perfectly possible for O(C)'s perception to exist without A knowing of that perception at all.

Example[50]

The Court of Appeal considered a claim by an infant claimant, who had been photographed covertly with a long-range lens by a photographer of an agency (BPL) whilst the claimant was in a public place with their parents. The claimant was, at the time, 19 months old, and sued by their litigation friends, their parents. The photographs were sold by BPL to the newspaper, which published some of them.

[50] The facts derive from the case of *Murray v Express Newspapers plc* [2008] EWCA Civ 446.

[3.64] The notion of A unknowingly owning something that is in the mind of O(C) does seem counterintuitive. But it is counterintuitive because of the fact that A has rights over O(C)'s perceptions (a point already considered at paragraph [3.35] ff), not because A is unknowing of their rights. A landowner may misunderstand the extent of their land, considering that their property is less extensive than in fact it is. Where C enters upon that land, they nevertheless do so as trespasser. Information has been defined as O(C)'s perception of A; A will not be able to say what anyone in the universe of O perceives about them, until (possibly) the information is used.[51]

[3.65] To focus on A's lack of knowledge of O(C)'s perception is to look at matters through the wrong end of the telescope. A's interest is in the protection of their privacy. A, like any human being, will have a keen sense of the importance of privacy generally, and their own privacy in particular. The fact that A's privacy involves the assertion of control over a perception that A may know nothing about is neither here nor there.

D. The right to exclude

[3.66] The right to exclude is an important incident of ownership.[52] In the case of tangible property, this right of exclusion is straightforward. As Fairfield puts it '[o]ne really easy way to tell others that you claim something is to pick it up – to possess it. That's why possession plays such a strong role in traditional property law. Possession signals to all others who encounter the resource that it is already claimed.'[53] The attributes of ownership – the rights of an owner – are easier to conceive because of the sheer *physicality* of tangible property.

[3.67] In the case of intangible property, the right to exclude is more nuanced. It involves an action by a claimant against a defendant, whereby the claimant either seeks to prevent the infringement of their rights by way of an injunction or obtains damages from the defendant in compensation for the infringement. This is how all intellectual property rights are enforced. Private information is no different. The point being made in this book is that the way in which the owner's right to exclude is enforced in the case of private information is by way of the Action.

[51] Often not even then, because use may be covert, not overt. Misuse by publication will be overt. Many misuses will, however, be covert. One of the points considered in Ch 10 is how A can actually find out whether C is infringing their rights in the case of covert infringement.

[52] See para [1.56].

[53] J Fairfield, *Owned: Property, Privacy and the New Digital Serfdom* (Cambridge University Press, 2017) 139.

E. The right to exploit

[3.68] The right to exploit was considered at paragraph [1.56]. The exploitation of property by an owner involves *monetising* the owner's rights, whilst *retaining* ownership. Many intellectual property rights are monetised in this way: the owner retains ownership, but licenses someone else to use their property. The owner of a patent need not exploit the patented invention themselves, but may license another to, for example, make goods using the patented invention. A scientist may invent a new drug, but license a pharmaceutical company to use that invention to manufacture the drug. (Of course, the scientist can sell the patent and transfer it to the pharmaceutical company: we will come to the right to transfer next.)

[3.69] Clearly, private information is licensable. A can reach an agreement with B whereby (gemerally in return for payment) certain (defined) private information belonging to A is permitted by A to be used (for defined purposes) by B. The licence, it is suggested, is the answer to the problem of surveillance capitalism so lucidly explained by Zuboff.

F. The right to transfer

i. Privacy is a personal right

[3.70] This is the third important right of an owner: to be able to transfer ownership to another.[54] Because private information is so personal to A, it is open to question whether private information is transferable at all.[55] That question is considered in Chapter 10. The only point worth making here is that the fact that English law holds that certain forms of property cannot (because they are so personal to the owner) be transferred does not cause the label 'property' to be inapt. It is simply that some forms of property cannot be transferred. As it happens, it is the conclusion of this book that private information *can* be transferred – but that question is considered in Chapter 10.

ii. The problem of duplication

[3.71] Transfer of private information implies a movement of property from A (the first owner) to a transferee, B, who succeeds to A's rights. That is what we typically take *transfer* to mean, a shifting of rights from transferor A to transferee B. Transfer in this sense is often not possible in the case of information.

[54] See para [1.56].

[55] In English law, intangible property is often referred to as a 'chose in action', and that is the appropriate classification of private information. It is well-established in English law that choses in action that are *personal* cannot be transferred: see Smith et al (n 42) Ch 21.

[3.72] Where there is communication of information from A to O(C), there is no transfer, only replication. The information is present in A and does not cease to be present simply because A has communicated the information to O(C).[56] Indeed, A may communicate the *same* information to many people, who all get their perceptions from the same source.

[3.73] Information is replicable, and this represents a significant point of difference between intangible property and tangible, physical, property, which is non-replicable. Fairfield calls this 'rivalrousness':[57]

> Rivalrousness means that if I have a thing, you don't. Imagine a vinyl record. If I give it to you, I don't have it anymore. We are rivals for its possession, hence the term. If an asset is non-rivalrous, both you and I can have it at the same time. Consider the same recording, but as an MP3. I can give you an identical copy of the MP3 without giving up my own copy. The MP3 is non-rivalrous.

Rivalrousness describes the *consequence* of an inability to duplicate. Non-rivalrousness describes the *consequence* of an ability to duplicate.

[3.74] Not all intangible property is capable of duplication. A debt can be transferred, not duplicated. But works generally protected by copyright (photographs, writing, etc) are clearly capable of duplication. Unless constrained, a party can make as many copies of the original work as they please. Non-rivalrous things can be copied with no derogation in quality at near-zero cost.[58]

[3.75] There is also an interesting relationship between tangible and intangible property, which is expressed very well by Fairfield:[59]

> Let's say I paint a picture. The actual picture and the copyright in the picture are two different things. A traditional distinction between the thing and the intellectual property rights that attach to it makes a lot of sense. Consider this book: you have the right to read it, take it with you, sell it to someone else, but not the right to make as many copies of it as you want and distribute it to anyone you wish. Ownership of a copy is separate from ownership of the copyright.

[3.76] The question for present purposes is whether the replicable or non-rivalrous nature of information renders it less likely to be property. The answer is that this characteristic does not affect the characterisation of private information as property, provided that the law creates a framework whereby that which

[56] Of course, it is perfectly possible for O(C)'s perception to be generated without communication from A (or anyone else): see the discussion in Section III of this chapter. Here, however, we are considering the case where A is choosing to sell and transfer their private information to C. That will almost certainly involve some form of communication.

[57] Fairfield (n 53) 148.

[58] ibid 148.

[59] ibid 24.

is non-rivalrous (or capable of duplication) is rendered rivalrous (or *legally* incapable of duplication). The reason transfer or sale of property is valuable (the seller can command a price) is because the thing sold is *scarce*. We want to create *scarcity*, because through scarcity the owner of the scarce thing can leverage the rights of ownership and monetise what has become their asset.[60]

[3.77] The law can render that which is intrinsically non-rivalrous into rivalrous property simply by creating a rule that where the non-rivalrous property has been transferred, the owner loses the right to use the property so transferred, even if the property is retained by the owner. Suppose A sells their private information to B, and agrees to 'transfer' it. In making this agreement, A cannot generally 'forget' their private information, but they *can* promise not to use it or by operation of law *lose* the right to use it.

[3.78] In this way, the economic effects of a transfer are proxied. Even though information is not, in reality, transferred, it nevertheless makes sense to use the term transfer when A sells their private information to B. One of the aspects of human and particularly legal reasoning is to deploy fiction or analogy in order to explain and regulate. Thus, even though a physicist will tell us that time is relative, for all practical purposes (so far, at least) we measure time by 'objective' fragments of hours, minutes and seconds.[61] When working with electronic documents, when we move a file from one electronic folder to another, we say are 'transferring' the file, even though we know that what is being done is something very different from the physical transfer of a document from one location to another.[62]

[3.79] A good example of the difficulties of matching reality to the labels attaching to legal mechanisms is *R v Preddy*,[63] a case in the criminal law

[60] I am indebted to Fairfield for this analysis: ibid 148–49.

[61] The opening words of W Newton-Smith, *The Structure of Time* (Routledge, 1980) at 1–2, make the point extremely well: 'There is perhaps no concept which we use more extensively and more happily in our non-philosophical moments than that of time. Virtually nothing is ever said or thought save with the use of this concept. This is not because we pay at least lip-service to time in the regular use of tenses but also because a whole host of important concepts have obvious temporal components. Not only is this concept used extensively, it is also used with facility. Children have no particular problem in acquiring a usable notion of time. And in everyday linguistic converse no one with the minimal normal linguistic competencies fails to grasp the meaning of utterances which make implicit or explicit use of the concept of time. However, we need only ask in a philosophical moment what it is we are talking about when we talk about time or the temporal aspects of things for the topic of our discourse to seem confused, complex and perplexing beyond comprehension. Often in desperation we make recourse to images, pictures, and metaphors in an attempt to make time comprehensible. Unfortunately these pictures usually have the effect of generating more mental cramps than they ease.'

[62] What generally happens if that the file is *rewritten* in a new location, and the old version either *deleted* or marked for *overwriting* when the need for space arises.

[63] *R v Preddy* [1996] AC 815.

concerning a defendant fraudulently obtaining advances from building societies, which advances were in some cases made by telegraphic or electronic transfer. The question arose as to whether such transfers amounted to the obtaining of 'property belonging to another'. Lord Goff answered this question in the negative:[64]

> The crucial question, as I see it, is whether the defendant obtained (or attempted to obtain) property *belonging to another*. Let it be assumed that the lending institution's bank account is in credit, and that there is therefore no difficulty in identifying a credit balance standing in the account as representing property, i.e. a chose in action, belonging to the lending institution. The question remains, however, whether the debiting of the lending institution's bank account, and the corresponding crediting of the bank account of the defendant or his solicitor, constitutes obtaining of that property. The difficulty in the way of that conclusion is simply that, when the bank account of the defendant (or his solicitor) is credited, he does not obtain the lending institution's chose in action. On the contrary, that chose in action is extinguished or reduced *pro tanto*, and a chose in action is brought into existence representing a debt in an equivalent sum owed by a different bank to the defendant or his solicitor.

[3.80] Whereas a layperson might very well say that the defendant had, indeed, obtained property belonging to another, the demands of the rule of law – particularly in criminal cases – require a high degree of correlation between the facts of the case and the specification of the crime. The same point arises when a party is seeking to effect an assignment – a transfer of intangible property. If X were to say to Y, 'I transfer to you £10 from my bank account' or 'I assign to you £10 from my bank account', there is a tension between X's stated intention (to assign or transfer £10) and the only mechanism by which this can be achieved which – for the reasons given by Lord Goff – is *neither* transfer *nor* assignment. The law must tread very carefully in allowing technicalities or linguistic shorthand to scupper intended and proper dealings.

[3.81] So, too, in the case of information. It is accepted that information is very hard to *transfer* in the ordinary sense. Clearly, that fact must have a bearing on the analysis. But whether this factor precludes the label of property or the existence of *in rem* rights in A over private information must be doubted; and equally, in this case at least, the use of the term 'transfer' is permissible.

[64] ibid 834.

4

Underpinnings and Rationale

In which: the hinterland to private information as property is explored, beginning with Warren and Brandeis' seminal article, traversing cognate areas of copyright and trade secret protection, before considering safeguarding of privacy through human rights and data protection.

I. Introduction and Overview

[4.1] So far, we have considered the emergence of the cause of action of misuse of private information;[1] and described and sought to define the nature of information.[2] The questions of what is *private* information and what constitutes the *misuse* of private information have only been touched upon, and (to manage expectations) are not addressed in any detail in this chapter.[3] This chapter does not seek to provide answers to these questions, but rather to provide context in which those answers can be placed. This chapter considers *why* privacy matters and the other ways in which privacy and personal data are protected other than through the proprietary tort of misuse of private information – the Action.

[4.2] This is, therefore, a somewhat wide-ranging chapter, unified by these broad themes. The approach is as follows.

(1) The seminal article of Warren and Brandeis[4] and the lessons that can be learned from it are considered first.[5]
(2) Moving on from the Warren and Brandeis analysis – or rather, the analysis of the analysis of Warren and Brandeis – the protection of private information is considered within the panoply of intellectual property rights in general and copyright in particular. A number of important and interesting similarities and differences exist between copyright and private information.[6]

[1] In Ch 2.
[2] In Ch 3.
[3] They are considered in Ch 6 (what is *private* information) and Chs 7 and 8 (what is *use* and *misuse* of private information by non-state and state actors respectively).
[4] S Warren and L Brandeis, 'The Right to Privacy' (1890) 4 *Harvard Law Review* 193.
[5] See Section II below.
[6] See Section III below.

(3) From there, the role of contract and the protection of privacy is considered, albeit very briefly, for it is the thesis of this book that *in personam* rights play an extremely limited role in the protection of privacy. This leads on to a consideration of some of the case law that supports an *in rem* analysis of the Action.[7]

(4) Thereafter the chapter explores the question of whether protection of privacy by way of property is actually *necessary* or *desirable*, given the role played by human rights law (in particular Article 8 of the European Convention on Human Rights (ECHR)) and data protection law (in particular the General Data Protection Regulation or GDPR[8]).[9]

II. Warren and Brandeis: *The Right to Privacy* and the Distinction between Expression and Perception

[4.3] Warren and Brandeis' *Harvard Law Review* article 'The Right to Privacy', was published in 1890.[10] Warren and Brandeis draw a fundamental distinction between the protections of publications that an author *chooses* to disseminate and the protection of privacy. There is an important interrelationship between the various intellectual property rights that exist in English law, including (so this book contends) private information.[11] They all protect different interests, but a key difference is that patents and copyright and trade marks are generally regarded as involving a desire in the owner to use, and often publish, the information; whereas, in the case of private information, the general view is that the owner wants to keep the information from public view. Of course, treating private information as property does enable the owner to monetise their property and in this private information is a lot like other intellectual property rights. But its other purpose – to inhibit third party use, to *exclude* – is really all about owner A trying to control how they are perceived in the wider world.

[4.4] Thus, Warren and Brandeis characterised the right to privacy as the right of the individual 'to be let alone'.[12] The right was seen as an incremental

[7] See Sections IV and V below.

[8] The GDPR is an emanation of European Union law which, post-Brexit, has been modified and incorporated into the law of the United Kingdom. There are many books dealing with the GDPR, and this book is not one of them. The GDPR will be considered – like the ECHR and copyright – as and when it assists in the analysis. For this reason, no distinction is drawn between the European Union and United Kingdom versions of the GDPR.

[9] See Sections VI and VII below.

[10] Warren and Brandeis (n 4).

[11] See Section V below, which considers some of the cases.

[12] Warren and Brandeis (n 4) 205.

development wrought by the common law and emanating out of older protections like remedies for physical interference with life and property.[13] In their view, the protection of privacy emanated out of the physical rights of protection anciently conferred by the common law:[14]

> These considerations lead to the conclusion that the protection afforded to thoughts, sentiments and emotions, expressed through the medium of writing or of the arts, so far as it consists in preventing publication, is merely an instance of the enforcement of the more general right of the individual to be let alone. It is like the right not to be assaulted or beaten, the right not to be imprisoned, the right not to be maliciously prosecuted, the right not to be defamed …

[4.5] When we come to consider the case law (in Section V below), we will see that the Action has its roots in many of these older protections, notably trespass, copyright and the protection of trade secrets.

[4.6] Warren and Brandeis thus saw the right of privacy as a right in A to prevent C from doing something; or else (where C has done that thing) a right in A to recover damages from C for having done it. They saw the action as a tort, but not as a tort protecting a property interest. A property right confers on A the right to exclude, similar to that articulated by Warren and Brandeis. But a property right does far more than this: it enables A to *exploit* their private information. If A owns their private information, A is not limited to a right to exclude, to be left alone, but may choose the manner in which their private information is used. This ability to exploit – including by way of transfer – is an essential component of the bundle of rights that vest in an owner. Warren and Brandeis came close to articulating a right of property, but did not quite get there:[15]

> The common law secures to each individual the right of determining, ordinarily, to what extent his thoughts, sentiments, and emotions shall be communicated to others. Under our system of government, he can never be compelled to express them (except when upon the witness stand); and even if he has chosen to give them expression, he generally retains the power to fix the limits of the publicity which shall be given them. The existence of this right does not depend upon the particular method of expression adopted. It is immaterial whether it be by word or by signs, in painting, by sculpture, or in music. Neither does the existence of the right depend upon the nature or value of the thought or emotion, nor upon the excellence of the means of expression. The same protection is accorded to a casual letter or an entry in a diary and to the most valuable poem or essay, to a botch or daub and to a masterpiece.

[13] ibid 193: 'Political, social, and economic changes entail the recognition of new rights, and the common law, in its eternal youth, grows to meet the demands of society. Thus, in very early times, the law only gave a remedy for physical interference with life and property, for trespasses *vi et armis*'.
[14] ibid 205.
[15] ibid 198–99.

> In every such case the individual is entitled to decide whether that which is his shall be given to the public. No other has the right to publish his productions in any form, without his consent.

[4.7] One can immediately see the link between privacy and copyright. The latter enables A to control the work which A has created, by preventing copies being made by C. The former enables A to be left alone, enforcing that right against C, without putting their work into the public domain. Notwithstanding this link, and the fact that copyright can in some cases further the interests of privacy, there is a tension between copyright and private information which means that copyright cannot do the work of the Action, and that the Action cannot do the work of copyright.

[4.8] The passage quoted above from Warren and Brandeis is also significant because its focus is on *expression* of thoughts, sentiments and emotions by A, rather than the *perception* of those thoughts, sentiments and emotions by C. This is another point at which the analysis in this book differs materially from that of Warren and Brandeis. If one pivots to the thesis here advanced – that it is the *perception* by C of A's information and the control of the *use* of that information by C vesting in A – then things begin to make a great deal more sense.

[4.9] First, one ceases to speak of A's 'thoughts, sentiments and emotions'. Privacy may embrace much more and much less than this, depending on the circumstances. Rather, one speaks of information in the mind of C, which (as a necessary element) must be private information pertaining to A. What matters is: (i) that which C perceives of A; (ii) how C has come by that perception; and (iii) what C intends to do with that perception or how they intend to use it.

[4.10] C's perception – provided that it remains internal to C – is not controlled by the law. We are still some distance from Orwell's Thought Police. What is controlled is C's ability to *use* that information external to themselves. Thus, there is a constraint on C in terms of the extent to which C may properly *use* A's private information. This distinction between *perception* and *use of perception* ('use', for short) is a helpful one that was articulated in Chapter 3 and which forms a theme throughout this book. But it should not be inferred that the distinction is altogether clear, even if it can be shortly stated. The distinction between perception, use and misuse is less straightforward than it might appear, as Chapters 7 and 8 show.

[4.11] The move away from A's *expression* of information to C's *perception* of information makes clearer the true ambit of the right to privacy. It does not matter if A has not expressed themselves *at all*. Take, for example, the long-distance photograph that C (a press photographer) takes of A (a famous person).

It is a stretch to say that A is expressing themselves, yet the right to privacy is (or ought to be) at least engaged. Similarly, suppose A's mobile phone is tracking their movements across space and time, providing that information to C, which C then sells for their own benefit. Again, A has not *expressed themselves*, unless merely carrying a mobile telephone on your person constitutes expression of self (which is to be doubted). What is significant is C's perception of A's conduct and C's use of that perceived information.

III. A Seamless Web: The Protection of Private Information and Other Intellectual Property Rights

A. Intellectual property rights generally

[**4.12**] Publication of information, if done in certain ways, and if that information meets certain pre-conditions, may become *property* in its own right. An invention may be the subject of a patent application and the grant of a patent in due course. Provided the information: (i) is published in the appropriate way; (ii) is an invention which, (iii) is properly original over the prior art and the knowledge of the skilled person (ie it is inventive), a patent may be applied for and granted.

[**4.13**] Patents are, for present purposes, not particularly interesting, because they are a very specialist form of communication of information, surrounded by a high degree of formality of process. That is true of many intellectual property rights. An exception, however, is copyright, which arises automatically on the creation of a 'work', without additional formality, and which embraces a number of the protections adverted to by Warren and Brandeis.[16] The thesis in this book can (and probably should) be translated into the language of intellectual property rights: in addition to patents, copyright, trade marks and database rights (to name a few) there exists a right over private information, a form of intellectual property protected by the proprietary tort of misuse of private

[16] The protection referred to in Warren and Brandeis (n 4) at 199–200 is copyright, and (in their analysis) it stands in contradistinction to the right of privacy: '... No other has the right to publish his productions in any form, without his consent. This right is wholly independent of the material on which, or the means by which, the thought, sentiment or emotion is expressed. It may exist independently of any corporeal being, as in words spoken, a song sung, a drama acted. Or if expressed on any material, as a poem in writing, the author may have parted with the paper, without forfeiting any proprietary right in the composition itself. The right is lost only when the author himself communicates his production to the public, – in other words, publishes it. It is entirely independent of the copyright laws, and their extension into the domain of art. The aim of those statutes is to secure to the author, composer, or artist the entire profits arising from production; but the common law protection enables him to control absolutely the act of publication, and in the exercise of his own discretion, to decide whether there shall be any publication at all. The statutory right is of no value, *unless* there is a publication; the common law right is lost *as soon as* there is a publication.'

information (ie the Action). Some of the limits of this intellectual property right can best be understood through an understanding of copyright.

B. The importance of copyright

[4.14] The distinction between the Action and the law of copyright is an important one. Although copyright has, as one of its functions, the ability to enable the holder of the right to commercialise the work, that is *not* its only function. Copyright serves also to protect and control the dissemination of works falling within the ambit of the law of copyright. Here we are principally interested in the latter function, but of course the distinction is by no means a watertight one. A poet may choose to keep their poem confined and unpublished or seek to leverage the poem commercially or artistically. The law of copyright will assist in both regards. However, as will be seen, copyright is now far more effective in enabling the monetisation of works by A than in the protection of A's privacy.

[4.15] If the thesis of this book is correct, and the Action enables A to control the use by C of C's perception of A's private information, then the parallels and differences between copyright and the privacy as property concept are important. Both involve the *publication* of *information* to a *third party*, in circumstances where that publication can be *controlled*. The real difference lies in the party who is entitled to enforce the right (as a lawyer would put it, the identity of the party in whom the ability to vindicate the property right inheres). As will be seen, in the case of the Action this is A, the person whose private information is in issue; in the case of copyright, the claimant is the creator of the work, even if the work involves A's privacy. To revert to the example of the photographer in paragraph [4.11], copyright in the photograph vests in the *photographer* not the *person photographed*.

C. Copyright, the furthering of commercial interests and the protection of privacy

[4.16] *Copinger and Skone James* makes the point that the economic significance of copyright has expanded dramatically 'through technological innovation and consequential new uses of works protected by copyright'.[17] The distinction

[17] G Davies et al, *Copinger and Skone James on Copyright*, Vol 1, 17th edn (Sweet & Maxwell, 2016) [1-01]. This is an old edition of *Copinger*, and none the worse for that. Where general statements of law are made, there is some virtue in looking to older statements of the law in the established texts, which is what has been done here.

between the furthering of commercial interests and the protection of privacy is explicitly drawn:[18]

> Works protected by copyrights and the rights related thereto discussed in this work are a constantly growing sector of the national economy and of world trade. In the modern world, the law of copyright provides the legal framework not only for the protection of the traditional beneficiaries of copyright, the individual author, composer or artist, but also for the investment required for the creation of works by the major cultural industries, the publishing, film, broadcasting and recording industries, and the computer software industry.
>
> Copyright is important not only to the individuals and industries which depend upon it for their livelihood but also impinges one way or another on the daily life of members of the public and business. Copyright protects a vast array of everyday items, including, for example on the private level, letters, photographs and home videos …

For the moment, the focus will be on the latter aspect.

D. Copyright and the protection of privacy

[4.17] Copyright arises automatically upon the creation of the work. There are no formalities regarding the creation of the right.[19] Copyright is an exclusively statutory right given against the copying of defined types of cultural, informational and entertainment productions, known as 'works'. Works are specifically described in sections 3–8 of the Copyright, Designs and Patents Act 1988, and comprise literary, dramatic and musical works,[20] databases,[21] artistic works,[22] sound recordings and films,[23] broadcasts,[24] and published editions.[25] The focus here will be on literary, dramatic and musical works (referred to as 'literary' works, for short), and with particular reference to the manner in which copyright can be said to protect privacy.

[4.18] The term 'literary' implies no requirement of any style or merit. Such qualitative assessments are not required when assessing the existence of

[18] ibid [1-01].
[19] M Smith et al, *Smith on The Law of Assignment*, 4th edn (Oxford University Press, 2026) [35.63].
[20] Copyright, Designs and Patents Act 1988, s 3.
[21] ibid s 3A.
[22] ibid s 4.
[23] ibid ss 5A and 5B.
[24] ibid s 6.
[25] ibid s 8: a 'published edition' means a published edition of the whole or any part of one or more literary, dramatic or musical works.

copyright.[26] The protection granted is wide. As *Copinger and Skone James* notes:[27]

> ... virtually every product of writing, speech or song is likely to be a literary work and a vast array of works have been protected as such, whether they are the product of substantial creative endeavour such as novels, newspaper articles or examination papers or more mundane things such as ordinary letters, written advertisements, rules for games or formulae. In this area of protected subject matter, the issue is usually whether the work is original or not, so that cases in which the point has been argued have been relatively rare. Leaving aside cases about compilations and tables, the following types of works have been protected: ordinary business letters; examination papers; a manual of instructions for a toy, being complete in itself; a form for use in correspondence courses; material included in a diary consisting of the months, dates and days, with a three-month calendar; a formula using symbols and numbers; and a programme and race card for greyhound racing. A host of other mundane works have been protected without any argument on the point, for example, trade circulars, consignment notes, the rules of a game and the rules of a trade association.

[4.19] The first owner of copyright is a person of significance when it comes to the protection of privacy, for it is the owner who has the initial entitlement to enforce the right. Unless the first owner is the party whose privacy needs protection, copyright is *not* useful as a protection when it comes to matters of privacy, as in such circumstances A would have to *acquire* the copyright to acquire the protection that comes with it.[28]

[4.20] In the case of copyright, the first owner is often the party *not* in need of privacy protection. The general rule is that the author is the first owner of the copyright,[29] and in the case of literary works the author is the person who creates the work.[30] In the case of literary works, this term is not further defined,[31] and this is because the answer is generally obvious. Copyright is concerned with the protection of original expression in some material form of ideas, information, etc and *not* with the ideas, information, etc themselves. The 'author' of a work is the person who originates the protectable elements of the work, whether it be the language used, dramatic incident, musical content or design.[32] Where the author acts through an agent (whether human or otherwise), the principal will be the author, not the agent.[33] It follows from this that

[26] *Copinger and Skone James*, Vol 1 (n 17) [3-36].
[27] ibid [3-41].
[28] As this work does in the case of private information, *Copinger and Skone James*, Vol 1 (n 17) at [5-01] draws a clear distinction between 'first owner' and 'subsequent transferee'.
[29] ibid [5-06].
[30] ibid [4-21].
[31] ibid [4-21].
[32] ibid [4-22].
[33] ibid [4-22].

the author will be a natural person.[34] It is also clear that the person who is the first owner of the copyright in a work may be quite different from the person who is the owner of the physical material or other medium on or in which the copyright work is first recorded or fixed.

[4.21] In terms of the implications for the law of privacy, copyright is a limited protector of A's privacy. Thus:

- Where A records their personal thoughts in their diary, then (whether the diary belongs to A or to C) copyright in the words used vests in A. A is thus able – as Warren and Brandeis anticipate – to control the use of their words by third parties.
- Similarly, suppose A writes a letter to C, recording their innermost thoughts. Whilst property in the physical letter may pass, and C will be entitled to read the words, C will not be entitled to publish them. However, the substance or gist of the words used by A are *not* protected by copyright. The privacy protection is thus more attenuated and confined to a restriction of the *copying* of the original material.
- Suppose C photographs A in circumstances where A would wish to assert some form of privacy protection. Here, C is the author, and A will gain no assistance though the law of copyright, although A may well have a legitimate privacy interest to protect, particularly if the photograph is in A's home (for example). This legitimate interest on A's part is not protected by the law of copyright. The position is a fortiori where A is photographed in the street or other public place.
- Suppose C's perception derives from something other than a 'work' – where C watches A or inspects their home. Here, copyright will not be engaged at all.

[4.22] None of this is to suggest that the law of copyright is deficient. It is simply that copyright serves to protect different interests. It is the interrelationship between two cognate forms of property – copyright and private information – that provides insight. This interrelationship is best explored by considering the key differences between copyright infringement and the Action.

[4.23] Whereas there may once have been an identity between the owner of the work (the first owner of copyright) and the party whose privacy requires protection, that alignment has lessened as technology has advanced. Prior to 1890, when Warren and Brandeis wrote their article, it might have been possible to say that there was a close identity between the author of a work and the party

[34] ibid [4-22].

whose privacy required protection. However, with the advent of photography, and other technologies, that alignment fractured. In the case of photography, it is the photographer (ie C) who is the first owner of the copyright in the picture, and the subject (ie A) is not protected (by copyright at least).[35]

[4.24] Copyright prevents the *copying* of the original work, and significant latitude is granted in terms of articulating the substance, without the form. Thus, there will be many respects in which the substance of A's private information *can* be communicated, without the form (which is protected) being copied at all. Here, again, the law of copyright does not protect A's privacy. The Action focuses C's perception, and A's ability to control its use. Copyright looks to the original work, and prevents others from profiting by copying that work without the copyright owner's consent.

IV. A Contractual Analysis of Privacy

[4.25] It is obvious, from the description so far, that the origins of first ownership in copyright and in private information lie far from the contractual. Indeed, the way in which first ownership comes into being *contradicts* a contractual analysis. What creates the right, in the case of copyright, is the *making* of the original by the first owner. In the case of private information, property lies in the perception, by C, of something relating to A that is private. These property rights come into being independently of contract. They exist not because A has agreed with B that A should have certain rights as against B. A's right lies against third parties C_1, C_2, C_3 to C_n because these parties are infringing A's property rights. The law of contract or (to use vaguer terms) agreement and consensus have nothing to do with the inception of a right to privacy, just as they have nothing to do with the inception of copyright.

[4.26] Warren and Brandeis rightly point out that using a contractual analysis as the foundation for a private law right of privacy is intellectually bereft and indefensible:[36]

> This process of implying a term in a contract, or of implying a trust (particularly where the contract is written, and where there is no established usage or custom), is nothing more nor less than a judicial declaration that public morality, private justice, and general convenience demand the recognition of such a rule, and that the publication under similar circumstances would be considered an intolerable abuse. So long as these circumstances happen to present a contract upon which such a term

[35] There was debate in the early days of photography as to whether the subject of the photograph ought to have rights ranking in priority to those of the photographer: see M Richardson, *The Right to Privacy* (Cambridge University Press, 2017) 63–64.

[36] Warren and Brandeis (n 4) 210–11.

> can be engrafted by the judicial mind, or to supply relations upon which a trust or confidence can be erected, there may be no objection to working out the desired protection through the doctrines of contract or of trust. But the court can hardly stop there. The narrower doctrine may have satisfied the demands of society at a time when the abuse to be guarded against could rarely have arisen without violating a contract or a special confidence; but now that modern devices afford abundant opportunities for the perpetration of such wrongs without any participation by the injured party, the protection granted by the law must be placed on a broader foundation …

[**4.27**] Warren and Brandeis are not just saying that the contract/trust analysis is *wrong*, although they are correct in this assertion. They go further and say that in light of 'modern' developments[37] the analysis is also *unworkable*. They are right in this, too. It is unworkable for the reasons given above. The need in A to protect their privacy derives not from what A knows or publishes about themselves, but from *other people's* perception of A, those persons not being limited to those that A might have direct interaction or bilateral relations with.[38] As Warren and Brandeis correctly note, privacy rights (like copyright) are 'rights as against the world'.[39]

[**4.28**] This is not to say that a contractual analysis is irrelevant to the law of information, confidentiality or privacy. Many rights that A may have against B will have a contractual basis:[40]

> The courts have frequently relied on contract to protect confidential information, especially in the period from around 1900 to 1945.

[**4.29**] Where A discloses confidential information to B on terms or in circumstances where A's cooperation is needed in order for B to perceive the information, the basis upon which such disclosure is made and such perception derived will often be contractual and certainly bilateral. But this is very far from explaining the intellectual basis for A's claim against anyone within the universe O who happens to misuse A's private information. But the existence of a right *in rem* does not prevent there being –*in addition* to the non-contractual right of privacy vesting in A as *owner* – additional rights vesting in A that sound in contract.

[37] Modern in 1890: Warren and Brandeis enumerate technological developments that render the need for a rethink of privacy at 195–96. The point they make is that privacy can no longer be bilaterally protected, as might have been the case before the technical innovations. The situation now is a fortiori.

[38] In this, there is a loose analogy with the trespass to the person with which Warren and Brandeis' essay begins (Warren and Brandeis (n 4) 193). The trespasser – C – may have no prior relationship with A and A's right not to be trespassed against is (it might be said) good against all the world. But A only has an accrued right against C, when C actually commits the trespass. The commission of the trespass represents that point in privacy cases where O(C) becomes C.

[39] Warren and Brandeis (n 4) 213.

[40] T Aplin et al, *Gurry on Breach of Confidence*, 2nd edn (Oxford University Press, 2012) [4.13].

[4.30] When it comes to the *transfer* of information or its *licensing*, contract assumes a much more prominent role. But that is precisely because transfer and licensing involve a bilateral relationship between A and B, whereby A promises to transfer information[41] or agrees the terms of a licence.

V. Juridical Support for a Property-based, Perception-based, Understanding of Privacy

A. Approach

[4.31] The juridical basis for the Action as being based on property, where the property right is defined by reference to the perception of those able to use (and so *misuse*) that information, has repeatedly been suggested in this book. It would be wrong to suggest that this is a completely innovative stance. There is no such thing as an original idea and the analysis is (if one looks for it) well-established in various strands of the case law, both past and present, which are considered in the following paragraphs.

B. A person's home is their castle

[4.32] The decision in *Entick v Carrington*[42] is important for two reasons. It is important, first, for the Diceyan[43] reason that the state can only act against the individual on the basis of specific legal authority. Second, it is a case that stresses the importance of privacy, at least within the confines of one's home: in short, this is a case where the link between privacy and property is very clearly articulated.[44]

[4.33] Dicey had a well-known antipathy or, perhaps, scepticism, towards general articulations of rights, quoting[45] the seventh article of the (then) Belgian constitution ('La liberté individuelle est garantie'),[46] before observing

[41] Transfers will almost always be preceded by a promise to transfer. This is the distinction between contract and conveyance, which is most clearly seen when buying and selling houses. The promise to transfer property binds the seller to pass that property over to the buyer; the conveyance represents the actual transfer or the performance of the promise to transfer.

[42] *Entick v Carrington* (1765) 2 Wils KB 275; 95 ER 807. See also Richardson (n 35) 2, 118.

[43] Albert Venn Dicey (1835–1922) was the leading constitutional scholar of his day and a great private international lawyer.

[44] R Clayton and H Tomlinson, *The Law of Human Rights*, 2nd edn (Oxford University Press, 2009) [12.118].

[45] A Dicey, *An Introduction to the Study of the Law of the Constitution*, 8th edn (MacMillan & Co, 1923) Ch V.

[46] ibid 202.

that '[t]he security which an Englishman enjoys for personal freedom does not really depend upon or originate in any general proposition contained in any written document',[47] because any incursion into personal freedom is prima facie illegal, unless justified by a specific law.[48] It will be suggested that this (at least nowadays) represents a naive view of the interplay between the state and individual liberty, and the extent to which (without prodding[49]) the common law will actually articulate rights protective of individual liberty. But this Diceyan view of the world continues to hold sway in English law's antipathy to bills of rights.[50]

[4.34] In *Entick v Carrington*, the plaintiff Entick brought an action for trespass for breaking and entering into his house and seizing his papers. The defendants – who were the King's Messengers – pleaded by way of justification a warrant of the Secretary of State which ordered them to search for the plaintiff and bring him, together with his books and papers, into safe custody before the Secretary of State to be examined. Lord Camden CJ considered that the critical question was the legal authority of the Secretary of State to make the warrant:[51]

> … we shall now consider the special justification, whether it can be supported in law, and this depends upon the jurisdiction of the Secretary of State; for if he has no jurisdiction to grant a warrant to break open doors, locks, boxes, and to seize a man and all his books, &c in the first instance upon an information of his being guilty of publishing a libel, the warrant will not justify the defendants …

[4.35] There was, in this case, no lawful basis for the defendants' actions:

> … if this is law it would be found in our books, but no such law ever existed in this country; our law holds the property of every man so sacred, that no man can set his foot upon his neighbour's close without his leave; if he does he is a trespasser, though he does no damage at all; if he will tread upon his neighbour's ground, he must justify it by law …

[47] ibid 202.

[48] ibid 203–204.

[49] In Ch 2, the point was made that the Action only evolved out of the action for breach of confidence because of the Human Rights Act 1998. Equity was said to have developed because of the increasingly static nature of the common law. Now, the rules of equity seem as static as those of the common law.

[50] These problems can be seen in the fact that it took the Human Rights Act 1998 and Art 8 of the ECHR to kick-start the Action: see Ch 2. As will be seen, the Protection of Freedoms Act 2012 does not, contrary to its title, protect our freedoms at all, but in fact entrenches and legalises a whole number of incursions into those freedoms. The Human Rights Act 1998 is the closest thing the United Kingdom has to a bill of rights.

[51] *Entick v Carrington* (n 42) 291; 817.

[**4.36**] The old constitutional law books make much of this case.[52] Apart from the point that 'one's home is one's castle'[53] – a point that informs a great deal of the law of privacy – *Entick v Carrington* enables the following two points to be made. First, it is a good example of Dicey's view of the rule of law. Heuston describes Dicey's position in the following terms and then points to *Entick v Carrington* as a 'great case' that stands as a concrete example of Dicey's thinking:[54]

> Let us then go back to Dicey himself and let us consider first of all what he said and then the more modern criticisms which have been made of his work. According to Dicey the doctrine of the concept of the Rule of Law had three aspects. First, 'it means the absolute supremacy or predominance of regular law as opposed to the influence of arbitrary power, and excludes the existence of arbitrariness, of prerogative, or even of wide discretionary authority on the part of the government. Englishmen are ruled by the law, and by the law alone; a man may with us be punished for a breach of the law, but he can be punished for nothing else'. This was put another way by one of the most distinguished authorities on the common law of the twentieth century, Sir John Latham, a former Chief Justice of Australia: 'It is not the English view of law that whatever is officially done is law – a view adopted by some jurists on the Continent of Europe – on the contrary, the principle of English law is that what is done officially must be done in accordance with law'. These two passages draw a contrast between the position in England and the position on the Continent. On the Continent there may be a general grant of power to the executive; the constitution may then endeavour to protect the private citizen from abuse of that power by guaranteeing certain fundamental rights to him. A general power is granted and then, against the possibility of abuse, there is erected the barrier of a Bill of Rights. The Continental constitution often recognises a 'police power', under which the government may act in a general way for the preservation of the public peace or safety. No such doctrines are recognised by the common law of England. With us a public authority must point, if questioned, to some specific rule of law authorising the act which is called in question. This is, of course, the principle governing the private law of contract and tort. We do not regard the character of an act as having been changed because the author of it is the government or some other public authority. There is no assumption, as there is or was in France, that the relationship of individual citizens to the state is governed by principles different from those which govern the relationship of one citizen to another. And, again, these principles are administered in the ordinary courts of the land, there are with us in general no special courts which govern the relationship between the citizen and the state. As Dicey said, powers whatever their extent must be exercised in accordance with the ordinary common law principles which govern the relationship of one Englishman to another.

[52] See the somewhat hyperbolic description in R Heuston, *Essays in Constitutional Law*, 2nd edn (Stevens, 1964) 35–36.

[53] For explicit judicial recognition of this, see Donaldson LJ in *McLorie v Oxford* [1982] 1 QB 1290: '"An Englishman's home is his castle" is one of the few principles of law known to every citizen ... The rule is, of course, subject to exceptions, but they are very few ...'. Again, those exceptions have expanded over time.

[54] Heuston (n 52) 35. The extract is taken from 33–35.

[4.37] Heuston is quoted at length because there is much that is contentious in what he says:

(1) The distinction between the 'Continental' and the 'English' way is (at least today) rather overstated. Other systems of law – including civilian systems – require that all acts against the interests of individuals (whether by the state or by another actor) be justified in law: England is certainly no special case. Moreover, modern English law is characterised by a large and increasing corpus of law that gives special powers to agents of the state, such that it is no longer possible to say that 'one law rules them all, and that that is the English common law'.[55] It is this development that has rendered administrative law (whereby there *is* judicial control over administrative action) so important and so pervasive: it reflects the exceptional position of the state vis à vis the individual.[56]
(2) The antipathy shown towards a bill of rights is also a little passé. Bills of rights do more than simply act as a bastion against the general powers of the state. We now have, of sorts, our own bill of rights, in the form of the incorporated ECHR; and it is the ECHR that has reinvigorated the common law in regard to privacy. We would not have the Action without the embedding into English law of Article 8 of the ECHR by the Human Rights Act 1998 (HRA 1998).[57]

[4.38] Nevertheless, this extensive reference to *Entick v Carrington* and Heuston's views on the rule of law are important because it remains true that where an individual's right is infringed, that individual will have a remedy against the infringer, unless specific cause can be shown to defeat the claim. This becomes important not only when a private person encroaches on *A*'s privacy, but also in the case of state encroachments on privacy.

[4.39] The second point emerging from *Entick v Carrington* is that it is important to note that the Diceyan vision of the rule of law only works where an individual's *rights* are infringed. It is a case of *ubi ius, ibi remedium*, and there will be no remedy where there is no right. As Heuston puts it, with specific reference to wire-tapping:[58]

> An important limitation on the principle in *Entick v Carrington* must, however, be noted. The principle assumes that the action of the administrator which has been

[55] We will see many examples of specific powers being handed to agents of the state in Ch 8 on the use and misuse of private information by state actors.

[56] The same is true of claims under s 6 of the Human Rights Act 1998: they operate vertically, enabling a person to claim against the state, not horizontally enabling one person to claim against another.

[57] One of the reasons for the antipathy towards bills of rights in some instances is the fact that it places unelected judges above elected representatives. All that need be said is that this is not the inevitable case. Indeed, if the United Kingdom were to withdraw from the ECHR, but maintain in force the HRA 1998, precisely this outcome would obtain.

[58] Heuston (n 52) 50.

> called in question infringes some legally protected interest of the private citizen. Yet upon investigation it may be decided by the court that no such legally protected interest has been infringed.

[4.40] At the time when Heuston was writing (1964), the general view was that wire-tapping did *not* infringe any rights of the individual.[59] The point can be made that if the Action is less extensive than suggested in this book, our privacy really is at risk, for the other protections that exist are not quite to the purpose.[60] The need for a right that can be infringed demonstrates the importance of some general articulation of individual rights (by way of a bill of rights, for instance), if only to provide some impetus to the common law to continue evolving and developing as technology and society themselves evolve and develop.

C. The old case law: Privacy and the evolving law of copyright

i. Prince Albert v Strange

[4.41] The headnote[61] in *Prince Albert v Strange*[62] records:[63]

> Where a workman, intrusted with copperplates for the purpose of taking impressions for the Plaintiff of etchings made by the latter, and not intended for publication, took impressions for himself, in violation of the trust, and sold the impressions to the Defendant, who published a catalogue of them, accompanied by remarks of his own: Held, that the Plaintiff was entitled at the hearing to a perpetual injunction to restrain the publication of the catalogue, and to a decree ordering the impressions to be destroyed; and that the Defendant was not entitled to a preliminary trial of his title at law.

[4.42] It should be noted that the defendant was only indirectly offered the impressions (via a pamphlet or 'Descriptive Catalogue'[64]) and did not directly obtain them from the plaintiff. In other words, this was a case where the right being asserted by A was not against B (ie it was *not* an *in personam* claim) but against C (it would appear by way of a claim *in rem*[65]). In other words, the cause

[59] ibid 50–52. Indeed, Heuston expresses the view (with concern) that interference with post was similarly not an infringement of a person's rights, and so not actionable.

[60] Copyright has been considered. We will be coming to the HRA 1998 and the GDPR later on in this chapter.

[61] A headnote is a summary of what the facts of a case are, and what that case decides, compiled by the law reporter. The first thing a student coming fresh to the law is told on embarking their studies by more senior students is that the headnote is all that needs to be read. It is dangerous advice, but can save a lot of time.

[62] *Prince Albert v Strange* (1849) 2 De G & Sm 652; 64 ER 293. On the case, see also Richardson (n 35) 40 ff.

[63] ibid 652; 293.

[64] ibid 685; 307.

[65] This was *not* the analysis in the judgment. That is one of the difficulties of the law in this area: there is remarkably little analysis.

of action appears to have been *in rem* in nature and not *in personam*. For the plaintiff (Prince Albert, the consort of Queen Victoria), the Solicitor-General contended that the injunction should be granted not because the plaintiff was in contractual relations with the defendant (he was not) nor because of the ownership of the etchings themselves (although the plaintiff was the owner). It is worth setting out the argument in some detail:[66]

> The importance of protecting the right of publishing a catalogue of objects of interest may be illustrated by many examples. About a century and a half ago the Earl of Arundel returned from the East with a collection of marbles of the most valuable description, which he presented to the University of Oxford. Their value chiefly consisted in the inscriptions which appeared upon them, casting light upon the chronology of Greece and ancient history generally. Can anyone doubt that a descriptive catalogue of those marbles would have been a most interesting work, of great value and great importance, and would have been productive of large profit? Would not this Court have restrained any person who had been permitted by the Earl of Arundel to examine the marbles from publishing a descriptive catalogue of them?
>
> Might a person go into the library of a literary man and give an account of any literary work on which he was engaged, or make a catalogue of all his manuscripts?
>
> Take the case of a chemist engaged in experiments from which most important results had been obtained. Would not the Court interfere to prevent the publication of the results derived from the skill and industry of such a chemist, by a person who had been permitted to witness the experiments? *Upon what principle does the Court interfere to prevent the publication of letters, or of recipes in medical science? Upon the principle that there is property in these things, and that the Court of Chancery will not permit another to derive a benefit by infringing the right to such property.*

[4.43] The reference to 'property' in the emphasised passage is significant. The reference is *not* a reference to the ownership, by the plaintiff, of the etchings themselves (although, as stated, the plaintiff *was* the owner of the etchings). That is clear from the example of the chemist, where the protected property was the demonstration of the experiments.[67] Equally, the 'stolen' catalogue of the library of the literary person is protected, whether the books in the library belong to the literary person or to others.

[4.44] The argument made explicit reference to copyright as being:

> not of a simple, but a complex, nature, involving two conditions, one of publication, and the other of exclusion. An author claims the right of multiplying the copies of his work, and of thus securing to himself present reputation and distant fame; and he also claims the advantage of excluding by statute law other persons from multiplying copies of the same work.[68]

[66] *Prince Albert v Strange* (n 62) 669–70; 301 (emphasis added).
[67] That is an example of a trade secrets case, another source that informs the Action.
[68] *Prince Albert v Strange* (n 62) 674; 303.

[4.45] The protected property in copyright is the 'work'. In the context of privacy, it is the 'private information', which (as has already been repeatedly stated) is defined as C's perception of information relating to A, which is classified as being private *to* A. At this point, the relevance of the ownership of the etchings becomes clear: ownership does *not* inform the right of action, but rather the *identity of the claimant*. If the claimant, the Prince Consort, had *not* been the owner of the etchings, it is difficult to see how he could properly have advanced the claim. Only the owner could have done, because (in this case) the fact of ownership caused the right of privacy to arise in that particular person. That does not mean that ownership of property is a *necessary* requirement for the right of privacy in all cases, nor even that it is in all cases a *sufficient* condition. The most that can be said is that in this case, ownership *was* sufficient to enable the Prince Consort to bring the claim.

[4.46] The argument before the court makes clear that the property analysis focuses not on the etchings, but on the impressions (also, sometimes, confusingly referred to as 'etchings') illicitly made therefrom. This is highly instructive:[69]

> There is another aspect in which the case may be regarded, and that is with reference to the mode in which the etchings were acquired. Supposing Mr Strange be as innocent as he declared himself, still, having derived possession through a person who had obtained the property by a breach of trust, he must take the property with all the infirmities in the title to it of the party with whom he agreed to participate in the profits. In *Bridgman v Green*, ... Lord Chief Justice Wilmot said of such a state of things, 'Let the hand receiving it be ever so chaste, if it came through such a corrupt and polluted channel, the obligation of restitution must follow'...
>
> But is such a case of innocence at all probable? What could Mr Strange have thought? Could he have believed that Mr Judge had obtained the etchings from a foreign potentate? It surely must have startled Mr Strange, as a respectable and intelligent man, doing an extensive business, to see the etchings in the possession of an individual whom he must have supposed to be one of the last persons in the world who could have come legitimately by them. Judge came to him, and described himself as connected with the press, and living at Windsor. He brought sixty-two engravings with him, purporting to be the productions of Her Majesty and Prince Albert. Did Mr Strange ask Judge any questions as to how he obtained them? Would that not naturally have been his very first inquiry under such peculiar circumstances? Here was a private individual presenting a collection of Her Majesty's and the Prince's etchings; and was it possible to suppose that Mr Strange asked him no questions, or that Judge could have given any sensible man an answer that would have borne the slightest scrutiny as to how he came by the property? A pawnbroker is prohibited from receiving a valuable article presented to him by a stranger (and especially so if the article is one that it is manifestly improbable that the party offering to pledge it could ever have legitimately obtained), without first making strict inquiries as to how

[69] ibid 678 ff; 304 ff.

> the person came into possession of it; and if a valuable article were offered to him at a very low price, and he abstained from asking the party bringing it any questions, it is a very fair inference to suppose that he was more anxious to get the article than scrupulous as to the means by which it was procured.
>
> Mr Strange says that he believed Judge purchased them from a workman named Middleton. The charge against Mr Strange is that he has sought to make use, for his own profit, of property which, although the paper or card on which it was impressed belonged certainly to Judge, was clearly the property of another. The designs, which alone gave the article its value, had been obtained from a person in a situation in life which could not enable him to be honestly possessed of these etchings. No reasonable person could have thought that Middleton, a mere journeyman pressman, had a right to the etchings, or could sell them for exhibition; and, consequently, the inference was perfectly irresistible that Strange must either have obtained them surreptitiously himself, or have agreed with Judge to make a matter of profit of them, knowing them to have been thus fraudulently obtained.
>
> The right of property has, therefore, in this instance, been manifestly invaded through the medium of a breach of trust. On this ground the case is peculiarly one within the jurisdiction of a Court of Equity, which can, consequently, interfere without putting the Plaintiff to establish his mere legal right, even if the Court should take a different view from that which we have submitted to it, and should consider the legal right subject to any doubt …

[4.47] There is an overt proprietary analysis here. The key question is 'What is the property?'. The original etchings, of which these were impressions, were not in play. The impressions were – like the paper on which the words of a letter are written – the property of the holder/recipient, in this case Mr Judge. Yet the argument was that the etchings could not properly be acquired by Mr Strange from Mr Judge, the owner of the paper.

[4.48] Although the language of property is used, including in particular knowledge of deficiencies of title, the peculiarity of private information is that its status as property depends upon its classification *as* private information.

[4.49] Put another way, it is only if the information is private that it can (at least in this context) achieve the label 'property'. It will only be property if: (i) it is information, by which is meant the perception of C, which (ii) relates to A (ie it is C's perception of A, directly or indirectly, that is in issue), which (iii) is private to A. Items (i) and (ii) are relatively easy to state; (iii) is much harder, because it is necessary to state the test by way of which the question of privacy is determined. Is the information private because A considers that to be the case? Or because C considers that to be the case? Or because the information meets and surpasses an objective standard of what is and what is not private? That is a question that will be considered when the meaning of 'privacy' is dealt with in Chapter 6. It is suggested, however, that the last alternative is the only serious option when it comes to testing for privacy, and that appears to be the approach that was advocated for by the Solicitor-General. The reason the definition of property and the propriety of the transfer are elided is because an objective understanding that A's private information is being used without justification is critical to *both* questions. Although not explicit in his argument, the Solicitor-General appears to have taken, nearly two centuries before this book, a perception-based analysis of privacy.

[4.50] Turning, then, from the argument to the approach adopted by the court, matters become less clear. The Vice-Chancellor (Knight Bruce, V-C) took the following approach.

[4.51] The starting point was that Mr Strange – C using our notation – was on notice that the 'etchings' he was being offered concerned the Prince Consort's – A's – privacy:[70]

> Now this is an answer difficult, I think, or impossible, to read, without being persuaded that, if the person whose answer it is did with fair meaning what he says he did, he acted in a very extraordinary manner indeed. That, being by business a publisher, by residence a Londoner, and of an age so mature as from the answer appears, he should have had the intentions which he ascribes to himself, and should nevertheless have printed and dealt with the pamphlet as he did, without any previous or accompanying communication to the Plaintiff, or any servant of the Plaintiff or of his Consort; should moreover have done so without obtaining or endeavouring to obtain information as to the origin or nature of Middleton's possession, or Jasper Tomsett Judge's title, should also, printing fifty-one, have printed only fifty-one, copies, breaking up then the type (this last fact not being represented as having taken place after the suit or after any remonstrance), does seem to me a combination of circumstances that no man could hear stated without surprise.

Quite clearly an objective approach is again being taken by reference to C's understanding of the facts.

[4.52] Having ascertained, in this way, that private information was at stake, the court was able to conclude that the information was being transmitted irregularly:[71]

> Whatever opinion ought to be formed, however, of his conduct, it is, I think, a proper and correct inference for every present purpose, from the materials before me on this motion, that the person called Middleton in the answer, by whatever process or means that individual had obtained the impressions acquired from him by Mr Jasper Tomsett Judge, had obtained them wrongfully as against the Plaintiff's Consort and the Plaintiff; that Mr Jasper Tomsett Judge did not gain any better title than Jasper Tomsett Judge …

[70] ibid 687; 308.
[71] ibid 688; 308–309.

[4.53] The analysis is 'on the money' to the extent that it sees private information as property. The case recognises that the rights being asserted by A are rights not against B (although such a claim did exist) but against C, a true third party with no bilateral *in personam* obligations owed to A. The reference to 'better title' is a reference to the chains of title by which property can be transmitted. This sort of dealing is considered in Chapter 11. The reference to 'better title' is thus understandable, but not quite correct. It overlooks the fact that this was not a case of transfer, but a case where A had an *in rem* claim against all those persons having a relevant perception of A's private property. That perception was not so much transferred as duplicated.[72]

[4.54] The protection conferred was explicitly based on privacy:[73]

> The Defendants' counsel say that a man acquiring a knowledge of another's property without his consent is not by any rule or principle which a Court of Justice can apply (however secretly he may have kept or endeavoured to keep it) forbidden without his consent to communicate and publish that knowledge to the world, to inform the world what the property is, or to describe it publicly, whether orally, or in print or writing.
>
> I claim, however, leave to doubt whether, as to property of a private nature, which the owner, without infringing on the right of any other, may and does retain in a state of privacy, it is certain that a person who, without the owner's consent, express or implied, acquires a knowledge of it, can lawfully avail himself of the knowledge so acquired to publish without his consent a description of the property.
>
> It is probably true that such a publication may be in a manner or relate to property of a kind rendering a question concerning the lawfulness of the act too slight to deserve attention. I can conceive cases, however, in which an act of the sort may be so circumstanced or relate to property such, that the matter may weightily affect the owner's interest or feelings, or both. For instance, the nature and intention of an unfinished work of an artist, prematurely made known to the world, may be painful and deeply prejudicial to him; nor would it be difficult to suggest other examples.

[4.55] The court drew an explicit contrast between the protection conferred by copyright and the protection being conferred in this case:[74]

> Even Mr Justice Yates said, in *Millar v Taylor*, 'Most certainly the sole proprietor of any copy may determine whether he will print it or not. If any person takes it to the press without his consent, he is certainly a trespasser, though he came by it by legal means, as by loan or by devolution; for he transgresses the bounds of his trust, and therefore is a trespasser.' And again, 'Every man has a right to keep his own

[72] The point is hidden because the court was here concerned with physical things – the catalogue and the impressions of the etchings. But the fact is that the originals, from which the catalogue and the etchings derived, remained in the Prince Consort's ownership and possession, and what the court was controlling was the duplication of the information that should (on the facts of this case) remain in the hands of the claimant and should not (absent consent) be more widely disseminated.

[73] *Prince Albert v Strange* (n 62) 689; 309.

[74] ibid 692 ff; 310 ff.

sentiments, if he pleases. He has certainly a right to judge whether he will make them public or commit them only to the sight of his friends. In that state the manuscript is, in every sense, his peculiar property; and no man can take it from him, or make any use of it which he has not authorised, without being guilty of a violation of his property'.

Now, this protection, by the common law, of literary compositions that have never been, with the consent of the author, the owner, generally published, cannot, I apprehend, be evaded by a translation (the case respecting Dr Burnett's treatise, mentioned by Lord Hardwicke, was, unless I mistake, upon a translation), by an abridgment, a summary, or even a review; for a review professes to treat of the general character of the work reviewed, to analyse or dissect it, and to shew from the contents some reason for the praise or dispraise which it may be the particular critic's task to disseminate.

A work lawfully published, in the popular sense of the term, stands in this respect, I conceive, differently from a work which has never been in that situation. The former may be liable to be translated, abridged, analysed, exhibited in morsels, complimented, and otherwise treated, in a manner that the latter is not.

Suppose, however – instead of a translation, an abridgment or a review – the case of a catalogue – suppose a man to have composed a variety of literary works ('innocent', to use Lord Eldon's expression), which he has never printed or published, or lost the right to prohibit from being published – suppose a knowledge of them unduly obtained by some unscrupulous person, who prints with a view to circulation a descriptive catalogue, or even a mere list of the manuscripts, without authority or consent, does the law allow this? I hope and believe not. The same principles that prevent more candid piracy must, I conceive, govern such a case also.

By publishing of a man that he has written to particular persons, or on particular subjects, he may be exposed, not merely to sarcasm, he may be ruined. There may be in his possession returned letters that he had written to former correspondents, with whom to have had relations, however harmlessly, may not in after life be a recommendation, or his writings may be otherwise of a kind squaring in no sort with his outward habits and worldly position. There are callings, even now, in which, to be convicted of literature, is dangerous, though the danger is sometimes escaped.

Again, the manuscripts may be those of a man on account of whose name alone a mere list would be matter of general curiosity. How many persons could be mentioned, a catalogue of whose unpublished writings would, during their lives or afterwards, command a ready sale.

The question, however, does not turn upon the form or amount of mischief or advantage, loss or gain. The author of manuscripts, whether he is famous or obscure, low or high, has a right to say of them, if innocent, that, whether interesting or dull, light or heavy, saleable or unsaleable, they shall not, without his consent, be published; and I think, as I have said, that to use a dishonest knowledge of them for the purpose of composing and publishing, and so to compose and publish a catalogue of them, amounts to a publication of them within the principle of the rule.

[4.56] The distinction between the rights conferred on an author by copyright and those that protect a person's privacy has already been stressed.

The discussion just set out makes clear that this distinction has been at the heart of the law in this area for a long time.

[**4.57**] In essence, the distinction is between a person's choice to publish (and to forsake privacy) or not to publish (and to maintain privacy). The choice must be that of the person to whom the material relates.

[**4.58**] Doubtless, in the time of this case, there was no means of intruding upon a person's private life *without* forcing this choice – of publication or non-publication – on that person. As Warren and Brandeis made clear, that choice has been abrogated by technology. Now it is possible to photograph or track or publish communications from A without A's involvement at all. There is a *mismatch* between A's ability to publish[75] (and have the protection of copyright) and A's ability not to publish (and have the protection of privacy). Although in some cases the choice still remains, privacy can be traduced without the person whose privacy is in issue having any choice or say in the matter at all.

[**4.59**] In *Prince Albert v Strange*, the consequences of the choice of publication/non-publication were clear. There was an ability to monetise through publication, with the consequent risk that what was published could be used by third parties within legal constraints. For instance, third parties might not be able to reproduce A's work but could *summarise* it or publish an *abstract*. That would not be permissible in the case where A had asserted their right *not* to publish at all.

[**4.60**] The consequence of the development of technology is that it is no longer possible to see privacy and copyright as two sides of the same coin. The protection of privacy necessarily must go far wider. It is suggested that this is the state of English law as it stands today.

[**4.61**] In the time of *Prince Albert v Strange* it was possible to see copyright as a means of *both* protecting the commercial interests of the creator of the original work *and* A's right to privacy. But, in truth, copyright and privacy serve inconsistent objectives, and it was always unlikely that one action could serve to protect both values.

[**4.62**] Thus, the first owner in the case of copyright ought to be the creator of the original work. That person is increasingly unlikely to be the person whose rights of privacy are engaged. The press photographer who, with a long lens, photographs the celebrity rightly owns the copyright in the image, but has no

[75] Or rather 'fix': the term 'publish' is not quite right if one is being technical about copyright. But the inaccuracy is immaterial for present purposes.

need of the law of privacy; the celebrity, on the other hand, clearly ought to have some form of protection from intrusion.

Example[76]

In the summer of 2012, the then Duchess of Cambridge was photographed sunbathing topless on a private terrace in France. The photographs were taken from a public road. When this came to be known, Clarence House commented:

'The incident is reminiscent of the worst excesses of the press and paparazzi during the life of Diana, Princess of Wales, and all the more upsetting to the Duke and Duchess for being so. Their Royal Highnesses had every expectation of privacy in the remote house.

It is unthinkable that anyone should take such photographs, let alone publish them. Officials acting on behalf of their Royal Highnesses are consulting with lawyers to consider what options may be available to the Duke and Duchess.'

The magazine *Closer* was unrepentant:

'One shouldn't over-dramatise these pictures. The reactions are a little disproportionate. What we saw in the pictures was a young couple that have just got married, who are in love, who are beautiful. She's a princess of the 21st century. They are on the terrace of a mansion in the south of France which is not far from a road along which cars pass without any problem. They are visible from the street.

She's a young woman who is topless just like the ones who can be seen on all the beaches of France and the world. It's a member of the British Royal Family. There have been pictures before that. Two weeks ago, there were the pictures of Prince Harry that had been published by the English press. So one shouldn't be hypocritical. And those pictures were degrading and far hotter than those that we're publishing. She's a topless princess. There have been others. It's really not new.'

The interests of the photographer and the subject of the photograph will often diverge, and different rights are engaged.

[**4.63**] Copyright is a protection against the copying of the original. If C were to illicitly read A's diary, which (let us suppose) confessed to an affair with another married person, C would be prevented by copyright from publishing extracts from the diary, but not from disclosing the fact of the affair.

ii. Abernethy v Hutchinson

[**4.64**] In *Abernethy v Hutchinson*,[77] it was held that where C attends A's oral lectures, C is not justified in publishing them for profit, and that an action by A would lie against C to recover the profits made. *Abernethy v Hutchinson*

[76] BBC News, 'Kate topless photos reaction' (14 September 2012), available at www.bbc.com/news/uk-19596681.

[77] *Abernethy v Hutchinson* (1825) 1 H & Tw 28; 47 ER 1313.

pre-dates *Prince Albert v Strange* by some decades, but is nevertheless appropriately considered *after* that later decision.

[4.65] The facts were that Mr Abernethy was a distinguished surgeon and a lecturer at the theatre of St Bartholomew's Hospital on the principles and practice of surgery. The attendees paid to attend – so there was clearly a contract involved. Mr Abernethy said this about the content of these lectures:[78]

> … these lectures were delivered by him, as from writings, the property of the Plaintiff, and composed by him, and which the Plaintiff had not yet printed or published, and that they were his own sentiments and language; that he had not authorised the publication thereof, or given such authority to any of the persons respectively attending the said lectures, or to any person or persons whatsoever; that he intended to print and publish his said course of lectures; that lectures had for a great number of years been delivered by the Plaintiff and by eminent persons his predecessors; and that, from the understanding and usage subsisting for a long space of time between the lecturer and the persons attending the same, no publication of lectures had ever been made by the persons attending them; that on the 9th of October 1824 was published a number or part of a periodical work called The Lancet, in which was described, as in the very words and figures thereof, in the name of the Plaintiff, the lecture which he had so as the aforesaid delivered on Monday evening, the 4th of October; that the said work held out to the public, that it then gave, and that from time to time it would continue to give, the Plaintiff's said lecture and lectures with minute fidelity …

[4.66] The Lord Chancellor, Lord Eldon, accepted that there were suggestions in the authorities[79] that a person, like Mr Abernethy, might 'have a property in sentiments and language, though not deposited on paper', 'but there has been no decision upon that point yet. And as it is a pure question of law, I think it would be going further than a Judge in equity should go, to say, upon that, that he can grant an injunction upon it, before the point is tried'.[80]

[4.67] Instead, Lord Eldon decided the case on an implied contract basis, namely an obligation in the defendants not to re-publish:[81]

> … where the lecture was orally delivered, it was difficult to say that an injunction could be granted upon the same principle upon which literary composition was protected; because the Court must be satisfied that the publication complained of was an invasion of the written work; and this could only be done by comparing the composition with the piracy. But it did not follow, that, because the information communicated by the lecturer was not committed to writing, but orally delivered, it was, therefore, within the power of the person who heard it to publish

[78] ibid 29–30; 1313.
[79] Notably, *Millar v Taylor* (1769) 4 Burr 2303; 98 ER 201.
[80] *Abernethy v Hutchinson* (n 77) 35; 1316.
[81] Lord Eldon framed the question at ibid, 35–36; 1316 and decided the issue at 39 ff; 1317 ff.

> it. On the contrary, he was clearly of opinion, that whatever else might be done with it, the lecture could not be published for profit. He had the satisfaction now of knowing, and he did not possess that knowledge when this question was last considered, that this doctrine was not a novel one; and that this opinion was confirmed by that of some of the Judges of the land. He was, therefore, clearly of opinion, that, when persons were admitted as pupils or otherwise to hear these lectures, although they were orally delivered, and although the parties might go to the extent, if they were able to do so, of putting down the whole by means of shorthand, yet they could do that only for the purposes of their own information, and could not publish for profit that which they had not obtained the right of selling … He had no doubt whatever that an action would lie against a pupil who published these lectures …

In other words, Lord Eldon saw this as a bilateral A versus B case, where A's rights against B arose *in personam*, in this case out of contract.

[4.68] The problem was that the publication was *not* by those attending the lectures, but by third parties to whom (it was inferred) those attending had communicated their notes. In other words, Lord Eldon was seeking to impose an *in personam* obligation on a *stranger* to that personal obligation. Whilst it might be easy to infer a contractual obligation not to publish as between the lecturer A and the persons paying to attend the lecture B_1 to B_n, creating a contractual obligation with a third party C, a stranger to the lecture, is obviously far harder.[82] Nevertheless, the Lord Chancellor concluded that an implied contract could arise in such circumstances:[83]

> How the gentlemen who had published them came by them, he did not know; but whether an action could be maintained against them or not, on the footing of implied contract, an injunction undoubtedly might be granted; because, if there had been a breach of contract on the part of the pupil who heard these lectures, and if the pupil could not publish for profit, to do so would certainly be what this Court would call a fraud in a third party. If these lectures had not been taken from a pupil, at least the Defendants had obtained the means of publishing them and had become acquainted with the matter of the lectures, in such a manner that this Court would not allow of a publication. It by no means followed, because an action could not be maintained, that an injunction ought not to be granted …

[4.69] The decision shows, quite clearly, the limits of both the copyright analysis of privacy and the limits – indeed, intellectual barrenness – of a contractual or *in personam* analysis of privacy rights. It is by no means clear that an action for infringement of copyright would have lain in this case.[84] There was no

[82] There was no suggestion that B were acting as agents of C, which would create bilateral relations between A and C.

[83] *Abernethy v Hutchinson* (n 77) 40–41; 1317–18.

[84] Even if, in this case, such an action could successfully have been brought, in other cases the rule would be easy to sidestep by summarising the essence of the lectures, without repeating them verbatim.

'work' to be copied. It can be debated whether – given the subject matter – this is better seen as a trade secrets case, and not a privacy case. At the end of the day, that distinction really does not matter, for this book will advance the thesis that trade secrets are (or can be) a form of private information.

[4.70] Whilst the contractual claim is easy to see as against the note-taking pupils, it is clear that the juridical basis for the injunction against the strangers was hard for the Lord Chancellor to frame. The point is that a contractual obligation operates *in personam* and binds only the person giving the promise. What the Lord Chancellor appears to have done, is held that there was some way in which A could claim against C. But the basis for that claim is obscure.

[4.71] Another of the interesting things about *Abernethy* is that there *was* publication, not (at least not unequivocally) protected by copyright, but which did result in a form of protection for Mr Abernethy. There are, thus, three categories of material that may need to be differentiated:

(1) *Material that is entirely unpublished.* In such circumstances, C will not have perceived A's private information absent some form of wrongdoing on C's part in order to gain perception of A's private information. Such wrongdoing is likely to be easy to use as the basis for A establishing a claim against C, either enjoining the use of such material or else obtaining damages.
(2) *Material that is published in a legally recognised regime.* Where, for instance, material is recognised as an invention (patentable) or as a work (protected by copyright) or as a business mark (protected as a trade mark or by the law of passing off), the rules of the game are well understood. Here, the law of privacy ought either to take a 'back seat' or else be jettisoned from the vehicle altogether. The existing legal regime ought to be all-in-all sufficient to protect the legitimate interests of both A and C.
(3) *Material that is not completely unpublished, but whose (limited) publication does not fall within any single legally recognised regime.* In practice, this is the borderline between copyrighted material and non-copyrighted material. It is clear from what we have seen that the mere fact that publication does not trigger copyright protection does *not* mean that there is no protection at all.

iii. Miller v Taylor

[4.72] In 1769, in *Miller v Taylor*,[85] the publishers of a work succeeded in establishing a common law (as opposed to statutory) copyright. The decision was reversed by the House of Lords in *Donaldson v Beckett*,[86] but the decision

[85] (1769) 4 Burr 2303; 98 ER 201.
[86] (1774) 2 Bro PC 129; 1 ER 837.

in *Miller v Taylor* is nevertheless of significance, even if bad law.[87] The case concerned the extent to which a form of common law copyright could exist beyond the limits of the statutory right conferred by the (then) Act of Queen Anne. It was found in *Miller v Taylor* that such a common law right did exist. The problem – and it may be the fault of the judgments or of the reporting of the judgments or both, it is hard to say which from the reports – is that no clear *ratio* beyond this can be discerned. Indeed, the law reports of this case demonstrate very well why the common law does not 'do' legislation. The clash of competing values is evident in the reports: the ability in an author to monetise their work versus the importance of diffusing productions of the mind as widely as possible. What is clear from the reports is that privacy was *not* very much in mind, but the importance of the common law not encroaching on the business of Parliament *was*. Thus, the report notes:[88]

> Whatever encouragement may be due to authors, the common law cannot, after the silence of ages, pronounce at once upon a new species of right, which has been hitherto property, not properly known. Bank notes are of a value well ascertained, and yet the common law did not adapt itself to that emergence of commerce; but it was for the Legislature to make the stealing it, or taking it by robbery, a felony … The statute of Anne was not declaratory of the common law, but introductive of a new law, to give learned men a property which they had not before.

[4.73] Then as now, copyright is a creature of statute, just as the Action is a creature of common law, aided in its development by Article 8 of the ECHR and the HRA 1998. It is better that the dual protections of copyright and privacy be kept separate. To be sure: they are closely related. But they protect different things, and a widening of the law of copyright is unlikely to solve issues relating to privacy.

iv. Fixation

[4.74] The limits of the law of copyright become important in terms of what publication is protected, and what is not. This is a question of 'fixation':[89]

> It is a long-established principle of UK copyright law the copyright does not subsist in a work unless and until the work takes some material form. This principle is known as the requirement of fixation. The reasons for this principle are practical. Since copyright is a form of monopoly in relation to the subject matter which is protected, there must be certainty as to what that subject matter is. This is necessary so as to be able both to prove the existence of the work and to establish what

[87] *Gurry* (n 40) [2.43].

[88] *Donaldson v Beckett* (1774) 2 Bro PC 129; 1 ER 837 at 139–40; 843.

[89] *Copinger and Skone James*, Vol 1 (n 17) [3-179]. More recently, see the latest edition of the volume, G Harbottle et al, *Copinger and Skone James on Copyright*, Vol 1, 19th edn (Sweet & Maxwell, 2025) [2-173]–[2-181].

> the work consists of, so that it can be judged whether the work has been copied or otherwise infringed. Fixation also provides a limit to the monopoly, ensuring that the protection accorded to the work does not extend beyond the expression of the work to the ideas or information contained or represented in it. This is necessary in holding a balance between the author's interests and society's interests. Further, fixation provides a defined moment when the work takes existence, essential for the purpose of applying the rules as to the status of its author.

[4.75] Fixation – and this passage in particular, describing it – provides real insight into the limits of copyright, and why it is not a remedy for invasions of privacy, save incidentally: (i) privacy needs to focus on the substance of what C perceives, whereas copyright looks to form, the copying of the original; (ii) the owner of the copyright is increasingly unlikely to be the person whose privacy needs to be protected; and (iii) privacy needs to focus on C's perception not A's fixation of their work. The point about the protection of privacy, and the Action that protects it, is that what is protected is emphatically *not* form of expression, but substance. Copyright, on the other hand, has priorities that are exactly inverted.

D. Privacy and trade secrets

[4.76] The emergence of the Action from the claim against breach of confidence has already been described.[90] There are a number of cases – in fact *Abernethy* is one – where copyright does not provide sufficient protection for trade secrets. The action for breach of confidence, described in Chapter 2, does, and has itself ancient origins. It is already clear from the discussion of the early copyright cases that the courts regarded protection of unpublished works (which, if published would be copyright) as also being in need of protection.

[4.77] *Morison v Moat*[91] is a trade secrets case decided a couple of years after *Prince Albert v Strange*. As *Gurry* notes,[92] the background facts are somewhat complicated, and the following is taken from *Gurry*'s helpful summary of the facts:[93]

> … James Morison invented [a] medicine, which proved a huge success. He entered a partnership in 1830 with Thomas Moat to exploit the invention, the partnership to last 20 years. Morison revealed the secret to Moat, and the latter undertook not to disclose it (on pain of a penalty of £5,000). In due course, the partnership was expanded to include the two plaintiffs, sons of James Morison. After five years,

[90] See Ch 2.
[91] (1851) 9 Hare 241; 68 ER 492.
[92] *Gurry* (n 40) [2.88].
[93] ibid [2.88].

> Moat died, and his share of the partnership vested in the defendant, William Crofton Moat, and an agreement was entered whereby he would simply be a sleeping partner, but with no role in the business. When the partnership was finally dissolved in 1851, the defendant started to advertise that he would sell the medicine. The plaintiffs sought injunctive relief, claiming that they were the owners of the secret, and the defendant claimed that he had learned it as a partner and that is was a partnership asset.

[4.78] The court held that the trade secret was not a partnership asset, and that the partnership's function had been limited to exploitation (with consent) of that asset, without the asset itself ever becoming an asset of the partnership. Although the decision could have been founded on a property analysis, the court (whilst not denying this as a possible analysis) was altogether more agnostic in its approach:[94]

> That the court has exercised jurisdiction in cases of this nature does not, I think, admit of any question. Different grounds have indeed been assigned for the exercise of that jurisdiction. In some cases it has been referred to property, in others to contract, and in others again, it has been treated as founded upon trust or confidence, meaning, as I conceive, that the court fastens the obligation on the conscience of the party, and enforces it against him in the same manner as it enforces against a party to whom a benefit is given the obligation of performing a promise on the faith of which the benefit has been conferred; but, upon whatever grounds the jurisdiction is founded, the authorities leave no doubt as to the exercise of it.

[4.79] Just as there is an important relationship between the protection of 'private' information and copyright, so too there is a similarly important relationship between 'trade secrets' and patents. In argument before the court, a contrast was made with the rights of the owner of a patent:[95]

> It was much pressed in argument, on the part of the Defendant, that the effect of granting an injunction in such a case as the present would be to give the Plaintiffs a better right than that of a patentee …; but what we have to deal with here, is not the right of the Plaintiffs against the world, but their right against the Defendant. It may well be that the Plaintiffs have no title against the world in general, and may yet have a good title against this Defendant …

[4.80] The contrast drawn is of interest and is suggestive of the existence of two different property rights. Assuming (which is by no means always going to be the case) the 'trade secret' to be patentable,[96] A will have the choice as to whether to patent the invention or not. If the patent route is taken, then A acquires a territorially and temporally limited monopoly, but must (as part of the so-called 'patent bargain') publish the invention for all to see. The patent is a

[94] (1851) 9 Hare 241, 255; 68 ER 492, 498.
[95] At 258–59; 500.
[96] The trade secret may not be an invention and so not patentable.

property right, 'good against all the world', with all the appurtenances of property – the ability to exclude, to exploit and to transfer. It does not follow that if A declines to patent (or cannot patent) they forfeit all legal protection and that the trade secret, even if not patented, is not property. The fact that A has not patented that which *could* have been patented says nothing about A's rights in circumstances where no patent has been granted or applied for.

[4.81] The position is that A's unpatented trade secret *can* constitute private information and *can* amount to a form of property. The court was right to observe that whereas the property rights of a patentee are *uniform*, the property rights of A over their trade secrets depend, in terms of their existence and extent, on the basis on which C acquired knowledge of the trade secret from A. In other words, what must be asked is the *basis* for C's perception of A's trade secret. Suppose C_1 finds out about A's trade secret by bugging A's premises. A ought to have a means, as against C_1, of restraining C_1 from using A's trade secret. On the other hand, suppose A has told C_2 about their trade secret in detail but in circumstances where no objective observer could appreciate a relationship of confidence to exist or any other constraint on C_2 so far as A's trade secret is concerned. It would be surprising if A had any claim against C_2, if C_2 chose to use the information vouchsafed them in these circumstances.[97]

[4.82] This example demonstrates that an absence of uniformity of right of action does not undermine the property analysis: it merely makes clear that the circumstances in which C perceives A's private information are critical to reaching an answer.

[4.83] *Seager v Copydex Ltd* is a seminal trade secrets case.[98] The claimant, Mr Seager, had invented a carpet grip, which he patented. He negotiated with the defendants with a view to marketing the grip, but nothing came of the negotiations. However, during the course of the negotiations, Mr Seager disclosed to the defendants the features of an alternative grip, not part of the patented design, which information was given to the defendants in confidence. When negotiations ended, the defendants made a carpet grip that was not infringing of Mr Seager's patent, but which embodied his non-patented alternative. They even gave this alternative grip the same name as that used by Mr Seager. Mr Seager claimed for an injunction and/or an inquiry as to damages. Mr Seager's claim failed at first instance but succeeded on appeal. The question is on what basis was that success achieved. The leading judgment was given by Lord Denning MR.

[97] On the other hand – and we will be coming to the important case of *Seager v Copydex Ltd*, where the facts were similar to the first of these cases – were A to have entered into a non-disclosure agreement with B, then A would have an *in personam* claim against B.

[98] *Seager v Copydex Ltd* [1967] 1 WLR 923.

[4.84] The judge held that Copydex honestly believed that the grip they had developed 'was their own idea; but I think that they must unconsciously have made use of the information which Mr Seager gave them'.[99] The judge made clear that where a defendant 'is proved to have used confidential information, directly or indirectly obtained from the plaintiff, without the consent, express or implied, of the plaintiff, he will be guilty of an infringement of the plaintiff's rights'.[100]

[4.85] Although these words seem consistent with a property analysis,[101] that was *not* Lord Denning MR's analysis:[102]

> The law on this subject does not depend on any implied contract. It depends on the broad principle of equity that he who has received information in confidence shall not take unfair advantage of it. He must not make use of it to the prejudice of him who gave it without obtaining his consent. The principle is clear enough when the whole of the information is private. The difficulty arises when the information is in part public and in part private. As, for instance, in this case. A good deal of the information which Mr Seager gave to Copydex was available to the public, such as the patent specification in the Patent Office, or the 'Klent' grip, which he sold to anyone who asked. If that was the only information he gave them, he could not complain. It was public knowledge. But there was a good deal of other information he gave them which was private, such as the difficulties which had to be overcome in making a satisfactory grip; the necessity for a strong, sharp tooth; the alternative forms of tooth; and the like. When the information is mixed, being partly public and partly private, then the recipient must take special care to use only the material which is in the public domain. He should go to the public source and get it: or, at any rate, not be in a better position than if he had gone to the public source. He should not get a start over others by using the information which he received in confidence. At any rate, he should not get a start without paying for it. It may not be a case for injunction or even for an account, but only for damages, depending on the worth of the confidential information to him in saving him time and trouble.

[4.86] Lord Denning's analysis is right in terms of outcome, but hopeless in terms of *why* that outcome pertains. The basis for A's claim against C is simply not addressed, save to assert the negative, that this is not a case of contract.[103]

[99] ibid 931.

[100] ibid 931, citing with approval the words of Lord Greene MR in *Saltman Engineering Co v Campbell Engineering Co* (1948) 65 RPC 203, 213.

[101] The word 'infringement' is significant, as are the words 'directly or indirectly', which implies rights against third parties.

[102] *Seager v Copydex Ltd* (n 98) 931–32.

[103] This is interesting, because a contractual analysis (based upon an implied contract between Mr Seager and Copydex) was in this bilateral case at least possible. But Lord Denning MR eschewed this analysis.

The position advanced in this book, it will come as no surprise, is that analysing the case in terms of C's perception of A's private information provides the intellectual basis for the right, and explains the nature of the Action.

[**4.87**] Buckley LJ similarly acquitted Copydex of 'any conscious plagiarism'[104] and allowed Mr Seager's appeal to succeed on a basis that is unsatisfactorily opaque:[105]

> ... the germ of the idea and the broad principle of the domed, V-shaped prong was, I am certain, implanted in their minds by the plaintiff at the confidential interview of March 13, 1962, and afterwards subconsciously reproduced and used, if only as a spring-board, to forestall the plaintiff with 'Invisigrip'. This is no reflection upon their honesty, but it does impinge the plaintiff's rights.

There the judgment ends.

[**4.88**] Winn LJ also allowed the appeal:[106]

> Unconscious plagiarism of ideas is no less common, I venture to think, than the phenomenon of multiple contemporaneous invention, of which counsel for the defendants spoke. To my own mind it appears that the proper conclusion to be drawn from all the material before the court, not by any means primarily from the direct evidence, is that the plaintiff did explain his 'Invisigrip' idea to Mr Boon and Mr Preston; that they absorbed what he told them; and were able to recall enough from their memories to indicate to Mr Sudbury and Mr Turl what they wanted them to produce. In doing so, they did not, I think, realise that they were infringing a duty of confidence: I think that they did infringe it. In so holding I do not imply any condemnation of Mr Boon or Mr Preston as dishonest men. Mr Preston made a most revealing statement at day 4, p. 9A, where he said: '... action for breach of confidence. I did not know such a thing existed ... the only problem was that we might infringe his patent'.

Again, the basis for the result is unstated.

[**4.89**] *Seager v Copydex Ltd* is significant because the distinction between the patented invention and the trade secret emerges so clearly from the facts. There was no question of patent infringement, Copydex were careful to avoid that. Copydex clearly regarded the information outside the scope of the patent as 'fair game'. The Court of Appeal unanimously disagreed. Yet the case is remarkably sparse as to the reason why Mr Seager's claim should succeed. Neither the judgments of Buckley nor Winn LJJ assist at all; Lord Denning MR asserts that 'he who has received information in confidence shall not take unfair advantage

[104] ibid 935.
[105] ibid 936.
[106] ibid 939–40.

of it': but that begs more questions than it answers. By what standard is the 'what is unfair' question to be measured? The following points seem to be of significance:

- There was no contract underpinning the obligation of confidence.
- The infringement of Mr Seager's (A's) rights by Copydex (B or C?, that is the question) was unintentional and unconscious. In this, Mr Seager's cause of action bore marked similarity to infringements of patents, where the infringement is no less of an infringement for being unconscious. Whilst in the case of copyright infringement some perception of the original work is required, a patent can be infringed without C knowing *anything* of the patent or the invention patented.
- There was no improper conduct on the part of B or C unless B or C's perception of A's idea somehow came to B burdened or fettered by A's rights. That – consistently with the thesis here advanced – is the only sound explanation for the outcome. B or C had perceived A's private information in circumstances where B or C was precluded from using that information.

[4.90] So, much as it might seem to be an *in personam* claim – where the bilateral relationship is between A and B – it can quite plausibly be contended that Mr Seager's claim against Copydex is better categorised as an *in rem* claim of A against C. What misleads us into an *in personam* classification is the fact that A's rights are not uniform against the world, they are moulded by C's perception. That subjectivity is unusual in property rights, but does not (it is suggested) detract from the correctness of the property analysis.

[4.91] Claims of confidence have been framed, found to exist and upheld many times since *Seager v Copydex*. In *Coco v AN Clark (Engineers) Ltd*, Megarry J articulated the elements necessary to found an action for breach of an equitable obligation of confidence as follows:[107]

> First, the information itself … must 'have the necessary quality of confidence about it'. Secondly, that information must have been communicated in circumstances importing an obligation of confidence. Thirdly, there must have been an unauthorised use of the information to the detriment of the party communicating it.

[4.92] Again, this formulation makes the claim appear much more *in personam* than is the case, particularly given the second requirement, that the information 'must have been communicated in circumstances importing an

[107] [1969] RPC 41 at 47. This formulation has been widely approved: *Attorney-General v Guardian Newspapers Ltd (No 2)* [1990] 1 AC 109 at 268; *Campbell v MGN Ltd* [2004] UKHL 22 at [13]; *OBG v Allen* [2007] UKHL 21 at [111]; *Primary Group v The Royal Bank of Scotland* [2014] EWHC 1082 (Ch) at [208]. See also L Bently et al, *Intellectual Property Law*, 6th edn (Oxford University Press, 2022) 1243–44.

obligation of confidence'. In *Primary Group v The Royal Bank of Scotland*,[108] Arnold J suggested a further requirement, namely that 'the unauthorised use of information was without lawful excuse'.

[4.93] The nature of the obligation of confidence has become clearer. Time was when a confidential relationship between A and B needed to be established.[109] The test is now that an obligation of confidence exists 'where confidential information is disclosed in breach of an obligation of confidence (which may itself be contractual or equitable) and the recipient knows, or has notice, that that is the case'.[110]

[4.94] This later case law makes the basis for the equitable obligation of confidence no clearer. An equitable obligation of confidence is a reversion to the discredited notion of the 'Chancellor's foot'.[111] What the courts are saying is that there is a breach of confidence where confidence is breached. Furthermore, the equitable nature of the cause of action sits ill with the relatively recent classification of the claim as tortious. Prior to this, as has been described, a number of different bases for the claim were articulated.[112] The pigeonholing of the action as tortious does not, however, solve the problem of the *nature* of A's rights, which turns on whether the tort is a proprietary tort protecting A's *in rem* claims against C or whether it simply enables A to vindicate a personal obligation owed to A by B.

[4.95] As noted at paragraphs [4.81]–[4.82], what misleads us into an *in personam* classification is the fact that A's rights are not uniform against the world. They are moulded by the 'relationship of confidence' between A and B (to deploy the label and the classification used in the cases) or they are moulded by C's perception and the manner in which that perception was derived (to use the analysis and classification in this book). This subjectivity does not detract from the correctness of the property analysis. The contention is reinforced, however, by the fact that the action of breach of confident affects third party C and is not just a bilateral right that A can assert against B. This is demonstrated by *Abernethy*, but also by the cases considered next.

[108] [2014] EWHC 1082 (Ch) at [208].

[109] Eg *A v B plc* [2002] EWCA Civ 337, [11(ix)]; Bently et al (n 107) 1262. This of course makes the 'contractual' or 'bialteral' *in personam* aspect much more evident.

[110] *Primary Group v The Royal Bank of Scotland* [2014] EWHC 1082 (Ch) at [210]–[211], [223]; Bently et al (n 107) 1262.

[111] John Selden said this of the law of equity: 'Equity is a roguish thing: for law we have a measure, know what to trust to; equity is according to the conscience of him that is Chancellor; and as that is larger or narrower, so is equity. 'Tis all one, as if they should make the standard for the measure we call a foot, a Chancellor's foot: what an uncertain measure would that be? One Chancellor has a long foot, another a short foot, a third an indifferent foot: 'tis the same thing in a Chancellor's conscience'.

[112] See the discussion in Ch 2.

E. Claims against third parties: A v C

i. An attempt at further classification

[4.96] Where A claims against B, seeking to restrain B from using A's private information, the basis for the cause of action will likely be *in personam* and (generally speaking) contractual. The problem – which arose in *Abernethy v Hutchinson* – is that where A seeks to claim against a person C the contractual analysis cannot hold. It is very difficult to articulate a *contractual* basis for A's claim against C, a 'stranger' to the contract. The analysis – in order to make sense – has got to be proprietary. The court in *Abernethy* erred in adopting a contractual analysis in a third party case.[113]

[4.97] A number of cases have held that A can have a claim against C, *Prince Albert v Strange* and *Abernethy v Hutchinson* both being examples. In these cases, the juridical basis for the claim is not clear, presumably because the judges could not actually identify that basis. As Bently et al note:[114]

> It was the case for many years that courts would struggle with justifying an obligation of confidence being imposed on a person who received the confidential information when that person was outside the initial confider-confidant relationship. The test set out in *Primary Group v The Royal Bank of Scotland* means that third parties, as well as those within any confidential relationship are bound by the knowledge/notice test. Thus, where information confidential to A is disclosed by B to C in circumstances where C knew or ought to have known that it was confidential to A then C is under an obligation of confidence to A. The obligation placed upon C may be not to disclose the information at all or to use the information for a particular purpose. In other words, the scope of the duty imposed on those receiving the information indirectly from the person owed the obligation can be as diverse as when it is received directly.

Obviously *something* is going on: but no-one has articulated *what* is going on.

[4.98] Before considering the cases, it is necessary to identify two ways in which a third-party claim may arise. The *first* is the case described by Bently in the passage at paragraph [4.97]. This is where there is a chain whereby B passes confidential information on to C in circumstances where B is under a duty of confidence, and C is aware of the facts that give rise to that duty. C is 'infected' by their knowledge of B's confidential obligations with their own duty of confidence to A. These types of case may be called 'chain' cases, because there is a link between C's duty of confidence and the manner in which C has received the confidential information from B.

[113] See paras [4.68]–[4.71], where the court's approach is criticised.
[114] Bently et al (n 107) 1265.

[4.99] This looks like a chain of *in personam* obligations, but it is not: C owes *nothing* to B: the duty of confidence is owed by C to A, not B. It is better to say that both B and C have perceived A's private information in circumstances (yet to be defined, but quite possibly different as between B and C) where their use of A's information is, in some way (also yet to be defined, and also likely to be different) limited. In this way:

(1) It does not matter that B's perception of A's private information does not arise through contract. We do not need to construct a bilateral obligation, because we can say that A's rights against B depend not on personal obligation, but on the fact that the circumstances in which B has obtained their perception of A restrict B's ability to use that information.
(2) When it comes to C, the question is exactly the same: are the circumstances in which C obtained their perception of A restrictive of C's ability to use that information? It may be that the manner in which B's perception has been obtained triggers an obligation of confidence, but that the manner in which B has communicated the same information to C is not sufficient to trigger a similar obligation in C.

[4.100] In this way, the problem of justifying an obligation of confidence on a third party, like C, is not to say that we are stretching B's bilateral obligations to A so as to extend them to C. We are saying that B is obliged to A in exactly the same way as C. In other words, the general position is that B is incorrectly classified (using our nomenclature, B should be classified as C_1), and this is really a case of A claiming against C_1 (the former B) and C_2 (the former C) by way of an *in rem* Action. In short, the bilateral analysis is jettisoned both as against the former B and the former C.

[4.101] The *second* case is simply a special case of the general position already discussed: what is the analysis where there is *no* kind of plausible bilateral relationship between A and the defendant that A claims against? In other words, there is no 'chain' A → B → C *at all*, just the fact that C – as in the Example at paragraph [4.62] – is capturing A's private information without any involvement or knowledge of A at all. The answer is the same as in the first case: a proprietary analysis resolves the problem of an absence of a bilateral relationship. The distance photographer C is not in any kind of bilateral relationship with A: rather, the constraints on C involve a consideration of the manner in which C is seeking to deploy or use the private information over A that they have captured.

[4.102] Although the difference between the first and the second case is illusory, the case law does observe the distinction, which needs to be respected for that reason. But the analysis in this book holds that there is *no distinction* between these types of case.

ii. 'Chain' claims

[4.103] *Primary Group v The Royal Bank of Scotland*[115] is the case which sought to articulate the manner in which information in B's hands, which B has passed to C, could be the subject of a claim by A against C. In other words, this is a case dealing with a 'chain' claim. The facts of the case are complex, and it is unnecessary to set them out. The claims before the judge (Arnold J) were direct, contractual, claims,[116] as well as direct, equitable, claims.[117] Additionally (and for present purposes significantly) indirect claims were brought, where A was claiming against C, not B. Arnold J said:[118]

> It follows from the statements of principle I have quoted above that an equitable obligation of confidence will arise not only where confidential information is disclosed in breach of an obligation of confidence (which may itself be contractual or equitable) and the recipient knows, or has notice, that that is the case, *but also where confidential information is acquired or received without having been disclosed in breach of confidence and the acquirer or recipient knows, or has notice, that the information is confidential. Either way, whether a person has notice is to be objectively assessed by reference to a reasonable person standing in the position of the recipient.*

[4.104] Two points arise:

(1) It is by no means clear that *notice* ought to be a part of the cause of action against B, let alone C. *Why* is notice relevant? That question can only be answered when the juridical basis for the claim is itself clear. But notice to C is conceptually quite close, albeit also quite different, from C's perception of A, and it may be that the issue is a linguistic or terminological one only.
(2) It is not clear whether Arnold J was framing a general obligation of confidence, such that (provided a third party has objective notice of confidentiality) an obligation of confidence exists. If that is the true reading of the emphasised words, then his is a statement of the existence of an *in rem* right vesting in A.

iii. 'No chain' claims

[4.105] In *Malone v Commissioner of Metropolitan Police*,[119] the plaintiff was prosecuted in the Crown Court, charged with handling stolen property.

[115] *Primary Group v The Royal Bank of Scotland* [2014] EWHC 1082 (Ch).
[116] ibid [175]. Where there is a contract, 'the ordinary principles of contract law apply to a claim for breach of a contractual obligation of confidence'. That is obviously correct.
[117] ibid [207]. Arnold J cited the decision of Megarry J in *Coco v AN Clark (Engineers) Ltd*, [1969] RPC 41 at 47.
[118] ibid [223] (emphasis added).
[119] *Malone v Commissioner of Metropolitan Police* [1979] 1 Ch 344. This was a case before the Police and Criminal Evidence Act 1984, which contains provisions regarding the exclusion of unlawfully obtained evidence. These provisions are considered in Ch 8, where the misuse of private

The plaintiff's telephone conversations had been intercepted on the authority of the Secretary of State's warrant. The conversations were to be relied upon, by the prosecution, in the criminal proceedings and the plaintiff, by these civil proceedings, sought to restrain their use, contending that their deployment without his consent was unlawful and that the plaintiff had a right of property, privacy and confidentiality in respect of telephone conversations on his telephone lines.

[4.106] The judge (Sir Robert Megarry V-C) made it clear that a very narrow form of interception of communications was before him:[120]

> I think that I should make it clear that the only form of telephone tapping that has been debated is tapping which consists of the making of recordings by Post Office officials in some part of the existing telephone system, and the making of those recordings available to police officers for the purposes of transcription and use. I am not concerned with any form of tapping that involved electronic devices which make wireless transmissions, nor with any process whereby anyone trespasses on to the premises of the subscriber or anyone else to affix tapping devices or the like. All that I am concerned with is the legality of tapping effected by means of recording telephone conversations from wires which, though connected to the premises of the subscriber, are not on them.

[4.107] A number of the plaintiff's arguments were based upon Article 8 of the ECHR.[121] These are not considered any further here. Article 8 is dealt with in more detail below, but it must be stressed that at the time of the decision in *Malone* the ECHR had yet to be 'brought home'[122] by the HRA 1998. The common law submission of the plaintiff was 'that it was unlawful for anyone to intercept or monitor the telephone conversations of another without the consent of that other. He rested this contention on the right of property, on the right of privacy, and on the right of confidentiality'.[123]

[4.108] The judge rejected the argument based on property briskly:[124]

> Mr Ross-Munro's first proposition rested in the first place on a right of property. To tap a person's telephone conversation without his consent, he said, was unlawful

information is explored. Two points are worth noting: (i) it is moot whether the evidence considered by Megarry V-C *was* unlawfully obtained in this case; and (ii) where evidence *is* unlawfully obtained, courts show a marked reluctance to exclude it, which is very much foreshadowed by this decision.

[120] ibid 355–56.

[121] The judge summarised the argument at ibid 356.

[122] By which is meant incorporating the ECHR into the domestic law of the United Kingdom. Prior to the HRA 1998, the ECHR was binding on the United Kingdom as part of European Union law, but did not form part of the domestic or municipal law of the United Kingdom. Because the United Kingdom played a leading role in the original drafting of the ECHR, the Blair government referred to this incorporation of the ECHR into United Kingdom law as 'bringing rights home': *Rights Brought Home: The Human Rights Bill* (1997) Cm 1782.

[123] *Malone v Commissioner of Metropolitan Police* (n 119) 356.

[124] ibid 357.

> because that person had rights of property in his words as transmitted by the electrical impulses of the telephone system, and so the tapping constituted an interference with his property rights. An analogy that he suggested was that the important part of a letter was the words that it contained rather than the paper that it was written on. I regret to say that Mr Ross-Munro found it difficult to persuade me that there was any reality in this contention, and he did not struggle long. I do not see how words being transmitted by electrical impulses could themselves (as distinct from any copyright in them) fairly be said to be the subject matter of property. At all events, no argument which even began to support such a proposition was put before me.

[4.109] Pausing there, it is worth noting that the form of property contended for (the electrical impulses) is very different to the form of property that this book suggests exists, which is based around human perception. There is no reference to information amounting to perception, and no attempt to limit the property right to private information. The link made by the judge to copyright harks back to the cases considered above.

[4.110] In support of a right of privacy and/or confidentiality, the plaintiff (unsurprisingly) relied upon (amongst many other authorities) the 1890 article of Warren and Brandeis.[125] The judge made the factual point that telephone conversations could not necessarily be regarded as private.[126] The point, which features in the judge's reasoning, as will be described, is a surprising and troubling one.

[4.111] The judge had few concerns about the fact that English law had not, to date, explicitly recognised a right of privacy:[127]

> I am not unduly troubled by the absence of English authority: there has to be a first time for everything, and if the principles of English law, and not least analogies from the existing rules, together with the requirements of justice and common sense, pointed firmly to such a right existing, then I think the court should not be deterred from recognising the right.

[4.112] He was, however, conscious that a court should not legislate in a new field,[128] and was particularly clear that the right to privacy contended for by the plaintiff was dangerously wide and therefore best left to the legislature:[129]

> One of the factors that must be relevant in such a case is the degree of particularity in the right that is claimed. The wider and more indefinite the right claimed, the

[125] ibid 357, 358. The article (n 4) is discussed in detail in Section II.

[126] ibid 360. Although this appears to have constituted only a background point to the judge's reasoning, it is odd nonetheless. Although there is a presumption that postcards are read when posted, and so their contents published, it is difficult to see how the same could be said for telephone calls. Presumptively, these ought to be regarded as private.

[127] ibid 372.

[128] ibid 372.

[129] ibid 373.

> greater the undesirability of holding that such a right exists. Wide and indefinite rights, while conferring an advantage on those who have them, may well gravely impair the position of those who are subject to the rights. To create a right for one person, you have to impose a corresponding duty on another. In the present case, the alleged right to hold a telephone conversation in the privacy of one's own home without molestation is wide and indefinite in its scope, and in any case does not seem to be very apt for covering the plaintiff's grievance. He was not 'molested' in holding his telephone conversations: he held them without 'molestation', but without their retaining the privacy that he desired. If a man telephones from his own home, but an open window makes it possible for a near neighbour to overhear what is said, and the neighbour, remaining throughout on his own property, listens to the conversation, is he to be a tortfeasor? Is a person who overhears a telephone conversation by reason of a so-called 'crossed line' to be liable in damages? What of an operator of a private switchboard who listens in? Why is the right that is claimed confined to a man's own home, so that it would not apply to private telephone conversations from offices, call boxes or the houses of others? If they were to be included, what of the greater opportunities for deliberate overhearing that they offer? In any case, why is the telephone to be subject to this special right of privacy when there is no general right? That is not all. Suppose that there is what for brevity I may call a right to telephonic privacy, sounding in tort. What exceptions to it, if any, would there be? Would it be a breach of the right if anyone listened to a telephone conversation in which some act of criminal violence or dishonesty was being planned? Should a listener be restrained by injunction from disclosing to the authorities a conversation that would lead to the release of someone who has been kidnapped? There are many, many questions that can, and should, be asked.

The judge could find no sufficient authority to support the right of privacy contended for, and the plaintiff's inability to frame answers to the questions the judge posed was obviously telling. The judge held that the claim to a right of privacy failed.[130]

[4.113] Turning to the separate contention of a right of confidence, the judge disposed of any argument that such a claim could be founded on contract,[131] and considered the position *apart* from any contractual right. The judge considered the three elements of the action for breach of confidence,[132] and rejected the plaintiff's claim for two reasons: (i) the tapped conversations were not confidential; and (ii) the interception of the calls was in the public interest. These points are considered in turn.

[130] ibid 375.

[131] ibid 375. The details do not matter, but clearly a contractual claim to confidence can (depending on the contract) be wider than a claim arising apart from contract. The point is there was no contract here, and so the plaintiff had to have recourse to other bases for his claim.

[132] ibid 375–76.

[4.114] The judge said that the tapped conversations were not confidential:[133]

> In the present case, the alleged misuse is not by the person to whom the information was intended to be communicated, but by someone to whom the plaintiff had no intention of communicating anything: and that, of course, introduces a somewhat different element, that of the unknown overhearer.
>
> It seems to me that a person who utters confidential information must accept the risk of any unknown overhearing that is inherent in the circumstances of communication. Those who exchange confidences on a bus or a train run the risk of a nearby passenger with acute hearing or a more distant passenger who is adept at lip-reading. Those who speak over garden walls run the risk of the unseen neighbour in a toolshed nearby. Office cleaners who discuss secrets in the office when they think everyone else has gone run the risk of speaking within earshot of an unseen member of the staff who is working late. Those who give confidential information over an office intercommunication system run the risk of some third party being connected to the conversation. I do not see why someone who has overheard some secret in such a way should be exposed to legal proceedings if he uses or divulges what he has heard. No doubt an honourable man would give some warning when he realises that what he is hearing is not intended for his ears; but I have to concern myself with the law, and not with moral standards. There are, of course, many moral precepts which are not legally enforceable.
>
> When this is applied to telephone conversations, it appears to me that the speaker is taking such risks of being overheard as are inherent in the system. As I have mentioned, the Younger Report referred to users of the telephone being aware that there were several well-understood possibilities of being overheard, and stated that a realistic person would not rely on the telephone system to protect the confidence of what he says. That comment seems unanswerable. In addition, so much publicity in recent years has been given to instances (real or fictional) of the deliberate tapping of telephones that it is difficult to 'envisage telephone users who are genuinely unaware of this possibility. No doubt a person who uses a telephone to give confidential informationto another may do so in such a way as to impose an obligation of confidence on that other: but I do not see how it could be said that any such obligation is imposed on those who overhear the conversation, whether by means of tapping or otherwise.

[4.115] With great respect, this conclusion is both troubling and surprising. What is determinative is not the general position of whether communications are or are not protected. That is a relevant background fact, but no more than that. What matters is the manner in which C's perception of A's private information is obtained. If, as the judge speculated, this arose because of A's excessively loud voice, which C overhead whilst standing in their (C's) own home, then A's claim ought to fail: A is speaking loudly in circumstances where they can be overheard by C who is neither trespassing nor eavesdropping. But if C's perception arises because of a deliberate act of interception of A's communications

[133] ibid 376.

by C, then the specific expectation of privacy *in that case* ought to have rather more weight than the judge allowed.

[4.116] The judge's second ground for rejecting the confidentiality claim is better, which was that the interception of the plaintiff's calls was in the public interest. The judge cited with approval the dictum of Lord Denning MR in *Fraser v Evans*:[134]

> It is merely an instance of just cause or excuse for breaking confidence. There are some things which may be required to be disclosed in the public interest, in which event no confidence can be prayed in aid to keep them secret.

[4.117] The judge went on to say:[135]

> If what is overheard, though confidential, is itself iniquity, it is plain that it is subject to no duty of confidence. But if there is merely a suspicion of iniquity, does that justify a deliberate overhearing by means of a tap? Even if from time to time the tap provides information about iniquity, does that justify a process of recording entire conversations, and listening to those recordings, when much of the conversations may be highly confidential and untainted by any iniquity? Further, if there is a reasonable suspicion of iniquity, can that suspicion justify tapping in order to find out whether the suspicion is well founded, if in fact the conversations are wholly innocent?
>
> I think that one has to approach these matters with some measure of balance and common sense. The rights and liberties of a telephone subscriber are indeed important; but so also are the desires of the great bulk of the population not to be the victims of assault, theft or other crimes. The detection and prosecution of criminals, and the discovery of projected crimes, are important weapons in protecting the public. In the nature of things it will be virtually impossible to know beforehand whether any particular telephone conversation will be criminal in nature. The question is not whether there is a certainty that the conversation tapped will be iniquitous, but whether there is just cause or excuse for the tapping and for the use made of the material obtained by the tapping.
>
> If certain requirements are satisfied, then I think that there will plainly be just cause or excuse for what is done by or on behalf of the police. These requirements are, first, that there should be grounds for suspecting that the tapping of the particular telephone will be of material assistance in detecting or preventing crime, or discovering the criminals, or otherwise assisting in the discharge of the functions of the police in relation to crime. Second, no use should be made of any material obtained except for these purposes. Third, any knowledge of information which is not relevant to those purposes should be confined to the minimum number of persons reasonably required to carry out the process of tapping. If those requirements are satisfied, then it seems to me that there will be just cause or excuse for carrying out the tapping, and using information obtained for those limited purposes. I am not, of course, saying that nothing else can constitute a just cause or excuse: what I am saying is that if these

[134] ibid 361. The decision in *Fraser v Evans* is reported at [1969] 1 QB 349, and the dictum is at 362.
[135] ibid 377.

> requirements are satisfied, then in my judgment there will be a just cause or excuse. I am not, for instance, saying anything about matters of national security: I speak only of what is before me in the present case, concerning tapping for police purposes in relation to crime.

[4.118] The exceptions to the right of privacy arising out of the public interest will be considered in due course.[136] It is sufficient for the moment to say that whilst the sentiment behind this restriction on confidentiality can readily be understood, the restriction is very widely framed by reference to the justification for phone tapping generally, rather than whether the particular fruits of the tap can or cannot be used.

[4.119] The public interest arguments are at their strongest when it is an organ of the state – say, the police – that is acting to uphold law and order. It is clear that privacy ought – at least to an extent – give way to this important public good. This is a large part of the consideration in Chapter 8.

[4.120] *Malone* is thus an unhelpful case. The bilateral claim A ↔ B was not open to A, and the various different ways in which the claim was framed – which included both claims based on property and claims based on privacy – failed.[137] To the extent that the failure was on public interest grounds, the decision is consistent with the thesis advanced in this book. But that was not the primary basis for the judge's decision, and *Malone* must be regarded as authority *against* this book's thesis. However, as will be seen, things rapidly moved on.

[4.121] *Francome v Mirror Group Newspapers Ltd* was a case where a private investigator (*not* the police) investigating breaches of Jockey Club rules tapped the telephone conversation of a jockey.[138] The leading judgment was given by Sir John Donaldson MR. The judge began by setting out the relevant facts:[139]

> The plaintiffs are husband and wife, the husband being the champion National Hunt jockey. The defendants are the proprietors of the 'Daily Mirror', its editor and two of its reporters. Someone – and we do not know his identity or that of his assistants – saw fit to plant what is popularly known as a 'bug' with a view to eavesdropping on any telephone conversations which were made to or from the plaintiffs' home. This was not official telephone tapping. Indeed it may not have been tapping in the strict sense at all, since it is common ground that it involved the use of

[136] This is an aspect of misuse or (more accurately) a case where the public interest renders a particular use *not* a misuse.

[137] It is interesting that *Seager v Copydex*, decided 10 years before, did not have more of an effect. That is probably because of the very different subject matter, and the fact that that case never actually articulated why Mr Seager won.

[138] *Francome v Mirror Group Newspapers Ltd* [1984] 1 WLR 892.

[139] ibid 894.

radio-telephony. It also had nothing to do with the 'Daily Mirror'. It is not clear for how long the 'bug' was in operation, but it was for not less than three months and may have been longer. The 'Daily Mirror' came into the story when the eavesdroppers offered to sell them 38 tapes of telephone conversations obtained by this means. In seeking to confirm the authenticity of the tapes, the reporter defendants approached Mr Francome and told him of their existence.

[4.122] There are a number of differences between this case and the facts of *Malone*, apart from the obvious one that this involved non-state actors:

- This was an application for interlocutory injunctive relief pending trial. The weight that can be given to interlocutory judgments, where the facts have yet to be established, is inevitably less than a judgment rendered after full trial.
- The interception of communications was by way of intrusion into the plaintiffs' home. Furthermore, the intercept or bug was not lawfully put in place.
- No claim was made against the planter of the bug, because the identity of that person was unknown. The defendants were third parties, who the unknown person had approached.[140] So, again, a contractually based claim or a claim otherwise *in personam* was not really open to the plaintiffs.

[4.123] The plaintiffs sought relief from the newspaper, a third party, and it was contended that both the unknown planter of the bug and the newspaper 'were under a duty to preserve the confidentiality of the plaintiffs' private conversations'.[141] The newspaper contended that there was no cause of action against them for breach of confidence, a proposition the judge regarded as 'surprising'.[142]

[4.124] The chief basis for the defence was the 'iniquity' defence which had succeeded before Megarry V-C in *Malone*.[143] The judge considered that there was no legal justification for the interception of the plaintiffs' communications, and that the 'iniquity' defence could not succeed. In this, it is important to note that the judge did not actually hold that the conduct in this case was in

[140] That being said, both the unknown person and the newpaper were strangers; in the nomenclature used in this book, they would be C_1 and C_2.

[141] *Francome v Mirror Group Newspapers Ltd* (n 138) 895.

[142] ibid 895.

[143] ibid 895: 'The defendants then go on to submit that whatever their obligations towards the plaintiffs upon grounds of confidentiality, they can rely upon the classic, but ill-defined, exception of what is quaintly called "iniquity". The basis of this exception is that whilst there is a public interest in maintaining confidentiality, there is a countervailing public interest in exposing conduct which involves a breach of the law or which is "anti-social".'

fact unlawful,[144] and the rejection of the iniquity defence needs to be seen in this light:[145]

> It is sometimes said, although to be fair to Mr Molloy he has not said it, that all are free to break the law if they are prepared to pay the penalty. This is pernicious nonsense. The right to disobey the law is not obtainable by the payment of a penalty or licence fee. It is not obtainable at all in a parliamentary democracy, although different considerations arise under a totalitarian regime.
>
> In saying this I nevertheless recognise that, in very rare circumstances, a situation can arise in which the citizen is faced with a conflict between what is, in effect, two inconsistent laws. The first law is the law of the land. The second is a moral imperative, usually, but not always, religious in origin. An obvious example is the priest's obligation of silence in relation to the confessional, but others can be given. In conducting the business of the courts, judges seek to avoid any such conflict, but occasionally it is unavoidable. Yielding to the moral imperative does not excuse a breach of the law of the land, but it is understandable and, in some circumstances, may even be praiseworthy. However, I cannot over-emphasise the rarity of the moral imperative. Furthermore, it is almost unheard of for compliance with the moral imperative to be in the financial or other best interests of the person concerned. Anyone who conceives himself to be morally obliged to break the law, should also ask himself whether such a course furthers his own interests. If it does, he would be well advised to re-examine his conscience.

[4.125] In this case, an interlocutory injunction was granted against publication:[146]

> In the instant case, pending a trial, it is impossible to see what public interest would be served by publishing the contents of the tapes which would not equally be served by giving them to the police or to the Jockey Club. Any wider publication could only serve the interests of the 'Daily Mirror'.

The other members of the Court of Appeal (Fox and Stephen Brown LJJ) gave short concurring judgments.

[4.126] *Francome* looks a bit like a 'chain' case, where C is enjoined because C knows (or ought to know) that B has behaved badly (ie infringing a bilateral obligation) *quoad* A. The problem with the decision is that there is no finding that B actually did infringe A's rights and so C cannot really have imputed to them B's 'naughtiness'. The decision is a remarkably conservative and unsatisfactory one. It would have been better to analyse the facts as a 'no-chain' case

[144] The conclusions at ibid 897 are couched in terms of there being a *risk* of the law being breached. This was because of the interlocutory nature of the hearing: the plaintiffs were seeking an injunction pending trial, and the question was whether they could show a 'good arguable case', not that they were right. The weight of this authority is therefore limited. As with most cases like this, the case never got to trial. Most of these cases are all about the interlocutory injunction.

[145] ibid 897.

[146] ibid 898.

where C was consciously invading A's privacy and where C's use of the perception that they had derived from B of A was indefensible. This would enable the court to identify C's true iniquity.

[4.127] In *Murray v Express Newspapers plc*,[147] the Court of Appeal considered a claim by an infant claimant, who had been photographed covertly with a long-range lens by a photographer of an agency (BPL) whilst the claimant was in a public place with their parents. The claimant was, at the time, 19 months old, and sued by their litigation friends, their parents.[148] The photographs were sold by BPL to the newspaper, which published some of them. The newspaper settled with the claimant; BPL sought to strike out the claim as disclosing no cause of action. The judgment of the court was handed down by Sir Anthony Clarke MR.

[4.128] The court stressed the importance of ascertaining precisely who the claimant was:[149]

> We do not think that the reality is that the parents seek through their son to establish a right to personal privacy for themselves and their children when engaged in ordinary family activities. The positions of parents on the one hand and children on the other hand are distinct. We will return to the relevant test in a moment but it seems to us that David may have a reasonable expectation of privacy in circumstances in which his famous mother might not. In our judgment the question in the action is whether there was an infringement of David's rights …

[4.129] The point is that the right of privacy vests in particular claimants, and it may well be – as here – that different rights of privacy need to be disentangled according as to the person asserting them. If privacy is all about our ability to control how the world sees us as individuals, then it must be right that just as C's perception of A is individual (or subjective) to C, so too (viewing matters from the other end of the telescope) is A's private information individual (or subjective to) A.[150] As the Court of Appeal noted:[151]

> … [t]he child has his own right to respect for his privacy distinct from that of his parents. While it is true that a small child of as little as 19 months is likely to be oblivious of the taking of a photograph of him (or her), at any rate if taken at a long range, and there is no suggestion that David suffered distress or harassment

[147] *Murray v Express Newspapers plc* [2008] EWCA Civ 446.

[148] The court stressed that it was important that the action was brought by the claimant's parents only on behalf of the claimant, and not on their own behalf (ibid [12]). This was an important distinction because the claimant's mother was famous and recognised that 'because of her fame the media are likely to be interested in her' (at [13]). The claimant's mother was the famous author JK Rowling.

[149] ibid [14].

[150] The contention advanced in this book is that privacy protects our ability to express ourselves.

[151] *Murray v Express Newspapers plc* (n 147) [16].

> as a result of the taking (or indeed publication) of the photograph, we do not think that it is quite right to describe the issue of principle as being 'whether the claimant who is not a public figure in his own right but is a child of one, is entitled to protection from being photographed in a public place even where a photograph shows nothing embarrassing or untoward but in which he is shown depicted with his parents.'
>
> Moreover, we do not agree that it is artificial for the parents to bring the action in the name of the child.

[4.130] The court also stressed the importance of context:[152]

> It may well be that the mere taking of a photograph of a child in a public place when out with his or her parents, whether they are famous or not, would not engage Article 8 ECHR. However, as we see it, it all depends upon the circumstances. We will return to the context below but it seems to us that the judge's approach depends too much upon a consideration of the taking of the photograph and not enough upon its publication. This was not the taking of a single photograph of David in the street. On the claimant's case, which must be taken as true for present purposes, it was the clandestine taking and subsequent publication of the photograph in the context of a series of photographs which were taken for the purpose of their sale for publication, in circumstances in which BPL did not ask David's parents for their consent to the taking and publication of his photograph. It is a reasonable inference on the alleged facts that BPL knew that, if they had asked Dr and Mrs Murray for their consent to the taking and publication of such a photograph of their child, that consent would have been refused.

[4.131] The use to which information is put lies at the heart of A's rights against C. This case is, *par excellence*, a no-chain case. There is no bilateral relationship between A and B on which A's claim against C can be built. We are therefore talking about A's rights 'against the world' O. Everyone in the chain in this case is either to be classed as O(C) or as C. The label B for any of the actors is wrong.[153] Had, in this case, C been a tourist, photographing a tourist attraction, in which David (the infant) had coincidentally appeared, and the photograph had simply formed part of a private photo album, then it is difficult to see any infringement of Article 8 of the ECHR (or, for that matter, any infringement of A's property rights), whether the parents (on David's behalf) consented or not. This case, however, lay at the other extreme.[154]

[152] ibid [17].

[153] The question of whether a person is to be classed as O(C) or C depends on whether they use their perception or not. In this case, obviously, the defendants *did* use their perception, and the Court of Appeal found that this was arguably (this was another interlocutory case) a misuse.

[154] The nature of BPL's business model appears at [18] of the judgment, and is material: '… BPL was described as a commercial picture agency that obtains, holds and licenses photographs for use in the media and runs a website which, subject to certain terms, permits photographs to be downloaded by publishers in return for fees …'.

[4.132] After setting out the prior case law in some detail, the court went on to articulate some general principles in terms of Article 8 of the ECHR. First, is there a reasonable expectation of privacy?[155] That, the court stressed, was an objective question to be answered by reference to the 'reasonable expectation of the person who is affected by the publicity'.[156] As Lord Hope put it in *Campbell v MGN Ltd*:[157]

> The question is what a reasonable person of ordinary sensibilities would feel if she was placed in the same position as the claimant and faced with the same publicity.

[4.133] The court considered that:[158]

> ... the question whether there is a reasonable expectation of privacy is a broad one, which takes account of all the circumstances of the case. They include the attributes of the claimant, the nature of the activity in which the claimant was engaged, the place at which it was happening, the nature and purpose of the intrusion, the absence of consent and whether it was known or could be inferred, the effect on the claimant and the circumstances in which and the purposes for which the information came into the hands of the publisher.

[4.134] The fact that the claimant was a child was an obviously relevant factor, which required a different approach because an infant (like David) 'has no obvious sensitivity to any invasion of his privacy'.[159] In such a case:

> The question whether a child in any particular circumstances has a reasonable expectation for privacy must be determined by the court taking an objective view of the matter including the reasonable expectations of his parents in those same circumstances as to whether their children's lives in a public place should remain private. Ultimately it will be a matter of judgement for the court with every case depending upon its own facts.

The physical awareness of the child could not be determinative, and the attitude of the parent might be material.[160]

[4.135] Assuming Article 8 of the ECHR to be engaged, the next question would be one of balancing A's right to privacy against C's right to publish. This, of course, engaged freedom of expression rights under Article 10 of the ECHR.[161]

[155] *Murray v Express Newspapers plc* (n 147) [35].
[156] ibid [35].
[157] [2008] EWCA Civ 446 at [99].
[158] *Murray v Express Newspapers plc* (n 147) [35].
[159] ibid [36], quoting from the speech of Lord Hope in *Campbell v MGN Ltd* at [100].
[160] ibid [38], the court noted that 'if the parents of a child courted publicity by procuring the publication of photographs of the child in order to promote their own interests, the position would or might be quite different from a case like this, where the parents have taken care to keep their children out of the public gaze.'
[161] ibid [40].

[4.136] In this case – and this was an interlocutory application to strike out the claim, not a trial determining the substantive rights and wrongs – the court considered it to be at least arguable that David had a reasonable expectation of privacy;[162] and similarly as regards the second, balancing stage.[163]

[4.137] *Murray* is a critical case. Even though there is a lot of reference in the case to Article 8 of the ECHR, it is not a human rights case. The ECHR and the HRA 1998 serve to curb excesses of state power over individuals. *Murray* was not a 'state power' case, but a battle between individuals, where A brought a privacy claim against non-state actor C. *Murray* is a case where the HRA 1998 and the ECHR are driving the common law forward, because of the courts' obligation themselves to have regard to the ECHR when developing English law.[164]

[4.138] Although it will be suggested that the 'balancing of rights' approach taken by the court in *Murray* is the wrong way of analysing A's rights, the case (even though interlocutory) is something of a landmark, because it is so clearly: (i) *not* a bilateral *A v B* case; (ii) *not* a breach of confidence case; and (iii) *not* an intellectual property (specifically copyright) case. It is supportive of the contentions in this book, even if the analysis of private information and privacy differs.

F. Drawing the threads together

[4.139] This has been a somewhat rambling stroll through some interesting cases, without any attempt to provide a comprehensive analysis. That will follow in later chapters. The point of the exercise has been to show that protection of private information has deep roots and that the case law is best understood as being based on an *in rem* property right, that is distinct from the actions of trespass, copyright and breach of confidence.

[4.140] Because of the evolution (through technology, and as described in Chapter 1) of the invasions into our privacy, the *Entick v Carrington* remedy of trespass is no longer fit for purpose. We cannot sufficiently protect our privacy

[162] ibid [45].
[163] ibid [49], [50], [58], [60].
[164] See HRA 1998, s 6(1): 'It is unlawful for a public authority to act in a way which is incompatible with a Convention right'. By s 6(3)(a), a 'public authority' includes a 'court or tribunal'. Thus, in a strange and negative way the courts must, in deciding cases, have regard to the ECHR, because it is 'unlawful' for them not to. A more positive way of putting it – eschewed by the 1998 Act – would be to proclaim the rights more positively, like the American bill of rights or Jefferson's ringing endorsement of rights: 'We hold these truths to be self-evident …'. The way in which the Human Rights Act 1998 is drafted is more than a little imbued with a Diceyan view of the world.

by relying on our ownership of our home. That is in part because many invasions of privacy occur *outside* the home. But it is also because many invasions of privacy occur *within the home* without engaging the law of trespass.

Example

In her book, Zuboff describes a project called the 'Aware Home', which was a 'smart' home which monitored its occupants, and reacted to their needs and desires accordingly. Precisely what the 'Aware Home' would do does not matter: the point is that to do all these good things, the 'Aware Home' harvested our private information.[165] The project's developers were well aware of this, and (according to Zuboff) there were three working assumptions:[166] 'first, the scientists and engineers understood that the new data systems would produce an entirely new knowledge domain. Second, it was assumed that the rights to that new knowledge and the power to use it to improve one's life would belong exclusively to the people who live in the house. Third, the team assumed that for all its digital wizardry, the Aware Home would take its place as a modern incarnation of the ancient conventions that understand 'home' as the private sanctuary of those who dwell within its walls.'

Whilst the first assumption has held good, the second and third assumptions have been falsified by events. There is no 'closed-loop' as regards our data, but that data is harvested and used by third parties, through smart devices like 'Nest' thermostats,[167] smart electricity meters[168] and devices like televisions and devices incorporating Apple's 'Siri' and Amazon's 'Alexa'.[169]

[4.141] The law has been sensitive to the need to protect certain classes of information which are unquestionably property. These are the intellectual property rights that have been referenced in this chapter. The patent is not apt to protect our privacy; but copyright certainly made a valiant effort to do so, thwarted (again) by technology. The law of copyright *could* have evolved to protect the interests not of the creator of the original work but additionally or alternatively the interests of the subject of the original work, as where subject A is photographed by photographer C. In all probability this would have resulted in a confused form of property, with conflicting rights of co-ownership: a path not taken for good reason.

[4.142] That left the protection of trade secrets and confidential matters *not* protected by intellectual property rights, as in the cases of *Abernethy v Hutchinson* and *Seager v Copydex*. Aided by the ECHR and the HRA 1998, we

[165] S Zuboff, *The Age of Surveillance Capitalism: The Fight for a Human Future at the New Frontier of Power* (Profile Books, 2019) 5–6.

[166] ibid 6.

[167] ibid 6–7; C Véliz, *Privacy is Power: Why and How You Should Take Back Control of Your Data* (Bantam Press, 2020) 8.

[168] Véliz (n 167) 9.

[169] ibid 11.

now appear to have a right of action – the Action – which renders private information property, and so gives A an *in rem* claim against C. It also appears that the Action has not only evolved out of the action against breach of confidence, but has also subsumed it. This statement anticipates the development of English law, which still maintains a distinction between the Action and breach of confidence. But when once the concept of *private* information has been unpacked (see Chapter 6), it will be clear that confidential information is private information, and the two causes of action cannot really be distinguished.

[4.143] The next sections consider whether the Action is *needed*, given the protections already afforded to us by human rights law and data protection law.

VI. Protection of Privacy by Way of Human Rights

A. The European Convention on Human Rights and the Human Rights Act 1998

[4.144] The European Convention on Human Rights and Fundamental Freedoms – generally referred to in this book as the ECHR – opened for signature in November 1950. The United Kingdom was an initial party to the ECHR. The ECHR – as a treaty between sovereign states – operates on the plane of international law, but the recognition of a right of individual petition under the ECHR opened the way for persons the subject of sovereign states themselves to petition in vindication of their rights under the ECHR. The European Court of Human Rights became operative in September 1958, when eight countries accepted its compulsory jurisdiction. The United Kingdom did not subscribe to the right of individual petition or compulsory jurisdiction until January 1966.[170] That opened the door for a number of cases against the UK state to succeed before the European Court of Human Rights where they had failed before the domestic courts because the ECHR was not incorporated into UK law.[171]

[4.145] The ECHR has been amended on a number of occasions (by Protocols). The most significant of these is the first Protocol, the Protocol to the Convention for the Protection of Human Rights and Fundamental Freedoms,

[170] Clayton and Tomlinson (n 44) [IN.09].

[171] The United Kingdom adopts a 'dualist' relationship to international obligations. As a nation state, the United Kingdom may sign up to and agree to be bound by a treaty, but that act has no effect on domestic or municipal law. If it is intended that the treaty have interal effects, then it is necessary to implement the treaty into domestic law. Prior to the HRA 1998, the ECHR was binding on the UK as a matter of international law but had no domestic (internal) effect. Hence the rather odd situation of English courts deciding cases by reference to a different rule-set to that of the European Court of Human Rights.

made in March 1952, which contains a number of substantive rights in addition to those enumerated in the ECHR, and which rights tend to be referred to as 'First Protocol' rights.

[4.146] Despite the subscription of the United Kingdom to the right of individual petition and compulsory jurisdiction, rights were not 'brought home' until the enactment of the HRA 1998. That is because the ECHR was, and is, a creature of public international law (albeit accessible by persons not normally recognised as having standing in international law[172]), such that in domestic litigation 'Convention rights' were only indirectly looked to, and not directly recognised as part of domestic law. The HRA 1998 incorporated certain 'Convention rights'[173] into the domestic law of the United Kingdom for certain purposes.[174]

B. Limited protection conferred

[4.147] A detailed enumeration of the *intra*-United Kingdom effects of Convention rights is beyond the scope of this work.[175] What is significant is that neither the ECHR (including any Protocols) nor its implementation into the law of the United Kingdom creates any direct horizonal legal relationship between natural and/or legal persons whereby one such person may enforce a Convention right against the other.[176] To use the language of the European Union, Convention rights are vertically effective (by natural or legal persons against the state) but not horizontally effective as between natural or legal persons *inter se*.

[4.148] This means that no matter how extensive the protections conferred by the ECHR and the HRA 1998, as between non-state actors (whether natural or legal persons) the extent to which the ECHR provides an effective protection is limited. Nevertheless, for present purposes, the ECHR is significant in two respects: first, as a controller of state power over the individual; second, as a source for common law development. Both of these aspects are considered further below. Before doing so, it is appropriate to identify the key provision in the ECHR for present purposes, which is Article 8 of the ECHR.

[172] Traditionally – but increasingly less so – public international law has been regarded as dealing with state relations. Now, it extends far further, to include relations with non-governmental organisations and even – as here – individual persons.

[173] Defined in the HRA 1998, s 1(1).

[174] HRA 1998, s 1(2).

[175] Convention rights are important to: interpretation (s 2 and ss 3–4); and the acts of public authorities (ss 6–10).

[176] J Morgan, 'Questioning the "True Effect" of the Human Rights Act' (2002) 22 *Legal Studies* 259; J Morgan, 'Privacy, Confidence and Horizontal Effect: "Hello" Trouble' (2003) 62 *Cambridge Law Journal* 444; D Milo, *Defamation and Freedom of Speech* (Oxford University Press, 2008) 4–5.

C. Article 8 of the ECHR

[4.149] Article 8 of the ECHR provides:

> (1) Everyone has the right to respect for his private and family life, his home and his correspondence.
>
> (2) There shall be no interference by a public authority with the exercise of this right except such as in accordance with the law and is necessary in a democratic society in the interests of national security, public safety or the economic well-being of the country, for the prevention of disorder or crime, for the protection of health or morals, or for the protection of the rights and freedoms of others.

[4.150] A number of points can be made in regard to Article 8. First, the right to respect for private and family life is both broad and ill-defined. Clayton and Tomlinson say this:[177]

> At the heart of the right of privacy lies the notion of personal liberty and autonomy. There is an enormous literature on 'privacy rights' in which a variety of different definitions of the scope of the rights have been suggested. In addition to the 'right to be let alone', privacy rights have been said to cover matters as diverse as an individual's dignity or moral integrity, the unauthorised circulation of portraits, the control of personal information, the establishment and development of emotional relationships with others and the freedom from media intrusion. The wide range of areas in which the right has been invoked have led to scepticism as to whether it is helpful to speak of a general 'right to privacy' at all. However, in analysing privacy rights it is important to distinguish between the 'human right' to privacy as against the state and the right to privacy as against private individuals or organisations. Although the two are closely connected, the range of the former has been greater than that of the latter because of the greater power of the state over all aspects of private life as compared to private organisations.

[4.151] Monti and Wacks are rather more blunt:[178]

> The notion of 'private and family life' is excessively wide. What could reasonably lie outside it? My private life is, in effect, my existence, my being. This provision is as ambiguous and indeterminate as the 'right to be let alone' that Warren and Brandeis invoked to describe the right to privacy in their celebrated essay, which … is the principal source of the confusion and incoherence.

This is harsh. Provided the values stated are used to inform more specific law – as in the case of the Action – there is no harm and real benefit in articulating the values by which we are governed. Where, however, a wide and nebulous value is used directly to empower judges, problems may arise. To this extent, Monti and Wacks have a point.

[177] Clayton and Tomlinson (n 44) [12.03].
[178] A Monti and R Wacks, *Protecting Personal Information* (Hart Publishing, 2020) 3.

[4.152] Clearly, a property right in 'private information' is different in conception to a right to respect for private and family life, home and correspondence. In short, it is informed by the underlying value articulated in Article 8 of the ECHR, but not defined by it. The scope of the Action will be informed by the nature of Convention rights, because of the obligation in the courts to take account of these rights, but not defined by it, because those rights only have a vertical (and no horizontal) effect.

[4.153] A property right is different in scope and operation from a human right, particularly in terms of the entities against whom it is enforceable. Human rights – including the right to a private and family life – are largely vindicated on a vertical basis, whereas property rights operate horizontally (including as against public authorities, but only in their 'private law' capacity[179]).

D. Remedies arising out of human rights infringements

[4.154] The remedies arising out of the incorporation of the ECHR into English law are stated in section 8 of the HRA 1998. Such remedies are explicitly limited to cases where the court finds that a 'public authority' has acted in a way which is incompatible with Convention rights. Thus, section 8(1) provides:

> In relation to any act (or proposed act) of a public authority which the court finds is (or would be) unlawful, it may grant such relief or remedy, or make such order, within its powers as it considers just and appropriate.

[4.155] Convention rights will often be asserted in judicial review proceedings and courts will be astute to tailor the relief granted in such proceedings to ensure that Convention rights are appropriately protected. That would be the case in any event, for judges are sworn to do right to all manner of people after the laws and usages of this Realm.[180] But, to make the assurance doubly sure, the HRA 1998 applies to courts just as it does to all public authorities.[181] It is perfectly possible for a Convention right to be asserted in proceedings other than judicial review proceedings, and the position as regards remedy will be no different.

[179] Recall the Diceyan philosophy that public bodies – state actors, as they are referred to in this book – are as much subject to the law as non-state actors, except where the law makes exceptional provision in regard to the rights and obligations of state actors. The problem, these days, is that there is a great deal of 'exceptional provision' in regard to state actors, such that the Diceyan philosophy no longer holds good in practice.

[180] To quote from the judicial oath taken by judges on appointment.

[181] See HRA 1998, s 6.

[4.156] Of course, the courts cannot act outside the law and cannot fashion remedies that are unknown to law. Section 8(1) enables a court to grant any relief or remedy *within* its power if it considers it just and appropriate to do so. What is significant about the HRA 1998 is that damages are available as a remedy. As Clayton and Tomlinson stress, '[t]he power to award damages under the HRA marks an important departure in English public law. Maladministration by public bodies does not entitle the injured party to compensation …'.[182]

[4.157] Nevertheless, the fundamental point is that the remedies under the HRA 1998 are *only* available against public authorities. In many cases A's privacy will be invaded by bodies that are not 'public authorities' within the HRA 1998, and A will therefore need a more extensive remedy in such cases. This (understandable) gap in the ECHR is filled by the Action, as Lord Hoffmann observed in *Campbell v MGM Ltd*:[183]

> What human rights law has done is to identify private information as something worth protecting as an aspect of human autonomy and dignity. And this recognition has raised inescapably the question of why it should be worth protecting against the state but not against a private person. There may of course be justifications for the publication of private information by private persons which would not be available to the state – I have particularly in mind the position of the media, to which I shall return in a moment – but I can see no logical ground for saying that a person should have less protection against a private individual than he would have against the state for the publication of personal information for which there is no justification. Nor, it appears, have any of the other judges who have considered the matter.

[4.158] It is worth also bearing in mind that using the Action against a state actor may offer a broader reach than a claim under the HRA 1998, section 8 or by way of judicial review. When we come to consider misuse of private information by state actors in Chapter 8, this point will be further considered.

E. A source for common law development

[4.159] As has been described, the HRA 1998 has been a driver of change in the common law, in particular in the development of the Action. That development was described in Chapter 2. Moreover, not only has the recognition of the Action largely been driven by the HRA 1998 and the ECHR, so too are aspects of its detailed scope and operation. It would be surprising if a cause of action, whose existence was informed by Article 8 of the ECHR, was not also

[182] Clayton and Tomlinson (n 44) [21.13].
[183] [2004] UKHL 22 at [50].

influenced in very granular ways by that Article, and indeed other Convention rights. This book does not purport to be a commentary on either the ECHR or the HRA 1998. However, to the extent the ECHR and/or the HRA 1998 inform the nature of the property right described in this book, reference will be made to this law as appropriate.

F. The fourth amendment

[4.160] The Fourth Amendment obviously has no application in the United Kingdom. But because there is a great deal of learning in the United States based upon the Fourth Amendment, it is appropriate now to consider this broad equivalent to Article 8 of the ECHR. The Fourth Amendment – made in 1791 – provides:

> The right of the people to be secure in their persons, houses, papers and effects, against unreasonable searches and seizures, shall not be violated, and no Warrants shall issue, but upon probable cause, supported by Oath or affirmation, and particularly describing the place to be searched, and the persons or things to be seized.

[4.161] Although privacy is not mentioned in the text, the Fourth Amendment is *all* about privacy; it simply approaches the subject matter in a different way. Where Article 8 of the ECHR is largely concerned with protecting privacy and thereby controlling state incursion, the Fourth Amendment is all about controlling state incursion and so protecting privacy. The difference in approach is illuminating. A few preliminary points can be made.

[4.162] The Fourth Amendment is inspired by the protection of physical papers articulated in *Entick v Carrington*.[184] Schulhofer, for instance, considers that the framers of the Fourth Amendment did not – as a matter of subjective drafting intent – consider that the Fourth Amendment extended to non-physical trespass:[185]

> … Eavesdropping was common in 1789, and there is no reason to think that the Framers viewed it as a violation of the Fourth Amendment. They recognised that prying eyes and ears could invade precious aspects of privacy …, but for them 'searches and seizures' implied a physical trespass.

[4.163] This construction of the Fourth Amendment – had it been maintained – would rapidly have rendered the protections conferred by it otiose in light of technological development. When, during Prohibition, wire-tapping or

[184] See para [4.32] ff.

[185] S Schulhofer, *More Essential Than Ever* (Oxford University Press, 2012) 38–39.

the interception of telephonic communications came to be used by the state, the US Supreme Court held that no warrant was required:[186]

> Prohibition brought the issue to a head. Roy Olmstead headed a syndicate that was importing illegal liquor into the United States. Without getting a warrant or showing any basis for their suspicions, federal agents tapped the phone lines to his house and listened to his telephonic conversations with associates. But the Supreme Court held that Olmstead could not object to this tactic, because there had been no 'search' and no 'seizure'. Chief Justice William Howard Taft acknowledged that the agents would have needed a warrant to open and read letters that the conspirators had sent through the mails. But tapping their phone conversations was different, he said, because the constitutional text protected only 'material things'. A letter 'is plainly within the words of the amendment … The letter is paper.' In contrast, he said, when the agents tapped Olmstead's phone, 'evidence was secured by the use of the sense of hearing and that only. There was no entry.' And as a result, no Fourth Amendment Safeguards were available at all.

[**4.164**] This approach was obviously unsustainable and gave rise to all kinds of absurd distinctions. Thus, placing a microphone against a wall without penetrating it so as to hear conversations within (a 'slap mike') did not infringe Fourth Amendment protections, but a 'spike mike', that penetrated the wall, did infringe.[187]

[**4.165**] The decision in *Olmstead* was overruled in *Katz*, where it was held that the Fourth Amendment protected people, not places.[188] On this point, the last word belongs to Justice Brandeis, who dissented in *Olmstead*:[189]

> … time works changes … Subtler and more far-reaching means of invading privacy have become available … Writs of assistance and general warrants are but puny instruments of tyranny and oppression when compared with wire-tapping … The makers of our Constitution … knew that only a part of the pain, pleasure and satisfaction of life are to be found in material things. They sought to protect Americans in their beliefs, their thoughts, their emotions and their sensations. They conferred, as against the Government, the right to be let alone … To protect that right, every unjustifiable intrusion by the Government upon the privacy of the individual, whatever the means employed, must be deemed a violation of the Fourth Amendment.

[**4.166**] The protections conferred by the Fourth Amendment are intended to prevent general – and so potentially arbitrary – invasions of privacy. The wording of the Fourth Amendment appears to require a high degree of specificity: 'no Warrants shall issue, but upon probable cause … particularly describing the place to be searched, and the persons or things to be seized'.

[186] ibid 116.
[187] ibid 118.
[188] ibid 118–19.
[189] Quoted in ibid 117–18.

[4.167] The expansion of the regulatory state has caused these apparently clear protections to be eroded, albeit with the best of intentions. Schulhofer describes the use of what he calls 'area warrants' in support of important public functions of the administrative state:[190]

> In the row houses and apartment towers of urban American, fire marshals and building inspectors often seek to search entire groups of homes on a routine basis, in order to check the safety of their electrical wiring and other systems. And city officials have long believed that a requirement of probable cause to suspect dangerous conditions in a particular home would make the building code virtually unenforceable. Responding to that view, the Supreme Court has held that health and safety inspectors can enter homes and apartments without permission, by using an 'area warrant' issued for an entire neighbourhood on the basis of some neutral enforcement principle.

[4.168] The road to hell is paved with good intentions, and it is a small step from ostensibly neutral 'administrative state'/'health and safety' inspections, to much more invasive searches. Schulhofer provides a host of other, much more dangerous, possible uses for the area warrant:[191]

> Suppose that building inspectors want to visit homes in a low-income neighbourhood to see whether any of them is being used as a 'crack house'. Suppose they want to check apartments in a public housing project to find out where firearms are being stashed. Should they be able to enter these residencies merely on the authority of an 'area warrant' – without any showing of probable cause that any particular apartment contains illegal drugs or weapons? What if a city wants to stop drivers on the highway and take samples of their blood and urine to determine whether any of them is using drugs or alchohol? Or suppose that police want to search all houses in a neighbourhood in order to locate a fugitive suspected of murder. All these situations pose potential threats to community health or safety. And all of them can be said to meet the vague Camara criteria – 'the public interest demands' that a dangerous condition be prevented and that enforcement techniques requiring probable cause may not achieve 'acceptable' results.

[4.169] The Fourth Amendment continues to draw from the notion that a person's house is their castle, and that they should be able to control what happens in their own homes, and that no-one else should tell them what to do there. Thus, Pitt said:[192]

> The poorest man may, in his cottage, bid defiance to all the forces of the Crown. It may be frail; its roof may shake; the wind may blow through it; the storm may enter; the rain may enter; but the King of England may not enter; all his force dares not cross the threshold of the ruined tenement.

[190] ibid 93–94.
[191] ibid 95–96.
[192] Quoted in ibid 22.

Similarly, Justice Scalia said,[193] '... in the home ... all details are intimate details'.

[4.170] When considering circumstances outside the home, the protections conferred by the Fourth Amendment attenuate,[194] in two ways in particular:

(1) The protection afforded to a person in public places is limited. After *Katz* recognised that reasonable expectation of privacy was the touchstone for the Fourth Amendment, the notion of what this entailed was curtailed:[195]

> A series of 'beeper' cases signalled the return to this outmoded conception of the Fourth Amendment. Unsurprisingly, the Court held that secretly placing an electronic signalling device inside a residence, in order to track movements there, qualifies as a 'search' and therefore violates the Fourth Amendment in the absence of a search warrant. But the Court reached the opposite conclusion when government agents were able to track a suspect's movements outside the home without disturbing any of his property. (They had simply planted a beeper inside a container that they delivered to him and then tracked as he drove away with it.) Of course, a person's movements on the street were not considered private in the eighteenth century. And even today, what a person does outdoors can be observed by anyone standing nearby. Seizing on these facts, and ignoring the capacity of electronic tracking to produce a detailed picture that was unimaginable in the eighteenth century, the Rehnquist Court held that use of a beeper to locate and track a suspect outdoors (in other words, searching for him) is not a 'search' in the constitutional sense.

(2) The protection afforded to a person who shares information that would otherwise be private is similarly limited:[196]

> The contemporary Court has also stripped away constitutional protection from information that citizens never expose to the general public at all. In a 1976 case, federal agents ordered bank officers to turn over all records pertaining to a depositor's checking and saving accounts. Of course, the records fell squarely within the terms of the Fourth Amendment; they were 'papers' of the traditional sort. And the bank, like most financial intermediaries, had pledged to keep them confidential. Yet the Burger Court exploited the flexible 'expectations' test to reduce the citizen's privacy protection. It held that a bank customer has no 'reasonable expectation of privacy' because he 'voluntarily' gives the information to the bank and therefore 'takes the risk' that bank employees will provide it to the government – even when the government forces them to do so.

[4.171] The Fourth Amendment has – as a result of a consideration of these issues – been reframed as mandating constitutional safeguards whenever

[193] Quoted in ibid 122.
[194] As Schulhofer puts it (ibid 122–23): 'Without expressly repudiating *Katz*, the Court has in effect reinstated the eighteenth century view that private information and private activity get little constitutional protection anywhere beyond a small inner sanctum – the four walls of the home'.
[195] Schulhofer (n 185) 123.
[196] ibid 123–24.

the government intrudes on a reasonable expectation of privacy.[197] Thus, the very differently framed Fourth Amendment comes very close, in its essence, to Article 8 of the ECHR.

[4.172] What is either reassuring or else alarming is that the trend towards the erosion of privacy – or, where no right of privacy exists, the non-recognition of privacy – is as evident in a country with an aggressive form of constitutional protection (the United States Constitution) as it is in a country with no particularly entrenched bill of rights at all, namely the United Kingdom.[198]

G. Conclusions

[4.173] The ECHR and the Human Rights Act operate in parallel with and act in support of the Action. They operate in parallel to the extent that they provide, as against public authorities, a claim (that may sound in damages or involve injunctive relief) *in addition* to the private law cause of action described here. There may be – almost certainly is – substantial overlap between these remedies, but that is explicable by virtue of the fact that the Action is the *only* remedy available against *non*-public authorities, where a claim under the Human Rights Act is not possible.

[4.174] The ECHR and the HRA 1998 operate in support of the Action in that they have informed and caused the development of this proprietary tort. Whether these protections go far enough is a matter for later. We need to understand the scope of the Action, and that will involve at least some consideration of Article 8 of the ECHR. One concern, however, is what the Fourth Amendment teaches: that our protections of privacy – whether expressed by way of the Fourth Amendment, Article 8 of the ECHR or the Action – still use as their starting point *Entick v Carrington*, with the inevitable corollary that privacy outside the home is an attenuated right. Obviously, to an extent, that has to be true: where we interact with other human beings in public places, privacy is a less protected value. But there is still the notion that privacy equates to secrecy,

[197] ibid 120.

[198] The difference is that the Supreme Court of the United States can strike down as unconstitutional primary legislation, as well as being the interpreter of the constitution that is the basis for striking down such primary legislation. Thus, in the power politics between the various functions of the state (legislative, executive and judicial) the judicial is very much 'top dog' in the United States. In the United Kingdom, the theoretical 'top dog' is the legislative branch, for no court may question an Act of Parliament. The most the HRA 1998 permits in regard to Acts of Parliament is to make a declaration of incompatibility under s 5 of that Act. Parliament is referred to as a 'theoretical top dog' because the executive controls Parliament: the Prime Minister is, practically speaking, defined as that person who can command a majority in the House of Commons.

and in the surveillance society that we live in that is a most dangerous notion. Veliz expresses this concern in the following words:[199]

> When discussing privacy in social settings, I have often encountered people defending the view that there is no claim to privacy in the public sphere. The thought is that, if something happens to someone while in the public sphere, or if some event or person belongs to the public sphere, they cannot be expected to enjoy privacy. The assumption is that the private sphere is the proper territory of privacy, or, in other words, that private, in the sense of privacy, is whatever is private, in the sense of belonging to the private sphere.

[4.175] This is the *Entick v Carrington* fallacy: that there is a line between the 'private' and the 'public' that privacy rights cannot cross. To be clear, this book suggests that any 'brightline' distinction between the public and private is indefensible; and that the distinction is probably not helpful at all. Of course, *where* our private information is harvested is a relevant factor, both in terms of defining whether information is indeed 'private' or, if private, whether it has been 'misused'. But a harder distinction than that cannot permissibly be drawn, as *Murray v Express Newspapers plc* shows.

VII. Data Protection

A. The data protection regime and its relevance

[4.176] Data protection involves control over the extent to which and the manner in which information about an individual may be used by others.[200] As Coppel notes, 'use' covers 'the complete life-cycle of information: acquisition, storage, organisation, retrieval, consultation, reliance, adaptation, copying, dissemination, publication, blocking, erasure and destruction'. This vast range of activity constitutes controlled use. This is also clear from Coppel's general description of the approach of data protection law:[201]

> Data protection law aims to protect the rights of identifiable living individuals ('data subjects') as regards anything done ('processing') with information relating to them ('personal data') by or on behalf of persons who determine how and for what purposes that information is used ('controllers'). It does so by imposing a range of continuing obligations on controllers and those acting on their behalf ('processors') in respect of all processing of personal data ('principles'), as well as conferring specific rights that data subjects can assert against a data controller.

[199] C Véliz, *The Ethics of Privacy and Surveillance* (Oxford University Press, 2024) Ch 3, quotation from 29.

[200] P Coppel, *Information Rights*, Vol 1, 5th edn (Hart Publishing, 2020) [7-001].

[201] ibid [7-002].

> Although these rights will often overlap with the ordinary conception of a right to personal privacy, there is no requirement that personal privacy be infringed in order for data protection obligations or rights to be infringed: the obligations and rights are inherent in the processing of personal data. Thus, data protection law recognises that where, for example, a controller has, without the consent of a data subject, abstracted his or her personal data, that data subject will have an actionable claim against the controller without needing to support that claim with an allegation of resultant pecuniary loss or resultant distress.

[4.177] The story[202] of data protection law begins with the Convention for the Protection of Individuals with regard to the Automatic Processing of Personal Data (Convention 108),[203] to which the United Kingdom subscribed,[204] and as a result of which the Data Protection Act 1984 was enacted.[205] In 1995, the European Parliament adopted Directive 96/45/EC, inspired by Convention 108, and based on Article 95 of the then-EC Treaty.[206] Data protection law continued to evolve,[207] culminating in the GDPR[208] and the Data Protection Act 2018 (DPA 2018) (which replaced the Data Protection Act 1998, which had itself replaced the 1984 Act of the same name). There is a further body of law contained in Directive (EU) 2016/680, the Law Enforcement Directive (LED).

[4.178] Prior to Brexit, these three legislative measures – GDPR, LED and DPA 2018 – covered 'the field of data protection in the UK'.[209] With the United Kingdom's exit from the European Union, the applicable law has changed or (more accurately) been modified. However, post-Brexit, the regime is substantially the same.[210] The DPA 2018 obviously remains in force, as amended from time-to-time; the GDPR forms part of 'retained' EU law;[211] and the LED is implemented by the DPA 2018.

[4.179] Coppel helpfully identifies four distinct regimes for the processing of personal data in the United Kingdom:[212] intelligence services processing of personal data;[213] processing of personal data by competent authorities for

[202] The history is a long and complex one, and this summary is drawn from Coppel (n 200). For those interested in a more detailed narrative, cross-references to Coppel (n 200) have been provided.
[203] ibid [7-008].
[204] ibid [7-009].
[205] ibid [7-009].
[206] ibid [7-012].
[207] ibid [7-013]ff.
[208] Regulation (EU) 2016/679 of the European Parliament and of the Council.
[209] Coppel (n 200) [7-034].
[210] ibid [7-046] describes the regime in overview.
[211] ibid [7-045].
[212] ibid [8-002].
[213] DPA 2018, Part 4. The GDPR has no role here.

law enforcement purposes;[214] processing of personal data that falls within the GDPR;[215] processing of personal data falling outside the GDPR.[216]

[4.180] The data protection regime – as this very brief overview demonstrates – is of some complexity, with four different regimes (meaning there are already 'demarcation' issues as between these regimes), each with their own complexities. As with the ECHR and the HRA 1998, it is no function of this book to describe these regimes. There are two reasons why they are considered at all:

(1) Unlike the HRA 1998, which operates in a manner complementary to the reification of private information described in this book, data protection might be said to be a rivalrous regime, which seeks in a 'top down' manner to protect individual rights, as opposed to a regime based on property which gives agency to individuals. In short, it might be said that an *in rem*, proprietary tort, serving to vindicate A's property over their private information, is duplicative of an existing statutory regime. To the extent that there is doubt over the existence of the regime propounded in this book, that doubt will be magnified if there is a rivalrous regime. This is a perfectly fair point, and one that needs to be addressed. To anticipate, it will be suggested that – just as with the ECHR and the HRA 1998 – the two regimes are not, in fact, rivalrous, but complementary.
(2) The data protection regime sheds light on the proprietary regime here under consideration. Reference will be made, as appropriate, to the GDPR regime in elucidating A's rights *in rem* over C.

[4.181] For these reasons, the consideration of the United Kingdom's data protection regime will be at a high level of abstraction, and the focus will be on the GDPR, even though the regime in the United Kingdom has moved on from this, post-Brexit. The differences are, for the purposes of this book, immaterial.

B. The GDPR regime

[4.182] The GDPR regime seeks to protect natural persons with regard to the processing of personal data.[217] The GDPR also contains rules regarding the free movement of data and its transfer outside the European Union.[218] These rules are of less significance for present purposes.

[214] DPA 2018, Part 3. This part implements the LED, and the GDPR has no role.
[215] GDPR and the DPA 2018, Part 2, Chapters 1 and 2.
[216] DPA 2018, Part 2, Chapter 3.
[217] GDPR, Art 1(1).
[218] ibid Art 1(1).

[4.183] The GDPR's protection is limited to 'natural persons'. The GDPR defines 'personal data' as:[219]

> … any information relating to an identified or identifiable natural person ('data subject'); an identifiable natural person is one who can be identified, directly or indirectly, in particular by reference to an identifier such as a name, an identification number, location data, an online identifier or to one or more factors specific to the physical, physiological, genetic, mental, economic, cultural or social identify of that natural person …

[4.184] The need for a data subject to be identifiable is readily apparent. The GDPR imposes specific obligations on 'processors' with regard to the personal data of data subjects. In some cases, the identity of the data subject affects the obligations of the processor. In this, the GDPR regime differs from the Action, which can involve obligations on C without A being identifiable at the time of the infringement of A's privacy.

[4.185] A processor of personal data is defined as 'a natural or legal person, public authority, agency or other body which processes personal data on behalf of the controller'.[220] The 'controller' is defined as:[221]

> … the natural or legal person, public authority, agency or other body which, alone or jointly with others, determines the purposes and means of the processing of personal data; where the purposes and means of such processing are determined by Union or Member State law, the controller or the specific criteria for its nomination may be provided for by Union or Member State law …

[4.186] The 'processing' of personal data means:

> any operation or set of operations which is performed on personal data or on sets of personal data, whether or not by automated means, such as collection, recording, organisation, structuring, storage, adaptation or alteration, retrieval, consultation, use, disclosure by transmission, dissemination or otherwise making available, alignment or combination, restriction, erasure or destruction.[222]

[4.187] Although these definitions are technical and somewhat complex, the regime is actually a straightforward one: it seeks to ensure that a data subject's personal data is processed by processors on behalf of controllers in accordance with certain standards. The GDPR sets out (in Article 5) a number of principles relating to the processing of personal data; and (in Article 6) more hard-edged rules regarding the lawfulness of processing.

[219] ibid Art 4(1).
[220] ibid Art 4(8).
[221] ibid Art 4(7).
[222] ibid Art 4(2).

[**4.188**] Beginning with the hard-edged rules, processing is only lawful if and to the extent that at least one of the following applies:[223]

(1) The data subject has given consent to the processing of their personal data for one or more specific purposes.
(2) Processing is necessary for the performance of a contract to which the data subject is party or in order to take steps at the request of the data subject prior to entering into a contract.
(3) Processing is necessary for compliance with a legal obligation to which the controller is subject.
(4) Processing is necessary in order to protect the vital interests of the data subject or of another natural person.
(5) Processing is necessary for the performance of a task carried out in the public interest or in the exercise of official authority vested in the controller.
(6) Processing is necessary for the purposes of the legitimate interests pursued by the controller or by the third party, except where such interests are overridden by the interests or fundamental rights and freedoms of the data subject which require protection of personal data, in particular where the data subject is a child.

[**4.189**] Before turning to the principles relating to the processing of personal data contained in Article 5 of the GDPR – which, of course, can only apply where the processing is lawful pursuant to Article 6 of the GDPR – it is worth noting the sheer width of this regime:

- Personal data is widely defined as that relating to a data subject. There is no qualitative threshold: A's email address (which A may *want* to publicise) will count as personal data, just as much as A's private information that A may very well wish to keep secret.
- Consistently with this book's approach to information (as constituting C's perception of A), personal data is simply that 'relating to' A.
- Processing personal data is so widely defined as to capture all forms of data handling, ranging from the handwritten list to the physical filing cabinet, to the personal electronic device to the most sophisticated organisations processing billions of pieces of information.
- Those involved in processing are the ministerial agents that actually *do* the processing (processors). Those at whose behest the processing occurred are 'controllers'.

[**4.190**] Apart from Article 2(2)(c) of the GDPR, the end result is that any natural person is likely to be both a data subject and (perhaps not in relation

[223] Quoting from ibid, Art 6.

to the same material) a processor/controller. C's use of emailing software – like Microsoft Outlook – would involve the processing of A's personal data, in the form of the emails of A_1, A_2, etc. Article 2(2)(c) of the GDPR provides an important limitation to the scope of the regime, providing that the GDPR does not apply to the processing of personal data 'by a natural person in the course of a purely personal or household activity'.

[4.191] Another important restriction on scope is Article 2(1) of the GDPR, which provides:

> This Regulation applies to the processing of personal data wholly or partly by automated means and to the processing other than by automated means of personal data which form part of a filing system or are intended to form part of a filing system.

[4.192] The width of the regime explains the breadth of the justifications under Article 6 of the GDPR for the processing of personal data. The GDPR regime gives with one hand (it is an extraordinarily inclusive or wide regime) but takes away with the other (the lawful justifications are correspondingly generous and render the regime much narrower).

[4.193] This is not an efficient form of regulation. Drawing the scope widely means that many people (both natural and legal) will have to consider the GDPR because it will likely apply to them, no matter how small or economically insignificant they are. This, of course, renders the principles relating to the processing of personal data of significance. It is the controller who is responsible for, and must be able to demonstrate compliance with, these principles.[224] The fact that most forms of use will be permitted does not reduce the regulatory burden.[225]

[4.194] The principles are as follows. Personal data shall be:[226]

(1) Processed lawfully, fairly and in a transparent manner in relation to the data subject.
(2) Collected for specific, explicit and legitimate purposes and not further processed in a manner that is incompatible with those purposes; further processing for achieving purposes in the public interest, scientific or historical research purposes or statistical purposes shall, in accordance with Article 89(1) GDPR, not be considered to be incompatible with the initial purposes.

[224] ibid Art 5(2).
[225] The central premise of this book is that our private information is important and requires protection. It is not being suggested that the GDPR is striving to regulate something unimportant. What *is* being suggested is that it is not a very good form of regulation. The GDPR runs to 99 articles. A commentary on the GDPR (C Kuner et al, *The E General Data Protection Regulation (GDPR): A Commentary* (Oxford University Press, 2020) is 1,393 pages long.
[226] Quoting from GDPR, Art 5(1).

(3) Adequate, relevant and limited to what is necessary in relation to the purposes for which they are processed.
(4) Accurate and, where necessary, kept up to date; every reasonable step must be taken to ensure that personal data that are inaccurate, having regard to the purposes for which they are processed, are erased or rectified without delay.
(5) Kept in a form which permits identification of data subjects for no longer than is necessary for the purposes for which the personal data are processed; personal data may be stored for longer periods insofar as the personal data will be processed solely for archiving purposes in the public interest, scientific or historical research purposes or statistical purposes in accordance with Article 89(1) subject to implementation of the appropriate technical and organisation measures required by this Regulation in order to safeguard the rights and freedoms of the data subject.
(6) Processed in a manner that ensures appropriate security of the personal data, including protection against unauthorised or unlawful processing and against accidental loss, destruction or damage, using appropriate technical or organisational measures.

[4.195] The GDPR contains a wealth of additional provisions to elucidate the above list, but these cannot be investigated here. However, something needs to be said about remedies for breach of the GDPR regime. As to this, the main responsibility for enforcing the GDPR lies with the Information Commissioner.[227] The Information Commissioner's functions can be summarised as follows:[228]

- carrying out international roles in relation to data protection;
- preparing codes of practice and guidance;
- carrying out consensual audits;
- carrying out other specific investigations by means of 'assessments', 'information notices', exercising powers of entry and search on warrants, etc;
- enforcing compliance by data controllers and processors by imposing 'enforcement notices' and 'penalty notices';
- dealing with complaints by data subjects;
- instituting criminal proceedings under the DPA 2018;
- reporting annually to Parliament;
- reviewing compliance.

[4.196] Private law claims can be brought by a data subject claiming that a controller or a processor, in processing their personal data, has not complied

[227] Coppel (n 200) Ch 44 and [44-001].
[228] Drawing on the helpful list set out in Coppel (n 200) [44-004].

with one or other of their continuing obligations or the data subject's rights. These actions are tortious, specifically for breach of statutory duty.[229]

C. Analysis

[4.197] The extent to which the GDPR data protection regime informs or elucidates the Action is considered as these points arise in the course of this book. These paragraphs consider the extent to which a data protection regime – such as the GDPR – can co-exist with the privacy regime for which this book makes a case, or whether there is such duplication or tension as to suggest limits on the proprietary tort here contended for.

[4.198] The two regimes in fact serve different functions and co-exist comfortably in parallel. As to this:

- The GDPR deals with the processing of personal data, which is data relating to a natural person (a data subject) which does not necessarily have the quality of privacy, which is the focus of the Action. The two regimes are thus, in terms of focus and function, very different. The GDPR looks to a natural person's personal data, without reference to the subject matter of that personal data. The Action looks to the protection of A's private information. Although that has yet to be defined (a pleasure that awaits the reader in Chapter 6), the meaning of private information is far narrower than the meaning the GDPR gives to personal data.
- The GDPR is concerned with the raising of standards of data processing generally. That explains its width, and the involvement of entities like the Information Commissioner. The processing of personal data is, rightly, perceived as of importance in this 'information society' and at least part of the objectives of the regime is to articulate and enforce standards. The protection conferred by the Action is much more concerned with the individual case, where A's privacy is infringed by C. Whilst such actions may, indirectly, have an effect on standards, their primary objective is to remedy the (hopefully) exceptional case where A's private information is unlawfully used (ie 'misused', the subject of Chapters 7 and 8).
- For this reason, the GDPR protects the personal data of natural persons: as will be seen, the Action has no such restriction. Equally, whereas the GDPR concerns data processing (albeit extremely widely defined), that is not a limitation that informs the Action.

[229] ibid [48-006] and, generally, Ch 48.

[**4.199**] Thus, the Action and the GDPR approach information from different ends of the spectrum. The Action starts with individual misuses, and it is an open question (which we will come to) how *aggregations* of data can sensibly be policed through the Action. By contrast, the GDPR begins (and, really, ends) with the general processing of data, viewing it largely divorced from subject matter and in the aggregate. That is not to diminish the importance of controlling information processing.[230] States in particular have *always* sought to collect information about their subjects and there is a certain legitimacy to this:[231]

> Historically surveillance, including mass surveillance, has always been a feature of power, and those who exert such power, irrespective of their particular ideology, have always relied upon the accumulation of information about their inhabitants, citizens or foreigners, to preserve their position.
>
> '[I]ntelligence organizations are neither the product nor a feature of any one particular form of government. All governments need intelligence upon which to base their decisions, be their posture defensive or offensive, be they are war or at peace. Intelligence gathering is just as natural to democracies as it is to dictatorships. Although totalitarian regimes very often misuse their intelligence services, notably by taking advantage of domestic surveillance capabilities, nevertheless every government, authoritarian or representative, needs information about neighboring countries in order to consider its options and make educated decisions.'

But this power must be controlled, particularly where: (i) information processing in bulk is so much cheaper and easier today than formerly (and that trend will continue); and (ii) the focus of the GDPR is more on private actors than state actors.[232]

[230] See para [1.17] and the Snowden Example referenced in that paragraph, which shows that aggregated metadata can produce individuated and personal information.

[231] Monti and Wacks (n 178) Ch 3, quotation from 35. The quotation within the quotation is from Rose Mary Sheldon's book *Intelligence Activities in Ancient Rome: Trust in the Gods but Verify*. For a more recent, but still paper-based, example, see T Garton Ash, *The File* (Harper Collins, 1997), which describes how the East German Stasi kept records.

[232] Of course public bodies are subject to the GDPR, but really only to the extent that they are truly equivalent to private actors. The regime in the United Kingdom differentiates between state and non-state actors. Intelligence services and law enforcement bodies have greater latitude than other bodies. To an extent, that is defensible, and this is why misuse of private information by state actors is treated separately (in Chapter 8) from misuse by non-state actors (in Chapter 7).

5

Economic Justification for a Proprietary Regime

In which: the importance and nature of economic analysis is stated; an economic analysis of the importance of property generally is undertaken; why 'reification' of private information is important; and the long-term disbenefits of failing to price factors of production appropriately considered.

I. An Introduction to Economic Analysis: Aggregation

[5.1] Section V of Chapter 3 set out the intellectual basis on which private information could be regarded as property. It was also suggested that this conclusion could be defended by reference to the decided case law[1] and justified in policy terms as being necessary to protect A's privacy, given the gaps in the other regimes that, to a limited extent, serve to protect A's privacy.[2] This chapter considers the importance of private information as property from an economic standpoint.[3]

[5.2] As Posner notes, economic analysis of law is not confined to anti-trust law but has been used (at least in American jurisprudence) to establish a framework for analysing the assignment of property rights and liability in economic terms.[4] The link between property rights and economics is a close one. In a world of scarce resources, economics is the study of how scarce resources are and should be allocated amongst rival claimants to those resources.[5] Property law articulates the processes by which property is allocated to an owner, what an owner's rights are and the circumstances in which an owner may divest themselves of ownership, typically through sale. In short, at the transactional level

[1] See para [3.51].
[2] See para [3.52] and Chapter 4.
[3] As foreshadowed in paras [1.63] and [3.52].
[4] R Posner, *Economic Analysis of Law*, 9th edn (Wolters Kluwer, 2014) 29–30.
[5] Economics has both analytic and normative aspects. It not only analyses how – in the real world – resources are allocated but also considers whether such allocation is optimal. This is not only a question of allocative efficiency but of fairness and the meeting of demand based on need and not just desire.

(where A sells something to B) the law provides the answer to the economist's question of who, in a world of scarcity, gets what; and what they can do with it, when they have it.

[5.3] Economics is not concerned with the individual transaction (which is the province of the law), but with the behaviour of *aggregates*, whether these be buyers or sellers or the transactions concluded between them. Thus, the economist will not be particularly troubled if, on the individual transaction level, A chooses not to sell to B or does sell, but at an under- or over-value.[6] The economist will be interested in the collective behaviour of sellers $A_{1 \dots n}$ and buyers $B_{1 \dots n}$. Such interactions between classes of seller and classes of buyer are what economists would call markets, which are no more than the cumulation of many individual but similar transactions between classes of buyer and seller. Since all individual transactions are susceptible of a legal analysis, economics might be said to be the study of the consequences of the aggregation of multiple, similar, *legal* transactions.

[5.4] So far, this book has considered the operation of generic rules[7] in the individual case: what rights does A have as against O(C), the person who perceives information that is personal and private to A? The benefits, in terms of protecting A's privacy are obvious; and they are best considered at the single transaction (or legal) level. Equally, the questions as to what constitutes 'private' information and 'misuse' of private information are also questions best addressed at the single transaction (or legal) level.

[5.5] However, the overall, societal, advantages and disadvantages of treating private information as property can only be considered at the aggregate level, through an economist's lens. This chapter considers the *aggregate* benefits and disbenefits of A's ownership of their private information. That consideration involves a radical change in standpoint for the reader – we are jumping from the micro-legal level (where the individual transaction is considered) to the macro-economic level (where the operation of classes of these individual transactions are under scrutiny). The dislocation begins with the 'externality', which is the first of a number of distinctly unlegal terms that the reader will be burdened with.

[6] Whatever 'value' may mean. A great of economic thinking concerns an understanding of cost, price and value and their inter-relationship. 'Value' is particularly intractable. A consumer surplus is a measure of how much a buyer values a particular product, because it represents the excess over price that the buyer would have paid for the product, but did not have to. Value is thus related to but different from price. When lawyers and economists have to assess a price without a market to reference, they tend (probably wrongly) to default to some assessment of value.

[7] Laws are – or should be – general, so that like cases are treated alike, and unlike cases treated appropriately differently according to the nature of their unalikeness. It is the function of courts to apply these general laws to the specific case before them.

II. The Externality

[5.6] In a sale between a vendor and a purchaser, the price is the means by which the efficient allocation of resource is determined. The purchaser is willing to pay the price, and the seller willing to sell at that price. The seller, in making the product they sell and that buyers wish to purchase, will have incurred costs (obtaining the factors of production that go to make the product sold) for which the seller will have paid a price to that seller's own suppliers. In the transactions between the seller and that seller's suppliers, price again informs the efficient allocation of resource. The seller must compete with other producers/sellers of other products for the scarce resources that comprise the factors of production.

[5.7] An 'externality' represents a cost or a benefit to society which is not recognised in the prices charged in a market economy. Meade provides the following definition:[8]

> An external economy (diseconomy) is an event which confers an appreciable benefit (inflicts an appreciable damage) on some person or persons who were not fully consenting parties in reaching the decision or decisions which led directly or indirectly to the event in question.

[5.8] In theory, as this definition shows, an externality can constitute a benefit to society that is not paid for. Instinctively, it might be felt that there is no problem in a transaction (sale/purchase) incidentally creating benefits for third parties, although matters are never quite as straightforward as they seem.[9] The definition here adopted is by reference to externalities that create disbenefits. The suggestion that externalities create costs represents an inaccurate use of language: it is precisely because externalities do *not* create costs that they represent a problem. For this reason, the term 'disbenefits' will be used, in preference to the term 'cost'.

[5.9] Externalities have a number of characteristics apart from the fact that they create disbenefits. The disbenefits tend to be borne by third parties and not by the parties to the transaction in question. This is because the parties to the transaction can often adjust the price to take account of the externality, although that is not always the case, and certainly is not the case with private information at present. The disbenefits of externalities also tend to be both subjective and difficult to pin down in terms of cost. As a result, externalities are difficult to control for or 'internalise' as a proper cost to a transaction as between buyer and seller.

[8] J Meade, *The Theory of Economic Externalities* (AW Sijthoff, 1973) 15.

[9] Problems can arise where one factor of production is priced too low, and the social problems that this causes can be immense. It will be suggested that this is a mischief that the 'reification' of private information prevents.

[5.10] Externalities should not generally arise between the parties to the transaction (the sale/purchase) because these parties get what they pay for and can choose not to transact. In theory, any benefits/disbenefits are paid for as costs in the price paid/received, and the producer/consumer surplus each party may achieve is an internalised outcome of the transaction.

[5.11] A consumer surplus arises when the price that consumers pay for a product or service is less than the price they would be willing and able to pay. Consumer surplus is subjective to the consumer in question: Buyer 1 may be able and willing to pay £10 for product P, but only has to pay £5. Buyer 1's consumer surplus is £5. Buyer 2 may value product P less, and only be prepared to pay £6 for product P. Buyer 2's consumer surplus (the price still at £5) is £1. The price that both buyers pay is the same, but their consumer surpluses very different.[10]

[5.12] Consumer surplus can be aggregated, and when economists speak of consumer surplus, it is usually a reference to the aggregate consumer surplus of all individual consumers. If it were possible to identify the monetary value each consumer attached to the product they had bought, the aggregate consumer surplus would be the difference between the price and each purchaser's value of the product purchased added together. Aggregate consumer surplus is a helpful term, provided it is not forgotten that individual consumer surplus is subjective and will vary from consumer to consumer. Also, because it is subjective, consumer surplus and (particularly) aggregate consumer surplus is generally a theoretical value, unascertainable in the real world.

[5.13] Producer surplus is the difference between how much a supplier would be willing to accept for a product versus how much they can receive by selling the product at the market price. Again, it is a measure that varies according to individual producer. The difference or surplus amount is the benefit a particular producer receives for selling the good in the market. Producer surplus turns on two factors: (i) relative efficiency between producers; and (ii) the extent to which, through product differentiation, any given producer can differentiate themselves from their competitors and by such differentiation induce consumers to pay more for their product.

[5.14] As with consumer surplus, producer surplus can be aggregated. Producer surplus is susceptible of a little greater certainty of calculation, because it is possible to achieve an understanding of industry, sector and individual costs.

[10] For a legal analysis of these economic terms see *Allergan plc v The Competition and Markets Authority* [2023] CAT 56 at [310] ff.

[5.15] If the market is functioning badly – by reason of an imbalance in market power[11] or because the market is badly structured[12] – it may be that there is a pricing 'mismatch' between what one party pays and another receives that can be said to create disbenefits. Excessive market power in a seller will result in consumer surplus being 'squeezed' with the producer surplus doing the squeezing. Some economists adopt a 'So what?' approach to this: all that is happening in the case of such squeezes is that the price is being adjusted upwards, and every £1 lost by the aggregate buyer class represents a £1 gained by the aggregate class of sellers. That is *not* the view espoused in this book. Even if the various levels at which the price can be set are Pareto efficient (a very doubtful point),[13] given that competition law exists to ensure value to consumers is maximised, the 'squeezing' of consumer surplus is something to be concerned about.

[5.16] Externalities in the buyer/seller relationship tend to involve an assertion that the market price is, in some way, not the 'correct' market price. In other words, there has been a 'squeeze' of the consumer surplus. Although abusive pricing (both too high and too low) is known to competition law, it is both rare and difficult to establish. That is because competition regulators and courts rightly consider the market price to be the 'correct' price because it is the outcome of market forces. Provided the market is operating efficiently (ie fairly in terms of market power between buyer and seller groups), its output – the price – should not be interfered with. Where the market is not operating efficiently, itself a hugely difficult question, then some form of intervention may be called for. The question, then, will be what shape that intervention should take.[14]

[11] Market power is controlled for in a variety of ways, most bluntly by competition law, which tends to focus on three areas where market power is illegitimately accrued. These three areas involve: (i) the control of mergers; (ii) the control of wrongful collusion between competitors (ie cartels); and/or (iii) the control of monopolistic abuses (referred to in the United Kingdom and the European Union as abuses of dominance).

[12] Much more subtly than competition law, markets can be well or badly designed. It is a mistake to assume that markets simply spring, fully-formed, out of nowhere. Markets are designed, whether intentionally or by a process of evolution, and can function well or badly depending upon whether the design is good or bad and/or whether evolutions in markets are beneficial or detrimental to competition. There is a close nexus between intentional design and the encouragement or discouragement of evolutionary trends in a market. On this, see A Roth, *Who Gets What and Why? The Hidden World of Matching and Market Design* (William Collins, 2015), in particular at 6–8.

[13] Pareto efficiency (Vilfredo Pareto, 1848–1923) describes an economic allocation where there is no feasible reallocation that can raise the welfare of one economic agent without lowering the welfare of some economic agent by the same amount. The example used here *looks* to be Pareto efficient, but given (i) uncertainties of measurement and (ii) the existence of externalities, it is almost bound not to be.

[14] The almost invariable response is some form of regulation or price control. This almost always adds transaction costs without actually solving the problem. After the event, competition law may be able to ride to the rescue. But – and we will be coming to this – in the case of underpriced private information, the answer is to propertise private information so that A gets a proper price for their private information.

[5.17] Disbenefits to third parties that rank as externalities are – by definition – paid for by neither party to the transaction that creates those disbenefits. They are (for that reason) not costs, but they *ought to be costs*.

[5.18] Externalities form a part of what is known as 'welfare' economics, which focuses less on how things are, and more on how things should be. Thus, the point about an externality is that it inflicts a disbenefit, generally on a third party, which – it is felt – ought to be paid for by the parties to the transaction. But, as has been noted, the same problem can arise as between the parties to the actual transaction, where consumer surplus is 'squeezed' and the price is wrong, not right.

[5.19] As can readily be appreciated, there is a high degree of *subjectivity* in the case of externalities. Indeed, there will generally be disagreement about what is, and what is not, an externality, as well as disagreement about the extent of the disbenefit created by it. Because of this subjectivity, disbenefits can be hard to define.

[5.20] Even if one takes a disbenefit which is *not* subjective – say pollution, resulting in climate change over the medium or long term – it is difficult to factor that disbenefit into transactions as a cost. This is because the consequences of the pollution, the disbenefit, are very hard to quantify, simply in causal terms, even accepting a consensus as to how pollution generally affects the environment and climate. Moreover, certainly in the context of climate change, and probably also in the case of other forms of environmental damage, the 'tragedy of the commons' renders the problem even harder to remediate. The tragedy of the commons arises where a commonly owned resource, that cannot sensibly be reduced to individual ownership, is abused by all. That makes many externalities extremely difficult to control for.

III. The Tragedy of the Commons

[5.21] In his seminal essay,[15] Hardin described the abuse of a common resource in cases where many have equal right of use. Each individual user will aim to maximise their profit. The outcome will be overuse and a destruction of resource. Cole explains Hardin's thesis as follows:[16]

> Hardin's 'The Tragedy of the Commons' (1968)[17] provides a useful starting point for analysing the ties between pollution and property in the real world. Its thesis is that

[15] G Hardin, 'The Tragedy of the Commons' (1968) 162 *Science* 1243.
[16] D Cole, *Pollution and Property* (Cambridge University Press, 2002) 5.
[17] Ie Hardin (n 15).

> resource depletion and pollution problems both stem from the incentives created by open-access (non-property) regimes, in which no one can exclude anyone else from using a given resource. Hardin demonstrates the problem with the simple example of a pasture open to unlimited grazing by all cattle ranchers. Assuming that all ranchers who might use the pasture are rational, each will seek to maximise his or her individual benefits from the pasture. Each will ask, '[w]hat is the utility to *me* of adding one more animal to my herd?' In other words, they will conduct a cost-benefit analysis to determine whether adding an additional animal to their herd on the commons will provide a net gain or loss. The benefit side of the equation is 'a function of the increment of one amimal.' According to Hardin, '[s]ince the herdsman receives all the proceeds from the sale of the additional animal, the positive utility is nearly +1.' The cost side of the equation is 'a function of the additional overgrazing created by one more animal.' These costs, however, are not borne solely by the rancher who adds one more head of cattle; rather, they are spread among all the ranchers who use (or might use) the pasture. Thus, 'the negative utility for any particular decision-making herdsman is only a fraction of -1'.

[5.22] Cole's interest in the tragedy of the commons arises in the context of pollution. But the problem of open-access non-property regimes is common. Ostrom begins her book with the following example:

> **Example**[18]
>
> Hardly a week goes by without a major news story about the threatened destruction of a valuable natural resource. In June of 1989, for example, a *New York Times* article focused on the problem of overfishing in the Georges Bank about 150 miles off the New England coast. Catches of cod, flounder, and haddock are now only a quarter of what they were during the 1960s. Everyone knows that the basic problem is overfishing; however, those concerned cannot agree how to solve the problem. Congressional representatives recommend new national legislation, even though the legislation already on the books has been enforced only erratically. Representatives of the fishers argue that the fishing grounds would not be in such bad shape if the federal government had refrained from its sporadic attempts to regulate the fishery in the past. The issue in this case – and many others – is how best to limit the use of natural resources so as to ensure their long-term economic viability. Advocates of central regulation, of privatization, and of regulation by those involved have passed their policy prescriptions in a variety of different arenas.

[5.23] Only a fool would deny the tragedy of the commons.[19] The tragedy, to be clear, arises out of the inevitable abuse of an open-access non-property regime. Hardin has wrongly been accused of pressing only one solution – private

[18] E Ostrom, *Governing the Commons: The Evolution of Institutions for Collective Action* (Cambrige University Press, 1990) 1. In the context of data, see A Sinnreich and J Gilbert, *The Secret Life of Data* (MIT Press, 2024) 172–75.

[19] As Cole (n 16) notes (at 15), the tragedy is less that of the commons, and more that of open-access non-property regimes. But that label is not very catchy.

ownership – to the problem of over-exploitation, and that is unfair.[20] Like Ostrom and Cole, Hardin recognises that there are many possible solutions – the problem is that one-size does not fit all (a solution may be good in one context, bad in another) and it is very difficult to differentiate 'good' solutions from 'bad' ones.[21]

[5.24] In the context of the economic analysis of private information, this book advances two propositions. First, that Zuboff's identification of the problem of 'surveillance capitalism' (described in Chapter 1) is of an externality arising out of the tragedy of the commons. Our private information is treated as a resource that is available, on a free-for-all basis, to anyone with the technology to capture it. Granted, there are *some* controls on the use of our private information, but these tend to relate to the publication of private information, not the other forms of (mis)use identified by Zuboff and described in Chapter 1. As a result, our information is over-used so as: (i) to intrude excessively into our private worlds; (ii) to generate massive producer surplus such that our consumer surplus is either non-existent or negative (because of the first factor identified, the invasion of our privacy).

[5.25] The second proposition is that the best solution to the problem identified by Zuboff is to render private information susceptible to ownership – or,

[20] Cole (n 16) 15–16.

[21] As Dahlman points out, the tragedy of the commons arises out of a failure to control the property rights over the common resource. That does not, however, mean to say that the solution is always to be found in the realm of *private property*. See C Dahlman, *The Open Field System and Beyond* (Cambridge University Press, 1980) 70–71: 'In their survey of the property rights literature, Furubotn and Pejovich therefore define the notion of property rights in the following manner "... property rights do not refer to relations between man and things, but, rather, to the sanctioned behavioral relations among men that arise from the existence of things and pertain to their use. Property rights assignments specify the norms of behavior with respect to things that each and every person must observe in his interactions with other persons, or bear the cost for nonobservance. The prevailing system of property rights in the community can be described, then, as the set of economic and social relations defining the position of each individual with respect to the utilization of scarce resources." Property rights, then, really refer to the rights of decision making with respect to an asset that are recognised within any given social setting. Property rights constitute a collection of social codes, legal remedies, and societal protection or sanctions. It follows, therefore, that the crucial distinction between capitalism and socialism is not so much state versus private possession, but the fact that, in a capitalistic system, a specific individual is allowed to make decisions that the government makes in a socialistic system. Related to this is the important notion of attenuation: all rights of usership or decision making, whether state or private, are always subject to certain limitations. There is no such thing as absolute ownership, not even in an economic system characterised by complete private ownership, for even a system with private ownership of scarce resources will prohibit certain actions in the interest of the community as a whole. For example, the right to use an implement to damage someone else physically has always been circumscribed in every known society. Sometimes, even in the most capitalistic societies, the right to damage others economically is also circumscribed by law. Thus, an owner who holds land in fee simple may still be prohibited from erecting certain structures on his land, or from putting the land to uses that have obvious side effects on his neighbors. What is to be understood by property rights is therefore not simply physical possession of an object, but the uses to which an economic asset can be put ...'.

more accurately, to recognise the full implications of the Action, which *already* treats private information as property.

IV. Controlling Disbenefits

[5.26] Many costs are inevitably incurred by the seller of a product. These costs relate to factors of production that inherently and in any economy have a cost. These costs are paid for by a seller in the course of producing the product; and transferred or passed on, through the price charged by the seller, to the buyer. Much of our law of contract and property is devoted to internalising these aspects of commercial activity so that factors of production are allocated, controlled and paid for in a legal environment. A market system depends upon a legal infrastructure to work.[22] Central to that infrastructure are contract, property, debt and money.

[5.27] Thus, some costs are 'internalised' into the price as an inevitable consequence of the market economy. They can never – unless a market economy moves away from its essence or fails to operate as it should – be externalities. The alternative is either anarchy (the seller steals what they need; and is stolen from) or a different form of economy, be it command or otherwise.

[5.28] Some costs are not, however, 'inevitable' in this sense. Externalities are a prime example. Externalities, as here defined, arise because they are *not* intrinsic to a market economy or are not properly taken into account in the interaction between demand and supply that generates price. Take, for example, the factor of production that is labour. In a pure market economy,[23] labour is simply a cost. In a properly functioning (that is to say, competitive) market economy, cost is squeezed by competition and (absent countervailing market power) labour costs (ie wages) will fall.[24] The operation of the price system thus involves what might be said to be an externality (in the form of wages that are 'too low') falling on a third party, the worker.[25] Sellers compete on, amongst other things, price. A seller is thus driven to minimise all costs, including labour costs, because that way (i) sales are maximised (because the seller can undercut their competitors

[22] There are other allocative systems which are not considered here. That is because our law is predicated on an economy that is (in material part) market-based. If ours was a command economy, the analysis would be different.

[23] In n 5, the point was made that economics has a normative aspect. The point is relevant here: of the four factors of production, only labour concerns human beings. For that reason, labour cannot only be regarded as a cost to be competed downwards by market forces.

[24] Re-reading JM Keynes, *The General Theory of Employment Interest and Money* (MacMillan, 1936), it is remarkable how the welfare economics aspect of labour takes a back seat.

[25] The value judgements involved are readily apparent. There is enormous and daily disagreement about what labour should be paid, and there is rarely consensus about the proper level of a wage. Even as regards something like the minimum wage there is no consensus.

on price) and (ii) profit can be maximised. This squeeze on costs is generally beneficial: but in the case of the worker the 'squeeze' of competition applies to the worker's wages.

[5.29] Paying labour a competitive wage that is nevertheless 'too low' by reference to other values is not an optimal outcome. Because labour involves human beings, it absolutely warrants special treatment. As a result of labour rights and trade union campaigns over the decades, the disbenefit of squeezing the price (or cost) of labour is controlled for by the creation of employment rights (including health and safety legislation), protection of the right to strike and pay control (including as regards the minimum wage). In this way, a disbenefit (poor conditions of employment) to a third party (the worker) is internalised as a cost paid for by the seller (the employer) and transferred (through the price of the products sold by the seller) to the buyer, the ultimate consumer of those goods.[26] Of course, problems arise when cheap labour costs in other jurisdictions mean that domestic production is rendered uncompetitive.

[5.30] Regulation – including, but not limited to, the criminal law – is one way in which an externality can be internalised into the sale/purchase transaction between the buyer and the seller. Other examples of such regulation are the control of emissions through carbon-emission purchase schemes and the control of pollution in rivers by strict liability offences. In these different ways, a disbenefit is (assuming the solution works) ameliorated through regulation. Often, but not always, the aim of that regulation is to create a cost that deters the disbenefit either through prohibition or licence. But there are other, more subtle, forms of regulation.[27]

[5.31] Two other means of control exist: taxation and third-party rights of action. It is possible, as an alternative to the criminal law or other forms of regulation, to tax undesirable externalities. The problem with such a course is that either the externality is precluded (thereby making the tax nothing more than an alternative to the criminal law or regulation) or it becomes an additional cost (paid for by the buyer, the ultimate consumer), which cost (as part of the price) finds its way into government coffers, where it may (or may not) be used to ameliorate the externality itself.

[5.32] In some cases, it is possible to hand agency to the affected third party, either by 'propertising' the source of the externality (ie rendering the third party the owner of it, with all the rights of ownership that go with property) or by

[26] 'Cost' does not necessarily mean a direct cost, although it can do so. The minimum wage is a direct cost because it forces the hourly rate of certain wage-earners up. Health and safety legislation, on the other hand, is an indirect cost. Complying with the rules will, generally speaking, have a cost.

[27] Tax, for example, considered further below; or consciously structuring markets so as to achieve certain results. On this, see Roth (n 12).

creating some cause of action not involving property rights. Both courses create a cost in the seller which either holds the third party harmless or renders the externality uneconomic when the underlying right is vindicated.[28]

V. Property Rights and Rights of Action as a Means of Controlling Externalities

A. Approach

[5.33] In this chapter, the focus is on rights of action and specifically property rights as a means of controlling externalities. Posner articulated the role that the law can play in internalising externalities:[29]

> A more direct antecedent of the economic approach to torts is the concept of social cost, or external cost, notably as articulated by Pigou. Using, among other examples, that of the locomotive that emits sparks which damage the crops of farmers located along the railroad rights-of-way, Pigou noted the potential divergence of social from private cost. The crop damage, he argued, was not a private cost to the railroad, and only private costs determine behavior. It was a social cost, however, because the farmer is a member of society as is the railroad. Therefore, unless some means were found to force the railroad to internalize the cost, there would be too much, or too careless, railroading.
>
> Perhaps because Pigou himself thought that the proper way to force the cost to be internalized was through a tax, and thus he did not discuss liability rules, Pigou's analysis of social cost was not applied to tort law until the Coase and Calabresi articles …

The point being made is that the creation of a cause of action by one party against another (whatever the nature of that claim) can serve the economic function of internalising into one party's costs an externality that *should be* internalised.

[5.34] The analysis here begins with an assessment of rights of action arising out of the disbenefits from the otherwise lawful use of real property or the invasion of the owner's own enjoyment of their land. These rights of action can be characterised as a response to disbenefits to third parties which are then

[28] See the essay 'The Problem of Social Cost' in R Coase, *The Firm, the Market and the Law* (University of Chicago Press, 1990) Ch 5. The efficiency by which rights can be vindicated is critical to any good regulatory regime, *whatever the mode of regulation chosen*. If a regulatory regime is put in place or rights conferred, but the regime is not properly enforced or the rights conferred are too expensive to vindicate, then the regime is worse than useless: (i) it costs money, (ii) to little effect, whilst (iii) misleading us into thinking the problem has been solved. It is important that we evolve, as an aspect of the rule of law, a measure to identify the extent to which a legal regime falls short, in that rights or obligations that should be enforced are not.

[29] R Posner, *The Economics of Private Law: The Collected Economic Essays of Richard A Posner*, Vol 2 (Edward Elgar, 2001) 92.

(through the development of a right of action in the third party) internalised as a cost to or right of action in the landowner.[30] This is the law of nuisance, which generates (in persons harmed by land use) a cause of action, resulting in a cost to the landowner if the landowner persists with the undesirable conduct. Nuisance is an example of a cause of action that does not vindicate an owner's rights but generates a purely *in personam* claim. After the law of nuisance, intellectual property rights are revisited as a prime example of where an externality is internalised by the recognition of a property right.

B. Nuisance and analogous cases

[5.35] Nuisance is a tort that responds to conditions or activities which unduly interfere with the enjoyment of land.[31] An actionable nuisance is incapable of exact definition,[32] and includes the form of liability formerly known as the rule in *Rylands v Fletcher*.[33]

[5.36] In a legal map, nuisance would lie contiguous to trespass over land, but its function and operation is very different to trespass. Trespass is a direct entry on the owner's land, and is actionable per se (ie without the owner having to show damage).[34] As such, it protects an incident of ownership – the right of an owner to exclude. Trespass is concerned with the protection of property rights against the world and is similar to the tort of conversion (which achieves the same function in the context of chattels).[35]

[5.37] There are various forms of nuisance, which will briefly be considered. They are: (i) public nuisance; (ii) private nuisance; and (iii) the rule in *Rylands v Fletcher*. Public nuisance was formerly a common law crime punishing acts or omissions which endangered the life, health, property, morals or comfort of the public or obstructed the public in the exercise or enjoyment of rights common to all His Majesty's subjects.[36] The crime was abolished by the Police, Crime, Sentencing and Courts Act 2022,[37] but a new statutory offence of more or less

[30] As Posner observes, '[a]n initially neglected aspect of Coase's article was his examination of actual English nuisance cases and his suggestion that the English courts had displayed a better (intuitive) grasp of the economics of the problem than had economists in the Pigovian tradition': Posner (n 29) 92.

[31] A Tettenborn (ed), *Clerk & Lindsell on Torts*, 24th edn (Sweet & Maxwell, 2023) [19-01].

[32] ibid [19-01].

[33] (1866) LR 1 Ex 265, affirmed (1866) LR 3 HL 330. The rule in *Rylands v Fletcher* used to be regarded as a distinct tort, but is now treated as a part of the law of nuisance: *Clerk & Lindsell on Torts* (n 31) [19-01] fn 4.

[34] *Clerk & Lindsell on Torts* (n 31) [19-02].

[35] The tort of conversion (and proprietary torts generally) are considered in Ch 10, Section II.

[36] *Clerk & Lindsell on Torts* (n 31) [19-03].

[37] Section 78(6); *Clerk & Lindsell on Torts* (n 31) [19-03].

similar scope – imposing criminal liability for acts or omissions which cause serious harm to the public or obstruct the public or a section of the public in the exercise or enjoyment of a right that may be exercised or enjoyed by the public at large – was inserted in its place.[38]

[5.38] The abolition of common law criminal public nuisance has not affected the civil liability of any person for the tort of public nuisance and it would appear that (despite the tort being parasitic on the crime, which has been abolished) the tortious right of action remains.[39] Public nuisance is actionable by persons who have been particularly affected by the nuisance.[40] The range of activities that can give rise to a public nuisance at common law is both vast and varied.[41]

[5.39] The essence of private nuisance is that it renders tortious a person's lawful conduct on their own land where that conduct affects the land of somebody else (a neighbour), whether by encroachment onto that land, physical damage to it or undue interference with the neighbour's comfortable and convenient enjoyment of their land.[42] Some of the classic nuisance cases concern nuisance by way of externalities such as pollution. These cases have been the subject of much consideration by those seeking to understand the manner in which civil liability can cause externalities to be internalised. The rule in *Rylands v Fletcher* concerns the escape from land of anything likely to do mischief if it escapes, even if that escape is not reasonably foreseeable.[43]

[5.40] The law of nuisance operates to internalise a wide range of externalities, in circumstances where the precise nature of the externality internalised is left to common law development, and where the range of claimants (third parties affected by the externality) is correspondingly wide. The law of nuisance is helpfully illustrative of how rights of action can be deployed to deal with adverse externalities.

[5.41] The law of nuisance operates purely as a right of action in tort. It operates *in personam*, not *in rem*, and cannot be classified as a proprietary tort.[44] There is no underlying property right which the tort serves to

[38] Section 78(1)(b); *Clerk & Lindsell on Torts* (n 31) [19-03].
[39] Section 78(8)(b); *Clerk & Lindsell on Torts* (n 31) [19-03].
[40] As to this, see *Colour Quest Ltd v Total Downstream UK plc* [2009] EWHC 540 (Comm) at [425] ff.
[41] *Clerk & Lindsell on Torts* (n 31) [19-04].
[42] ibid [19-05].
[43] ibid [19-45]–[19-46].
[44] The nature of proprietary torts is considered in Ch 10, Section II. As with all labels, so too here: there is difficulty in defining what is captured by the label, and difficult distinctions can arise. It is only where the resolving of such difficulties advances the analysis that it is worth actually doing so. Here, there is room for debate, but it is not a very helpful debate to have.

protect – unlike trespass (land), conversion (chattels) or infringement (claims in respect of intellectual property rights). The tort is a *response* to an event that injures the claimant, and although transferable as a right of action, is not property in any recognisable sense.

C. Intellectual property rights

[5.42] There are some cases where the externality cannot be internalised simply by the recognition of a right of action, but by the recognition of a property right that is buttressed by rights of action protecting the owner of that property right. Intellectual property rights are a good example. A form of intangible property is defined in terms of how it is created and transferred, and incidental rights of action are recognised to enable the owner to vindicate their rights when their property rights are trespassed upon or infringed.

[5.43] Intellectual property rights are far more than mere permissions. A permission enables the right holder to do something they otherwise could not do (such as pollute). Permissions may be transferable and so have some of the hallmarks of property. But permissions do not create claims against third parties,[45] and at most remedy externalities which harm society as a whole without generating claims against specific individuals.

[5.44] By contrast, intellectual property rights recognise a property right vesting in certain identifiable persons (owners) and entitle those persons to enforce those rights *in rem* against all the world. Provision is also made, as with most property, for the transfer and licensing of intellectual property. Unlike with land and chattels, where ownership and property rights are an almost inevitable corollary of their existence, the need for intellectual property rights is not immediately self-evident, tends to evolve over time, and follows the recognition of property rights in land and chattels.[46] There is no inevitable *need* for intellectual property rights, but their recognition is important because they serve to address significant externalities that would otherwise arise. Thus, the patent furthers technical development in a society by requiring the publication of the invention, but encourages the research and development work and innovation of the inventor by giving a limited statutory monopoly to the inventor, whereby the inventor can prevent or control third parties from using the invention without their permission. Put crudely, it might be said that the externality that is remedied is to prevent third parties from being enriched by exploiting

[45] Take the example of a general prohibition on pollution, but subject to a permissive licence. A person who pollutes without a licence may be stopped by the regulator or by the criminal law, but not at the suit of a holder of a licence to pollute.

[46] See, further, M Smith et al, *Smith on the Law of Assignment*, 4th edn (Oxford University Press, 2026) Ch 34.

for nothing someone else's work and incidentally disincentivising industrial espionage. But that in fact misstates the genius of the patent bargain, which encourages innovation in two directions: first, the inventor's efforts are protected by the monopoly grant, and many inventors might be deterred from the costs of inventive effort if there was a liberty to 'freeriders'; but second, innovation in wider society is encouraged by the dissemination of the invention which – if it is sufficiently useful – has to be paid for in the shape of the acquisition of a licence. The monetisation of inventions itself encourages research and development in what becomes a virtuous circle.

[5.45] The justification for copyright is twofold. It protects the misuse of the creator's work without the creator's consent, which (as described in Chapter 4) does have implications for privacy. But the requirement of consent to use copyrighted material also enables the creator to *monetise* their work, either by sale or by licence. Particularly in this media age, where entertainment is business, the effort behind screenplays, music, books, etc needs and deserves protection.[47]

[5.46] What was – or absent the recognised right, would be – an externality is *fully internalised*, in the sense that the property becomes a product to be bought or sold, like any other. Rights in property are not inherent: they are *legal constructs*. Of course, the assertion of rights over tangible property (real or moveable) is much more intuitive than the assertion of rights over that which is intangible. That is because of their *physicality*. If a tangible, physical thing has value (which will be because in some way it is scarce), then almost inevitably we will intuit that it can be owned. Some physical things are different – the sea, cadavers, human beings, possibly animals – but the general rule that physicality informs property law holds good. In the case of intangible property there is, *ex hypothesi*, nothing physical to inform the content of the applicable law. The property, because it is intangible, is actually defined by law. There would be no patent without a conscious decision to create, out of *nothing*, a property right. In the case of all intangible property, it is the law that does the 'heavy lifting' and our initial intuition is that such matters are *not* property.

[5.47] Our intuition is soundly based. One of the real problems of intangible property is that unconscious infringement is all too easy. If I see a bicycle in the street, and I know it is not mine, then I will also know that it should not be interfered with.[48] By contrast, an inventor coming to an invention second (after the first inventor has patented the invention) can infringe the prior

[47] There are again controversial aspects: should *machine code* be copyright? But this in no way detracts from the basic importance of the property right.

[48] Of course, there are always exceptions: (i) the bicycle may have been abandoned by its owner, and be 'looking' for a new owner (probably to dispose of it); (ii) the bicycle may have been chained to my railing, in which case I will have a limited power of removal.

right, even unconsciously. That is why any major organisation commencing a research project will (before doing much else) run an extensive patent- and technology-search, just to see if the research project is patentable and so capable of monetisation. These are, or can be, enormous and front-loaded costs. They are transaction costs that arise out of intangibility: they are, at one and the same time, indefensible and necessary.

VI. The 'Reification' of Private Information

A. The distinction between creating positive benefits and the elimination of disbenefits

[5.48] The effect of creating property 'out of nothing' – which is a fair description of how intellectual property works – gives the owner the ability to *exclude* and gives the owner the ability to *exploit*. There is, additionally, the ability to transfer, on which there will be less focus in this section. These are all direct benefits to A, the owner.

[5.49] Whether private information should be property is a normative question.[49] The benefits of creating property out of nothing can be assessed in two ways: (i) the positive benefit that is conferred on A, the putative owner of the right; and (ii) the avoidance of wider societal disbenefits (externalities).

[5.50] So far (in Chapters 1–4) the focus has primarily been on the former, the direct benefit to A, which benefit is briefly recapped below. Reverting to the distinction drawn in paragraph [5.5] between the micro-legal aspect and the macro-economic aspect, the direct benefit to A is essentially a question of law. The focus of this section is to consider the latter, economic, question, that of wider societal benefit. Specifically, the question is whether the internalisation of the externality that Zuboff described as 'surveillance capitalism' and Fairfield as 'digital serfdom' is a worthy policy objective.

B. Positive benefits to A: A recap

[5.51] A's ability to *exclude* enables A (within certain limits) to control how their private information is used. This is a bulwark against invasions of privacy. The ability to *exploit* is similarly important. Thus, intellectual property rights like patents and copyright protect forms of property *other than* private

[49] ie we are not considering what the law is, but what it should be. Put another way, the thesis of this book is that private information *is* property. The point here being made is that this is, in policy terms, defensible.

information. Article 8 of the European Convention on Human Rights (ECHR) might overlap with the protection of private information as property but really only as regards A's remedies against C when C is a public authority. As against non-public authorities, the ECHR does not, of itself, assist, although it does inform the Action, which is A's primary source of protection. The GDPR is concerned with data processing standards, and not the protection of privacy, although there may be some overlap. In short, these regimes do not, particularly, duplicate the regime for the protection of private information considered in this book. The law of property has something to add in terms of preventing invasions of A's privacy.

[5.52] More to the point, anyone who perceives A's private information ought to be controlled in how that information is monetised or used. Increasingly, private information is the staple of *making money*, which C does at the expense of A. The Action enables the protection of A's interests in giving A the choice as to how their private information is used, and taking it away from C. Like the owner of any property, it is A who should be able to determine whether their private information is used and, if so, the manner in which it is used. Put another way, where A's private information is a valuable asset, it is A who should primarily be involved in the exploitation of that asset. The best way of achieving this – as with intellectual property rights – is to ensure that private information is property.[50] This leads directly to the wider benefits of this reification, which will now be considered.

C. Elimination of disbenefits: Externalities and private information

i. The thesis stated

[5.53] The thesis that will be advanced in the following paragraphs is this: that where a factor of production (here, private information) is priced too low, disbenefits (typically in the shape of externalities) arise. The point is that not only is there no such thing as a free lunch, but where (contrary to expectation) a free lunch appears to be offered, it is pernicious, not beneficial, even to the person receiving the free lunch.

[50] See also J Fairfield, *Owned: Property, Privacy and the New Digital Serfdom* (Cambridge University Press, 2017) 3–4: 'The act of owning works considerable social magic. Private property performs an important role in balancing the parts that citizen, corporation, and state play in relation to one another in modern society. Well-defined property rights spur investment. By controlling resources, owners may control their own destinies (or at least attempt to do so). Furthermore, owners can order their surroundings to their liking by modifying their property … the control over surroundings that basic ownership supplies is linked to the democratic value of self-determination … Property also works economic magic …'. That economic magic is considered and in part explained in H De Soto, *The Mystery of Capital* (Black Swan, 2001): property can act as security to finance business ventures, and a stable system of property – properly distributed – enables economic activity.

[5.54] Although they (erroneously) use it as an example against the capitalist system and the market economy generally, Monbiot and Hutchison articulate very clearly the *inefficiencies* and *disbenefits* that arise where something is obtained for nothing:[51]

> While capitalism's origins are disputed, we believe there is a case for tracing them to the island of Madeira, 320 miles off the west coast of north Africa. Madeira was first colonised by the Portuguese in the 1420s. It was a rare example of a genuinely uninhabited island. The Portuguese colonists treated it as terra nullius: a 'blank slate'. They soon began clearing it of the resource after which it was named: madeira is Portuguese for wood.
>
> At first, forests on the island were felled to meet the need for timber – which had been all but exhausted in Portugal and was in high demand for shipbuilding – and to clear land for raising cattle and pigs. In other words, the original colonists simply extended the economy with which they were familiar. But after a few decades, they discovered a more lucrative use of Madeira's land and trees: producing sugar.
>
> Until that point, economies had remained, at least in part, embedded in religious, ethical and societal structures. Land, labour and money tended to possess social meanings that extended beyond the value that could be extracted from them. In medieval Europe, for instance, feudal economies – while highly oppressive – were strongly connected to both the Church and a codified social system of mutual obligation between large landowners and their serfs or vassals.
>
> On Madeira, as the geographer Jason Moore has shown, a form of economic organisation developed that was in some respects different from anything that had gone before. On this newly discovered island, the three crucial components of the economy – land, labour and money – were detached from any wider cultural context, and turned into commodities: products whose meaning could be reduced to numbers in a ledger.
>
> Onto the blank slate of Madeira's land, the colonists imported labour in the form of slaves, first from the Canary Islands 300 miles to the south and then from Africa. To finance their endeavours, colonists imported money from Genoa and Flanders. Each of these components – land, labour and money – had been stripped of their social meanings before. But arguably not all in the same place, at the same time.
>
> By the 1470s, this tiny island became the world's biggest source of sugar. The fully commoditised system that the Portuguese created was astonishingly productive. Using slave labour, freed from all social constraints, the colonists were able to produce sugar more efficiently than anyone had done before. But something else was new – the amazing speed at which productivity peaked and then collapsed.
>
> Sugar production on the island peaked in 1506, just a few decades after it began. Then it fell precipitously, by 80 per cent within twenty years – a remarkable rate of collapse. Why? Because Madeira ran out of madeira. Stoking the boilers needed to refine and process a kilogram of sugar required 60 kilograms of wood. The enslaved

[51] G Monbiot and P Hutchison, *The Invisible Doctrine: The Secret History of Neoliberalism* (Allen Lane, 2024) 8–10.

labourers had to travel further and further afield to find this wood, extracting it from ever steeper and more remote parts of the island. In other words, more labour was needed to produce the same amount of sugar. In economic terms, the productivity of labour collapsed, tumbling fourfold in twenty years. In tandem, the forest clearance drove several endemic Madeiran animal species to extinction. The island-wide disturbance of forest eco-systems was sufficiently serious that the first of several major extinctions of endemic molluscs occurred in the early sixteenth century, the result of 'rapid and large scale change in the habitat, from woodland to grassland'.

[5.55] A number of lessons can be learned from this narrative of a depressing tale, albeit not the lessons that the authors seek to press upon the reader. There is a sense, throughout this passage, that economic systems are detached from the societies that produce the entrepreneurs who exploit the economic opportunities of the world. But economic systems cannot be detached from the societies and legal systems out of which they arise. Put another way, Madeira was only *res nullius* because the Portuguese legal system so classified it. Quite different rules could have been applied to the colonists. The creation of a limited (and extremely harmful) 'free-for-all' was a matter of choice, not inevitability.[52]

[5.56] The 'free-for-all' was limited. Madeira did not contain all the factors of production necessary to make sugar. Labour had to be imported and (as we will come to) slave labour was itself hugely damaging because it was not reflective of the true cost of that labour.[53] Other factors of production, and the funding for it, would have had a proper economic cost.[54]

[5.57] The (limited) 'free for all' was a *choice*, *not* an inevitability. The nation state involved in the affairs of the island – Portugal – *chose* to treat the island as

[52] Non-action of other state players will also have played a role. Madeira was obviously within Portugal's 'sphere of influence' at that time.

[53] Slavery cannot be defended on moral grounds. Obviously. But that is not the point being made here. Following the valuable analysis in E Williams, *Capitalism & Slavery* (Andre Deutsch, 1964), the point is that slavery is indefensible on economic (as well as moral) grounds. The moral grounds are obvious, the economic grounds rather less so. See also D North and R Thomas, *The Rise of the Western World* (Cambridge University Press, 1973) 20, where the same point (that slavery is uneconomic) is made differently: '… Some might ask why in feudal times the lords did not simply make slaves of the peasants, owning them outright. For one reason, it was not difficult for an oppressed peasant to flee to a neighbouring castle where he might hope for a better bargain, since labor was scarce and lords were in competition for its use. Second, it would have been costly to direct and supervise slaves in the many types of tasks involved in making the self-sufficient manor a viable economic system. In short, slavery was not the most efficient system when (1) the costs of enforcement were high, and (2) the costs of supervision were high relative to the alternative of serfdom.' As stated, this is a different point to that made by Williams and in this chapter. The point that will be made (and it is Williams' point) is that even if the costs of slavery are less than alternative costs of providing labour, not rewarding labour is in the wider economic sense bad business.

[54] Money – presumably *debt* – is not simply imported at no cost: there will have been a charge for the monies lent by Flanders and Genoa.

res nullius;[55] and therefore chose to create a market that prioritised the immediate short-term over the longer-term. There was no reason why a proper price could not have attached to the trees, so as to encourage more efficient long-term use of a scarce resource.[56] The cost of the end-product might have been greater:[57] but producers would have been incentivised to seek *genuine* efficiencies (eg burning less wood to produce the sugar) rather than the false economy of simply asset-stripping what should have been treated for what it was, a valuable and scarce resource.

[5.58] Underpricing a factor of production also results in the inefficient use of other factors of production. Take airport check-in processes or supermarket tills: both of these processes have been automated not necessarily because they result in a better consumer outcome but because capital (tools) is cheaper than labour (workers).[58] This may be an optimum outcome but it does beg the question of what outcome would pertain if workers were taxed less, and capital taxed more. The odious practice of slavery makes the point very well in the

[55] It might be said that the *res nullius* finding was one of international law, but that is both meaningless and wrong. The fact is that *Portugal* exercised dominion over the island, to the exclusion of others. Where there was a dispute about territorial control, that manifested itself politically and militarily and was not resolved by international law. Williams says this about the partition of the New World by Spain and Portugal (Williams (n 53) 3–4): 'When in 1492 Columbus, representing the Spanish monarchy, discovered the New World, he set in train the long and bitter international rivalry over colonial possessions for which, after four and a half centuries, no solution has yet been found. Portugal, which had initiated the movement of international expansion, claimed the new territories on the ground that they fell within the scope of a papal bull of 1455 authorising her to reduce to servitude all infidel peoples. The two powers, to avoid controversy, sought arbitration and, as Catholics, turned to the Pope – a natural and logical step when the universal claims of the Papacy were still unchallenged by individuals and governments. After carefully sifting the rival claims, the Pope issued in 1493 a series of papal bulls which established a line of demarcation between the colonial possessions of the two states: the East went to Portugal and the West to Spain. The partition, however, failed to satisfy Portuguese aspirations and in the subsequent year the contending parties reached a more satisfactory compromise in the Treaty of Tordesillas, which rectified the papal judgment to permit Portuguese ownership of Brazil. Neither the papal arbitration nor the formal treaty was intended to be binding on other powers, and both were in fact repudiated. Cabot's voyage to North America in 1497 was England's immediate reply to the partition. Francis I of France voiced his celebrated protest: "The sun shines for me as for others. I should very much like to see the clause in Adam's will that excludes me from a share of the world" …'. The presumption of these leaders is – through modern eyes – breathtaking. What is clear is that these nations were dividing the world between them, with disagreement and rancour and war. Whoever won had the right to determine how these territories would be governed. In the case of Madeira, this was Portugal.

[56] The same point underlies misguided attempts to permit collusion in competitive markets so as to promote environmental values. Absent proper market design, collusion will result in inefficient use of resource.

[57] It is debatable whether the price to the ultimate consumer would have been any different. The effect would likely have been to reduce the (exorbitant) profits of the producers.

[58] In both airports and supermarkets, there is now a high-degree of depersonalisation in the checking in of luggage and in the scanning of products being purchased. The number of staff employed is much less, and their role changed from serving the customers to intermediating between annoyed customers and non-functioning technology. It is likely that the reason this course has been taken is not to improve the consumer experience, but to save costs.

context of British colonial possessions up to the American War of Independence in 1776. The point is made beautifully by Williams:[59]

> According to Adam Smith, the prosperity of a new colony depends upon one simple economic fact – 'plenty of good land'. The British colonial possessions up to 1776, however, can broadly be divided into two types. The first is the self-sufficient and diversified economy of small farmers, 'mere earth-scratchers' as Gibbon Wakefield derisively called them, living on a soil which, as Canada was described in 1840, was 'no lottery, with a few exorbitant prizes and a large number of blanks, but a secure and certain investment'. The second type is the colony which has facilities for the production of staple articles on a large scale for an export market. In the first category fell the Northern colonies of the American mainland; in the second, the mainland tobacco colonies and the sugar islands of the Caribbean. In the colonies of the latter type, as Merivale pointed out, land and capital were both useless unless labour could be commanded. Labour, that is, must be constant and must work, or be made to work, in co-operation. In such colonies the rugged individualism of the Massachusetts farmer, practising his intensive agriculture and wringing by the sweat of his brow niggardly returns from a grudging soil, must yield to the disciplined gang of the big capitalist practising extensive agriculture and producing on a large scale. Without this compulsion, the labourer would otherwise exercise his natural inclination to work his own land and toil on his own account. The story is frequently told of the great English capitalist, Mr Peel, who took £50,000 and three hundred labourers with him to the Swan River colony in Australia. His plan was that his labourers would work for him, as in the old country. Arrived in Australia, however, where the land was plentiful – too plentiful – the laborers preferred to work for themselves as small proprietors, rather than under the capitalist for wages. Australia was not England, and the capitalist was left without a servant to make his bed or fetch him water.

[5.59] The point is that labour – in contrast to the other factors of production (with the possible exception of entrepreneurship) – involves more than the provision of a specific product at a specific price. Labour has *agency*, and that needs to be respected, because labour is a misleading reference to the human being as worker (in contradistinction to the human being as consumer). Thus, labour (because it comprises human beings) will value freedom of action and choice in a way that is alien to other factors of production. Labour is deserving of rights and of respect that other factors of production do not deserve.

[5.60] Moreover, where factors of production are wrongly priced, the market gets distorted. Either a venture fails (Mr Peel's venture to Australia, where he paid agents, who *became* free to act differently, too little to retain them in the new circumstances that pertained); or it succeeds too well, as in Madeira and in the slave-owning colonies, where the efficient use of resource is discouraged.

[59] Williams (n 53) 4–5.

ii. Zuboff's 'behavioural surplus'

[5.61] This is the point made by Zuboff, namely that surveillance capitalism arises because the producers of data services are acquiring their factor of production – data – too cheaply. Zuboff refers to this as 'behavioural surplus', and it worth understanding what she means by this.

[5.62] Zuboff begins by describing what she terms the 'behavioural value reinvestment cycle', where users using Google's search engine provide, through their use, data that enables Google to improve that service.[60] As Zuboff describes it,[61] '[i]n this cycle only behavioural data needed for service improvements are rendered. These are reinvested in the user experience.' It is unnecessary to describe the clever ways in which Google makes search outcomes better by monitoring the information that users input, but there is an obvious defensibility in Google using the data in this way.[62] Zuboff describes the situation in the following terms:[63]

> … at this early stage of Google's development, whatever Search users inadvertently gave up that was of value to the company they also used up in the form of improved services. In this reinvestment cycle, serving users with amazing Search results 'consumed' all the value that users created when they provided extra behavioural data. The fact that users needed Search about as much as Search needed users created a balance of power between Google and its populations. People were treated as ends in themselves, the subjects of a nonmarket, self-contained cycle that was perfectly aligned with Google's stated mission 'to organize the world's information, making it universally accessible and useful …'

[5.63] According to Zuboff, things went wrong when Google discovered 'behavioural surplus'.[64] According to Zuboff, '[s]urveillance capitalism begins with the discovery of behavioural surplus. More behavioural data are rendered than required for service improvements. This surplus feeds machine intelligence – the new means of production – that fabricates predictions of user behaviour. These products are sold to business customers …'.[65]

[5.64] What Google is selling, using this 'surplus' data, is what is still called 'advertising', but which is in fact selling connections between users of Google's products and those who pay Google for 'screen space' on Google's web pages. This is all proprietary and highly confidential, and this description will no doubt

[60] See S Zuboff, *The Age of Surveillance Capitalism: The Fight for a Human Future at the New Frontier of Power* (Profile Books, 2019) 70 (Fig 1: The Behavioural Value Reinvestment Cycle).
[61] ibid 70.
[62] Whether it is in fact and in law defensible is for later.
[63] Zuboff (n 60) 70.
[64] See ibid 97 (Figure 2: The Discovery of Behavioural Surplus).
[65] ibid 97.

be off the mark in the details because it is being written only by reference to publicly available materials. The following is a rough outline of what appears to be the case.

[5.65] Google has relations with third parties, who want to buy space for their advertisement. Price will usually involve an element of 'pay per click'. For every click on the advertisement, the advertiser gets an interested person moved to their web location. And Google gets a tiny sum of money. In every case, a mini-auction – conducted in tiny slivers of time – takes place. The auction does not simply look at the price Google is promised per click but by reference to Google's assessment of how many clicks there are going to be. Back to Zuboff to explain her take on this:[66]

> Rival search startup Overture had developed an online auction system for web page placement that allowed it to scale online advertising targets to keywords. Google would produce a transformational enhancement to that model, one that was destined to alter the course of information capitalism. As a Bloomberg journalist explained in 2006, 'Google maximises the revenue it gets from that precious real estate by giving its best position to the advertiser who is likely to pay Google the most in total, based on the price per click multiplied by Google's estimate of the likelihood that someone will actually click on the ad.' That pivotal multiplier was the result of Google's advanced computational capabilities trained on its most significant and secret discovery: behavioural surplus …

[5.66] What Google is doing is monetising a combination of users' data – what we do online, monitored and harvested ('rendered') – and Google's human predictive technology.[67] A user doing 'this' (whatever 'this' may be) is more likely than others to also do 'that' (where 'that' is choosing to click on one ad in preference to another ad). In this way, the interests of Google and the advertiser are aligned: both want the maximal number of clicks. What is being delivered is our attention, using our data, and this encourages our purchase of the product being advertised.

[5.67] We like this: most people prefer targeted, rather than non-targeted, advertisements. But we should, at least, be aware of how this outcome is achieved, and of how our data (in combination with Google's know-how) is

[66] ibid 76–77.

[67] Zuboff refers to this as a product, 'prediction products', where the deliverable is a forecast of what people will 'feel, think and do: now, soon and later': ibid 96. As Zuboff explains, Google is concerned to protect its intellectual property, but this is not the same as protecting our privacy. Zuboff notes at 96, 'These methodologies are among Google's most closely guarded secrets. The nature of its products explains why Google repeatedly claims that it does not sell personal data. What? Never! Google executives like to claim their privacy purity because they do not sell their raw material. Instead, the company sells the predictions that only it can fabricate from its world-historic private hoard of behavioural surplus.'

being monetised. Our increasingly great on-line activity is being monitored. Both the privacy implications and the monetary returns to Google (and other big-data companies) are vast.[68]

[5.68] Fairfield makes the same point as Zuboff, but in a different way. His point is that in permitting the law of contract to prevail over the law of property, we enable those who provide services by way of licence to dictate the agenda far more than they should be able to.[69] Fairfield proposes a radical curtailing of the power embedded in the software copyright licence:[70]

> Jailbreaking ownership will be challenging, but not impossible. We can do it by accomplishing four tasks. First, we must restore ownership rights to individual property owners and update property rights for the digital age. Second, we must constrain the reach of contracts and make it clear that intellectual property licences have limits. Third, we must make some limited adjustments to laws governing owner modification of smart property, and to the means by which consumer disputes are handled by the judicial system. And fourth, we must advance and develop technology that makes decentralised property systems not just possible but practical. No single element will work alone, but together they can snap the chains restricting modern forms of ownership.

[5.69] Fairfield's proposals are much more wide-ranging and ambitious than the limited thesis of this book, which is that private information is property. For that reason, treating private information as property achieves only some of Fairfield's objectives, namely a protection of privacy and an economic empowerment accorded to the owner of private information. Nevertheless, it is a start down Fairfield's battle against our digital serfdom, and not an insignificant one. If private information is property, which must be *acquired* by users other than A either by way of transfer or by way of licence, then proper economic value attaches to that information.

[5.70] Zuboff's 'behavioural surplus' is the way in which undertakings like Google make money out of the 'free' services that they provide to us users. It is not wholly persuasive that the original entrepreneurs behind Google were proposing to incur significant costs in providing a search engine free at the point of use without in some way having those costs reimbursed and making a profit. Larry Page and Sergei Brin may very well be altruistic and keen to further the common good of humankind, but they also need to live and to have the means of repaying the obligations incurred in setting up a venture like Google. In other words, the need to make a return will have been integral to the thinking at

[68] ibid 87–88.

[69] See the quotation at para [1.66].

[70] Fairfield (n 43) Ch 8 ('Jailbreaking Ownership'). The quotation is a summary of his proposals at 187–88.

Google, and rightly so. This is the foundation of an entrepreneurial society. So how are 'free' services like search engines, digital maps, email and social media monetised? It is necessary at this point to introduce the 'two-sided market'.

[5.71] Two-sided markets – not a good label, but unfortunately one that has stuck – are typically[71] different product markets operating off a single 'platform' run by a single undertaking. It is best to start with an example. The newspaper that sells content to readers and advertising space to advertisers is a nice, low-tech, example. The newspaper is the platform, which deploys two products, content and advertisement. The undertaking that owns the newspaper is the seller of *both* products. The buyers are: (i) on the one side, readers; and (ii) on the other side, sellers of other products who want to advertise in order to sell those products. The sellers will only pay for advertising if there is a sufficiently large, interested, group of readers. The larger this group of potential buyers of product, the more interest there will be in the advertising product. Essentially, what the newspaper is selling is reader attention.

[5.72] How best to maximise reader attention? Obviously, content is important (different content will attract different reader types). But so too is price. Many newspapers – the sort, in pre-iPad days, that commuters would pick up at the station to read on the train home – were 'free' to readers, because that widened the readership base, and made the advertisement product more valuable.

[5.73] The markets only make sense when viewed together.[72] To the reader, the free newspaper looks like an unalloyed benefit – even altruistic. That is, until the reader realises that in the context of the advertising market, they (the reader) are the product. This is obvious to anyone thinking about it, but the privacy implications are minimal or nil. The reader is simply giving of their attention, and they can choose to throw the newspaper away or follow up on

[71] In *BGL (Holdings) Ltd v The Competition and Markets Authority* [2022] CAT 36, [90], it was noted that the definition of two-sided markets was elusive: 'Although the term "two-sided market" is a term of economic art, it carries with it a high degree of uncertainty of concept, making it a difficult subject for analysis and – unsurprisingly – a difficult subject for the purpose of market definition. The paper that really set the two-sided ball rolling was by Jean-Charles Rochet and Jean Tirole entitled "Two-sided markets: an overview". They defined this type of market in the following "you know it when you see it" way: "... Two-sided (or more generally multi-sided) markets are *roughtly* defined as markets in which one or several platforms enable interactions between end-users, and try to get the two (or multiple) sides 'on board' by appropriately charging each side. That is, platforms court each side while attempting to make, or at least not lose, money overall ..."'.

[72] Sometimes the markets operating off the platform need to be seen and considered as separate entities and sometimes they need to be considered together. The appropriate approach depends on the question at issue. Whatever the approach, the existence of a 'network effect' between the various markets operating off a single platform cannot ever be disregarded. See further *BGL (Holdings) Ltd v The Competition and Markets Authority*, [2022] CAT 36, [115]–[119].

an advertisement.[73] In other words, in accepting the free product, the reader is not allowing their private information to be obtained – they are merely giving of their attention.

[5.74] The Google model is exactly like this, only more invasive. In using the free services offered – the search engine, the map/navigation service, the information about local services like restaurants – we give up our data, which Google monetises through its 'prediction products', using what Zuboff terms 'behavioural surplus'.

[5.75] As with Fairfield, the thesis being advanced in this book is rather more modest than Zuboff's passionate critique of surveillance capitalism. The thesis here is that the data that Google uses – whether to provide outstanding free product to us or whether to provide outstanding advertising services in which we are the product –is something that Google cannot use without A's consent if it consists of A's private information. And that consent may be withheld by A.

iii. The consumer surplus 'squeeze'

[5.76] The consumer surplus, the producer surplus and the way in which one 'squeezes' the other was considered at paragraphs [5.11]–[5.15]. The use of our private information by data behemoths is no more than a case of consumer surplus 'squeeze', albeit rendered more complex by the two-sided market through which social media services[74] and advertising services[75] are sold.

[5.77] The consumer – A, the owner of private information – is induced to give up their private information in return for a service that they desire and which is offered to them 'free'. Of course, 'free' means no price being paid in monetary terms. But there is a price, which is the facilitation (by the very use of the social media service) of the extraction of A's private information.

[5.78] Viewed on its own, the market for social media services between A_1, A_2, A_3 … A_n (on the one side, all 'buyers') and C, the counterparty providing those social media services (and so a 'seller'), looks very odd. C is providing a valuable and costly to produce product without any monetary return.

[73] Advertisement is largely disregarded by economists. The notable exception is L Moor, *Communication and Economic Life* (Polity Press, 2022) Ch 3. Given the amount of money spent on advertising, it is surprising that the matter does not receive greater attention. Advertising is plainly the lubricant by which buyers are informed of products and put in touch (directly or indirectly) with sellers. Although we may very well claim not to be influenced by advertising, that claim is gainsaid by the vast sums spent on advertising by hard-nosed sellers.

[74] A compendious term intended to refer to all the benefits we get – search engines, navigation, social interaction, etc.

[75] A compendious term intended to refer to the advertising products sold to third parties so that they may better sell their products, whatever those products might be.

The market for social media services only makes sense when the other side of the two-sided market is considered – the market for the sale of advertising services by C to sellers of products looking for buyers of those products, who are or include A_1, A_2, A_3 … A_n.

[5.79] C, quite rightly, gets paid a lot of money for its advertising services. Rightly so, because these are sophisticated and useful products. The costs of producing these services (both the social media services and the advertising services) are unknown, but they are likely to be high. It is known that entities in the position of C are *now* making very large profits, having endured years of development and its associated costs.

[5.80] But the question of the existence of a producer surplus cannot be excluded, and a producer surplus may exist. If so, then that means that the consumer surplus of A_1, A_2, A_3 … A_n is being 'squeezed'. The 'squeeze' is not easy to spot, because the producer surplus exists (if it exists) in the advertising market, whereas the impairment of the consumer surplus exists (if it exists) in the social media market. The way in which the squeeze manifests itself is that the 'price' that A_1, A_2, A_3 … A_n receive in that market (the social media market) is too low, meaning that C's costs (in both markets) are also too low.

[5.81] How, it might be asked, can the A_1, A_2, A_3 … A_n consumer surplus be too low, when A_1, A_2, A_3 … A_n are paying *nothing* for the services they receive? Answer: A_1, A_2, A_3 … A_n should be paid a price for the private information they give up, and if that private information is given up and used without their consent, then that constitutes a misuse of A_1, A_2, A_3 … A_n's private information and an infringement of their property rights by C.

[5.82] The thesis being put forward is: that A is not being paid sufficiently or at all for the use of their private information; that this constitutes a misuse of A's property; and that this misuse is actionable by A against C by way of the Action.[76]

iv. The problem of consent obtained

[5.83] The answer that C (say, Google or Meta) would give to A is that in using the social media services of C, A is consenting to the use by C of A's private information – assuming that the information is indeed private. A is thereby – if we are accepting the thesis that private information is property – *licensing* to C the ability to use their (A's) data. Such consent or the terms of the licence are drawn in very wide terms.

[76] A lot of questions are being begged here. Is the information 'private'? Is C's use, even without A's consent, a 'misuse'? These are all questions we will come to, but the context in which they are going to be considered matters greatly.

[5.84] At this stage, the argument of C (as the user of A's private information) that A has consented to the use is simply being noted. The point is that (i) even if the information is private, (ii) and even if it constitutes property vesting in A, (iii) A has no Action because C is not misusing A's property, because C has A's consent. So the Action will fail. It will be necessary to consider this argument in the context of a full understanding of what is *private* information, and what constitutes *misuse* of private information. Both of these are discussions that are to come. For the present, a limited number of points are made.

[5.85] Consent is, in many cases, illusory. Zuboff makes the point with force when discussing 'pernicious' terms of service agreements:[77]

> ... Legal experts call these 'contracts of adhesion' because they impose take-it-or-leave-it conditions on users that stick to them whether they like it or not. Online 'contracts' such as terms-of-service or terms of use agreements are also referred to as 'click-wrap' because, as a great deal of research shows, most people get wrapped in these oppressive contract terms by simply clicking on the box that says 'I agree' without ever reading the agreement. In many cases, simply browsing a website obligates you to its terms-of-service agreement even if you don't know it. Scholars point out that these digital documents are excessively long and complex in part to discourage users from actually reading the terms, safe in the knowledge that most courts have upheld the legitimacy of click-wrap agreements despite the obvious lack of meaningful consent.

[5.86] That consent – widely extracted – is abused, at least on occasion:

Example[78]

Why did Google's Gmail, launched in 2004, scan private correspondence to generate advertising? As soon as the first Gmail user saw the first ad targeted to the content of her private correspondence, public reaction was swift. Many were repelled and outraged; others were confused. As Google chronicler Steven Levy puts it, 'By serving ads related to content, Google seemed almost to be revelling in the fact that users' privacy was at the mercy of the policies and trustworthiness of the company that owned the servers. And since those ads made profits, Google was making it clear that it would exploit the situation.

Example[79]

Meta's Beacon was an information distribution system linked to Facebook. One user described the effects of this in the following terms:

'I purchased a diamond engagement ring set from overstock in preparation for a New Year's surprise for my girlfriend ... Within hours I received a shocking call from one of my best friends of surprise and 'congratulations' for getting engaged (III) Imagine my horror when I learned that overstock had published the

[77] Zuboff (n 60) 48–49.
[78] ibid 47.
[79] Recounted in ibid 48.

details of my purchase (including a link to the item and its price) on my public Facebook newsfeed, as well as notifications to all of my friends. ALL OF MY FRIENDS, including my girlfriend, and all of her friends, etc ... ALL OF THIS WAS WITHOUT MY CONSENT OR KNOWLEDGE.[80] I am totally distressed that my surprise was ruined, and what was meant to be something special and a lifetime memory for my girlfriend and I was destroyed by a totally underhanded and infuriating privacy invasion. I want to wring the neck of the folks at overstock and facebook who thought this was a good idea. It sets a terrible precedent on the net, and I feel that it ruined a part of my life.'

[5.87] Control over 'contracts of adhesion' or 'standard form terms' is difficult.[81] It is possible to police unreasonably wide terms (here: where wide consent to use private information is obtained) by various forms of consumer protection,[82] but all this does is re-package the fundamental question of difficulty, which is 'when is A's private information *misused*?'. The better approach is to ensure that instead of overlaying an unsatisfactorily wide consent with an unsatisfactorily nebulous form of consumer protection, we have a system that ensures that consent is voluntarily given. This is an intractable question, but it will be suggested that recognising private information as property enables it to be satisfactorily answered. This question – fundamentally one of licensing – is addressed in Chapter 11.

[5.88] This chapter is not the appropriate point to discuss private information, licence negotiation and price. The only point that needs to be stressed is that absent genuine consent from A, any price will not be reflective of proper market forces. The providers of innovative products (as Google clearly is) might say that the imposition of genuine consent will make the establishment and development of new products harder. Imagine a start-up having to navigate the rapids of consent from potential users A_n. The difficulties – and the costs (which will be incurred 'up-front' – are obvious. In order to establish the network effects to make a social media and advertising market viable, one has to start small and think big. But, having thought big, and having achieved the thought, the changed market conditions ought to be reflected in the value that the seller of the private information (A) is receiving. We end where we began,[83] with the point that markets are made and need to be designed. Or as Zuboff puts it:[84]

A précis of Piketty's extensive research may be stated simply: capitalism should not be eaten raw. Capitalism, like sausage, is meant to be cooked by a democratic society

[80] It is to be anticipated that some form of consent was extracted in the user agreement whereby Facebook's services were subscribed to.
[81] The problems are well articulated in M Radin, *Boilerplate: the Fine Print, Vanishing Rights, and the Rule of Law* (Oxford University Press, 2013) Ch 1.
[82] See ibid, Part IV.
[83] See para [5.15] and in particular n 12 to that para.
[84] Zuboff (n 60) 43–44.

and its institutions because raw capitalism is anti-social. As Piketty warns, 'A market economy ... if left to itself ... contains powerful forces of divergence, which are potentially threatening to democratic societies and to the values of social justice on which they are based'.

[5.89] The thesis in this volume goes further: raw capitalism, without legal underpinnings, cannot work. It is for society to choose what the underpinnings of markets should be. In this case, it is the thesis of this book that one of those underpinnings is that our private information is our property; and that attaching proper value to it benefits us all.

D. The long-term benefits of 'proper' pricing

[5.90] The point has been made that the undervaluing of factors of production is damaging to the economy as a whole and is as much an evil as excessive pricing, which is more obviously problematic and sub-optimal. The point was made that slavery is not merely wrong, but inefficient. Both Zuboff and Fairfield suggest that we are digital slaves or serfs, and so the analogy with slavery is perhaps less extreme than might be the case in other circumstances. The analogy is not pressed here. The point being made is that the underpricing of factors of production is damaging because it is *inefficient*.

[5.91] Suppose, then, a slave-based economy producing a product (P_1) in competition with a non-slave-based economy producing a similar product (P_2). Demand for P is a not elastic, comprising a demand for 100,000 units per annum whether the price materially goes up or down. Apart from labour, the costs of producing P_1 and P_2 are the same (40*x*, *x* being the common currency of both economies). However, the slave-based economy's labour costs are 10*x* (being simply the cost of feeding and housing the slaves, who have no agency), whereas the non-slave based economy's labour costs are 50*x*, because this economy pays its workers well, and needs to have attractive workplaces for them, because in this economy, the workers might choose to work elsewhere (a choice labour is denied in the slave-based economy). It will be assumed that these labour costs of 50*x* in the non-slave-based economy comprise 25*x* in wages (direct costs) and 25*x* in the costs associated with employing a contented workforce (indirect costs, eg a safe place of work; staff canteen, etc).

[5.92] The capacity for the production of P_2 is such that P_2 can meet all demand (ie produce 100,000 units of P_2), whereas the slave-based economy can maximally produce 50,000 units of P_1. That is because keeping labour in the economy is difficult: most workers in the slave-based economy are keen to move to the non-slave-based economy, and to work there in better conditions for better pay.

[5.93] The slave-based economy will want to sell all 50,000 units of P_1 that it can produce at the highest price it can. That price will be informed by the pricing of the non-slave-based economy, whose costs are higher, at 40*x* plus 50*x* plus a reasonable rate of return of 10*x*.[85] Say a price of 100*x* for each unit of P_2.[86] The slave-based economy's costs are 40*x* plus 10*x*. But the slave-based economy will not sell at 60*x* (a more than reasonable rate of return), but at the *highest price below its competitor* that enables all 50,000 units of P_1 to be sold. Say a price of 90*x*.

[5.94] So, the cost/price schedule of the two economies will look something like this:

	Slave-based economy producing P_1	**Non-slave-based economy producing P_2**
[1] Unit costs apart from labour	40*x*	40*x*
[2] Labour unit costs	10*x*	50*x*
[3] Total cost: [1] + [2]	50*x*	90*x*
[4] Price	90*x*	100*x*
[5] Profit per unit: [4]–[3]	40*x*	10*x*
[6] Total profit (on sales of 50,000)[87]	2,000,000*x*	500,000*x*
[7] Total wages received by workers	None	1,250,000*x*[88]

Considering this example, the problem with models is that the more realistic they get, the less useful they are, because what they teach becomes encumbered by nuance and qualification and doubt. This model is undoubtedly artificial: but none the worse for that. A number of lessons can be learned.

[5.95] The gross domestic product of the slave state is higher (at 2m *x*) than that of the non-slave state (at 1.75m *x*). This underlines the dangers of attaching too much weight to metrics.[89] The slave state is only achieving this level of

[85] The reasonable rate of return, or normal profit, is the return that needs to be generated to keep the entrepreneur in the market, selling product P_2.

[86] The price of P_2 of 100*x* comprises (i) non-labour costs of 40*x*, (ii) labour costs of 50*x* and (iii) a return to the entrepreneur of 10*x*.

[87] Remember: the total demand for P_1 *and* P_2 is 100,000 units.

[88] Ie 25*x* (the unit cost wage paid) multiplied by 50,000 units. The other labour-related cost, that of providing good work conditions, is not treated as a monetary benefit to the workers, and not included in this figure.

[89] Measures like GDP are all very well as guides, but they need to be treated with caution. Thus, in an economy with high inflation, GDP will probably rise (unless inflation is adjusted for, itself no mean feat). Equally, technology may make things cheaper (computers regularly fall in price; and the advent of digital photography certainly made photography cheaper), with the result that GDP falls even though people are better off. In this case, the slave-owning state's GDP is merely a reflection of that state's ability to undercut the non-slave-owning state.

GDP by charging up to but just below the price of the non-slave state. In other words, inter-state competition is constraining what the slave state can charge for its product; that somewhat undermines the value of GDP as a metric of success in this case.

[5.96] What is much more telling is the way in which GDP is distributed in the non-slave state. The costs of the sellers in the non-slave state are higher because labour is a cost. Pricing a factor of production wrongly – non-competitively – is not merely bad morals but bad business. The non-slave state achieves *almost* the GDP of the slave state whilst also: (i) spreading the profits earned more equitably; and (ii) providing a form of competion that constrains the abuses of the slave state if it were a monopoly.

[5.97] The model does not seek to proxy the states' tax revenue, but it seems quite likely that the non-slave owning state will be able to raise more in tax by taxing the income of workers and the profit of sellers than a tax based simply on seller profits (as would be the case in the slave-owning state).

[5.98] Even so, the factor of production that is labour is far better off in the non-slave-based economy. Not only are the workers paid, but they have agency to choose to work elsewhere, with the result that (assuming demand for labour) wages and work conditions will be forced upwards.

[5.99] More importantly for present purposes, and less obviously, the gains out of selling product P are more evenly distributed in the non-slave-based economy than in the slave-based economy, where profit is concentrated in the entrepreneur. It is trite that that will result in different, and objectively better, spending patterns.

[5.100] Extrapolating this to private information and the Action, it is clear that the Action is the mechanism whereby improper extractions of value from the class comprising A_1 to A_n is controlled for. The point is that the Action obliges C to consider what A's private information is actually worth. It enables the class of A to demand proper value from C. The benefit to A is obvious; the overall societal benefit is less evident, but nevertheless clearly present.

6

Private Information

In which: the essence of privacy is considered and existence of a subset of information – private information – is postulated and defined as perceptions of O(C) that are (i) personal to A and (ii) private to A; and exploring what these two elements ('personal' and 'private') mean.

I. The Story So Far …

A. Information and the private information subset

[6.1] *Information* has been defined as the perception of something within the mind of a human being.[1] That definition is both broad and subjective. It is *broad* because perception, even when considered in relation to a single person within the universe of O, embraces many distinct perceptions or many distinct pieces of information. It is *subjective* because perception is, inevitably, unique and specific to the person who perceives. If (as is here contended) perception is something going on in the mind of a human being, then the class of persons comprising O can include only natural persons.[2]

[6.2] *Private information* is a subset of *information*. The qualifier *private* narrows the *information* that is of interest for the purposes of the Action. The definition of the qualifier *private* is of importance because it articulates those circumstances in which A *may be able to* (not *will*) exercise dominion or control over O(C)'s *use* of their perception. The purpose of this chapter is to describe the nature of the qualification *private* or (to put the same point differently) to define the ambit of this subset of information.

B. Perception and the different ends of a telescope

[6.3] The thesis that is advanced in this book is that, like beauty, private information is in the eye of the beholder, O(C). As will be seen, whilst the test

[1] See generally Ch 3.
[2] See para [1.40].

for whether O(C)'s perception is of A's private information is not entirely subjective, the starting point is O(C)'s perception, which is subjective to O(C). If many people – $O(C)_1$ to $O(C)_n$ – perceive the same thing, it is almost certainly going to be the case that those perceptions will differ. Each of $O(C)_1$ to $O(C)_n$ is looking at the world through the eyepiece of their own telescope.[3] Inevitably, the resultant perceptions will be different.

[6.4] This makes private information an *odd* form of property. Unlike with tangible property, where there is an obvious scarcity based upon physicality, there will be as many perceptions of private information as there are perceivers. In an earlier chapter, the notion of replicability or rivalrousness was encountered.[4] As Fairfield puts it, '[r]ivalrousness means that if I have a thing, you don't'.[5] If A owns a table, no-one else can own that particular table. It is their table. They and only they can exercise the prerogatives of ownership (to exclude, to exploit, to transfer) not primarily because of the law but because of the physical dominion physical possession brings. All the law is doing is following through on the inevitable consequences of physicality. It is not possible to 'clone' the table.[6]

[6.5] Most intellectual property is non-rivalrous. It can be copied or duplicated, often perfectly, often at little expense. The law apart, there is no reason why two people cannot discover the same invention and both exploit it. The law apart, there is no reason why one person cannot copy and exploit another person's original work. What the law does is define 'out of thin air' something that the law then says is property, giving the owner of that property rights of action that render that property rivalrous.[7]

[6.6] Because there are as many perceptions as there are perceivers, private information is subjective to the perceiver in the manner described at paragraph [6.4].[8] The perceptions of $O(C)_1$ to $O(C)_n$ insofar as they relate to something

[3] Ie their perception based upon what their senses and their reasoning tell them, whether that perception is assisted by technology or not.

[4] See paras [3.73]–[3.77].

[5] J Fairfield, *Owned: Property, Privacy and the New Digital Serfdom* (Cambridge University Press, 2017) 148.

[6] This is why English law draws a distinction between choses in possession and choses in action, the distinction zoning in on how the rights of an owner are enforced (whether by possessory remedy or 'action', ie litigation). See M Smith et al, *Smith on the Law of Assignment*, 4th edn (Oxford University Press, 2026), Ch 2 and [2.54] in particular.

[7] See para [3.77]. Thus, actions for infringement of a patent or for breach of copyright ensure that that which is non-rivalrous is rendered rivalrous, not because it is intrinsically so, but because the law makes it so.

[8] That makes the classification of private information as non-rivalrous technically questionable, because each perception is unique. This is another instance where form (the label) should not drive the substance. In reality, private information is non-rivalrous, because it can be replicated, even if (because subjective) that replication will be less than perfect. Clearly, private information is not like

A has said will not be identical, but subjective to each of $O(C)_1$ to $O(C)_n$. The notion of a chimeric form of property is unusual, possibly even unique.[9] However, that is no reason why chimeric property cannot be property in English law. The essential requirements were set out at paragraph [1.46] and comprise: (i) identifiability of subject matter; and (ii) identifiability of the owner, particularly the first owner. There is no reason why chimeric property cannot satisfy these requirements: but it is certainly unusual, if not unprecedented.

[6.7] So far, we have been looking through the telescope from the observers' point of view: $O(C)_1$ to $O(C)_n$. But not only do the observers have different perceptions, but so too does the subject of the observation, A. O(C)'s telescope is trained not necessarily on A, but on private information relating to or personal to A. A will have their own perception of self. The object of the law of privacy is to enable A to control (to a degree: the right is not absolute) how they relate to the world,[10] it is obvious that A will have a perception of self, which will not necessarily be the same as that of any of $O(C)_1$ to $O(C)_n$. This, too, needs to be factored into the definition of private information. The perception of the *perceived* is no less important than the perceptions of the *perceptor(s)*.

C. Perception, use and misuse

[6.8] Having explored the relationship between *private information* and *information*, the former being a subset of the latter, and identified a difficult interplay between differing perceptions of the same thing, it is necessary to consider the relationship between *private information perceived* by O(C) and the *misuse of private information* by C.[11]

[6.9] The labels used for the *dramatis personae* featuring in this work are (hopefully) helpful rather than unhelpful.[12] Sometimes (perhaps misleadingly) different labels are attached to the same person. Thus, in the present context, O(C) and C are the *same* natural person. The label attaching to that identical person changes because perception does *not* constitute use, let alone misuse. There is no arguable basis for A to suggest that O(C) is infringing their rights, for the Action looks to the use of (A's) private information. If O(C) does not

our hypothetical table, which cannot be replicated save by making another, identical copy, which will, no matter how carefully made to look the same as the original, still constitute a second table.

[9] The chimera of Greek mythology was a creature comprised of different animal parts – the body of a lion, the head of a goat and the tail of a serpent. That is a fair description of the different perceptions of $O(C)_1$ to $O(C)_n$.

[10] This point has been touched on already, but is considered fully in Section II of this chapter.

[11] The distinction between perception and use is articulated at paras [3.41]–[3.42].

[12] Most of the characters – A, B, O, C and U – are introduced in paras [1.37]–[1.44]. O(C) is introduced in paras [3.46]–[3.48].

cross the line between *perception* and *use*, then no Action is maintainable. The two labels for the same person are intended to make clear the distinction between: (i) all of the people theoretically exposed to an Action (ie O), many of whom will have no perception of A at all; (ii) the persons within the universe O who are more tangibly exposed to an Action because they have some perception of A, but who are nevertheless 'safe' because they are not using their perception (ie O(C)); and (iii) those people who are exposed to an Action because they are using their perception, and where the critical issues are whether the perception is of A's private information and whether the line between *use* and *misuse* has been crossed (ie C). This chapter is littered with references to O(C) and to C, which was considered better than imposing a spurious uniformity, by only using one of these labels.

[6.10] Where C *uses* A's private information, there is a much more than theoretical risk that A has an arguable claim against C, hence the change in label from O(C) to C. That is not to say that every use by C of A's private information represents an instance where A can even arguably suggest that C has infringed A's rights. Some uses of A's private information will unquestionably be legitimate. In such cases, not even an arguable claim will result from C's use of that information. However, because the Action is relatively new, and there is not that much case law exploring the boundary between *use* and *misuse*, it is fair to say that until the law has bedded down, A will find it relatively easy to frame an Action against C. As a body of precedent develops, however, the boundary between use and misuse will become clearer. That is in part the genius of the common law: judicial decisions do not just decide the case in hand, they also provide a steer for future cases. Questions of use and misuse, and the borderline between the two, are for later consideration.[13]

D. The 'gatekeeper' function of 'private' information

[6.11] This chapter considers the 'private' in private information. The limitor 'private' serves as an important 'gatekeeper' to control the scope of the Action. If C's perception is *not* of A's private information, then A's Action against C will end (ie fail) at this point. Questions of use and misuse simply cannot arise because A must, as a necessary condition of success, show that C's perception is of information that is private to A.

[6.12] The elements of the Action are becoming clearer. We are concerned with information (defined in Chapter 3) that is private to A (the element considered in this chapter) where that information is used by C (and not merely

[13] In Ch 7 (misuse by non-state actors) and Ch 8 (misuse by state actors).

perceived by C) and where that use can be characterised as a *misuse* (the element considered in Chapters 7 and 8).

[6.13] The gatekeeper function of private information controls the scope of the Action. Define privacy narrowly, and the circumstances in which A can bring an arguable Action concerning misuse of information narrow accordingly. Put another way, if information fails to satisfy the *private to A* test, then no matter how egregious C's misuse of the information, no Action will lie.

[6.14] This book suggests a wide definition of private information. That is for two reasons:

(1) If privacy is all about enabling A to control how they relate to the world, then a wide definition of private is apt. The notion that privacy or private information are concepts defined by reference to *subject matter* is explored and dismissed in Section II of this chapter. Whilst, clearly, it can never be said that the nature and quality of O(C)'s perception is irrelevant – that would be an indefensible proposition, not advanced here – it is wrong to seek to define private information by reference to subject matter *only* (eg sexual peccadillos or confidential information or misconduct) or by reference to the effect that publication might have on a person in A's position (eg a propensity to embarrass or humiliate or distress). These are *not* irrelevant factors, far from it, but they are not the *essence* of what constitutes private information.
(2) One aspect of control is to *prevent* misuse. But if A's private information is A's property, then – as owner – A has the right not merely to exclude, but to exploit. A can, for instance, license C to do something which would otherwise be a misuse. This is also a form of control, and the economic case for private information to constitute property was made in Chapter 5. That economic case also points in the direction of a wide definition of private information.

[6.15] It is all very well to say that private information should be given a wide meaning. The gatekeeper function of private information requires that the definition, even if it is wide, be clear. The law values – or should value – certainty. Predictability of outcome is an essential aspect of the rule of law.[14] The law must be predictable, so that A and C know where they stand; and so that O(C) will know what lines they can and cannot cross.

[6.16] The definition of private information is considered in Sections III and IV of this chapter. Even before its precise definition can be considered, it is

[14] J Raz, *The Authority of Law: Essays on Law and Morality* (Oxford University Press, 1985) Ch 11.

necessary to locate private information that is protected by the Action amongst other forms of information protection. There are a number of regimes, well-established in English law, where information is already protected *as property*: patents and copyright being the leading examples. Equally, although it may be debated whether the law of defamation involves information at all,[15] defamation is obviously a regime that is at the least congruent with the protection of private information. It also provides a great deal of helpful learning by way of legal analogy to the operation of Action. Section III considers the relationship between the Action and other information rights that A may have.

[6.17] Section IV of this chapter then considers in detail the definition of *private information*, differentiating between the two central characteristics of what is 'private', namely that O(C)'s perception be *personal* to A and that it be *private* to A. Section IV also deals with the problem, already identified in paragraphs [6.4]–[6.7], that private information as defined in this book can comprise a myriad of perceptions of different people $O(C)_1$ to $O(C)_n$, as well as owner A themselves.

E. Bilateral relations A ←→ B are of no interest

[6.18] It will, by now, be abundantly clear that thesis of this book is that A has *in rem* rights over their private information. Private information is property. For this reason, purely bilateral relations as between A and B are of no interest for present purposes. They will become of interest when we come to consider the transfer of private information by A or the licensing of that information by A, for such transactions or dealings can only be achieved by way of contract, which is *par excellence* a bilateral relationship.

[6.19] That being said, the relationship between A and C can or could be described as 'bilateral' because C has a perception of A. Self-evidently, the relations that exist as between A and C are critical to the classification of C's perception as being of private information relating to A, and also to the identification of the borderline between *use* and *misuse*. This relationship between A and C (or O(C)) is not what this book describes as 'bilateral'. A trespasser coveting a landowner's land and entering upon it without consent, might be said to have a bilateral relationship with the landowner. But this is a mischaracterisation. The fact is that the label 'bilateral' *misdescribes* the relationship that exists

[15] The essence of defamation is a false publication damaging to reputation. Falsity is central. However, it has already been noted (at paras [3.21]–[3.23] that it is a fool's errand to seek to define 'information' by reference to qualitative standards. It will therefore be suggested that there is a close relationship between the protection of private information and the protection against reputationally damaging publications, but that these actions are also distinct in nature.

between the owner of property and the rest of the world, namely that if a person belonging to the class of O infringes upon A's rights as owner, then that person (C) is exposed to a claim by the owner. That claim might very well be described as bilateral, but the underlying rights of the owner that generate the claim certainly are not. The bilateral nature of the Action is the reason why many people might, incorrectly, classify the rights that the Action vindicates as *in personam* and not *in rem*.

II. Privacy is Subject Matter Neutral

[6.20] Earlier drafts of this work sought to define private information by reference to subject matter (eg this information is confidential or it relates to intimate matters) or by reference to the reaction (putative or actual) of A on publication (eg this information would/did harm or embarrass A if/when published). Whilst it is right to say that both these factors – subject matter and A's (likely) reaction – are relevant to a consideration of what is private and what is not, these matters are not so much definitive of what is private, but rather aspects of an altogether more fundamental definition. It is suggested that focusing on these factors, instead of seeing them as aspects of something deeper, is distracting and unhelpful.[16]

[6.21] Warren and Brandeis defined the right to privacy much more generally as a right *to be left alone*.[17] Obviously, this can be neither an *unqualified* right nor an *absolute* right, but it is a *general* right not specific to any particular type or kind of information. Just as copyright is engaged no matter what the quality of the copyrighted material, so too it is with private information. Zuboff refers to the right to sanctuary:[18]

> The human need for a space of inviolable refuge has persisted in civilised societies from ancient times but is now under attack as surveillance capital creates a world of 'no exit' with profound implications for the human future at this new frontier of power.

This captures the essence of Warren and Brandeis' notion of privacy very well, as essentially a negative right – to prevent incursions into A's private space. Intuitively, this seems right: property is characterised by the right it confers on an owner to *exclude* – and exclusion is, essentially, negative.

[16] A Monti and R Wacks, *Protecting Personal Information* (Hart Publishing, 2020) 9–10, take a different view. They contend that a neutral definition of privacy is so broad as to be effectively meaningless.

[17] See para [4.4].

[18] S Zuboff, *The Age of Surveillance Capitalism: The Fight for a Human Future at the New Frontier of Power* (Profile Books, 2019) 21.

[6.22] But property has its positive side also, in the ability of an owner to sell or license, and this important aspect of private information should not be lost sight of. It follows that privacy – and so private information and the property rights associated with it – needs to be seen in a broader and more positive context. The various phases of threats to privacy have been described.[19] The differences between those phases reflect the increasing difficulty of a person to shape how they are perceived by the world. As Woods-Marsden notes, 'How a person constructs the relations between an "I" and its world is *the* crucial factor in self-presentation, whether in life or art'.[20] In this relationship, the *person* is central:[21]

> Our (seemingly natural) conception of the self is in actuality a construct with a long and varied social history. According to the anthropologist Mauss, the category of the 'person', the idea of the 'self', developed slowly over many centuries and always in relation to contemporary social history. Different cultures held different notions of the self at different times, the construction of each being connected to the culture's particular form of social organisation.
>
> The notion of a persona, the Latin translation of the Greek prosopon, meaning the mask used in drama, is the character type of role that the mask represented. A key moment in this development for the Western world may have occurred in ancient Rome, when a person's given role – the mask or persona – was made the locus for a theory of general rights and duties as a legal 'person' and a citizen of the State. Thus, the Romans established the notion of the 'person' as a basic fact of law. All freemen of Rome were Roman citizens, and all had a civil persona. Only the slave was excluded from the right to a persona: servus non habet personam, 'he has no personhood, he does not own his body, nor has he ancestors, name, cognomen, or personal belongings'.
>
> To this notion of a 'person' with citizenship and other rights, Christianity later added the concept of an inner conscience and inner life. Even the slave, albeit not in possession of his own body, was given a soul. The foundation, then, of the modern individual is this notion of a 'person', bearing on the one hand a civic identity derived from Roman law and on the other a conscience and soul bestowed on it by Christianity.

[6.23] Given the centrality of personality, the importance of a person's right to control *how* they are perceived becomes evident. A right to privacy (as understood by Article 8 of the European Convention on Human Rights (ECHR)) is critical to preserving the element of *sanctuary* identified by Zuboff. The law of defamation controls the publication of *false* information about A. Copyright, to an extent, enables A to shape how they present themselves, by ensuring that

[19] See paras [1.3]–[1.19].

[20] J Woods-Marsden, *Renaissance Self-Portraiture: The Visual Construction of Identity and the Social Status of the Artist* (Yale University Press, 1998) 13.

[21] ibid 13. It is quite likely that there is a social element to this, and this book adopts (consciously and unconsciously) the standpoint of a modern Western democracy. Monti and Wacks (n 17) 62–63 make this point by reference to Japan's different and yet similar approach to privacy.

their original 'work' cannot be copied without consent. Private information as property both protects the element of sanctuary *and* buttresses the way in which A can positively (or proactively) present their persona to the world by *permitting* certain uses of their private information by a third party. This ability is not without its limits, for there are other values that may oppose an unfettered right to privacy and an unfettered ability to control how private information is used. Freedom of expression, for example, protects the right of O(C) to articulate their perceptions, including the perceptions O(C) have of A.

[6.24] In *R (Wood) v Commissioner of Police of the Metropolis*,[22] Laws LJ put the point as follows:[23]

> [21] The notion of the personal autonomy of every individual marches with the presumption of liberty enjoyed in a free polity: a presumption which consists in the principle that every interference with the freedom of the individual stands in need of objective justification. Applied to the myriad instances recognised in the Article 8 ECHR jurisprudence, this presumption means that, subject to the qualifications I shall shortly describe, an individual's personal autonomy makes him – should make him – master of all those facts about his own identity, such as his name, health, sexuality, ethnicity, his own image, of which the cases speak; and also of the 'zone of interaction' (the *Von Hannover* case, 40 EHRR 1, [50]) between himself and others. He is the presumed owner[24] of these aspects of his own self; his control of them can only be loosened, abrogated, if the State shows an objective justification for doing so.[25]
>
> [22] This cluster of values, summarised as the personal autonomy of every individual and taking concrete form as a presumption against interference with the individual's liberty, is a defining characteristic of a free society. We therefore need to preserve it even in little cases …

[6.25] Privacy as property is thus not solely or simply concerned with the protection of secrets, although that is a purpose it does serve, Privacy as property is concerned with matters far more important and far more wide-ranging: the manner in which we are able to show ourselves to the world.[26] In a world

[22] *R (Wood) v Commissioner of Police of the Metropolis* [2009] EWCA Civ 414.

[23] Although Laws LJ dissented in the result, this statement is of general value. Dyson LJ and Lord Collins (the other judges) did not appear to disagree in their judgments.

[24] It is not suggested that Laws LJ was finding that personal information is property, but the phrase is a telling one, nonetheless.

[25] This was a case under the HRA 1998, s 6 against a state entity, not a private claim against a private individual.

[26] Privacy is thus closely related to how we interact with others and a right to anonymity. S Spaulding, *How We Understand Others* (Routledge, 2020) 7–8 proposes that our interactions with others involve 'mindreading': 'Suppose Lawrence agrees to meet you at your office at 11 am, and by 11:10am he has not come to your office. The standard mindreading story holds that we are inclined to explain Lawrence's behavior by figuring out what his beliefs and desires are. We might consider the possibility that Lawrence desires to meet with you but has a false belief about the meeting time or location. Or perhaps Lawrence desires to meet with you, has a true belief about

where the publication and wide dissemination of information is both easy and (more-or-less) instant, this right is crucial. Privacy is subject matter neutral because it is for A to say, within the limits permitted by law, how they should be perceived by their fellow persons in the world we all inhabit. That right in A has two hallmarks of property: the ability to exclude; and the ability to exploit.[27]

III. Privacy in Context: Other Information Regimes

A. Introduction: Cognate regimes considered

[6.26] It is important that the Action dovetail with other information-protecting torts. This section considers those torts and their relationship with the Action. The interaction between A's remedies needs to be carefully considered. In an ideal world, each remedy (patent, copyright, defamation, the Action, etc) would have its own clearly demarcated 'sphere of influence', with no overlap or duplication. Anyone who has had to consider the sometimes fraught and complex interplay between parallel claims in contract and in tort will appreciate both the difficulty of avoiding duplication, and the complexities that duplication can give rise to.

[6.27] Duplication of remedies is, thus, a problematic area. Take, for example, the interplay between copyright infringement and the Action. The interrelationship between copyright and privacy was considered in Section III of Chapter 4. There is an extremely close relationship between the two, but (because they serve to protect different values) copyright almost certainly does not operate as a constraint on the scope of the Action, although it does inform our understanding. In short, the same act can trigger or be the subject of distinct legal claims (infringement of copyright and the Action). Similarly, Fairfield's example of the picture, which is both a tangible object and an original work, subject to copyright.[28] The owner of the picture may be a different person to the owner of the copyright. This will be the case where someone purchases a picture from

the scheduled meeting time and location, but something urgent has come up and he cannot come to your office. Or perhaps Lawrence has a true belief about the scheduled meeting time and location but does not desire to meet with you. Through a process of theorizing or simulating, or a combination of both, you determine which of these belief/desire combinations is most plausible and attribute them to Lawrence. This explanation allows you to predict Lawrence's future behavior – perhaps he will show up late, send an apologetic email after the urgent situation is resolved, or simply avoid contacting you altogether.' This mindreading is very much what data giants do algorithmically. This underlines the importance of anonymity, and its close relationship with privacy: A Sinnreich and J Gilbert, *The Secret Life of Data* (MIT Press, 2024) 57.

[27] See, further, C Véliz, *The Ethics of Privacy and Surveillance* (Oxford University Press, 2024) Ch 3 and 47–50.

[28] See para [3.75].

an artist. The ownership of the physical object transfers to the purchaser; but copyright in the work does not (unless itself transferred). A thief who steals the picture and then circulates copies of it infringes the owner's right to have the property and the artist's copyright.

[6.28] The example of the long-lens photographer described at paragraph [4.62] is worth repeating. The photograph is an original work, and the copyright will vest in the photographer. The photographer will be able to prevent third parties from duplicating the image. Assuming that the photograph is private information relating to A, in parallel with the photographer's rights, A will have their own rights with regard to the use of the photograph, including as against the photographer themselves. If the photographer misuses the photograph, then (as C) they will be exposed to an Action capable of being brought by A.

[6.29] The same matter may be both copyright *and* private information, owned by different people. That is a complex, but not an undesirable, outcome. It means that a genuine third party (ie someone who is not A and not the photographer) will have to negotiate with two people if they want to use the photograph: this third party will need a licence from the photographer (regarding copyright) and a licence from A (regarding the use of A's private information).

[6.30] The co-existence of different remedies concerning information assists in articulating the boundaries of each. In articulating the boundaries of cognate information regimes, the scope of the Action (and in particular the definition of private information) becomes clearer. Even where there is overlap of remedy, as is the case with copyright, the reasons for that overlap are informative.

The following regimes fall to be considered: (i) patents; (ii) copyright; (iii) defamation; (iv) database rights.

B. Patents

[6.31] The grant of a patent for an invention is the grant to the patentee for a limited period of a monopoly right in respect of that invention. The monopoly confers on the patent-holder the right to exclude others from using the invention and to exploit it themselves (including by way of licence to others). Where A is the inventor, it is A who chooses whether or not to seek the protection of a patent. Where A does so, the information relating to the invention is published, a part of the 'patent bargain' that exists between the inventor/patentee and the state. Where this occurs, A cannot properly advance a claim against C for misuse of private information. The invocation of the patent process renders the information underlying the invention *not private*. A, to be clear, is not without protection: but A's protection lies in an action for infringement of the patent, and A does not have an alternative remedy for the misuse of private information.

[6.32] Matters are different where A chooses *not* to patent their invention, whatever the reason may be. Where A adopts this course, the information underlying the invention may very well receive the protection of the Action because it can be private information belonging to A. This, indeed, is what happened in *Seager v Copydex*.[29]

C. Copyright

[6.33] Copyright differs from patent protection in that patent protection must be *sought*, whereas copyright simply *arises* out of the conduct of the first owner of the copyright. In many cases, the same information will be subject to protection both under copyright and the Action. That is because although for a time it appeared that copyright might serve as a protection of privacy, in fact it protects the maker of an original work, who may not be the person whose privacy needs protection. Copyright and privacy serve different objectives, and it is not surprising that the same (or very similar) information can generate two claims – an Action and a claim for copyright infringement.[30]

D. Publication of false information that would be private if true: Defamation

i. The distinction between privacy and defamation

[6.34] Just as there is a clear distinction between A's rights under the law of (say) copyright and A's ownership of private information, so too there is an essential distinction between the use of A's private information by C and the publication by a defendant of false information that relates to A. This is the province of the law of defamation. Warren and Brandeis, when speaking of the limits to the right of privacy, consider the relationship between private information and false statements in the following way:[31]

> The truth of the matter published does not afford a defence. Obviously, this branch of the law should have no concern with the truth [or][32] falsehood of the matters published. It is not for injury to the individual's character that redress or prevention

[29] See Section D of Ch 4.
[30] See Section D of Ch 4.
[31] S Warren and L Brandeis, 'The Right to Privacy' (1890) 4 *Harvard Law Review* 193, at 218.
[32] The original article says 'of', but that must be a typographical error.

> is sought, but for injury to the right of privacy. For the former, the law of slander and libel provides perhaps a sufficient safeguard. The latter implies the right not merely to prevent inaccurate portrayal of private life, but to prevent its being depicted at all.

[6.35] The law of defamation is concerned with the protection of a person's reputation.[33] As *Gatley* notes, there is a close relationship between the protection afforded by the law of defamation and the protection afforded by the law of privacy.[34] The essential line of demarcation is that whereas privacy is concerned with the protection against the use of private information that may or may not be *true*, defamation is concerned with injury to reputation through publication of *falsehood*. To insist on too rigid a demarcation between truth and falsity in information cases is a mistake.[35] Certainly, it is no part of the definition of information in this book that the information perceived by O(C) must be a 'true' perception, whatever that might be. That, as has been described, opens the way for state control over what is, and what is not, information.

[6.36] But it must be the case that a *dishonest* perception (ie one that O(C) does not subjectively hold) cannot be O(C)'s perception. If O(C) is, in effect, lying about their perception, the lie is not their perception (it is a false statement): the lie simply masks their truly held perception. This is a limit to the scope of the Action yet to be explored in the cases, but it can easily be seen that this case (the lied about perception) is one best handled by the law of defamation rather than the Action – although, of course, it is perfectly possible for a defendant to defame A without appreciating that what is said is false.

[6.37] The borderline between private information and defamation is thus a difficult one. The critical distinction lies not so much between truth and falsity (although, as will be seen, *truth* is important in defamation, as a defence) as in the difference between *reputation* and *privacy*. Reputation can be *legitimately* damaged, as where a true but reputationally damaging thing is published. That would preclude a successful defamation action, but still leave open a claim for misuse of private information. The Action protects A with regard to the

[33] R Parkes and G Busuttil (eds), *Gatley on Libel and Slander*, 13th edn (Sweet & Maxwell, 2022) [1-002]. This work treats actions in defamation as sounding *in personam*. Damage to reputation is closer to a personal injury claim than a proprietary (*in rem*) claim. But, given the fluidity of the border between *in rem* and *in personam*, the contrary argument can be made: see D Milo, *Defamation and Freedom of Speech* (Oxford University Press, 2008) 27–28; J Townshend, *A Treatise on the Wrongs Called Slander and Libel*, 3rd edn (Baker, Voerhis & Co, 1877) Ch 3.

[34] *Gatley on Libel and Slander* (n 31) [1-004]: 'Disparate explanations of the importance of reputation have been proffered by scholars and others, resting on such values as honour, dignity and property. The matter has resurfaced in a new guise in recent times, as attempts have been made to explain the coverage of reputation – a quintessentially public matter – by the Article 8 ECHR right to respect for privacy'.

[35] See paras [3.21]–[3.22]. See, further, Véliz (n 28) 87–91.

(mis)use of information by C (and that use is not confined to use through publication, but can be far wider) that is private and true.

[6.38] According to *Gatley*:[36]

> ... a statement is defamatory when it harms or tends to harm a person's reputation. However, there is no wholly satisfactory common law definition of the term. Three formulae have been particularly influential: (1) would the imputation tend to 'lower the plaintiff in the estimation of right-thinking members of society generally'? (2) would the imputation tend to cause others to shun or avoid the claimant? and (3) would the words tend to expose the claimant to 'hatred, contempt or ridicule'? Of these, it is the first that is in most common usage.

[6.39] Defamation refers collectively to the torts of libel and slander. The torts of libel and slander are committed when a person publishes words or matter to a third party containing an untrue imputation that harms the reputation of the claimant.[37] If the publication is made in permanent form or is broadcast or is part of a theatrical performance, the publication is libellous, which is a tort that is actionable per se and without proof of special damage.[38] Where the publication assumes a more transient or less widely transmissible form, the publication is slanderous,[39] and damage arising out of the publication must be pleaded and proved.

ii. The relationship between true statements and defamatory ones; and the relationship between misuse of private information and defamation

a. The problem stated

[6.40] The relationship between misuse of private information and defamation is more complex than the relationship between misuse of private information and (i) patents and (ii) copyright, where the boundaries are more easily discernible. This is for a number of reasons, which are now explored.

b. Claims pleaded in the alternative

[6.41] The defamation torts are in essence torts of strict liability, although that has been qualified in certain cases by the Defamation Act 2013.[40] It remains

[36] *Gatley on Libel and Slander* (n 33) [1-007].
[37] ibid [1-005].
[38] ibid [1-005]. Although s 1 of the Defamation Act 2013 requires – as a condition of actionability – that serious harm has been caused or is likely to be caused to a claimant's reputation by the publication complained of.
[39] *Gatley on Libel and Slander* (n 33) [1-005].
[40] ibid [1-008].

the case, however, that the claimant does not need to plead falsity: rather the truth of the publication is a defence to the claim brought by A against the defaming defendant. Truth (or 'justification') is a complete defence to the torts, even if the publication is made with a deliberate or malicious desire to injure the claimant.[41] Justification will only be established at the end of the trial,[42] and it would be an extremely confident claimant who would rely only on defamation where an Action could also arguably lie. There will be many cases where the claims can be pleaded in the alternative, and where it will be appropriate for the A to run both an Action *and* a defamation claim.

[6.42] More fundamentally, and as considered in paragraphs [6.35]–[6.37], the definition of information as perception does not differentiate between the true and the false perception. Information can be *false* and *still be information*. If that is right, then the defamation torts and the Action ought *both* to be available to A where:

(1) In the case of defamation, there has been publication of something defamatory of A.
(2) In the case of the Action, there has been a misuse of information (ie the *same* publication) personal to and private to A.

[6.43] We have encountered duplication causes of action before. As in the case of the long lens photographer, it is perfectly possible for the *same* act – C photographing A – to give rise to (i) a copyright vesting in C (so that C can prevent all the world, including A, from copying their original work, the photograph) and (ii) an Action, vesting in A, where by A can prevent all the world, including C, from misusing their image, as recorded in the photograph). But in the case of defamation actions and the Action, the same act (publication/misuse) gives rise to a claim by the same claimant A against the same defendant.

[6.44] This duplication of remedy is inevitable, and perhaps not even undesirable. Take, for example, 'deepfake' images, where A's face is placed on a naked body to create a damaging pornographic image of A. The use of A's image in this context ought to be seen as a misuse and (provided the image is not obviously so false as to be impossible to believe of A) also defamatory.[43]

[41] ibid [1-009].
[42] As has been repeatedly noted, trials resolve disputed allegations.
[43] The law in this area is difficult and (as is too often the case) further law is proposed instead of considering whether the existing law can adapt. On 7 January 2025, the Ministry of Justice indicated that the government was to make 'creating sexually explicit "deepfake" images a criminal offence'. I Kalpokas and J Kalpokiene, *Deepfakes: A Realistic Assessment of Potentials, Risks and Policy*

The problem of parallel claims is, therefore, unavoidable for more than just the reason that A may want to cover their bases by pleading arguable alternative claims. Privacy and defamation may very well be run in tandem, with success achievable not in the alternative, but cumulatively.

[6.45] The problems with parallel *non-alternative* claims are, however, multiple and in an ideal world should be avoided. As recognised by Warren and Brandeis, the law of defamation *itself* strikes an uneasy and difficult balance between freedom of expression and the protection of reputation. As *Gatley* puts it:[44]

> The task facing legislators and judges in the design and implementation of defamation law involves reaching an appropriate accommodation between individual rights and societal interests in both freedom of expression and reputation. Under s 3(1) of the Human Rights Act 1998, legislation must be read and given effect in a way which is compatible with Convention rights, so far as it is possible to do so. As public authorities, the courts must themselves not 'act in a way which is incompatible with a Convention right'. The result is that defamation law, whether based on statute or the common law, must be interpreted and applied in a rights compliant manner. Clearly, this involves assigning a value to the right to freedom of expression embodied in Article 10(1) ECHR. Equally, it involves acknowledging the interest in the protection of reputation which is mentioned in Article 10(2) ECHR and in certain circumstances is guaranteed by Article 8(1) ECHR …

[6.46] The Action creates an additional threat to freedom of expression. Given that the Action is *itself* based on the ECHR, these various rights – freedom of expression, protection of reputation, protection of privacy – will have to be read consistently *inter se*, but that is easier said than done.

[6.47] Matters are different where a defaming defendant seeks to invoke the defence of 'fair comment' or opinion; or publication in the public interest. These will be considered next.

Regulation (Springer, 2022) 2, 666–67 describe the challenges: 'Even in cases where the harm caused by deepfakes appears to be obvious, victims can often find it extremely difficult to put the perpetrators to account. That is the case, notably, with non-consensual deepfake pornography. Even when laws against "revenge porn" exist, they are unlikely to help because the actual body of the victim (except for the face) is not shown …; moreover, in the US, the pornographic nature of such synthetic recordings would not suffice unless the content is deemed obscene, particularly if laws against non-consensual pornography do not exist at a State level … However, even the latter could be ineffective, again, primarily because the only body part of the victim in the video is their face ….' The problem is the intersection between freedom of expression, 'truth' or 'falsity' of the images and consent. One can see how the law of defamation might struggle; and the challenges in drafting an effective criminal prohibition are not to be underestimated. But if (as here) privacy is defined as the right to control how one is presented to the world, then the deepfake is a paradigm instance where private information is being misused.

[44] *Gatley on Libel and Slander* (n 33) [1-011].

iii. The defence of fair comment

[6.48] The common law defence of 'fair comment' was abolished by section 3(8) of the Defamation Act 2013 and a new, statutory, defence of 'honest opinion' introduced in section 3 of that Act. The defence of honest opinion obtains where the defendant makes a statement of opinion,[45] indicating the basis for that opinion (whether in specific or general terms),[46] in circumstances where an honest person could have held that opinion on the basis of:

(1) Any fact which existed at the time the statement complained of was published.[47]
(2) Anything asserted to be a fact in a privileged statement published before the statement complained of.[48] A privileged statement is one that is a publication on a matter of public interest,[49] a peer-reviewed statement in a scientific or academic journal,[50] a report of court proceedings protected by absolute privilege[51] or a report protected by qualified privilege.[52]

[6.49] The question for present purposes is not so much the limits to a claimant's ability successfully to press a claim in defamation (for that, reference should be made to *Gatley*, which explores the limits of the defence in detail) but rather how an expression of opinion interrelates with the law of privacy.

[6.50] An opinion can be based on private information and to that extent the expression of the opinion by C represents a *use* of private information that might amount to a misuse actionable in the hands of A. That would be so even if the private information were *true* and the opinion expressed defensible in defamation terms.

[6.51] If *untrue*, then the issue ought primarily to be one of defamation and not privacy. That is the point of the section 3 defence: it enables a defamatory opinion to be defended if it is based on existing facts (this is like the defence of justification, and those facts obviously must be *true*) or on 'privileged statements'. Privileged statements are unlikely to be *private information*. But the section 3(4)(a) 'facts' can be, and it must follow that even if C can defend a statement of opinion under section 3, the statement may be based on private

[45] Defamation Act 2013, s 3(2). The defendant must in fact hold that opinion. Although the burden of proof is on the claimant, if the defendant does *not* hold the opinion, the defence fails: Defamation Act 2013, s 3(5) and also s 3(6).
[46] ibid s 3(3).
[47] ibid s 3(4)(a).
[48] ibid s 3(4)(b).
[49] ibid s 4.
[50] ibid s 6.
[51] ibid s 14.
[52] ibid s 15.

information that C has no right to use in this way. In this way, an action in defamation might fail, but a claim asserting the Action succeed.

iv. The public interest

[6.52] The background of this defence to an action in defamation is set out in *Gatley*, and that background is adopted here. The defence is as important in privacy cases as it is in defamation cases, and there is every reason to expect that the defence will operate similarly in both. That question is considered later. Here, the public interest defence in a defamation action (only) is considered:[53]

> Legal recognition of the potential value of widespread communication on matters of public interest was slow to develop in the common law. Instances of protection were isolated and infrequent. There was no general privilege for 'fair information on a matter of public interest', although the courts were occasionally willing to admit in theory of 'extreme cases where the urgency of communicating a warning [was] so great, or the source of the information so reliable, that publication of suspicion or speculation [was] justified.

[6.53] In *Reynolds v Times Newspapers Ltd*,[54] the House of Lords recognised a defence based on whether a defamatory publication was defensible in the public interest. That defence was then recast in statutory form in section 4 of the Defamation Act 2013,[55] which provides that it is a defence to an action for defamation for the defendant to show that:[56]

(1) The statement complained of was, or formed part of, a statement in a matter of public interest.[57]
(2) The defendant reasonably believed that publishing the statement complained of was in the public interest.[58]

In considering this defence, the court must consider all the circumstances of the case.[59]

v. Some unresolved difficulties

[6.54] The foregoing discussion shows that the interaction between defamation and privacy is complex. Although the law of defamation is extremely useful in assisting in demarcating the limits of the law of privacy, fine distinctions are

[53] *Gatley on Libel and Slander* (n 33) [16-001].
[54] [2001] 2 AC 127.
[55] The *Reynolds* defence was abolished by the Defamation Act 2013, s 4(6).
[56] Defamation Act 2013, s 4(1).
[57] ibid s 4(1)(a).
[58] ibid s 4(1)(b).
[59] ibid s 4(2). Certain aspects are specifically mentioned in sub-ss 4(3)–(5).

going to have to be drawn in future cases, and overlap is likely to be the rule and not the exception.

Example[60]

In late January 2024, sexually explicit AI-generated deepfake images of American musician Taylor Swift were proliferated on social media platforms 4chan and X (formerly Twitter). The images led Microsoft to enhance Microsoft Designer's text-to-image mode to prevent future abuse. Several artificial images of Swift of a sexual or violent nature were quickly spread, with one post reported to have been seen over 47 million times before its eventual removal. These images prompted responses from anti-sexual assault advocacy groups, US politicians, Swifties, Microsoft CEO Satya Nadella, among others, and it has been suggested that Swift's influence could result in new legislation regarding the creation of deepfake pornography.

[6.55] Clearly, this is a black-and-white case which should never have happened, and no doubt multiple infringements of many laws (including criminal) occurred. It is not the purpose of this book to resolve these issues, but this Example demonstrates the importance of the law in this area, and the need for the law to be clear. A few issues arise:

(1) There may have been copyright in the images of Ms Swift that were used, and this may have resulted in a civil remedy for copyright infringement. But that remedy may not have been Ms Swift's (the copyright may not have vested in her).
(2) It is suggested that the deepfake images in this case would have been defamatory. That must be the case if there could be any question of a person actually believing the images to be genuine, for obvious reasons.
(3) But suppose that no-one was taken in by the deepfakes, in the sense that no-one actually believed that Ms Swift was implicated or involved or (in any real sense) represented in these publications. In such a case – and this might occur with an inexpertly done fake (a 'shallow-fake' or an 'obvious-fake') – it would appear that a defamation action might not necessarily succeed. Yet it would be odd and unsatisfactory if there were no remedy. Of course, specially created remedies – both criminal and civil – can be crafted, but given the rapid developments of technology, it would be better if the common law (or common law accretions to and developments of statute) could evolve to keep up. It is suggested that an Action would lie here, and that the Action fills an important gap unfilled by copyright and defamation law.
(4) Other complexities arise. Suppose an obvious fake is created to make a political or satirical point?

[60] See 'Taylor Swift deepfake pornography controversy', https://en.wikipedia.org/wiki/Taylor_Swift_deepfake_pornography_controversy, accessed 21 August 2025.

Example[61]

A teacher who held a placard depicting Rishi Sunak and Suella Braverman as coconuts has been found not guilty of a racially aggravated public order offence. Marieha Hussain, 37, had denied the prosecution's allegation that the placard she held at a pro-Palestine protest was 'racially abusive'. She carried a picture showing the faces of the then Prime Minister and Home Secretary superimposed on coconuts under a palm tree in November 2023. Hussain's defence said the placard was satirical and humorous. She denied the charge and was acquitted at Westminster magistrates' court. Outside court after the hearing, the teacher, of High Wycombe, Buckinghamshire, said: 'The damage done to my reputation and image can never be undone'.

In this case, there could be no question of 'deep-fakery'; but the defamation and privacy questions – although perhaps as easily resolvable as the criminal offence in this case – are clearly not easy ones generally.

E. Database rights

i. Forms of intellectual property protection

[6.56] The database right is an innovation of the European Union[62] that has been retained post-Brexit as part of the law of the United Kingdom. It is this right that is considered in these paragraphs, but it should be noted that the Copyright, Designs and Patents Act 1988 protects databases as a separate class of literary work. Thus:

- A database is defined as a collection of independent works, data or other materials where these are arranged in a systematic or methodical way and are individually accessible by electronic or other means.[63]
- A literary work consisting of a database is original if, and only if, by reason of the selection or arrangement of the contents of the database, the database constitutes the author's own intellectual creation.[64]

[6.57] The self-standing database right arises where there has been substantial investment in obtaining, verifying or presenting the contents of the database.[65]

[61] N Badshah, 'Pro-Palestinian protester cleared of racial offence over "coconut' placard" (*The Guardian*, 3 September 2024), www.theguardian.com/uk-news/2024/sep/13/pro-palestine-protester-cleared-racial-offence-coconut-placard-sunak-braverman, accessed 21 August 2025.

[62] Directive 96/9/EC on the legal protection of databases, implemented in the UK by the Copyright and Rights in Databases (Amendment) Regulations 1997, SI 1997/3032.

[63] Copyright, Designs and Patents Act 1988, s 3A(1).

[64] ibid s 3A(2).

[65] G Harbottle et al, *Copinger and Skone James on Copyright*, Vol 2, 19th edn (Sweet and Maxwell, 2025) Ch 21.

In Case C-444/02, *Fixtures Marketing v OPAP*, the Court of Justice of the European Union said that classification as a database depends on the existence of a collection of 'independent' materials,[66] that is to say, materials which are separable from one another without their informative, literary, artistic, musical or other value being affected.[67]

[6.58] Classification of a collection as a database then requires that the independent materials making up that collection be systematically or methodically arranged and individually accessible in one way or another. While it is not necessary for the systematic or methodical arrangement to be physically apparent, the collection should be contained in a fixed base of some sort, and include technical means such as electronic, electromagnetic or electro-optical processes or other means, such as an index, a table of contents, or a particular plan or method of classification, to allow the retrieval of any independent material contained within it.[68]

[6.59] A database is principally defined 'in terms of its function'.[69] The Directive is intended 'to encourage the development of systems performing a function of "storage" and "processing" of information'.[70]

[6.60] Both the copyright and the database right protect the owner of the database (the original work, in copyright terms) from other people copying their database. These rights are transmissible, but apart from this, the property rights conferred are largely negative, ie the owner can prevent infringing uses. What is not made clear is the extent to which the database right (or copyright in a database) authorises use of collections of individual – discrete – pieces of data.

ii. Implications

[6.61] The point of a database is to enable the parsing of collections of information for particular – and, generally speaking, commercial – purposes. Obviously, this implies *use* and the potential for *misuse*. The question that arises is the extent to which individual pieces of private information, collected into a database, can be used through the medium of the database itself. A number of points emerge.

[66] There is no lower limit as to the size of the collection: see Case C-444/02, *Fixtures Marketing* EU:C:2004:697 at [24]. Nor does it matter from where the materials derive: ibid at [25]–[26].

[67] ibid at [29]. The subject matter of the materials does not particularly matter. Certainly, it can extend to sporting activity materials: ibid at [23].

[68] ibid at [30].

[69] ibid at [27].

[70] ibid at [28].

[6.62] It is perfectly possible for a database to be used to store homogeneous but individual private information, where the database is simply used to access an individual's (private) information *as such*. Suppose, for example, a database of intimate details of many individuals is used to market products to those individuals. All that the database is doing is *facilitating* access to private information that the database owner had in any event, even without the database. The use of a database cannot, in such cases, render what would be a *misuse* of information lawful. As in the case of the long lens photographer, there will simply be two property rights in play – A's Action against C, and C's database right or copyright.

[6.63] Suppose, however, an aggregation of private data gives rise to conclusions that can be drawn because of an analysis (by the database owner) of that aggregate. Suppose it is possible to say that persons with certain attributes are more likely to buy a certain product, be moved by a particular issue (for voting purposes) or commit a certain offence such that, based upon that *aggregate* analysis, *individually targeted steps* can be taken as against specific persons: for example, certain advertisements shown, certain prices imposed, or certain articles or polling questions sent, or certain communications intercepted. The reason this case is a difficult one is because the targeting arises out of a *combining* of discrete pieces of private information, where the combining is itself original and done through the efforts of the database owner. It is harder to say that such use of information constitutes *misuse* because it is harder to see the connection between A (the claimant in the Action) and the aggregated information put together by C. Of course, if this sort of aggregation precludes the Action, then Zuboff's 'surveillance capitalism' is uncontrolled. As was noted above, 'private' information performs a 'gatekeeper' role. It was suggested that, for that reason, a 'wide' (albeit clearly defined) definition of 'private' information ought to be adopted. This is a clear case where a narrow definition of 'private' will close out many cases where an Action ought to lie.

[6.64] There will be many variants on the aggregation theme, for data can be manipulated in so many ways, to achieve many different goals. The purpose of considering database rights is to identify one area where technological development is rendering data which, in the past, would have been useless, useful and valuable. Database rights are, it must be suggested, very much yesterday's news, in a world where 'artificial intelligence' is rapidly developing: these machines use our data in ways unknown even to their operators, producing outcomes that startle (in both good and bad ways). The point being made here is that we should not, without very careful consideration, conclude that the fact that information personal to A_1 is aggregated with information personal to $A_2 \ldots A_n$ precludes A_1 from contending that the information remains private to A_1, such that, if misused, A_1 has an action against aggregator C.

iii. Analysis

[6.65] Just as the long lens photographer rightly ought to own the copyright in their photograph of A, so too ought the compiler of a database to be able to protect their work, whether through copyright or database right. These rights are good against all the world (*erga omnes*), including A. A cannot copy or use C's photograph or database without consent: A's privacy rights do not confer rights over C's property: they confer rights over A's property, which is C's perception and misuse of private information that relates to A.

[6.66] It will be suggested that aggregation of private information of many people in no way prevents an Action being asserted against the aggregator of such data. It is true that the Action will face greater difficulty, not least because it will be very hard to understand precisely how A's private information is actually being used in a complex system. But that is very much a matter of practice and procedure – the procedural rules of Court need to be sufficiently robust to ensure that A (or the class $A_1 \ldots A_n$) can effectively vindicate their rights. This is a matter for Chapter 10. Nor is the topic presently under consideration one of *misuse*. Many uses of aggregated data will be just that: *uses*, without crossing the line to *misuse*. This is a matter for Chapters 7 and 8.

[6.67] It is also clear that aggregation involves a very complex manifestation of O(C) or C. A's private information is likely to be gathered from many sources, most of which will not even amount to legal persons: they will simply be machines, like our mobile devices, that report on us. The aggregation of such data is also likely to be achieved simply through machines, again without human input. It may even be the case that the use to which such data is put is done without human involvement. In short, it is perfectly possible for the gathering, processing and use of A's private information to be achieved by machines that are not legal persons and not natural persons. The legal challenges to ensuring that $A_1 \ldots A_n$ can effectively vindicate their rights are formidable. Again, this is not a topic for now, but is the subject matter of Chapter 9.

[6.68] The proposition being considered now is thus very narrow. We speak of information flows, and information can certainly be analogised to a river, which starts small (at source), grows at is accretes more data, and while it flows and grows aggregates, analyses and uses. In truth, these functions are very hard to separate, and there is (absent the distinctions between perception/use/misuse) no particular need to do so. The proposition is whether a droplet of data or information, personal and private to A, ceases to be so merely because it is aggregated with millions of other droplets of data that form the data flow. There is no reason why this should be the case, and every reason why it should be, given that aggregated data can effectively be disaggregated and used to produce very specific information that is specific to A. The Example at paragraph [1.17] shows how easily the droplets of data forming a flow of information can be disaggregated and analysed so as to provide very specific information about A. It would be perverse if aggregation should preclude any prospect of bringing an Action. When considering aggregated data flows, the concern should be less with the identification of particular 'drops' of A's private information and much more with the question of what outputs the aggregated data can be used to generate that are personal and private to A. In other words, one looks not to the drops that form the river, but to the river itself. At the risk of stretching the analogy too far, if the river injures A, even though the individual droplet would not, A's claim remains. This is no more than a colourful articulation of the differences between perception and use. The uses that A's data is put to will be the most cogent answer to the question of whether the Action should lie. For this reason, the privacy 'gateway' needs to be wide, even if the misuse hurdle is a stringent one.

IV. Private Information Defined

A. Some preliminary questions

i. Perception is too subjective to establish

[6.69] When analysing the information (that is to say the perception) in the mind of O(C), the critical question is what attributes must O(C)'s perception have in order to render it A's private information?

[6.70] The starting point, one might think, ought to be C's perception. Immediately the difficulties begin. It is not possible for us to know what is going on in C's mind and, moreover, it is important that C's freedom of thought is protected from inquiry.[71] It would appear, therefore, that the very subjectivity of information as perception prevents its further legal exploration. The prospect of successfully bringing an Action would appear to be dead before it is even begun.

[6.71] This, however, is too pessimistic a view. Law is, if nothing else, a practical and pragmatic discipline. The key element in the Action – what will drive A to bring proceedings – will *not* be O(C)'s perception, but C's misuse (or threatened misuse) of A's private information. It is with the *overt* – the use or misuse – that we must begin, because the Action is all about the control of use, not the control of perception.

[6.72] So we start with the *manifestation* of C's perception, and immediately it is possible to shift our consideration from the subjective to the

[71] See paras [3.37]–[3.40].

objective: what C has done (or threatened to do, in the case of a *quia timet* action). In some cases, the use or misuse will be overt and easy for A to recognise: if C, the photographer with a long lens, covertly photographs A, A will not (necessarily) know this at the time of image capture. But A will certainly know when their photographs are spread across the front page of a tabloid newspaper or (more likely) across the Internet.

[6.73] The Internet is a good example of the practical difficulties that privacy, defamation and copyright actions (to name but three) throw up. It may be very hard to identify *who* is doing the publishing. The same is true of aggregated data: A may not know *how* (or even *if*) their private information is being used. These are real, practical, difficulties, to which we will return in Chapter 10. For the present, they will be parked, and we will content ourselves with having at least turned C's hidden and unknowable, subjective, perception into something overt in the form of C's use of their perception. Whilst it may be hard to identify what the use is, that is a procedural problem to be remedied through development and deployment of proper court procedures;[72] the starting point is nevertheless use/misuse.

[6.74] By taking 'backbearings' from C's use or misuse, it is possible (by way of backward extrapolation) to ascertain what C's perception must have been. Use of perception – by definition occurring after the perception has been gained by C – will say a great deal about the nature of C's anterior perception.

ii. C's perception need not derive from A

[6.75] Although the perception in C must, in some way, relate to A in order to be A's private information, it does not matter whether that perception derives from A or whether it has been obtained by other means. Thus, information will be no less private to A if it derives from A's diary (which C has read, illicitly or otherwise) or if it is an image captured without A's knowledge or consent. C's perception may emanate from sources other than A. There is no requirement that the perception be communicated by A to C.[73]

B. Two elements of private information

i. The two elements laid out

[6.76] When once O(C)'s perception – to the extent it is relevant to A's claim – has been identified and defined, the question then arises as to how

[72] Such procedures already exist.
[73] See the definition of information in Section III of Ch 3.

that perception in O(C), now identified, is to be characterised. It is, to be sure, *information*, but is it A's *private information*?

[6.77] In order for O(C)'s perception to be A's private information, two requirements have to be met or the perception must have two characteristics:

(1) The perception must be of *private* information.
(2) The private information must be A's.

These are distinct elements, and they are considered separately below.

ii. Back to objective and subjective: Different standpoints for analysing private information

[6.78] Our sense of privacy will diverge. A_1 may be an 'open book', happy for all the world to know everything about them. A_2 may be a closed book, with an obsessive sense of their own privacy. It would be unfair on C to impose on them the privacy equivalent of the 'thin skull' rule that exists in personal injury cases. The 'thin skull' rule, also known as the 'eggshell skull' rule, is a legal principle that holds that a defendant is liable for the full extent of a claimant's injuries, even if those injuries are more severe than would be expected, due to a pre-existing condition or weakness of the claimant. The defendant takes their victim as they find them.[74]

[6.79] Whilst this rule is fair enough in the context of personal injury, it will not do in the case of the Action. C is entitled to be able, by careful navigation of what they do with their perceptions, to avoid an Action by A against them. So it will not do for A's subjective view of what they hold private to govern. O(C) needs to be protected from A's over-developed sense of privacy.

[6.80] At the other extreme, it would be wrong for C's subjective views as to A's rights of privacy to determine the scope of A's privacy rights. If C were a hardened, insensitive and unimaginative person, it would likely be the case that they would have a peculiarly narrow view of A's rights of privacy. It will not do for C's subjective view to inform the scope of the Action.

[6.81] The two elements of private information – (i) private information that is (ii) personal to A – can therefore be considered from and answered by reference to different standpoints, ranged along a spectrum. Five different

[74] The same holds in aspects of the criminal law. If X punches Y, X may be lucky, and Y will not be seriously injured. But if Y is vulnerable or simply falls badly, and dies, then a punch that would otherwise have led to an assault charge leads to manslaughter.

standpoints can usefully be identified to resolve the two characteristics of 'private' that we have identified:[75]

(1) *A's subjective standpoint*. According to this approach, the two questions are determined by reference to A's subjective (honestly held) views, without any objective control. If A honestly believes the information to be private and honestly believes that that private information is their information, then (on this basis) that is sufficient for the requirements to be satisfied. It will readily be appreciated that this is no tenable basis for any law of private information, and it does not represent the law. Because they must adjudicate by reference to objective criteria, courts are (certainly in the civil law) instinctively against the purely subjective.[76]
(2) *An objective assessment based upon a reasonable person in the position of A*. This approach is subjective to the extent that it is based on facts and matters in the knowledge of A, but those facts and matters are assessed objectively. For example, O(C) may have a perception that does not appear to relate to A at all but – to the objective observer in A's shoes – it is clear, knowing what A knows, that the perception *does* relate to A.
(3) *An objective assessment based upon O(C)'s perception only*. Here the only matter under objective consideration is O(C)'s perception. When determining whether that perception is of A's private information, *only* that perception is considered. Facts within the knowledge of A or O(C) are not considered, even on an objective basis.
(4) *An objective assessment based upon a reasonable person in the position of O(C)*. This is the approach described in (2), only from O(C)'s standpoint, not A's. For example, O(C) may have derived their perception of A from a chain of people who have communicated the same information from $O(C)_1$ to $O(C)_2$ to $O(C)_3$ to (our ultimate person of interest) O(C). Are the circumstances by which O(C) obtained the information relevant to the questions here under consideration, albeit on an objective basis? It is, of course, a tacit assumption of this approach that O(C)'s perception can be separated from the manner in which that perception was obtained. That is an assumption which is entirely workable: whether it is desirable or represents the present law is an altogether different question, to which we will come.
(5) *O(C)'s subjective standpoint*. This is the flipside of (1), where O(C)'s subjective (but honest) beliefs determine the answers to the two requirements

[75] Doubtless, if one is imaginative, a longer list could be compiled. But that would not be helpful.
[76] Indeed, even subjectivities like intention are given an objective patina. Thus, it is often said that a person intends the natural and probable consequences of their actions. This is not an objective test – the court will want to understand the person's *actual* state of mind – but if I tie another person to a chair and cut their throat, then it will take a great deal to persuade a court that I did not subjectively intend very serious harm to that person.

here under consideration. For the reasons given, this is an unacceptable approach that does not represent the law.

[6.82] These five different standpoints may be referred to as (i) 'Subjective A', (ii) 'Objective A', (iii) 'Neutral Objective', (iv) 'Objective O(C)' and (v) 'Subjective O(C)'. For the reasons given, (i) and (v) do not need to be considered further. The others all represent reasonable articulations of what the law might be, and will be considered further. They will be referred to by these labels.

[6.83] There is a final standard, which is simply this: the court determining the Action decides the question objectively on the basis of the evidence before it at the time of trial. This is what courts do when resolving questions of fact. This test is simply referred to as 'Court-Determined Fact', and the determination is made at the time of trial (or more specifically when judgment is handed down based upon the evidence received during the course of the trial).

C. Overview: The test for determining whether information is 'private' information

[6.84] Recognising that the question of *standpoint* is critical to determining what is, and what is not, private information, but leaving consideration of that question to detailed discussion later on, the test for private information is a twofold one, as suggested above. The information (or perception) that O(C) has must be both *personal* to A and *private* to A. It is perfectly possible for information:

- to be private information, but not personal to A. In other words, it is *someone else*'s private information;
- to be personal to A, but *not* private (whether to A or anybody else).

The two requirements are distinct: and both must be satisfied in order for the perception of O(C) to qualify as A's private information.

[6.85] The test for what is private information will be satisfied where the following four cumulative requirements are met:

(1) The information is *personal* to A, when tested for *objectively* by the court on a Court-Determined Fact[77] basis.
(2) A is a person, whether natural or legal. This is a question of law: is A a person capable of asserting legal rights?

[77] Court-Determined Fact is defined at para [6.83].

(3) The information is *private* to A, when objectively considered from A's point of view (ie the Objective A standard considered at paragraphs [6.81]–[6.82]). This is a different and additional requirement from the requirement that the information be personal to A.
(4) A reasonable person, standing in the position of O(C), would know, or on reasonable inquiry ought to know, that the information is both (i) personal to and (ii) private to someone.[78] Both of these questions are determined according to the Objective O(C) standard described at paragraphs [6.81]–[6.82].

[6.86] These elements will now be considered in greater detail. The consideration of these points will be in the following order. First, the nature of A as claimant will be considered, and specifically whether A can be a legal person as well as a natural person (Section IV.D). Second, the question of whether the putative defendants to A's claim, O(C), must (by reason of the nature of how information has been defined) be a natural person only (Section IV.E). Third, the requirement of information being *personal* to A is considered (Section 4.F). Fourth, and finally, the requirement that the information be *private* is considered (Section 4.G).

D. The nature of A

i. The point at issue

[6.87] It is obvious that A must have legal personality. Procedurally that is necessary in order for A to bring a claim. More fundamentally, privacy is an attribute of a person, and it is impossible to see questions of privacy arising in relation to inanimate objects. But, as we have seen,[79] the law differentiates between natural and legal persons. The harder question is whether the Action can *only* be brought by a natural person and *not* by a legal person. The data processing obligations arising out of the General Data Protection Regulation (GDPR) serve to protect only *natural* persons.[80] Leaving on one side the question of whether information relating to non-natural persons can ever be 'personal' information or 'private' information, there is the anterior question of whether this is a cause of action that should be limited so as to exclude non-natural persons as claimants altogether.

[78] As will be considered in greater detail, it is not necessary for C to know exactly who A is, even to an Objective (C) standard. All that is needed is for C is appreciate, to this standard, that the perception is personal to and private to *some person*.
[79] See para [1.38].
[80] See paras [4.182]–[4.183].

[6.88] The question, therefore, is this: Is the right to claim for misuse of private information a cause of action unavailable to non-natural persons and only available to natural persons?

ii. The 'personal to A' test does not answer the question

[6.89] It is quite clear that a perception can relate just as much to an undertaking[81] as it can to a human being. This is not a reason for limiting the cause of action to claimants who are human beings. Whether a non-natural person A can have private information relating to them is a matter that we will come to. Clearly, one would expect that there will be more private information with regard to natural persons than non-natural persons, but it would be a bold assertion to state that a non-natural person cannot own private information *because* they have no capacity for privacy. The exclusion of non-natural persons therefore needs to be approached at a level of policy: ought the cause of action to extend to such persons as claimants?

iii. Extension of the cause of action to non-natural persons

[6.90] Natural persons – human beings – have always been regarded as being capable of possessing legal rights and of being subject to legal obligations.[82] Legal persons are *constructs*, and their possession of rights and their subjection to obligations *in their own right* and *independently of natural persons* was at one time extraordinarily contentious, and is still regarded as one of the most extraordinary economic innovations of the last few centuries.[83] The three great characteristics of the typical[84] legal person are described as follows:[85]

> The most powerful economic power of the day finally brought together the three big ideas behind the modern company: that it could be an 'artificial person', with the same ability to do business as a real person; that it could issue tradable shares to any number of investors; and that those investors could have limited liability (so they could only lose the money they had committed to the firm).

[81] ie a firm or a corporation, U.

[82] There are, obviously, questions of capacity that arise, both due to age and mental capacity. But these are derogations from the general case that need not concern us.

[83] J Micklethwaite and A Wooldridge, *The Company: A Short History of a Revolutionary Idea* (Phoenix, 2005) at 8–9, and in particular: 'The company has been one of the West's great competitive advantages. Of course, the West's success owes much to technological prowess and liberal values. But Lowe and Gladstone ushered in an organisation that has been uniquely effective in rendering human effort productive'.

[84] Being creatures of law, companies can be created with whatever characteristics law-makers care to attribute to them. Company law has, at its core, a political element. See Micklethwaite and Wooldridge (n 82) at 60: '… no matter how much modern businessmen may presume to the contrary, the company was a political creation …'.

[85] ibid 5.

[6.91] It is trite to say that companies have (and ought to have, for the concept to be meaningful) the 'same ability to do business as a real person'. But the extent of the recognition of a legal person's rights goes well beyond this. In *Jameel v Wall Street Journal Europe Sprl*,[86] the issue was whether a trading company, itself conducting no business but with a trading reputation in England and Wales, could (as any natural person could) recover general damages for libel without pleading and proving that the publication complained of had caused them special damage.[87] The conclusion was that there was no difference between different types of person, and the approach of the Court of Appeal in the far earlier decision of *South Hetton Coal Co Ltd v North Eastern News Association Ltd* was endorsed:[88]

> Then, if the case be one of libel – whether of a person, a firm, or a company – the law is that damages are at large. It is not necessary to prove any particular damage; they jury may give such damages as they think fit, having regard to the conduct of the parties respectively, and all the circumstances of the case.

[6.92] Generally speaking, corporations (under English law at least) are regarded as having the capacity to have rights and be subject to obligations that are co-extensive with the putative rights of and obligations of natural persons, including as to human rights.[89] That extends to a claimant's reputation, which seems anomalous. That point was made by the two dissenters in *Jameel*, Lord Hoffmann and Lady Hale.[90] Lord Hoffmann noted:[91]

> In the case of an individual, his reputation is a part of his personality, the 'immortal part' of himself and it is right that he should be entitled to vindicate his reputation and receive compensation for a slur upon it without proof of financial loss. But a commercial company has no soul and its reputation is no more than a commercial asset, something attached to its trading name which brings in customers. I see no reason why the rule which requires proof of damage to commercial assets in other torts, such as malicious falsehood, should not also apply to defamation.

[6.93] The point being made by these dissenters is that some rights of natural persons do not similarly vest in legal persons, or only do so on an attenuated basis. The right to privacy can easily be seen as falling within this class. In *Campbell v MGM Ltd*,[92] Lord Hoffmann (again) stated that '[w]hat human rights law has done is to identify private information as something worth

[86] *Jameel v Wall Street Journal Europe Sprl* [2006] UKHL 44.

[87] This is how the question was put in the leading judgment of Lord Bingham in ibid [11].

[88] *South Hetton Coal Co Ltd v North Eastern News Association Ltd* [1894] 1 QB 133 at 139 (per Lord Esher MR).

[89] See, generally, A Kulick, 'Corporate Human Rights?' (2021) 32 *European Journal of International Law* 537.

[90] *Jameel v Wall Street Journal Europe Sprl* (n 85); Lady Hale's dissent is at [152]–[158].

[91] ibid [91].

[92] *Campbell v MGM Ltd* [2004] UKHL 22 at [50].

protecting as an aspect of human autonomy and dignity'. Similarly, in the earlier Court of Appeal decision in *Douglas v Hello! Ltd*, Sedley LJ said this in support of recognising what became the Action:[93]

> What a concept of privacy does, however, is accord recognition to the fact that the law has to protect not only those people whose trust has been abused but those who simply find themselves subjected to an unwanted intrusion into their personal lives. The law no longer needs to construct an artificial relationship of confidentiality between intruder and victim: it can recognise privacy itself as a legal principle drawn from the fundamental value of personal autonomy.

[6.94] As constructs of law, legal persons do not enjoy dignity or personal autonomy. However, the ability to bring a claim for misuse of private information should not be limited to natural persons, even if (practically speaking) it may well be that information relating to a corporation (for example) cannot or can only in rare cases be *private* information. In other words, the Action should be open to a legal person as claimant, even if in practice such an Action would rarely be available on the facts.

[6.95] The approach in *Jameel* strongly suggests that a claim for misuse of private information is in theory maintainable by a non-natural (legal) person. That is consistent with the ECHR and in particular Article 8 of the ECHR.[94] The point is relevant because the Action explicitly draws on the ECHR. There is, of course, no reason why the Action cannot evolve. But if (as is the case) the ECHR protections extend to non-natural persons, then it would be surprising if the Action denied its origins and limited the beneficiaries of the Action in a manner not consistent with the ECHR. The question whether non-natural persons can or should enjoy human rights under the ECHR is a vexed one, and the answer appears to be that it depends upon the right in question.[95] Article 34 of the ECHR provides that the Court may receive applications from any person, non-governmental organisation or group of individuals claiming to be the victim of a breach of their Convention rights, making it clear that ECHR rights *can* apply to non-legal persons (as Article 1 of Protocol 1 of the ECHR (protection of property) undoubtedly does).

[6.96] The better view is that A can be a non-natural person or – put another way – information can be *personal* to a non-natural person. Thus, for instance, it is quite possible for O(C) to perceive information regarding A's share price

[93] *Douglas v Hello! Ltd* [2001] 1 QB 967 at [126].

[94] Art 8 ECHR protection has been afforded to companies in certain circumstances, including a right to protection of their home and correspondence. The European Court of Human Rights has canvassed the possibility that a legal person may rely on the right to respect its home, which has been held to include business premises.

[95] Kulick (n 95).

or A's corporate headquarters. Such information obviously specifically relates to – in the terminology here used, is *personal* to – that non-natural person A. Whether such information can be *private* is another matter, considered further below.

E. The nature of O(C)

[6.97] The counterintuitive point advanced in this book is that O(C) and, ultimately, C, can *only* be a natural person; and cannot be a legal person.[96] That is because a purely legal person cannot *perceive*: only a human being can do that.

[6.98] This is a counterintuitive conclusion because it suggests that an undertaking can never be a defendant to the Action, when it is precisely corporations who encroach most upon our privacy. For the present, all that will be said is that this conclusion is forced by the definition of information that has been adopted in this book. If information is perception, perception is only possible in a human being.

[6.99] Notwithstanding that O(C) must be a natural person, and that the universe of O can only comprise natural persons, undertakings can and are nevertheless capable of being defendants to A's claim where A seeks to bring an Action. There is a wealth of case law supporting such a conclusion. The way in which the circle is squared is by recognising that non-natural persons can only act through human agents. As will be explored in Chapter 9, which deals with this aspect of liability, the states of mind and actions of such human agents can be attributed to the principal U of such agents, thereby rendering them liable. The position is, therefore, that U, a legal person, can properly be a defendant to an Action brought by A, but that the mechanisms by which U is rendered liable are sufficiently complex to warrant distinct consideration after the more straightforward questions relating to natural persons as defendants have been dealt with.

F. The information must be personal to A

i. The nature of the requirement

[6.100] This is not the same as the information being A's *private* information. The requirement is more akin to *standing* in public law, in that there must be something in O(C)'s perception that singles A out from the body of other

[96] See paras [1.39]–[1.40].

persons who are not A. In order to frame a claim against O(C), A must be able to show that the information contained in O(C)'s perception relates to A. The point here is that there is a vast array of perception in the mind of O(C) that has nothing to do with A: the sunset that O(C) saw last night, and wrote a poem about or filmed, and so on. What A will have to show is that O(C)'s perception relates specifically to A and is not generic. It is not enough for the perception to be of all the world *including* A. That said, it may be that O(C)'s perception relates to a class of person (a family, for example, or the members of a club) and that the appropriate claimants are A_1, A_2, and A_3, the members of that class. Doubtless, like other forms of property, private information can be jointly owned as between A_1, A_2, and A_3.[97] For the moment, the point that is being made is twofold:

(1) O(C)'s perception may be *generic*, in that it relates to no specific person at all. In such a case, there are no constraints on O(C)'s use of the information arising out of the Action (although, of course, other constraints on O(C) may exist).
(2) O(C)'s perception may be *personal* to someone other than A. In such a case, it is simply that the proper claimant is not A, but someone else.

[6.101] For these purposes, the first case is of greater interest than the second. The second is concerned with the identity of the claimant, and not with the meaning of what is private information. The first case – not personal information at all – means that no claim will ever get off the ground. This needs to be considered further.

ii. The borderline between personal and generic

[6.102] The question, therefore, is the borderline between the *personal* and the *generic*. It is perfectly possible for information to be personal to A without A being identified or identifiable.

Example[98]

In September 2010, 18-year-old Tyler Clementi, a freshman at Rutgers University, was filmed secretly through his bedroom while making out with another man. The video, taken by his roommate, was then distributed through Twitter and among students at his school. When Tyler had a second date, a group of students organised a viewing party to watch footage from a hidden camera. Tyler was ridiculed. His sexuality was exploited for fun. After the incident, he jumped to his death into the Hudson River.

[97] This is another matter on which the law in quite undeveloped, even as regards other forms of intangible property.
[98] I Cofone, *The Privacy Fallacy* (Cambridge University Press, 2024) 1.

[6.103] This is an instance where Tyler's privacy was clearly invaded. The point of deploying the Example at this stage is that Tyler's privacy would be no less invaded if none of the 'Peeping Tom' viewers *knew* Tyler's identity; nor even if it were not possible to identify Tyler's name at all. The point is that the perception of the Peeping Toms in this case was personal to the human being in the recorded and transmitted footage and (had Tyler commenced an action under English law) it would have been no defence for the various Cs to say 'I have no idea who that was, and there was no way I could find out'. The fact is that the multiple C perceptions that existed in this case *all* comprised information that was personal to this student (and, to anticipate, private to that student). In short, the student A would have a claim against each and every C, whether C was able to identify A by name or not. As noted at paragraph [6.85], the test for whether information is personal to A is tested for on a Court-Determined Fact basis. Taking all the facts into account, the court must ask and answer after a trial: 'Is this perception personal to A?'.

[6.104] To this extent, there is a divergence between the GDPR (which obliges certain processing standards) and the protection conferred by the Action. The GDPR refers to information relating to an identified or identifiable natural person. Although the Action requires that the information to be *personal* to A, that can be established at any time as a Court-Determined Fact based upon evidence adduced at the trial of the Action.

[6.105] However, there comes a point where the class within which A sits is so large that, although it can be said that O(C)'s perception relates to A, it relates to so many others that it cannot be said to be personal to A, but generic. Thus, suppose O(C)'s perception relates to lawyers (and A is a lawyer), or to ginger-haired persons (of which A is one), or men (and A is or perhaps identifies as a man). In all of these cases, O(C)'s perception is not one that can be said to be personal to A.

[6.106] Defined classes can be extremely large and still be certain in that the class members are identified or identifiable.[99] In other words, the requirement that the perception be personal to A is not described by the borderline between persons unknown and unknowable and persons identified or identifiable. It may very well be that the class of person involved in O(C)'s perception is identified or identifiable (in that it can, with certainty, be said of any given person that they are within or without the class), and yet the perception will still not be personal to A. What is *personal* to A thus does not depend upon identifiability *sensu stricto*. That may be a relevant factor, but it is certainly not

[99] For instance, when defining the beneficiary of a discretionary trust; or when identifying a class for purposes of certifying collective proceedings.

determinative. It might be very difficult to identify the person in the Example at paragraph [6.102] (Tyler) without that person actually coming forward. That should be no bar to the Action.

iii. Analogous cases

[6.107] A better way for testing whether O(C)'s perception is personal to A is to draw upon the test for standing in judicial review. This is characterised by the need to show 'sufficient interest' or to meet the 'victim test' or to be a person particularly aggrieved.[100]

[6.108] As with all analogies, legal or otherwise, one must tread warily, particularly when applying public law in a private law, property, context. A is only a victim if C misuses A's private information. We have yet to consider the question of use/misuse and are at the stage of working out whether – assuming misuse – A can properly suggest that they have a right to bring the Action. In short, we are considering the 'gatekeeper' function of 'private' information. A is only a 'victim' if there has been misuse, and there can only be misuse if private information personal to A has been misused. Referring to a 'victim test' and to A as a victim thus tends to involve a circularity or a question-begging process. One cannot assert that information is personal to A merely because A has a legitimate grievance in regard to the misuse of the information. On the other hand, if misuses are regularly not susceptible to the Action because of the way in which 'private' information is conceived, then it is likely that the concept has been drawn too narrowly.

[6.109] Section 31(3) of the Senior Courts Act 1981 refers to an applicant for judicial review needing to have 'a sufficient interest in the matter to which the application relates'. A can have a 'sufficient interest' in O(C)'s perception *without* being a 'victim'. Before considering further the question of 'sufficient interest', it is necessary to ask why we are drawing upon this public law analogy to answer what ought to be a straightforward question of property. The reason analogy is important is because this is *not* a straightforward question of property. It is a difficult and contentious question of property.

[6.110] The prevailing – and, it is suggested, correct – view is that information generally *cannot* be property. The prevailing – and, it is also suggested, correct – view is that *certain types* of information (patents, copyright, etc) *can* be property. The question is whether private information can be property. It is intellectually straightforward to see tangibles as comprising property

[100] See generally on judicial review, M Fordham, *Judicial Review Handbook*, 7th edn (Hart Publishing, 2020) P38, referring to s 31(3) of the Senior Courts Act 1981.

and correspondingly easy to differentiate between the *thing* and *rights in the thing*. That distinction does not exist in the case of intangible property, where the property only exists by virtue of a legal definition. As a result that (intangible) property and the rights in that property are incapable of differentiation, both being exclusively defined by the law. In the case of tangible property, one can point to or identify the thing without having to have recourse to the law.

[6.111] There is nothing tangible in terms of A's private information and, as has been described,[101] the problem with private information is that it exists in as many minds as there are perceptors, including not just $O(C)_1$ to $O(C)_n$ but also A. This is a chimeric form of property capable of wide application. It is inevitable that reifying or propertising A's private information involves a potentially serious incursion into O(C)'s personal freedom. That is why it is so important that the nature and ambit of A's rights be clear and clearly defined.

[6.112] Absent a tangible starting point to the property inquiry, we must ask ourselves how certain perceptions of O(C) might be identified as being of such relevance to A that it is proper for the law to impose constraints on O(C)'s use of that information at the instance of A, it being recognised that such constraints are in no way absolute, depending (as they do) on the further categorisation of the perception as *private information* and the use as constituting *misuse*.

[6.113] But we should also not overstate the extent to which this reification is heterodox. A person who unknowingly copies someone else's patented invention will be enjoined and liable to damages (even if they had no knowledge of the patented invention); and a person who infringes another's copyright (even if advertently, having seen it and forgotten the seeing) is similarly exposed.

[6.114] In short, all that is being said is that the public law concept of standing is an excellent starting point for the defining of information that is personal to A. With that cautionary introduction, the lessons from public law are as follows.

[6.115] The term 'sufficient interest' is a helpful one, in and of itself. It implies that there is a distinction between A and the rest of the world, that entitles A to bring a claim, and the rest of the world not. This is putting the point in a very binary fashion, and the potential for information to be personal to two or more persons – A_1 and A_2 – is an obvious one. But that is a secondary question. The point of the 'sufficient interest' test is that it *differentiates* A from others.

[101] See para [6.6].

[**6.116**] It is doubtful that what constitutes 'sufficient interest' in the public law context can be anything other than a loose guide to what constitutes property in the private law context. Considering standing in the public law context, Sedley J stated:[102]

> Public law is not at base about rights, even though abuses of power may and often do invade private rights; it is about wrongs – that is to say, misuses of public power; and the courts have always been alive to the fact that a person or organisation with no particular stake in the issue or the outcome may, without in any sense being a mere meddler, wish and be well placed to call the attention of the court to an apparent misuse of public power. If an arguable case of such misuse can be made out on an application for [permission], the court's only concern is to ensure that it is not being done for an ill motive. It is if, on a substantive hearing, the abuse of power is made out that everything relevant to the [claimant]'s standing will be weighed up, whether with regard to the grant or simply to the form of [remedy].

[**6.117**] This statement concerned the grant of permission for judicial review, and it serves as a helpful contrast to what the court's approach would be in a private information case. In such a case, the court would be concerned to ensure that the claim was being brought by the correct party – the party whose rights have arguably been infringed – and no-one else. Private claims are not like judicial review, which:

> is a constitutional guarantee of protection under the rule of law, and the courts secure the scope of judicial review required by the rule of law. It can be contrary to the rule of law and the public interest for there to be a 'lacuna'; where 'public law wrongs' by public authorities would be left unsupervisable by the courts because no person has standing'.[103]

In the private law context, if the proper claimant does not wish to bring a claim, then the court should (in accordance with the rule of law) respect that decision.

[**6.118**] A claimant will have sufficient interest only if the perception of O(C) is specific to A, singling them out from others. This is similar to the rule in defamation cases, where a member of a class can only claim if the defamatory words can be said to point to them:[104]

> The law of defamation does not allow an individual to sue in respect of words directed only at a group. Where the words complained of reflect on a body or class of persons generally, such as lawyers, clergymen, publicans or the like, no particular member of the body or class can maintain an action. 'If', said Willes J in

[102] *R v Somerset County Council, ex p Dixon* [1998] Env LR 111 at 121.
[103] Fordham (n 107) [38.2].
[104] *Gatley on Libel and Slander* (n 33) [8-009].

Eastwood v. Holmes, 'a man wrote that all lawyers were thieves, no particular lawyer could sue him unless there was something to point to the particular individual'. As this statement makes plain there is no special rule about 'class libel', it is simply a question of whether a reasonable reader could conclude that the claimant as an individual was pointed at and the broader the 'class' the less likely this is:

> 'The only relevant rule is that in order to be actionable the defamatory words must be understood to be published of and concerning the plaintiff. It is irrelevant that the words are published of two or more persons if they are proved to be published of him, and it is irrelevant that the two or more persons are called by some generic or class name. There can be no law that a defamatory statement made of a firm, or trustees, or the tenants of a particular building is not actionable, if the words would reasonably be understood as published of each member of the firm or each trustee or each tenant.'

[6.119] Obviously, we are not talking about defamatory statements published by a defendant, but about a perception in the mind of O(C) (which, admittedly, will have had to have been used in order to generate even the potentiality of a claim). Nevertheless, the defamation analogy assists in suggesting that there must be something in the perception that connects the perception to A specifically.

iv. Differentiating between rival claimants

[6.120] The distinction between the generic and the personal does not (as a matter of logic) prevent information from being personal to more than one person. The generic does not begin at two. Where information is or appears to be personal to more than one person, a number of additional questions fall to be considered:

- Is this a case of rival claims (where the relevant information relates to A_1 and not A_2) or a case where both A_1 and A_2 have a claim because the information is personal to both of them? It is very difficult to debate these questions in the abstract, and much will depend on the information in question.
- Assuming the information is personal to A_1 and A_2, the question arises as to how it is held. The law recognises two forms of co-ownership, the joint tenancy and the tenancy in common. (Confusingly, these labels apply to all kinds of property, not merely tenacies.) The distinction between these two forms of co-ownership is somewhat technical, but it seems clear from the nature of private information that the information must be held in a form of joint tenancy, rather than a tenancy in common, such that A_1 and A_2 can only litigate and deal together, rather than individually. The tension between a joint tenancy and a tenancy in common lies in the tension between the inflexibility, but predictability of the former, and the flexibility, but unpredictability of the latter. Although there is no learning on co-ownership in the

context of information, the problems of assertion of title and management are well-understood in the context of land.[105]

v. The problem of aggregation

[6.121] This question was touched upon in the context of databases. If information relating to A is genuinely submerged into the aggregate, such that only the aggregate data remains, then it is right to say that that data cannot be personal to A. However, this will rarely be the case.[106] Persons compiling aggregates will almost always want their work to be auditable or replicable, and this is likely to be the case to make the data commercially usable. Suppose a doctor is undertaking a statistical study seeking to ascertain a causal link between a particular phenomenon and a particular illness – say, to take an old and obvious case, the link between smoking and cancer. If a statistical case is being made, then the headline data will have to show the broad statistical correlation. Any properly-based scientific inquiry will want its conclusions to be capable of 'audit'. That will require access to the individual cases that comprise the aggregate. Similarly, any commercial venture will need to be able to identify its market. Even where the data is deliberately rendered unauditable, it is clear that with a modicum of processing power and thought, aggregated data can easily be disaggregated and rendered specific to A.

[6.122] Furthermore, if one takes the operation of algorithmic systems, these operate at the level of mass data and yet can be used in a very personal way. The sort of predictive products described by Zuboff are aggregations of data that are nevertheless also personal to A because they can be used in relation to A specifically. It must be borne in mind that publication is only one possible use of private information. It is the one that makes the drawing of the line between the personal and the generic the hardest, as can be seen from the defamation cases. As *Gatley* notes,[107] the defamatory words published must be of the claimant, of A:

> To succeed in an action for defamation, the claimant must not only prove that the defendant published the words and that they are defamatory: he must also identify himself as the person defamed. 'No writing whatsoever it to be esteemed a libel unless it reflects upon some particular person'. It is an essential element of the cause of action for defamation that the words complained of should be published 'of the plaintiff'. There is no cause of action, for instance, if words are defamatory of the claimant's relatives, unless they refer to and reflect on the claimant.

[105] S Bridge et al., *Megarry & Wade: The Law of Real Property*, 9th edn (Sweet & Maxwell, 2019) [12-032]–[12-033]. In the context of intangible property and co-ownership, see Smith et al (n 6) Ch 2 Section E.

[106] See, again, the Example at para [1.17].

[107] *Gatley on Libel and Slander* (n 33) [8-001].

> It is usually clear enough that the words are published of the claimant because he is named in the statement and the defendant intends to refer to him, but neither of these elements is necessary or determinative. The question in all cases is whether the hypothetical reasonable reader would understand the words to refer to the claimant, subject to the qualification that where the words are published to persons who have special knowledge, the issue will be decided by reference to what reasonable persons possessing that knowledge would understand by them …

[6.123] Use through publication is not the only way perception can be used, and is perhaps an outlier as our society stands at present. Most of the cases to date litigated on privacy involve publication, but (as has been described in Chapter 1) the third phase of privacy involves much more than this. But whether the use is personal to A is actually (if it is detected) quite an easy test to apply: the question is whether the use directly affects A, whether through predictive searching, dynamic pricing, or otherwise. The starting point for defining private information ought always to be the use to which the private information is put.

vi. The question of standpoint

[6.124] The question of whether information is personal to A is to be assessed on a Court-Determined Fact basis.[108] That implies that the question of whether information is personal to A is determined after the event by reference to facts established at the trial of the Action.

[6.125] At first blush, this seems unfair to O(C). Why should the identity of the claimant in the Action be tested for and determined long after O(C) has acquired their perception of A and actually used that perception? Given that the Action constrains the ability of C to use their perception, one might think that a different time (eg the time the perception is used) and a different test (eg the Objective O(C) test described at paragraphs [6.81]–[6.82] ought to be used.

[6.126] These alternatives to the Court-Determined Fact approach are to be rejected. Recall the case of Tyler (the Example at paragraph [6.102]), whose privacy was clearly invaded by various Cs who may very well neither have known nor cared about Tyler's identity. The fact is that at the time of the misuse of their perception, C would have known that *someone's* privacy was being invaded, and that is all C needs to know in order to enable them to behave in a legally compliant manner and avoid exposure to an Action. Whether the claimant who ultimately brings the Action is the right claimant is something for trial.

[108] See paras [6.81]–[6.82] (defining 'Court-Determined Fact') and para [6.85] (stating the test for what is *personal* to A).

[6.127] The point about the 'personal to A' test is twofold:

(1) It serves to exclude the generic perception, which relates to no specific person at all.
(2) In the case of perceptions that are personal to *someone*, it ensures that the correct person (here: Tyler or Tyler's estate) is bringing the Action.

These are both matters that can be determined after the event, at trial, on a Court-Determined Fact basis without in any way prejudicing the interests of defendant C.

G. The information must be private to A

i. Introduction

[6.128] If a straightforward definition of privacy were possible, it would already have been stated earlier on in this book. The definition is not straightforward because privacy has little to do with the protection of secrecy or confidentiality (although it does protect those interests), and everything to do with A's right to control how they are perceived by the world.[109] It is thus not possible to define privacy by reference to either subject matter or A's presumed reaction if the private information were used in a certain way. Both of these factors are relevant to the definition of 'private', but they are only two elements in a multifactorial evaluation. The definition of 'private' is 'multifactorial' in nature, which is lawyer-speak for 'vague'.

[6.129] Before turning to the multifactorial elements that go to define that which is 'private', the following points can be made (largely by way of reiteration of what has gone before):

- What is at issue is *information*, which we define as O(C)'s perception of something that is *personal* to A which is *also* – the quality now under discussion – *private* to A.
- The quality of information that is personal to and private to A is further understood by the interrelationship between the Action and other information regimes considered in Section III of this chapter.
- Attempts in the case law to describe A's rights are for the most part circular. The test that has been framed (largely through the case law considering Article 8 of the ECHR) is that A's privacy rights are engaged where A has a 'reasonable expectation of privacy'.[110] This does not assist but represents the starting point for the analysis.

[109] See Section II of this chapter.
[110] *Murray v Express Newspapers plc* [2008] EWCA Civ 446 at [45]. Different tests are used: in *R (Wood) v MPC*, [2009] EWCA Civ 414 at [24], Laws LJ also referred to a 'legitimate expectation of privacy'.

ii. HRH Duchess of Sussex v Associated Newspapers Ltd

[6.130] In *HRH Duchess of Sussex v Associated Newspapers Ltd*,[111] the essential principles governing the Action, including the reasonable expectation of privacy test, were expressed by Warby J in the following terms:[112]

> [30] At stage one the question is whether the claimant enjoyed a reasonable expectation of privacy in respect of the information in question. One way the question has been put is to ask whether a reasonable person, placed in the same position as the claimant and faced with the same publicity, would feel substantial offence. There must be something of a private nature that is worthy of protection. In some cases, the answer will be obvious; but the methodology is to make a broad objective assessment of all the circumstances of the case. These include (1) the attributes of the claimant, (2) the nature of the activity in which the claimant was engaged, (3) the place at which it was happening, (4) the nature and purpose of the intrusion, (5) the absence of consent and whether it was known or could be inferred, (6) the effect on the claimant and (7) the circumstances in which and the purposes for which the information came into the hands of the publisher … If the information, or similar information about the claimant, is in the public domain, or is about to become available to the public, the court must have regard to that. In such a case, it is a matter of fact and degree as to whether the legitimate expectation of privacy has been lost. Privacy rights can survive a degree of publicity for the information or related information.
>
> [31] At stage two, the question is whether in all the circumstances the privacy rights of the claimant must yield to the imperatives of the freedom of expression enjoyed by publishers and their audiences. The competing rights are both qualified, and neither has precedence as such. The conflict is not to be resolved mechanically, on the basis of rival generalities. The court must focus intensely on the comparative importance of the specific rights being claimed in the particular case; assess the justifications for interfering with each right; and balance them, applying a proportionality test. The court must have regard to the extent to which it is or would be in the public interest for the material to be published. The decisive factor at this stage is an assessment of the contribution which the publication of the relevant information would make to a debate of general interest. Other factors to be weighed in the balance are the subject matter, how well-known the claimant is, the claimant's prior conduct, and editorial latitude. When examining the demands of free speech, the court should be slow to interfere in respect of matters of technique, form and detail; it should defer, to the extent appropriate on the facts, to professional expertise and judgment of journalists and editors.

There are many issues with this framing of the Action. Setting these out enables a far better understanding of what 'private' information actually is.

[111] [2021] EWHC 273 (Ch) (first instance, Warby J) and [2021] EWCA Civ 1810 (Court of Appeal).

[112] ibid at [30]–[31]. Sir Geoffrey Vos MR noted that this summary was 'not much disputed before us' (at [34]), which ranks as a measure of endorsement.

a. The test for what is 'private' is exceedingly narrow

[6.131] The definition centres on the reaction of a reasonable person in the position of A. Thus, the essence of the test for privacy is:

> ... whether a reasonable person, placed in the same position as the claimant and faced with the same publicity, would feel substantial offence ...

[6.132] This focuses exclusively on two elements that are undoubtedly relevant to defining 'private' – (i) subject matter ('substantial offence') and (ii) A's reaction (a reasonable person in the position of A) – but misses the wider picture of what privacy really is.[113]

b. The relationship between 'private' and 'misuse' is not clearly stated

[6.133] Throughout this book, the distinction has been stressed between: (i) information that is private; and (ii) the misuse of that information. The very name of the Action – misuse of private information – makes this essential dichotomy clear. This book suggests a property analysis of private information, which *Duchess of Sussex* does not address. The failure to do means that the nexus between the two elements of privacy and misuse is never clearly articulated. Although it is clear from the case that the putative reaction of A to C's use of their (C's) perception links the 'private' with the 'misuse', the nature of this link is missed. The link – which is A's rights as an owner of property – will be considered next. For the present, it is worth mentioning the difficulties that a non-property analysis brings with it:

- This approach misses the point that it is perfectly possible for A's private information to be used by C in circumstances where that use is lawful. The conflation of private with misuse means that the very important borderline between lawful use and unlawful misuse is missed.
- Equally, the critical role of 'private' information as the gatekeeper of the Action is lost. This is important. This book suggests a wide definition of private information (so that A's interests can properly be protected), where the Action is prevented from being unduly wide by the use/misuse distinction considered in Chapter 7. Even so, the creation of a sub-set of information that is private information is very significant in controlling the ambit of the Action.

[6.134] It might be said that the definition of privacy ought to be as narrow as suggested in *Duchess of Sussex*. But that dismisses the wider privacy concerns that have been articulated by many – Warren and Brandeis, Fairfield and Zuboff to name but a few.

[113] As to which, see Section II of this chapter.

c. There is a tacit assumption that the only misuse of private information is its publication

[6.135] Of course, publication can constitute a misuse of A's private information. Publication is probably the most overt form of misuse of private information. It was also the most ubiquitous in the second phases of threats to our privacy, where it is possible for C to record a person's private life, whether by image or in words, and to circulate that record to many people across the world.[114] A focus on publication was obviously, and rightly, the trending concern when Warren and Brandeis were writing in 1890. But things have moved on in the intervening years, and the threats to our privacy now are altogether more insidious, covert and intrusive.[115] Although (mis)use is the subject matter of Chapters 7 and 8, the point needs to be made that misuse comes in all shapes and sizes, including digital surveillance, which involves no publication at all. The framing of the Action in the *Duchess of Sussex* case is of no help when it comes to misuses other than publication; and the 'reasonable expectation of privacy' test framed is quite clearly calibrated by reference to this particular form of misuse only.

d. There is a mistaken view that the only value in opposition to privacy is freedom of expression

[6.136] The essence of the two-stage test articulated in *Duchess of Sussex* is that: (i) one first considers whether privacy has been invaded (stage 1); (ii) next, one considers whether the interests of freedom of expression of C outweigh A's privacy interests (stage 2). This approach is in line with the approach that should be taken when considering infringements of Article 8 of the ECHR, but it is insufficient when considering A's rights in respect of the Action and misuses of private information generally. As to this:

(1) A's control over their private information as perceived by C is (as has been repeatedly stressed) not unlimited. C's unused perception cannot be controlled by the Action at all.
(2) Not all *uses* by C of A's private information constitute *misuses*. One of the factors, as we shall see, that goes to defining the line between *use* and *misuse* is, unsurprisingly, freedom of information, but this does not involve a balancing of opposing values. That is because the effect of the Action is to give agency (or control) to A as regards their private information through the law of property. Viewed in this way, C's freedom of expression is substantially less prejudiced than *Duchess of Sussex* would have us

[114] See paras [1.4]–[1.7], where the second phase is described.
[115] See paras [1.8] ff, describing the third phase. It is an error to speak of publication as the only form of misuse of our private information. Misuse *may* involve publication: but publication is just one form of misuse.

believe: if C wants to use A's private information, then there is nothing to stop C from asking A's permission to publish their private information. Of course, there may be some cases where C ought to be permitted to publish without A's consent and without paying for the privilege. These cases fall on the *lawful* side of use, and not on the *unlawful* side of misuse.

(3) Seeing the value of privacy as standing in straightforward opposition to freedom of expression is to miss the essential point of the Action. What is more, in many cases, the Action does not stand in opposition to freedom of expression at all but enables freedom of expression. Take the case where there is a limited group of people – A_1 to A_9 – who for legitimate purposes wish to discuss a matter frankly and confidentially. Suppose one of their number – A_5 – in breach of this understanding, wishes to publish these discussions to all the world. A_5 becomes C, and claimants $A_{1\text{-}4}$ and $A_{6\text{-}9}$ ought to be able to bring an Action preventing this publication. In this way, freedom of expression is protected, not inhibited.

e. Final points

[6.137] The following general points can be made in regard to the *Duchess of Sussex* case:

(1) In a negative way, the case considerably assists in the framing of the definition of privacy.

(2) An Article 8 approach is not consistent with the operation of the Action. The concept of privacy in Article 8 of the ECHR, although of course informing the meaning of 'private' in the Action, does no more than that. The role of the Action as a proprietary tort enables a far wider understanding of that which is 'private', without encroaching on C's freedom of expression rights under Article 10 of the ECHR.

(3) Following on from this, it is plain that the conception and definition of what is 'private' in *Duchess of Sussex* is unduly narrow.

(4) The conflation of 'private' with 'misuse' misleads. In paragraph [30] of the *Duchess of Sussex* decision (set out at paragraph [6.130]) a number of relevant factors are listed:

  (i) The attributes of the claimant.
  (ii) The nature of the activity in which the claimant was engaged.
  (iii) The place at which it was happening.
  (iv) The nature and purpose of the intrusion.
  (v) The absence of consent and whether it was known or could be inferred.
  (vi) The effect on the claimant.
  (vii) The circumstances in which and the purposes for which the information came into the hands of the publisher

  Factors (iv), (vi) and (vii) (at least) do not seek to address what is *private* but rather address the question of *(mis)use*.

iii. A positive definition of 'private'

[6.138] Without falling into the trap of conflating 'private' with 'misuse', there is, nevertheless a nexus between the two concepts. This needs to be identified. There is a relationship between A's privacy as protected by their rights of ownership and C's infringement of those property rights in misusing A's property. The essence of ownership is *control*. If information generally is *not* property, then it is the quality of 'privateness' that causes that which is not property (information generally) to become property (in the form of private information). From this it follows that the scope of what is 'private' must be determined by the extent of A's legitimate property interests, the extent of which in turn is defined by the reach of A's control over information (ie perception) in the hands (or, rather, the mind) of another, C.

[6.139] The reach of A's control is defined by the nature of privacy, which we have already discussed in Section II. To repeat the words of Laws LJ in *R (Wood) v MPC*, 'an individual's personal autonomy makes him the master of all those facts about his own identity'.[116] The reach of A's control is defined by this interest. The test for privacy is whether, as regards *any use* to which C may put information that is personal to A, there arises a reasonable expectation that A should be entitled to a level of control over that information. In short, the circular test for privacy – 'private information is private if there is an expectation of privacy' – is abandoned, and a reasonable expectation of control test substituted for it. Thus, the circularity is broken and the test for privacy becomes, *Is there a reasonable expectation in A that a given use of certain information ought to be subject to A's control?*

[6.140] This represents a significant broadening of the test for what is private. That broadening is defensible given the values that privacy seeks to protect. The essence of privacy is the need for control over information that is personal to A and it represents a light touch test, given the uses to which our personal information is now being put. The breadth of the test is supported by the fact that it is so easily monetised and that private information (which is, in essence, information that is *personal to A*) is used as a raw material, a factor of production. Generally speaking, the entrepreneur will expect to pay a price for the factors of production used in the making of products. The mischief of undervaluing factors of production was explained in Chapter 5. There is every reason why the predictive products described by Zuboff, where they are based on our data, should involve payment for that data to the data subject.

[6.141] The point can be tested in the following way, by reference to 'dynamic pricing' done by reference to A's personal information. The consumer surplus was defined at paragraphs [5.11]–[5.12] and represents the difference between

[116] *R (Wood) v Commissioner of Police of the Metropolis* (n 19) at [25].

the price actually paid by the buyer and the higher amount that the buyer would have been able and willing to pay for a product, had they been required to do so. In other words, the buyer in fact paid £10 for the product, but would and could have paid £15. The buyer's consumer surplus is £5. The sellers in the market will want, if they can, to appropriate this consumer surplus, and convert it to their own producer surplus. They can do so if they: (i) have a means of pricing differentially (which, in these days of Internet purchase, is easy); and (ii) have the data to enable differential pricing (in other words, they can predict how much the buyer is prepared to pay).[117] Obviously, the data used to make this prediction will be personal to A. But is it *private*? That is a value judgement, but really it admits of only one answer. *Of course*, it is private. Buyers and sellers, in a market economy, should not know the other's bottom line, because that subverts the price system. The information is private because it is confidential to A and valuable.

Example[118]

You are late for a meeting. (How would the seller know? Your calender and your current GPS location as well as current traffic data.) Your car is low on gas. (How would the seller know? If you have a smart car, it can report the data. If you have just a cell phone and a credit card, an algorithm can track your miles travelled and tie that to the last time you bought gas.) The question, then, is how much a seller might charge for gas, knowing that you are late, desperate, and that its gas station is the only one in range. Having shrunk the mass market for gas to the specific conditions that currently drive your decisions to buy, the seller can avoid competition in a mass market. You are a market of one.

[**6.142**] In short, the general rule ought to be that information that is personal to A is *also* private where either it is relevant to the way in which A wants to present themselves to the world and/or where it has economic value, in that it enables O(C) to monetise it.

iv. The 'control' test expanded

a. A recapitulation and an overview

[**6.143**] Once again, to recap. The test for privacy is based upon the question of whether A has a reasonable expectation of control. There will presumptively be a reasonable expectation of control on the part of the reasonable person in the position of A where A would reasonably want to control the release of the information and/or where A reasonably wants to participate in the economic

[117] See J Fairfield, *Owned: Property, Privacy and the New Digital Serfdom* (Cambridge University Press, 2017) 89–94; A Bernasek and D Mongan, *All You Can Pay: How Companies Use Our Data to Empty Our Wallets* (Nation Books, 2015), generally but in particular Chs 1, 2 and 4.

[118] Fairfield (n 117) 98.

exploitation of the information. The control test is intended to be flexible, future-development-proof and capable of evolving without having to be comprehensively re-written as technology or society change.[119] In short:

> Information is private to A where that information is (i) personal to A and (ii) where a reasonable person, in the position of A, would have a reasonable expectation of control over the use or exploitation of the information.

[6.144] It is obvious why the Objective A standpoint described at paragraphs [6.81]–[6.82] is adopted. The law of privacy seeks to protect A's interests. It follows that A's standpoint is the relevant one. Of course, for reasons that have also been explored, the Subjective A standpoint is to be rejected. Whilst A's interests need to be reflected in the control test, it goes too far to permit a genuine, but excessive, desire in A to protect their privacy to operate in constraint of C. Moreover, an objective test is predictable, which is necessary so that O(C) can (if they so desire) avoid infringing A's property rights.

[6.145] The control test can be particularised by reference to a number of further (more specific) factors. These factors are set out below, and then expanded upon in the paragraphs that follow.

- *Confidentiality or ubiquity.* Although there is a misconceived equation of privacy with secrecy, nevertheless the confidentiality of the private information or the extent to which it is publicly known matters.
- *The nature or characteristics of A.* To the extent different, or distinguishable, from the first characteristic, this is plainly relevant.
- *The manner in which O(C) obtained or derived the perception.* Was the perception derived from circumstances that were permissive (ie A allowed the access) or public (ie where A ventured out into domains that carried no expectation of privacy)? Or did O(C) act in some improper or wrong way to obtain their perception?
- *The nature of the perception.* By which is meant, subject matter *sensu stricto*. Some subject matters are obviously more sensitive than others.
- *Whether the production of the information was obtained compulsorily.* There is a significant difference between: (i) private information imparted voluntarily and spontaneously; (ii) private information imparted pursuant to an obligation voluntarily entered into; and (iii) private information extracted compulsorily, through force of law.

These factors are now variously considered.

[119] In other words, the test operates a unifying criterion, much as the unified duty of care in *Donoghue v Stevenson* operated.

b. Confidentiality and 'ubiquitousness'

[6.146] The essence of the tort of breach of confidence is the protection of confidential information conveyed by one person to another in circumstances which impose an obligation on the recipient to respect the confidentiality of the information. There is a clear link between some degree of secrecy and the obligation of confidence.

[6.147] That link does not define the scope of privacy protection. As Schulhofer makes clear, it is a myth to associate privacy with secrecy or confidentiality.[120] Discussing the Fourth Amendment, Schulhofer makes the following point:[121]

> Everyone understands the principle that the Fourth Amendment should prevent government officials from rummaging through your private diary without good reason. But this natural idea easily leads to the dangerous notion that the Fourth Amendment therefore should not protect anything you willingly reveal to others. It was this notion that led a federal appeals court, in an opinion by Judge Richard Posner, to hold that the Fourth Amendment does not require a sheriff to obtain a warrant before seizing and towing away a person's mobile home. As long as the sheriff did not go inside, Judge Posner reasoned, the officer did not see anything that was not already exposed to the public.
>
> This is far too narrow a view, and the Supreme Court rightly (and unanimously) rejected it … As the Court recognized, the Fourth Amendment protects us from unjustified government actions that disturb our peace and transquility, not only from those that interfere with secrecy. The language of the amendment is explicit on this point, affirming 'the right of the people to be secure in their persons, houses, papers and effects.'

[6.148] The private information of A is almost always deployed by A in some way – often involving O(C)s. Private information is not about secrecy, it is about the right in A to control the use, by O(C), of A's private information.[122] As Schulhofer puts it:[123]

> Only a hermit can lay claim to complete secrecy. For anyone who wishes to inhabit the world, daily life inevitably involves personal associations and the information we exchange within them. Relationships give meaning to our lives and define a large part of who we are. To insist that information is private only when it remains completely secret is preposterous. Indeed, personal information often becomes more

[120] S Schulhofer, *More Essential Than Ever* (Oxford University Press, 2012) 6.

[121] ibid 6–7.

[122] As Schulhofer says in relation to the Fourth Amendment (ibid 130): 'The notion that shared information should have no Fourth Amendment protection has *always* been untenable, because privacy has never been equated with mere secrecy. It is something much more important: the *right to control* knowledge about our personal lives, the right to decide how much information gets revealed to whom and for which purposes.'

[123] ibid 130.

> valuable when we share it confidentially with chosen associates who help us pursue common projects. As Judge Richard Posner puts it, 'productive independent thinking almost always requires bouncing ideas off other people.' Though shared, the information remains private until we relinquish control and expose it to the public.

[6.149] Privacy is thus – and for these reasons – about control of use and that point in time at which A chooses to relinquish control of their private information. Once again, Schulhofer puts it well:[124]

> The idea that privacy means secrecy is too narrow even when we think only about personal information, like the contents of a journal. Suppose I give you my diary and urge you to read it. No one would think you are violating my privacy when you do so. The reason is that privacy is not about the information itself, no matter how personal it may be. Instead, this aspect of privacy – informational privacy – is about my right to control what others see, and in this example I have given you my permission. Although the diary is no longer completely secret, it remains private, in the sense that I (and others whom I trust) still have the right to control who can see it.

[6.150] It will be noted that consent is not specifically listed in this attempt to define private information. That is because consent does not *define* private information but rather serves as a defence to what would otherwise be an invasion of privacy. Where A has, in the exercise of their property rights, transferred their private information to O(C) or licensed its use, then O(C) steps into the shoes of the owner and has (derived from A) the positive *right* to use the information. In other words, the information is not any the less private or personal to A, it is simply that A's rights over their property have been transferred or licensed to another (B).

[6.151] Consent is not relevant to the definition of what is or what is not private. Consent must be distinguished from 'ubiquitousness'. Where the private information is ubiquitous, it is not private. Thus:

(1) The publication of an invention pursuant to patent law cannot constitute private information.
(2) Depending on the extent to which publication has been licensed, the publication of a 'gist' or summary will not be a publication of private information nor yet an infringement of copyright.
(3) There may be other circumstances where information that is personal to A and would otherwise be private to A is nevertheless not private information even though A has not consented to C's specific use of the information. That not because the information is not secret, but because, through legitimate channels, it is information that has become well-known.

[124] ibid 8.

This is referred to as information in the public domain, when considering *confidential information*, but the point is as valid in the context of private information.[125]

[6.152] Equally, the notion of exhaustion in the context of copyright can helpfully be deployed. Copyright exhaustion – in the United States, the 'first sale' doctrine – has been described as:[126]

> one of the most fundamental principles of copyright law. Under this doctrine, the copyright holder must accept that copies, or the originals of copyrighted works, and other subject matter lawfully placed into circulation by or with the authorisation of the rights holder, through the sale or in any other form of transfer of ownership, are subsequently distributed by the lawful owner of those copies or originals, if the rights holder received proper remuneration for the initial distribution.

Thus, where the owner of copyright causes 100,000 copies of their work to be printed and sold, the next sale of these copies (even at a far higher price) is not something that can be objected to. In the context of physical property, that is a remarkably obvious proposition. The copyrighted work can be onsold but not reproduced.

[6.153] The same thinking can be applied to digital property, but the problem of replication immediately surfaces. Is it permissible for a person buying (say) a digital book or software to replicate the item across many devices, including (say) other people's? The problem that the ability to replicate gives rise to is that the common-sense basis for the doctrine of exhaustion becomes distorted. Where a seller is seeking to maximise the revenue of (say) their electronic book or software or film, replication is a real problem, which tends to dealt with by the creation of technical barriers to replication.[127]

[6.154] In the context of private information, the issues raised by exhaustion are helpful by way of analogy. Once private information has been put into circulation or has public currency A's rights might be said to be 'exhausted'.

c. The nature and subject matter of the perception

[6.155] Apart from ubiquity, the nature of the information itself is a most significant factor. There is obviously a relationship between privacy and ubiquity

[125] L Bently et al, *Intellectual Property Law*, 6th edn (Oxford University Press, 2022) 1250–59.
[126] P Mezei, *Copyright Exhaustion: Law and Policy in the United States and the European Union* (Cambridge University Press, 2018) 1.
[127] Thus, a subscription to the streaming of films or music tends to be limited not merely to certain users (which is hard to control for) but also certain devices (far easier to control for).

that is intermediated by subject matter. As Lord Goff noted in *Attorney-General v Guardian (No 2)*, when speaking about the duty of confidence:[128]

> I have expressed the circumstances in which the duty arises in broad terms … to include certain situations, beloved of law teachers – where an obviously confidential document is wafted by an electric fan out of a window into a crowded street, or where an obviously confidential document, such as a private diary, is dropped in the public place, and is then picked up by a passer-by.

[6.156] This reveals that subject matter is itself a complex question, defined by reference to at least three, interrelated, strands. Most literally, subject matter refers to just that: the substantive content of the information. But that substantive content is coloured by two other matters:

- The party to whom the information relates – that is, the nature and qualities of A. The point is that the same subject matter will have different privacy implications according to the nature and qualities of A. It is here that the distinction between A as a natural person and A as a legal person is most likely to tell.
- The manner of the dissemination of the information colours its privacy. It is here that there is the closest link with ubiquity. The privacy implications will be different depending on whether the information was voluntarily published by A or stolen from A by another.

d. Voluntary and involuntary extraction of private information

[6.157] The involuntary extraction of information from A or about A is highly material to the question of both privacy and (as we shall see) misuse. It seems clear that if A is *obliged with no choice* to provide information to O(C), then two things follow: (i) the information so provided ought to be regarded as private; and (ii) the question of whether C's subsequent use of the information so obtained is legitimate depends upon the reasons why C was given the power to compel information from A. This second point will be considered in Chapters 7 and 8: the point is that C's right to use the information that have obtained ought to be limited to the proper purpose for which it has been extracted. This relates to the use/misuse borderline; but of course that borderline is only relevant if the information extracted is classified as private.

[6.158] The point here being made is that the power to extract information about A (whether from A directly or from a third party who has information about A) is a strong indicator that the information is private to A.

[128] *Attorney-General v Guardian (No 2)* [1990] AC 109, 281–82.

v. Time of assessment

[6.159] It would obviously be inappropriate to assess the question of privacy *after* O(C) had made use of the perception. It might be thought that privacy ought to be assessed at that point in time immediately prior to O(C)'s use of the information, and this is probably a good starting point.

[6.160] But it would be wrong to consider this as the *only* time for assessment. In this day and age, it is possible for information to be transmitted to many people very quickly, and O(C)'s (mis)use may follow thick and fast on the use or misuse of others. To an extent that has been true since the time of Warren and Brandeis' article, but the position today is much more extreme, where (for example) a 'tweet' can be posted, liked by others, and then reposted.

[6.161] It is therefore suggested that the time for assessing whether information is private to A ought to be a flexible one that is part of the privacy evaluation itself. In other words, when considering whether something is or is not private, the court must explicitly address and consider the point in time at which this question must be resolved.

vi. Standpoint

[6.162] The test for determining whether information is private was set out in brief at paragraph [6.85], and contains four elements. The first and second of these (numbers (1) and (2)) have already been considered. The third and fourth (numbers (3) and (4)) need to be addressed in light of the multifactorial test for privacy that has been considered in the foregoing paragraphs.

[6.163] The second element provides that whether information is private to A should be objectively considered from A's point of view (ie the Objective A standard considered at paragraphs [6.81]–[6.82]). This is a different and additional requirement from the requirement that the information be personal to A. This is consistent with *Murray v Express Newspapers plc*,[129] which makes clear that the Objective A Standpoint is to be adopted.[130] Whether something is private to A can only be considered from A's standpoint, but that consideration must be objective and not subjective to A.[131]

[6.164] O(C) might object that this takes into account facts and matters that O(C) may not know and may be unable to ascertain, even after undertaking diligent inquiry. These concerns are dealt with by the fourth element, which

[129] See n 110.
[130] See paras [6.81]–[6.82].
[131] See the third element of the test set out at para [6.85].

holds that information will only be regarded as personal to A and private to A *if* a reasonable person, standing in the position of O(C), would know, or on reasonable inquiry ought to know, that the information is both (i) personal to and (ii) private to *someone*. It is not necessary for C to know exactly who A is, even to an Objective (C) standard. All that is needed for C's interests to be sufficiently protected is for C is appreciate, to this standard, that the perception is personal to and private to *some person*. Thus, both of these questions are determined according to the Objective O(C) standard described at paragraphs [6.81]–[6.82].

vii. Sharing private information; the significance of 'consent'

[6.165] Two cases can be differentiated. The first is where A, with no intention of sharing their private information, nevertheless must do so in order themselves to enjoy their property. For example, A may write a diary, but do so electronically, saving the file on the 'cloud'. Inevitably, this involves interaction with O(C), the provider of the cloud service. Almost inevitably, this interaction will involve some form of agreement with O(C). If that agreement does no more than state the services that O(C) is providing, and permits O(C) to use A's information only to provide those services that A is seeking from O(C), no particular problem arises. But what if the agreement with O(C) goes further, and permits O(C) to use this information for their *own* purposes? To what extent must A parse the contract between themselves and O(C) and determine the extent to which the information that A commit to the 'cloud' is going to be appropriately used? Or can A rely upon their tortious claim under the Action whatever the agreement might say?

[6.166] The second case is where A does more than merely require O(C) to perform a specific service, but shares the substance of the private information with O(C) – as where A asks O(C) to read their private diary with a view to getting comments before A chooses to publish it. Here O(C) is invited into A's circle of confidence; and the question is the extent to which O(C) can use A's private information.

[6.167] Both cases look very much like the bilateral relationship that arises in cases of breach of confidence, and certainly these cases can be analysed in this way. But that is to create a distinction between breach of confidence and misuse of private information that is unhelpful. After all, proprietary torts do not draw this distinction, because it is an unnecessary and an unhelpful one. In other words, it is far better to see information sharing as feeding into the questions of (i) 'Is this information, that is personal to A, also private to A?' and (ii) 'Has O(C) misused that information?', rather than being characterised as elements of, say, the tort of breach of confidence. These two (very different) cases are considered in this light.

[6.168] The second case is easier than the first: it turns upon precisely what the arrangement between A and O(C) is understood to be. Clearly, A inviting O(C) into their circle of confidence injects a bilateral element into their relationship. This does not affect the quality of privacy, but it is relevant to the uses to which O(C) can put the perceptions that they have consensually obtained from A. All that is being said is that these dealings between A and O(C) do not render that which was private not private, but the dealing may have significant bearing on the legitimate uses to which O(C) may put their perception. The point thus is relevant to the question of (mis)use rather than privacy.

[6.169] The first case is harder. A may have no real choice but to use O(C)'s services. A will often contract on O(C)'s standard terms and conditions, which may not be reviewed, and which may – in addition to containing rights that are substantively more extensive than they should be –contain procedural obstacles (eg jurisdiction and choice of law clauses in favour of O(C)). Moreover, A may give no thought to the fact that the service they are buying from O(C) is enabling O(C) to access and use particularly sensitive information. Technology is increasingly complex and pervasive, and so intrusive, in terms of how our information is used. A may not even understand that they need to examine the terms of a contract with O(C) with particular care so far as their private information is concerned.

Example[132]

> … on September 13, 2016 … the *Chicago Tribune* reported that a class action lawsuit had been filed on behalf of tens of thousands of people against the makers of WeVibe, a popular couples' erotic massage device. WeVibe was discovered to have been extracting the most intimate data possible from the device: date and time of each use, level of vibration intensity, vibration mode or pattern selection, even the temperature of the device and the email address of the user. The data were apparently collected for the purposes of market research. The manufacturer of WeVibe – a company called Standard Innovation – was able to do this as a technical matter because the device was web enabled, controlled wirelessly by a smartphone application, called We-Connect. Standard Innovation buried software in the device that communicated the intimate details to We-Connect, and We-Connect then secretly forwarded the details to SI's own servers. SI claimed the *legal* right to do this because of terms hidden deep within the app's software licence …

[6.170] At this stage, a number of somewhat obvious points need to be articulated:

- The consent of A to the use of their private information is hugely relevant, not merely to the question of use or misuse, but also to the very question

[132] Fairfield (n 117) 2–3.

of whether the information is private or not. If A elects to put personal and private information on a social media webpage open to all, that information will cease to be private and duplication by members of O will be permitted use and not misuse. That is so, even if there is no contractual term governing matters. It is simply the combination of (i) voluntary publication by A, combined with (ii) publication in a manner that renders the information ubiquitous.

- Similar and perhaps similarly difficult questions arise where A shares to a lesser extent, but permits someone else to use more widely, as where on social media A consents to the use of their photographs by O(C) going well beyond what is needed in order for the photographs to be presented on the Internet.
- Obviously, one can see that A, in such cases, has property rights which are capable of protection by way of the Action. The problem is how can A's property rights in their private information avoid being 'trumped' by the specific contractual provisions drafted by O(C) permitting such use, either in the form of licence or even transfer. In such cases, C's response to A's claim against them may not be to assert that A has no property in the information, but to assert that A has exercised an owner's rights to allow C to use the information. The outcome is that contract trumps property, using A's rights as owner against them.

[6.171] This difficulty has yet to be addressed. Consent to use of property and the transfer of property is a complex question, particularly in the case of intangible property. The topic is considered in Chapter 11, which considers A's rights, as the owner of private information, to both licence and transfer that information to B. Inevitably, licensing and transfer involve some form of bilateral relationship between A and B.

viii. Have privacy and misuse been conflated?

[6.172] The 'trap' of conflating 'private' with 'misuse' was mentioned in paragraph [6.138]. The question that this chapter ends on is whether that trap has successfully been avoided. The control test described in paragraphs [6.139] and [6.143] might be said to equate 'private' with 'misuse'. If something is private where A has a reasonable expectation of control over the use or exploitation of the information, then where such reasonable expectation of control exists, and C (without A's consent) uses the information, there is inevitably misuse on the part of C.

[6.173] This is not conflation of two tests that should be distinct, but merely a reflection of the Hohfeldian truth that where A has a right, C has a correlative duty.[133] The test of 'privateness' defines A's rights, whereas the concept of 'misuse' characterises C's infringement of A's rights. There has to be a correlation between right and infringement, but rights are 'forward looking' and infringements 'backward looking'. Thus, A has a property right against the world without there being any infringement of that right by anyone at all. A has a right in the abstract, but no right to bring an Action because there has been no arguable infringement. It would be absurd to deny this proposition, because otherwise A would have nothing to license and nothing to transfer, both of which are rights of the owner of property. They exist independently of any infringement of A's property rights. Thus, A's property rights may be said to be forward looking, because they control the future conduct of the universe of persons O.

[6.174] Infringement by contrast is backward looking: the question then is not 'What rights does A have?', but 'Has C infringed those rights?', which involves specific consideration of C's conduct. An analysis of the right must focus on *predictability*. It is necessary, in order to achive this, to articulate the drivers of the reach of A's right, and the factors that inform its extent, so that A can understand their rights and O(C) can (attempt to) respect them in advance of infringing.

[6.175] Infringement is much more granular or specific. It involves consideration, after the event, of specific acts (here, uses) by C that involve the potentiality of A's property rights being interfered with. The exercise is a retrospective one.

[6.176] The beauty of the common law is that retrospective decisions serve to inform the nature of A's prospective rights. There is an interplay between right and infringement or privacy and misuse. This chapter has sought to explain the reach of A's rights. The next chapters consider perception, use and misuse, first in the case of non-state actors (Chapter 7) and then in the case of state actors (Chapter 8).

[133] For a description of Hohfeld's analysis of interests, see Smith et al (n 6) Ch 2 Section B(2).

7

Misuse: Non-State Actors

In which: C's misuse of A's private information is considered, in circumstances where C is a 'non-state' actor; the boundary between perception and use is articulated, and an extended meaning of 'perception' stated; the boundary between use and misuse is considered, and the various factors that inform whether use is misuse in the case of non-state actors are set out.

I. Different Treatment of Non-State and State Actors

[7.1] Article 8 of the European Convention on Human Rights (ECHR) protects A's privacy as against state actors, but not as against non-state actors.[1] For this reason, it can be said that Article 8 has 'vertical' but not 'horizontal' effect.[2] That does not take into account the fact that Article 8 has *indirectly* had 'horizontal' effect by inspiring the development of the Action, as described in Chapter 2. Nevertheless, it remains the case that as against non-state actors, actions under the Human Rights Act 1998 (HRA 1998) are not possible, and that the main protectors of privacy in this context are data protection regimes and the Action.

[7.2] Because Article 8 has 'vertical' effect, it might be thought that the Action has no role to play as against state actors. This is not correct: whilst it may be the case that A has a claim against a state actor under the HRA 1998, that does *not* mean to say that the Action is irrelevant so far as state actors are concerned. Indeed, it will be suggested that even as against state actors, A may find it advantageous to bring an Action, either in addition to a claim under the HRA 1998 or as a self-standing claim without direct reliance on the HRA 1998.

[7.3] Although the distinction is here drawn between 'state actors' and 'non-state actors', this is simply the terminology that this book has chosen to adopt: it has the benefit of clarity. However, the true distinction in terms of the application of the HRA 1998 lies in classifying the powers that *any* actor – public or

[1] See para [4.157].
[2] See para [4.147].

private, state or non-state – exercises, which may either be of a public nature or a private right common to all persons in England. As regards state actors (referred to in the HRA 1998 as 'public authorities'), the HRA 1998 imposes an obligation to act compatibly with the ECHR.[3] A public authority includes 'any person certain of whose functions are functions of a public nature'.[4] The Act also provides that '[i]n relation to a particular act, a person is not a public authority … if the nature of the act is private'.[5]

[7.4] Thus, the HRA 1998 takes a functional approach. If an act is private, the 1998 Act does not apply, even if the body in question looks like a public body. On the other hand, if an act involves a public function, it will be subject to the HRA 1998 even if the actor appears to all intents and purposes to be a private body. Since articulating this distinction is a mouthful, this book will refer simply to 'state' and 'non-state' actors, as a convenient (if slightly inaccurate) shorthand.

[7.5] Actions against non-state actors are considered first, in this chapter, for the following reasons:

(1) The position as against non-state actors is more straightforward than is the case with state actors. It makes sense to consider the easier case first. The reason Actions against state actors are complex is because (in the public interest) state actors are given powers that non-state actors do not have, and these powers include the power to invade our privacy. Where a state actor operates within such powers, there is obviously a strong argument that the Action will fail, because however clearly the information is A's private information, the state's actions are unlikely to amount to an infringement of A's property rights, because the infringement is justified by the exercise of public law power (or state-sanctioned power). In short, infringements of A's private information will generally constitute lawful *use* and not unlawful *misuse* for this reason.
(2) Since the line between lawful *use* and unlawful *misuse* is more straightforward in the case of non-state actors, the consideration of non-state actors in this chapter precedes the consideration of state actors in Chapter 8.
(3) Since the Action is the only effective way in which A can protect their privacy as against non-state actors, and since the concerns about invasions of privacy principally concern such actors – particularly in 'phase 3'[6] – it also makes sense to begin with the Action as a control over 'surveillance capitalism'.

[3] HRA 1998, s 6(1).
[4] ibid s 6(3)(b). This articulates the point already made. A private actor is, in such a case and to this extent, a public actor.
[5] ibid s 6(5).
[6] See para [1.8] ff.

A's Action against non-state actors is, therefore, the paradigm case: and we will begin there. Misuse by state actors, which builds on this chapter, is dealt with in Chapter 8.

II. Perception, Use and Misuse

A. Overview, nomenclature and assumptions

[7.6] The subject matter of this chapter is the borderline between legitimate use of private information by O(C) and illegitimate misuse of private information by C. It is assumed, for the purposes of this chapter, that O(C)'s/C's[7] perception is of private information of A. The question of misuse involves consideration of two borderlines. The first is the distinction between *perception* and *use*. The second is the distinction between *use* and *misuse*.

[7.7] O(C) and C are designators of the same person, having the same perception of A. It is simply that the descriptor O(C) shows that there is no arguable claim that can be brought by A against O(C), whereas in the latter instance C is a defendant or potential defendant. The line between the designation O(C) and C is difficult for two, related, reasons. First, the lines between (i) *perception* and *use* and (ii) *use* and *misuse* are intrinsically difficult. That is the subject matter of this chapter. Second, and this will be touched upon again in Chapter 10, A can name C as a defendant to a claim without establishing conclusively that their (A's) rights have been infringed. A cause of action like the Action involves the pleading of specific *allegations* in proceedings, which are then resolved by a court, unless they are compromised. So the designator C does not refer to someone *necessarily* liable to A, but rather to someone against whom A can bring a claim to trial, at which trial A may (or may not) succeed. The point is that it is courts that determine disputes, not the parties. All the parties do is make assertions that the court adjudicates upon. Put another way, for A to assert that C has infringed their privacy amounts to no more than an arguable claim; when once the court has adjudicated in A's favour (if it does so), the position is entirely different – A has a judgment in their favour against C which can be enforced.

[7.8] When discussing the borderline between perception and use, reference will be made to O(C), for if there is no use by O(C) of A's private information, there is no arguable case that A can make against O(C). (This involves an over-simplification: the borderline between perception and use is not clear-cut, and it may very well be the case that: (i) A has an arguable case that O(C) has used and not merely perceived A's private information; *and* (ii) an arguable case that O(C)'s (arguable) use constitutes misuse. In which case the proper label

[7] They are the same person: see para [6.9].

for O(C) is in fact C.) Nevertheless, when considering the perception/use borderline, reference will be made to O(C). When we move on to consider the use/misuse borderline, reference will be made to C. It is not a completely defensible position, but it does importantly highlight the need to protect O(C)'s freedom of thought. Before we move on to the two borderlines that are considered, it is stressed again: O(C) and C are the *same* person; and that person is a non-state actor.

B. Two borderlines

[7.9] Consideration of *misuse* involves consideration of two lines of demarcation or 'borderlines'. The first is the borderline between perception and use. Perception in O(C) is not actionable by A, no matter how private the information. That much is clear if 'perception' bears its normal meaning of something in the mind of O(C), which has no external manifestation. On this basis, any manifestation of O(C)'s perception becomes *use*. Although this is consistent with the plain meaning of these words, it will be suggested (and, of course, there is no authority on point, given the state of development of the Action) that this is too narrow a protection of O(C)'s own freedoms, in particular Article 9 of the ECHR (freedom of thought, conscience and religion) and Article 10 of the ECHR (freedom of expression). Suppose O(C) writes a diary, strictly privately kept, and records their perception as an entry in that diary. It is suggested that this 'use' ought not to be classified as such but ought rather to be protected as 'perception', even though that is not the natural meaning of the word. The perception/use borderline thus contains within it hidden complexities.

[7.10] The second borderline is the borderline between use and misuse. Not every use by C of C's perception of A's private information constitutes an infringement of A's rights. Some uses by C of their perception are legitimate and A will in those cases have no claim in relation to them. It is only when the line between use and misuse is crossed that C infringes A's rights. Again, where that line is to be drawn is matter that is less straightforward than one might wish.[8]

C. Two points left for later

[7.11] Two further matters are parked for consideration in later chapters:

(1) *Non-natural persons.* In order to understand the perception/use and the use/misuse borderlines, the issue of *non-natural* persons is left

[8] A start on articulating this line has already been made in defining 'privacy' in Chapter 6. This chapter takes that analysis further.

unaddressed. It will be recalled that the universe O must – because of the nature of information – only comprise *natural persons*;[9] but that the consequence that a legal person cannot be liable for a misuse of A's private information is obviously unsustainable and not the correct legal position. However, it is better to consider the use/misuse borderline independently of, and in advance of, the question of the liability of an undertaking under the Action. O(C) and C are natural persons (and non-state actors). The complex question of the liability of undertakings is for Chapter 9.

(2) *Quia timet relief.* The circumstances in which A can obtain an injunction for threatened misuse of private information will obviously be informed by what constitutes misuse. In order to obtain a *quia timet* injunction, additional factors will have to be shown, which are best considered separately, when once the notion of misuse of private information has been articulated. Accordingly, the discussion in this chapter will be by reference to *uses* and *misuses* of A's private information, and not *threatened* misuses. The circumstances in which a *quia timet* injunction can be obtained is one of the topics considered in Chapter 10.

III. The Boundary between Perception and Use

A. The utility of the distinction

[7.12] The starting point is that a perception in O(C) of information that is both personal and private to A is not in any way actionable without *use* on the part of O(C). Whilst it may be said that A has property in the perception, in just the same way as A might be said to own land, there is no possible infringement of A's rights without *use*, just as where A's land is untrodden by anyone there is no trespass. The point is *not* that A has no rights in this case: the point is that those rights are not even arguably infringed. In just the same way, a landowner cannot stop another *looking* at their land, admiring the landscape, provided the land is not entered upon. The landowner's rights are not any the less. It is simply that they have not been infringed.[10]

[7.13] Even use of the perception by C is not enough to enable A's claim to succeed: it must be shown that the use is a misuse. Not all uses are misuses, and that borderline is considered later. The point here is that *unused* perception is an inevitable corollary of freedom of thought and a vital basis for freedom of expression.

[9] See paras [6.97]–[6.99].
[10] A very good example is the *Victoria Park Racing* case considered at paras [1.60]–[1.61].

[7.14] There is some suggestion in the case law that this borderline is less helpful than is being suggested here. *R (Wood) v Commissioner of Police of the Metropolis*[11] concerned photographs taken of Mr Wood by the police for the purposes of their duties.[12] The submissions to the Court of Appeal 'drew a distinction between the *taking* of the photographs and the *retention* of the images',[13] which Laws LJ claimed not to find helpful, at least in this case.[14] Contrary to Laws LJ's views, the distinction *is* a helpful one, and what underlies it is precisely the distinction between perception and use that is here being articulated. Framing the question in these terms, the first question becomes whether the *taking* of a photograph is *perception* or *use*. A second question is similar – is *retention* (without doing anything more) of the photograph *perception* or *use*? Considering these two points together, it can persuasively be suggested that the mere taking of photographs is a matter of perception, not use. Clearly, the use of one's own senses is perception, even if those senses are enhanced (eg by the use of binoculars or a telescope). Does the recording of the image on the camera make any difference? Assuming the image just stays there, in the camera, it can be argued that this remains a case of perception. As Laws LJ noted in *Wood*, 'the taking of photographs in a public street involves no element of interference with anyone's private life and therefore will not engage Article 8(1) ECHR, although the later publication of such photographs may be a different matter'. This a clear and helpful articulation of the perception/use divide.

[7.15] In *Campbell v MGM Ltd*,[15] where the model Naomi Campbell was photographed in a public street leaving a narcotic addiction therapy session, Lord Hoffmann drew a similar distinction:[16]

> [73] In the present case the pictures were taken without Ms Campbell's consent. That in my opinion is not enough to amount to a wrongful invasion of privacy. The famous and even the not so famous who go out in public must accept that they may be photographed without their consent …
>
> [74] But the fact that we cannot avoid being photographed does not mean that anyone who takes or obtains such photographs can publish them to the world at large.

Similarly, Lord Hope said:[17]

> The photographs were taken of Miss Campbell while she was in a public place, as she was in the street outside the premises where she had been receiving therapy. The taking of photographs in a public street must … be taken to be one of the ordinary

[11] *R (Wood) v Commissioner of Police of the Metropolis* [2009] EWCA Civ 414. Although this case involved a claim under Art 8 of the ECHR against a state actor, the reasoning in the case is of general interest.

[12] This was, therefore, a state actor case, and we will come back to it in Ch 8.

[13] *R (Wood) v Commissioner of Police of the Metropolis* (n 11) [29] (per Laws LJ).

[14] ibid [29], although Laws LJ did in fact use the distinction in his consideration of the arguments.

[15] *Campbell v MGM Ltd* [2004] UKHL 22.

[16] Cited with approval by Laws LJ at *Wood* (n 11) [31].

[17] *Campbell v MGM Ltd* (n 15) [122].

> incidents of living in a free community. The real issue is whether publicising the content of the photographs would be offensive ...

[7.16] For the present, the concern is less with *where* the line between perception and use is to be drawn, and more with its *existence*. The foregoing passages can be read as simply an attempt to articulate the borderline between use and misuse. But that is not the tenor of the words used. Reading them, these judges had in mind that there were certain acts which were *neither* misuses *nor* uses. The question then is what label one attaches to this 'not use'. The label used in this book (consistent with what is defined as information) is *perception*. The label and the perception/use distinction both matter because of the importance of O(C)'s freedom of thought (Article 9 of the ECHR).

[7.17] When it comes to O(C)'s freedom of expression (Article 10 of the ECHR), we are talking about use and have transited to the use/misuse borderline. Thus, the emphasis on the fact that the *published* photographs of Ms Campbell and Mr Wood were taken in public goes (because the *publication* in the press was clearly use not perception) to the use/misuse line, not the perception/use line. Suppose, for example, someone illicitly trespassed onto property in order to take the photographs: if nothing was done by C to *use* the photographs, then it is suggested that the mere perception, even if recorded in a camera, would not infringe A's rights of privacy,[18] although any use would be liable to be classified as a misuse by virtue of the trespass.

[7.18] When considering misuse, the starting point is C's use of the information, *not* C's perception. In *Wood*, Laws LJ stated that the 'real issue is whether the taking of the pictures, along with their actual and/or apprehended use, might amount to a violation'.[19] This is exactly the point: C has a certain perception, and the question is whether the use (in light of all the circumstances, including how the perception was derived) is proper or improper.

[7.19] Turning to the question of retention and where retention falls in terms of the perception/use borderline, it might be suggested that there can be no difference between taking a photograph and retaining it. If one is perception, both ought to be. That was the position of Laws LJ in *Wood*:[20]

> It might be thought that if (as I would hold) the mere taking of the pictures does not engage Article 8(1) ECHR, there follows a wholly separate question: whether their retention and intended use might do so. But I do not think this is the right way to analyse the case. I stated earlier, at [29], that the supposed distinction between the taking of photographs and the retention of the images is in the end unhelpful for the

[18] Other rights might be infringed, for instance, trespass.
[19] *R (Wood) v Commissioner of Police of the Metropolis* (n 11) [38].
[20] ibid [39].

> purpose of ascertaining the reach of the Article 8 ECHR right. We have seen that the defendant's policy is that 'cameras are deployed overtly … officers should clearly identify themselves as police officers or police staff and not hide the fact that they are filming'. This is certainly as it should be; if it were done covertly, there would be other very substantial arguments to consider which in this case do not arise. As it is, the subject here, the claimant observes who is taking his picture and knows it is a police photographer. He is bound to assume that the picture will be kept, and that it will, or at least might, be used for a police purpose. Mr Grodzinski submitted that if the taking of the pictures is not itself any interference with the claimant's Article 8(1) ECHR right, it cannot become so by reason of the pictures' potential use; but this I think is too simplistic. The subject's complaint absent any question of intimidation or harassment is that his image is being recorded by State authorities, an act to which he does not consent, which he believes to be unjustified, and whose precise purpose is unknown to him. The police operation, from the taking of the pictures to their actual and intended retention and use, must in my opinion be judged as a whole. Accordingly I am inclined to agree with Mr Westgate's submission recorded by the judge below as follows:
>
> 'It is impossible … to compartmentalise the taking of the photographs without regard to the circumstances in which they were taken, the purposes of their retention, whether, for example, it is intended thereby to identify the individual and whether there is proper and certain legal control over the photography as a whole. He submits that here the claimant's identity was discovered and there was a degree of systematic gathering of information about CAAT[21] activity and its members. He pointed also to evidence from the claimant's solicitor of other occasions when members of CAAT have been similarly photographed.'

[7.20] Laws LJ concluded, looking at the matter as whole, that whilst there was no 'rigid class of case in which, once it is shown that the state actions complained of (such as taking photographs) are expected and unsurprising, Article 8 ECHR cannot be engaged',[22] in this case there was enough to engage Article 8:

> … it is important to recognise that State action may confront and challenge the individual as it were out of the blue. It may have no patent or obvious contextual explanation, and in that case it is not more apparently rational than arbitrary, nor more apparently justified than unjustified. In this case it consists in the taking and retaining of photographs, though it might consist in other acts. The Metropolitan Police, visibly and with no obvious cause, chose to take and keep photographs of an individual going about his lawful business in the streets of London. This action is a good deal more than the snapping of the shutter. The police are a State authority. And as I have said, the claimant could not and did not know why they were doing it and what use they might make of the pictures.

[21] The organisation to which the applicant, Mr Wood, belonged, and which was the subject of police interest.

[22] *R (Wood) v Commissioner of Police of the Metropolis* (n 11) [44]. The converse was also true: surprising and unexpected actions would not automatically engage Art 8 of the ECHR.

[7.21] Unlike the other two Judges (Dyson LJ and Lord Collins), Laws LJ considered that Article 8(2) rendered what would otherwise be an infringement not. That question is not directly in point at the present, for what is being considered is the perception/use borderline. Here, it is suggested that the dismissal of this distinction was an error.

[7.22] Separating perception from use is valuable because it enables there to be a clear focus on the question that follows: namely 'Is the use a misuse?'. In this case, if it is right to say that the mere taking of photographs is not even use, then one must consider what additional factors need to exist in order to render the case one of use. Then, in the light of that analysis, it is possible to focus on whether the use (if it *is* a use) constitutes a misuse.

[7.23] In this case, the conclusion that this was a case of *use* seems impossible to avoid. The police were taking the photographs for a distinct purpose, namely to keep track of members of an organisation that they were interested in. That is far more than perception.

[7.24] The question of whether retention constitutes use is returned to in Chapter 8,[23] but an answer is attempted now. Retention of information *without intended use* falls within perception, not use. Thus, if O(C) takes lots of photographs, stores them in an album or on a hard drive or on a cloud, with the intention of looking only at these photographs themselves, then this looks like perception. If, on the other hand, the photographs are catalogued by reference to name with a view to identifying individuals through face recognition software, then this is *use*, even if the use is only *intended* and does not actually take place.

[7.25] The question that then follows is whether that use (if it is a use) amounts to a misuse: although the Article 8(2) of the ECHR exemption is not directly read across into the Action, it is relevant in defining what constitutes misuse. Laws LJ identified a number of factors relevant to the question of misuse: (i) Mr Wood's acquiescence or consent; (ii) the overreaching of the police in terms of how they were tracking a group of interest to them, but in circumstances where the police were not actually breaking the law; (iii) precisely what the police would do when tracking the group.

[7.26] The point is that perception means (or ought to mean) something more than what is purely internal to C. It is a linguistic stretch, but a perception remains a perception even though it has an external manifestation. The problem is that the borderline based internal to C/external to C is much more straightforward than differentiating between different external manifestations of O(C)'s internal perception.

[23] Public records are an important aspect of state perception/use/misuse.

B. Perception does not really mean perception: It can be externally manifested

[7.27] The core meaning of *perception* is the case where C holds information in their mind and does nothing with it save think about it. In such a case, there is unequivocally no use. The question is, where C does something external with the perception, whether that *inevitably* implies use or whether it is necessary to stretch the meaning of perception to certain limited external manifestations of C's perception in order to achieve the appropriate balance between A's interest in privacy and C's own freedoms.

[7.28] It will be rare for perception to be limited to the case of no external manifestation. C will in many cases *do* something with their perception. Unless that doing is purely internal to C, it may very well look like use. By way of example, what happens where C, for their own personal use, writes information down or incorporates it in a database? What is the position where, when doing so, C utilises a third-party provider, because the information is stored in a cloud, online? Provided that C is only using external means to store their perception for later use and recollection, what is being suggested that such use (and *senso strictu* it *is* use) is *better* classified as a case of perception. Thus, there are a number of cases – including this – where the meaning of perception needs to be 'stretched' so as properly to articulate the borderline between perception and use.

[7.29] A label should not be allowed to dictate the substance of the law. The use of the term *perception* has been helpful, because it has enabled us to understand that information is primarily understood as *someone's perception of something*.[24] The term perception may not be the best, but it is the term alighted upon in this book. The 'internal to C' nature of perception is part of the 'baggage' that comes with the ordinary meaning of the word. All this means is that the term or label adopted is not quite apposite to the matter being articulated, and the precise meaning of the label needs to be further refined, even though that means translating a word of ordinary English into a term of art. That is what is being done now. The label is just that – a convenient shorthand for a line of demarcation that is not without its complexity.

C. The perception/use boundary elucidated

i. Rationale for reinterpreting 'perception'

[7.30] The question, then, is how far is the concept of 'perception' (or 'non-use') to be stretched? Obviously, this is an area that is ripe for legal development,

[24] See the discussion on Ch 3.

and it would be surprising if the areas considered below constituted a complete articulation. The Action is clearly undeveloped and must be allowed to evolve. The rationale for extending the meaning of perception beyond the purely internal is this: if a 'use' is reclassified as a 'perception', there is no prospect of A contending that C is liable under the Action. Misuse implies use, and if we are reallocating what might otherwise be regarded as use into the realm of perception, which is not actionable, we are limiting A's rights of action. In short, we are considering the extent to which A's rights should be limited in order to ensure O(C)'s rights are sufficiently protected.

[7.31] It will be suggested that uses that are incidental to O(C)'s perception ought to be regarded as exactly that – incidental to perception, and therefore not use. It has been repeatedly emphasised that C's perception is unimpeachable in law. Freedom of belief and thought, at the most fundamental level, preclude this being actionable. Uses incidental to C's perception should not even arguably amount to *misuse*. Defining these uses as a 'non-use' and so extending the meaning of perception achieves this objective.

[7.32] There are two 'non-uses' which, it is suggested, should operate to stretch the meaning of perception for the purposes of the Action:

(1) *Retention without use.* On any view,[25] the case where C photographs A but does nothing with the image recorded except keep the photograph or image with no intention of using it in any way ought not to amount to use. Of course, an intended use can be enjoined if a misuse.[26]
(2) *Internal affairs, where C is part of a complex organisation U.* Anticipating a future discussion in the context of undertakings (in Chapter 9), the question arises as to whether O(C) is liable if, within the context of an organisation's internal affairs, and consistent with O(C)'s duties to and in that organisation, O(C) communicates their perception *internally*.[27]

These two 'non-uses' are considered as extensions to the meaning of perception in the following paragraphs.

ii. Extension 1: Personal use by O(C) of A's private information is better classified as perception

[7.33] The law in this area is undeveloped, but even where information is personal and private to A it would be unduly invasive to C to restrain C from

[25] The same should be true, *mutatis mutandis*, of information other than photographs. The camera image is illustrative, not definitive.

[26] In other words, if A fears that C will use the material to infringe A's rights, then *quia timet* relief is possible.

[27] This is the so-called 'internal management rule': see eg *Royal British Bank v Turquand* (1865) 6 E&B 327; 119 ER 474.

all external acts regarding this information. There are not merely freedom of expression issues, but wider issues regarding liberty of the subject. A similar issue arises in the case of copyright. *Copinger and Skone James* notes:[28]

> Chapter III of Pt I of the 1988 Act, containing over 60 sections, permits certain acts which would otherwise amount to copyright infringement. Since the 1988 Act was originally enacted, various sections have been added and a large number of amendments made in order to comply with European legislation. These 'permitted acts' are in general designed to balance the interests of copyright owners with the public interest, and some of the provisions show up important conflicts between the two. More generally, the permitted acts should be viewed alongside the requirement of the taking of a 'substantial part' in relation to infringement and the restrictive way in which some of the exclusive rights of the copyright owner are drawn, in particular the exclusive right to perform a work, which only applies to performances in public …

[7.34] Similarly:[29]

> The law has never allowed a defendant to escape liability on the grounds that they have not copied the claimant's work exactly; less than complete copying has always been an infringement. In this, it has been said that the underlying rationale of the law of copyright is to protect and adequately reward the interests of authors and copyright owners and to prevent others from unfairly appropriating the benefit of the effort, skill and labour which went into a work's creation. On the other hand, it has never been the law that copying of any part of a work, no matter how small, is unlawful; copyright should not be allowed to become an instrument of oppression and extortion …

[7.35] Just as in the case of copyright, there must be a level of 'give and take' between privacy and other fundamental freedoms. On this basis, purely private use is not capable of being misuse and should for that reason be classed as perception. Private use is the external manifestation of C's perception but where no third party gets to perceive the information. Thus, if C keeps a handwritten diary for private purposes or records their perceptions in some similar way, C is entitled to do so. (Of course, if C fails to take reasonable care of what is still A's private information, there will be liability: see further below.)

[7.36] Private use includes cases where C uses a third-party provider for the recording of their perception. These days a great deal of data is held in this way, and to differentiate between a handwritten diary and a typed diary saved to a 'cloud' is irrational. As will be seen, such third-party providers will themselves be obliged to protect A's privacy, and the only way they will be able to do so is by respecting the limits that O(C) is subject to in order to respect A's privacy.

[28] G Harbottle et al, *Copinger and Skone James on Copyright*, Vol 1, 19th edn (Sweet and Maxwell, 2025) [8-01].

[29] ibid [6-43].

The fact that there may be a contractual term between O(C) and the third party regarding the information will be no protection to that third party.

[7.37] Suppose that O(C) has a contract with C[30] (a cloud-storage provider) for the provision of data storage. Suppose also that C's standard terms and conditions state that C may use the data so stored by O(C) for any and all purposes. If the data that O(C) stores (unwisely, it would seem, but then who reads standard terms and conditions?) is not private information at all, or only information personal to and private to O(C), then C may have a good defence if O(C) were to object to C's release of their private information for publication to the Daily Bugle online.[31] However, matters are very different if the information that O(C) stores is information that is personal to and private to A. O(C) is safe from the Action A might bring, because they have not strayed beyond perception (in the wider sense here being considered). But C, who *are* using A's private information will have no such defence; and also no contractual defence, for A will not have licensed the use by C of what is *their* information.

[7.38] There is thus a strong case for saying that retention without intended use and without actual use is 'only' perception and does not count as use. However, the limits of this need to be carefully considered:

(1) C, for reasons described, can only be a natural person. It would be concerning if this exception extended to undertakings. As will be seen from Chapter 9, retention by undertakings is differently treated.
(2) It is quite possible to maintain records with the intention of accessing them as and when the need arises. This is not 'non-use' retention in the sense here being used but constitutes actual use. Where that need involves dealing with the information in a manner that involves third parties, then we are no longer within the realms of perception, but have crossed the line to use. Suppose C retains CCTV footage so that if a crime is committed on their property, the footage can be reviewed and passed to the police. If no crime is committed, the footage is retained unused. This is not retention, but contingent use – and cannot be classed as perception, even in its wider sense.

iii. Extension 2: Internal affairs, where C is part of an undertaking

[7.39] Undertakings, and their exposure as defendants to an Action, is the subject matter of Chapter 9. Chapter 9 considers the extent to which C's thoughts, words and deeds can be attributed to undertaking U so as to render U

[30] In this example, O(C) and C are clearly different persons.
[31] Whether there is in fact a good defence is considered further in Ch 11.

liable to an Action brought by A, that liability arising because the relationship C(U) renders U liable for C's conduct.

[7.40] This attribution of C's conduct to U means that a gloss to the meaning of 'perception' is possible, extending it. The gloss is obviously closely tied to the analysis in Chapter 9, but it is necessary to anticipate.

[7.41] Where C is acting as part of an undertaking U and is using information pursuant to undertaking U's legitimate internal management, it is better to focus on the attribution of C's conduct to U than on C's individual conduct. The question is really one of who is liable to A under the Action, C or U or both?

[7.42] Where C is perceiving and using A's personal information pursuant to their duties to U (as, say, an employee), acting within the 'scope of their employment' (as the lawyers would say[32]), then C's use or misuse of A's personal information should not necessarily be treated as C's wrongdoing, but as that of U. There are two different cases that are described in Chapter 9, and summarised here:

(1) *Vicarious liability.* This is where C commits all elements of the Action, enabling A to claim against C. In other words, C has perceived information personal to and private to A, and has not merely used it, but misused it. In these circumstances, C is liable to A. But, if C is part of undertaking U, the relationship C(U) may be sufficient to render U *additionally* liable to A. A thus has two claims: (i) against C (primary liability); (ii) against U by virtue of the C(U) relationship (secondary or vicarious liability).
(2) *Primary liability by way of attribution.* Now suppose a more complex case. C_1, C_2 and C_3 are all employees of Undertaking U, which is engaged in a process of misusing the private information of A_1 to A_n. C_1 harvests the private information of A_1 to A_n, C_2 processes it and C_3 uses it in circumstances amounting to misuse. It may be that A_1 to A_n can argue that there is an infringement of the Action at each stage of the process, and that the Action is maintainable against each of C_1 to C_3. But that seems like quite a fragile claim, particularly if (as will be suggested is the case) the conduct of C_1 to C_3 can be attributed to U such that *even if* no individual action is maintainable against C_1 to C_3, the cumulative conduct of C_1 to C_3 renders U personally liable to A. In this case, U is the primary defendant, and C_1 to C_3 are not liable at all.

[7.43] In the second case, C_1 to C_3's use of A's information should not be regarded as use by the Cs at all, *provided that* there is a claim against undertaking

[32] The basis for attribution is complex, and not examined further here. See Ch 9.

U by virtue of the C(U) relationship that subsists. This gloss to the concept of perception focuses explicitly on the undertaking U that is overall in charge of the process by which A's private information is misused. It localises liability in the enterprise that is monetising (or otherwise benefiting) from A's private information. In such circumstances, the cogs in the machine (C_1 to C_3) should not be exposed to an Action by A. An extended definition of 'perception' achieves this. As will be seen in Chapter 9, there is a great deal of law (drawn from other areas) that supports this reasoning.

IV. The Boundary between Use and Misuse

A. A recap: The 'control' test

[7.44] In Chapter 6, the concept of private information personal to A was explored. At paragraph [6.143], the following test was expounded:

> Information is private to A where that information is (i) personal to A and (ii) where a reasonable person, in the position of A, would have a reasonable expectation of control over the use or exploitation of A's private information.

[7.45] There is a nexus between A's right of control and C's infringement of A's rights by misusing A's private information. Where A has no reasonable expectation of control, C's use is just that: legitimate use. Where A has a reasonable expectation of control, C's use (absent A's consent: see Chapter 11) constitutes a misuse and an infringement of A's rights. As noted in Chapter 6, this is no more than the Hohfeldian parity between A's right and C's obligation.

[7.46] As Lord Atkin noted in *Donoghue v Stevenson*,[33] speaking of the duty of care in tort:

> [i]t is remarkable how difficult it is to find in the English authorities statements of general application defining the relations between parties that give rise to the duty. The courts are concerned with the particular relations which come before them in actual litigation, and it is sufficient to say whether the duty exists in those circumstances. The result is that the courts have been engaged upon an elaborate classification of duties as they exist in respect of property, whether real or personal, with further divisions as to ownership, occupation or control …

[7.47] Whilst it is understandable how courts can vanish down the rabbit hole of excessive classification and complexity, the genius of the common law is, on occasion, to be able to look to unifying general principle, borne out of the detail. To quote Lord Atkin once more, '[a]t present I content myself with

[33] *Donoghue v Stevenson* [1932] 1 AC 562, 579.

pointing out that in English law there must be, and is, some general conception of relations giving rise to a duty of care, of which the particular cases found in the books are but instances'.[34]

[7.48] Although well-known, Lord Atkin's classic statement of principle deserves quotation:[35]

> The liability for negligence, whether you style it such or treat it as in other systems as a species of 'culpa', is no doubt based upon a general public sentiment of moral wrongdoing for which the offender must pay. But acts or omissions which any moral code would censure cannot in a practical world be treated so as to give a right to every person injured by them to demand relief. In this way rules of law arise which limit the range of complainants and the extent of their remedy. The rule that you are to love your neighbour becomes in law, you must not injure your neighbour; and the lawyer's question, Who is my neighbour? receives a restricted reply. You must take reasonable care to avoid acts or omissions which you can reasonably foresee would be likely to injure your neighbour. Who, then, in law is my neighbour? The answer seems to be – persons who are so closely and directly affected by my act that I ought reasonably to have them in contemplation as being so affected when I am directing my mind to the acts or omissions which are called in question.

[7.49] Although a general duty to avoid injuring A's rights of privacy is *not* being contended for – we are in the realms of *property* not *obligation* – Lord Atkin's words support an approach that presumes a property right in private information perceived by C, which right is *infringed* where the control test is met.

B. Two cases of misuse: Inadvertent/negligent and deliberate/intentional

[7.50] Two cases of misuse now need to be considered. There are here termed 'inadvertent misuse' and 'deliberate misuse'. Inadvertent misuse arises where C does not intend to use A's private information, but (inadvertently) causes that information to be misused. For example, C_1 takes an intimate photograph of A with their mobile phone and inadvertently sends it not to A but to C_2. Another example: C, for legitimate reasons, keeps and processes information about A_1 to A_n. Unfortunately, C's systems are insufficiently robust, and a rogue, C_1, is able to 'hack' into C's systems and 'steal' the private information about A_1 to A_n. C's liability for inadvertent misuse is considered in Section V of this chapter.

[7.51] Deliberate misuse arises where C's use of the information is not inadvertent but deliberate. There is no accidental 'leak': the use was deliberate or

[34] ibid 580.
[35] ibid.

intended. It must be stressed that C does not have to be subjectively aware that their perception is of A's private information. The definition of private information is not subjective: it is objective. Where C publishes A's private information deliberately, it is no answer to A's claim for C to assert that they were subjectively unaware that the information was (i) personal to A or (ii) private. These questions were considered in Chapter 6, and the analysis is not repeated here. C's liability for deliberate misuse is considered in Section VI of this chapter.

C. The 'public interest' and 'chains of title'

[7.52] Two further discrete areas related to the use/misuse discussion are set out at the end of this chapter:

(1) First, the extent to which what would otherwise be a misuse by C can nevertheless be justified 'in the public interest'. This is considered in Section VII.
(2) Second, the extent to which a later recipient of A's private information is affected by the Action. Take the case where C_1 has perceived A's private information, and misused it, in circumstances where that misuse is the passing of the information on to C_2. To what extent is C_2 liable under the Action? This is considered in Section VIII.

V. Inadvertent Misuse

A. Meaning

[7.53] Inadvertent misuse is the outcome where C has breached their obligation to look after A's private information. It is the liability that obtains if – in breach of this obligation – A's private information is inadvertently (without deliberation) used. This, it is suggested, is an obligation analogous to 'bailment'.[36] If C fails to protect private information in their control, then there will be liability for its misuse (ie inadvertent publication) if the information is private to A. In framing this obligation, the law relating to the Action can appropriately draw on the law of bailment.

[7.54] By definition, inadvertent use of information cannot be deliberate. All other non-inadvertent uses of information will, to some extent, be deliberate or intentional. The obligation to look after information – to avoid the accidental

[36] Bailment is a legal relationship where one party (the bailee) temporarily possesses personal property belonging to another party (the bailor). Bailment can only operate by analogy here, because it applies to tangible property only, whereas private information, being intangible, cannot be possessed. On bailment generally, see N Palmer, *Palmer on Bailment*, 3rd edn (Sweet & Maxwell, 2009).

use of information that is in fact private – is not a strict one. Liability does not attach to C for the accidental misuse of private information, provided C has acted with reasonable skill and care. Where such reasonable skill and care is lacking, liability to A may attach, assuming the information used is private and personal to A. It will be noted that this type of misuse – accidental, but negligent – triggers liability provided the requirements of (i) information that is (ii) personal to A and (iii) private are met.

B. The obligation to look after personal information: An analogy with bailment

[7.55] As Palmer makes clear, bailment and the tort of conversion protect tangible and not intangible property.[37] It is not suggested that an action for breach of bailment nor a claim in conversion can lie in relation to private information. The remedy, as ought to be obvious by now, is the Action. But what constitutes 'misuse' can helpfully be informed (by analogy) by the law of bailment. In particular, the duties on C to protect A's private information from misuse (eg inadvertent publication) is one that is very close to the obligations of a bailee to their bailor.

[7.56] There are many different forms of bailment, and it would be unwise to draw the analogy too tightly. Several points can be noted. The position of C will generally be closest to that of an unrewarded custodian of goods,[38] for as a general proposition C has no control over what they perceive and should not be subject to unduly onerous obligations to A. Palmer notes that '[a]ccording to Holt CJ, a depositary whose misconduct is neither fraudulent nor wilful is liable only for gross neglect of the chattel',[39] but that there is a march towards a higher standard 'to exercise reasonable care, having regard to all the circumstances of the case'.[40] Provided the fundamental importance of ensuring C is not unduly constrained in their freedom of thought and expression, it perhaps does not

[37] ibid [30-001], [30-003]–[30-004]. In particular, in *OBG v Allan* [2007] UKHL 21, the House of Lords made clear that the tort of conversion did not serve to protect intangible property. As Palmer notes (at [30-006]), '[t]his decision raises a serious bar to the extension of bailment to intangibles. If conversion (which can be committed by a defendant who is not in possession) does not apply to intangible matter, such material might well fall beyond a claim for breach of bailment, to which relationship possession is regarded as crucial. Moreover, even if the orthodox limitation of bailment to tangible property were in principle reversible, one might argue that the main statutory cause of action available to a bailor, that of conversion, under section 2(2) of the Torts (Interference with Goods) Act 1977, would remain unavailable in this context. The question would then arise whether a discrete action for breach of bailment could produce a remedy for invasions of entrusted intangible property that was at odds with, and could overleap, the denial of a remedy in conversion …'.

[38] Palmer (n 36) Ch 10.

[39] ibid [10-005].

[40] ibid [10-008].

matter how the standard is expressed, but (given the human rights questions) a standard of gross neglect is probably better as a starting point.

[7.57] Where there is a relationship of borrowing, the duties of the borrower are higher.[41] Where there is some form of bilateral relationship between A and C, as where C's perception has been obtained with A's consent and C's perception has been derived by way of that consent, the standard of care is likely to be – and should be – higher. According to Palmer, the duties of a borrower are 'fourfold: to take proper care of the chattel, to use it for the purpose for which it was lent, to return it at the appointed time and to restore it in a proper condition'.[42] The duty is a high one, as Lord Holt noted in *Coggs v Barnard*:[43]

> ... the borrower is bound to the strictest care and diligence ... because the bailee has a benefit by the use of them, so as if the bailee be guilty of the least neglect, he will be answerable ... Bracton says, the bailee must use the utmost care, but yet he shall not be chargeable, where there is such a force as he cannot resist.

[7.58] Where there is involuntary bailment, Palmer notes that the involuntary bailee whose conduct does not amount to conversion will only rarely be liable for any loss or damage occurring to the goods.[44] Nevertheless, this conventional view is regarded as too low a standard and has been criticised. Palmer suggests that:[45]

> ... an acceptable compromise would be to extract from the involuntary bailee a variable standard of care according to what is reasonable in all the circumstances of the case ...

Involuntary bailment is a difficult analogy here, since of course conversion does not apply in the case of intangibles.

[7.59] As has been noted, analogy is at the same time both helpful and dangerous. Relying on analogy and conscious of a dearth of law in this area, although misuse of private information will often involve a conscious decision by C to use information that they perceive, and whilst it is clear that mere perception cannot constitute either use or misuse, there is an important middle ground where information is inadvertently or accidently used, such that A's property rights in their private information are infringed.

[7.60] Most cases of use or misuse will involve elements of deliberation, as where the information is deliberately used (whether or not there is a state of

[41] ibid Ch 12.
[42] ibid [12-022].
[43] *Coggs v Barnard* (1703) 2 Ld Raym 909; 92 ER 107, 111.
[44] Palmer (n 36) [13-006].
[45] ibid [13-012].

mind as regards whether the information is personal to and private to A). The question is whether in inadvertence cases the mere fact of use is enough (strict liability) or whether some mental element is required (eg negligence).

[7.61] Normally infringements of property rights result in a form of strict liability – the invasion of the right is enough to engender liability, without any need for an intention to infringe or lack of reasonable care.

[7.62] In the case of non-deliberate (inadvertent) misuse, it is important that there be a controlling limiting factor like negligence. Otherwise there is likely to be a constraint on freedom of expression and other important rights of C. Bailment thus provides a helpful analogy to draw upon.

[7.63] It is not right – given the nature of information – to frame any duty around not 'damaging' the information. It is impossible damage an intangible, particularly where one is speaking of a perception in C. However, the duty can be framed around use and control. Where information is private and personal to A, there is a duty on C, who perceives it, not to misuse that information inappropriately when it is under their control. That includes taking reasonable steps to ensure that the information is kept safe from abuse or misuse, including by others. Naturally, what constitute 'reasonable steps' is going to be very fact dependent.

VI. Deliberate Misuse

A. Deliberation

[7.64] As should be clear from the foregoing discussion, deliberation simply means that the use of the private information was not inadvertent or accidental. Deliberation does not imply knowledge or intention to infringe on the part of C. The *only* question is whether the (deliberate) use is justified or whether it constitutes a misuse.

B. Getting granular about 'misuse'

[7.65] Misuse, as we have seen, is determined by the control test articulated at paragraph [7.44]. As a general test it provides high level guidance to judges seeking to determine the individual case. But the guidance is, inevitably, high level, because the test is a general one. The question is whether greater granularity can be injected into the definition of misuse so as to aid predictability and legal certainty without unduly undermining the importance of deciding each case on its own facts and without rendering the test overly complex. This tension between general legal certainty and justice in the individual case is perennial.

[7.66] The factors that are relevant to an assessment of whether A has a reasonable expectation of control can briefly be enumerated (this is done immediately below in paragraph [7.67]), and further articulation is not particularly productive, save in the last of these factors (number (5)), which deserves significant expansion.

C. Factors going to the 'control' test

[7.67] The five factors which serve to inform the application of the control test can be stated as follows:

(1) *Confidentiality or ubiquity.* Although there is a misconceived equation of privacy with secrecy, nevertheless the confidentiality of the private information or the extent to which it is publicly known matters.
(2) *The nature or characteristics of A.* A will have characteristics which, if objectively ascertainable, will render a reasonable expectation of control greater or less.
(3) *The nature of the perception.* By which is meant, subject matter *sensu stricto*. Some subject matters are obviously more sensitive than others.
(4) *Public or private space, overt and covert 'harvesting' of perception.* Several interlocking factors arise here:
    (i) Was C's perception obtained in circumstances where A was observed in a public space or in a private space?
    (ii) Assuming a *public space*, was the collection of data overt or covert? Overt collection of data is the case where A is at least aware that information about them is being captured. Even where A is in principle aware, A is most unlikely to have more than an abstract idea that their information is being harvested and used. A CCTV notice displayed in a public place or a car park may (as part of the conditions of use) say that data is collected, or a software upgrade on a mobile phone might say that personal information is collected, but A will probably not know what data will be gathered, how it is retained, or how it is used. A will find it difficult to obtain these details.
    (iii) More problematic are those cases where A does not even know of the harvesting of information, as in the case of the long-lensed photographer, or the app that tracks movements, etc, or the covert intelligence gathering of the intelligence services. In such cases, A cannot even begin to protect themselves from their private information being collected.
    (iv) Even where the information capture is overt, the capture may not readily be avoidable. The question must be whether A can realistically either object to the capture or else (if so advised) avoid the capture.

(5) *The manner in which C obtained or derived the perception: the relationship between A and C.* This factor considers whether the perception in C derived from circumstances that were permissive (ie A allowed the access) or public (ie where A ventured out into domains that carried no expectation of privacy).

[7.68] There is no need to expand upon factors (1)–(4): obviously, they are factual in nature, and the weight that attaches to them will turn on the facts. There is some overlap between factor (4) and factor (5). These two factors are, however, considering different aspects of C's perception. Factor (4) is looking at where A was when the perception was harvested. If in a public place, then A's right of control will be more attenuated than if the harvesting occurred in a private space. In a public place, A's powers of control will vary. Factor (5) – which warrants and receives expansion below – considers the *relationship* between A and C and describes how that relationship informs the control test. Four different relationships can be identified:

- *Transfer or licence by A.* The private information may have been transferred or licensed by A to C, in which case the question is whether C's use falls within the proper scope of that which A has conveyed or licensed to C.
- *Ancillary to work C is providing to A.* Although there is (in this case) no explicit formal conveyance or licence, the use to which C is putting A's private information is necessarily incidental to the performance of a service (or supply of a product) which either: (i) C is obliged to perform for A; or (ii) A is *voluntarily* using.
- *Lawful capture of information, but for C's own purposes.* Leaving on one side the question of A's privacy (which is the question at issue), the private information has been lawfully captured by C and is being used by C for their *own* purposes (which may or may not be commercial).
- *Unlawful capture of information.* The private information has been unlawfully captured by C (disregarding any question of privacy itself).

These four different relations are worthy of further consideration, which follows now.

D. The relationship between A and C: Four cases

i. Transfer or licence; and the question of consent

[7.69] Warren and Brandeis refer to consent as a limitation on A's right of privacy.[46] Consent is obviously relevant to C's ability to use A's private information: were

[46] S Warren and L Brandeis, 'The Right to Privacy' (1890) 4 *Harvard Law Review* 193, 218.

A to claim against C for infringement, consent would be a 'defence'. But the term has been placed in inverted commas for a reason. To call consent a defence, or even a limitation on A's rights, is to mistake the essential fact that A, in transferring their property to C, or in licensing C in their use, is *exercising the rights of an owner*. There is, in this case, a bilateral relationship between A and C – really A and B to use the designations in the *dramatis personae*[47] – whereby A is no longer entitled to complain of C's actions either (i) because A is no longer the owner; or (ii) because A has licensed B to do precisely that which B is doing. There may be disputes about the validity and scope of the transfer or the licence, but (assuming such disputes do not exist or are resolved in favour of C) A really has nothing to say by way of complaint. A has consented, and there is an end to it. The 'defence' of consent is really a reflection of A's exercise of their ownership rights.

[7.70] These matters of transfer and licence are considered in Chapter 11. For the present, what must be noted is the obvious relevance of this point to the question of misuse. Absent A exercising the rights of an owner, C would be infringing. But because A has exercised their rights as owner of private information to transfer or to exploit, B's (as they become) use is a legitimate use because A has exercised their rights as owner and thereby consented to B's use of A's private information.

[7.71] It is at this point that it needs to be stressed just how dangerously slippery the question of consent can be: for 'consent' is often used by a defendant as a means of defeating A's claim where A has *not* exercised their rights as an owner so as to enable the defendant's use.

[7.72] It is very important that we do not confuse A's exercise of their rights as owner so as to enable C to do something they could not otherwise do (the case presently under consideration), and the case where C is doing something they can lawfully do, but which A is at best acquiescing in. There is an enormous difference between acquiescence and consent and an unfortunate tendency to elide the two. This is best exemplified by reference to (of all things) car parks.

[7.73] Data as regards car registration and the images from CCTV cameras are used in combination by the owners of *private* parking places in order to police parking infractions. In other words, we are watched through CCTV and when we infringe the rules by parking for too long or in the wrong place, a private body (the owner of the car park or their agent) will examine those images,[48] find the offending car's registration mark, and obtain the details of the registered 'keeper'[49] from the Driver and Vehicle Licensing Agency (DVLA).

[47] See paras [1.37]–[1.44].
[48] This will likely be done automatically, by image recognition, but nothing turns on this.
[49] The DVLA's register is not one of ownership, and provides no assurance as to title.

[7.74] The parking infringement is enforced by access to two types of information about A: the CCTV image (which renders the number plate) and the registration data (which renders the identity of the registered keeper of the car). In neither case has A specifically consented to their data being used by C, the owner of the car park.

[7.75] The DVLA is a state entity and so its use of A's data falls for consideration in Chapter 8. But it is relevant for the purposes of this example. Drivers and the operators of motor vehicles are obliged to provide information to the DVLA. The DVLA's annual report and accounts describe its role as follows:[50]

> We are one of the most advanced large scale digital organisations in government.
>
> We are proud to be a centre of excellence for IT and digital skills and the majority of the services we provide are available digitally. We deal with billions of digital interactions every year which support a wide range of customers, stakeholders and businesses.
>
> We are responsible for maintaining accurate records of more than **52 million** drivers in Great Britain and more than **46 million** vehicles across the United Kingdom. We are also responsible for the collection and enforcement of Vehicle Excise Duty (VED), with **£7.8 billion** passed to HM Treasury during this reporting year.
>
> Those who own or drive a vehicle need to regularly use our services. Our customers rely on us to make sure those services are quick and easy to use. Whether they need to tax their vehicle, renew a driving licence, tell us about a medical condition, change their address on a driving licence and vehicle registration certificate, order a duplicate registration certificate, buy a personalised registration number or register a brand new or imported vehicle, it can all be done online.
>
> In addition to our day-to-day dealings with the public, which is the majority of our customer transactions, we work closely with a wide range of stakeholders. Close collaboration with industry, charities, the police, medical professionals and other government departments enables us to develop services that work for them. It also allows us to securely share information to support digital services across government and to help combat driver and vehicle-related crime.

[7.76] This information sharing includes providing to privately run car park operators the registered address for vehicles that breach the parking conditions:

> **Example**[51]
>
> The DVLA provided this response on 8 May 2012 to a Freedom of Information request by Mr Watson:
>
> Dear Mr Walton,

[50] DVLA, *Annual Report & Accounts 2023–2024*, HC 533, at 6.

[51] This example derives from a Freedom of Information request made of the DVLA regarding the sale of driver personal details, which is set out at www.whatdotheyknow.com/request/dvla_selling_personal_informatio, last accessed 21 August 2025.

Thank you for your email of 30 April about the release of information to third parties. We are responding to you under routine business and not through the terms of The Freedom of Information Act 2000.

We will answer your questions in turn, Questions 3 & 4 are answered together –

1. Under what authority is the DVLA allowed to pass on or sell personal details to third parties, without first seeking permission from the people whose data it wishes to sell?

The law allows the DVLA to disclose vehicle keeper information to those who can demonstrate a reasonable cause for requiring it. Reasonable cause is not defined in legislation but the Government's policy is that it should relate to the vehicle or its use, following incidents where there may be liability on the part of the driver. Guidance on what constitutes reasonable cause is published online at www.direct.gov.uk/motoring.

The release of information under this legislation is not based on the consent of the data subject. Regulation 27 provides a legal gateway for the release of information. Disclosure in these circumstances does not breach the Data Protection Act and the Information Commissioner's Office is fully aware that data held on the DVLA's records is released in this way.

The fees levied by the DVLA for Fee Paying Enquiries are set to recover the costs of processing requests and ensure that the cost is borne by the requester and not passed onto the taxpayer.

2. Why does this practice not contravene the data protection act?

The most recent audit by the Information Commissioners Office judged the DVLA's procedures to offer high assurance that processes to mitigate the risks of non-compliance with the Data Protection Act are in place.

3. The private parking business is unregulated and riddled with poor practice and inappropriate enforcement, the business does not exist to regulate parking, it is merely a means to issue 'fines' to motorists. The fact that the DVLA facilitates this practice makes it complicit in this disgraceful and dishonest behaviour. So what is the justification for the DVLA in allowing these companies access to personal data?

4. It is well known (and proven) that in some cases, the information is being accessed by disreputable companies or those with criminal connections, so why are there no safeguards in place to ensure this does not happen?

It is the motorist's choice to park a vehicle on private land and their responsibility to ensure that they do so in accordance with the terms and conditions set out on signage at the entrance and around the car park. The DVLA considers it to be a reasonable cause for businesses and landowners to receive vehicle keeper details where there has been an alleged breach of these terms and conditions. I am sure you will appreciate that if this were not the case, motorists would be able to park with disregard for the law or the rights of the landowner without fear of being held to account for their actions.

The DVLA has a range of measures in place to ensure that all companies are subject to the appropriate controls and safeguards. All car parking companies requesting keeper data must be members of a DVLA Accredited Trade

Association, which has a mandatory code of practice that all members must adhere to. The British Parking Association (BPA) is the appropriate Accredited Trade Association for the parking industry and its code of practice is published on their website at www.britishparking.co.uk.

The BPA code of practice must be adhered to by all members in order to maintain their membership. The code of practice is strictly monitored by the BPA, as this is a condition of their accreditation. If they fail to police their code they could lose their accreditation and their members would lose their ability to request DVLA data.

5. I have never given my permission to the DVLA to allow my personal details to be passed on or sold to third parties and I strongly object to this practice. How do I stop the DVLA from passing on my personal details?

To help ensure that personal data obtained in the process of registering a vehicle is processed fairly, the DVLA advises vehicle keepers of how their data will be used and where it may be disclosed. The information leaflet INS 160 contains an explanation on the release of data. This information is also contained on the website at www.dft.gov.uk/dvla/data

The Agency would not be able to justify withholding personal information from third parties able to demonstrate reasonable cause without evidence that such disclosure would cause unwarranted and substantial distress or damage.

In exceptional circumstances, when an individual is at particular risk, a marker may be put against a record to highlight this risk to the staff member considering the request for information. In these circumstances, the individual concerned may be contacted before the data is disclosed in order to bring the request to their attention. However, for DVLA to put a marker on the vehicle record, they would be required to supply evidence to support their request and supply the registration mark(s) of their vehicle(s).

If you wish to have this marker added to your record(s), you should write to Vehicle Enquiry Section, DVLA, Longview Road, Morriston, Swansea SA99 1AJ. You will need to provide the vehicle registration mark(s) of your vehicle(s). I should point out that any marker would apply only to the specific vehicle(s) requested. Should you later become the registered keeper of another vehicle, you would be required to inform the Agency separately of the need to add the marker to the new vehicle record.

[7.77] It is clear from this that the DVLA regarded the data provided to it as 'its' information, which it could monetise within broad limits. This event – in 2012 – was done by a responsible state actor that had considered its obligations under the ECHR and the GDPR. The DVLA's then justification that 'reasonable cause' to disclose information included that the information 'should relate to the vehicle or its use, following incidents where there may be liability on the part of the driver' is a justification to provide a speeding car's registered address to the police for investigation and prosecution; but to enable a private, commercial, entity to levy a parking fine seems to be stretching the point.

[7.78] There were obviously some doubts as to the propriety of this, for this case has now been placed on a statutory footing. That makes matters worse, not better, because what was questionable initially becomes established orthodoxy, without examination of the underlying values or issues. The somewhat euphemistically named Protection of Freedoms Act 2012 renders that which was questionable unquestionably lawful. The Explanatory Notes at the end of the Protection of Freedoms Act 2012 explain the thinking. The 2012 Act put on a statutory basis a number of information-related matters that had previously been dealt with at common law or left altogether unarticulated.[52] The Explanatory Notes state:

> [218] … the scheme[53] provides that, subject to certain conditions being met, the keeper or hirer of a vehicle may be liable for any unpaid parking charge that has arisen as a result of either: the driver of the vehicle having entered into a contract with a landowner and/or another person authorised to require payment of parking charges on the land in question; or, through the driver of the vehicle committing a trespass or other tort on land where parking is prohibited. The scheme is based on the legal analysis that a driver of a vehicle by parking on private land either expressly or implicitly accepts the landowner's offer to park (or that of a parking company acting as the landowner's agent), or prohibition on parking and agrees to comply with any terms and conditions (including any parking charges and the associated enforcement mechanism for those charges) advertised on a notice board at the entrance to and within the land. The driver may commit a trespass by parking on private land without permission or, if the terms and conditions of any agreement which the driver has implicitly accepted and not adhered to, then the driver may be in breach of that agreement. In either situation, whether the existence of a contract can be established or, alternatively, if the driver can be shown to have committed a tort, the Schedule envisages a situation where the vehicle can be 'ticketed' for charges due under the terms of that contract or for the pre-estimated damages resulting from the trespass.
>
> [219] Under the current law, parking providers wishing to enforce charges against drivers are able to obtain the details of the vehicle keeper from the DVLA if they are able to show 'reasonable cause' for wanting the information (so as to satisfy regulation 27(1)(e) of the Road Vehicles (Registration and Licensing) Regulations 2002 (SI 2002/2742)). A parking provider managing parking in accordance with industry best practice has reasonable cause to seek from the DVLA the keeper details of a vehicle in respect of parking related charges that have not been paid. The DVLA requires parking companies requesting keeper details for parking enforcement purposes to be members of an accredited trade association (the British Parking Association's

[52] In this way, our rights were silently eroded. What might, once, have been arguable as an unlawful infringement is – under the guise of the 'Protection of Freedoms' Act – rendered lawful or at least less unlawful. The lawfulness of these practices have not often been litigated, although that appears to be changing as car park owners increasingly seek to extract value from their property.

[53] Set out in the Protection of Freedoms Act 2012, s 56 and Sch 4.

Approved Operator Scheme is the only trade association currently so accredited). Whilst landowners and agents may seek to recover unpaid parking charges from vehicle keepers, as the law is currently understood to stand, any parking contract will be between the driver of a vehicle and the parking provider and any tort is committed by the driver of the vehicle. Accordingly, the keeper may not be liable in law for the charges incurred if he or she was not the driver at the time.

It is significant is that there is no express consideration of questions of privacy at all, even though privacy is the raison d'être of the 2012 Act.[54] Note also the references to 'consent', which is the matter presently under consideration.

[7.79] The same approach or attitude can be discerned in relation to C's culling of images of registration marks from CCTV. The use of CCTV in privately owned but publicly accessible spaces (eg car parks, shopping malls, etc) is not unlawful, but that fact does not necessarily justify using it in this way. It is concerning that the privacy issues of culling CCTV images and accessing DVLA data were not weighed against the understandable desire of a commercial parking operator to receive as many parking fines as possible, as cheaply as possible.[55] Clearly, when it conflicts with other values, privacy comes off second-best: even when the competing value is the private enforcement of parking penalties.

[7.80] What is concerning – and the reason for the present discussion – is how *consent* is used as the primary justification for the outcomes described. Consent is something that is emphasised in the Explanatory Notes to the Protection of Freedoms Act. If A chooses to park in C's car park, A will either do so without consent (and so trespass) or do so with consent, in which case a contract will generally arise (although of course C could simply give permission without a contract[56]). Where there is a contract, it may well contain provisions regarding C's use of A's private information. The terms and conditions – no doubt in small print online or on a board in the car park[57] – might articulate A's consent to being filmed on CCTV; and might even go so far as to provide A's consent to the release to C of information held by DVLA. It is, at this stage, important to

[54] The Explanatory Notes say at [20] that the Act was passed pursuant to the Coalition Government's 'commitment to introduce a "Freedom" Bill'. Whether the objective of the 2012 Act was to protect or enhance freedoms or circumscribes them is unclear, but the effect has been one of circumscription.

[55] The Explanatory Notes do not even articulate the position that there is a privacy question at all. It could be argued that the registration mark captured (along with other images) by CCTV and the keeper details kept by DVLA are *not* private information. That would be a surprising position, but would explain why there is no discussion of the weighing of competing interests. But even that position remains unarticulated.

[56] But we are not interested in gratuitous access to parking for present purposes.

[57] M Radin, *Boilerplate: the Fine Print, Vanishing Rights, and the Rule of Law* (Oxford University Press, 2013) 161–66 highlights the problems of consent that effectively deprive contract of its moral force as a creator of obligation.

differentiate between *consent* to the use of private information and *acquiescence* in the use of private information.

[7.81] At the end of this long example, we have arrived at an important distinction between *consent* and *acquiescence*:

- *Consent* refers to the case where A either transfers or licenses their private information to another, C. Consent so understood is considered in Chapter 11. Where there is such a transfer or licence then C obviously has a complete 'defence' to any claim A may bring, provided the use is within the scope of the transfer/licence. The parking terms and conditions that make express provision for the use of A's private information hypothesised in this paragraph are instances of *consent*.
- *Acquiescence* refers to the less formal case where A is aware of and in some sense acquiesces in C's use of their information, but neither transfers nor licenses the use of the private information. Thus, where the parking terms and conditions make no provision for the use of A's private information (so that this is not a case of consent), it might nevertheless be said that A was accepting of the steps that C might take to enforce any unpaid parking charges. Cases of *acquiescence* do not constitute a complete defence to any Action that A might bring. But acquiescence *does* come into play as a factor in determining whether a particular use constitutes a *misuse*. In other words, acquiescence is informative of the use/misuse borderline, whereas consent is determinative.

[7.82] Consent authorises a specific person to use A's personal information in a specific way. The consent has very precise limits or a very circumscribed ambit which will depend on the interpretation (or, as lawyers would say, 'construction') of the instrument of transfer or of the licence. Acquiescence is much less specific in nature. It articulates A's relationship to their own private information and the extent to which they are acknowledging that in the give-and-take of the modern world even information that is correctly classified as A's private information can be used by C without infringing A's rights. There is, in this regard, a link between A's privacy and A's participation in the quotidien affairs of the world which informs the ambit of what constitutes legitimate use by C.

[7.83] Take the use of a photograph of A as part of a 'deepfake' pornographic image created and published by C. It has already been suggested that the photograph used in this context is A's private information, and it is suggested that this would be a clear case of misuse on the part of C. But if C used the same photograph to publicise their restaurant, and A happened to be in the background of the picture enjoying a meal on C's premises, then this would be a much more marginal case. The important point is that these are not cases of 'consent', but fall into one or other of the three other categories we are coming to.

[7.84] The use or misuse of private information is significantly informed by the relationship between the private information and the use to which it is put. That link can sometimes best be described as acquiescence, and that is a helpful term *provided* acquiescence is in no way equated with consent.[58] By way of another example, A, a season ticket holder to Arsenal FC, will have to submit a good deal of personal information simply to access the ground (which these days is by way of electronic pass) – name, address, email address, mobile phone number, billing details, etc. A will provide this information voluntarily, because A wants to get to their seat through the electronic turnstiles at the ground. If Arsenal FC use the information only for these purposes, then A will have no grounds for complaint even if there is no contractual consent. But suppose Arsenal FC (without A's *consent*) seeks to monetise A's footballing enthusiasm by selling A's details and the fact that A is an Arsenal supporter to third parties interested in selling other products to A. Here, A's acquiescence in that specific use is less self-evident.

[7.85] Acquiescence is thus a slippery concept, as the car park example shows. To revert to that example, consent by A cannot be the justification for C's use of A's private information in at least two cases, no matter how wide the terms and conditions for car park use are drawn. Thus:

- In the case of trespass (where the driver simply enters upon C's property intending to infringe A's rights), C will certainly have rights against A but whether an implied contract comes into being is rather less open and shut. If there is only trespass, then A's consent to the use of their private information will not have been forthcoming.
- In many cases, the driver of the vehicle will not be the registered keeper, and C will have no way of knowing whether the driver is the registered keeper or whether the driver is someone other than the registered keeper. If A is not the driver but is the registered keeper, A will not be consenting to the use of their private information when the driver comes to use the car park. At most, the driver will be consenting to the use of *their* private information, but their private information will not include the details of the car's registered keeper. Thus, the car park owner will be requesting information of the DVLA using CCTV footage where consent is not established, and the DVLA will be providing that information without any assurance of actual consent.

[7.86] The basis for subordinating privacy to debt collection in this car park example can only be because of an unarticulated combination of (i) acquiescence and (ii) a sense that A's privacy interests rank second to C's interests in

[58] As with 'perception', the moment it becomes a term of art, it moves away from its central meaning, because defining its exact parameters (the 'penumbral' issues that hard questions throw up) inevitably means the focus is not on the core meaning, but on the borderlines between perception and non-perception and acquiescence and non-acquiescence.

debt collection. It is suggested that neither of these points can, without more, justify the outcome.

[7.87] Staying with CCTV, but moving from the car park to the shopping centre, the blurring of the acquiescence/consent line can again be illustrated. Many cases are presented as cases of consent, when they are no such thing, and where even the acquiescence of A is attenuated or tenuous.[59] Suppose a shopping mall states that the public spaces are subject to 24-hour CCTV. It might very well be said that A, by entering the shopping mall, is (i) consenting to be watched and (ii) consenting to whatever use the images are being put to. The second proposition (ii) simply does not follow from A's entry into the mall at all, but even proposition (i) cannot be right without exercising a baleful constraint on A's freedoms. If we are defining privacy as the ability to shape how the external world sees us and how we choose to present ourselves to the external world, then surely A ought to allowed to wander about in public without thereby 'consenting' to being watched. A should not be put to the choice of a hermit-like existence that is private or a normal life in public spaces, where privacy is set at naught.

[7.88] The answer is that this CCTV case is *not* one of consent at all, but one of acquiescence. Acquiescence will justify a narrow range of uses by C, but C cannot (simply by drawing up a wide policy of how CCTV is going to be used) automatically justify as a proper use every case falling with that policy. To be

[59] Sections 29–36 of the Protection of Freedoms Act 2012 make provision for the issuing of a Code of Practice for surveillance camera systems, together with the establishment of a 'Surveillance Camera Commissioner' to encourage compliance with the Code of Practice. The *Surveillance Camera Code of Practice* was issued in June 2013 under s 30 of the 2012 Act. It sets out (at [2.6]) various 'guiding principles', all of which are unexceptionable but vague:

'1. Use of a surveillance camera system must always be for a specified purpose which is in pursuit of a legitimate aim and necessary to meet an identified pressing need.
2. The use of a surveillance camera system must take into account its effect on individuals and their privacy with regular reviews to ensure its use remains justified.
3. There must be as much transparency in the use of a surveillance camera system as possible, including a published contact point for access to information and compaints.
4. There must be clear responsibility and accountability for all surveillance camera activities including images and information collected, held and used.
5. Clear rules, policies and procedures must be in place before a surveillance camera system is used, and these must be communicated to all who need to comply with them.
6. No more images and information should be stored than that which is strictly required for the stated purpose of a surveillance camera system, and such images and information should be deleted once their purposes have been discharged.
7. Access to retained images and information should be restricted and there must be clearly defined rules on who can gain access and for what purposes such access if granted; the disclosure of images and information should only take place when it is necessary for such a purpose or for law enforcement purposes ....'

Public bodies like local authorities publish their policies in accordance with this guidance. The justifications are broadbrush and there is a pretty standard 28-day retention policy. Most CCTV feeds go to a central control centre as well as to the police.

sure, the ambit of the policy and the extent of its publication are relevant to acquiescence, but: (i) acquiescence does not equate to consent; and (ii) it is only one factor going to whether C's use is lawful or not.

[7.89] One point that emerges out of this discussion is that the right of privacy tends to be undervalued when weighed against countervailing considerations. A's privacy gives way to the car park owner's commercial interests; it also gives way to the owner of the shopping centre's desire to have information about, and so control, their premises through CCTV observation. These interests of C are legitimate, but legitimacy does not mean that there is no misuse. Put another way, privacy should not only be respected where there are no countervailing interests in play, in other words where valuing it is essentially cost-free, because nothing is being given up. Properly valuing privacy has a cost: information is useful and those uses confer benefits, whether they be economic (in terms of how social media behemoths, like Google and Meta, use our information or parking companies recover fines) or public (in terms of law and order and national security). Rigorously enforcing how private information can be used has a cost that can usually be clearly articulated. The problem is that when that cost is articulated, it almost always causes A's rights of privacy to be subordinated to those other interests. It may be that the appreciation that A has property rights, not simply human rights, will cause privacy to be valued more.[60]

[7.90] Often, invasions of privacy are justified on grounds of 'security'. This, as will be seen, is a major theme when we come to state misuse in Chapter 8. But security or safety is also deployed as a justification in cases of non-state misuse, and it is as well to remind ourselves of what Benjamin Franklin said in 1775: 'Those who would give up essential Liberty, to purchase a little temporary Safety, deserve neither Liberty nor Safety'.[61]

[7.91] Monti and Wacks quote a 'security guru', Bruce Schneier, who puts the point in this way:[62]

> If you set up a false dichotomy, of course people will choose security over privacy – especially if you scare them first. But it's still a false dichotomy. There is no security without privacy. And liberty requires both security and privacy. The famous quote attributed to Benjamin Frankin reads: 'Those who would give up essential liberty to purchase a little temporary safety, deserve neither liberty nor safety'. It's also true that those who would give up privacy for security are likely to end up with neither.

[60] This is the point made in Chapter V: undervaluing a factor of production is in the long-run detrimental not merely to the interests of A but to the interests of society as a whole.

[61] Quoted in A Monti and R Wacks, *Protecting Personal Information* (Hart Publishing, 2020) 66.

[62] Quoted in ibid 66.

[7.92] There is benefit in requiring the closer justification for the use by C of A's private information. The borderline between use and misuse is immensely important in articulating why a use is (or is not) a misuse. The use/misuse borderline frames the debate as to the extent to which privacy is worth protecting. Critically, that borderline will be drawn differently to the line drawn by Article 8(2) of the ECHR:

- Article 8(1) enshrines the right to respect private life and famil life, home and correspondence. Not only is this value extremely vague, it is also a value different from A's rights over their private information, both in terms of nature (the distinction is between human rights and property rights) and in terms of ambit (Article 8(1) protects against state encroachment on private life, whereas private information controls C's use of A's private information).
- Article 8(2) makes clear that the *state* may encroach upon A's Article 8(1) rights where such limitations are 'prescribed by law and are necessary in a democratic society in the interests of public safety, for the protection of public order, health or moral, or for the protection of the rights and freedoms of others'. Article 8(2) has very little to do with those cases where non-state-actor C is using/misusing A's private information. Of course, C has rights under the ECHR (eg freedom of expression: Article 10 of the ECHR) but it is noteworthy that neither the car park example nor the shopping centre example engage questions of freedom of expression.

[7.93] This has been a long journey to make a short point. Absent consent within the parameters of Chapter 11, consent *cannot* be relied upon as a justification by C to convert a misuse into a use. Acquiescence has no such properties: it is one of several factors to be taken into account when applying the control test. The weight that acquiescence has will depend on factual circumstance, but will diminish progressively through each of the next three cases which we now turn to consider.

ii. Where the use to which C is putting A's personal information is necessarily incidental to performance

[7.94] Acquiescence is at its strongest where even though there is no formal transfer or licence on A's part conferring rights on C, the use to which C is putting A's personal information is necessarily incidental to the performance of a service or supply of a product which either C is obliged to perform for A, or A is *voluntarily* using.

[7.95] In some cases, in order to obtain a product from C, A must surrender private information about themselves. For example, in order to obtain insurance, the proposer (the intended insured, A) is under a duty of full and frank disclosure to insurer C, who needs this information in order to evaluate the risk and to determine whether A's insurance proposal should or should not be accepted. A runs the risk of having their policy or claim avoided or invalidated or reduced where a material fact is not disclosed. Of course, proposer A does not have to obtain insurance,[63] but *if* they want the product unimpaired by potential future problems with cover, they will have to disclose a great deal of information. In the case of health insurance or medical insurance, this is likely to involve the disclosure of a great deal of private information. Even if there is no contractual agreement between A and C as to C's ability to use A's private information, insurer C's use of A's information *to evaluate the risk and to decide whether or not to insure A* is obviously legitimate, and it can be said that A is acquiescing in this. But were C thereafter to sell A's information, so provided, to someone else, to enable that person (say) to sell another product to A, then A is not acquiescing.

[7.96] From C's perspective the control test in this sort of case boils down to this:

- C is providing a service or selling a product to A.
- That process involves capturing some of A's private information.
- C will be safe from an Action by A where the use to which C puts that information is necessarily incidental to the provision of the service or sale of the product.

[7.97] This approach applies equally in the non-commercial context. Suppose A participates in the work that charity C does. Where the use of A's private information is necessarily incidental to this relationship between A and C, then that is legitimate. But where C begins to use A's private information for other purposes, C moves into the next case: the lawful capture of A's private information, where its use is not necessarily incidental to the relationship A ←→ C. In such cases, the acquiescence factor weighs significantly less than where C's use is necessarily incidental to A's relationship with C.

iii. Lawful capture but use for C's own purposes

[7.98] Where A's private information has lawfully been captured by C, C's use of that perception for their own purposes is not necessarily an infringement of A's rights under the Action. It is important to avoid the trap of concluding that there is misuse in every case where C is using A's private information purely for their own purposes, in circumstances where that use is not incidental to what A is asking C to do.

[63] Albeit, in the case of motor insurance, the choice will generally involve choosing not to drive a car.

[7.99] This question of use for C's own purposes arises in the car park and shopping centre examples that have already been considered. This book will not presume to anticipate the answers to the difficult questions that arise out of C's use of A's information. It is enough that the framework in which the question of privacy must be addressed has been articulated.

[7.100] Rather, a different case is going to be considered, namely the case where A communicates something to C in circumstances where there is no commercial (or other purposive) relationship between A and C. Take the letter written by A to C. Although property in the physical letter passes from A to C, the copyright in the words written vests in A. It is A, not C, who is entitled to reproduce the words written, and if C were to do so, A would be able to prevent that, relying upon their copyright. The constraints on C arising out of the law of copyright are significant, but C can do a great deal with content of the letter without infringing copyright. The letter can be shown – if not copied – to third parties and the gist published. Absent a privacy right, and assuming no bilateral agreement or understanding between A and C sufficient to trigger a duty of confidence, C is at liberty to do precisely this.

[7.101] The question which arises is the extent to which the Action operates as a constraint on C. Put another way, can C (subject to the law of copyright) use the content of A's letter unconstrained or do some uses cross the line into *misuse*? It is clear that there is a line that can be crossed.

Example[64]

The claimant, who was a member of the royal family, wrote a letter to her father, the existence of which later became public when it was mentioned in an article in a magazine published in America. Subsequently, large parts of the letter were included in articles published by the defendant newspaper group. The claimant brought a claim against the defendant for misuse of private information and breach of copyright, contending that the letter contained private matters of no legitimate public interest. In its defence to the claim, the defendant alleged inter alia that the claimant had written and sent the letter with a view to it being read by third parties and/or disclosed to the public, had intended to publicise the letter at a future date and had briefed the contents of the letter to the publishers of a book about her and that, therefore, she had not had a reasonable expectation of privacy in the letter. At first instance, and on appeal, the claim to infringement of the Action was upheld.

[7.102] Letters are a particularly clear example where the Action may assist A. The ambit of the Action, however, extends further.

[64] These are the facts of *HRH Duchess of Sussex v Associated Newspapers Ltd*, [2021] EWCA Civ 1810, taken from the headnote of [2022] 4 WLR 81.

Example[65]

The claimant, a well-known entertainer who had promoted his Christian beliefs in books and in his public appearances, became the subject of an investigation by a police force in relation to an allegation of an historical sexual offence. The police gave advance notice of a search of the claimant's home to a broadcaster. The broadcaster's subsequent television coverage of the search was prominent and extensive, and included footage of the search taken from a helicopter. The claimant, against whom no charges were brought, commenced an action against the broadcaster and the Chief Constable of the police force, claiming, inter alia, that they had violated his right to privacy under Article 8 of the ECHR. The Chief Constable accepted liability, apologised, and paid the claimant damages and costs, but the broadcaster contended that the claimant did not have a legitimate expectation of privacy in relation to the fact of the investigation and the fact of the search of his home; and that, in any event, even if his Article 8 rights were engaged, they were outweighed by the broadcaster's right to freedom of expression under Article 10 of the Convention. The claimant succeeded in the action.

[7.103] Both the Duchess of Sussex and the Cliff Richard cases involved no illegality on the part of C (apart from the point under consideration, namely whether private information had been misused). In each case, A could point to no self-standing illegality on the part of C apart from the Action itself, but (equally clearly) C was (in both these cases) using A's private information for their own purposes. The question is whether there was a misuse of that private information on the part of C within the meaning of the Action. In each case, C was not using A's private information because that use was necessarily incidental to the commercial or other relationship subsisting between A and C. Indeed, it is clear that suggestions of acquiescence by A in C's use would be difficult to sustain. C was (in each case) thus driven to rely upon other factors in support of the propriety of their use. In each case, those factors were insufficient to avoid the use being designated as a misuse.

[7.104] The Action is likely further freedom of expression in cases where there is a closed circle of communication between a limited number of participants. Suppose a WhatsApp group is established between A_1 to A_n for the purposes of discussing a defined topic or subject matter, on the basis of mutual confidence. Suppose then that one of the group of As – let's call them C_1 – chooses for their own purposes to use the communications between the members of the group by passing these communications on to C_2. Assuming the communications to comprise information personal to and private to A_1 to A_n, the question is whether such use by C_1 constitutes a misuse – and indeed, whether any use by C_2 can similarly be characterised.

[65] These are the facts of *Richard v British Broadcasting Corpn* [2018] EWHC 1837 (Ch), taken from the headnote of [2018] 1 Ch 169.

[7.105] Given that A_1 to A_n will most certainly not be acquiescing in C_1's use of their private information – C_1 will have been breaching the confidentiality within the group – the case for misuse is strong. Not only is the private information of the group being misused, but there is a significant threat to freedom of expression. We present ourselves differently in different contexts, and provided other laws are not infringed (eg unlawful conspiracy, etc) there is every reason why expectations of privacy furthering freedom of speech ought to be protected. This is one of those cases where the values of privacy and freedom of expression are not in opposition but are mutually supporting.

Example[66]

Ms Higgs was a teacher employed by Farmor's School. In October 2018, the head of the School was emailed by a parent (whose anonymity was protected[67]) complaining that Ms Higgs had expressed 'homophobic and prejudiced views', requesting an investigation. There was nothing intrinsically unlawful in Ms Higgs' views nor was it suggested that Ms Higgs had expressed those views directly to the students in her care. In other words, the complaint focused on lawful (if, perhaps, controversial, even disagreeable) views expressed outside the workplace. Ms Higgs was suspended pending the investigation, disciplinary charges were brought, and Ms Higgs was summarily dismissed for gross misconduct. Ms Higgs took the matter further, and the Court of Appeal considered Ms Higgs' rights under Article 9 of the ECHR (freedom of thought) and Article 10 (freedom of expression), as well as provisions in the HRA 1998 and the Equality Act 2010.

The School defended its conduct by – amongst other things – asserting that its course was justified to protect the School's reputation. This was rejected by the Court of Appeal at [156]ff and the dismissal was found to be unlawful.

All this has nothing to do with the nature of the Action. Significantly, Ms Higgs' Article 8 (privacy) rights were not considered by the Court of Appeal (the point seems not to have been argued), even though Ms Higgs' views had been expressed on a private Facebook account. Although it was accepted that it was significant that Ms Higgs' views were expressed 'in a forum which is not in the workplace, is not controlled by the employer, and which has a limited number of members' (at [153]) and that 'the posts were published in a forum which had nothing to do with the School, and would be likely to be seen by only a small number of people not all of whom would know of [Ms Higgs'] connection with it' (at [154]), weight was also placed on the fact that 'there is no guarantee that Facebook posts will only be seen by those to whom the owner of the account gives access' (at [154]).

Here, it is suggested, lies an error: there *is* a guarantee that private posts will be protected from wider circulation. That guarantee is the Action. The operation of the Facebook account was not further explored in the case, and it may be that the parent's original complaint to the School was *not* a misuse of private information within the meaning of the Action. But this is certainly not self-evident.

[66] *Higgs v Farmor's School* [2025] EWCA Civ 109.
[67] Ibid, see para [9] of the decision.

Example[68]

Health Minister Andrew Gwynne MP was dismissed as a minister because of offensive and abusive WhatsApp messages sent (and received) by him. It is not known who C was in this case, and the WhatsApp group was, in any event, clearly quite a large one. There may have been no understanding of confidence between the members of the group. Misuse within the sense of the Action would therefore appear weak: but what is significant is that questions of privacy in the context of lawful if offensive and regrettable communications were never even raised.

iv. Unlawful use by C for their own purposes

[7.106] So far, we have considered:

(1) The case where C uses A's private information pursuant to a right conferred on them by A as the owner.
(2) The case where C uses A's private information for purposes necessarily incidental to furthering a relationship between A and C in which A is the voluntary participant.
(3) The case where C uses A's private information for their own purpose.

[7.107] In all these three cases, leaving on one side any infringement of the Action (which is the point under consideration),[69] C has been acting *lawfully*. The question at issue is whether C's otherwise lawful conduct renders C nevertheless liable under the Action. The present case is different: C's use of A's information is independently unlawful, without considering the Action at all.

[7.108] Where a non-state actor has used A's private information where this information has been captured unlawfully, it will be very hard to avoid the conclusion that C's use is a misuse and that A will successfully be able to bring an Action. The answer *may* be different in the case of state actors (a matter for Chapter 8), but non-state actors, who are not above the law, cannot generally assert some kind of public interest in the actions.[70] Thus, for instance, where C's perception derives from a trespass to A's home (say, by planting a listening device), it will be difficult to justify *any* use of that perception on the part of C.

[68] L Nathoo and Z Fatima, 'Health Minister Andrew Gwynne sacked over messages' (*BBC News online*, 9 February 2025), www.bbc.com/news/articles/c5y7zperkelo, last accessed 21 August 2025.

[69] The illegality argument cannot be used in a circular fashion. It cannot be said that C has misused A's private information, therefore has acted unlawfully, and so is guilty of misusing A's private information.

[70] See *Francome v Mirror Group Newspapers Ltd* [1984] 1 WLR 892, considered at paras [4.121]–[4.125].

E. A *de minimis* requirement for misuse

[7.109] Before concluding this section on deliberate misuse, it is necessary to say something about appreciability. In order to found a claim by A against C there needs to be an appreciable misuse of the perception or (put another way) the infringement must reach 'a certain level of seriousness'. In *R (Gillan) v Commissioner of Police of the Metropolis*,[71] Lord Bingham stated:

> It is true that 'private life' has been generously construed to embrace wide rights to personal autonomy. But it is clear Convention jurisprudence that intrusions must reach a certain level of seriousness to engage the operation of the Convention, which is, after all, concerned with human rights and fundamental freedoms, and I incline to the view that an ordinary superficial search of the person and an opening of bags, of the kind to which passengers uncomplainingly submit at airports, for example, can scarcely be said to reach that level.

[7.110] Although this case concerned the HRA 1998, and we are here concerned with an infringement under the Action, the same sort of filter must apply. A matter may be insufficiently serious because the perception is trite or insignificant, the use minor or trivial or the misuse – the infringement – marginal, or any combination of these three factors. These are all matters of judgement.

VII. The 'Public Interest'

[7.111] Warren and Brandeis articulated a series of 'limitations' to the right to privacy,[72] the first of which was that '[t]he right to privacy does not prohibit any publication of matter which is of public or general interest'.[73] They envisaged this as a broad limitation on A's right of privacy, drawing on 'the analogy, in the law of libel and slander, of cases which deal with the qualified privilege of comment and criticism on matters of public and general interest'.[74]

[7.112] The 'public interest' should inform the borderline between use and misuse, but is unlikely to be a significant factor so far as non-state actors are concerned. We are not, in the case of the Action, concerned with the balancing of two competing values. It is true that Articles 8 (privacy), 9 (freedom of thought), 10 (freedom of expression) and Article 1 of Protocol 1 (protection of property) of the ECHR all inform the operation of the Action, but these values

[71] *R (Gillan) v Commissioner of Police of the Metropolis* [2006] 2 AC 307 at [28].
[72] Warren and Brandeis (n 46) 214ff.
[73] ibid 214.
[74] ibid 214.

are already 'baked-in' to the Action, and there is no need for a separate 'public interest' test.

[7.113] Thus, the Action protects a right of property in A which has already been defined as described in this book. A has a property interest in C's perception of A's private information. The Action is the means by which A's Article 1 Protocol 1 rights are protected.

[7.114] C's right of freedom of thought, conscience and religion under Article 9(1) of the ECHR is protected because the Action does not impinge upon C's perception. The significance of the perception/use borderline is that C's rights under Article 9(1) of the ECHR receive very significant protection under the Action. When it comes to C's manifestation of their religion or beliefs, protected in a qualified way under Article 9(2) of the ECHR, two points can be made. First, it is difficult to see how A's private information can be necessary for C's manifestation of their religion or beliefs. Second, the use/misuse borderline properly draws the line between legitimate use and illegitimate misuse by reference to the factors already described, and there is no warrant for any adjustment of that borderline by reference to C's Article 9(2) rights.

[7.115] The same is true of C's rights under Article 10 of the ECHR (freedom of expression). Freedom of expression is an ECHR-protected right, but that right is not an absolute one and is circumscribed by various factors, one of which is A's property in their private information. Just as C cannot 'express themselves' by infringing A's copyright, so too C cannot 'express themselves' by infringing on A's private information unless the use is a proper one. Again, there is no warrant for redrawing the use/misuse borderline by reference to Article 10 of the ECHR.

[7.116] The reference to 'fair comment' in defamation actions by Warren and Brandeis is, it is suggested, misconceived. The point about fair comment is that it acts as a defence where defamatory comment is based on facts which are true. If the underlying facts are A's private information, then a 'fair comment' defence based on those facts cannot, in and of itself, justify the use of that private information.

[7.117] Finally, as regards constraints on C's use of A's private information, *whatever* that use may be, it must always be borne in mind that, unlike in human rights cases, A has the rights of an owner, and is able to transfer or license their property to C. Put another way, if C has a wish, because of their own commercial or other interests, to use A's private information, then (as is the case with *all* property) C must negotiate with A for the right to use that property. This represents no more than the normal operation of the market economy, where a scarce resource (here, A's private information) is allocated to those who want to have that resource by reference to price. The fact that private information is intangible property is neither here nor there: all intellectual property rights are intangible, and C (if they wish to use A's patented invention or copyrighted original work) must pay the price. Private information is no different.

[7.118] In *Enderby Town Football Club Ltd v The Football Association Ltd*,[75] Lord Denning famously said:

> All these are cases where the judges have decided, avowedly or not, according to what is best for the public good. I know that over 300 years ago, Hobart CJ said the 'public policy is an unruly horse'. It has often been repeated since. So unruly is the horse, it is said that no judge should ever try to mount it lest it run away with him. I disagree. With a good man in the saddle, the unruly horse can be kept in control. It can jump over obstacles. It can leap the fences put up by fictions and come down on the side of justice ...

There will always be a role for public policy in the use/misuse borderline. But, it is suggested, that role is very limited.

VIII. 'Chains of Title': The Position of C_2

[7.119] So far, we have been considering the case where C_1 has a perception of information that is personal to and private to A, which C_1 misuses. Let us suppose that C_1's misuse consists in conveying their (C_1's) perception to C_2. Obviously, given these assumptions, C_1 will be liable to A if A brings an Action. What we are here interested in is C_2's liability to A under the Action.

[7.120] As to this, the answer is that C_2 can be liable to A under the Action, but only where the following conditions are met. The test for what is private information, expounded in Chapter 6, must be satisfied as regards C_2. Thus: (i) the information must be personal to A when tested for objectively by the court on a Court-Determined Fact basis; (ii) the information must be private to A, when objectively considered from A's point of view; and (iii) a reasonable person, standing in the position of C_2, would know, or on reasonable inquiry ought to know, that the information is both personal to and private to someone (even if that person is not known to be A).

[7.121] Thus, the control test, as we call it, is applied anew to C_2 at the point when C_2 themselves do more than merely perceive A's private information. C_2 cannot be prevented from *perceiving* that which C_1 has (in breach of

[75] *Enderby Town Football Club Ltd v The Football Association Ltd* [1971] Ch 591 at 606–607.

A's rights under the Action) communicated to them, but C_2 does not have to use that perception, and any use by C_2 may constitute a misuse according to the factors already discussed. In particular, were C_1 to tell C_2, 'Don't worry, A has transferred their private information to me' or 'Don't worry, A has licensed that private information to me, and I am entitled to sub-license to you', then C_2 is perfectly capable of checking the correctness of C_1's assertions, and should do so. If C_1 asserts an entitlement to use A's property (whether by transfer or licence), it is incumbent upon C_2 to ascertain that C_1 holds the rights they assert they have.

[7.122] Where C_1 purports to be using A's private information as necessarily incidental to work C_1 is doing for A, pursuant to a relationship between A and C_1, then C_2 must ask themselves whether (because they are a subcontractor of C_1 or otherwise involved in C_1's supply to A) their (C_2's) use is similarly necessarily incidental to the work that they are doing. Again, it is incumbent upon C_2 to investigate the reasons why their use falls on the right side of the line.

[7.123] The final two cases are much more straightforward. If C_2, whilst behaving lawfully, is nevertheless using A's private information to their own ends, they must ask themselves (by reference to the factors already outlined) whether such use in fact constitutes misuse. Where C_2's user is unlawful (whether because it is clear that C_1 is infringing on A's rights or otherwise unlawful), then the position is clearer still (or *a fortiori* as the lawyers would say).

8

Misuse: State Actors

In which: the issue of misuse is explored in the context of state actors; the 'control' test applied in the case of non-state actors is revisited and reframed as a 'proper purpose' test; instances of state power and the manner of its exercise are explored; and an approach to misuse of state powers articulated.

I. Approach

[8.1] It would be surprising if the analysis of misuse by state actors were to be fundamentally different from the analysis of misuse in the case of non-state actors. This chapter accordingly tracks and draws upon large chunks of the analysis in Chapter 7. Thus, the essential distinctions between perception, use and misuse remain important, as do the two borderlines that these distinctions imply: (i) the borderline between perception and use; and (ii) the borderline between use and misuse. Equally, the two ways in which private information can be misused by C – inadvertent misuse and deliberate misuse – are as relevant to state actors.

[8.2] That being said, there are material differences between state and non-state actors. If there were not, then the treatment of misuse would not have been split across two chapters. Although, in (Diceyan) theory, the legal position of state actors is the same as that of non-state actors, that is becoming increasingly untrue, both in terms of the additional powers that are conferred on state actors and in terms of the controls over state actors. Some of the additional powers – those most illustrative of encroachments on or threats to our private information – are considered in this chapter. The controls – other than the Action, which is the subject matter of this book – are in essence judicial review and the Human Rights Act 1998 (HRA 1998), both of which are only considered to the extent relevant to an understanding of the Action. These matters are considered in Section II.

[8.3] Section III – somewhat provocatively entitled 'privacy as a second-order value' – considers the relationship between competing values: privacy on the one hand; and the reasons why special powers are conferred on the state on the other, which is to protect other important values too numerous to list here.[1] This is an important, balancing value judgement, and it is one that is not made in this book. The extent to which privacy is protected or not protected is a matter for citizens and government – and the view of any individual, including the author of this book, is not worth articulating. Rather, Section III considers: (i) the extent to which it is right to say that privacy is a second-order value when set against other values; and (ii) if this is the case, why that is so. The second insight is particularly valuable when we come to consider the future of private information and privacy protection (in Chapter 12).

[8.4] The starting point for the consideration of the Action and the state actor is the *power* that is conferred on state actors to do certain things. These powers are wide and invasive, although subject to control. A key limitor or constraint on these powers is that they must be used for a proper purpose, and that purpose is one that is defined by the conferral or existence of the power itself. This is the content of Section IV below, which considers the powers of state actors, and the constraints that exist on their use.

[8.5] Having considered these matters, the issue of misuse of A's private information by state actor C can properly be explored. That is done from Section V to the end of the chapter. Section V reverts to a matter touched upon in previous chapters, and postponed until Chapter 9, namely the questions of the liability of non-natural persons under the Action. Section VI considers the relevance of the perception/use/misuse divide (articulated in paragraph [8.1]) in this context. Section VII considers the distinction between inadvertent and deliberate misuse which was first articulated in Chapter 7 in connection with non-state actors: the same distinction needs to be considered in the case of state actors. Inadvertent misuse is not specifically considered in this chapter, because (as will be described) the law is the same for state actors as it is for non-state actors. However, the same is not the case as regards deliberate misuse: although the definition of deliberate misuse is similar for state as for non-state actors, the test for what constitutes misuse is different in the case of state actors. The reason for this, and the nature of the test that *does* apply, are considered in Section VIII.

[8.6] Section IX considers the various factors that arise when determining whether a use of A's private information is in fact a misuse by a state actor. Finally, Section X considers a variant on the 'chains of title' theme considered in Section VIII of Chapter 7. To be clear, the Chapter 7 analysis holds good in the case of state actors, when they pass information on to others, whether state or

[1] It is trite that over the last decades, the state has grown because it is providing more services to people in the jurisdiction. That often involves the conferring of additional powers.

non-state actors. Section X considers the related question of the responsibility of a third party to A, where that third party is asked by state actor C to provide information, not about themselves but about A.

II. The Diceyan View: *Entick v Carrington* ... Again

[8.7] The constitutional theory expounded by *Entick v Carrington* is that there is no difference in principle between non-state actors and state actors.[2] They are all the same under the law; there is no 'special' treatment of state actors. The only differences are where specific powers are conferred on particular persons. The trend has been to confer ever more specific powers on state organs, with the consequence that the Diceyan model is honoured more in the breach. The doctrine remains technically true but is increasingly not a protector of our civil liberties, but the basis upon which they are lawfully infringed.[3] This expansion of state power is reflected in the rise of judicial review as a guardian of the rights of the individual against the abuse of public power.[4]

[8.8] Some of the specific powers conferred on state actors to interfere in the lives of citizens and other persons within the power of the state are described in this chapter in order to illustrate general points regarding the Action as it affects state actors. In *Entick v Carrington*, the claimant won because the Secretary of State lacked a legal justification for their act.[5] These days, Parliament has chosen to confer on other state bodies considerable powers that go well beyond the powers that the law confers on non-state actors, including natural and legal persons.

[8.9] The dogma that civil liberties under English law are not protected through constitutional guarantees but subsist in the unencroached remnant where our rights are not affected is maintained in form but invalidated in substance. Any non-state actor can still do what a person is not constrained by law from doing, and every state actor is obliged to act according to the law. But two significant caveats need to be entered as regards the doctrine.

[8.10] First, the doctrine does not do anything to prevent or constrain encroachment by the state into our individual liberties when this is done

[2] The decision in *Entick v Carrington*, and its constitutional significance, is described at paras [4.32]–[4.40].

[3] This assumes a definition of 'civil liberty' independent of what civil liberties a legal system confers as a matter of law.

[4] I Hare et al, *De Smith's Judicial Review*, 9th edn (Sweet & Maxwell, 2023) [1-017].

[5] See para [4.35].

pursuant to lawful process. The doctrine may have had greater relevance when the role of the state was limited,[6] but the doctrine is less relevant when the state's functions are ever expanding, even where that expansion is for very good reason. To be clear, an expanding state (or at least the services provided by an expanding state) is what people want and society expects. As AJP Taylor remarked, before the First World War, the encroachment of the state on our lives was *de minimis*.[7] But that absence of encroachment was because we lacked a serious welfare state and serious healthcare provision (to name but two now critical state functions). Additionally, the burdens of policing and protecting our national security have increased. As a result, there are a whole series of incursions into our privacy spread across multiple institutions and multiple statutes and jurisdictions, all done with the best of intentions[8] without any particular regard for our general civil liberties – the HRA 1998 (to which we will come) notwithstanding.

[8.11] Second, the doctrine does not enable rights hitherto unrecognised to be protected.[9] It is significant – and precisely illustrative of the problem – that the Action grew not out of the common law (which tried but failed to create a

[6] The opening words of AJP Taylor, *English History 1914–1945* (Oxford University Press, 1965) 1 are telling: 'Until August 1914 a sensible, law-abiding Englishman could pass through life and hardly notice the existence of the state, beyond the post office and the policeman. He could live where he liked and as he liked. He had no official number or identity card. He could travel abroad or leave his country for ever without a passport or any sort of official permission. He could exchange his money for any other currency without restriction or limit. He could buy goods from any country in the world on the same terms as he bought goods at home. For that matter, a foreigner could spend his life in this country without permit and without informing the police. Unlike the countries of the European continent, the state did not require its citizens to perform military service. An Englishman could enlist, if he chose, in the regular army, the navy, or the territorials. He could also ignore, if he chose, the demands of national defence. Substantial householders were occasionally called on for jury service. Otherwise, only those helped the state who wished to do so. The Englishman paid taxes on a modest scale: nearly £200 million in 1913–14, or rather less than 8 per cent of the national income. The state intervened to prevent the citizen from eating adulterated food or contracting certain infectious diseases. It imposed safety rules in factories, and prevented women, and adult males in some industries, from working excessive hours. The state saw to it that children received education up the the age of 13. Since 1 January 1909, it provided a meagre pension for the needy over the age of 70. Since 1911, it helped insure certain classes of workers against sickness and unemployment. This tendency towards more state action was increasing. Expenditure on the social services had roughly doubled since the Liberals took office in 1905. Still, broadly speaking, the state acted to help those who could not help themselves. It left the adult citizen alone …'; W Hanlon, *The Laissez-Faire Experiment* (Princeton University Press, 2024).

[7] See n 6.

[8] Most governments of the last 20–30 years have promised to wage a 'war' on 'red tape', and all have failed. That is because we have drafters of legislation of great skill and good, not bad, intentions behind the legislation our elected representatives choose to pass. The consequence is that when one examines individual pieces of legislation, the rules look not like 'red tape' but are sensible and capable of cogent justification. So the corpus of rules grows and grows.

[9] See para [4.39]. Thus, if the state is at liberty to intercept communications or photograph people in a public place because there is no right in the citizen to object, then the state does not require specific authority in law. State actors are entitled to do what non-state actors can do. If C is entitled to follow A over a city's public spaces, then so too can a police officer.

privacy right) but out of the European Convention on Human Rights (ECHR) and the HRA 1998.[10]

[8.12] The result is that there are no significant constitutional controls enabling our courts to deal with technological changes of the sort that so worried Warren and Brandeis in 1890. It is no coincidence that our law of privacy is at its most effective when existing rights (eg trespass to our homes) are engaged, because the encroachment on our privacy is protected by other means. Where we have no rights – walking through a shopping centre being filmed by CCTV whose data is processed and used in ways we can only imagine – our law is (at least as presently enforced) correspondingly ineffective. If the police or a private person choose to invade our privacy where it is not protected by other means, that invasion is likely to be sanctioned. Indeed, where there is a so-called statutory protection of our rights, on closer examination what is happening is a legitimisation of the invasion, not its prevention.[11]

[8.13] What, then, of the HRA 1998? Does that fill the civil liberties vacuum left by *Entick v Carrington*? The short answer is that it does not. The HRA 1998 acts as a very good control over the content of legislation, both primary and secondary. Although the HRA 1998 cannot affect primary legislation, save by making a declaration that the legislation is incompatible with the ECHR,[12] we live in a society governed by the rule of law, and our Parliament and executive are careful to ensure that primary law is HRA 1998 compliant. Declarations of incompatibility are, correspondingly, extremely rare. Secondary legislation gets an altogether tougher scrutiny, by the courts, if not by the legislature. That is because, unlike primary legislation, administrative action (including the framing of secondary legislation) is subject to judicial review, now bolstered by the 'rights brought home' by the HRA 1998. We can thus be confident that the powers conferred on state actors by primary and secondary legislation are very likely to be ECHR compliant. Thus, where the police enter your home and search it, or where your communications are intercepted by MI5, or where bulk data including your data is analysed by GCHQ (all powers considered further in this chapter) we can be confident that the controls over the *conferring* of such powers are robust in general terms. The controls regarding their *exercise* are perhaps less robust, and this is where the Action may be of significance. But the Action is of little or no significance as regards the *conferring* of powers in the first place.

[8.14] The focus of this chapter is thus on the role of the Action in controlling the use or exercise of power by state actors, where this use involves our

[10] As to which, see Ch 2.

[11] The Protection of Freedoms Act 2012 is an excellent case in point. The Act does not protect our freedoms but rather embeds in primary legislation encroachments on our liberties.

[12] See HRA 1998, s 4.

private information. As we shall see, the controls apart from the Action are rather less robust when it comes to controlling the *use* to which information harvested by such incursions into our privacy is put. The legislation and the ECHR tend to focus on the harvesting of information (or, in the language of this book, the gathering of perceptions relating to A) as opposed to the use to which such information is put. This is the province of the Action: the Action protects A against misuse of their private information by state actors in ways not achievable by either the HRA 1998 or (for that matter) wider judicial review.

III. Privacy as a Second-order Value

A. The thesis

[8.15] Privacy is a right that we all claim to value. It is a protected right under the ECHR, although that protection is qualified.[13] Under the ECHR, privacy receives a qualified protection because it is rightly recognised that it may have to give way to other values. The point being made here is not that there are *no* circumstances where privacy must give way to other values (privacy is certainly not an absolute value), but that it tends to give way too easily. The following paragraphs provide a few examples of this. The section then concludes with an attempt to explain why privacy tends to be under-protected when stood against other values.

B. Instances

i. Privacy versus national security

[8.16] Obviously, national security is a critical value to protect. Ward and Blundell summarise the law in the United Kingdom in the following terms:[14]

> 4.02 The Human Rights Act 1998 ('HRA 1998') gives effect in UK law to the rights set out in the [ECHR], some of which are unqualified and some of which are qualified ie may lawfully be interfered with on specified grounds set out in the Convention. Article 8 ECHR guarantees the right to respect for private and family life, home and correspondence. It is a qualified right and may lawfully be interfered with on national security grounds (amongst others). Article 8 ECHR is likely to be engaged when the Agencies exercise covert surveillance powers. Interference with property may also engage Article 1 of the First Protocol, which guarantees the right to peaceful enjoyment of possessions. This chapter considers the statutory framework under which

[13] See Art 8(2) of the ECHR.

[14] R Ward and D Blundell, *National Security: Law, Procedure and Practice*, 2nd edn (Oxford University Press, 2024).

covert surveillance or property interference activity can be authorised and conducted compatibly with the ECHR.

4.03 The framework is to be found in three statutes the Intelligence Services Act 1994 ('ISA 1994'), the Regulation of Investigatory Powers Act 2000 ('RIPA 2000') and the Investigatory Powers Act 2016 ('IPA 2016'). These statutes do not impose a requirement to obtain a warrant or authorisation where one is available. However, there is an expectation that a warrant or authorisation will be obtained in such circumstances, and a failure to do so is likely to result in public criticism by the principal oversight body, the Investigatory Powers Commissioner's Office ('ICPO'), which will treat the failure as a 'relevant error' within the meaning of IPA 2016 and the relevant Codes of Practice. Depending on the circumstances, a failure to obtain a warrant or authorisation might also result in liability to pay civil damages (eg for trespass); prosecution for a criminal offence (eg unlawful interception of communications or computer interference); the lodging with the Investigatory Powers Tribunal ('IPT') of a complaint and/or a claim under s 6 of the HRA 1998; or a ruling in criminal proceedings that evidence obtained by reason of the unauthorised conduct is inadmissible or that the proceedings should be stayed.

[8.17] The starting point for national security protection is the gathering of data regarding those who would wish to undermine or who are in fact undermining our national security. Because it is difficult to identify such people out of the mass of law-abiding and loyal non-state actors, mass gathering of information is the norm. Inevitably that involves incursions into our privacy.

Example[15]

The British government has ordered Apple to grant it secret access to its customers' encrypted cloud storage data using controversial surveillance powers known as the 'Snoopers' Charter', in a move that could weaken security for iPhone users all over the world.

Last month the US tech group received a 'technical capability notice' under the UK Investigatory Powers Act, requiring the iPhone maker to create a 'back door' to its encrypted iCloud storage service, according to people familiar with the matter.

The move would enable law enforcement and security services to tap iPhone backups and other cloud data that is otherwise inaccessible, even to Apple itself. The law has extraterritorial powers, meaning UK law enforcement could access the encrypted data of Apple customers anywhere in the world, including in the US.

The UK's demand is the latest flashpoint in a long-running battle between the tech industry and law enforcement over the use of encryption in messaging apps and storage services.

Billions of people worldwide rely on encryption in apps provided by tech companies including Apple, Google, Meta and Signal to secure their personal data.

[15] 'UK orders Apple to give it access to encrypted cloud data' (*Financial Times*, 7 February 2025) https://www.ft.com/content/57b391a0-c531-4cde-a5e9-c5d60b21a161.

> However, security and law enforcement officials argue it shields criminals, terrorists and child abusers, making it harder to gather digital evidence for prosecutions and intelligence critical for national security.
>
> A Home Office spokesperson said: 'We do not comment on operational matters, including for example confirming or denying the existence of any such notices.' Apple declined to comment.
>
> The *Washington Post* first reported the UK's order to Apple.
>
> 'Using technical capability notices to weaken encryption around the globe is a shocking move that will position the UK as a tech pariah, rather than a tech leader', said Meredith Whittaker, president of the Signal Foundation, the non-profit that runs the secure messaging app. 'If implemented, the directive will create a dangerous cyber-security vulnerability in the nervous system of our global economy.'
>
> The UK Investigatory Powers Act, dubbed the 'Snoopers' Charter' by critics when it was passed in 2016, was updated last year in the final weeks of the Conservative government before July's election.
>
> Under the legislation, which has been widely criticised by human rights campaigners and privacy activists as well as Silicon Valley tech companies, recipients of technical capability notices are not allowed to acknowledge their existence or warn users that their security had been weakened, unless the Secretary of State grants permission to do so.

[8.18] In this case, even the existence of the technical capability notice – the fact that it has been made – cannot be acknowledged. The party against whom the notice is directed can have the decision reviewed, but that party is *not* the party whose private information is liable to be accessed at some point in the future. Such persons – A_n – have no say. The reason for the secrecy is that some of A_n will be criminals or terrorists who should not be forewarned of the creation of 'back door' access. But that is precisely the point: privacy rights are subordinated to other interests.[16]

ii. Privacy versus admissibility of evidence in court processes

[8.19] The doctrine of the fruit of the poisonous tree is well known in the procedural law of the United States. It holds that evidence improperly obtained may be excluded from use in criminal (and sometimes civil) proceedings, including (in the most extreme versions of the doctrine) further evidence obtained through the use of improperly obtained evidence (hence the reference to fruit of the poisonous tree).

[16] The relevant statutory provisions for technical capability notices are in secondary legislation, made under ss 253 and 267 of the IPA 2016, specifically The Investigatory Powers (Technical Capability) Regulations 2018, SI 2018/353. The Explanatory Note at the end of the statutory instrument notes that '[a] full impact assessment has not been produced for this instrument as no, or no significant, impact on the private, voluntary or public sectors is foreseen'.

[8.20] There is an obvious conflict between privacy and due process. Mellifont puts the point (speaking from the standpoint of an Australian lawyer) as follows:[17]

> When a court is presented with illegally or improperly obtained evidence, it is faced with the fundamental dilemma of trying to resolve the tension between conflicting principles. On the one hand there is the public interest in convicting the wrongdoer on proof beyond a reasonable doubt. Conviction of the guilty is more likely when all relevant and reliable evidence is admitted in the trial process than when some or all of such evidence is excluded. The credibility of the criminal trial process 'depends substantially on a genuine attempt being made to establish the facts on the basis of which the final decision is made'. The public interest in admitting all relevant evidence which will have a rational and probative value in the determination of the material facts is explicitly recognised by the High Court. It is this general principle which 'gives rationality, coherence and justification to our system of evidence.
>
> On the other hand, there is the public interest in ensuring that the integrity of the court process is maintained, that misconduct in law enforcement officials in their investigative activities is deterred and that the rights of the citizen are upheld.

[8.21] The value in admitting improperly obtained evidence is well expressed in this passage. The value in *excluding* such evidence is put rather less well. The value is expressed as one of ensuring that the police and other investigatory bodies stick to the law. It is significant that the protection of the privacy of non-state actors is not mentioned at all by Mellifont, given that the process of seeking evidence usually involves some form of trespass into our privacy.

[8.22] As Giannoulopoulos notes, '[i]n contrast to Greece and the United States, where a long tradition of constitutional protection of the right to privacy transverses [sic] the legal system, recognition of the right to privacy is a recent phenomenon in English and French law'.[18] Arenson comments that:[19]

> … the 'fruit of the poisonous tree' doctrine has been severely emasculated in America and rejected altogether in Australia. Yet if the paramount purpose of the aforementioned exclusionary rules and discretions is that of deterrence, how does one explain this emasculation and rejection? If, for example, the police beat a confession out of a person who is arrested on suspicion of murder and the confession (primary evidence) is later ruled inadmissible on the ground that it was obtained involuntarily, should the prosecution be permitted to adduce evidence of the deceased's body (derivative evidence) which was discovered solely as a result of the inadmissible confession? If so, does this frustrate or further the paramount interest in deterring police misconduct?

[17] K Mellifont, *Fruit of the Poisonous Tree: Evidence Derived from Illegally or Improperly Obtained Evidence* (The Federation Press, 2010) 1.

[18] D Giannoulopoulos, *Improperly Obtained Evidence in Anglo-American and Continental Law* (Hart Publishing, 2020) 88.

[19] K Arenson, 'Rejection of the Fruit of the Poisonous Tree Doctrine in Australia: A Retreat from Progressivism' (2011) 13 *University of Notre Dame Law Review* 17 at 18–19.

> The obvious answer is the former because the police have gained a forensic advantage as a direct result of their misconduct.

Again, the justification of the rule is deterrence more than the protection of privacy.[20]

[8.23] English law does not have a 'fruit of the poisoned tree' doctrine, and is also (apart from confessions) pretty relaxed about the admission into criminal proceedings of evidence that comprises private information obtained improperly by the police.[21] The approach of our legal system is *not* to regard this as an Article 8 (privacy) question *at all*, but as an Article 6 (fair trial) matter:[22]

> The Convention was already relevant to a judge's exercise of his discretion under section 78(1) PACE before the coming into force of the Human Rights Act 1998 on 2 October 2000. It has become increasingly important since then.
>
> Breach of Article 8 ECHR (right to respect for private life) is, of itself, irrelevant to questions of admissibility at trial. The issue is whether Article 6 ECHR (the right to a fair trial) has been breached: see *Khan v. United Kingdom*, in which is was held that a violation of Article 8 ECHR did not mean that there had been a violation of Article 6 ECHR. In *R v. P*, in which *Khan* was considered, Lord Hobhouse said that Article 6 ECHR does not entitle a defendant:
>
> 'to have unlawfully obtained evidence excluded just because it was so obtained. What he is entitled to is an opportunity to challenge its use and admission in evidence and a judicial assessment of the effect of its admission upon the fairness of the trial as is provided for by section 78.'
>
> No general principle of common law or of EU law prohibits the use of unlawfully obtained evidence, although it might be excluded in the exercise of judicial discretion …

[8.24] This places no value on privacy at all: the private information can be used in court proceedings provided those court proceedings are 'fair'. It may be that some degree of privacy can be maintained through the court process by not openly publishing the private information or by sitting in private, but that is not the point. The point is that the improperly obtained (ergo in breach of a protected right of privacy) private information is being used in the court process. The invasion of privacy point would be as valid if court processes in this country were entirely secret (undesirable for altogether different reasons).

[20] Of course, it is recognised that the extorted confession is not an invasion of privacy. But the search of a home conducted pursuant to an irregular search warrant that results in the obtaining of evidence is.

[21] The police unsurprisingly have considerable powers to obtain information, a great deal of which has the potential to be private. Equally unsurprisingly, these powers are carefully controlled in terms of when and how they may be exercised. There are times when those safeguards are breached, and the information improperly obtained. PACE contains a provision – s 78 – permitting the exclusion of 'unfair evidence'.

[22] H Malek (ed), *Phipson on Evidence*, 20th edn (Sweet & Maxwell, 2022) [39-21].

[8.25] The reason for this approach is that it lies ill in the mouth of an accused – A in this instance – to assert privacy over information that may help convict them. But the same point can be made as regards the use of A's private information in court processes where A is a witness or where the proceedings are civil only.[23] The point is that we consider the integrity of our court processes – that the court adjudicate upon the best evidence – as significantly more important than protecting A's private information from use.

iii. Retention of records

[8.26] For reasons that have been described,[24] retention of A's private information by C in circumstances where that retention is *not* a form of contingent use constitutes perception and not use. On the other hand, records that are retained on the basis that they will be used in certain contingencies constitutes use. CCTV footage and other forms of record – which will be referenced where there is need, but not otherwise – thus constitute use and not perception.

[8.27] In the case of CCTV the only constraint on use is a Code of Practice issued under the Protections of Freedom Act 2012.[25] Such Codes tend to be widely drawn but usually contain a limit on retention time. Thus, the London Borough of Redbridge's CCTV code of practice[26] provides that '[r]ecorded media not subject to any further legal or civil action will be retained for a maximum period of 31 days'.[27]

[8.28] The police have a wide variety of powers regarding fingerprinting,[28] taking impressions of footwear,[29] taking of intimate samples,[30] taking of non-intimate samples,[31] and taking of DNA.[32] These processes all generate *information* about A, whether by themselves or in conjunction with other evidence/material. In other words, the sample is not information in its own

[23] In civil proceedings, the position is altogether more fluid, turning on the overriding importance of fairness: *Phipson on Evidence* (n 22) [39-36].

[24] See paras [7.33]–[7.38].

[25] See paras [7.78]–[7.79].

[26] Available at https://www.redbridge.gov.uk/crime-and-public-safety/cctv/cctv-code-of-practice/, last accessed 25 August 2025.

[27] ibid at [9.4].

[28] M Zander, *Zander on PACE: The Police and Criminal Evidence Act 1984*, 9th edn (Sweet & Maxwell, 2023) [5-120]–[5.125].

[29] ibid [5-126]–[5-127].

[30] ibid [5-128]–[5-133]. Intimate samples are samples like blood, semen, other tissue fluid, saliva, pubic hair or a swab taken from a person's body orifice: ibid [5-129].

[31] ibid [5-134]–[5-138]. Non-intimate samples are samples like hair samples (other than pubic hair), nails, body samples (including mouth, but not other body orifices): ibid [5-134].

[32] ibid [5-190]. DNA is different from the previous description of samples because it is liable to be derived from them. Thus s 65 of PACE defines a 'DNA sample' as any material that has come from a human body and consists of or includes human cells.

right, but it serves to generate information – perceptions in C – that are almost certainly going to be private.[33] That is not least because they have been acquired compulsorily, pursuant to statutory powers.

[8.29] Something that has only much more recently come to the fore is how samples are *used* after they have been acquired by the police (whether lawfully or not). The lawful or unlawful acquisition of samples may affect the use to which they may be put but – as has already been observed – the fruit of the forbidden tree is not something many jurisdictions are particularly firm on excluding – even the United States. In terms of use, the following points are of note.

[8.30] There is, in the United Kingdom, a National DNA Database (the NDNAD). Zander describes it as follows:[34]

> The National DNA Database (NDNAD) was established in 1995. The Protections of Freedoms Act 2012 section 23 inserted section 63AA into PACE which places the National DNA Database on a statutory footing. The section requires DNA profiles taken under PACE or in connection with an investigation to be recorded on the relevant database. As at the end of 2020 the Database held 6,079,575 subject DNA profiles and 631,122 crime scene profiles for England and Wales. This equates to an estimated 5,179,022 individuals. UK holdings total 6,678,369 subject profiles and 660,240 crime scene profiles, or an estimated 5,672,343 individuals.

[8.31] In Zander's words, section 63A of the Police and Criminal Evidence Act 1984 (PACE) 'provides for the checking of biometic data – fingerprints, footwear impressions, intimate and non-intimate samples, and profiles derived from DNA samples – against existing records. Such a search is defined as a "speculative search". It applies in regard to anyone who has been arrested on suspicion of involvement in a recordable offence or who has been charged with or informed they will be reported for such an offence'.[35]

[8.32] Section 63D of PACE provides for the destruction of fingerprints and DNA profiles.[36] These must be destroyed if it appears they were unlawfully taken,[37] and may or may not be retained if lawfully taken according to a set of detailed and complex provisions under PACE. There is little to be gained by setting these out: the point to be derived is that the power to retain is very specific, and unhelpfully so, because it confers powers without any weight being given to different privacy interests. Thus, there is no real consideration given

[33] This is clear, for example, from the definition of 'DNA profile' in s 65 of PACE. A 'DNA profile' is any information derived from a DNA sample.

[34] Zander (n 28) [5-142].

[35] ibid [5-139].

[36] ibid [5-151].

[37] PACE, s 63D(2).

to the interrelationship between: (i) the taking of samples; (ii) the recording of samples; (iii) the retention of samples; and (iv) their other use going beyond recording and retention (being uses in any event); and (v) A's privacy. The powers simply say what they say.

[8.33] The provisions according to which records of fingerprints, footwear impressions, DNA samples and profiles derived from such samples are required to be destroyed[38] were introduced into PACE (and other legislation) by the Protection of Freedoms Act 2012 (PFA 2012). These amendments followed the decision of the European Court of Human Rights in *S and Marper v United Kingdom*,[39] holding that the provisions in PACE (and equivalent legislation for other parts of the United Kingdom) permitting the blanket and indiscriminate retention of DNA from unconvicted criminals violated Article 8 of the ECHR. Although there was a legislative response in the form of sections 14–23 of the Crime and Security Act 2010, these provisions were never brought into force, and were repealed by the PFA 2012, which put in place the provisions here described.

[8.34] Records provide an excellent example of the tension between privacy and other needs, values and interests. The point about records is that they *record* and they are most useful if they are permanent, whether for the purposes of the investigation of 'old' cases or for the purposes of research or for the purposes of historical record.

Example[40]

Peter Sullivan was jailed over the 1986 killing of Diane Sindall. He was acquitted and released, aged 68, in 2025, having spent 39 years in prison. The Criminal Cases Review Commission had referred Mr Sullivan's case to the Court of Appeal after fresh testing found a DNA profile pointing to an unknown attacker in semen samples preserved from the crime scene. The Court of Appeal admitted the new DNA evidence and quashed Mr Sullivan's conviction.

Example[41]

Ryland Headley, aged 92, was convicted in 2025 of the rape and murder of Louisa Dunne in 1967, nearly 60 years earlier. The case was re-examined in 2023, when it was considered that DNA testing had sufficiently improved to warrant testing Mrs Dunne's clothing. Presciently, the clothing had been sealed and retained to await such improvements. The testing produced a viable DNA 'hit', which processed through the DNA database, and found to match a DNA sample compulsorily provided by Mr Headley to the police in 2012 in relation to an alleged offence

[38] For a detailed explanation, see the Explanatory Notes to the PFA 2012 at [22]–[25].

[39] *S and Marper v United Kingdom* [2008] ECHR 1581.

[40] BBC News online, 'Man jailed for 1986 murder acquitted after 38 years' (*BBC News*, 13 May 2025) https://www.bbc.com/news/articles/ce809e3gd1xo, last accessed 25 August 2025.

[41] *BBC online*, 1 July 2025, https://www.bbc.com/news/articles/c24vvdp371jo, last accessed 31 August 2025.

that did not result in a charge. It would appear that the DNA sample from Mr Headley was just within the permitted retention period.

Similarly, medical records may be of assistance both in terms of medical treatment in the individual case and wider medical research.

[8.35] A policy of destruction is thus understandable and yet potentially quite counter-productive because the information has (or may have) a use well beyond its date for destruction. The problem is one of trust: if a record is kept for ever, A's protection is never absolute, for there is a fine line between retention without intended use and retention for a use that has yet to be articulated. Self-evidently, the records here under consideration would fall within the latter case and would constitute 'use' within the meaning of the Action.

[8.36] The problem is particularly acute in the case of material obtained in relation to innocent people when the police are investigating crime. The chief argument against retention is the fear that the retained private information will be misused. Destruction is the safest course to prevent that. Yet this may be too simplistic a response. Tell someone that the state is introducing identity cards, and there is uproar.[42] Suggest the centralised control of state information about individuals, and there is suspicion and rejection. Yet the amount of data held on us collectively by state entities is vast, but unknown. We do not know by which entities information is held, what that information is, and how it is intended to be used. There is much to be said for central retention of all (state actor acquired) information, but subject to strict controls. Perhaps a single, independent, organisation that holds all information the state has, controls the issue of search warrants and other state powers regarding the obtaining of information, and controls access. Access could be one-off (for the purposes of an investigation) or by way of standing order (repeat prior approved demands, eg for tax authorities). Citizens could ask for an audit of what was held on them and would be told unless (in clearly articulated exceptions, eg national security) they should not be.

[8.37] Our society's attitude towards state-retained information will be returned to in Chapter 12. The point for present purposes is that there is a significant link between retention, use and misuse. The fact that retention may be use and misuse is supported by the 'right to be forgotten'. Obviously, that right attaches to use, generally for publication, and there is no inevitable overlap between a narrow form of retention and a use that is, or ought to be, part of the right to be forgotten.[43] Where private information is harvested and retained and used, an interesting question for privacy law is whether use can become misuse over time. Thus, information used on Day 1 may amount to legitimate use, but

[42] These issues are taken up further in Ch 12, including questions of identity cards.

[43] As to this, see generally P Lambert, *The Right to be Forgotten*, 2nd edn (Bloomsbury Professional, 2022).

by Day 100, becomes misuse. In the context of the right to be forgotten, Lambert refers to:[44]

> [o]ne of the problems facing individuals is that information, once online, can become almost permanent. At least that is the common perception. This can have implications for the remainder of their life …

[8.38] It is not simply publication, but digital memory and automation that is problematic:[45]

> A further developing issue relates to how digital memory may be utilised in an automated manner. Elena Esposito refers to 'algorithmic memory' and RtbF issues. She notes for example and by way of contextualisation, that '[w]hat distinguishes digital memory is … its ability to process information without understanding'. There are increasing risk and safety considerations which mirror the interests sought to be protected via RtbF …

[8.39] The General Data Protection Regulation (GDPR) contains a qualified right to erasure, the so-called right to be forgotten or RtbF.[46] As with so many of these 'rights', they are so qualified, so hedged and subject to so many exemptions that their utility may be questioned.

[8.40] Clearly, misuse has a temporal quality, such that something used may, over time, morph into a misuse. The problem is that protecting our privacy through deletion is too blunt a tool. In the first place, it may rightly be asked whether, in this electronic age, information can ever, truly, be deleted. It is perfectly possible to capture a 'snapshot' of the Internet at a specific moment,[47] and it is to be doubted whether any of the data behemoths can actually delete specific information across all backups and safeguards. Indeed, it would be somewhat alarming if they could.

iv. Mission creep

[8.41] The dangers of 'mission creep' – where powers conferred for one purpose are then used for other purposes – are almost inevitable.

> **Example**[48]
>
> Campaigners say councils are using RIPA powers to catch 'low-level' offenders and disregarding the public's right to privacy.

[44] ibid [3.2].
[45] ibid [3.3].
[46] P Coppel, *Information Rights*, Vol 1, 5th edn (Hart Publishing, 2020) [10-023]–[10-028].
[47] See, for example, the Internet archive called the 'Wayback Machine' which, if you subscribe, permits access to the World Wide Web at any point in time back to 1996. The archive (in June 2025) contained 835 billion web pages.
[48] 'Revealed: anti-terror snooping law used for fly-tippers and parking' (*The Guardian*, 8 August 2021) www.theguardian.com/world/2021/aug/08/revealed-anti-terror-snooping-law-used-for-fly-tippers-and-parking, last accessed 25 August 2025.

> Councils have used controversial surveillance legislation to combat 'low-level' offences, such as the misuse of blue badge parking permits, fly-tipping and benefit fraud, an *Observer* investigation has found.
>
> The Regulations of Investigatory Power Act (RIPA) 2000 gives certain public bodies the right – under limited circumstances – to conduct surveillance activities, including for crime prevention and national security purposes.
>
> At least 70 councils in England and Wales were authorised to use RIPA powers between January 2018 and March 2021 to gather evidence via cameras, street surveillance and informants or undercover officers.
>
> The law restricts local authorities in England and Wales to use the surveillance powers only to investigate crimes that carry a prison term of at least six months, unless they relate to the sale of alcohol or tobacco products to underage buyers.
>
> However, as revealed through a bulk of freedom of information (FoI) requests, a number of councils used the legislation to clamp down on what privacy campaigners described as 'low-level offences' that did not result in custodial sentences.
>
> In 2018, Wandsworth council used the act to launch three undercover operations into people deceitfully using a lost or stolen blue badge permit to park in a controlled parking zone. The offenders were prosecuted and given community orders, fined or ordered to do unpaid work. A council spokesman said all three cases impacted disabled and vulnerable elderly people and involved serious offences of fraud, which carry a maximum sentence of 10 years.
>
> Sandwell council, meanwhile, deployed covert surveillance tactics to monitor 'physical locations' and scour Facebook to try to identify the suspected sellers of counterfeit Nike training shoes worth £900. The suspect was cautioned and no criminal charges were brought.
>
> Elsewhere, RIPA powers were used by Anglesey county council to investigate the sale of 'possibly dangerous cosmetics', while other local authorities were authorised to check whether people were fraudulently claiming benefits. For example, in 2019, Blackpool council granted the Department for Work and Pensions access to its CCTV system to try to identify suspected 'benefit fraud'.
>
> Dozens of other operations were related to fly-tipping, with a number of councils using cameras to catch individuals dumping waste at known hotspots.

C. Why is privacy a second-order value?

[8.42] The problem in weighing the protection of privacy against other interests is that information is intrinsically *useful* whereas using private information does not (in most cases) in any easily definable way damage A. Privacy is an important, but qualified right. The problem is that every time privacy is pitted against some other value – perhaps not even a very important value – it seems to lose. That, it is suggested, is because the harm to A of an infringement of their privacy (particularly when it does not involve publication to the outside world[49]) is not particularly easy to identify or quantify. Even if some harm is identified, then this is seen (perhaps rightly – these are value judgements) as a price to be paid for the furthering of other values.

[8.43] The Examples at paragraph [8.34] show the importance of data and records. In the first Example (Mr O'Sullivan) the acquittal of an innocent man was secured in 2025 on the basis of DNA collected in 1986. In the second Example (Mr Headley) a conviction was secured in 2025 on the basis of DNA obtained in 1966 compared against a sample obtained in 2012. A policy of destruction can, as these cases demonstrate, be very damaging and it may be that a more nuanced approach, permitting retention, but controlling use, would be preferable.

[8.44] It may also be that seeing private information through the lens of the ECHR, even in the case of state actors, misses the bigger picture. As was described in Chapter 5, one of the economic justifications for the reification of private information is that it is – in the long-run, and perhaps even in the medium term – beneficial for non-state actors to pay a proper price for the information that they use. In other words, if A is given the opportunity to license the use of their private information to C (a non-state actor), then not only does A benefit (in monetising their rights), but so too does C (because C is forced to consider *why* A's information is valuable to them and how they are going to use it); and so too does the wider economy (because the whole point about price is that it serves as an allocation mechanism). In other words, reifying private information makes private information a scarce resource and (counterintuitively) by increasing C's cost-base, actually makes for greater efficiencies all round.[50]

[8.45] The question is whether the same is true in relation to state actors. Does the fact that the state extracts a great deal of information from us without payment to us make the state less, rather than more, efficient? This is another point that is reverted to in Chapter 12. It is a distraction in this chapter, which is concerned with state-actor-misuse of private information. However, the following issues need to be raised at this stage, because they inform the question of misuse.

[49] There is here an unhelpful analogy to the law of defamation, which turns on harm to reputation through the publication of material to the world. Often, infringements of privacy are seen as the publication to the world of sensitive information about A. This book asserts a wider meaning of privacy, as involving any misuse (through publication or otherwise) of private information.

[50] Recollect the exploitation of the island of Madeira (at paras [5.54]–[5.60]), which is mistakenly blamed on the market economy. That is misconceived. The failure was a failure on the part of the state to put in place a properly working market economy.

[8.46] In Chapter 7, reference was made to a state actor (the DVLA) selling *at a price that simply covers its (the DVLA's) costs* A's private information to private car park operators, who use that information (together with their own CCTV footage) to levy fines on users of car parks:[51]

Example[52]

Ms Rosey Hudson, was taken to court by Excel Parking Ltd, who sought to recover from her parking fines of £1,906 levied pursuant to 10 Parking Charge Notices. Ms Hudson had paid for her parking on these 10 occasions but had breached the 'five minute' rule laid down in Excel Parking Ltd's terms and conditions. These rules required payment within five minutes of entry to the car park, otherwise the user was liable to a fine.

The system works in this way: entry to the car park is electronically recorded by Automated Number Plate Recognition (ANPR) and the owner's details obtained from the DVLA. The level of the charge by the DVLA to Excel Parking Ltd is not known, but the five minute rule enabled Excel Parking Ltd to charge not the £3.30/day rate, but £100 (a price by way of fine) payable within 28 days.

Ms Hudson's position was that it was difficult – generally speaking because of a weak mobile phone signal – actually to pay within five minutes.

The registered keeper of the car (in this case, Ms Hudson) of course receives no payment from the DVLA for the provision by the DVLA of her name and address, to Excel Parking Ltd, even though this information enables the car park provider to levy a fine of £100. If the DVLA charged a proper rate, and paid the owner of the information a proper rate, it is likely that it might be more economic for car park owners to revert to the employment of car park attendants.

[8.47] The fact that private information is provided effectively for free shows precisely the sort of mischief described in relation to the island of Madeira in Chapter 5.[53] The car park owner obtains what would appear to be an unjustified producer surplus; the user of the car park has their (already limited[54]) consumer surplus eradicated; and the DVLA (arguably) misuses the user's private information, and ought to be accountable. The reason this happens is because A's information is regarded as *valueless* when (as can be seen from this example) it is actually *extremely valuable*.

[51] See paras [7.75]–[7.79].

[52] 'Woman hit with eye-watering £1,906 fine for taking 5 extra minutes to pay for parking' (*Nottingham Post*, 1 December 2024), https://www.nottinghampost.com/news/local-news/woman-hit-eye-watering-1906-9758330, accessed 25 August 2025.

[53] See paras [5.54]–[5.60].

[54] This is a case where the consumer surplus is hard to calculate. No-one really uses a car park for the pleasure of it. The car park is incidental to other objectives, whether getting to work or something else. It is a necessary part of a broader objective. That is why the conduct of the car park operator needs to be carefully controlled, ideally by market forces. The ability to charge excess profits because the parked car is a prisoner of circumstance is a market abuse that needs to be controlled. Of course, regulation is always an option, but the point here is that it may not be the most efficient option.

[8.48] Too often wide powers are granted and exercised, with significant incursions into privacy, without any proper use being made of the information derived. If information has a price, it becomes valued and is only sought when there is an identified need. If a resource is 'free', it is abused: in the case of information, this means one asks for too much, *receives it*, and never properly processes it because the effort is too great. It is an extreme and desperately sad case, but the case of the 'Southport killer' is instructive:

Example[55]

Axel Rudakubana, who pleaded guilty to the killing of three children, was 'referred to the anti-extremism programme Prevent on three separate occasions between 2019 and 2021', yet nothing was done. The Counter-Terrorism and Security Act 2015 imposes on certain 'specified authorities' (which include schools) a duty to prevent people being drawn into terrorism.[56] That involves a duty to co-operate between authorities, which includes a communication of private information. The problem is that the duty is widely drawn, and the objectives unclear. Protection of privacy should not be seen as simply obstructive of other public benefits, but as a means of sharpening the purpose of the intrusion so that the intrusion is truly effective. The words of the Prime Minister in light of Rudakubana's conviction are telling:[57]

'The perpetrator was referred to the Prevent programme on three separate occasions – in 2019 once and in 2021 twice … Yet on each of these occasions, a judgement was made that he did not meet the threshold for intervention, a judgement that was clearly wrong and which failed those families. And I acknowledge that here today.'

[8.49] Although the prevailing view is that state actors are best held to account for misuses of private information through the HRA 1998, it may be that the better remedy (in some cases at least) is the Action. As has been seen, Article 8 of the ECHR tends to give way to other values, and the Action has a far broader scope, focusing not on immediate invasion of privacy (the collection of the information) but on its use or misuse. If it is correct that attaching value to something – here by making it property – promotes a better use[58] of that information, then the Action has a great deal to contribute to the wider public good. This point will be returned to in Chapter 12: but this is why *this* chapter focuses on misuse of private information by state actors.

[55] 'Southport killer admitted carrying a knife more than 10 times' (*BBC News*, 21 January 2025) https://www.bbc.co.uk/news/articles/ce8j453e7z1o, last accessed 25 August 2025.

[56] Counter-Terrorism and Security Act 2015, s 26.

[57] Speech given on 20 January 2025.

[58] An economist would use the term 'efficient', meaning a better allocation of resources. That is not what is meant here. Rather, a broader point is being made. If private information is not valued, it is abused. It is obtained for free, but without purpose or focus. Purpose and focus matter because they make for the provision of better services. In short, this is not a 'free market' argument, but an 'improvement of public service' argument.

IV. The Powers of State Actors

A. Private powers exercised for public purposes

[8.50] One of the effects of the approach to state actors in *Entick v Carrington* is that state actors have all the powers of non-state actors plus any specific additional powers conferred on them by law. Thus, a police officer may photograph someone in a public place, without relying on any specifically conferred power because this is a right any non-state actor has.[59] Equally, a police officer may shadow or follow a suspect in a public place, without any specific power being conferred.

[8.51] The fact that a person is a state actor does not deprive them of their rights as a private individual (obviously), and also does not preclude them from using those rights in the furthering of their state actor roles (less obvious, but also the case).[60]

B. Public powers

i. Definition

[8.52] 'Public powers' – in contrast to the 'private powers' just discussed – refers to powers specifically conferred on an actor for a public purpose. Such powers:

- Are conferred on a particular person or body, for reasons of societal interest or benefit. There is a collective reason for the conferring of such powers, justifying the singling out of an actor or undertaking for the receipt of power that non-state actors do not have.
- Usually involve safeguards in terms criteria that must be met before the power can be exercised. This follows from the fact that additional power over other people has been created and conferred.

[59] See, for example, *R (Wood) v MPC* [2009] EWCA Civ 414.

[60] Although unnecessary, this doctrine is usually reiterated in legislation. Thus, RIPA 2000, s 80 provides for a general saving for lawful conduct in the following terms: 'Nothing in any of the provisions of this Act by virtue of which conduct of any description is or may be authorised by any warrant, authorisation or notice, or by virtue of which information may be obtained in any manner, shall be construed – (a) as making it unlawful to engage in any conduct of that description which is not otherwise unlawful under this Act and would not be unlawful apart from this Act; (b) as otherwise requiring – (i) the issue, grant or giving of such a warrant, authorisation or notice, or (ii) the taking of any step for or towards obtaining the authority of such a warrant, authorisation or notice, before any such conduct of that description is engaged in; or (iii) as prejudicing any power to obtain information by any means not involving conduct that may be authorised under this Act.' See, to similar effect, IPA 2016, s 270(1) and Sch 9, para 10.

- Often require a court (or other body) to sanction in advance the exercise of the power or at least exercise after-the-event control through review. Such controls may be internal (eg a senior police officer may give authority to a junior officer to exercise a power) or external (as in the case of a minister or a court). External control is better in the sense that it is properly independent and will minimise the risk of 'group-think' or confirmation bias, but problematic in that an external reviewer may not understand the environment in which the state actor is operating (for instance, the day-to-day pressures of keeping track of terrorist suspects).

ii. A sampling approach

[8.53] There are too many powers to be individually listed. What follows is a selection of the sorts of public powers that are conferred. The consideration begins with some police powers, moves on to the powers of the intelligence services, and then considers more generally information collection powers just to show the *reach* of the state. A couple of powers are dealt with in some detail, to give a feel for how these powers are conferred, and the limits on their exercise that are imposed. The analysis grows more staccato as it progresses. The point of this book is not exhaustively to list and analyse all powers, but to provide a basis by way of which privacy issues and the operation of the Action can be considered.

iii. General ECHR compliance

[8.54] It is also not the purpose of this book to assess whether the powers conferred on the state are HRA 1998 compliant. It is not the thesis of this work that the statutory powers here considered (or, indeed, those not here considered) are per se inconsistent with A's human rights. All of these powers, being powers of the state, are susceptible to challenge by way of the ECHR, and it will be taken as read that – in the abstract – these powers are ECHR compliant. The focus is much more on the lawfulness or otherwise of the *exercise* (or *use*) of a lawful power in the individual case.

[8.55] For example, Clayton and Tomlinson describe the process for the issuing of search warrants in the following terms:[61]

> Applications for search warrants by police officers must be made in accordance with the procedure laid down in section 15 of the Police and Criminal Evidence Act 1984 ('PACE'). An application must be supported by an 'information' in writing. The warrant must specify the name of the person who applies for it, the date on which it is

[61] R Clayton and H Tomlinson, *The Law of Human Rights*, 2nd edn (Oxford University Press, 2009) [12.123].

> issued, the enactment under which it is issued, the premises to be searched and the articles or persons to be sought. The execution of warrants by police officers is governed by section 16 of PACE. The constable must, if the occupier is present, identify himself, produce the warrant and supply a copy. If the occupier is not present, a copy of the warrant must be left at the premises. A warrant does not permit a 'general search' of the premises: a search under warrant may only be a search 'to the extent required for the purpose for which the warrant was issued'. The warrant must be endorsed, stating whether the articles which were sought we found and what other articles were seized. The safeguards imposed by sections 15 and 16B of PACE are 'stringent in effect'. Any search which is not carried out in accordance with these provisions will be unlawful. Thus, searches have been held to be unlawful where copies of the schedules to the warrants were not supplied to the applicant at the time of the search and where the enactment under which the warrant was issued was not specified.

[8.56] This passage makes clear that an argument that the search warrant process was generally an infringement of Article 8 of the ECHR would be doomed to fail. But it also makes clear that a failure to abide by the provisions regarding searches might result in liability (including, no doubt, civil liability for trespass[62]). It cannot be said that simply because powers are in general terms HRA 1998 or ECHR compliant, that the *exercise* of these powers is, in each and every case, unimpeachable. It is quite possible to misuse a power that has been properly conferred.

[8.57] Thus, to carry on with the example of magistrate-issued warrants, Clayton and Tomlinson note:[63]

> The provisions of PACE in relation to warrants are, in general, in conformity with the Convention. An issue may arise, however, as to whether the procedure for the issue of search warrants by magistrates conforms to Article 8, because the procedure is arguably little more than a 'rubber stamping exercise', with refusals being exceedingly rare. A warrant does not show the grounds on which it was issued and the 'information in writing' is usually formal in nature. Justices have no clear obligation in domestic law to give reasons for the grant of a warrant or to keep a record of proceedings. This makes legal challenges extremely difficult. If a warrant is issued without proper grounds, then the person whose property is searched has no remedy in domestic law absent malice. No action for malicious procurement of a search warrant has been successful in England in modern times. These factors lead Feldman to conclude:

[62] R Clayton and H Tomlinson, *Civil Actions against the Police* (Sweet & Maxwell, 1992) 213–22, in particular 220–22.

[63] Clayton and Tomlinson (n 61) [12.126]. The are other instances where questions of HRA 1998 compliance of state actions might arise: see, for example, the invention of common law (ie non-statutory) closed material processes in *R (Haralambous) v Crown Court at St Albans* [2018] UKSC 1; and the consideration of the requisite due process where the Competition and Markets Authority exercises its statutory powers under ss 28 and 28A of the Competition Act 1998 in *R (Competition and Markets Authority) v The Competition Appeal Tribunal* [2024] EWHC 904 (Admin).

> one is left with an impression that justices of the peace do not provide the independent judicial scrutiny of proposed entries and searches under warrants which is needed to ensure that interferences with the right to respect for a person's private life and home are justified ... The formal trappings of scrutiny are there, but the substance is sadly lacking in most cases.
>
> As a result, it is arguable that the procedure for the grant of search warrants is in breach of Article 8 ...

[8.58] One point that is worth flagging now, because it will be returned to, is that the controls over the powers considered below tend to relate to their initial exercise whereby private information is *captured* and say less about how such captured information is *used*. Thus, to deploy the perception/use borderline considered in Chapter 7, the capturing of private information through the use of a power can be equated with C's perception of A's private information; whereas the later use of that perception – by state actor C or someone that state actor C passes that information on to – is: (i) likely to be use as that term is understood in this book; and (ii) the true area of interest when it comes to the Action, which focuses on the use/misuse borderline, and not on perception. If it is the case that the controls over powers conferred on state actors focus principally on initial capture (perception) rather than subsequent use (use/misuse), then the Action has an important role to play in controlling excessive incursions into our private lives.

iv. Police powers

a. Powers of search when executing an arrest warrant (PACE, section 17)

[8.59] Section 17 of PACE confers, amongst other powers, a power on a constable[64] to enter and search any premises for the purpose of executing a warrant of arrest issued in connection with or arising out of criminal proceedings.[65] This power of entry and search does not require a search warrant[66] and is limited in the following respects:

- It is only exercisable if the constable has reasonable grounds for believing that the person they are seeking is on the premises.[67]
- 'Premises' are widely defined in PACE as including 'any place' and in particular includes any vehicle, vessel, aircraft or hovercraft and any tent or

[64] Uniformed or otherwise. PACE, s 17(3) identifies some powers exercisable only by a constable in uniform, but these specific powers are not so limited.

[65] PACE, s 17(1)(a)(i). There are a number of other aspects to the section which also confer a power to enter, but which are not considered.

[66] That process exists and has been touched upon. This example has been chosen because it involves the constable operating without specific judicial authority to search: there is no search warrant, but a warrant for arrest.

[67] PACE, s 17(2)(a).

moveable structure.[68] However, where the premises consist of two or more separate dwellings, the power to enter is limited to those dwellings where the constable has reasonable grounds for believing that the person whom they are seeking may be,[69] including 'common parts'.[70]

b. Powers of seizure: PACE, section 19

[8.60] 'Search' does not authorise 'seizure', which is separately provided for in section 19 of PACE, which provision is entitled 'general power of seizure, etc'. Section 19 confers on a constable who is lawfully on any premises[71] the power to seize anything on the premises if:

- They have reasonable grounds for believing that it has been obtained in consequence of the commission of an offence and it is necessary to seize it in order to prevent it being concealed, lost, damaged, altered or destroyed.[72]
- They have reasonable grounds for believing that it is evidence in relation to an offence that they are investigating or any other offence and it is necessary to seize it in order to prevent the evidence being concealed, lost, altered or destroyed.[73]

[8.61] These days, a great deal of potentially relevant information will be held on electronic devices, doubtless protected by some form of security (password, face recognition, fingerprint, etc). In such cases, section 19(4) of PACE provides:

> The constable may require any information which is stored in any electronic form and is accessible from the premises to be produced in a form in which it can be taken away and in which it is visible and legible or from which it can readily be produced in a visible and legible form if he has reasonable grounds for believing –
>
> (a) that –
>
> (i) it is evidence in relation to an offence which he is investigating or any other offence; or
>
> (ii) it has been obtained in consequence of the commission of an offence; and
>
> (b) that it is necessary to do so in order to prevent it being concealed, lost, tampered with or destroyed.

[8.62] As noted above, it is assumed that these powers are compliant with Article 8 of the ECHR. They have not been challenged. Indeed, the limitations

[68] ibid s 23.
[69] ibid s 17(2)(b)(ii).
[70] ibid s 17(2)(b)(i).
[71] ibid s 19(1). The power of seizure is thus much wider than simply in relation to PACE, s 17. It entitles seizure pursuant to a number of powers.
[72] ibid s 19(2).
[73] ibid s 19(3).

of the exercise of the powers seem reasonable and (although power specific) equate to the much more general protection conferred in the United States by the Fourth Amendment.

[8.63] The limits imposed on the powers matter when the width of those same powers is considered. Thus, when executing a warrant for the arrest of a particular person for a particular offence (which is what must be specified in a warrant), a constable may enter premises to effect the arrest. In doing so, the constable's powers extend as follows:

- The constable may search the premises, subject only to the restriction on dwelling and common parts. The constable may not – absent specific separate justification – search *another* dwelling.
- The search is not limited to the possessions of the person whose arrest is being sought. That would be a difficult limitation to impose on a constable. The search, therefore, will be general one, across all parts of the dwelling or premises, irrespective of *whose* personal information is being searched.
- The protections on third party privacy are limited to reasonable grounds for believing that the evidence is related to *a crime*, not necessarily the crime that informed the warrant. Thus, the risks to those on the same premises as the subject of the warrant are high, even in their own home. Unlike in the United States, it is *not* necessary to show probable cause against A in order to enter and search A's dwelling. It is enough that X, the subject of the warrant, is on the premises (or rather that the constable reasonably believes that to be the case).

[8.64] Section 19 of PACE envisages even very sensitive material being seized. That is clear from section 19(6), which gives special protection for material subject to legal privilege:[74]

> No power of seizure conferred on a constable under any enactment (including an enactment contained in an Act passed after this Act) is to be taken to authorise the seizure of an item which the constable exercising the power has reasonable grounds for believing to be subject to legal privilege.

c. Search without arrest warrant (PACE, section 17)

[8.65] Section 17(1)(b) of PACE provides that a constable may enter and search any premises for the purpose of arresting a person for an indictable offence. Powers of arrest are stated in section 24 of PACE and arise in relation to the following circumstances.

[74] Lawyers will know, but non-lawyers may not know, that the law confers enormous protection on a person's interactions with their lawyer for the purposes of obtaining legal advice. Here, the protection is limited to a constable's reasonable grounds for belief.

[8.66] *Offences about to be committed or in the process of being committed.* In these cases:

(1) A constable may arrest without warrant anyone who is about to commit an offence or anyone who is in the act of committing an offence. Provided the guilty acts are being committed or about to be committed, no foundation is required for constable to exercise their power: no belief of any kind is required (although this case must be extremely rare).
(2) A constable may arrest without warrant anyone who they have reasonable grounds for suspecting to be about to commit an offence or to be committing an offence. Provided the reasonable grounds for suspicion exist in the mind of the constable, it is not necessary for the guilty act actually to be committed.

[8.67] *Past offences.* In these cases:

(1) Where a constable has reasonable grounds for suspecting that an offence has been committed, they may arrest without warrant anyone who they have reasonable grounds to suspect of being guilty of it.
(2) If an offence has been committed, a constable may arrest without warrant anyone who is guilty of the offence or anyone they have reasonable grounds for suspecting to be guilty of it.

Once again, it is possible to arrest someone *guilty* of an offence or where an offence *has in fact been committed* without reasonable suspicion, but where no offence has been committed or an offence has been committed but not by the person arrested, reasonable suspicion on the part of the constable is required.

[8.68] 'Reasonable suspicion' exists where a person thinks that there is a possibility, which must be more than fanciful, that the relevant matter is satisfied.[75] This is not a high threshold. It follows that a constable may lawfully be on A's premises in a variety of cases, many of which may have nothing to do with A. Yet the powers of search and seizure are as wide as they are in the case of arrest pursuant to a warrant.

d. Search of premises on arrest (PACE, section 32)

[8.69] Section 32(2)(b) of PACE provides that where a constable arrests a person at a place other than a police station, if the offence for which that person has been arrested is indictable, then the constable has the power to enter and search any premises in which that person was when arrested or immediately before that person was arrested for evidence relating to the offence.

[75] R Card, *Card and English on Police Law*, 16th edn (Oxford University Press, 2022) [4.41].

[8.70] The power to search premises where the person was arrested appears to duplicate section 18 of PACE. But the power to search premises where the arrested person was immediately before arrest under section 32 of PACE is different to the power under section 18 of PACE. The power conferred by section 32(2)(b) is 'only a power to search to the extent that is reasonably required for the purpose of discovering ... any such evidence'.[76]

[8.71] The important point about these powers is that they enable a constable lawfully to be on the premises and so trigger the wider search and seizure powers described above.

e. Fingerprinting and biometric evidence

[8.72] As noted at paragraph [8.28], the police have a wide variety of powers regarding fingerprinting,[77] impressions of footwear,[78] taking of intimate samples,[79] taking of non-intimate samples,[80] and taking of DNA.[81] In all of these cases, the same issues arise. It is, before any question of use/misuse arises, necessary to evaluate the extent to which such samples or evidence constitute private information. It is suggested such samples or evidence will generally be of A's private information (although that would have to be established at trial).

[8.73] Recalling the distinction between information *personal to* A and *information private to* A,[82] the samples are – self-evidently – *personal* to A. Whether they are *private* to A is a harder question, but the answer is likely to be 'Yes', even in less intrusive cases like non-intimate samples. That is because the samples are being obtained for a reason, and that reason is – or ought to be – for the purposes of a police investigation. The critical question – 'Is the information private?' – depends upon the process (investigation) of which the sample-taking is a part.

[8.74] Going back to the analysis of what constitutes information[83] and the question of whether information in an unread book is information, or whether

[76] PACE, s 32(3).

[77] Zander (n 28) [5-120]–[5.125].

[78] ibid [5-126]–[5-127].

[79] ibid [5-128]–[5-133]. Intimate samples are samples like blood, semen, other tissue fluid, saliva, pubic hair or a swab taken from a person's body orifice: ibid [5-129].

[80] ibid [5-134]–[5-138]. Non-intimate samples are samples like hair samples (other than pubic hair), nails, body samples (including mouth, but not other body orifices): ibid [5-134].

[81] ibid [5-190]. DNA is different from the previous description of samples because it is liable to be derived from them. Thus s 65 of PACE defines a 'DNA sample' as any material that has come from a human body and consists of or includes human cells.

[82] See Ch 6.

[83] See Ch 3.

(in order to be information) it must be perceived by someone: this book favours the latter understanding (although the former is a perfectly proper definition). On this basis, all the taking of a sample does is generate a potential for generating *information* about A, whether by itself or in conjunction with other evidence/material. The sample is *not* information in its own right, but it serves to generate information – perceptions in C – that are almost certainly going to be private.[84] That is not least because they have been acquired compulsorily, pursuant to statutory powers, which is a material factor when considering both privacy and misuse. This is reflected in the fact that the (compulsory) obtaining of this information (by which is meant the sample that leads to the perception that is information) is controlled. It is unnecessary to go into the detail, but the police are rightly constrained by the samples that they may acquire from A. Obviously, those controls are informed by the duties of the police to investigate crime. That is why these powers exist.

v. National security

a. Introduction

[8.75] The statutory framework was summarised in paragraph [8.16]. There are three statutes which matter: (i) the Intelligence Services Act 1994 (ISA 1994); (ii) the Regulation of Investigatory Powers Act 2000 (RIPA 2000); and (iii) the Investigatory Powers Act 2016 (IPA 2016). These three Acts confer a number of surveillance powers on the 'Agencies', as they are referred to.[85]

b. Property warrants (ISA 1994, section 5)[86]

[8.76] The Secretary of State may, on application by one of the Agencies, issue a warrant authorising entry on or interference with property or with wireless telegraphy, the effect of which is to render the entry or interference lawful. The warrant must specify the action to be taken and the property or wireless telegraphy concerned. The warrant may only be issued where the Secretary of State is satisfied that the entry or interference is necessary for the purpose of assisting the Agency in carrying out its statutory functions and is proportionate to what the entry or interference seeks to achieve. It is obviously important to consider whether the end could be achieved by other means, and a property warrant is not required where the Agency could lawfully act in any event. Warrants last for six months but may be renewed.

[84] This is clear, for example, from the definition of 'DNA profile' in PACE, s 65. A 'DNA profile' is any information derived from a DNA sample.

[85] See Ward and Blundell (n 14) Ch 3 on the various agencies and their legal basis of operation. The Agencies are MI5, the SIS (colloquially, MI6), and GCHQ.

[86] Ward and Blundell (n 14) [4.04]–[4.08].

c. Directed surveillance authorisations (RIPA 2000, part II)

[8.77] Directed surveillance is (covert) surveillance[87] undertaken in relation to a specific investigation or operation which is likely to result in the obtaining of private information about a person and is conducted otherwise than by way of an immediate response to events or circumstances, the nature of which is such that it would not be reasonably practicable for an authorisation to be sought for the carrying out of the surveillance.[88] Private information includes any information relating to a person's private or family life.[89] Directed surveillance may include interception of communications sent by or intended for a person who has consented to the interception and no interception warrant is in place.[90] Ward and Blundell summarise the effect of such authorisations:[91]

> A directed surveillance authorisation may be granted by members of specified public authorities of a prescribed office, rank or position. Anything done in accordance with such an authorisation is lawful for all purposes. A directed surveillance authorisation lasts for three months. An authorisation may be renewed, in which case the renewal authorisation will last for six months. An authorisation must be cancelled when it is no longer needed or ceases to meet the statutory criteria.

d. Intrusive surveillance warrants (RIPA 2000, part II)[92]

[8.78] A warrant must be granted by the Secretary of State but does not require the approval of the Judicial Commissioner. Warrants last for six months, may be renewed, and must be cancelled when no longer needed or when they cease to meet the statutory criteria. Intrusive surveillance is covert surveillance 'carried out in relation to anything taking place on residential premises or in a private vehicle, which involves the presence of an individual on the premises or in the vehicle or is carried out by means of a surveillance device'.[93]

e. CHIS authorisations (RIPA 2000, part II)[94]

[8.79] 'CHIS' stands for Covert Human Intelligence Resources. A person is a CHIS if they establish or maintain a personal or other relationship with a person for the covert purpose of facilitating the doing of anything that involves:

- covertly using such a relationship to obtain information or to provide access to any information to another person; or

[87] See the definition in Ward and Blundell (n 14) [4.17].
[88] ibid [4.18].
[89] RIPA 2000, s 26(10).
[90] Ward and Blundell (n 14) [4.20].
[91] ibid [4.17].
[92] ibid [4.21]–[4.26].
[93] ibid [4.22].
[94] ibid [4.27]–[4.37].

- covertly disclosing information obtained by the use of such relationship or as a consequence of the existence of such a relationship.[95]

[8.80] A CHIS authorisation may be granted by members of specified public authorities of a prescribed rank, office or position. Anything done in accordance with such an authorisation is lawful for all purposes. Originally this provided protection only from *civil* and not *criminal* liability.[96] However, the Covert Human Intelligence Sources (Criminal Conduct) Act 2021 inserted into RIPA 2000 authorisation of criminal conduct by way of a criminal conduct authorisation, which must be notified to a Judicial Commissioner.[97]

f. Data

[8.81] This is where we move from 'traditional' forms of information gathering to the collection of data in a manner akin to the approaches of non-state entities, as described by Zuboff.[98] Of course, unlike in the case of surveillance capitalism, the purpose of such powers is not the making of money, but the use of data (both mass and individuated) in order to predict the conduct of terrorists and others to commit acts against the law.

[8.82] The law in this regard was restated in the IPA 2016. The 2016 Act 'gave the Agencies no significant new capabilities but instead provided an updated legal basis for those they already had'[99] (or may have had[100]). The reason for the need for a restatement was the disclosures of Edward Snowden.[101]

[8.83] The legal provision made by the IPA 2016 may helpfully be summarised as follows:[102]

> The IPA 2016 makes provision for both 'targeted' and 'bulk' powers. The targeted powers may be used to obtain information about particular individuals. The bulk powers permit the obtaining of large volumes of data, which can then be 'mined' or examined for information relating to individuals or activities of concern. The Act enables the Secretary of State to issue bulk interception warrants, warrants for the bulk acquisition of communications data, bulk equipment interference warrants, and bulk personal dataset warrants. These warrants may be issued only to the Agencies.

[95] ibid [4.27].
[96] ibid [4.33].
[97] ibid [4.36]–[4.37].
[98] See paras [1.8] ff and [6.61] ff.
[99] ibid [4.39].
[100] As in the case of the PFA 2012, the 2016 Act makes clear powers that may have been more debatable prior to the enactment of the legislation.
[101] Ward and Blundell (n 14) [4.39]. The concerns regarding bulk powers have resulted in a number of challenges, which are described at ibid [4.41]–[4.47].
[102] ibid [4.40].

One of the safeguards imposed by the Act is that the selection for examination of bulk data is limited to operational purposes that appear on a list maintained by the Agency heads. An operational purpose may be added to the list only with the approval of the Secretary of State and the list must be reviewed at least annually by the Prime Minister. A bulk warrant may be issued only if the Secretary of State considers that the examination of material under the warrant is or may be necessary for operational purposes specified on the warrant, which must be purposes that appear on the list.

[8.84] The statutory provisions are both complex and extensive. The powers are all subject to a 'double-lock' mechanism, requiring a warrant by the Secretary of State approved by a Judicial Commissioner. What follows is a summary of the key areas.

[8.85] *Interception.* There is a general prohibition on interception. Generally speaking, the interception of a communication in the course of its transmission by means of a public or private telecommunication system or a public postal service is unlawful.[103] The IPA 2016 provides a variety of lawful bases by which interception can take place.

[8.86] *Retention notices.* The Secretary of State may issue a 'retention notice' requiring a telecommunications or postal operator to retain relevant communications data if they consider this necessary and proportionate for one or more of the purposes for which communications data may be obtained,[104] which include: (i) the interests of national security; (ii) the purpose of preventing and detecting crime; and (iii) the interests of the economic well-being of the United Kingdom insofar as those interests are also relevant to the interests of national security.[105]

[8.87] *Inappropriate use of bulk data.* An Agency may not select from the product of a bulk interception warrant the communications sent by or intended for an individual known to be in the British Islands at the time. The Secretary of State may issue a targeted examination warrant authorisiing such selection if they consider that essentially the same tests are met as for a targeted interception warrant. These provisions are necessary to ensure that the requirements for the obtaining of a targeted interception warrant are not circumvented by the selective and targeted use of bulk data.[106]

[103] ibid [4.48]–[4.51].

[104] ibid [4.65].

[105] ibid [4.63]. There is also provision for 'national security notices' and 'technical capability notices'. The former is a notice requiring a telecommunications operator to take such specified steps as the Secretary of State considers necessary in the interests of national security. The latter is issued where the Secretary of State considers it necessary for securing that the operator has the capability to provide any assistance which they may be required to provide in relation to warrants that may be issued in the future.

[106] ibid [4.61].

[8.88] *Targeted equipment interference warrants.* Such warrants permit the interference with electronic devices in order to obtain information. The warrant is issued by the Secretary of State. The warrant may authorised both physical interference with equipment and remote interference, as well as any conduct necessary to do that which is expressly authorised or required by the warrant. The warrant will enable the monitoring, observing or listening to a person's communications or other activities and recording anything monitored, observed or listened to.[107]

[8.89] *Bulk Interception Warrants.* A bulk interception warrant is issued on the application by one of the Agencies (typically, GCHQ) the purpose of which is the interception of overseas related communications and/or the obtaining of secondary data from such communications. Overseas related communications are those sent or received by individuals outside the British Isles (although the counterparty may be within the British Islands). The point of this limitation is to prevent warrants whose primary purpose would be intercepting communications between people within the British Islands. The Secretary of State may issue such a warrant if satisfied that the warrant is necessary in the interests set out at paragraph [8.84]. The warrant must set out specified operational purposes, and intercepted content or secondary data may not be selected for examination unless the examination is necessary for one or more of the operational purposes specified in the warrant. These warrants last for six months but are renewable.[108]

[8.90] *Bulk Acquisition Warrants.* By issuing a bulk acquisition warrant, the Secretary of State authorises or requires the person to whom it is addressed to acquire bulk communications data from a telecommunications operator and to select the acquired data for examination. These warrants may be granted in similar circumstances and on similar terms to bulk interception warrants (see paragraph [8.87], but the focus will be on the acquisition of domestic communications ie between persons within the British Isles.[109] The relevant code of practice is illuminating.[110]

[8.91] The warrants are exercisable against 'telecommunications operators', being persons who offer or provide a telecommunications service to persons in the United Kingdom or who control or provide a telecommunication system which is wholly or partly in or controlled from the United Kingdom.[111] Warrants extend to 'Internet-based services such as web-based email, messaging applications and cloud-based services'.[112]

[107] ibid [4.66]–[4.72].
[108] ibid [4.73]–[4.74].
[109] ibid [4.75].
[110] See Home Office, *Bulk Acquisition of Communications Data Code of Practice* (updated 6 June 2025), available at the gov.uk website.
[111] ibid [2.1], [2.2].
[112] ibid [2.4].

[8.92] Warrants extend to the capture of systems data and content. Content, of course, is going to be individual to the parties to the communication, and therefore not susceptible of proper use under a bulk acquisition warrant. In theory, therefore, a bulk acquisition warrant ought not to extend to content. The trouble is that the content may *also* be systems data, and to this extent may be subject to capture and use. The dividing line between 'bulk' and 'individual' is thus a remarkably difficult one to draw, as section 261 of the IPA 2016 shows:[113]

> **261 Telecommunications definitions**
>
> (1) The definitions in this section have effect for the purposes of this Act.
>
> Communication
>
> (2) 'Communication'… includes—
>
> (a) anything comprising speech, music, sounds, visual images or data of any description, and
> (b) signals serving either for the impartation of anything between persons, between a person and a thing or between things or for the actuation or control of any apparatus.
>
> Entity data
>
> (3) 'Entity data' means any data which—
>
> (a) is about—
>   (i) an entity,
>   (ii) an association between a telecommunications service and an entity, or
>   (iii) an association between any part of a telecommunication system and an entity,
> (b) consists of, or includes, data which identifies or describes the entity (whether or not by reference to the entity's location), and
> (c) is not events data.
>
> Events data
>
> (4) 'Events data' means any data which identifies or describes an event (whether or not by reference to its location) on, in or by means of a telecommunication system where the event consists of one or more entities engaging in a specific activity at a specific time.
>
> Communications data
>
> (5) 'Communications data'… means entity data or events data—
>
> (a) which is (or is to be or is capable of being) held or obtained by, or on behalf of, a telecommunications operator and
>   (i) is about an entity to which a telecommunications service is provided and relates to the provision of the service,

[113] The quotation is kept as short as possible, and no effort is made to construe it. The point being made is the rather cruder one going to the breadth of the information that may be captured under these warrants.

(ii) is comprised in, included as part of, attached to or logically associated with a communication (whether by the sender or otherwise) for the purposes of a telecommunications system by means of which the communication is being or may be transmitted, or
(iii) does not fall within sub-paragraph (i) or (ii) but does relate to the use of a telecommunications service or a telecommunication system,

(b) which is available directly from a telecommunication system and falls within paragraph (ii) of paragraph (a), or
(c) which—
(i) is (or is to be or is capable of being) held or obtained by, or on behalf of, a telecommunications operator,
(ii) is about the architecture of a telecommunication system, and
(iii) is not about a specific person

but (subject to subsection 5A) does not include any content of a communication or anything which, in the absence of subsection 6(b), would be content of a communication.

(5A) In subsection (5), the words after paragraph (c) do not apply to relevant subscriber data.

(5B) In subsection (5A) 'relevant subscriber data' means entity data, other than data comprised in a recording of speech, which—

(a) constitutes any or all of the content of a communication made for the purpose of initiating or maintaining an entity's access to a telecommunications service, and
(b) is about an entity to which that telecommunications service is (or is to be) provided.

Content of a communication

(6) 'Content' … means any element of the communication, or any data attached to or logically associated with the communication, which reveals anything of what might reasonably be considered to be the meaning (if any) of the communication, but—

(a) any meaning arising from the fact of the communication or from any data relating to the transmission of the communication is to be disregarded, and
(b) anything which is systems data is not content.

Other definitions

(7) 'Entity' means a person or thing.

[8.93] Section 158 is the legal basis for the issue of a bulk acquisition warrant. The warrant may only require the production, etc of 'communications data', and so excludes content, because that – by definition – is individual. Quite why a definition of such abnormal complexity is required when the distinction between metadata and content is actually straightforward to understand and where there is supervision of the issue of warrants by judicial commissioners is difficult to understand.

[8.94] The code of practice attempts to make the statutory definition clearer, as follows:

> [2.7] For the purposes of the Act, communications may comprise two broad categories of data: systems data and content. Some communications may consist entirely of systems data. Section 261(6)(b) makes clear that anything which is systems data is, by definition, not content. When permitted by the Act, certain data may also be separated from the remainder of a communication in circumstances where, if it were so separated, it would not reveal anything of what might reasonably be considered to be the meaning (if any) of the communication. This is identifying data. Systems data and identifying data may be obtained by interception or equipment interference warrants under Parts 2, 5 and 6 of the Act.
>
> [2.8] [Communications data] is a subset of systems data. Section 261(5) is clear that, even though systems data cannot be content, [communications data] is limited to data which does not reveal anything of what might reasonably be considered to be the meaning of the communication, excepting any meaning arising from the fact of the communication or transmission of the communication. That is, any systems data which would, in the absence of section 261(6)(b), be content, cannot be [communications data].

[8.95] *Bulk Equipment Interference Warrants.* Ward and Blundell describe this type of warrant as follows:[114]

> A bulk EI warrant, like a bulk interception warrant, may only be issued on application by one of the Agencies, and its main purpose must be the obtaining of 'overseas-related' communications, equipment data, or information ie the communications sent or received by or the information of people outside the British Islands. The provisions relating to these warrants are materially identical to the provisions for bulk interception warrants. Bulk EI warrants last for six months, but are renewable. A warrant must be cancelled when no longer necessary or proportionate or when the examination of material obtained under it is no longer necessary for any of the specified operational purposes. Persons exercising functions relating to bulk EI must have regard to a Code of Practice issued by the Secretary of State.

[8.96] *No bulk processing save when there is legal basis.* The IPA 2016 defines bulk personal datasets as a set of information that includes personal data relating to a number of individuals, in circumstances where the majority of the individuals are not, and are unlikely to become, of interest to the Agency in the exercise of its functions, but where (after initial examination of the contents) the Agency retains the set for the purpose of the exercise of its functions and the set is held, or is to be held, electronically for analysis in the exercise of those functions.[115] The IPA 2016 provides for two kinds of warrant, 'class' warrants

[114] Ward and Blundell (n 14) [4.76].
[115] IPA 2016, s 199.

(which authorise multiple similar bulk personal dataset analyses)[116] and 'specific' warrants (which authorise one specific bulk personal dataset analysis).[117]

vi. The reach of state powers into the private sphere: The need for data and information

[8.97] Sturge makes the important point that information or data counts, matters:[118]

> The act of counting people can be greatly significant in its own right. At some point around the nineteenth century, the verb to 'count' started to be used as 'to matter'. It makes sense that we would use the same word – why would we go to the trouble if we didn't think it did. The act of enumerating things – and specifically people – is recognition that we find them important and worthy of being noticed. A development since the 1990s is the collecting of data on people's personal characteristics, for the reason that recognising an identity – be that related to sexual orientation, ethnicity or belief – is a means of bestowing dignity, which itself is considered a key element in a fulfilled existence. Going further back in time, we can see how collecting data on the working classes, people living in poverty and on the terrible housing and sanitary conditions of whole swathes of the population not only acknowledged their existence but made it clear something had to change.
>
> But there is a dark side to this. Counting people is only a positive form of recognition if people agree with the way they are being labelled and sorted, and with the reason for their information being collected. Unfortunately, there have been many instances in which this was not the case. In our official statistics, people have been counted as 'lunatics', 'idiots' and 'feeble-minded' with what we can hardly imagine was a thorough medical assessment. They have been labelled as paupers, lower class, semi-criminal, illegitimate, degenerate, aliens, half-breeds and pagans based on someone else's idea of what is acceptable, normal or desirable. The classifications used in counting can encourage a view that some people are lesser than others – sometimes quite literally, to the extent that they are counted as less of a human being. Refusing to count people in the way they would like to be acknowledged can be a formal kind of slap in the face.

[8.98] Sturge is here talking about perception, not use. But the point is that perceptions are gathered by the state in order to be used.

[8.99] Sturge articulates very clearly the sheer usefulness of data,[119] and this is not the case merely at the aggregate level, but at the individual level: revenue authorities, competition authorities, health authorities, all have powers

[116] ibid s 204. There is statutory provision in the IPA 2016, s 202 which states certain circumstances in which the Agency *must* apply for a specific warrant.
[117] ibid s 205.
[118] G Sturge, *Sum of Us: A History of Data in the UK* (Bridge Street Press, 2025) 14–15.
[119] ibid generally.

to command information from us in order to pursue their proper purposes. Schulhofer too makes clear the importance of information in the service of the administrative state.[120]

C. Powers, purpose and use

[8.100] The big difference between powers conferred on non-state actors and powers conferred on state actors is the question of proper purpose. We call powers conferred on non-state actors *rights* rather than *powers* to reflect the fact that non-state actors have agency within limits, and those limits are defined by rights/powers, whether of individual actor or of third parties. Thus, an individual has the right to choose where to walk, what to say, how long to work, subject to constraints both legal and economic. Within those constraints, the individual is not compelled to act for a particular purpose but is free to choose their own course. This is no more than (limited) self-determination.

[8.101] By contrast, state actors do not have rights in this sense: they have powers. Those powers have particular purposes; and those purposes constrain how the powers may lawfully be exercised. There is a very close relationship between power and discretion. Power gives a basis for doing something, but the power does not have to be exercised at all, and there is certainly no unconstrained ability to use the power howsoever the holder wishes. Power involves choice or discretion, and that discretion must be exercised lawfully. Supperstone and Goudie provide the following helpful list of cases where, in a judicial review context, the courts have considered the borderline between proper and improper purposes:[121]

> **Improper purposes**
>
> Under this heading examples show a wide range of impropriety from the technical, arising from a misconstruction of a statutory power, to collateral or ulterior purposes clothed thinly with the veil of the statutory purpose. The former include planning cases in which the protection of tenants was held to be an improper purpose in the licensing of a caravan site, and a requirement to construct a road as a condition of planning permission was held to be an unlawful collateral obligation. The 'misplaced philanthropy' cases involving payment of improperly generous wages and subsidising public transport are also examples of intrinsically legitimate objects that simply lacked statutory authority. Many cases involve the pursuit of purposes at variance with the policy of the relevant legislation or directly opposed to it. Examples

[120] S Schulhofer, *More Essential Than Ever* (Oxford University Press, 2012) Ch 5; and see para [4.160] ff which consider this question through the prism of the Fourth Amendment.

[121] M Supperstone and J Goudie, *Judicial Review*, 2nd edn (Butterworths, 1997) 5.40–5.41. The examples are drawn from all areas of public decision-making, and are not privacy-specific. The point is to illuminate generally how discretion is articulated by reference to purpose.

include a refusal to raise rents, and an allocation of a local authority's entire required rent increase to a single unoccupied house, in order to avoid the requirements of legislation authorising or requiring increased rents for the properties concerned.; the exercise of a prerogative power to remove the designation of an airline under a bilateral international agreement in order to defeat the purpose of the regulatory statute; use of a prerogative power to introduce a new scheme for criminal injuries compensation inconsistent with a scheme enacted by Parliament but which had not been brought into effect by a commencement order; refusal to exercise a discretion to refer a dispute to a committee of investigation to avoid political embarrassment; fixing high overtime rates for shop workers to force shops to close earlier in the evening; and removing local authority-appointed school governors to secure compliance with the authority's policy for the school. An example of an ulterior purpose, albeit benign, is the leading case of *Webb v Minister of Housing and Local Government*,[122] where a power of compulsory purchase for coastal protection was used ostensibly for the permitted purpose but in reality (as inferred, amongst other things, from the width of the strip of land acquired) to enable the construction of a promenade. Improper political purposes occasionally feature in successful challenges, as in two cases involving opposition to Mr Rupert Murdoch's activities. Use of a broad discretionary licensing power to enforce the payment of money to the Crown without Parliamentary sanction has also been held to involve an unlawful purpose. On the other hand, the House of Lords, overruling the Court of Appeal, has upheld the use of a power of compulsory purchase in a way designed to create price control over development land.

[8.102] A good formulation of discretion and its policing is to be found in the trusts case (ie *not* a public law case at all) of *Karger v Paul*, a decision of the Supreme Court of Victoria.[123] This case concerned a widely-drawn power exercisable by the trustees 'in their absolute and unfettered discretion'. The court nevertheless held that the essential component parts of even so widely drawn a discretion were to act: (i) in good faith; (ii) with a real and genuine consideration of the matter; (iii) in accordance with the purposes for which the discretion was conferred:

> ... it is open to the court to examine the evidence to decide whether there has been a failure by the trustees to exercise the discretion in good faith, upon real and genuine consideration and in accordance with the purposes for which the discretion was conferred. As part of the process of, and solely for the purpose of ascertaining whether there has been any such failure, it is relevant to look at evidence of the inquiries which were made by the trustees, the information they had and the reasons for, and manner of, their exercising their discretion. However, it is not open to the court to look at those things for the independent purpose of impugning the exercise of discretion on the grounds that their inquiries, information or reasons or the manner of the exercise of the discretion, fell short of what was appropriate and sufficient. Nor is it open to the court to look at the factual position established by the evidence, for the independent purpose of impugning the exercise of the discretion

[122] *Webb v Minister of Housing and Local Government* [1965] 1 WLR 755.
[123] *Karger v Paul* [1984] VR 161, 164.

> on the grounds the trustees were wrong in their appreciation of the facts or made an unwise or unjustified exercise of discretion in the circumstances. The issues which are examinable by the court are limited to whether there has been a failure to exercise the discretion in good faith, upon real and genuine consideration and in accordance with the purpose for which the discretion was conferred. In short, the court examines whether the discretion was exercised but does not examine how it was exercised.

[8.103] Sturge's point (in the passage quoted at paragraph [8.97]) is a powerful statement as to why information and privacy matter: they go to being *seen* or being *counted*. Indeed, Sturge's framing of the issue is very close to the definition of privacy adopted in this book. Nevertheless, the mere collection of information, without more,[124] falls on the side of *perception* and is not actionable under the Action. It is the use/misuse borderline that counts, and the suggestion in this chapter is that proper purpose is a key element in differentiating between a use that is legitimate and a use that is illegitimate. This is a point that will be returned to when we come to frame the test for misuse of private information by a state actor.

V. Liability of Non-natural Persons

[8.104] This chapter continues with a focus on C being a natural person, a human being. Of course, it is recognised that state actors will almost inevitably be undertakings and/or legal persons of one form or another. Generally speaking (police powers are a notable exception, which tend to be conferred on the officer not the undertaking) special powers are conferred on entities that are undertakings – MI5, the SIS, GCHQ (ie the Agencies) and so on. Nevertheless, even these entities have to act via human beings, and the starting point of the Action – the perception of C – continues to mean that consideration of the liability of undertakings has to be postponed (until Chapter 9) after the easier case of A versus C has been resolved.

VI. The Perception/Use/Misuse Divide Continues to Hold Good

A. Exercise of a state power tends to equate to perception, not use

[8.105] There is a temptation to elide perceptions obtained through the exercise of a power with liability or non-liability under the Action. This false elision manifests itself in two ways:

- There is an instinct to conclude that perceptions obtained pursuant to the lawful exercise of a power means that no Action can lie.

[124] Although retaining for the purpose of contingent access is use, not perception.

- There is also an instinct to conclude that perceptions obtained pursuant to an unlawful exercise of power will involve a successful claim under the Action.

[8.106] Neither proposition is true. The equation of the (un)lawfulness by which a perception has been obtained is, to be sure, a factor that is relevant, but it is very far from being determinative. The reason the elision is false is because, just as in the case of non-state actors, the perceptions of state actors do not trigger the Action, even if there has been an abuse of power.[125] What matters is the use to which the perception is put, and whether that use crosses the line into misuse. Just as in the case of non-state actors, perception is protected, albeit for different reasons. In the case of the non-state actor, protection of perception is necessary to protect that actor's human rights; in the case of the state actor, perception (ie the obtaining or harvesting of information) is controlled for through the limits on the exercise of the power. The Action has no role in regard to the *acquiring* of perception, but serves to police the *use* of perceptions obtained through the use of state powers.

[8.107] Suppose a police officer mala fide enters upon A's property, searches it, and uplifts A's diary, and even reads it. Suppose, further, the officer transmits A's private information to their superior to consider. All of this involves the perception of C (and his superior[126]), and A is far from having a strong claim under the Action. A is far from establishing *use*, which is the critical point for actionability. In short, A would be at serious risk of being struck out before trial.

[8.108] Of course, C may well be exposed to an action in trespass.[127] But that is not the topic of this book. We are interested in the Action, and it is clear that an unlawfully obtained perception remains just that – a perception, insufficient to support a successful Action. Unlawfulness in the obtaining of the perception may be a relevant factor in the perception/use borderline, but it is (at most) a factor. The converse, however, also holds good. The fact that C's perception has been lawfully obtained says nothing about the lawfulness of any subsequent use by C of that perception.

[125] What is being postulated is not a 'technical' abuse of power: the point holds good even in the case of an egregious abuse of power.

[126] This would (or might be, depending on how the law treats mala fides in this context) be a case of 'internal communication', as to which, see paras [7.39]–[7.43]. It might be said that a communication within an organisation by a mala fide employee to a bona fide recipient takes the case out of perception and into use. Again, this is an area ripe for further development.

[127] Clayton and Tomlinson consider the efficacy of such actions in controlling abuse of police power, and conclude that the efficacy of such actions is minimal: Clayton and Tomlinson (n 62) 13–17. That may well be the fate of the Action. Only time will tell. See also Clayton and Tomlinson (n 61) [12.134].

B. Asking the right question: The importance of the use/misuse divide

i. The wrong question

[8.109] Focusing upon *use* rather than *perception* means that the dichotomy between a lawful and an unlawful exercise of power is much less clear cut. Suppose an entirely indefensible, egregious, mala fides abuse of power by a police officer (as set out in paragraph [8.107], for example). Whilst A may have a cast-iron claim for trespass to property or person and an ability to recover their physical property (through conversion: although there is very little law on this), police officer C's conduct will not trigger an arguable claim under the Action because we are still in the realms of perception, not use. Similarly, where the state actor is acting *within* the proper exercise of a power – whether that is a state or non-state power – then it is tempting to say that A has no claim *because there has been no infringement* in the exercise of the power. It is not right to say in absolute terms that A has no claim. It is very likely that there will have been no trespass, but we are not concerned with trespass. In order to determine whether the Action is engaged, once again, we need to look to the point of use, not the point at which perception obtains.

ii. Specific statutory defences

[8.110] Specific statutory defences need to be read in this light. It is odd to see specific statutory defences being framed in the context of specific state powers. One would think that staying within scope would be all that was needed (and, generally speaking, certainly with police powers, that is all there is).

[8.111] But in some cases, the point will have been anticipated in statute. There may be statutory defences in place that bite even where the power has been abused. In other words, there has been what would (but for a statutory defence) be an infringement. It seems extraordinary that what is a non-compliance with the conditions for the exercise of a power should nevertheless be incapable of vindication. Yet there are some provisions that come close to this limit. Section 27 of RIPA 2000 provides:

> (1) Conduct to which this Part applies shall be lawful for all purposes if –
>
> (a) an authorisation under this Part confers an entitlement to engage in that conduct on the person whose conduct it is; and
> (b) his conduct is in accordance with the authorisation.
>
> (2) A person shall not be subject to any civil liability in respect of any conduct of his which –
>
> (a) is incidental to any conduct that is lawful by virtue of subsection (1); and
> (b) is not itself conduct an authorisation or warrant for which is capable of being granted under a relevant enactment and might reasonably have been expected to have been sought in the case in question.

(3) The conduct that may be authorised under this Part includes conduct outside the United Kingdom.

[8.112] Provisions such as this are troubling because the exclusion of civil liability needs to be closely justified. Given that the power is granted by statute, it is difficult to see what the exemption actually adds when one is acting within the scope of the power. Section 27(1)(a) of RIPA 2000 is superfluous, and it is noteworthy that 'ordinary' police powers do not contain such exemptions. The conferring of the power is enough. Section 27(1)(b) at least makes it clear that if the conduct is *not* in accordance with the authorisation, then the exemption does not apply.

[8.113] Section 27(2) of RIPA 2000 has been criticised for being 'almost impenetrable'. McKay states:[128]

> No civil liability arises out of the conduct authorised under Part II or which is incidental to it and 'is not itself conduct an authorisation or warrant for which is capable of being granted under a relevant enactment and might reasonably have been sought in the case in question'. This latter element of what would limit civil liability is almost impenetrable but appears to extend to conduct that cannot in fact be authorised under 'a relevant enactment' (RIPA, and the Intelligence Services Act 1994, and the Police Act 1997) even if there may have been a reasonable expectation that such an authorisation (one that could not in fact be given) should have been sought …

[8.114] This, for the reasons given by Ward and Blundell, goes too far. Section 27(2)(a) and (b) of RIPA 2000 are cumulative and, properly construed, the provision can be understood:[129]

> RIPA 2000 provides, in section 27(2), that a person shall not be subject to any civil liability in respect of conduct which is incidental to properly authorised directed or intrusive surveillance and is not conduct for which a warrant might reasonably have been expected to be sought. Accordingly, a person may not be sued for trespass and/or under section 6 HRA 1998 for entering land or premises in the course of a properly authorised directed surveillance operation, where it would not have been reasonable to expect a property warrant to be sought because it was unforeseeable that the entry would be required. This might be the case, for example, where surveillance officers are following a suspected terrorist who unexpectedly enters private land, and the officers need immediately to enter the land in order to keep the suspect in sight and achieve the purposes of the surveillance operation.

[8.115] Whilst this is all very interesting from a civil liberties point of view, in terms of the Action it may be that defences or exclusions such as this can be

[128] S McKay, *Covert Policing*, 2nd edn (Oxford University Press, 2015) [6.80].
[129] Ward and Blundell (n 14) [4.07].

sidestepped as irrelevant because of their focus on the conduct by which the perception was obtained rather than the use that was made of a perception improperly obtained. Whether the Action can be maintained in the face of a statutory exclusion will depend on: (i) the nature of the state power conferred; and (ii) the width of the exclusion. Where the power extends to permitting a specific form of use (as in the case of bulk personal data sets), the exclusion will almost certainly be effective. Where the power confers a right to *harvest* but is silent as to *use*, then the Action is unlikely to be excluded. That does not mean that all uses of the information are precluded: that would be absurd. What this means is that careful consideration will have to be given as to the use/misuse borderline. The Action will successfully lie in the latter case (misuse), but not the former (use).

[8.116] It is not being said that the lawfulness or the unlawfulness of the conduct is irrelevant to the use/misuse borderline. Far from it. What is being said is that (i) the distinction is not determinative, because (ii) the relevant act that informs infringement under the Action is *not* the act whereby the perception was obtained but the acts whereby the information was used.

VII. Inadvertent and Deliberate Misuse

[8.117] In Chapter 7, Section IV.B, two forms of misuse of private information were articulated: (i) inadvertent misuse;[130] and (ii) deliberate misuse.[131] That distinction holds good in the case of state actors. There is no reason why the liability of a state actor for the inadvertent misuse of private information should not be exactly the same as that of a non-state actor. For that reason, inadvertent misuse is not considered further in this chapter, and the reader is referred to Chapter 7, Section V.

[8.118] On the other hand, the test for the deliberate misuse of private information is different in the case of state actors for reasons we will come to. As in the case of non-state actors, 'deliberate misuse' means no more than that use of the private information was not inadvertent or accidental. Deliberation does not imply knowledge or intention to infringe on the part of C. However, the 'control' test espoused at paragraph [7.44] in the case of misuse by non-state actors is not apt to control for misuse of private information by state actors. The reason for this and the nature of the test that applies in the case of state actors are the subject of the next section.

[130] Ch 7, Section V.
[131] Ch 7, Section VI.

VIII. The Test for Misuse in the Case of State Actors

[8.119] The test for misuse in the case of non-state actors was set out at paragraph [7.44]. It was labelled the control test. To recap: information is private to A where that information is personal to A and where a reasonable person, in the position of A, would have a reasonable expectation of control over the use or exploitation of A's private information. There is an infringement of A's rights where C, a non-state actor, deliberately uses A's private information without A's consent in circumstances where A has a reasonable expectation of control.

[8.120] Why is this test insufficient in the case of a state actor? It is best to begin with the test that (it is suggested) does apply to state actor C, and then to justify this resort to a different test. The control test, in the case of state actors, can helpfully be inverted so that it is reframed in the following way:

> Would a reasonable person standing in the position of C and at the time of C's use of A's private information conclude that C's use was a misuse, bearing in mind that A has a reasonable expectation of control over their private information?

[8.121] At first sight, this appears to be a circular, and so substantially meaningless, test. Use is misuse when the reasonable person holds that it is. For the reasons set out below, it will be suggested that the test not, in fact, meaningless, and that it is preferable to the control test in the case of state actors.

[8.122] Expressing a test by reference to A's reasonable expectation of control misses the point that in the case of state actor powers, A has no control nor any reasonable expectation of it. C, as a state actor, has many powers in respect of which A has no agency. When considering, for instance, police powers of search, the whole point of these powers is that they can be exercised as against an involuntary party. A has no control. A test framed in terms of A's reasonable expectation of control is meaningless, because the compulsory nature of the powers means that A can have no reasonable expectation of control.

[8.123] On the other hand, all state actor powers are conferred on those actors *for a reason*. These powers exist to serve the wider good; they have a public purpose. In this, they differ from the rights of information use of non-state actors, who (within the limits of the law) ought to have free agency to act in their *own* interests. In the case of the non-state actor, that actor ought to be free to act as they wish, provided they do not, in doing so, infringe another's rights or the law more generally. A's reasonable expectation of control is a perfectly comprehensible constraint on non-state actor C.

[8.124] Where a power has a purpose, the line between use and misuse arises out of the power's proper purpose. That is a matter of statutory construction, and a state actor has a duty to exercise their power properly: this involves patrolling the state actor's discretion, which was considered at paragraphs [8.101]–[8.103]. It will rarely be the case that a state actor will be *obliged* (with no choice/discretion) to exercise a power. All powers involve *choice* and a properly framed discretion that informs choice. Thus, every choice to exercise a power by state actor C involves a consideration of whether the power should be exercised that is (i) real and genuine, (ii) done in good faith and (iii) where the purposes for which the power was conferred is specifically considered by C. It is suggested that no matter how widely drawn a power, these considerations inevitably arise.

[8.125] The 'proper purpose test' (as it will be called, in contradistinction to the 'control test') thus focuses on the reality of the case, namely that it is C (and not A) that understands the various factors that underlie the choice in C to exercise the power that has been conferred on them. The nature of these factors, and the weight accorded to them, will depend on the nature of the power and the circumstances of the case. However, one factor that will be a constant presence is the need to weigh A's rights. It is here that the control test makes a belated entrance. One of the factors that C *must* weigh is A's right of privacy, and this explains the last phrase ('bearing in in mind that A has a reasonable expectation of control over their private information') of the proper purpose test.[132]

[8.126] One of the differences between a state actor and a non-state actor is that C *qua* state actor is under a positive duty, owed to A, to consider whether any given use of A's private information is justifiable. It is not suggested that a failure to consider this is actionable in itself (just as a breach of a duty of care is not actionable without harm) and it is not suggested that there is any kind of negligence threshold to the Action. It is simply that a public body, a state actor, is obliged to exercise its powers properly. That is the reason judicial review applies to state actors, but not to non-state actors.

IX. What Constitutes Deliberate Misuse of A's Private Information?

A. Overview

[8.127] Before each and every use of A's private information, state actor C is obliged to consider whether that particular use of their perception of A is in all the circumstances reasonable. As with any discretion, no matter how widely drawn, C must exercise that discretion: (i) in good faith; (ii) with real and genuine consideration; (iii) considering the purposes for which the power was conferred.

[132] Bear in mind that '[i]t is unlawful for a public authority to act in a way which is incompatible with a Convention right': HRA 1998, s 6(1).

[8.128] The mere fact that a proposed use is beneficial is not enough to justify the use. Take the 'mission creep' illustration at paragraph [8.41], where powers under RIPA 2000 were used in relation to 'low-level' offences. This is doubtless a worthy objective, but the state actors in this case were not *obliged* to exercise these powers (ie they had a discretion) and so they had to weigh the justifiability of the proposed use against A's right of privacy (ie Article 8 of the ECHR) and also A's property rights (ie Article 1 of Protocol 1), bearing in mind that A owns their private information.

[8.129] There are thus two specific human rights in play. The Article 8 right to a private life has already extensively been considered, and will not be considered further. Article 1 of Protocol 1 requires a little further consideration, which it receives below. Thereafter, the manner in which C should exercise their discretionary power is 'structured' so that a degree of legal predictability is imposed.

B. Property rights and the ECHR

[8.130] Let us begin by placing the inquiry in context. We are dealing with private information that is personal to A and within C's perception. C is, for these purposes, assumed to be a natural person who is also a state actor.[133] C has *used* that perception – otherwise the inquiry would not have got this far. In this context, it is clear that A has a property right in their private information that is deserving of and entitled to protection, but only in the case of *misuse*. That is the concept we are seeking to elucidate in the case of the state actor.

[8.131] Article 1 of the First Protocol of the ECHR provides:

> (1) Every natural or legal person is entitled to the peaceful enjoyment of his possessions. No one shall be deprived of his possessions except in the public interest and subject to the conditions provided for by law and by the general principles of international law.
>
> (2) The preceding provisions shall not, however, in any way impair the right of a state to enforce such laws as it deems necessary to control the use of property in accordance with the general interest or to secure the payment of taxes or other contributions or penalties.

[8.132] The paradigm of property is land and chattels.[134] The wording of Article 1 of the First Protocol implies a physical limitation to the protected right by the use of the term 'possession', which clearly suggests physicality.

[133] The approach being taken is that complexities need to be addressed one by one and not mixed up. The question of undertakings, and their exposure to the Action, is considered not here, but in Ch 9.

[134] Clayton and Tomlinson (n 61) [18.07].

Nevertheless, Article 1 Protocol 1 is not so limited. Even under English law, property includes intangible property:[135]

> ... anyone using the English language in its ordinary signification would ... agree that 'property' is a word of very wide import, including tangible and intangible property. But he would surely deny that any one of those rights which in in the aggregate constituted ownership of property could itself and by itself be aptly called 'property' ...

[8.133] This is a reference to Honoré's 'bundle of rights' theory of property. Clearly, only 'bundles' that meet the notion of 'ownership' can result in the conclusion that that which is owned is property. There are cases where the line can be difficult to draw:[136]

> The relationship between 'property rights' and benefits conferred by the State is not straightforward. State incentives, subsidies, grants and welfare benefits are, potentially, extremely valuable and, arguably, constitute property. American jurisprudence recognizes a very wide range of rights as 'property' attracting the protection of the 'due process' clause: an interest in State benefits will be 'property' if there is an 'entitlement' to such benefits ...

It would appear, from those instances where intangibles have been recognised as 'possessions' under Article 1 Protocol 1, that it is no stretch for 'possessions' to include information.[137]

[8.134] If, as is suggested, private information is property protected under the ECHR, then state actors must give the right due regard, independently of any question of privacy. Of course, the second paragraph in Article 1 Protocol 1 provides the usual qualification that the right is not absolute but qualified. Nevertheless the value attaching to property rights is a factor that must be taken into account when considering the state actor and their exposure to an Action. In other words, the HRA 1998 and the ECHR have not only inspired the development of the Action itself,[138] but also its application to state actors.

C. Structuring the discretion

i. A focus on past infringements

[8.135] It will be assumed that A is claiming damages for a past infringement of their rights, rather than seeking prospective injunctive relief to prevent an

[135] *Belfast Corpn v OD Cars* [1960] AC 490, 517.
[136] Clayton and Tomlinson (n 61) [18.09].
[137] Instances are set out in Clayton and Tomlinson (n 61) [18.25], including intellectual property rights, rights under a retirement annuity contract, a well-founded claim under the criminal injures compensation scheme and a claim for the repayment of VAT paid in error.
[138] As to which, see Ch 2.

infringement. Remedies are considered in Chapter 10. As will be seen, two of the remedies available to A are damages and an injunction. For the sake of simplicity, a past infringement and a claim in damages will be considered in this chapter.

ii. Time of assessment = Time of alleged misuse

[8.136] The time of assessment of C's alleged infringement of A's rights is that point in time at which C transitions from merely perceiving to making use of perception. At that point – having articulated the use that has been made of A's private information – it is possible meaningfully to ask whether that use amounts to a misuse sufficient to enable A to begin an Action and to succeed in it.

[8.137] It has repeatedly been stated that use rather than perception is the critical factor. Indeed, this is how we intuitively approach privacy infringements. This was the approach taken by Laws LJ in *Wood* regarding police photography.[139] It is also the approach taken in the case of Automatic Number Plate Recognition (ANPR) data. The Police UK website provides the following description.

> **Example**[140]
>
> We use ANPR (Automatic Number Plate Recognition) technology to help detect, deter and disrupt criminal activity at a local, force, regional and national level. This includes travelling criminals (those using the road network to avoid being caught), organised crime groups and terrorists.
>
> ANPR provides lines of enquiry and evidence in the investigation of crime and is used by forces throughout England, Wales, Scotland and Northern Ireland.
>
> **How it works**
>
> As a vehicle passes an ANPR camera, its registration number is read and instantly checked against database records of vehicles of interest.
>
> Police officers can stop a vehicle, speak to the occupants and, where necessary, make arrests.
>
> ANPR has proved to be important in the detection of many offences, including locating, for example, people wanted for arrest or missing witnesses, stolen vehicles, uninsured vehicles and uncovering cases of major crime.
>
> **How data is stored**
>
> A record for all vehicles passing by a camera is stored, including for vehicles that are not known to be of interest at the time of the read.
>
> At present, ANPR cameras nationally submit on average around 60 million ANPR 'read' records to national ANPR systems daily.
>
> ANPR data from each police force is stored together with similar data from other forces for one year.

[139] See para [7.19].

[140] See https://www.police.uk/advice/advice-and-information/rs/road-safety/automatic-number-plate-recognition-anpr/, last accessed 25 August 2025.

[8.138] Control over ANPR data is by way of 'soft law' guidance, in combination with GDPR obligations. Thus, there is 'guidance' entitled *National ANPR Standards for Policing and Law Enforcement.*[141] This makes clear that 'ANPR operates under a complex framework of legislation of general application, including the Data Protection Act 2018, UK General Data Protection Regulation … and common law'.[142] ANPR may be used for 'law enforcement purposes', defined as 'the prevention, investigation, detection or prosecution of criminal offences or the execution of criminal penalties, including the safeguarding against and the prevention of threats to public security',[143] or for 'other Policing Purposes and Public Benefit'. Thus:[144]

> LEAs may [use] the NAC for operational purposes relating to individual and public safety including in collaboration with other public authorities. For example, those partners with accountability for traffic management and road safety.
>
> Data may be processed independently by the LEA or other public authority using shared collection equipment … such that each are independent controllers for the processing that they undertake, or statistical information may be provided by the LEA devoid of personal data. In all cases a Memorandum of Understanding (MOU) must be in place setting out the arrangements for compliance with these standards.

NAC is the National ANPR Capability, whereas LEAs are Law Enforcement Agencies listed in Annex A. As well as the law enforcement agencies one might expect to see listed (like police forces), Annex A contains some surprises and lists the Department for Work and Pensions, the DVLA, the Environment Agency, the Food Standards Agency, HMRC, the Medicines and Healthcare Products Regulatory Agency, trading standards, and the Pensions Regulator.

[8.139] The focus, throughout, is on use not perception. The important consequence is that materially the same perception may be used differently, and that one use may be a misuse, whereas another may not be. In the case of state actors, *why* the information is being used is critical. The point may be illustrated as follows: suppose two bodies (say, the police and the Pensions Regulator) both use ANPR to obtain A's address from the DVLA. The police do so because A is reasonably suspected of a serious offence, and they want to track them down and need A's address for this purpose. The Pensions Regulator do it because they want to correlate age and type of car with place of residence of people considered according to age. The police use is clearly not a misuse. The Pensions Regulator use is much the harder case, even if the research is well-intentioned and objectively important.

[141] Version 3.3 (2024), last accessed 25 August 2025.
[142] Paragraphs under Section 6.
[143] ibid Section 6.2.
[144] ibid Section 6.3.

[8.140] The problem is that – staying with ANPR for the moment – the *use* to which the data may be put is not clearly articulated and appears to be both unmonitored and vague. The guidance on the standards says:[145]

> **Policy**
>
> All LEAs that connect to, or have access to, the NAC must have an up to date written policy in place for the access, management and use of ANPR data, including provisions for audit, which must be consistent with Compliance and Audit Standards.
>
> Access to ANPR data must be proportionate to the circumstances of that access and taking account of the impact on the fundamental rights and freedoms of individuals.
>
> **Data access management**
>
> Authorised members of LEAs may access and use data within the NAC to the extent that this is compliant with the DPA in the circumstances of each case, without reference to a controller unless otherwise required within the terms of NASPLE.

[8.141] The problem is that when one reviews the policy documents that explain how information is going to be used, generalities abound. Rather than having a policy that is vague and general, it is far better for there to be an obligation on a state actor to consider the justifiability of the use, at the time of use, in each given case. That, it is suggested, is the true state of the present law.

iii. Structuring the discretion

[8.142] The factors relevant to determining whether a use of A's private information by state actor C constitutes a misuse of A's property and so an infringement of the Action is determined by reference to the following factors.[146]

a. Proper public purpose as at the time of use

[8.143] State actors act in the public interest. Generally speaking, the purpose of state actors – what they are there to do – is defined in law. It is possible for private information to be used *improperly* even though the purpose is well-intended and beneficial in the round. It is quite possible for there to be 'misplaced philanthropy'. Were the police to use their powers of entry and search for reasons other than prevention and detection of crime, it would be necessary for that exercise of power to be closely justified. That is why the 'fly-tipping' example considered at paragraph [8.41] looks like a misuse. The powers

[145] ibid Section 10.2.

[146] There will no doubt be other factors. Certainly, this list is not intended to be a closed list, and the individual case will doubtless throw up other relevant factors.

under RIPA 2000 are conferred essentially for the protection of national security, and it is very difficult to fit the prevention of fly-tipping into the true purposes of the 2000 Act. Where the use is in fact an improper purpose, there will be a misuse on the part of C, and liability under the Action.

b. Weight of proper purpose

[8.144] A purpose can be proper, and yet lightweight. In other words, the use is for a proper purpose, but the purpose is not weighty. There are crimes of greater or lesser seriousness, and national security risks of greater or lesser moment. This is a relevant factor when considering whether a use is lawful when set against other values – notably A's right of privacy under Article 8 of the ECHR[147] and A's right to property under Article 1 Protocol 1. Obviously, C is a natural person. We will be coming to the liability of the organisation in which C sits in Chapter 9. But where the use is by an undertaking, the overall objectives of the undertaking need to be considered. The more closely aligned the use is to the undertaking's purposes, the clearer the indicator is that this is not a case of *misuse*.[148]

c. The lawfulness of the obtaining of the perception

[8.145] Where the perception was unlawfully obtained, this will be a relevant factor in determining whether C's use of A's private information is a misuse. Note that this is only a relevant factor, not a determinative one. As has been described, there are many cases where an unlawfully obtained perception has nevertheless lawfully been used.[149]

d. Alternative ways of proceeding

[8.146] It may be possible to achieve the same end through alternative means which do not involve using A's private information. This is a relevant factor; its weight will turn on the extent to which this alternative course is practical and cost effective.

[147] Obviously one does not consider the Action in this – that would be circular and self-fulfilling. But ECHR rights *have* to be taken into account.

[148] See, for instance, *Jones v University of Warwick* [2003] EWCA Civ 151. The claimant had suffered an injury at work. Her employers engaged the services of private inquiry agency, who undertook surveillance of her, because there was a suspicion that she was exaggerating the impact of the injury. The surveillance involved deception and secret filming. The claimant sought to have the evidence excluded from the subsequent litigation. That application failed, and the question of balance was not considered by the Court of Appeal.

[149] See, for instance, the 'fruit of the forbidden tree' doctrine, which is rejected in English law.

e. Unjustifiable opacity in cases of overt surveillance

[8.147] There are many cases where A will know that their information is being harvested, but not *why*. McKay refers to this as 'overt' surveillance.[150] The best example is CCTV. There is a natural tendency in public bodies not to explain what they are doing. That is particularly so in the case of information use. Partly this is because it is difficult, ex ante, to describe possible future uses. But partly it is to avoid accountability. CCTV is probably the best example of overt surveillance: these days, there is usually signage stating that CCTV is in use, but the proposed uses are either not specifically stated, or impossible to find, or, when found, are remarkably vague. Take the following, hypothetical, example.

Example

Suppose a local authority has CCTV cameras around a children's playground, which are face-recognition enabled, and which enable identification of persons from their images.[151] The local authority uses this information to: (i) report serious crime to the police; (ii) track down and prosecute people who drop litter other than in designated bins, and (iii) monitor speech so that persons expressing undesirable or illegal speech can be dealt with. None of these uses is specifically identified, but there are signs saying 'We use CCTV to keep you safe',

[8.148] It is suggested that the failure to articulate use clearly is a factor that is indicative of misuse. Thus, in this case, the failure to state the uses of the CCTV footage (and its capabilities) is an indicator of misuse, as and when it is uncovered. Of course, there will be many reasons for secrecy, good and bad. Often, the police and the national securities agencies will be reluctant to disclose their modus operandi for fear of tipping off the very people they are investigating. But a bad reason for opacity is to stifle an Action. Means of ascertaining the uses to which overt surveillance is put and whether it amounts to covert surveillance are considered in Chapter 10. The point here being made is that where there is overt surveillance and opacity in terms of use, state actor C is under a heightened obligation to consider A's interests, because A cannot take steps to protect themselves from unknown misuses. Should A find themselves in a position of knowledge, then A ought to be entitled to rely on C's opacity in support of the contention that there has been a misuse of their private information.

[150] McKay (n 128) Ch 5, Section F.

[151] This is by no means far-fetched, and is almost certainly being deployed in some areas at the time of writing. See K Hill, *Your Face Belongs to Us: The Secretive Startup Dismantling Your Privacy* (Simon & Schuster, 2023). The website of the Metropolitan Police (https://www.met.police.uk/advice/advice-and-information/fr/facial-recognition-technology/, last accessed 25 August 2025) states: 'Facial Recognition (FR) technology can be used in a number of ways by the Met, including to prevent and detect crime, find wanted criminals, safeguard vulnerable people, and to protect people from harm – all to keep the people we serve safe'.

f. Covert harvesting of information

[8.149] In the case of overt surveillance, A will at least know that they are being surveilled, although they may not know much more than this. The covert gathering of information presents different challenges. Where the exercise of the power is overt – where A can see the CCTV or has actually been required to provide the information through the exercise of a power on them[152] – A will at least know that there is a state use of their information that can be followed up and investigated. In the case of extraction of information from A, A will at least *know* what information has been provided to C.[153]

[8.150] The problem with the covert gathering of information is that A will not even know that the information has been obtained unless and until it is *overtly* used (eg in a criminal prosecution[154]). A will have nothing to pursue. This lack of information in A represents a real inequality of arms which clearly diminishes the efficacy of A's ability to vindicate their rights, whether through the Action or otherwise.[155]

[8.151] Clearly, there will be many cases where the demands of (usually national security) will require the covert gathering of private information; and safeguards exist in terms of the need for warrants to be approved. But as the Apple case demonstrates,[156] the veil of secrecy is often drawn very widely. Although it is very much an incomplete solution, it is suggested that in the case of use of covertly gathered private information, the obligations on the state actor are particularly high and particularly anxious consideration must be given to the interests of A.

g. Acquiescence

[8.152] Generally speaking, state powers are exercised or capable of being exercised without A's consent. Because of a concern about authority, or because our society prides itself on 'policing by consent', we may very often be asked to render up our private information 'voluntarily', and we may

[152] For instance, where there is an investigation by an authority which requires A to provide information.

[153] The assumption is that it is A who is being compelled to provide the information. The case where someone other than A is obliged to provide information that is A's without A's consent is more closely analogised to covert gathering of information. But there may be liability in the third party, which is considered further below.

[154] In fact, this may very well not happen. Section 56 of the IPA 2016 bars the use or disclosure of a targeted interception warrant in legal proceedings. Where this evidence favours the prosecution, then this is a self-denying ordinance which can be accepted. But what if the information is useful to the defence of A? On this tricky area, see Ward and Blundell (n 14) [4.52]–[4.61].

[155] These questions of efficacy of remedy are considered in Ch 9.

[156] See para [8.17].

do so. This, emphatically, is not consent, and should not even be treated as acquiescence.[157]

h. Does A have to be coerced?

[8.153] So far, we have been considering cases where state actor C is using their powers of coercion to obtain information either without A's knowledge at all or without A's consent. In many cases, this will be appropriate. But not in all. In considering whether misuse exists, a property analysis assists. As has been described, A's property in their private information is a matter that a public authority needs to respect by virtue of the combination of the HRA 1998, section 6 and Article 1 of Protocol 1 to the ECHR. A good test for misuse is to ask the question: 'Should the state entity be paying A for the use of their information?' In the case of police investigation and national security, the answer is likely to be 'No'. Where the DVLA is providing A's data to enable a private parking operator to fine users for breach of the 'five minute rule', the answer probably ought to be 'Yes'. To be clear, what is being suggested, for the present, is merely a test for misuse, based upon the principle that underpayment for valuable property is a form of expropriation that is not not merely likely to amount to an ECHR infringement, but also in the long run economically bad.[158]

i. Conclusions

[8.154] All these factors go to an assessment of how defensible C's use of A's private information is. They inform the *legitimacy* of the use. Against this must be set the rights and interests of A. The test is whether a reasonable person, in the position of C, would consider the use a misuse bearing in mind A's reasonable expectation of control over their private information. Thus:

(1) The factors so far considered go to the legitimacy of the use of the power, the motivating force impelling C to use the power. In many cases, if C asks

[157] Schulhofer (n 120) 59–60 describes the problem of the 'so-called consent search' extremely clearly: 'After an officer makes a traffic stop, for example, it is not unusual for her to ask permission to check the trunk. Usually she will do so *before* making a formal arrest, so that the driver – still hoping to be let off with just a warning – will have every incentive to cooperate. The officer simply says something like "Mind if I have a look in the trunk?" Most motorists acquiesce, but not necessarily because they are eager to give permission. More often they either fear the consequences if they object or believe that in any event they have no right to refuse. Indeed, in may cases the driver submits, knowing that when the officer opens the trunk, she will see a large bundle of drugs, packages and stacked in plain view. In such circumstances, it is difficult to believe that the driver felt he had a meaningful choice.' This is an outstanding example of privacy ranking second to other interests. If, in such circumstances, the officer discovers a stash of drugs, surely the answer is that *of course* they must take it further. The more nuanced response is to say that this is only true where the offence is serious.

[158] See Ch 5.

the question, the answer will be that the power ought *not* to be exercised because there is (for example) a disproportionality between the end (the use) and the exercise of the power.

(2) If, however, C considers, in light of the nature of the power and the nature of the use, that the use is proper, and has reached a view as to its weight, C must then weigh this interest in exercising the power against the damage this does to A's interests.

(3) This, to be clear, is an obligation on every state actor by virtue of section 6 of the HRA 1998, which provides in section 6(1) that '[i]t is unlawful for a public body to act in a way which is incompatible with a Convention right', save where (in section 6(2)) the public authority has no choice but to infringe. A key question for the state actor to consider is whether the state actor could have taken a different, non-infringing, course.

(4) In every case, there will be two human rights in play. The first is the right to the protection of property under Article 1 of Protocol 1. There are many ways in which the weight of this right can be assessed, but a good question to ask (it is suggested) is whether the state actor is entitled to take (ie use without consent) A's property without paying for it. The second right is the right to privacy, and the extent to which A has a reasonable expectation of control. This imports into the analysis the factors that were considered in Chapter 7, Section VI. These factors cannot be imported unquestioningly, for there significant differences between a state actor and a non-state actor. Nevertheless, state actor C will be obliged to consider the extent of any interest A will have in controlling their private information.

iv. The balance between public and private interest

[8.155] A's interests in their privacy and in the protection of their property are not really private interests at all. They are public values which the state is obliged to protect. When considering the exercise of state power, the balance is not as between public right and private right, but between two conflicting *public* rights.

[8.156] Viewed in this way, it is wrong to say that the private interest must always give way to the public interest, for that is to mischaracterise the nature of A's interests. Warren and Brandeis thus went too far in suggesting that the public good always overrode the private interest in privacy:[159]

> The right to privacy does not prohibit the communication of any matter, though in its nature private, when the publication is made under circumstances which would render it a privileged communication according to the law of slander and libel.
>
> Under this rule, the right to privacy is not invaded by any publication made in a court of justice, in legislative bodies, or the committee of those bodies; in municipal

[159] S Warren and L Brandeis, 'The Right to Privacy' (1890) 4 *Harvard Law Review* 193 at 216–17.

> assemblies, or the committees of such assemblies, or practically by any communication made in any other public body, municipal or parochial, or in any body quasi public, like the large voluntary associations formed for almost every purpose of benevolence, business, or other general interest; and (at least in many jurisdictions) reports of any such proceedings would in some measure be accorded a like privilege. Nor would the rule prohibit any publication made by one in the discharge of some public or private duty, whether legal or moral, or in conduct of one's own affairs, in matters where his own interest is concerned.

Although the Action is unquestionably a private law remedy, when brought against a state actor the Action serves to protect important public interests.

X. Demands for Information from Third Parties

[8.157] Most of the national security powers described in this chapter involve state actor C obtaining A's private information from a third party, usually a telecommunications operator. An excellent example is the bulk acquisition warrant, where the production of information pertaining to A comes from a telecommunications operator operating within the United Kingdom.

[8.158] Of course, such third parties must obey the law. If information can compulsorily be acquired by the state, and the third party has no agency to refuse, then it must comply. And if it is obliged to keep the provision of information a secret from A, then this rule also needs to be complied with.

[8.159] However, where the third party has *agency* – choice – it must bear in mind its own exposure to an Action by A. If the third party has a choice in terms of compliance or a right of challenge, it must consider whether the use of A's private information in disclosing that information to state actor C in itself constitutes a misuse of that information, as described in Chapter 7.

9

Undertakings, Mass Data Collection and the Protection of Privacy

In which: the exposure of the undertaking to an Action brought by A is explained, though the law of attribution and vicarious liability; the protection of A's private information is considered when located within the operations of undertakings; and the question of non-human processing of private information is addressed.

I. The Issue Stated

A. The paradigm case

[9.1] So far, the discussion of the component elements of the Action has focused on the case where A claims against C, where C is a natural and not a legal person. It has been stressed that this is the paradigm case, because if information is perception, then non-natural persons cannot perceive, and so they cannot, without more, be a defendant to A's claim. It is important to stress the 'without more', because it is certainly *not* being suggested that the Action cannot reach undertakings. What this chapter discusses is the process of *how* undertaking U can be rendered susceptible to an Action brought by A.[1]

B. The importance of the law of attribution

[9.2] It is not possible to speak of perception without starting first with natural persons. At the same time, questions of attribution and vicarious liability render possible the liability of non-natural persons for infringements of A's rights under the Action. It is not being suggested that the only defendants to A's claim can be natural persons, and that non-natural persons somehow get a 'free pass'. That would be a remarkable, counterintuitive – indeed perverse – outcome.

[1] The concept of an undertaking (U) was described at paras [1.40]–[1.41].

[9.3] The liability of non-natural persons is more complex and is based upon, but derived from, the liability of C, a natural person. Where C, a natural person, perceives and uses information within a broader undertaking – whether that is a corporation having legal personality in its own right or an entity, like a partnership, that does not – the Action operates differently, attributing C's perception of and use of A's private information to the undertaking. In other words, C's perception, use and misuse, whilst not that of undertaking U, is attributed to undertaking U so as to render it liable.

[9.4] The 'undertaking' is a helpful European Union concept, which is adopted in this book, but used in a slightly different sense to the European one. In Case C-41/90, *Höfner and Elser v Macroton GmbH*,[2] the Court of Justice of the European Union stated that 'the concept of an undertaking encompasses every entity engaged in an economic activity regardless of the legal status of the entity and the way in which it is financed'. The undertaking thus references economic activity without particular regard to legal structure or personality. Strictly speaking, C (acting on their own) could be an undertaking, and to that extent this book uses a narrower definition. The aim is to consider the case where C is part of undertaking U, but C is not, in and of itself, an undertaking. The relationship between C and U is described as C(U). Undertaking U will likely involve multiple actors like C – C_1 to C_n – and one of the question addressed in this chapter is how the perceptions and actions of multiple agents (C_1 to C_n) of an undertaking can *all* be attributed to that undertaking.

[9.5] Whilst the *perception* of A's private information must vest in a natural person (C), this does not prevent an undertaking U from being liable in the Action by virtue of C's knowledge or statements or actions being attributed to U (which relationship is described as C(U)). That liability can arise either by way of vicarious liability of C(U) for C's tort or by way of primary liability of C(U) through the attribution of C_1, C_2, to C_n's conduct and states of mind to U. The nature of these two very different forms of attribution – (i) 'vicarious liability' and (ii) 'primary liability through attribution' – will be considered in this chapter.

C. Machine-only operation

[9.6] There is further complexity which is not resolved – or at least not wholly resolved – by the law of attribution. In many cases, information about a group of persons – A_n – will be assimilated or harvested or collected through the use of technology without human involvement. Thus, Google's predictive products

[2] EU:C:1991:161 at [21].

assimilate the inputs of A, aggregate them, and make predictions about A using that aggregate data. Although these processes are highly confidential (and not known to the author, save in the most general of terms), it is likely that these processes operate without any human involvement. Similarly, a state actor like one of the Agencies may require the production of reams of data, which is then processed by machine and the output simply used to inform an investigation without very much or even any human input. Again, devices using the Alexa and Siri operating systems will use our inputs and deploy them without human involvement.

[9.7] In these cases, it is artificial to speak of C having any perception of anything. C will therefore have nothing capable of attribution to U so as to render U liable to A. The process of machines rendering information, one machine to another, or one programme to another, without any human engagement, resulting in a use of private information without human engagement is also tackled in this chapter. To be clear: there is a liability in U, but it does not arise either by way of (i) 'vicarious liability' or (ii) 'primary liability through attribution', but (iii) by deployment of the liability for inadvertent misuse that was considered in Chapter 7, Section V and Chapter 8, Section VII. The difficult question here under consideration is the nature of the legal response where a tool – admittedly, an extremely sophisticated tool – assembles and uses perceptions. Such sophisticated tools are not autonomous, and they probably ought not to be called 'artificial intelligence'. They are just sophisticated tools, but they are quite capable – in and of their own right – of capturing information about A and then using it, without any human involvement. U ought to be responsible through the Action for any use amounting to a misuse. That question is considered at the end of this chapter.

D. The structure of this chapter

[9.8] This chapter is structured around three sections, in addition to this introduction. Section II considers theories of attribution in more or less abstract terms; Section III considers attribution in the specific context of the Action; and Section IV deals with autonomous operation of tools and how liability under the Action arises in this case.

II. The Law of Attribution

A. Overview

[9.9] This section considers vicarious liability and primary liability through attribution. In the civil law, these are the only two routes by which a non-natural person can be made liable. In the criminal law – not considered here – attribution works differently, and not by way of useful legal analogy. Although there is a suggestion that vicarious liability operates in the criminal sphere much as it does in the civil,[3] this is an untenable proposition. Of course, a statutory offence can be framed however the lawmaker wishes, but if one takes the general position of an offence that is not specifically corporate, the notion of vicarious liability becomes untenable because it involves – for no good reason – the attribution of a crime committed by one person to another, which is unjust, even if the defendant is an undertaking. Liability under the criminal law must be personal, and it is in principle wrong to attribute one person's crime to another.[4]

[9.10] Within the civil law, some commentators have a threefold classification of attribution: (i) vicarious liability; (ii) primary liability by way of attribution; and (iii) something called 'direct liability'.[5] It is difficult to see any distinction between 'primary liability by way of attribution' and 'direct liability'. As this form of attribution is neither capable of clear articulation nor capable of differentiation from primary liability by way of attribution, it is a classification not used (and not considered) in this book. The two bases for an undertaking's liability – (i) vicarious liability; and (ii) primary liability by way of attribution – will now be considered.

B. Vicarious liability

[9.11] In a case of vicarious liability, all of the elements of a tort (the Action or other civil wrong, known to English lawyers as 'torts' (wrongs) and a 'delict' to lawyers in civil law jurisdictions) are committed by a single, human, actor C, but another person (typically C's employer, and here U) is vicariously liable for the actions of C. In this type of case, there are two defendants: (i) the primarily liable defendant C; and (ii) the secondarily liable defendant U, liable by virtue of the relationship C(U). This type of case is an 'easy' case, because although the conceptual bases for vicarious liability are hotly contested and unclear, there is no *fragmentation* of the elements comprising the tort, no distribution of these elements amongst different actors. All of the elements that lead to liability are unified in a single actor C. Vicarious liability imposes secondary liability on another U by virtue of the relationship C(U) between C and U.

[9.12] The law of vicarious liability causes a secondary defendant (U) to be liable for the wrong (generally a tort) of a primary defendant (C). The primary

[3] N Hawke, *Corporate Liability* (Sweet & Maxwell, 2000) [3-06].
[4] See A Pinto and M Evans, *Corporate Criminal Liability*, 4th edn (Sweet & Maxwell, 2021) [2-005].
[5] See, for example, Hawke (n 3) Chs 2, 3 and 5.

defendant (C) remains liable, but does not have to be joined to the action.[6] It has been noted that the doctrine is or seems anomalous because it conflicts with two fundamental principles of tort law: (i) a person should only be liable for loss and damage *they* caused by their *own* acts and omissions; and (ii) that liability should be fault based.[7]

[9.13] Consideration of the doctrine is made all the harder because its rationale is controversial.[8] Traditionally, where C was doing the bidding of U, liability was imposed on U because U was morally responsible for the harm C did, U having requested the deed. As Pollock and Maitland noted:[9]

> We may take for granted that the man who commands a trespass, which is committed in obedience to his command, is himself a trespasser. About this our law of the thirteenth century and of much earlier times had no doubt whatsoever … what is done by a man's command may be imputed to him as though it were his own act.

[9.14] As organisations became more complex, so too a 'command' theory of vicarious liability became less tenable. The case where the master commands the servant to do a wrong is easy. The case where the master commands the servant to do something which can be done lawfully, but which the servant chooses to do unlawfully is altogether more difficult. More to the point, the very notion of a 'command' from the master 'executed' by the servant is at odds with a modern business enterprise. As Gray notes:[10]

> As the size of business enterprise grew, it became less likely that a master would specifically authorize particular actions of a servant. The master and the servant were more remote from each other than was the position at the time the doctrine was first conceived.

[9.15] The doctrine of various liability came to extend to the unintended consequences of intended acts and processes, provided the acts of the servant C were in some way of 'benefit' to the master U.[11]

[9.16] The doctrine could (just about) still be justified by the maxim *qui facit per alium facit* per se.[12] The basis for the doctrine, at this point, was well expressed by Salmond:[13]

[6] In many cases of medical negligence, where a patient has been injured by a doctor, it is considered 'bad form' to sue the doctor, and most claims are directed to the hospital employing the doctor only.

[7] A Gray, *Vicarious Liability: Critique and Reform* (Hart Publishing, 2018) 5.

[8] ibid 48, refers to the 'evident inability of the United Kingdom courts to agree upon a consistent rationale for the imposition of vicarious liability'.

[9] Quoted in ibid 7.

[10] ibid 9.

[11] ibid 9–10.

[12] 'Who does something through another does it himself'.

[13] In his *The Law of Torts*, quoted by Gray (n 7) 31.

> It is clear that the master is responsible for acts actually authorised by him: for liability would exist in this case, even if the relation between the parties were merely one of agency, and not one of service at all. But a master, as opposed to the employer of an independent contractor, is liable even for acts which he has not authorised, provided they are so connected with acts which he has authorised that they may rightly be regarded as modes – although improper modes – of doing them. In other words, a master is responsible not merely for what he authorised his servant to do, but also for the way in which he does it … On the other hand, if the unauthorised and wrongful act of the servant is not so connected with the authorised act as to be a mode of doing it, but is an independent act, the master is not responsible: for in such a case the servant is not acting in the course of his employment, but has gone outside of it.

[9.17] Problems arose where the doctrine imposed liability on U where U was *not* benefited by the acts of C, as where C perpetrates a fraud on a third party which employer U would not countenance and had expressly forbidden. Here even the 'in the course of employment' test becomes strained. Where there is intentional wrongdoing on the part of C which is only tangentially attached to the 'course' or 'scope' of employment, there either should be no vicarious liability or a different test is required.[14]

[9.18] In *Lister v Hesley Hall Ltd*[15] the House of Lords considered whether the employers of a warden of a school boarding house could be vicariously liable for his acts of sexual abuse against boys in his care. *Clerk & Lindsell* comments on the case as follows:[16]

> … Their Lordships noted that the *Salmond* test was unhelpful in cases involving intentional wrongdoing, particularly where the employee sets out to benefit himself. Instead they looked to the close connection between the acts in question and the nature of the employment. As Lord Steyn put it, the key test was whether the tort was 'so closely connected with his employment that it would be fair and just to hold the [employer] vicariously liable'. Applying this test to the facts in *Lister* it was held that, rather than the employment merely furnishing an opportunity to commit the sexual abuse, the connection between the employment and the torts was very strong. As Lord Steyn observed: 'the reality was that the County Council were responsible for the care of the vulnerable children and employed [the warden] … to carry out that duty on its behalf. And the sexual abuse took place while the employee was engaged in nduties at the very time and place demanded by his employment'. Thus, he concluded, the sexual abuse was 'inextricably interwoven with the carrying out by the warden of his duties'.

[9.19] This framing of the rational basis for vicarious liability resonates with the distinction drawn in some Australian decisions, where it is held that the

[14] As noted in A Tettenborn (ed), *Clerk & Lindsell on Torts*, 24th edn (Sweet & Maxwell, 2023) [6-29].

[15] *Lister v Hesley Hall Ltd* [2001] UKHL 22.

[16] *Clerk & Lindsell* (n 14) [6-29].

provision of the *opportunity* to C to commit the wrongful act is not enough to render U liable, but that if the *occasion* for the commission of the wrongful act is provided, vicarious liability can arise.[17] In *DC v Prince Alfred College Inc*, the distinction between opportunity and occasion was framed thus:[18]

> It may be sufficient to hold an employer vicariously liable for a criminal act committed by an employee where, in the commission of that act, the employee used or took advantage of the position in which the employment placed the employer vis-à-vis the victim. In determining whether the apparent performance of such a role may be said to give for the wrongful act, particular features [are relevant]. They include authority, power, trust, control and the ability to achieve intimacy with the victim. The latter feature may be especially important. Where in such circumstances, the employee takes advantage of [their] position with respect to the victim, that may [suggest] the wrongful act should be regarded as committed in the course or scope of employment ... [rendering] the employer vicariously liable.

[9.20] But there are some cases where even the occasion theory cannot easily explain liability. In *Mohamud v Wm Morrison Supermarkets plc* an employee at a filling station refused a request by a customer to print out some documents, expressing the refusal in racist and offensive language. The employee then proceeded to assault customer by their car, having to be restrained by a supervisor.[19] It is difficult to understand the basis for U's vicarious liability in this case. The doctrine has spread its wings very widely indeed.

[9.21] The general approach to cases of vicarious liability was stated by Lord Phillips JSC in *Various Claimants v Catholic Child Welfare Society*.[20] Lord Phillips propounded a two-stage test as to when C also causes a secondarily liable defendant U to be liable:[21]

> ... Hughes LJ rightly observed that the test requires a synthesis of two stages: (i) The first stage is to consider the relationship of [C] and [U] to see whether it is one that is capable of giving rise to vicarious liability. (ii) Hughes LJ identified the second stage as requiring examination of the connection between [U] and the act or omission of [C]. This is not entirely correct. What is critical at the second stage is the connection that links the relationship between [C] and [U] and the act or omission of [C] ...

[9.22] More specifically, the paradigm relationship C(U) between C and U that gives rise to potential vicarious liability on the part of U is the relationship between employer (U) and employee (C).[22] The reasons for this were as follows:[23]

[17] Gray (n 7) 68–69. Needless to say, this is a *very* fine distinction.
[18] *DC v Prince Alfred College Inc* [2015] SASC 12 at 159–60.
[19] *Mohamud v Wm Morrison Supermarkets plc* [2016] UKSC 11, commented upon by Gray (n 7) 41–42.
[20] *Various Claimants v Catholic Child Welfare Society* [2012] UKSC 56.
[21] ibid [21]. See the description of the test in *Clerk & Lindsell* (n 14) [6-01].
[22] *Various Claimants v Catholic Child Welfare Society* (n 20) [47].
[23] ibid [35].

> The relationship that gives rise to vicarious liability is in the vast majority of cases that of employer and employee under a contract of employment. The employer will be vicariously liable when the employee commits a tort in the course of his employment. There is no difficulty in identifying a number of policy reasons that usually make it fair, just and reasonable to impose vicarious liability on the employer when these criteria are satisfied: (i) the employer is more likely to have the means to compensate the victim than the employee and can be expected to have insured against that liability; (ii) the tort will have been committed as a result of activity being taken by the employee on behalf of the employer; (iii) the employee's activity is likely to be part of the business activity of the employer; (iv) the employer, by employing the employee to carry on the activity will have created the risk of the tort committed by the employee; (v) the employee will, to a greater or lesser degree, have been under the control of the employer.

[9.23] This bases vicarious liability firmly on the rationale of 'enterprise liability'.[24] However, the employer-employee relationship is not the only relationship capable of generating vicarious liability:[25]

> … Where the defendant and the tortfeasor are not bound by a contract of employment, but the relationship has the same incidents, that relationship can properly give rise to vicarious liability on the ground that it is 'akin to that between an employer and an employee' …

[9.24] The second stage is the connection linking C's wrong (for which they are primarily liable) to the relationship between C and U. It is necessary 'to identify whether the workman was working on behalf of an enterprise or on his own behalf and, if the former, how central the workman's activities were to the enterprise and whether these activities were integrated into the organisational structure of the enterprise'.[26]

[9.25] Summing up, it is the commission, by C, of a wrong (not *necessarily* a tort[27]) that is the critical pre-condition for attribution of liability to U. Unless such a wrong is committed, there can be no primary liability in C and so no secondary liability in U. Put this way, it is clear that vicarious liability is premised on the theory of the 'employee's tort' and not the 'employer's tort', where the tort is committed by virtue of the employee's acts being attributed

[24] On this, see Gray (n 7) Ch 5.

[25] *Various Claimants v Catholic Child Welfare Society* (n 20) [47].

[26] ibid [49].

[27] In *Majrowski v Guy's and St Thomas' NHS Trust* [2006] UKHL 56, it was made clear that C's wrong did not have to be a tort in the strict sense. The doctrine might be invoked in connection with equitable wrongs and breaches of statutory duty, provided these were capable of grounding an award in damages.

to the employer.[28] There are at least two difficulties with the 'employer's tort' theory:

(1) It is clear law that under the doctrine of vicarious liability, properly understood, any immunity enjoyed by the employee who committed the wrong would also apply to the employer.[29]
(2) The law is prepared to attribute acts of agents to principals, but much less so states of mind. This does not particularly signify in the case of wrongs committed negligently – there is nothing that needs to be attributed by way of state of mind – nor, for the same reason, in cases of strict liability. But an *intentional* wrong requires the attribution to U of the subjective state of mind of C. Attribution of states of mind, whilst possible, is rare. Thus, cases like *Lister v Hesley Hall Ltd*[30] are very hard to explain unless the juridical basis for the doctrine is that of 'employee's tort', which is then attributed, hook, line and sinker, to undertaking U.

[9.26] The approach taken in this book is that the *key* distinction between vicarious liability and primary liability through attribution (to which we will come next) is this question of attribution. In the case of *vicarious liability*, it is C who commits the tort and who is liable. U is rendered liable only because the relationship C(U) renders it desirable, as a matter of policy, to create a second defendant against whom the claimant can claim additionally or alternatively. Primary liability through attribution (as the label implies) renders U primarily liable: it is U that commits the wrong or does the legal act. Where U is a legal person, an abstraction, it obviously can think and say and do *nothing*, save by way of others. The law attributes certain thoughts and words and deeds of C_1 to C_n to U. If, taken together, these attributed thoughts and words and deeds are sufficient to render U liable to the claimant, then that liability is a primary one in U. None of C_1 to C_n need have committed any legal wrong at all.

C. Primary liability by way of attribution

i. The difference between vicarious liability and primary liability by attribution

[9.27] Vicarious liability simply creates another defendant. Primary liability by way of attribution does not. Undertaking U is primarily liable but only by virtue of acts and/or states of mind of others (C_1 to C_n) that are *attributed* to

[28] This is another controversial area. See, for instance, Gray (n 7) 35, 58–59.
[29] ibid 34–35.
[30] *Lister v Hesley Hall Ltd* (n 15).

U. Whilst U can itself be a natural person,[31] the importance of attribution is that it can locate liability in non-natural or legal persons, and the discussion in this chapter will focus on that case. Non-natural persons can only act through agents. Primary liability by way of attribution is, therefore, of significant importance. It is a part of the law of agency and extends beyond the 'master-servant' relationship that continues to constrain vicarious liability.[32]

[9.28] Unlike with vicarious liability, what is under consideration here is the case where different elements of a tort,[33] done by different actors, are attributed to a single undertaking U who is thereby primarily and not secondarily liable. U may be primarily liability by way of attribution through the attribution of different elements of the tort from different people. Thus, the elements of liability may be *fragmented* across multiple actors (C_1, C_2, C_3 etc) which, when combined in U result in U being liable even though none of C_1, C_2, C_3 are. The elements that have to be satisfied to render U liable emanate (or can emanate) from different sources. In other words, liability can arise where the elements of the tort are not unified in a single person, but are distributed across a number of persons, as where one person (C_1) perceives private information and another person (C_2) (mis)uses it. Of course, in order for C_2 to be able to use (or misuse) the information, it must be transmitted by C_1 to C_2, which implies use of the information by C_1. However, such use does not constitute *misuse* (and so C_1 may not be liable)[34] and C_2 may be a non-natural person unable to perceive and so not capable of misuse themselves. Alternatively, the non-natural person C_2 may themselves transmit the information to natural person C_3 who then uses it in a manner that would constitute an infringement *if only* C_1's perception were attributed to C_3. This is not an uncommon case – even outside the realms of privacy law – and one suspects that very many claims in tort are framed against non-natural defendants where liability is imposed based upon the attribution of thoughts, words and deeds[35] of others to the primarily liable defendant, but without particular consideration of the significance of this.

[31] There is no reason why the thoughts or words or deeds of one human being cannot be attributed to another. Indeed, that is exactly how agency works. The reason we are focusing on U is because (absent vicarious liability) this is the *only* way U can be rendered liable under the Action.

[32] See H Bennett, *Principles of the Law of Agency* (Hart Publishing, 2013) [1.18]–[1.21] and Ch 10.

[33] The principle operates more widely, but we are interested in how U can be made liable to A, who is bringing an Action against U, which is a tort, a civil wrong.

[34] For the reasons described in paras [7.39]–[7.43].

[35] The trifurcation between thoughts, words and deeds is well established in moral thinking, as well as English law. Take, for example, Wesley's hymn (New English Hymnal 235) referencing '... all I think or speak or do' or the Book of Common Prayer's confession of sins, which refers to sinning '... in thought and word and deed'.

ii. An illustration: Lewis v Carmarthenshire County Council

[9.29] This form of liability is well illustrated by the decision of the House of Lords in *Lewis v Carmarthenshire County Council*.[36] A four-year-old boy attending a nursery school under the management of the defendant county council strayed from the school premises onto a public highway. The plaintiff's husband, who was driving a lorry, in his efforts to avoid the child, struck a telegraph pole and was killed. The plaintiff sued the county council for damages, alleging that the death of her husband was caused by the negligence of a school teacher (a Miss Morgan) in failing to take proper steps to prevent the child from straying onto the highway. The claim was thus based upon the vicarious liability of the county council (U) for acts of its servant, Miss Morgan (C).

[9.30] The trial judge – Devlin J – found for the plaintiff and awarded her damages. The Court of Appeal affirmed that decision, but with some reluctance. The reluctance arose out of doubts as to whether Miss Morgan had indeed been negligent, as Devlin J had found. On appeal, the House of Lords unanimously held that Miss Morgan had *not* been negligent.[37] However, with the exception of Lord Oaksey, who dissented, their Lordships held that the *county council* had been negligent. In other words, the case translated from one of vicarious liability to one of primary liability by way of attribution. Lord Goddard stated:[38]

> I cannot bring myself to lay blame for this tragic accident on Miss Morgan. But this does not conclude the matter so far as the appellants are concerned. They maintain a nursery school and an infant school on these premises. In the former they accept the care of children from three to five years and in the latter those of five to seven. During the time when the child was in their care he is found outside the school premises wandering in the street. That, in my opinion, clearly calls for an explanation from the appellants. They have only shown that the child left the room in the temporary absence of the teacher and so got into the playground. In the playground he would have been safe at least from traffic risks. All we know is that the gates must have been open or so easy to open that a child of three or four could open them. True, the nursery children are put, when out of school, into the playpen, but infants from five to seven play in the playground. If it is possible for children of that age, when a teacher's back may be turned for a moment, to get out into a busy street this does seem to indicate some lack of care or of precautions which might reasonably be required. There is no analogy between a school playground and the home in this respect. At any rate, no satisfactory explanation had been given for this child being found in the street at a time when he was in the care of the appellants, and for this reason I would dismiss the appeal.

[36] *Lewis v Carmarthenshire County Council* [1953] 1 WLR 1439 (CA); [1955] 1 AC 549 (HL).
[37] ibid (HL) 559 (per Lord Oaksey), 561–62 (per Lord Goddard), 564 (per Lord Reid), 568–69 (per Lord Tucker).
[38] ibid 562.

[9.31] Lord Reid stated:[39]

> ... I am of opinion that the appellants were negligent. However careful the mistresses might be, minor emergencies and distractions were almost certain to occur from time to time so that some child or children would be left alone without supervision for an appreciable time. The actions of a child of this age are unpredictable, and I think that it ought to have been anticipated by the appellants or their responsible officers that in such a case a child might well try to get out onto the street and that if it did a traffic accident was far from improbable. And it would have been very easy to prevent this, and either lock the gates or, if that was thought undesirable, to make them sufficiently difficult to open to ensure that they could not be opened by a child so young that it could not be trusted alone on the street ...

[9.32] Lord Tucker stated:[40]

> My Lords, such an occurrence [ie the child getting onto the road] I think calls for an explanation from the appellants. Not because the facts and circumstances are exclusively within their knowledge – a theory to which I do not subscribe – but because it was an event which should not have happened and which prima facie indicates negligence on the part of those in charge of the child just as much as the presence of a motor-car on the foot pavement prima facie points to negligence on the part of the driver.

Lord Tucker found that 'the appellants failed altogether to show that the child's presence in the street was not due to any negligence on their part or on that of those for whom they are responsible'.[41]

[9.33] Lord Keith stated:[42]

> ... the appellants, in my opinion, have failed to give any explanation that would excuse them from the prima facie inference of carelessness that arises from the children having escaped onto the road. Whether the inference is one of lack of proper supervision, or lack of safeguards against very small children escaping through doors and gateways onto the street does not, in my opinion, matter. I would say there was a presumption of negligence here that the appellants have failed to discharge.

[9.34] *Lewis* is a decision showing that hard cases make bad law, although in this case the law is not so much *bad* as *unarticulated*. A number of points can be made.

[9.35] It would be interesting to review the pleadings in this case.[43] It would appear that the House of Lords – for readily understandable reasons – substituted for a *vicarious liability* a form of *primary liability* aggregating different elements

[39] ibid 563–64.
[40] ibid 568.
[41] ibid 569.
[42] ibid 571.
[43] To be clear, this has not been done.

of the tort and attributing them to a single person, the council. The pleadings, one imagines, would have set out the negligence of Miss Morgan and asserted that the defendant authority was vicariously liable for her actions. That was the basis for Lord Oaksey's dissent. He made clear that the only case before the courts had been based on the negligence of Miss Morgan:[44]

> Both the courts [ie Devlin J in the King's Bench Division and the Court of Appeal] have based their judgments on the negligence of Miss Morgan, but some of your Lordships are of opinion that, though Miss Morgan was not negligent, yet the appellants were negligent for allowing the gate into the lane to be left unlocked. It is true to say that in particulars delivered on October 20, 1952, it was alleged that 'one of the mistresses ... failed to see that the gates leading from the school premises to the highway were closed'. But the case was not fought on this issue. In fact, the gates were closed but not locked. No question was asked of the headmistress as to why the gates were not locked. None of the judges who has heard the case has based his judgment on an obligation on the appellants to keep the gates locked and the matter is not relied upon in any of the reasons to the respondent's printed case.
>
> I think, therefore, that the case ought to stand or fall upon the issue of Miss Morgan's conduct, and, in my opinion, it cannot be decided in favour of the respondent without inferentially holding that education authorities are bound to keep children under constant supervision throughout every moment of their attendance at school, which, in my opinion, is to demand a higher standard of care than the ordinary prudent schoolmaster or mistress observes.

[9.36] Viewed through the lens of vicarious liability, if Miss Morgan had failed to supervise the boy not out of a dereliction of duty but because *other duties* (a child that had hurt themselves) had (in her judgement) a higher calling upon her time and attention, then she was not negligent and there would be no primary liability to which vicarious liability could attach. Lord Oaksey formed the view that it was 'perfectly natural that Miss Morgan would never have thought that the children would wander out of the school into the yard, much less go out through the gate into the lane. As she said, they were trained children who had been in the school for over a year'.[45] In these circumstances, Lord Oaksey considered that Miss Morgan had not been negligent; and so the claim against the local authority had to fail.

[9.37] Although English law has, in the competition law arena, come close to adopting a form of enterprise liability based on the *undertaking*, no such doctrine exists apart from this limited (European Union law-based) instance.[46] Instead, the English law approach is somewhat unarticulated but does allow

[44] *Lewis v Carmarthenshire County Council* (n 36) 559.
[45] ibid 559.
[46] As to this, see generally P Whelan, *Parental Liability in EU Competition Law* (Oxford University Press, 2023).

different elements of the same tort to be aggregated in certain circumstances so as to render a single principal liable. The outcome in *Lewis* can only be explained by such a combining in circumstances where the presence of a child on the road was – at the level of the enterprise – *res ipsa loquitur*.[47] That, it is suggested, is the only explanation for the decision in *Lewis*.

[9.38] Absent vicarious liability, the liability under the Action of non-natural persons will be: (i) primary (*ex hypothesi*); and (ii) (also *ex hypothesi*) fragmented, by which is meant that the components of liability arise piecemeal through the actions of the defendant's agents, in circumstances where none of them are liable, but where, by a process of cumulation, the undertaking is.

[9.39] That being said, it is quite possible for vicarious and primary liability to subsist in the same case or for judges to disagree as to whether a case *is* one of primary or secondary liability.[48] Yet the distinction is an important one, for obvious analytical reasons. Take the facts of *Lister* – vicarious liability for the intentional acts of an employee[49] – and assume that the House of Lords had drawn the line for imposition of vicarious liability differently (such that no secondary liability on the part of U was possible), but was open (as in the case of *Lewis*) to consideration of primary liability on the part of employer U. Suppose the abusive tendencies of the employee would have been apparent on reasonable examination when the employee was appointed, and the supervision of the employee at work was negligently non-existent. It is easy to see how primary liability could be found in such a case, by attributing to the employer the *negligent* acts of agents *other than* the employee committing the wrong.[50] This is exactly what happened in *Carmarthenshire*, albeit that there was no real factual consideration of how the little boy had escaped from the school premises.

iii. Demarcating thoughts and words and deeds

a. Deeds

[9.40] The trifurcation between thoughts and words and deeds matters in terms of how attribution works. Deeds are positive acts or actions by a human actor. They are to be distinguished from omissions, which tend to be legally relevant only where there is a *duty* to act. Of course, the borderline between acts and omissions is in itself less than clear cut, and lawyers will often seek to characterise omissions as acts, because that avoids the need to show a duty to act in order for an omission to qualify as legally relevant and capable of attribution.

[47] 'The thing speaks for itself', in this case meaning that something had so obviously gone wrong, that negligence could be inferred simply from the facts of the accident.

[48] Gray (n 7) 68; *Carmarthenshire v Lewis* is itself an excellent example.

[49] Considered at para [9.18].

[50] In other words, U would be primarily liable for the failure to 'vet' the employee on appointment and for the failure to supervise that employee at work.

b. Words

[9.41] Words are statements. Again, there are two difficult borderlines that need to be identified:

- *Different types of statement*. There is a clear distinction between the positive statement and what is impliedly said. Again, lawyers will seek to cast silence as a positive representation, relying upon context (X positively said *this*, and thereby implied *that*) or upon what was said in the past *becoming* incorrect (X said this in the past, it was a continuing representation, and when it became false, X had a duty to speak or else was guilty of misrepresentation).
- *Are statements acts?* In one sense, of course, they are: it is not a misuse of language to refer to the *act of speaking*; and it is perfectly possible for an *act* to constitute *speech*. Nevertheless, the law draws a distinction between acts and speech, which therefore informs the distinction being drawn here. There are at least two reasons why the distinction matters:

    (i) Speech does not tend to harm or – put another way – does harm in ways that the law is, or ought to be, slow to respond to. This is very much a policy question, but we have seen that freedom of expression is a protected right under the European Convention on Human Rights. This is a material distinction between acts and speech, and it is harder for an action in relation to speech to succeed than one in relation to acts.[51]

    (ii) Relatedly, acts typically will do very specific harms: if I push you, and you fall over, your bruises are down to me. There are, of course, exceptions (like psychiatric injury, which the law finds difficult to limit) but the general rule holds good. Speech, on the other hand, very rarely results in physical injury (the best example is the person shouting 'Fire' in a crowded theatre, resulting in a stampede that injures people), and usually results in forms of loss ('pure economic loss') that the law is reluctant to compensate for without the existence of special circumstances.

c. Thoughts

[9.42] Thoughts include (some) states of mind, knowledge and perception (in the sense used here). In the criminal law, the distinction would be between the *actus reus* (the act: here deed and words, eliding the distinction just drawn) and

[51] Indeed, until the seminal decision of the House of Lords in *Hedley Byrne & Co Ltd v Heller & Partners Ltd* [1964] 1 AC 465 there was no general liability for harm arising out of negligent misstatement, whereas a general liability for harm arising out of negligent acts had been established for many years, a fragmented liability being unified by the seminal decision of the House of Lords in *Donoghue v Stevenson* [1932] 1 AC 562. Even today, the laws regarding negligent acts and negligent speech are very different.

the *mens rea* (the mental state that some crimes require[52]). Again, mental states need to be parsed quite carefully.

[9.43] Cases of strict liability arise where the act alone involves legal consequence. In a case of strict liability, the defendant infringes the law by their act alone. Put in criminal law terms, simply doing something has a consequence amounting to an infraction of the law. Strict liability is rare (it tends to exist in regulatory areas like health and safety), because we consider that legal consequence ought only to attach to acts over which we have some form of agency. In strict liability cases, even an act that could not have been avoided has consequences.

[9.44] At the other end of the scale lie cases where an act, in order to be consequent, needs to be accompanied by a subjective state of mind, typically *intention* or *recklessness*. Here, the party doing the act is only afflicted by legal consequence where there is a high degree of agency, where to an appreciable extent, the defendant *chooses* to do that act which has legal consequence.

[9.45] Lying between these two extremes are what might rather oddly be called objective states of mind, states of mind that the actor ought to have which (had they done so) would have meant that the act would not have occurred. The best instance of this is negligence. Where the actor fails to act as a reasonable person, in that position, would have acted, they can be said to be negligent. This involves limited agency: the actual actor did what they did because they fell below the standard of conduct of the reasonable person. But, because they were not the reasonable person (or, at least, not at the relevant moment in time), they lacked the ability to choose not to do the act. Thus, where a driver runs someone else over, they will not be civilly liable for the injuries of the victim unless the accident occurred through the negligence of the driver; ie the driver, on the occasion of the accident, failed to drive according to the standards of the reasonably competent driver.

D. How attribution works

i. Anthropomorphisis

[9.46] It is probably unavoidable to anthropomorphise the undertaking. How helpful this is, is a different matter. Denning LJ said this in *HL Bolton (Engineering) Ltd v Graham & Sons Ltd*:[53]

[52] Serious offences, like murder, require intention.
[53] *HL Bolton (Engineering) Ltd v Graham & Sons Ltd* [1957] 1 QB 159 at 170–73.

> … A company may in many ways be likened to a human body. It has a brain and a nerve centre which controls what it does. It also has hands which hold the tools and act in accordance with directions from the centre. Some of the people in the company are mere servants and agents who are nothing more than hands to do the work and cannot be said to represent the mind or will. Others are directors and managers which represent the directing mind and will of the company, and control what it does. The state of mind of these managers is the state of mind of the company and is treated by the law as such …

[9.47] Denning LJ was drawing a distinction between the attribution of deeds (relatively easy) and the attribution of states of mind (harder), with statements no doubt sitting between these two extremes on this particular spectrum. It is most convenient to begin (counterintuitively) with the hardest instance of attribution, that of state of mind.

ii. States of mind

a. Where no attribution is needed

[9.48] In cases where liability is strict (as in the case of the Action and indeed most cases of infringement of intellectual property) as well as those cases where an objective state of mind only is required (ie negligence), questions of attribution of state of mind do not arise or arise only to a limited extent. Liability for the deliberate misuse of private information is strict.[54] However, in order for undertaking U to be liable, C's perception (a state of mind) will have to attributed to undertaking U, as well as the act of misuse.

b. The general rule of attribution: Agency basis

[9.49] In the words of Denning LJ in *HL Bolton (Engineering) Ltd v Graham & Sons Ltd*:[55]

> … here the intention of the company can be derived from the intention of its officers and agents. Whether their intention is the company's intention depends on the nature of the matter under consideration, the relative position of the officer or agent and the other relevant facts and circumstances of the case …

As will be seen, this context-sensitive approach very much foreshadows the approach of Lord Hoffmann in *Meridien*, a case we will come to.

[9.50] The test for attribution of states of mind (as opposed to acts) has been framed in many cases. In *Lennard's Carrying Co Ltd v Asiatic Petroleum Ltd*,[56]

[54] See the analysis of deliberate misuse of private information in Chapters 7 and 8.
[55] *HL Bolton (Engineering) Ltd v Graham & Sons Ltd* (n 53) 170–73.
[56] *Lennard's Carrying Co Ltd v Asiatic Petroleum Ltd* [1915] AC 705.

the question arose as to the application of section 502 of the Merchant Shipping Act 1894, which provided that the owner of a British sea-going ship shall not be liable to make good to any extent whatever 'any loss or damage happening without his actual fault or privity' where any good or merchandise taken in or put on board his ship are lost or damaged by reason of fire on board the ship. Viscount Haldane LC used language so evocative that it is in danger of becoming a straitjacket not a guide:[57]

> My Lords, a corporation is an abstraction. It has no mind of its own any more than it has a body of its own; its active mind and directing will must consequently be sought in the person of somebody who for some purposes may be called an agent, but who is really the directing mind and will of the corporation, the very ego and centre of the personality of the corporation …

[9.51] The implication of this passage – not helped by the later reference to boards of directors or persons with authority co-ordinate with boards of directors – is that only people at the apex of the organisation can be that organisation's 'active mind and directing will'. Significantly, Lord Dunedin – who gave a concurring opinion – propounded a much less memorable but more flexible test:[58]

> The real question therefore turns upon what is ton be the application of the words [in section 502] to a metaphysical conception like an incorporated company who cannot act directly themselves.
>
> My Lords, I do not know that a case will ever arise in which that will need to be treated as a purely abstract proposition. I do not think it arises in this case, and I certainly incline to the opinion that it will be found always to depend upon the particular facts of the case. If I was bound to decide affirmatively in this case, I should be inclined to think that there was enough known about Lennard to show that, to use the appellants' learned counsel's own phrase, he was the alter ego of the company. He was a director of the company. I can quite conceive that a company may be entrusting its business to one director may be as truly represented by that one director, as in the ordinary senses it is represented by the whole board. I am quite sure that you cannot at least put as a general proposition in law that it is true that nothing will ever be the actual fault or privity of an incorporated company unless it is the actual fault of the whole board of directors.

[9.52] Questions of attribution are determined not by a one-size-fits-all test, but by a consideration of the individual circumstances read in the context of the relevant legal provision requiring a particular state of mind in a particular actor. The term 'controlling mind' is itself issue-dependent, and any sense that the controlling mind is always located at the organisational apex is simply

[57] See eg Hawke (n 3) [2-04]: 'Regrettably, the statement of principle here has undoubtedly resulted in a fairly crude, generalised, development of the jurisprudence down the years of the century …'.

[58] *Lennard's Carrying Co Ltd v Asiatic Petroleum Ltd* (n 56) 715–16.

to over- or mis-state the true legal position. This is the message of the Privy Council's decision in *Meridian Global Funds Management Asia Ltd v Securities Commission*, where Lord Hoffmann clarified *Lennard's* case as follows:[59]

> The phrase 'directing mind and will' comes of course from the celebrated speech of Viscount Haldane LC in *Lennard's Carrying Co Ltd v Asiatic Petroleum Co Ltd* [1915] AC 705, 713. But their Lordships think that there has been some misunderstanding of the true principle upon which that case was decided. It may be helpful to start by stating the nature of the problem in a case like this and then come back to Lennard's case later.
>
> Any proposition about a company necessarily involves a reference to a set of rules. A company exists because there is a rule (usually in a statute) which says that a persona ficta shall be deemed to exist and to have certain of the powers, rights and duties of a natural person. But there would be little sense in deeming such a persona ficta to exist unless there were also rules to tell one what acts were to count as acts of the company. It is therefore a necessary part of corporate personality that there should be rules by which acts are attributed to the company. These may be called 'the rules of attribution'.
>
> The company's primary rules of attribution will generally be found in its constitution, typically the articles of association, and will say things such as 'for the purpose of appointing members of the board, a majority vote of the shareholders shall be a decision of the company' or 'the decisions of the board in managing the company's business shall be the decisions of the company'. There are also primary rules of attribution which are not expressly stated in the articles but implied by company law, such as 'the unanimous decision of all the shareholders in a solvent company about anything which the company under its memorandum of association has power to do shall be the decision of the company': see *Multinational Gas and Petrochemical Co v Multinational Gas and Petrochemical Services Ltd* [1983] Ch 258.
>
> These primary rules of attribution are obviously not enough to enable a company to go out into the world and do business. Not every act on behalf of the company could be expected to be the subject of a resolution of the board or a unanimous decision of the shareholders. The company therefore builds upon the primary rules of attribution by using general rules of attribution which are equally available to natural persons, namely, the principles of agency. It will appoint servants and agents whose acts, by a combination of the general principles of agency and the company's primary rules of attribution, count as the acts of the company and having done so, it will also make itself subject to the general rules by which liability for the acts of others can be attributed to natural persons, such as estoppel or ostensible authority in contract and vicarious liability in tort.
>
> It is worth pausing at this stage to make what may seem an obvious point. Any statement about what a company has or has not done, or can or cannot do, is necessarily a reference to the rules of attribution (primary and general) as they apply to that

[59] *Meridian Global Funds Management Asia Ltd v Securities Commission* [1995] 2 AC 500 at 506–507.

> company. Judges sometimes say that a company 'as such' cannot do anything; it must act by servants or agents. This may seem an unexceptionable, even banal remark and of course the meaning is usually perfectly clear. But a reference to a company 'as such' might suggest that there is something out there called the company of which one can meaningfully say that it can or cannot do something. There is in fact no such thing as the company as such, no *ding an sich*, only the applicable rules. To say that a company cannot do something means only that there is no one whose doing of that act would, under the applicable rules of attribution, count as an act of the company.
>
> The company's primary rules of attribution together with the general principles of agency, vicarious liability and so forth are usually sufficient to enable one to determine its rights and obligations. In exceptional cases, however, they will not provide an answer. This will be the case when a rule of law, either expressly or by implication, excludes attribution on the basis of the general principles of agency or vicarious liability. For example, a rule may be stated in language primarily applicable to a natural person and require some act or state of mind on the part of that person 'himself', as opposed to his servants or agents. This is generally true of rules of the criminal law, which ordinarily impose liability only for the actus reus and mens rea of the defendant himself. How is such a rule to be applied to a company?
>
> One possibility is that the court may come to the conclusion that the rule was not intended to apply to companies at all; for example, a law which created an offence for which the only penalty was community service. Another possibility is that the court might interpret the law as meaning that it could apply to a company only on the basis of its primary rules of attribution, ie if the act giving rise to liability was specifically authorised by a resolution of the board or an unanimous agreement of the shareholders. But there will be many cases in which neither of these solutions is satisfactory; in which the court considers that the law was intended to apply to companies and that, although it excludes ordinary vicarious liability, insistence on the primary rules of attribution would in practice defeat that intention. In such a case, the court must fashion a special rule of attribution for the particular substantive rule. This is always a matter of interpretation: given that it was intended to apply to a company, how was it intended to apply? Whose act (or knowledge, or state of mind) was for this purpose intended to count as the act etc of the company? One finds the answer to this question by applying the usual canons of interpretation, taking into account the language of the rule (if it is a statute) and its content and policy.

This is an important articulation of the law, and one that does not so much overturn *Lennard's* as explain it.[60] Attribution is a function of agency.

c. Attribution of perception specifically

[9.53] It is the attribution of perception that is the question here under consideration. Perception of private information is central to the Action, and the question that arises is how (as a matter of law) C's perception is attributed

[60] Hawke (n 3) [2-43].

to the non-human undertaking U. A great many of the cases dealing with attribution of knowledge within undertakings concern cases of insurance. This is not particularly surprising, because insurance cases involve the duty of utmost good faith on the part of an assured when making an insurance proposal to the insurer.[61] In the insurance context:[62]

> In the case of corporate assureds or brokers, their knowledge is that of those who are sufficiently concerned with the operation of the company and the activity at hand, whether it be the operation of the interest insured, the placing of the insurance or the making of a claim. The question whose knowledge will be attributed to the company will also depend on the nature of the insurance …
>
> If an individual's knowledge is attributed to a company, such knowledge is said to be actual knowledge. The knowledge of these natural persons is attributed to the company, either by virtue of agency or by the doctrine of imputation associated with the 'directing mind and will' of the company.

The distinction drawn between agency and imputation is one without a difference, following *Meridien*. As per Lord Hoffmann, one collapses into the other.

[9.54] What is attributed depends upon all the relevant circumstances, but with particular reference to duties to report information and duties to receive reports of information. But it is important: (i) not to be too prescriptive; and (ii) to bear in mind the insurance context of these cases. In *Fitzherbert v Mather*,[63] the plaintiff took out insurance with the defendant on 21 September 1782 on a cargo of oats. The policy was placed on the basis of information provided by (it was found) the plaintiff's agent, one Mr Thomas. Thomas failed to tell the plaintiff what he knew *before* 21 September, namely that the cargo was lost. As a result, Buller J held that the policy was void:[64]

> Though the plaintiff be innocent, yet if he build his information on that of his agent, and his agent be guilty of a misrepresentation, the principal must suffer. It is the common question every day at Guildhall, when one of two innocent parties must suffer by fraud or negligence of a third, which of the two gave credit? Here it appears that the plaintiff trusted Thomas; and he must therefore take the consequences.

[9.55] Similarly, in *Gladstone v King*,[65] the question was whether the captain of a ship should have communicated to the shipowners the fact that his ship had been driven onto a rock, but had got off without appearing to have suffered material damage. It was held that there was a duty on the captain to communicate, and that his knowledge was therefore that of the

[61] P MacDonald Eggers and S Picken, *Good Faith and Insurance Contracts*, 4th edn (Informa Law, 2018) [7.98]. See also, for a statutory framing of the duty, the Marine Insurance Act 1906, s 18(1).
[62] MacDonald Eggers and Picken (n 61) [7.107].
[63] *Fitzherbert v Mather* (1785) 1 TR 12; 99 ER 944.
[64] ibid 16; 946–47.
[65] *Gladstone v King* (1813) 1 M & S 35; 105 ER 13.

shipowners. Lord Ellenborough CJ noted that 'what is known to the agent is impliedly known to the principal'[66] and Le Blanc J observed that the antecedent damage was something which 'the captain was bound to communicate to his owners'.[67]

[9.56] Non-insurance cases, although rarer, are to similar effect. Thus, in *Ranger v Great Western Rly Co*,[68] it was alleged by the appellant/plaintiff, Mr Ranger, that he had been induced to enter into a contract by the fraud of the respondent/defendant, Great Western Rly Co. The Lord Chancellor rejected the question of fraud, but stated the following general principle:[69]

> Strictly speaking, a corporation cannot itself be guilty of fraud. But where a corporation is formed for the purpose of carrying on a trading or other speculation for profit, such as forming a railway, these objects can only be accomplished through the agency of individuals; and there can be no doubt that if the agents employed conduct themselves fraudulently, so that if they had been acting for private employers, the persons for whom they were acting would have been affected by their fraud, the same principles must prevail where the principal under whom the agent acts is a corporation.

[9.57] *Dresser v Norwood* was a case of identity as between contracting parties, which mattered because one party wished to assert a set-off against the other. It is unnecessary to consider the facts, but a broad statement regarding the attribution of knowledge was made: the knowledge of the agent, as to identity, 'howsoever acquired, is the knowledge of the principal'.[70]

d. The fraud exception

[9.58] The 'fraud exception' is not something that needs particular discussion in the context of attributing C's perception to U, but for completeness the point is briefly articulated. The question is to what extent can an agent's fraud be imputed to their principal? In *Re Hampshire Land Co*,[71] this question was addressed and answered:[72]

> The case is very much more like the one which both Mr Bramwell Davis and Mr Jenkins had to admit was an exception to the general rule that they sought to lay down, for they admitted that if Wills had been guilty of a fraud, the personal knowledge of Wills of the fraud that he had committed on the company would not have been knowledge of the society of the facts constituting that fraud; because common sense at once leads one to the conclusion that it would be impossible to infer that the

[66] ibid 37–38; 15.

[67] ibid 38–39; 15. See also, to similar effect, *Proudfoot v Montefiore* (1867) lr 2 QB 511, 521–522; *Bawden v The London, Edinburgh and Glasgow Insurance Co* [1892] 2 QB 534.

[68] *Ranger v Great Northern Rly Co* (1854) 5 HLC 72; 10 ER 824.

[69] ibid 86–87; 830.

[70] *Dresser v Norwood* (1864) 17 CB (NS) 466, 481–482. See also, to similar effect, *Tanham v Nicholson* (1872) LR 5 HL 561, 567–68; *Baldwin v Casella* (1872) LR 7 Exch 325, 326–27.

[71] *Re Hampshire Land Co* [1896] 2 Ch 743.

[72] ibid 749–50.

> duty, either of giving or receiving notice, will be fulfilled where the common agent is himself guilty of fraud. It seems to me that if you assume here that Mr Wills was guilty of irregularity – a breach of duty in respect of these transactions – the same inference is to be drawn as if he had been guilty of fraud. I do not know, I am sure, whether he was guilty of actual fraud; but whether his conduct amounted to actual fraud or to breach of duty, I decline to hold that the knowledge of his own fraud or of his own breach of duty is, under the circumstances, the knowledge of the company.

[9.59] English law has subsequently got itself in a right mess in terms of what knowledge can and what knowledge cannot be attributed to a principal pursuant to the so-called 'fraud exception'. It is unnecessary to consider the details, because (as has been noted) the fraud exception is not relevant when it comes to attributing C's perception of A which (whilst it may or may not have been obtained fraudulently) is simply a perception and not any part of a fraud by C against U.

[9.60] The 'fraud exception' does, however, matter when it comes to understanding the limits of attribution. There is a clear line to be drawn between the attribution of states of mind and the attribution of acts and statements. The 'fraud exception' sheds light on the approach that courts take to attribution of states of mind generally.

iii. Attribution of deeds

a. A problem stated

[9.61] We move from one extreme to another, from states of mind to deeds. Statements, lying somewhere between states of mind and deeds in the attribution spectrum, are considered last. The law regarding the attribution of deeds to principals is difficult for a number of related reasons:

- The doctrine of vicarious liability serves to confuse. The doctrine makes it seem like C's deeds are being attributed to U, when in fact the law creates a secondary liability in U (secondary to C's primary liability). Vicarious liability is not a case of attribution at all: but appearances can serve to mislead, as evidenced by the confusion surrounding 'employee's tort' versus 'employer's tort' referenced at paragraph [9.25].
- Although the doctrine of vicarious liability is wide, it is nevertheless clearly circumscribed. Assuming that the rationale for vicarious liability is 'enterprise liability', then the limits of the doctrine are described by the limits of the enterprise. The point is that those limits in no way inform the circumstances in which C's deeds can be attributed to U when considering U's primary liability by way of attribution.
- It is quite clear that the deeds of agents, not just servants, can be attributed to U, and that it is agency that informs attribution more than anything else. Thus, the 'scope of authority' test remains of significance, in a way long forgotten in the case of vicarious liability.

[9.62] One complicating factor is that deeds tend only to come to courts' attention where they affect third parties. In the case we are here considering, that of complex undertakings, much is going on 'under the bonnet' *within the undertaking*, but without any particular manifestation in the outside world. Where C_1 communicates their perception to C_2, who then misuses that perception, the communication from C_1 to C_2 is not going to register with an outsider because it is internal to U and not visible to the outside world. Even C_2's misuse may be invisible, as in the case of use by way of data processing.

b. Attribution in the case of the outside world

[9.63] *Bowstead and Reynolds* says this:[73]

> Where a person P, by words or conduct, represents or permits it to be represented that another person, A, has authority to act on P's behalf, P is bound by the acts of A with respect to anyone dealing wth A as an agent on the faith of any such representation, to the same extent as if A had the authority that A was represented to have, even though A had no such actual authority.

[9.64] This is the doctrine of ostensible authority, it being taken as read that this consequence follows where there is actual authority. So, if U tells C to do something and that something affects A, then C's deed is attributable to U both where the authority existed and where it was represented to have existed by U.

[9.65] To be an agent:

- The agent must have been instructed to represent the principal.
- The agent must not merely stand in the principal's shoes, but must act for the principal.
- The result of the agent so acting is to affect legal relations between the principal and a third party.[74]

[9.66] Although this definition does not deal with ostensible (or lacking) authority, it is valuable because it makes clear that agency is not to be equated purely with the conclusion of contract. Of course, agents are regularly tasked with concluding contracts on behalf of their principal and the conclusion of a contract very obviously does affect the principal's legal relations. But the agent who drives the principal's vehicle on the principal's business is no less an agent; it is simply that their function of driving tends not to affect the principal's legal

[73] P Watts and F Reynolds, *Bowstead and Reynolds on Agency*, 23rd edn (Sweet and Maxwell, 2024) [8-009].

[74] Adapted from R Powell, *The Law of Agency*, 2nd edn (Pitman, 1961) 4.

relations *except where something goes wrong*. The driver who on their principal's business runs another down will have their act attributed to the principal. Usually, it will be the agent who will have been negligent and so such cases tend to be pleaded as cases of vicarious liability. But there are cases where the act of the agent does not involve negligence on the part of *that agent*, but where the act was rendered negligent through the acts of another, different agent. This would be the case where the individual act causing the injury is not negligent, but where the principal's wider system has culpably broken down.

Example

Suppose driver X, acting in the course of their employment by undertaking U, runs over pedestrian Y in circumstances where X did not drive negligently. However, the accident was caused by defective brakes in the vehicle, and those defective brakes existed because of U's failure to have the vehicle serviced. Had the vehicle been serviced, the defective brakes would have been rectified. The act of X in running over Y and the negligent failure to have the vehicle serviced will be attributed to U, who will be primarily liable to Y.

Indeed *Lewis* was exactly this case.

c. Internal management

[9.67] So far, we have been considering the case where the act of the agent impacts upon a third party. Of course, where there is misuse of A's private information by C on behalf of U that will be the case. But there is likely to be a great deal done internally, as where C_1 does something, a process to which C_2 adds and so on, all of C acting for U. As has been described, the acts of C will not, if they are part of the internal processes, be uses by C. But they will be attributable to U as and when A is affected by U's putative misuse. What is the basis for such attribution? There are two facets to this, discussed in turn.

[9.68] The first is the doctrine of the presumption of regular internal management, first stated in *Royal British Bank v Turquand*.[75] Turquand was the official manager of a coal mining and railway company and he was sued on a bond given by the company to the plaintiff bank to secure its drawings on current account. The bond was given under the seal of the company and signed by two directors and the secretary, but the company alleged that under the terms of its registered deed of settlement the directors had power to borrow only such sums as had been authorised by a general resolution of the company, and in this case no sufficiently specific resolution had been passed. The court held that even so – despite these irregularities – the company was bound by the bond:[76]

[75] *Royal British Bank v Turquand* (1856) 6 E & B 327; 119 ER 886.
[76] ibid 332; 888.

We may now take for granted that the dealings with these companies are not like the dealings with other partnerships, and that the parties dealing with them are bound to read the statute and the deed of settlement. But they are not bound to do more. And the party here, on reading the deed of settlement, would find, not a prohibition on borrowing, but a permission to do so on certain conditions. Finding that the authority might be made complete by a resolution, he would have a right to infer the fact of a resolution authorising that which on the face of the document appeared to be legitimately done.

[9.69] This case concerned a contract, but the point is a general one. Where it appears that there has been a process within an organisation by which the end product is a wrong done by the undertaking, any person claiming in regard to that wrong should not be prevented from a successful claim by an assertion on the part of the undertaking that the undertaking's own internal processes were such that the wrong should never have been committed.

[9.70] The second facet concerns the doctrine of 'common employment', which precluded an injured employee from obtaining compensation from their employer where their injuries were caused by the actions of another employee.[77] The high-water mark of this doctrine is the decision in *Priestly v Fowler*,[78] which is cited because it shows how far 'enterprise liability' has come since that decision. In that case, one servant of a master (a butcher, as it happened) through their negligence injured another. The court, driven essentially by reasons of policy, limited the injured employee's claim to a claim *against the other employee personally*. Lord Abinger CB said this:[79]

If the master be liable to the servant in this action, the principle of that liability will be found to carry us to an alarming extent. He who is reponsible by his general duty, or by the terms of his contract, for all the consequences of negligence in a matter in which he is the principal, is responsible for the negligence of all his inferior agents. If the owner of the carriage is therefore responsible for the sufficiency of his carriage to his servant, he is responsible for the negligence of his coach-maker, or his harness-maker, or his coachman. The footman, therefore, who rides behind the carriage, may have an action against his master for a defect in the carriage owing to the negligence of the coach-maker, or for a defect in the harness arising from the negligence of the harness-maker, or for drunkenness, neglect, or want of skill in the coachman; nor is there any reason why the principle should not, if applicable in this class of cases, extend to many others. The master, for example, would be liable to the servant for the negligence of the chambermaid, for putting him into a damp bed; for that of the upholsterer, for sending in a crazy bedstead, whereby he was made to fall down while asleep and injure himself; for the negligence of the cook, in not properly cleaning the

[77] Gray (n 7) 21; D Bennett (ed), *Munkman on Employer's Liability*, 17th edn (LexisNexis, 2019) [1.13]–[1.25].

[78] *Priestly v Fowler* (1837) 3 M & W 1; 150 ER 1030.

[79] ibid 5–7; 1032–33.

copper vessels used in the kitchen; of the butcher, in supplying the family with meat of a quality injurious to the health; of the builder, for a defect in the foundation of the house, whereby it fell, and injured both the master and the servant by the ruins.

The inconvenience, not to say the absurdity of these consequences, afford a sufficient argument against the application of this principle to the present case. But, in truth, the mere relation of the master and the servant never can imply an obligation on the part of the master to take more care of the servant than he may reasonably be expected to do of himself. He is, no doubt, bound to provide for the safety of his servant in the course of his employment, to the best of his judgment, information, and belief. The servant is not bound to risk his safety in the service of his master, and may, if he thinks fit, decline any service in which he reasonably apprehends injury to himself: and in most of the cases in which danger may be incurred, if not in all, he is just as likely to be acquainted with the probability and extent of it as the master. In that sort of employment, especially, which is described in the declaration in this case, the plaintiff must have known as well as his master, and probably better, whether the van was sufficient, whether it was overloaded, and whether it was likely to carry him safely. In fact, to allow this sort of action to prevail would be an encouragement to the servant to omit that diligence and caution which he is in duty bound to exercise on the behalf of his master, to protect him against the misconduct or negligence of others who serve him, and which diligence and caution, while they protect the master, are a much better security against any injury the servant may sustain by the negligence of others engaged under the same master, than any recourse against his master for damages could possibly afford.

[9.71] The days of masters and servants and small households and businesses are long gone, and the idea that an undertaking discharges its duty to one employee merely by ensuring that another is duly appointed died long ago. In *Wilsons & Clyde Coal Co Ltd v English*,[80] decided a century after *Priestly v Fowler*, the House of Lords had to consider a personal injury claim by an employee against a company that owned five collieries. The company's board of directors appointed an agent to run the collieries, who in turn selected a mine manager for each colliery (these appointments being approved by the board), with all subordinate officials being selected and appointed by the mine manager. All were tasked with ensuring the workplace was safe, and it was contended on behalf of the defendant company/employer that although the company owed a duty of care to its servants to provide a reasonably safe system of working, that duty was discharged if the company delegated their duty to competent subordinates. Any negligence in the provision of such a system would then be the negligence of such delegates and for this negligence – under the doctrine of common employment – the company would not be liable. The argument – this time – was rejected. Lord Thankerton stated the general point as follows:[81]

It seems to me that the fallacy in the appellant's argument lies in the view that the master, being under a duty to take due care in the provision of a reasonably safe

[80] *Wilsons & Clyde Coal Co Ltd v English* [1938] 1 AC 57.
[81] ibid 64–65.

> system of working, is absolved from that duty by the appointment of a competent person to perform the duty. In my opinion, the master cannot 'delegate' his duty in this sense, though he may appoint someone as his agent in the discharge of the duty, for whom he will remain responsible under the maxim r*espondeat superior*. It therefore becomes necessary to examine the nature and limits of the doctrine of common employment.

[9.72] The employer is responsible for the system and for the performance of the employees within that system, both individually and *inter se*. It is actually very difficult to differentiate between: (i) a negligent system; (ii) the negligent performance of a single employee (the vicarious liability case); and (iii) the 'concert party' of two or more employees acting negligently as a collective, but within a system that is defensible. Attribution of acts to the undertaking means that these distinctions become irrelevant. That is the legal approach that has pertained since at least *Wilsons & Clyde Coal*. Thus, Lord Macmillan stated:[82]

> In this appeal your Lordships have to consider and accommodate the spheres of operation in the law of master and servant of two competing doctrines, the doctrine of vicarious liability and the doctrine of common employment. According to the former, a master is responsible for the negligence of his servant acting within the scope of his employment; according to the latter a master is not: esponsible for the negligence of his servant causing injury to a fellow-servant. Both doctrines are well established in the law. It is obvious that they may come into conflict. If a servant is injured by the negligence of a fellow-servant acting within the scope of their common employment, the former doctrine would impose liability on the master, while the latter doctrine would exculpate him. The question is, Which of these two principles is applicable to the present case?
>
> Now I take it to be settled law that the provision of a safe system of working in a colliery is an obligation of the owner of the colliery. He cannot divest himself of this duty, though he may –and, if it involves technical management and he is not himself technically qualified, must –perform it through the agency of an employee. It remains the owner's obligation, and the agent whom the owner appoints to perform it performs it on the owner's behalf. The owner remains vicariously responsible for the negligence of the person whom he has appointed to perform his obligation for him, and cannot escape liability by merely proving that he has appointed a competent agent. If the owner's duty has not been performed, no matter how competent the agent selected by the owner to perform it for him, the owner is responsible.
>
> But then it is said the if the person injured in consequence of the non-performance of the owner's duty by the owner's agent is an employee of the owner there is no redress, because the agent is engaged in a common employment with the injured party and the latter took the risk of the negligence of his fellow-employees. To this the conclusive answer is that the agent engaged in discharging the owner's duty the owner of providing a safe system of working in the mine is not engaged in a common

[82] ibid 74–75.

> employment with the ordinary workmen in the mine. He is not collaborating with them. He is performing the duty of the owner, not the duty of an employee. The doctrine of common employment implies that the employment must be common. The owner of a colliery is not engaged in a common employment with the miners who work in the colliery, and the agent carrying out the obligations of the owner is not collaborating with the workmen in the mine. Consequently the defence of common employment is not available to the mine-owner where an accident occurs to an employee in the mine through the negligent performance of the owner's duty by the person appointed by the owner to perform that duty for him; for such agent of the owner and the injured workman are not in this respect engaged in a common employment.

The doctrine of common employment reaches, as regards persons *within the undertaking*, the same conclusion as in *Turquand*: the acts of agents are attributable to the undertaking.

[9.73] All the law leads in the same direction. Acts done by agents in the course of their employment – including by way of 'ostensible authority' – are attributable to the undertaking.

d. Statements

[9.74] Statements have – ever since *Hedley Byrne* – occupied a peculiar position in English law. That is because, in contrast to acts, statements are made all the time, in circumstances where free speech is a protected right. The law needs to be peculiarly on guard when it comes to imposing liability for statements. The law is characterised by a marked differentiation between fraudulent, negligent and innocent misrepresentation, but it is suggested that this differentiation operates at the level of liability not attribution. In short, it is in the framing of the primary liability that the issue arises, not in the context of attribution. Put another way, C's statement will be attributed to U in just the same way as C's deed. Whether that statement triggers a liability in U depends on the other requirements for a successful cause of action being satisfied.[83]

[9.75] It must not be forgotten that *Hedley Byrne & Co Ltd v Heller & Partners Ltd* itself was a case where the statement of C was attributed to U.[84] The facts were these: Hedley Byrne & Co Ltd were a firm of advertising agents, whose customer, Easipower Ltd, had placed some business with them. The proposal was for a campaign involving the expenditure of around £100,000 (a lot of money in 1957, when these events took place), and Hedley Byrne became doubtful of Easipower's financial position. They sought a banker's report, and approached their bank, the National Provincial Bank Ltd, to obtain this. A

[83] These will not be discussed: this is not a book on liability for misrepresentation.
[84] *Hedley Byrne & Co Ltd v Heller & Partners Ltd* [1964] 1 AC 465.

person at a branch of that bank contacted a certain Mr L Heller at the bank at which Easipower banked, Heller & Partners Ltd. A representation as to the company's financial standing was made orally over the telephone, but there was before the courts an agreed note of what was said. This then culminated in an exchange of letters as follows. The first, from National Provincial Bank to Heller & Partners Ltd:

> Dear Sir
>
> We shall be obliged by your opinion in confidence as to the respectability and standing of Easipower Ltd, 27 Albemarle Street, London W1 and by stating whether you consider them trustworthy, in the way of business, to the extent of £100,000 per annum advertising contract.
>
> Yours faithfully

To this, Heller & Partners Ltd responded:

> Confidential
>
> For your private use and without responsibility on the part of this bank or its officials.
>
> Dear Sir
>
> In reply to your inquiring letter of 7th instant, we beg to advise
>
> 'Re E … Ltd'
>
> Respectably constituted company, considered good for its ordinary business engagements. Your figures are larger than we are accustomed to see.
>
> Yours faithfully
>
> Per pro Heller & Partners Ltd

[9.76] It is unnecessary to go into the details of the law of negligent misstatement. Quoting from the headnote:

> … A negligent, though honest, misrepresentation, spoken or written, may give rise to an action for damages for financial loss caused thereby, apart from any contract or fiduciary relationship, since the law will imply a duty of care when a party seeking information from a party possessed of a special skill trusts him to exercise due care, and that party knew or ought to have known that reliance was being placed on his skill and judgment …

[9.77] The reference to 'him' and 'his' disguises the fact that this was a claim between corporate undertakings and that there was no question of vicarious liability. The fact is that questions of assumption of responsibility by the defendant and reliance by the claimant can – where there is a corporate undertaking – only be resolved by wholesale (unaddressed) attribution of thoughts and words and deeds of C to U. Cases concerning misstatement are peculiarly good at showing this general truth: but it is a general truth, and it is better to look for those cases where there is no attribution of thoughts and words and deeds rather than to frame the general rule the other way round.

iv. Cumulation

[9.78] The decision of the House of Lords in *Lewis*[85] stands as clear authority that the elements of liability of an undertaking can derive from different agents, none of whom would individually be liable, but whose conduct in thought and word and deed viewed cumulatively and attributed to the undertaking renders the undertaking U, but not the agents (C), liable. It is this fact that makes primary liability by way of attribution so different from vicarious liability. *Lewis* is interesting and unusual because it shows the fault-line between vicarious and primary liability. Normally, in cases of primary liability, attribution is taken as read where it is the thoughts or words or deeds of an agent acting within the scope of their authority (actual or ostensible) that are being attributed. That is as much the case where there is a single agent in play (C) as where there are many (C_1 to C_n).

[9.79] However, cumulation is a dangerous doctrine if read too widely. The law must be careful against spreading the net of primary liability too broadly. This may happen for a variety of reasons.

a. Mixing and matching agents

[9.80] In *Re Marseilles Extension Ry Co, ex p Crédit Foncier and Mobilier of England*,[86] two directors of Company A were also directors of Company B, and both companies employed the same solicitor. It was sought to attribute the knowledge of the directors and solicitor in their capacity as agents of Company A to Company B (and vice versa) and cumulate that knowledge with their knowledge derived as agents of Company B. The court rejected any such argument. Mellish LJ said:[87]

> … I cannot think that, because he was a common director to the two companies, we are on that account to say that the one company has necessarily notice of everything that is within the knowledge of the common director, and which knowledge he has acquired as director of the other company. It appears to me, that a director is simply a person appointed to act as one of a board, with power to bind the company when acting as a board, but otherwise having no power to bind them …

[9.81] The judge was demarcating between knowledge acquired by a director in one capacity (as director of Company A) and knowledge acquired by the same director in a different capacity (as director of Company B). There can be

[85] Discussed at para [9.29] ff.
[86] *Re Marseilles Extension Ry Co, ex p Crédit Foncier and Mobilier of England* (1871) LR 7 Ch 161. Affirmed in this regard in *Re Hampshire Land Co* [1896] Ch 743.
[87] *Re Marseilles Extension Ry Co* ibid 168–69.

no cumulation in such a case, because the agent is acting in different capacities. That is as true where a person acts as agent for several principals as where the agent has information in their capacity as agent and in their capacity as their own person, as James LJ noted in the same case:[88]

> I cannot understand how a director of a company going to borrow money from another company can put the company from whom he borrowed it in any different position from that in which a joint stock bank would be placed by a director of it asking a loan for himself. Is it to be imputed to the banking company that they have knowledge of everything the director knows about his own private affairs? Such a proposition seems to be most unreasonable.

[9.82] Thus, the question of an agent's scope of authority becomes significant. *Bradley v Riches* concerned the attribution of a solicitor's knowledge to his client:[89]

> … You must, in the first place, look at what are the circumstances of the case as to knowledge. If the circumstances of the case are such as in the ordinary course of business between solicitor and client they are, then the solicitor must be assumed to have communicated the fact to his client, and the knowledge of the agent is, to use the language of Lord Chelmsford in *Espin v Pemberton*, the imputed knowledge of the client. It appears to me to be clear that that presumption or imputation is a thing which the client cannot be allowed to rebut.

[9.83] The limits of the doctrine were carefully explored in *Blackburn, Low & Co v Vigors*, where courts of differing instances differed.[90] In the Court of Appeal, Lord Esher MR (who dissented) stated as a general proposition:[91]

> The law does not hold that for every purpose the principal is to be deemed to know whatever becomes known to an agent of his in the course of the agent's employment.

[9.84] It will readily be seen that this is a narrower approach than simply the 'ordinary course of business' test propounded in *Bradley v Riches*. The Court of Appeal was overruled in the House of Lords, but on the straightforward basis of the limits of the agent's authority. Lord Halsbury LC stated:[92]

> … A broker is employed to effect a particular insurance. While so employed he receives material information – he does not effect the insurance and he does not communicate the information. How is it possible to suggest that the assured could rely upon the communication to the principal of every piece of information acquired by any agent through whom the assured has unsuccessfully endeavoured to procure

[88] ibid 170.

[89] *Bradley v Riches* (1878) 9 ChD 189, 195–96.

[90] *Blackburn, Low & Co v Vigors* (1886) 17 QBD 553 (Court of Appeal) and (1887) LR 12 App Cas 53 (House of Lords).

[91] ibid (CA) 556.

[92] In a long passage at ibid 535–39, only part of which is set out here.

> an insurance? I am unable to accept the criticism by the Master of the Rolls upon the proposition that the knowledge of the agent is the knowledge of the principal. But in this case I think that the agency of the broker had ceased before the policy sued upon was effected …

[9.85] An agent's words and deeds are, relatively straightforwardly, attributed to their principal. It is *wrong* (as has been repeatedly emphasised) to regard this as a form of vicarious liability.[93] Attribution by way of agency extends beyond the employee, to the independent contractor.[94] The agent's acts are readily attributed to the principal. Thus, where an agent or multiple employees are guilty of a negligent act, what is attributed is the *act* and no state of mind *at all*. It is the falling short of the act from the standard of the reasonable person that constitutes the test for liability.

b. Nexus between attributable matters

[9.86] In *Armstrong v Stain*,[95] an agent made a representation to the plaintiffs that was untrue. It was a material representation and, on the basis of it, the plaintiffs acted to their detriment (in buying a house in reliance upon the representation). The agent's principal did not authorise the agent to make the representation, and did not know that it was being made, but *did* know of facts which rendered it untrue. In other words, had the principal made the statement themselves to the plaintiffs, they would have been guilty of a fraudulent misrepresentation. The plaintiffs claimed damages for fraudulent misrepresentation against both principal and agent, on the basis that the knowledge of the principal could be combined with the statement of the agent so as to render one or other or both defendants liable. This claim failed. Singleton LJ held that 'at least since the year 1889, it has not been open to any court to find for the plaintiff in an action for fraudulent misrepresentation unless there is proof of fraud or dishonesty'.[96] This was so at least where principal and agent were two natural persons. As regards non-natural persons, Singleton LJ said:[97]

> Difficulties may arise in a claim against a company which can only speak or act through its agents or officers, but if an officer of a company writes and represents that which is untrue when many other officers of the company know the true facts, it may well be found that he made the representation without belief in its truth, or that he made it recklessly, careless whether it was true or false. That must depend on the evidence. In the case before us the principal is an individual; it was the agent which made the representation which was false. The judge negatived fraud on the part

[93] Cf *Clerk & Lindsell* (n 14) [6-89].
[94] ibid [6-89].
[95] *Armstrong v Stain* [1952] 1 KB 232.
[96] ibid 243. Birkett and Romer LJJ reached similar conclusions.
[97] ibid 244.

of both. In those circumstances an action for fraudulent misrepresentation cannot succeed against either.

[9.87] The point in the case of human actors is straightforward. Where actual dishonesty is required, it must vest in a single person.[98] In *Armstrong v Stain*, the principal knew the facts and the agent made the representation. Fraud was thus negatived on the part of both. In the case of the corporate undertaking, this is an area where the same point must apply. For dishonesty or fraud to arise, the same 'controlling mind' must make the statement and know it to be false.[99]

III. Application of these Principles in the Case of the Action

A. Introduction

[9.88] It is now necessary to consider the application of the rules of attribution (both those of vicarious liability and primary liability by way of attribution) in the case of the Action. By way of summary, the case of vicarious liability is straightforward. This is the case where C commits the tort comprising the Action so as to be primarily liable, but acts (in doing so) as the servant of U, thus triggering a secondary liability in U. The only live question in such cases is whether the relationship C(U) is sufficient to render U vicariously liable.

[9.89] Primary liability by way of attribution is the harder case, where the elements of the Action are fragmented across multiple actors – C_1 to C_n in circumstances where, if all of these fragments are assembled together and attributed to a single undertaking U, liability will exist. Two things, it is suggested, are clear in this case: (i) it is vital for the credibility of the Action for U to be exposed to liability for corporate misuse of A's private information; yet (ii) it is as vital for the credibility of the Action that the liability net not be cast too wide. It will be suggested that the rules regarding primary liability by way of attribution articulate a 'Goldilocks' course, which imposes liability, but which also appropriately controls the scope of that liability, so that the net is not cast too widely.

[98] *Derry v Peek* (1889) 14 LR App Cas 337. In an action for deceit, the claimant must prove actual fraud, which exists when it is shown that a false representation has been made knowingly or without belief in its truth or recklessly, without caring whether it be true or false. A false statement made through carelessness and without reasonable ground for believing it to be true may be evidence of fraud but does not necessarily amount to fraud.

[99] The law regarding undertakings in competition law is different, but similarly complex: see Whelan (n 46) Ch 15.

B. Vicarious liability of U for C

[9.90] Where C is an employee of U, acting within the scope of their employment, and in doing so infringes the Action, then not only will C be liable, but so too (under the principle of vicarious liability) will U. This is the straightforward case and adds nothing to what has been said about C's liability in previous chapters. There is nothing more to be said.

C. The action and primary liability by way of attribution

[9.91] The operation of the rules of attribution in the context of undertaking U's primary liability under the Action is best articulated as a series of propositions, drawing upon the statement of the various legal principles articulated in this chapter. These propositions are set out below. The undertaking said to be liable will be referred to as U. The actors across whom the elements of the Action are fragmented are referred to as C_1 to C_n. It will be assumed that if all of these fragments were to be assembled together and attributed to U, U would itself be liable under the Action (even though there would be no arguable claim against any of C_1 to C_n).

i. C_1 to C_n must all be agents of U, acting within the scope of their authority (actual or ostensible)

[9.92] There can be no attribution of a thought or word or deed unless C is the agent of U. Save where the contrary is stated, it will now be assumed that C_1 to C_n are all agents of U, acting within the scope of their authority (actual or ostensible).

ii. Where C_1 has derived a perception of A's private information as agent of U and uses that perception for the purposes of U, then this is not 'use' by C_1 nor is it 'use' by U provided the perception remains internal to U

[9.93] This proposition contains within it a number of aspects that need to be unpacked. Where C_1 'uses' A's private information purely for the internal purposes of U, then C_1 is not using that information with the meaning of the Action.[100] Suppose C_1 is a photographer employed by U to take celebrity photographs. C_1 takes photographs of A which (let it be assumed) constitute A's private information. If C_1 do their duty to U and file the photographs on U's server or with C_2 (another of U's agents) for processing by C_2, then this is not use

[100] See paras [7.39]–[7.43].

by C_1 of A's private information. The same is true of C_2 if C_2, within the scope of their authority, themselves file the photographs. There will be a presumption of regularity in all of this: following the rule in *Turquand* and the present position regarding common employment, U is responsible for the proper internal operation of the undertaking.[101]

[9.94] On the other hand, if C_1 (or C_2), acting *outside* the scope of their authority, publish A's photographs in a daily newspaper, then they will be exposed to an Action by A for which U will not necessarily be vicariously liable[102] and not liable in a primary capacity at all.[103]

[9.95] Returning to the case of agents C_1 and C_2 acting within the scope of their authority, what is the legal position of U? The answer is that the perceptions of A's private information that C_1 and C_2 have will be attributed to U, as indeed will be their acts (the taking and filing of the photographs).

[9.96] Subject to the consideration at paragraph [9.97] ff, whether these acts constitute misuse is a question that would have to be answered by reference to the control test (non-state actors: Chapter 7) or the proper purpose test (state actors: Chapter 8). In this case, retention of the photographs by U would be use but perhaps not misuse. Publication would, on the facts of this case, almost certainly amount to misuse on the part of U.

iii. The perception/use borderline in the case of undertaking U

[9.97] We have reached a point where the perceptions of C_1 and C_2 are attributed to U, as are their actions. The question for U is whether the combination of these perceptions and actions renders U even arguably exposed to an Action by A. This involves consideration of a novel question, namely the perception/use borderline within an undertaking. This has not been considered so far in this book and represents a novel legal question.

[9.98] Describing this question as a further articulation of the perception/use borderline is an error and risks confusion. As has repeatedly been stressed, undertakings can only perceive through others, and to refer to 'perception' in the context of both C and U is analytically unsound and asking for trouble.

[101] See paras [9.67]–[9.73].

[102] That will depend upon the breadth of the doctrine. It is certainly broad, and vicarious liability certainly could not be excluded in this case. But this, it will be recalled, is a secondary and not a primary liability in U.

[103] Where C is acting for themselves, they are generally not acting as an agent: the requirement described at para [9.92] would not be satisfied.

[9.99] It is better to change the terminology and to differentiate between 'purely internal operations', which do not count as use for the purposes of the Action, and use. Thus, a purely internal operation within U is treated – for the purposes of the Action – like perception, such that there is (in the case of a purely internal operation) not even an arguable case for bringing an Action. For the reasons set out below, it is suggested that the category of purely internal operations that do not amount to use within the meaning of the Action is a vanishingly small one. The following sub-paragraphs parse the question of purely internal operations by considering a series of cases, beginning with the clearest instances of use, and ending with those (rare) cases where it will be possible to suggest that the case is one of purely internal operations.

(1) Cases where the use of private information 'crosses the line' between internal and external deployment are straightforward. Where U causes A's private information to be deployed so that it can be perceived by an agent *external* to U, then this is quite obviously not a purely internal operation. Thus, where an act by C, attributable to U, involves non-internal use, ie a use *external* to U, there can be no question of such use amounting to a purely internal operation. If U's business involved the selling online of a catalogue of photographs of A_1 to A_n taken by photographers C_1 to C_n in relation to some of which A_1 has a reasonable expectation of control,[104] then U will (if A_1's photographs are published without A_1's consent) have infringed A_1's rights and will be exposed to a claim under the Action. This is an easy case, involving the overt use of A_1's private information in circumstances where the use equates easily to misuse (given the assumptions of the example). It cannot be said that this is a case of U's purely internal operations.

(2) Where U retains a catalogue of photographs as a record, the question becomes a little (but not very much) harder. It has been suggested that a record kept by C (a natural person) without any intended contingent use is perception, not use.[105] In the case of a natural person, this is justifiable, for the reasons given in paragraphs [7.33]–[7.38]. However, this rationale does not apply to an undertaking, which cannot act in a purely personal capacity. Undertakings always have a purpose. They will not record perceptions with no purpose in mind. Again, therefore, this is not a case of U's purely internal operations.

(3) What of the case where there is no intention, on the part of U, ever *overtly* to use the perceptions of C that are attributed to it? Again, it is very unlikely that this could be a case of U's purely internal operations. Most instances of 'surveillance capitalism', where U is analysing mass data of A_1 to A_n will

[104] ie the control test described at para [7.44] is satisfied.
[105] See paras [7.33]–[7.38].

(i) be internal to U but (ii) will nevertheless be *uses* of private information. A use of private information does not have to be *overt* for it to constitute a use. Since undertakings – whether non-state or state – almost always have a purpose, it is very hard to suggest that any perception of C that is attributed to U is not a use. It may be that there are exceptions to this general rule, but the fact is that where U records a perception of C, U will be doing so (i) in order to provide a good or service or perform a function, (ii) in order to do work preparatory to the provision of a good or service or to perform a function or (iii) to store the information because it may be useful at some point in the future. These instances are all uses and not purely internal operations.

(4) It thus would appear that the class of purely internal operations is actually an empty set, and that where a perception of C is attributed to U, that is inevitably a use. The only case where it might safely be said that there is no use, only a purely internal operation, is where C has a perception which they hold for U because they have been acting as U's agent but where C does *nothing* with that perception, save to retain it within their brain.

[9.100] In conclusion, it would be a very rare case for a perception in C attributable to U not to constitute a use of the private information by U. Of course, whether that use constitutes a misuse is a separate question, to which we now turn.

iv. The use/misuse borderline in the case of undertaking U

[9.101] Here, we are back in familiar territory. It is the borderline between purely internal operations and internal use that is new in the case of undertakings. Misuse has been described in Chapters 7 and 8, and the nature of the distinction between use and misuse is the same for a non-state undertaking U as it is for non-state actor C; and the same is true of state undertaking U and state actor C. The difference is that whereas, in the case of C, perception, use and misuse combine in the same person C, in the case of undertaking U it is possible for different agents to have their states of mind and actions all attributed to U, with the result that U is primarily liable under the Action.

v. Combination

[9.102] Because the fraud exception (whereby the dishonesty of a fraudulent agent cannot be attributed to U) will generally not apply, there is no reason why the perceptions and acts of multiple agents cannot all be attributed to U, thereby rendering U liable under the Action if that combination satisfied all the requirements of the Action.

IV. Non-human Processing

A. How is data used? The role of machines

[9.103] Data is easily manipulable by non-human means. Much of the data that is handled by undertakings like Google will not involve *any* perception on the part of any of undertaking U's agents, C_1 to C_n. Indeed, it is perfectly possible for even the use of such machine-based perception to be machine-based, such that A's private information is used without any human involvement *at all*. Clearly, this presents problems when it comes to the attribution of thoughts and words and deeds to U. Machines fit badly into the schema that has so far been advanced, which concerns the interaction between human and non-human actors, where the thoughts and words and deeds of the former are attributed to the latter. We do not have a system of rules dealing with the interaction between a non-human agent and a non-human principal.

[9.104] Three scenarios will be considered:

- *Scenario 1.* Harvesting of information using machines without human intervention, but where the information so gathered is submitted to human control prior to any use.
- *Scenario 2.* Information is harvested through human actors, who then input or facilitate the input of their perception(s) into a system, which then uses the data without further human involvement.
- *Scenario 3.* A system of gathering and use of private information that is altogether devoid of human input. Private information is gathered and used without any human intervention.

B. 'AI' = Autonomous intelligence not artificial intelligence

[9.105] The term 'artificial intelligence' is not a meaningful one. Computers are never going to have – or even understand – our values, even if they can proxy them or imitate them to a high level. It may very well be that an artificial intelligence can paint a respectable version of something that Van Gogh could have, but did not himself, paint, basing itself on the corpus of work that Van Gogh *did* paint. But the artistic genius, what drove Van Gogh to paint, what differentiated him from other impressionists, and indeed, what differentiated impressionists from the schools that preceded them – that creativity does not exist in the form of artificial intelligence. *If* artificial intelligence *is* intelligent, it will be intelligent in a different way, which we will doubtless struggle to understand, not (necessarily) because it is more advanced, but because it is different. This is because machines do not sense in the way we do. Shylock was right, in *his* case, when he asked: 'If you prick us, do we not bleed?' *Bleed* is precisely what machines do *not* do. They do not feel pain. Jealousy, and rage, and love, and respect: these are all closed books to the machine. If it looks like a machine is experiencing these things, it is only because it is playing the imitation game very well.

[9.106] The label 'artificial intelligence' is thus pointless. The relevant distinction, to which attention ought to be paid, lies between the *autonomous* machine and the machine that acts *as the tool of a natural person*. There are now, and will continue to be, many cases where extremely sophisticated tools are *used* by a person to deliver a good or service. Doubtless the range and usefulness of machines as tools is expanding. What is *not* expanding is the 'agency' model, by which responsibility for machine 'failure'[106] is attributed to a human being. The agency model refers not to the law of principal and 'human' agent, but simply to the fact that if a person (natural or legal) uses a tool, they bear responsibility for any adverse consequences arising out of that use. A bad labourer cannot blame their tools: rather, the tools represent the acts of the labourer, no matter how sophisticated the tool in question.

[9.107] The agency model just described – where a person is responsible for the tools they choose to use – is not the only way in which the law can deal with intelligent tools. An alternative model (not hitherto adopted by our legal system) could treat sophisticated tools *not* as tool, but as *autonomous* intelligence. This concept will briefly be considered.

[9.108] The point about human beings is that they are capable of being regulated through rules, and our systems of governance and regulation rest on this basic fact. Hart draws a distinction between merely convergent behaviour by a group of persons and behaviour by a group of persons that is convergent *because* the group is following a rule.[107] An alien observing conduct of cars at traffic lights would see causality and convergent behaviour – a red light, the traffic stops; a green light, and it proceeds, but the alien would not necessarily understand the *why* of the causality. There is no physical force emitting from the red light (or anywhere else) to prevent the traffic from moving, merely an internalised respect for the law in the drivers. Our alien would have to be remarkably embedded in and sympathetic towards our psychology to understand that in

[106] Failure is unlikely to be the right term, when it refers to the machine. Generally speaking, machines act by deliberation. Of course, there may be cases where there is a defect (a computer overheats, and causes a fire), but that it not the sort of failure we are interested in here. We are interested in the machine that – because it has been programmed in this way – determines that a driverless car should kill one rather than seriously injure 10. It may be that the circumstances giving rise to this choice are accidental, but the choice itself will be informed by an algorithm that will operate deliberately and not accidentally. When we speak of failure, we should speak of the failure of the human operator that gave the machine the opportunity to act.

[107] HLA Hart, *The Concept of Law* (Oxford University Press, 1961) 8.

many cases we *choose* to follow the law; and our choice to do so is informed by many factors, including (but very much not limited to) risk of non-compliance, punishment and its consequences.

[9.109] The question is whether a machine can differentiate between that which they *can* do (drive through a red light) and that which they *ought to do* (stop at the red light, and allow other traffic to pass). Unpacking this question, two sub-questions arise:

(1) One must first ask whether it is in fact possible to encode legal norms so that they are not built into a machine's architecture and do not describe the machine's operation but are *external* to the machine and are *referred to by the machine as binding on it*. An external rule would mean that third parties – our lawmakers – could legislate for machines.
(2) Second, and this is really the flipside of the first issue: even if laws could be encoded so as to be machine readable, would this notion of voluntary obedience to a norm be computable? Rules are not binary Yes/No norms, but nuanced, and obedience is typically qualified and not absolute. If I, as a car-owner, have to MOT my car on 1 June, I will probably only start thinking about complying with this obligation in the course of May. If something stops me getting an MOT in time (my busy-ness at work, no slots at the garage), I will deal with that eventuality and take a degree of risk of non-compliance and penalty. The machine, on the other hand, will compute risks, and if there is a calculable risk that even on 2 June of the previous year, the car having just passed its MOT, some circumstances may pertain to prevent the car returning for next year's MOT, the machine may not allow the car ever to leave the MOT centre.

[9.110] The point is that we cannot take for granted that following laws is quite as straightforward as one might initially think. But, assuming this *is* possible, a new form of corporation could be envisaged to give legal personality to autonomous machines.[108] There is nothing odd in recognising legal persons – we have done this for centuries – nor in investing them with the ability to assume the rights and obligations of human beings. It would be quite possible to create an 'AI corporation' that invested the machine with legal autonomy, translating it from being a tool of another to being an autonomous agent. But we are far away

[108] Possibly, autonomous intelligence could just be given legal personality, but that would be a mistake. Given that we are not treating machines as the equivalent of the human being, but rather as the equivalent of the corporation, the operations of the autonomous intelligence need to be controlled. The solution ought to be some form of 'AI corporation'. As to this, see K Low et al, 'Property/Personhood and AI' in E Lim and P Morgan (eds), *The Cambridge Handbook of Private Law and Artificial Intelligence* (Cambridge University Press, 2024) Ch 14; and R Brownsword, 'Treating AI as a Legal Person: Simply a Means to a Regulatory End?' in H-W Micklitz and G Vettori (eds), *The Future of the Person* (Hart Publishing, 2025) Ch 11.

from this. For the present, our agency models will have to do; and on that basis, the three scenarios outlined above are considered.

C. Agency and machines

i. Scenario 1

[9.111] The starting point is that where C uses a tool, they are responsible for the consequences. This is easiest to discern in the case of Scenario 1, where the machine M harvests data, which is then used by C. C will be responsible for the information provided by M, and C's actions in *using* that information will be attributable to undertaking U. Of course, it is unlikely that C will acquire any perception of the information processed. The real question will be whether the information is properly safeguarded and reviewed before it is used. The case thus looks much more like a case of inadvertent misuse, where there is a negligence liability in U.[109] Thus, in Scenario 1, if C takes the information produced by M and it is deployed by C in a manner that results in an infringement of A's privacy, C's acts will be attributable to U, and U will be liable under the Action is there has been a negligent use of A's personal information.

ii. Scenario 2

[9.112] Scenario 2 arises where human actor C harvests the information and then allows machine M to use it in some way. C's acts are attributable to U, including C's conduct in allowing M 'off-the-leash'. Again, the case is one of inadvertent misuse.

iii. Scenario 3

[9.113] Scenario 3 is no more than a combination of Scenarios 1 and 2, although rather more *Space Odessey* in flavour. But the 'HAL9000' M will still be a tool – needing of electricity and subject of control – for which U, through its agents C_1 to C_n, will be responsible.

[109] See the consideration of inadvertent misuse in Ch 7, Section V.

10

Vindication

In which: A's ability to vindicate an infringement of their rights under the Action is explored; the distinction between substantive and adjectival (procedural) law is considered, and the importance of procedural law stressed, and then considered under various topics, namely: (i) the relationship between right and remedy; (ii) pleadings; (iii) the remedies of damages and injunction, with particular reference to damages for infringement of property rights; (iv) collective proceedings; (v) 'international' questions; and (vi) getting information out of potential defendants.

I. The Process of Enforcing an Owner's Rights is not Unimportant (or Boring)

[10.1] Vindication describes an owner's ability to prevent – or be compensated for – the infringement of their property rights. This chapter is to do with the mechanics of bringing an Action, where A is the claimant and C and/or U are the defendants. There is a tendency (particularly amongst academic lawyers) to regard practice and procedure as the 'boring' side of the law, with the 'excitement' lying on the side of the substantive law. Whilst it is unsurprising that the initial focus, even in the case of lawyers, will be on substantive rights – what A can claim against C or U or (put the other way round) what must C or U render to A – a strong case can be made for the fundamental importance of process and procedure when it comes to A seeking to have their rights adjudicated upon and determined. This chapter is all about how A vindicates their owner's right to exclude C and/or U from their property, their private information. This is the whole point of the Action.

[10.2] This is a book dealing with private information as property. It does not pretend to be a complete procedural guide. This chapter does, however, aim to underscore key procedural (or 'adjectival') aspects of the Action, both so that it can be better understood and so that a complete (if broadbrush) picture of the Action is given. This process considers the following areas, set out below.

A. *Ubi jus, ibi remedium*

[10.3] The maxim where there is a right, there is a remedy can be inverted to say that where there is a remedy, there a right must exist. That, given the Diceyan view of English law that still – notwithstanding the European Convention on Human Rights (ECHR), the Human Rights Act 1998 and the expansion of legislation generally – prevails, is the better way of seeing the English legal landscape, and it underlines the important nexus between the nature of the Action as a procedure for the bringing of claims and A's substantive rights. This nexus is considered in Section II, which describes the nature of the Action and its status as a 'proprietary tort'.

B. Pleadings

[10.4] At the commencement of every civil action, the parties set out their allegations or claims in the form of 'pleadings' or 'statements of case'. These documents enable the issues between the parties to be listed, and areas of factual and legal disagreement to be identified. Pleadings allow for proper case management – what documents should be disclosed, what witnesses called – in order for the case to be tried efficiently and effectively. Section III, which sets out what A needs to plead in order to bring an arguable claim to trial, and what C and U need to assert in order to defend themselves, is an excellent way of drawing the threads of previous chapters together, providing a synthesis of what has previously been considered in greater detail.

C. A's remedies where the action is infringed

[10.5] Closely related to Sections II and III is the question of remedy, which is considered in Section IV. Since *remedy* is what A is principally concerned with, it may be surprising to the reader to find consideration of this important topic buried in one of the later sections of one of the later chapters of this book. But just as the scope of an action describes the claimant's rights (here, the Action defines what rights A has against C and/or U), so the claimant's rights (A's rights under the Action) define what the claimant can oblige the defendant to do. It is not possible to address the remedy that A can seek without being clear on the ambit of A's rights. Section IV focuses on three main areas: (i) A's remedy in damages, and in particular how damages for an infringement of the Action are assessed or quantified; (ii) A's remedy in terms of injunctive relief, by which A can obtain a court order preventing C or U from using A's private information, thereby limiting the extent to which damages have to be paid; and (iii) the remedies available to A before trial and adjudication of their claim (as where

C or U threaten to infringe A's rights and A, by way of a *quia timet* injunction, seeks to stop the infringement before it starts).[1]

D. Collective actions and group litigation

[10.6] One of the problems that A will face when contemplating bringing a claim against C/U will be the relationship between the damages that A is likely to recover and the costs of bringing the Action.[2] In most cases, the relationship between likely recovery and cost (even if successful) will make it pointless for A to bring a claim. One way of addressing this 'enforceability gap' (where A has rights in theory, but not in practice) is by way of the collective action, where claimants with a common interest or similar claims collectively bring Actions against C/U, thereby multiplying the damages recoverable and spreading the costs so that it actually becomes efficient to bring the claim. England has a nascent collective proceedings regime, which is briefly described in Section V.

E. Questions of private international law or the conflict of laws

[10.7] So far, discussion of the Action has left transnational or international questions completely out of account. These issues are addressed in Section VI. It is not the case that English courts have a kind of universal jurisdiction over the misuse of A's private information. Suppose A is habitually resident in the United States, and C's misuse of A's private information occurs only in the United States, where C is also habitually resident. It is unlikely, in this case, that A would be able to commence an Action against C in an English court (the court would either not have jurisdiction or would decline to exercise that jurisdiction). If A were able, in some way, to bring proceedings in an English court, it is unlikely that that court would apply English law to A's claim: the applicable law would almost certainly be the law of the relevant State in the United States. It will readily be appreciated that infringements of A's rights will often have an international dimension, and questions of jurisdiction and applicable law are important facets of the Action that need to be considered.[3]

[1] The consideration is limited to damages and injunctive relief. As with other intellectual property rights, other remedies will likely be available to A, such as an account of C/U's profits. These remedies are not considered further in this book.

[2] Particularly when the risks of losing are factored in. The general rule in English law – unlike the rule that prevails in the United States – is that 'costs follow the event' or (put in plain English) if claimant A loses the Action against C/U, then not only does A bear their own legal costs, but also they must pay C/U's own (reasonably incurred) legal costs.

[3] As in the case of damages, it will only be possible to delineate what is a complex area of law.

F. Disclosure or 'discovery'

[10.8] A theme that runs through this chapter is that one of the many difficulties that A will face is the informational asymmetry that will often exist between A and C/U. Particularly in cases of 'surveillance capitalism', A will not know how C/U is actually using A's private information – if indeed, C/U is doing so at all. If A is able to plead a claim against C/U, then in the course of proceeding to trial, A will receive disclosure of relevant documents from C/U, including documents that are *adverse* to C/U's claim or *helpful* to A's claim against C/U. This is one of the real advantages of litigating in English courts (although it is also a major costs centre). But A will only receive disclosure (or 'discovery', as it used to be known in this jurisdiction, and is still known in the United States) if they can plead an arguable claim. In many cases, A will require disclosure in order to do this. Thus, in many cases, A will be in a 'chicken and egg' situation, where they need disclosure to plead an arguable case, but can only plead an arguable case with disclosure. Section VII does not consider disclosure during the course of an Action, but considers the narrower, but in this context important, question of what information A can obtain from C/U prior to commencing an Action at all.

II. The Action as a Form of Proprietary Tort

[10.9] There is a circuity in asserting that something is property and identifying the cause of action by which A can vindicate those so-called property rights. The Romans said *ubi ius, ibi remedium*: where there is a right, there is a remedy. But the point can equally be put the other way round: where there is a remedy, there must be a right. The remedy *creates* the right. The thesis advanced in this book is that the Action, like the tort of conversion, constitutes a 'proprietary tort', providing A with a remedy for the infringement of their property rights. A's rights are proprietary because of the reach of the Action (eg enabling claims against C and U, not just B). Hence the term proprietary tort.

[10.10] The nature of the Action is considered by reference to the (it is suggested analogous) tort of conversion, which protects ownership in chattels. If I seek to recover my car from someone who has purchased it from the thief who stole it from me, I will be relying on the tort of conversion.

[10.11] Roman law knew a specific right of action whereby an owner could recover their property: the *rei vindicatio*.[4] English law has no such equivalent but protects or allows an owner to 'vindicate' their property rights through various tortious causes of action. Chattels are protected through the tort of

[4] See B Nicholas, *An Introduction to Roman Law* (Oxford University Press, 1962) 100.

conversion, which protects possession rather than ownership *sensu stricto*; and trespass protects interests in land. Thus English law turns to the law of tort to protect proprietary interests:[5]

> A common objection to Conversion is that it is a poor substitute for a *vindicatio* action which enables a dispossessed individual to claim his asset *in specie* from the defendant. The common law lacks any such action, and this is regarded by some as a failing. Far from being a compromise made to compensate for a common law deficiency, the law of torts' solution to the problem of dispossession is actually far more sophisticated than anything the law of property could easily achieve. The primary reason for this is that, by focussing on what one has lost rather than what one is owed, tort can provide protection for a wider range of parties than merely the 'ultimate' owner. What is more, the common law position is, in its entirety, closer to the Roman structure than unfavourable comparisons between Conversion and the *vindicatio* would suggest …

[10.12] It is tempting to call conversion a 'proprietary action',[6] and that is a temptation to which it is entirely appropriate to succumb. Conversion and the Action can be differentiated from other torts which lack the proprietary aspect that conversion and the Action have by reference to the *range* of potential defendants that are liable or potentially liable. In the case of conversion, anyone who, without justification, interferes with the claimant's chattel can be claimed against. The action lies against not merely a single defendant, but anyone interfering with the chattel. Similarly, with the Action. Anyone who misuses A's personal information is liable to A. This is in essence why the label proprietary action or action *in rem* is justified. Compare a personal injury claim: the injured claimant can sue the person who injured them and – within the confines of secondary liability – anyone who is vicariously liable for *that* defendant's tort. This is a personal action, operating *in personam*. A proprietary action permits the claimant to claim against a range and succession of persons, not merely (say) the original taker of the thing but subsequent recipients of the thing, even if those recipients had nothing to do with the claimant, but only interfered with that which they did not own. Thus, the Action is maintainable by A against *anyone* misusing A's private information.[7]

[10.13] The differences between conversion and the Action arise out of the intangible quality of personal information. Whereas conversion is informed by the

[5] S Green and J Randall, *The Tort of Conversion* (Hart Publishing, 2009) 54–55.

[6] We take the point – indeed, we adopt it – made in S Douglas, *Liability for Wrongful Interference with Chattels* (Hart Publishing, 2011) 62–64 that the tort of conversion in a number of respects operates not as *vindicatio*, but in an altogether more wide-ranging and sophisticated way. That makes the label 'proprietary action' more apposite, not less.

[7] The case of the long-lens photographer – described at para [4.62] – is the most straightforward illustration of the reach of the Action. There is no relationship *at all* between claimant A and photographer/defendant C. A may not even know that their image has been captured. Yet if C misuses this information, by publishing it or threatening to publish it, an Action will lie.

physical nature of a chattel, the Action must (like all claims concerning intellectual property) first define the nature of the property rights that A has. Hence the detailed explanation in earlier chapters of slippery concepts like 'private', 'information', 'perception' and 'use'. Leaving on one side the problems thrown up by intangibility, the analogy with conversion is clear. In *Seager v Copydex*,[8] an early case concerning an action for breach of confidence, the link with the tort of conversion was explicitly drawn, albeit in the context of the assessment of damages:[9]

> Now a question has arisen as to the principles on which the damages are to be assessed. They are to be assessed, as we said, at the value of the information which the defendants took. If I may use an analogy, it is like damages for conversion. Damages for conversion are the value of the goods. Once the damages are paid, the goods become the property of the defendant. A satisfied judgment in trover transfers the property in the goods. So here, once the damages are assessed and paid, the confidential information belongs to the defendants.
>
> The difficulty is to assess the value of the information taken by the defendants. We have had a most helpful discussion about it. The value of the confidential information depends on the nature of it. If there was nothing very special about it, that is, if it involved no particular inventive step, but was the sort of information which could be obtained by employing any competent consultant, then the value of it was the fee which a consultant would charge for it: because in that case the defendants, by taking the information, would only have saved themselves the time and trouble of employing a consultant. But, on the other hand, if the information was something special, as, for instance, if it involved an inventive step or something so unusual that it could not be obtained by just going to a consultant, then the value of it is much higher. It is not merely a consultant's fee, but the price which a willing buyer – desirous of obtaining it – would pay for it. It is the value as between a willing seller and a willing buyer …

[10.14] This is, to be clear, a decision about the quantification of a claim where confidentiality has been breached. That said, it is not possible sensibly to quantify a loss without clearly articulating that which has been lost. Here, the analysis of the Court of Appeal is explicitly proprietary: information is regarded as property, to be bought and sold.[10]

III. Pleadings

A. The function of pleadings

[10.15] The purpose of pleadings – or statements of case, as they are now known – is to define the ambit of the dispute that is to be resolved by the court.

[8] *Seager v Copydex* [1969] 1 WLR 809.
[9] ibid 813 (per Lord Denning MR).
[10] See T Aplin et al, *Gurry on Breach of Confidence*, 2nd edn (Oxford University Press, 2012) [4.84], where the point is made that damages were assessed 'as if there was an infringement of property'.

A pleading is neither evidence nor a legal submission. Rather, it sets out in a series of allegations or 'averments' a party's position on the elements that comprise a cause of action or a defence to a cause of action. Pleadings are responsive documents: the claimant goes first, followed by the defendant and the procedural rules make provision for later pleadings like replies and rejoinders. As the sequence progresses, these become increasingly rare.

[10.16] A cause of action comprises 'every fact which it would be necessary for the plaintiff to prove, if traversed,[11] in order to support his right to the judgment of the court'.[12] All pleadings, apart from the first (by the claimant) are responsive documents. Thus, in regard to an averment in a claimant's statement of case, a defendant may respond by saying that the averment is 'admitted' (not in issue), 'not admitted' (in which case the claimant is obliged to prove the point, but the defendant is not themselves going to lead evidence) or 'denied' (the point is in dispute, and the defendant is running a positive case in opposition to that of the claimant).

[10.17] In this way, a court can manage the proceedings through to trial, knowing what issues are in dispute and so what disclosure is required and what evidence is going to be needed to resolve the points at issue. Typically, as a case proceeds to trial, the pleadings become less important: by the time of trial, they ought to have served their function.

B. The difference between averments and findings

[10.18] Particularly in an area of law that is developing – both because of societal change and because the law lags behind such change and is constantly trying to catch up – the distinction between an *allegation* that can proceed to trial and a *determination* of that allegation (whether successful or not) is of particular importance. Much of what has been said in previous chapters about the nature of information, the nature of privacy and the nature of misuse has been expounded by reference to principle, analogy and the limited case law actually on point. That will almost certainly change in the future, for privacy and the use and abuse of our data are issues that will not go away.

[10.19] The consequence is that many of points that A could articulate in support of their claim against C/U might be regarded as *arguable* but not necessarily as *right*. The Action is a private law right of action, and so a chose

[11] A traverse means that the averment is either not admitted or denied by the defendant. If a point of fact that is pleaded is admitted, then it does not have to be proved.

[12] *Coburn v Colledge* [1897] 1 QB 702, 706–707.

in action.[13] A private law right of action is no more than that – a *right* to bring a claim before a court for adjudication. The right of action is supported by a claim form and a statement of case, to which a defendant responds (ie 'pleadings') and – provided the claim is arguable, the litigation process proceeds via disclosure, witness statements and expert reports (as necessary) to trial.

[10.20] In order to be sustainable, a claim form and statement of case – hereafter generally referred to as the claim or A's claim – must plead a cause of action, which comprises every fact which it would be necessary for the claimant A to prove in order to support their right to the judgment of the court.[14] Provided the necessary facts are pleaded, and those allegations meet the (low) standard that must be passed to avoid the action being struck out at an interlocutory stage, the claim will proceed to trial.

[10.21] It is the difference between an (arguable) averment and a court determination that informs many of the references in previous chapters to a claim being 'arguable'. This is not a lawyer's equivocation, but a reflection of the fact that it is courts that determine disputes: the parties merely advocate their cases before the court.

C. The elements of the action

[10.22] The elements of the Action have been considered at length in previous chapters. By way of recapitulation:

- An Action by A will lie against C where C has used A's private information in such a way as to constitute a misuse of that private information.
- Information is defined as C's perception of something.[15] That information will be A's private information where it is: (i) personal to A; and (ii) private to A.[16]
- Information will be *personal* to A where it is not generic, but is specific to A in particular.[17] That is tested for on a Court-Determined Fact basis as at the time of the use by C.[18]
- Information will be private to A where it satisfies what has been described as the 'control test'.[19] Information is private to A where a reasonable

[13] M Smith et al, *Smith on The Law of Assignment*, 4th edn (Oxford University Press, 2026) Ch 4.
[14] *Coburn v Colledge* (n 12); Smith et al, ibid, [4.22]–[4.23].
[15] See Ch 3.
[16] See Ch 6.
[17] See para [6.100] ff.
[18] See para [6.85].
[19] See para [6.139].

person, in the position of A, would have a reasonable expectation of control over the use or exploitation of A's private information. That is tested for both by reference to the Objective A standard[20] *and* the Objective O(C) standard.[21]

- The question of misuse will very much depend on the nature of the defendant. Is the defendant a natural person (C) or an undertaking (U)? Is the defendant a state or non-state actor? As to this:
  - (i) In the case of non-state actor C, the issue of misuse is the flipside of the control test: would C, according to the Objective C standard, appreciate that a reasonable person in the position of A would have a reasonable expectation of control over the use or exploitation of A's private information?[22]
  - (ii) Where C is a state actor, the test for misuse is different, reflecting the fact that C has power over A's private information that can override the control test, but where that power must be exercised for a proper purpose. Accordingly, the test for misuse changes to the 'proper purpose' test: would a reasonable person standing in the position of C and at the time of C's use of A's private information conclude that C's use was a misuse, bearing in mind that A has a reasonable expectation of control over their private information?[23]
  - (iii) It may be that undertaking U is in a position of secondary liability – that is to say, is vicariously liable for C's infringement of the Action. Where the 'master/servant' test is met,[24] A can claim against C or U or both. Often – cases of injunction aside, where different considerations apply – it will be appropriate for A to proceed only against the party with 'deep pockets', undertaking U.[25]
  - (iv) State actor or non-state actor, it may be that A cannot frame a claim against C at all, because no single natural person satisfies all the requisite elements of the Action – yet there has still been a misuse of A's private information. The question here is whether A can establish primary liability against undertaking U by attributing to a single undertaking the thoughts and words and deeds of that undertaking's agents, so as to render the undertaking liable, even though the individual agents themselves are not.[26]

[20] See para [6.85].
[21] See para [6.85].
[22] See para [7.44].
[23] See para [8.120].
[24] See Ch 9.
[25] In medical negligence cases, it is regarded as 'bad form' to claim against a negligent doctor as opposed to the hospital that employs them.
[26] See Ch 9.

The question of remedy is one for Section III: remedies have, so far, only been touched upon, even though it is for the remedy that A will be bringing their claim under the Action.

D. Pleading the case

[10.23] Pleading a case is an art. All cases have strengths and weaknesses, and a good lawyer will anticipate, in their pleading, the difficulties that may be faced at trial, and endeavour to begin to address them.

[10.24] The starting point for A's statement of case will be the use or threatened use that they either want to be compensated for or else want stopped before any harm can be done. That will involve A: (i) asserting precisely what is complained of; and (ii) alleging that this matter, of which complaint is made, is not a case of perception, but one of use.

[10.25] One of the problems that A will face is the fact that covert (mis)uses of private information are hard to detect. This is why most reported cases concerning the Action relate to publication in the media.[27] This has resulted in a skewing of the understanding of the true nature of the Action. But this skewing of the case law towards certain types of infringement of the Action serves to underline the real difficulty that will be faced by A, which is working out whether their private information is being used *at all*. The essence of 'surveillance capitalism' is that A's private information is monetised without advertisement or overt use in systems of great complexity which are (rightly) regarded by their operators as systems or processes themselves proprietary and confidential. The challenges faced by A in such cases in even beginning to frame a case are enormous, yet identifying this use is a necessary preliminary to articulating all of the other elements of the Action.

[10.26] How, then, is the law to deal with cases of covert infringement of A's rights in their private information? It must be recognised that many cases are likely to go undetected and so unchecked by someone who has a claim but cannot even articulate it to the low standard of arguability. A great deal will turn on the ability of persons sufficiently conversant with the processes and the technology to be able to reason backwards from certain occurrences. Suppose a

[27] See, for instance: *Prince Albert v Strange* (1849) 2 De G & Sm 652, 64 ER 293 (para [4.41] ff); *A v B plc* [2002] EWCA Civ 337 (para [2.9]); *Campbell v MGN* [2004] UKHL 22 (para [2.11]); *Murray v Express Newspapers plc* [2008] EWCA Civ 446 (para [4.127] ff); *Richard v British Broadcasting Corpn* [2018] EWHC 1837 (Ch) (para [7.102]); *HRH Duchess of Sussex v Associated Newspapers Ltd* [2021] EWCA Civ 1810 (para [7.101]).

class of person – A_1 to A_n – regularly receives advertisements that are targeted at them in circumstances where the only source for the information that informs the targeting is (let us be completely hypothetical here) A's artificially intelligent fridge, that not only keeps food cool, but listens for instructions for the ordering of food for delivery from A's local supermarket. Assembling a dataset to enable a reverse inference to be drawn between the listening fridge, A's conversations in their home, and the use of those conversations will be hard, but not impossible. Although in the past reluctant to admit statistical evidence, English courts are now much more amenable to receiving such evidence. Thereafter, as is considered further in Section V, there are procedures by way of which A can seek information from a putative defendant *before* commencing proceedings. But these processes of pre-Action disclosure require A to know *something* about what is going on.

[10.27] The focus on *use* (assuming this can arguably be stated) enables the pleading then to articulate the other points that are likely to be in issue, which will have to be pleaded (even if they are subsequently admitted by the defendant). These points will relate to A's standing to make the claim, and the basis for the defendant's alleged liability.

[10.28] Starting with standing – A's right to bring the claim – A will have to aver why that the (alleged) use involves information that is personal to them. If the information is not personal to A then no matter how egregious the misuse, this will not be A's claim to bring. Thereafter, A will need to aver that a reasonable person in the position of A would consider the information private to A. This averment will be based on the Objective A standard, but the pleader will be alive to the need to plead misuse and to show that according to the Objective C standard, C would have appreciated that the information was private to A. A good pleading will recognise the synergies here, and this part of the pleading will lay the groundwork for the allegation of misuse.

[10.29] Moving on to the misuse, it will first be necessary to identify the intended defendant. Is this a case of a single, natural, person C infringing A's rights or a case of an undertaking U doing so? The two cases are very different:

- If this is a claim against natural person C, then all of the elements of the Action will have to be united in that person – perception, use and misuse. The question of vicarious or secondary liability in U only arises for pleading once the primary case against C has been set out. The question then is whether the C(U) relationship is sufficient to generate secondary (vicarious) liability in U.
- If this is a claim against undertaking U, then the pleader's job becomes at once harder and easier. Harder, because A will almost certainly know nothing about the internal processes of U, and so will not be able to plead to

> the specific thoughts and words and deeds of U's agents (C_1 to C_n) which, if attributed to U, render U primarily liable. Easier, because A will be able to rely on the presumption of internal regularity[28] and (again) will be able to deploy reverse inference. To revert to the intelligent (but over-listening) fridge, if a correlation can be shown between the fridge's operation and the use of A_1 to A_n's private information, then the inference that undertaking U organised itself to achieve this outcome can be drawn (at least to the level of arguability so as to enable disclosure in due course).

[10.30] Thereafter, the facts and matters relied upon in support of C and/or U's misuse of A's private information will have to be pleaded. This will be a matter of setting out the relevant facts going to either the 'control' test or the 'proper purpose' test. Pleadings tend to be light on the nature of A's loss and damage. In other words, loss and damage is asserted in only the most general terms. That is not good practice, and in the case of licence fee damages is liable to cause the claim to fail. It is to the question of remedies, including licence fee damages, that we now turn.

IV. Remedies

A. Approach

[10.31] This section considers the key aspects of the remedies that A can call upon if their Action succeeds. The general rule that damages are compensatory is stated first. Then the difficulties in assessing compensatory damages are identified and addressed, including in particular the problem of subjectivity in the award of damages. Thereafter, a very particular form of compensatory damage – licence fee damages – is considered, before moving on to the related questions of final and interlocutory injunctive relief.

B. The compensatory principle

[10.32] A civil action is intended to compensate the claimant, not punish the defendant. In the context of the law of obligations, including so-called 'equitable wrongs', compensation means:

> the award of a sum of money which, so far as can be so, is equivalent to the claimant's loss. The loss may be pecuniary (that is, a loss of wealth) where the equivalence to the claimant's loss can be precise; or non-pecuniary (for example, pain, suffering and loss of amenity; loss of reputation; and mental distress generally) where the sum to

[28] See, generally, Ch 9.

> be awarded as compensation cannot be precisely equivalent to the loss and where the only way to ensure consistency of awards is through conventionally accepted tariff of value.[29]

[10.33] In the case of a tortious claim, such as the Action, the measure of loss (and we are talking about damages, here) is '... that sum of money which will put the party who has been injured, or who has suffered, in the same position as he would have been in if he had not sustained the wrong for which he is now getting his compensation or reparation'.[30] In a jury action, *Phillips v South Western Rail Co*,[31] Field J put the point in his summing up to the jury as follows:

> You cannot put the plaintiff back again into his original position, but you must bring your reasonable common sense to bear, and you must always recollect that this is the only occasion on which compensation can be given. [The plaintiff] can never sue again for it. You have, therefore, now to give him compensation, once and for all. He has done no wrong; he has suffered a wrong at the hands of the defendants, and you must take care to give him full fair compensation for that which he has suffered.

[10.34] The interlocutory injunction made permanent is in many cases the perfect remedy to achieve compensation for A, rather than damages,. That is because the injunction stops the wrong before it has started, and renders assessment of damages not just otiose, but impossible (because the misuse that would cause the damage is stopped). Damages and not the injunction are, nevertheless, the default remedy for a number of reasons.

[10.35] As has been described, A will very often not know until after the event that their right to control the use of their private information has been infringed. An injunction enjoining or preventing the unlawful use of private information will come too late, at best only preventing future harm (assuming the harm to be continuous and not a 'one-off') and not being capable of remediating past harm. In such cases, damages for past harm to A will be the only effective remedy.

[10.36] A remedy for an infringement of the Action should only be granted after a trial, where A has established that the defendant has infringed their

[29] A Burrows, *Remedies for Torts, Breaches of Contract, and Equitable Wrongs*, 4th edn (Oxford University Press, 2019) 35.

[30] *Livingstone v Rawyards Coal Co* (1880) 5 App Cas 25 at 39; J Edelman (ed), *McGregor on Damages*, 22nd edn (Sweet and Maxwell, 2024) Ch 2.

[31] The direction given by Field J is reported in J Munkman, *Damages for Personal Injuries and Death*, 4th edn (Butterworths, 1970) 5. On appeal, Field J's direction was approved: *Phillips v South Western Rail Co* (1879) 4 QBD 406 at 407, but without setting out in full Field J's direction. It is not known where Munkman derived the quotation. The old books, which contain citations to the cases where juries still assessed damages, are instructive: see Munkman Ch 1.

rights. It takes time to bring a claim to court, even if A is well-informed about the defendant's intended infringement and sufficiently well-financed to bring an Action quickly. Even with a following wind, A is unlikely to get a judgment within a year (and that is disregarding any post-trial challenges, like appeals, which can stretch matters out still further).

[10.37] It is possible to obtain interim relief – including injunctive relief – *before* judgment. The interlocutory injunction is a well-known form of protection, but it is intrinsically unsatisfactory, coming as it does *before* the trial of the very issue in dispute. The circumstances in which an interlocutory injunction will or will not be granted are illuminating in terms of demonstrating why the default remedy is damages. An interlocutory injunction will not be granted where damages provide an adequate remedy, precisely because of the very real desire to avoid pre-judging a dispute unless such pre-judgment is essential in the interests of justice. That will generally only occur where the threatened infringement is so awful or damaging to A's interests that monetary compensation will not in any real sense be compensatory. The interlocutory injunction can then be made permanent if A's Action succeeds at trial.

[10.38] It will be suggested that in the case of proprietary torts like the Action, where the Action serves to protect a proprietary interest vesting in A, the interplay between damages and injunctive relief is far more complex, in that the injunction is *not* the most appropriate remedy. In many cases, where owner A is more interested in *monetising* their property, damages will inevitably be the better remedy. This point is considered further below.[32]

C. How does one assess compensatory damages?

[10.39] The injunction is a pleasingly straightforward remedy because it avoids the awkward question of how one assesses in monetary terms the level of a compensatory award. Obviously, the point is to hold the claimant harmless against the wrong that has been done to them, and in some cases a monetary award is capable of being truly compensatory. If, for instance, a defendant has destroyed my new car, which I have just purchased from the garage, the starting point (and probably the finishing point) for an award of damages is the cost of replacing the car. In any case where what has been lost can be replaced by the purchase of something, compensatory awards are straightforward. But straightforward cases are actually very rare, as the following examples demonstrate.

[32] See para [10.70] ff.

i. The property may be irreplaceable or non-fungible

[10.40] Suppose the defendant in the hypothetical case just postulated destroys not my car, but my 'priceless' Van Gogh. There is no possibility of replacement, and establishing a 'market' value can only be achieved by looking at the prices achieved on sale by (in this order) other Van Goghs, other Impressionists, other valuable schools of art like the Old Masters and valuable works of art generally for which public values have been obtained. It may be that I get an award of £50 million (which seems to be the average going rate for a Van Gogh, judging by reported sales), but it is difficult to say that that is a truly compensatory award for two reasons: (i) even applying an objective test, by looking at past sales, the award could be defended at materially different levels: £45 million to £55 million are all defensible figures, and prices for Van Goghs at much more and much less than £50 million can be identified; (ii) the claimant will feel their loss subjectively, and an award of £50 million is liable not to be compensatory because the claimant's sense of loss is *subjective to the claimant*.[33] Compensatory damages for property only truly work where there is a market, not merely to establish value, but to enable the claimant to obtain a true replacement for what they have lost. Thus, damages in sales of goods cases, where there generally is a market, are straightforward. The more unique the property in question, the less easy it is to calculate the compensatory award.

ii. Non-pecuniary loss in personal injury cases is not really susceptible of a compensatory award

[10.41] Personal injury cases involve awards that have a pecuniary and a non-pecuniary element. The pecuniary element, although technically tricky to calculate, can properly be a compensatory award. Suppose, as in the case of Hare's *Tragedy At Law*, an intoxicated judge runs someone over, injuring the victim's 'knuckle-joint of one finger which may entail its amputation'.[34] Ordinarily, the difference between the claimant's earnings absent the accident and the claimant's earnings without a finger would be relatively modest. Damages would be assessed by reference to that difference (the 'multiplicand') multiplied by the number of years over which the claimant would work (the 'multiplier'), reduced for early receipt (because damages tend to be paid up-front, whereas the earnings are received over the years).[35] Should the claimant have a particular vocation rendering the use of a finger particularly lucrative – in *Tragedy At Law*,

[33] Damages tend to be objectively assessed so as to maintain consistency and a degree of predictability of outcome. There is no reason why damages cannot be assessed by reference to the claimant's *subjective* sense of loss, but this is a very uncertain metric. As will be seen, even objective measures of loss are remarkably subjective when they come to be assessed by a court.

[34] C Hare, *Tragedy At Law* (Faber and Faber, 1942) 58.

[35] See *McGregor* (n 30) [5-050]–[5-062], Ch 41(IV) and (V); Munkman (n 31) 13–14 and Ch 2.

the victim/claimant is 'the best-known pianist alive'[36] – the loss of earnings will be all the greater. It is the non-pecuniary loss – pain and suffering (ie the pain of the injury) and 'loss of amenity' (simply not having a finger, the loss of the pleasure of playing the piano, to stick with the *Tragedy at Law* example) that require compensation, but where assessment in monetary terms is not possible.[37] What the courts do is create their own benchmark, whereby injuries are assessed by reference to previous awards.[38] As Munkman puts it:[39]

> In principle, damages for the injury itself are intended to be like all other damages: an equivalent in money – so far as the nature of money admits – for the loss sustained. The problem for the court, therefore, is to place a *fair value* on the lost limb or eye, or whatever the injury is. This does not mean that you value the totality of the harm, positive and negative, which the loss has entailed, the loss of the good things of life and the positive infliction of pain and distress. While this must vary from case to case, the loss of a limb has similar effects for the majority of mankind, so apart from earning capacity one would expect rather similar damages for the loss of the same limb. It is this consideration which justifies classifying awards according to the type of injury.

[10.42] In effect, the court is setting a 'price', by reference to other cases, which determines the compensation that a claimant having suffered a personal injury receives. Loss of a leg is worth so many pounds; if the claimant is a claimant who enjoyed amateur football, the loss of amenity will be higher, but still related to the basic 'value' of the loss of a leg. The monetary award is – viewed in the abstract – entirely arbitrary. Viewed in the context of prior decisions, the award of damages can be contextualised, and so rationalised and rendered predictable.

iii. Defamation damages are essentially subjective

[10.43] It is obvious that damages for defamation will be hard to assess in any meaningful way. *McGregor* identifies:

> three regular, although sometimes overlapping, heads of damage: (i) injury to reputation; (ii) injury to feelings; (iii) the head which is unfortunately described by the label 'vindication', a type of damages which has elsewhere been rejected and which, as we will see below, should be understood as compensation to avoid the future consequences of present and future injury to reputation and feelings because to the extent that damages are awarded to vindicate they can thus reduce the amount needed to compensate for future pecuniary and non-pecuniary loss.[40]

[36] Hare (n 34) 57.

[37] See Munkman (n 31) 14–23.

[38] Thus, there are works like *Kemp and Kemp: Quantum of Damages* (Sweet & Maxwell, looseleaf) that analyse past awards and provide a baseline for assessing future awards. In this way, a degree of consistency can be maintained. Using such materials, it is remarkable how accurately a lawyer expert in the field can predict the outcome of a court's quantification of loss.

[39] Munkman (n 31) 17–18.

[40] *McGregor* (n 30) [47-031].

[10.44] Heads (i) and (ii) are even more subjective than 'pain and suffering' and 'loss of amenity' in personal injury cases. Head (iii) is quantified by reference to the level of monetary award needed to 'vindicate' the claimant. As Lord Hoffmann put it in *Gleaner Co Ltd v Abrahams*:[41]

> The damages must be sufficient to demonstrate to the public that the plaintiff's reputation has been vindicated. Particularly if the defendant has not apologised and withdrawn the defamatory allegations, the award must show that they have been publicly proclaimed to have inflicted a serious injury.

In the earlier House of Lords' decision of *Broome v Cassell & Co*,[42] Lord Hailsham said that the claimant 'must be able to point to a sum awarded by a jury sufficient to convince a bystander of the baselessness of the charge'.

D. The problem of subjectivity

[10.45] There is thus a clear tension between the general (and uncontroversial) principle that civil damages are compensatory and the implementation of that principle in the specific case. The broad division between pecuniary and non-pecuniary loss has already been mentioned. As regards the latter, it is generally accepted that losses classified under this head are not susceptible of measurement in monetary terms *at all*, and that any figure which the assessor of damages arrives at cannot be other than artificial.[43] Artificial is not the same as subjective. Subjectivity can be avoided, although the artificiality cannot, by setting out reasoned awards on damages, and imposing on cases a kind of comparative rationality. Thus, in personal injury cases, there is enough of a body of reported case law to enable a capable practitioner to predict the 'value' of the non-pecuniary aspects of a personal injury claim.

[10.46] By contrast, there is a misplaced confidence in lawyers that pecuniary losses can objectively be assessed and truly be 'compensatory'. Burrows explains why this confidence is generally misplaced. Referring to the difficulties in assessing pecuniary losses, Burrows says:[44]

> ... while in some cases compensation for monetary loss is mathematically obvious and exact (for example, pre-trial expenditure), in most instances the uncertainties of what would have happened but for the wrong, and of what will happen in the future, make the assessment of even the loss of monetary income (eg loss of earnings)

[41] *Gleaner Co Ltd v Abrahams* [2003] UKPC 55 at [55].
[42] *Broome v Cassell & Co* [1972] AC 1027 at 1071.
[43] *Wright v British Railways Board* [1983] 2 AC 773 at 777 (per Lord Diplock); Burrows (n 29) 36. It follows that there is a high level of policy involved in such awards, which tends not to be articulated (at least by the courts): see E Quill and R Friel (eds), *Damages and Compensation Culture: Comparative Perspectives* (Hart Publishing, 2019). generally, but in particular Ch 5 on the approach of Canadian courts to personal injury compensation.
[44] Burrows (n 29) 36.

> problematical. Similarly, while reliance on market values is often the most accurate method of assessing pecuniary loss for, for example, property damage, any attempt to put a value on anything, other than money itself, involves some approximation. So the distinction is not between losses where the compensation is precise and losses where it is imprecise. Rather, it is between losses which are of wealth, and can therefore readily be translated into money, and other losses.

[10.47] One can now see the reluctance of policy-makers to move away from jury trials in certain kinds of civil action. Defamation trials were, until relatively recently, the province of juries, and juries used to determine damages in a far wider array of cases. In this way, even if artificiality and subjectivity cannot be avoided, the award of damages receives the imprimatur of a collective of a claimant's and defendant's peers, rather than of a single judge.

[10.48] Subjectivity – as well as artificiality – is particularly rife when one comes to what are variously referred to as 'licence fee' or 'negotiating' or 'user' damages. Such damages are intimately linked to infringements of proprietary torts. They are therefore of particular importance in the case of the Action.

E. Licence fee damages

i. A difficult head of loss

[10.49] *McGregor* makes the point that this form of damage is intractable:[45]

> A mark of the difficulty in comprehending a doctrine can be the difficulty in giving it a meaningful label. The form of damages that is described in this chapter as 'licence fee damages' is a good illustration of this. These damages have been described as *Wrotham Park* damages, after a leading case where they were awarded for a claim that was treated as equivalent to a breach of contract. They have also been described as 'negotiating damages' to describe one method, but not the only method, by which the damages are calculated, namely a hypothetical negotiation. They have also been described as 'user' damages and, until the alternative conception was rejected in 2019, as 'restitutionary' damages.

[10.50] The difficulty is that 'licence fee damages' – the label that will be used in this book as the one that best captures this head of loss[46] – are arguably not a form of compensatory damage at all, because these damages are awarded in cases where *either*: (i) the claimant has suffered no damage to be made good at

[45] *McGregor* (n 30) [15-001].

[46] The label is controversial because it suggests that licence fee damages are only available where an owner's rights are infringed. It is clear that licence fee damages are available in other cases: *One Step (Support) Ltd v Morris-Garner* [2018] UKSC 20 at [95(6)]–[95(12)]. Since the Action is concerned with the infringement of an owner's rights, the implication does no harm precisely because an owner's rights *are* infringed.

all; *or* (ii) that damage is so low that it is considered that a higher award is justified. This captures the controversial nature of licence fee damages nicely.[47]

[10.51] When extended beyond the protection of an owner's property interests, licence fee damages are problematic because they are (at least arguably) non-compensatory. In *One Step (Support) Ltd v Morris-Garner*,[48] the Supreme Court imposed limits on the extent to which licence fee damages were available for breach of contract. It is unnecessary to debate this question further, since the Action is a proprietary tort that protects an owner's interest, specifically (in the case of licence fee damages) the owner's right to exploit their property. It is for this reason that licence fee damages is a label that this book is very comfortable with. The operation of licence fee damages is best explained by reference to various different proprietary torts, other than the Action.

ii. Licence fee damages and proprietary torts

a. Trespass

[10.52] Take the case of a trespasser to A's land: the trespasser infringes A's rights of property, but may occasion the property owner no loss in terms of actual damage to A's property. Nevertheless, under the tort of trespass, the owner will still be able to recover damages, even where there is no physical or otherwise manifested damage that the claimant could point to. Damages in the case of trespass may be assessed in the following ways:

- *Physical damage.* This is the most closely related measure to the ordinary tort measure, where the damage to the owner's property is made good. The measure of damages is generally the amount by which the value of the land has been diminished, not the cost of restoration;[49] the costs of repair and reinstatement exceeding diminution in value may be awarded where these are reasonable in all the circumstances.[50]

[47] Similar controversy arises in the case of the 'reliance' versus 'expectation' measures of damage in cases of breach of contract. Contractual damages are (as in the case of tortious claims) compensatory, and the object of the award is to put the claimant in the position they would have been in had the contract been properly performed by the defendant. This measure – the so-called 'expectation' measure – rightly does not protect the claimant from the loss-making contract. If it can be shown that the claimant would have made no profit or even made a loss out of the contract, then no damages can be recovered. The claimant is not entitled to recover their expenditure in performing their side of the failed bargain – the so-called 'reliance' measure of loss. However, in at least two cases, a claimant has successfully recovered the reliance measure because the expectation measure of loss was too speculative to be calculated, and the court therefore defaulted to the reliance measure: *McRae v Commonwealth Disposals Commission* (1950) 84 CLR 377; *Anglia Television Ltd v Reed* [1970] 1 QB 60.

[48] *One Step (Support) Ltd v Morris-Garner* (n 46) at [95(6)]–[95(12)]; *McGregor* (n 30) [15-019]–[15-026].

[49] A Tettenborn (ed), *Clerk & Lindsell on Torts*, 24th edn (Sweet & Maxwell, 2023) [18-67].

[50] ibid [18-69].

- *Cases of benefit to the infringer, but no loss to the owner.* This is the case of licence fee damages. As *Clerk & Lindsell* notes, a claimant in trespass is entitled to recover damages even though they have sustained no actual loss. To recover substantial damages, the claimant must have a more than transitory interest in the land, but where there is such a substantial interest, damages may be quantified by reference to the price that the defendant ought to have paid for the benefit they took. In such cases, damages are fixed in accordance with the price the defendant would have had to pay to do the acts complained of had they negotiated for permission to do them.[51]

The hypothetical negotiation is one way in which it is said that licence fee damages can be assessed.[52] It is, in fact, a flawed method of assessment, for reasons we will come to.

b. Patents

[10.53] The owner of a patent will exploit it in one of two ways: (i) by utilising the monopoly themselves; or (ii) by permitting others to use their invention under licence.[53] In the second case, damages in the case of the infringement of the patent are assessed by reference to the amount which the infringer would have had to pay according to the terms of the licence that would normally be granted by the patent owner.[54] The first case, where the owner exploits the patent without licensing, is harder. The owner can, of course, recover provable loss, as where the owner has sold less than they otherwise would.[55] In the alternative, the owner can recover on a 'reasonable royalty basis'.[56] It is clear that these damages are not 'restitutionary', but compensatory for the infringement of an owner's rights.[57]

c. Copyright

[10.54] Damages for the infringement of copyright follow a similar scheme:

(1) *Lost profit.* Where the owner exploits their copyright to their own profit, and the infringement diverts sales from the owner to the infringer, the owner may obtain damages by reference to the profit that would have accrued but

[51] *Bocardo SA v Star Energy UK Onshore Ltd* [2010] UKSC 35; *Clerk & Lindsell* (n 49) [18-65], [18-66].

[52] See para [10.86].

[53] D Campbell (ed), *Terrell on the Law of Patents*, 20th edn (Sweet and Maxwell, 2024) [23-77].

[54] ibid [23-77].

[55] This is akin to physical damage to land, but will be hard to prove: ibid [23-79], [23-82]ff.

[56] *Watson, Laidlaw & Co Ltd v Pott, Cassels and Williamson* (1914) 31 RPC 104 at 120; ibid [23-79].

[57] *Coventry v Lawrence* [2014] UKSC 13; *Terrell on the Law of Patents* (n 53) [23-80].

for the infringing act.[58] This is the ordinary measure of damages in tort; and similar to the case where an owner's land has been damaged by another's trespass.

(2) *Lost royalty.* Where the owner exploits their property by licensing it to others, the damages in the case of infringement will usually be calculated by reference to the amount that the infringer would have had to pay instead of acting illegally.[59]

(3) *No lost profit and no normal royalty. Copinger and Skone James* says this about the case where there is no loss of profit demonstrated, but also no normal royalty rate payable:[60]

> In such a case it is for the claimant to adduce evidence to guide the court. The evidence may consist of the practice in the trade or other trades, expert opinion, evidence as to the profitability of the right and any other factor on which the judge can decide the measure of loss. The ultimate process is one of judicial estimation of the available indications. In this third group of cases, the court is seeking to assess the price which could reasonably have been charged for a licence.

iii. Licence fee damages compensate for the owner's loss of the ability to exploit

[10.55] An owner's essential rights have been described in this book as the right to exclude, the right to exploit and the right to transfer or alienate. We will come to the right to transfer or alienate in Chapter 11. The right to exclude includes an owner's right to enjoy, and where this is what an owner wishes to do with their property, the injunction or ordinary compensatory damages (ie non-licence fee damages) will be the appropriate remedy.[61] Licence fee damages most closely correlate to an owner's right to exploit. In one of the early cases on licence fee damages, *Watson Laidlaw & Co Ltd v Pott, Cassels and Williamson*,[62] Lord Shaw said:

> It is not exactly the principle of restoration, either directly or expressed through compensation, but is the principle underlying price or hire. It plainly extends – and I am inclined to think not infrequently extends – to patent cases. But, indeed, it is not confined to them. For whenever an abstraction or invasion of property has occurred, then, unless such abstraction or invasion were to be sanctioned by the law, the law ought to yield a recompense under the category or principle, as I say, or price or hire. If A, being a liveryman, keeps his horse standing idly in the stable, and B, against his

[58] G Harbottle et al, *Copinger and Skone James on Copyright*, Vol 2, 19th edn (Sweet & Maxwell, 2025) [24-300].

[59] ibid [24-301].

[60] ibid [24-302].

[61] Included in the right to exclude are remedies against damage to or the destruction of the property in question.

[62] *Watson Laidlaw & Co Ltd v Pott, Cassels and Williamson* (n 56) at 119.

wish or without his knowledge, rides or drives it out, it is no answer to A for B to say: 'Against what loss do you want to be restored? I restore the horse. There is no loss. The horse is none the worse; it is better for the exercise'.

[10.56] The same point is made in *One Step (Support) Ltd v Morris-Garner*:[63]

(1) Damages assessed by reference to the value of the use wrongfully made of property (sometimes termed 'user damages') are readily awarded at common law for the invasion of rights to tangible moveable or immovable property (by detinue, conversion or trespass). The rationale of such awards is that the person who makes wrongful use of property, where its use is commercially valuable, prevents the owner from exercising a valuable right to control its use, and should therefore compensate him for the loss of the value of the exercise of that right. He takes something for nothing, for which the owner is entitled to require payment.
(2) Damages are also available on a similar basis for patent infringement and breaches of other intellectual property rights.

F. Injunctive relief

i. Overview

[10.57] An injunction may be sought as a final remedy after a trial or as an interlocutory remedy pending trial. Usually, the two go together and, in a privacy case, it will often be difficult to maintain a claim to a final injunction without having the benefit of interlocutory protection. That is because where the information that is said to be private is used before the outcome of the trial, a final injunction may have no purpose, at least where the misuse is overt.

[10.58] Injunctions are thus often obtained on a *quia timet* and interlocutory basis. They can be obtained against 'persons unknown' or 'against the world' (*contra mundum*), which is important given that it may not be known who, exactly, is misusing A's private information. The consideration in this section begins with the final injunction, then considers interlocutory injunctions before dealing with injunctions against 'persons unknown'.

ii. Final injunctions

[10.59] An injunction is an equitable remedy, and the grant of a final injunction is ultimately a matter of the court's discretion, exercised judicially. One of the key questions to be considered is whether the claimant should be left to their alternative remedy in damages. Damages are available to a claimant as of right;

[63] See above n 47 at [95].

the injunction is available where: (i) a right to a remedy has been established; and (ii) the injunction is the proper remedy in the circumstances of the case.[64]

[10.60] Provided it is seen as no more than guidance, and provided it is recognised that there are other factors, such as the claimant's conduct and laches (delay), the guidance of AL Smith LJ in *Shelfer v City of London Electricity Lighting Co* is sound. Although the judge was considering the circumstances in which damages could be awarded in lieu of an injunction, the guidance is also helpful when considering whether an injunction should be granted at all:[65]

> ... it may be stated as a good working rule that:
>
> (1) If the injury to the plaintiff's legal rights is small,
> (2) And it is one which it is capable of being estimated in money,
> (3) And is one which can be adequately compensated by a small money payment,
> (4) And the case is one in which it would be oppressive to the defendant to grant an injunction:
>
> then damages in substitution for an injunction may be given.[66]

iii. Interim relief: American Cyanamid

[10.61] The leading case on the granting of an interim injunction is the now venerable decision in *American Cyanamid Co v Ethicon*,[67] a decision of the House of Lords dating from 1975. A claimant will need to show the following in order to persuade a court to grant interim relief.

a. Serious question to be tried

[10.62] Interlocutory injunctions are sought at the early stages of litigation, sometimes even before the proceedings have formally been commenced. There is, generally speaking, no ability in the court to anticipate the likely outcome of the trial: it is a fundamental assumption of the English system of justice that the trial is the best way of resolving legal disputes. That being the case, any attempt to resolve a dispute in advance of trial is going to be flawed.[68] A 'serious issue

[64] D Bean et al, *Bean on Injunctions*, 15th edn (Sweet and Maxwell, 2025) [2-02] ff.

[65] *Shelfer v City of London Electricity Lighting Co* [1895] 1 Ch 287 at 322–323.

[66] As is clear from its terms, this passage considers the use of Lord Cairns' Act to award damages in lieu of an injunction, whereas the question here is the reverse: should an injunction be granted in place of damages? It is suggested that the factors identified are material either way.

[67] *American Cyanamid Co v Ethicon* [1975] AC 396.

[68] As Lord Diplock put it at ibid 406–407: 'The evidence available to the court at the hearing of the application for an interim injunction is incomplete. It is given on affidavit and has not been tested by oral cross-examination. The purpose sought to be achieved by giving to the court discretion to grant such injunctions would be stultified if the discretion were clogged by a technical rule forbidding its exercise if on that incomplete untested evidence the court evaluated the chances of the claimant's ultimate success in the action at 50 per cent or less, but permitting its exercise if the court evaluated

to be tried' is a low bar, and unless the evidence adduced 'fails to disclose that the plaintiff has any real prospect of succeeding in his claim for a permanent injunction at the trial',[69] this stage will be passed. In rare cases, the court might properly go into the merits in a little greater detail:[70]

> If the extent of the uncompensatable disadvantage to each party would not differ widely, it may not be improper to take into account in tipping the balance the relative strength of each party's case as revealed by the affidavit evidence adduced on the hearing of the application. This, however, should be done only where it is apparent on the facts disclosed by evidence as to which there is no credible dispute, that the strength of one party's case is disproportionate to that of the other party. The court is not justified in embarking on anything like a trial of the action on conflicting affidavits in order to evaluate the strength of either party's case.

b. Inadequacy of damages to either side

[10.63] The point about an injunction is that it stops the defendant from doing something. The point about an interim injunction is that in advance of trial, the defendant is stopped from doing something that they might very well be entitled to do (ie if the claim fails at trial). Obviously, when seeking to justify interlocutory relief, the claimant will make clear what damage or harm they will sustain, unless the court enjoins the defendant. If that damage or harm can properly be compensated for in damages (ie monetary compensation is sufficient), then an injunction will probably not be appropriate. But the position of the defendant also needs to be taken into account. As a matter of course, as the 'price' of the injunction, the claimant will be obliged to offer an 'undertaking in damages' to the defendant, undertaking to hold the defendant harmless against all loss sustained by the granting of the injunction should it prove, at trial, that the injunction should not have been granted. Of course, the defendant may well say that damages awarded pursuant to the undertaking would be insufficient to compensate them, and it is at this point that the court will balance not the merits of the claim, but the adequacy of damages on either side:[71]

> The court should go on to consider whether ... if the claimant were to succeed at the trial in establishing his right to a permanent injunction, he would be adequately compensated by an award of damages for the loss he would have sustained as a result of the defendant's continuing to do what was sought to be enjoined between the time of the application and the time of the trial. If damages ... would be an adequate remedy, and the defendant would be in a financial position to pay them, no interim

his chances at more than 50 per cent ... there is no such rule ... The court no doubt must be satisfied that ... there is a serious question to be tried ...'.

[69] ibid 408.

[70] ibid 409.

[71] ibid 408.

injunction should normally be granted, however strong the claimant's claim appeared to be at that stage.

[10.64] Conversely: (i) if damages would not adequately compensate the claimant; and (ii) the claimant is in an financial position to give a satisfactory undertaking as to damages; and (iii) an award of damages pursuant to that undertaking would adequately compensate the defendant in the event of the defendant succeeding at trial, the injunction will likely be granted. In practice, it is the cases lying in the middle which are the trickiest. The key question was articulated in *Evans Marshall & Co v Bertola SA*: 'Is it just, in all the circumstances, that a [claimant] should be confined to his remedy in damages?'[72]

c. The balance of convenience

[10.65] As Bean et al note:[73]

> By definition, once the investigation has reached this third stage, the decision of the court, whether in favour of or against an injunction, will inevitably involve some disadvantage to one or the other, which damages cannot compensate. The extent of this 'uncompensatable disadvantage' either way is a significant factor in determining the balance of convenience.

The balance of convenience really involves weighing relative injustices to the parties. A factor that is often taken into account is the status quo:[74]

> Where other factors appear to be evenly balanced it is a counsel of prudence to take such measures as are calculated to preserve the status quo.

d. Special cases

[10.66] The court is obviously obliged to recognise that there may be other special factors to be taken into consideration in the particular circumstances of individual cases.[75]

iv. Quia timet *injunctions*

[10.67] In many cases, an interlocutory injunction will be granted *quia timet* ('because he fears'). In short, the injunction is granted to prevent the occurrence of an actionable wrong in advance of its occurrence (or repetition).[76] There is no

[72] *Evans Marshall & Co v Bertola SA* [1973] 1 WLR 349 at 379.
[73] Bean et al (n 64) [3-26].
[74] *American Cyanamid* (n 67) at 408.
[75] See para [10.62].
[76] Bean et al (n 64) [1-01]; S Gee, *Commercial Injunctions*, 7th edn (Sweet and Maxwell, 2021) [2-045]. As to the jurisdiction to grant these, see ibid [12-014]–[12-017]. The freezing order is, in a sense, a form of *quia timet* relief, although intended to ensure that any judgment ultimately obtained is not valueless.

fixed or absolute standard for measuring the degree of apprehension of a wrong. The factors that will have to be considered are:[77]

- whether the injunction sought is final or interlocutory;
- the degree of irremediable[78] harm that the injunction will avoid or prevent – in short, the gravity of the harm or likely consequences of the to-be-enjoined act;
- the likelihood of the wrongful act being committed.

v. Injunctions against persons unknown

[**10.68**] Both interim and final injunctions may be made against an unknown class of persons. Clearly, questions of notice, joinder and challenge loom large in such cases, but the power exists, and it has been deployed when protecting intellectual property rights from infringement. The principles were stated in *Vastint Leeds BV v Persons Unknown*,[79] affirmed after some to-ing and fro-ing on final orders in *Barking and Dagenham LBC v Persons Unknown*.[80] A more extreme version of an injunction against persons unknown is the injunction 'against the world' (*contra mundum*).

G. Remedies and the action: Drawing the threads together

i. The degree of agency in A

[**10.69**] As claimant under the Action, A will have a higher degree of agency than the defendants C and/or U. Thus, it is for A to choose *whether* to bring an Action at all, against whom and – to a rather more limited extent – what remedies to seek from C/U. A's agency is at its highest just before A issues proceedings against C/U. Most claimants do not appreciate that the moment proceedings have been issued, they cede control over their dispute to the court, which determines not merely the substance of the dispute between A and C/U, but also the manner in which the dispute is to be determined, including questions of cost allocation between litigants.[81]

[77] See further Gee (n 76) [2-045]–[2-048]; *Vastint Leeds BV v Persons Unknown* [2018] EWHC 2456 (Ch); *Barking and Dagenham LBC v Persons Unknown* [2022] EWCA Civ 13; *Wolverhampton City Council v London Gypsies and Travellers* [2023] UKSC 47.

[78] Ie the fact that damages will compensate is a relevant factor.

[79] *Vastint Leeds BV v Persons Unknown* (n 77).

[80] *Barking and Dagenham LBC v Persons Unknown* (n 77). See also *Wolverhampton City Council v London Gypsies and Travellers* (n 77).

[81] Costs are a critical aspect of any litigation. Generally speaking, in the English jurisdiction: (i) costs 'follow the event', that is, the loser must bear their own costs and also pay those of the winner; and (ii) costs payments are staged, not saved up until the end. Thus, the 'winner' in terms of a particular hearing (on, say, disclosure) may very well not be the winner of the overall dispute. Legal

ii. The choice between exclusion and exploitation

[10.70] A will (hopefully) have a clear idea of what they are seeking to achieve by way of the Action. Those who have read this far, will appreciate that the remedy that A seeks will not necessarily be an injunction. A is the owner of their private information, and they can exercise control over C/U's (mis)use of that information. A's rights as owner comprise not merely the right to *exclude*, but also the right to *exploit*.[82] The right to transfer is less of an issue for the purposes of this chapter. The right of *exclusion* harks back to privacy as secrecy and A's right to control how A presents to the world.[83]

[10.71] If A is concerned to *control* information flow about themselves, then an interlocutory injunction and a claim seeking a final injunction is the way to go, with compensatory damages for the harm done to A very much a poor second alternative. On the other hand, if A is concerned with the wrongful exploitation by C/U of A's asset, their private information, then an injunction (final or interlocutory) will be of less interest to A. A will want damages and will seek the higher measure of ordinary compensatory damages or licence fee damages. Although A has a right to damages, and a strong claim to choose the measure of those damages, the choice is not unfettered. A court is perfectly able to refuse to assess damages on a particular basis, although of course that refusal must be justified and grounded in law.

iii. Remedies supportive of A's right of exclusion: The injunction

[10.72] The decisions of the Administrative Court and the Court of Appeal in *Ministry of Defence v Global Media and Entertainment Ltd* show just how wide-ranging interlocutory injunctive relief can be.[84] Although this is a case of inadvertent misuse in circumstances where U was seeking injunctive relief in order to protect A's rights, which U had infringed, the case is nevertheless instructive of the power and reach of the interlocutory injunction. The facts, to the extent they matter, were described by Court of Appeal.[85] The claim arose:

> from the fact that someone working for the UK Government made an unauthorised disclosure of secret information of a kind that would put lives in jeopardy if it fell into the wrong hands. The Ministry of Defence (MoD) later learned that the existence of

costs in England are high, and in many cases – unless the parties manage a settlement – litigation can end up being about costs.

[82] See para [1.56].

[83] See Ch 6, Section II.

[84] There are a number of decisions arising out of this matter. Of present interest is the decision of the Court of Appeal [2024] EWCA Civ 838 (overturning the decision of Chamberlain J to discharge a '*contra mundum*' injunction: [2024] EWHC 1220 (KB)) and the later decision of Chamberlain J – not appealed – eventually to discharge the injunction: [2025] EWHC 1806 (Admin).

[85] [2024] EWCA Civ 838 at [2].

> such a data incident had become known to journalists and others and at least some of the information itself was in unauthorised hands. Fearing further disclosure, the MoD brought proceedings for an injunction. It applied in private for orders against the world at large. The judge who was dealing with urgent injunctions at that time in the King's Bench Division, Robin Knowles J, granted an interim injunction which prohibited any person disclosing information about the incident. He also made an order for a 'super-injunction', prohibiting disclosure of the fact that an injunction had been sought and granted.

[10.73] This is (obviously) an extreme case. As Chamberlain J noted:

> the grant of a super-injunction in the circumstances of this case gave rise to serious free speech concerns. The information to which it related was highly relevant to a series of policy decisions being taken by Government about how to safeguard those whose safety had been jeopardised by the release of the dataset. The grant of a super-injunction had the effect of completely shutting down the ordinary mechanisms of accountability which operate in a democracy. This led to what I described as a scrutiny vacuum.[86]

[10.74] There is also a peculiarly toxic combination of making an injunction against all the world whilst not telling the world that it is enjoined and (if it breaches the order) liable to contempt proceedings. Where an injunction is granted against a named defendant C, it is perfectly possible to restrain C from publishing A's private information *and* to oblige C not to disclose even the fact of the injunction. Such an order is capable of being complied with by C. Where an injunction is against 'persons unknown' or 'against the world at large' (*contra mundum*) and there is a prohibition about disclosing that order, the risks of innocent breach of the order are high.[87]

[10.75] It is not proposed to consider 'super-injunctions' any further. The ability, however, to enjoin persons unknown or the world at large is of great significance to A,[88] who may well know that there is a risk of their private information being misused, whilst having at the same time no idea who C/U might be. In *Bloomsbury Publishing Group plc v Newsgroup Newspapers Ltd*,[89] several copies of an unpublished book (this was another JK Rowling case, and the book in question was *Harry Potter and the Order of the Phoenix*) were removed

[86] [2025] EWHC 1806 (Admin) at [10].

[87] Unnamed defendants – whether 'persons unknown' or the 'world at large' become party to the proceedings by the very act of infringing the order made: *Vastint Leeds BV v Persons Unknown* (n 77) at [22]–[24]. In these circumstances, one might think that knowing or having the means of knowing that such an order has been made is of particular importance for reasons other than freedom of speech and political engagement. As was noted in *Vastint* at [25] 'person unknown' orders need to be drawn with particular care.

[88] On these types of order, see further N Moreham and A Speker (eds), *The Law of Privacy and the Media*, 4th edn (Oxford University Press, 2024) [15.100]–[15.107].

[89] [2003] EWHC 1205 (Ch).

from the printers without authority and were offered for sale to the press by an unidentified person or persons. The publishers obtained an interlocutory injunction against 'persons unknown'. This, of course, was a case where the right to exploit was being protected, but the same jurisdiction will operate to protect the right to exclude, so as to ensure that information A wishes to keep from the world is kept from the world.

[10.76] Generally speaking in the case of persons unknown, injunctions are granted in wide terms at the beginning of proceedings and then, as those proceedings continue (if they do – often these cases end at the interlocutory stage) so too do particular 'target' defendants emerge, who are then specifically named and identified in the course of the proceedings. This is necessary not least because in our adversarial process it is important to have a defendant in court for the claimant's claims properly to be tested and resisted. That involves identifying specific persons from the universe of persons unknown who will actually turn up.

iv. Where no injunction is granted: Damages for a seeking to exclude

[10.77] A will want an injunction either: (i) because publication to the world is not desired and A wants to keep their private information to themselves; or (ii) because A is seeking to exploit their private information, and C/U's intended misuse is better prevented by injunction than by damages because damages are going to be speculative. We will come to the latter case next. This section addresses the damages that A can expect to receive where: (i) their private information is misused; (ii) no injunction has been granted; but (iii) A's right to exclude is being infringed (ie A is not seeking to monetise their private information but would rather it was not misused).

[10.78] It may be asked why A might not get the injunction they would ordinarily seek in these circumstances. There are many reasons for this: (i) A may come to court too late for an injunction to be effective, because the misuse has already occurred: the horse has bolted, whilst A is seeking to shut the stable door; (ii) A may not be able to *afford* to obtain an interlocutory injunctions. Such injunctions are only ever granted on the condition that A undertake to hold C/U harmless against all adverse consequences should (after a trial) it prove to be the case that the interlocutory injunction was wrongly granted. This 'undertaking in damages', as it is called, can be a large (albeit contingent) financial commitment, and one that an individual claimant will want to think hard about giving; (iii) there may be weightier issues of freedom of expression or other public interest values that render it inappropriate to grant an injunction; or (iv) A may have themselves behaved in a manner that renders it inappropriate for the court to grant injunctive relief (which is a discretionary remedy).

[10.79] In such cases, A will be left to a claim in damages under the Action and – given that A is unlikely to be exploiting their private information in this case – licence fee damages are unlikely to be apt. A will thus be driven to ordinary compensatory damages. These damages are best classified as 'non-pecuniary' and, whilst damages for emotional distress or disappointment, embarrassment or humiliation can be awarded,[90] there is obviously a subjectivity that needs to be controlled for. As the jurisdiction develops, it is to be hoped that (just as in the case of personal injury) predictability can be introduced through the setting of a 'price' by reference to other cases.[91] Damages in defamation cases will also be a good guide. Indeed, many of these privacy cases have damage to reputation as a head of loss.[92]

[10.80] In *Mosley v News Group Newpapers Ltd*, Eady J considered the damages to be awarded where a newspaper had published video footage of the claimant's engagement in sexual activity with prostitutes. An injunction would serve no practical purpose (too late, the horse had bolted).[93] On the question of damages, Eady J articulated the relevant principles.[94] He noted (the judgment dates from 2008) that there had been relatively few awards of damages for infringement of privacy, and 'they have all been pitched at relatively modest levels compared with some defamation awards'.[95] He recognised the link between privacy cases and defamation cases:[96]

> Because both libel and breach of privacy are concerned with compensating for infringements of Article 8 ECHR, there is clearly some scope for analogy. On the other hand, it is important to remember that this case is not directly concerned with compensating for, or vindicating, injury to reputation. The claim was not brought in libel. The distinctive functions of a defamation claim do not arise. The purpose of damages, therefore, must be to address the specific public policy factors in play when there has been 'an old fashioned breach of confidence' and/or an unauthorised revelation of personal information. It would seem that the law is concerned to protect such matters as personal dignity, autonomy and integrity.

[10.81] Eady J noted that 'it is reasonable to suppose that damages for such an infringement may include distress, hurt feelings and loss of dignity.[97]

[90] *Jarvis v Swan Tours Ltd* [1973] 1 QB 233; *Farley v Skinner* [2001] UKHL 49; Moreham and Speker (n 88) [12.124]–[12.138].

[91] See para [10.42].

[92] As in the case of Cliff Richard (see the Example at para [7.102]), where Sir Cliff expressly sought damages for the damage to his reputation caused by the BBC's broadcast of a police search in connection with the investigation of historic sex offences: *Richard v British Broadcasting Corpn* [2018] EWHC 1837 (Ch) at [334]–[346].

[93] *Mosley v News Group Newpapers Ltd* [2008] EWHC 687 (QB).

[94] *Mosley v News Group Newpapers Ltd (No 3)* [2008] EWHC 1777 (QB) at [212]–[231].

[95] ibid [212].

[96] ibid [214].

[97] ibid [214].

Furthermore, damages could (as in the case of defamation[98]) contain an element of vindication, to mark the infringement of a right.[99]

[10.82] In an important passage, the judge said:

> [215] It has to be recognised, of course, that at first sight these notions [of distress, hurt feelings, loss of dignity] appear somewhat incongruous when introduced in the present context. But, as I have already said in the context of liability, one must beware of being distracted by considerations which relate purely to taste or moral disapproval. One should be careful not to dismiss matters going to personal dignity because a particular sexual activity or inclination itself may seem undignified. After all, sexual activity is rarely dignified. That is far from saying, however, that intrusions into a person's sexual tastes and privacy cannot infringe the right to dignity protected by Article 8 ECHR.
>
> [216] The Strasbourg jurisprudence demonstrates the contrary. Thus it is reasonable to suppose that damages for such an infringement may include distress, hurt feelings and loss of dignity. The scale of the distress and indignity in this case is difficult to comprehend. It is probably unprecedented. Apart from distress, there is another factor which probably has to be taken into account of a less tangible nature. It is accepted in recent jurisprudence that a legitimate consideration is that of vindication to mark the infringement of a right: see eg *Ashley v Chief Constable of Sussex* [2008] 2 WLR 975 at [21]–[22] and *Chester v Afshar* [2005] 1 AC 134 at [87]. Again, it should be stressed that this is different from vindication of reputation (long recognised as a proper factor in the award of libel damages). It is simply to mark the fact that either the state or a relevant individual has taken away or undermined the right of another – in this case taken away a person's dignity and struck at the core of his personality. It is a relevant factor, but the underlying policy is to ensure that an infringed right is met with 'an adequate remedy'. If other factors mean that significant damages are to be awarded, in any event, the element of vindication does not need to be reflected in an even higher award. As Lord Scott observed in Ashley, '... there is no reason why an award of compensatory damages should not also fulfil a vindicatory purpose'.
>
> [217] If the objective is to provide an adequate remedy for the infringement of a right, it would not be served effectively if the court were merely to award nominal damages out of distaste for what the newspaper had revealed. As I have said, that should not be the court's concern. It would demonstrate that the judge had been distracted from the main task. The danger would be that the more unconventional the taste, and the greater the embarrassment caused by the revelation, the less effective would be the vindication. The easier it would be for the media to hound minorities.
>
> [218] These are the elements which need to be recognised in an award of damages in this field but, of course, they must be proportionate and not open to the criticism of arbitrariness: see eg *Tolstoy Miloslavsky v United Kingdom* (1995) 20 EHRR 442. It has been recognised since the Court of Appeal decision in *John v MGN Ltd* [1997] QB 586 that there must be a readily identifiable scale in the field of defamation so as

[98] See para [10.44].
[99] ibid [217].

> to avoid, as far as possible, the vices pointed out in Strasbourg. The guidance there provided can to that extent be transferred to the present environment. Thus, it will be legitimate, in particular, to pay some attention to the current levels of personal injury awards in order to help maintain a sense of proportion.
>
> [219] It is common knowledge that general damages for pain and suffering are relatively low compared to awards made in the past in respect of some of the more serious defamation claims. In recent years, however, the practice has developed of acknowledging informally a ceiling in the libel context, broadly geared to that in personal injury awards …

v. Licence fee damages: Where A is seeking to exploit their private information

a. Difficulties in assessing licence fee damages

[10.83] Where A is seeking to *monetise* their private information, C/U's misuse deprives A of their ability to exploit that which is theirs. Whilst it may be the case that other remedies will get A more,[100] licence fee damages are a very natural remedy.[101] Such damages constitute a pecuniary loss and are measured by reference to A's lost opportunity – the 'opportunity cost'. Economists define opportunity cost as the cost of something in terms of an opportunity foregone. Where C/U has misused A's property, by (for instance) monetising it without A's consent, A has been deprived of the opportunity of bargaining with C/U so as to negotiate the terms of the licence by which C/U may (with A's consent) use A's property.

[10.84] Licence fee damages compensate for such pecuniary loss. There is a sense that because these damages are pecuniary, they are susceptible of straightforward objective calculation. Where there is a market so that comparable transactions can be drawn upon, or where the right that has been infringed is effectively fungible, there will be no difficulty in assessing licence fee damages.

[10.85] Problems arise, however, where there is no market. As *McGregor* rightly notes:[102]

> In some cases, the exercise will be very difficult or impossible. For instance, it will not be appropriate to conduct a hypothetical negotiation where no reasonable claimant would grant a licence for the activity undertaken by the defendant. In any event, apart from cases where there is a clear and established market rate for a licence, the exercise of the hypothetical negotiation will not be a matter of precision. The award will often be one where there are a range of possible answers so that a Court of Appeal will not readily intervene. This is particularly so where the decision is one of a specialist judge, such as one in the intellectual property area.

[100] Ordinary compensatory damages may get A more, and there are other remedies (for instance an account of profits) that will not be considered further here.
[101] For cases in the privacy context, see Moreham and Speker (n 88) [12.116]–[12.123].
[102] *McGregor* (n 30) [15-043].

[10.86] Where there is no market, the courts have had resort to a test based upon a hypothetical negotiation:[103]

> Several of the recent cases have explored the nature of the hypothetical negotiation called for in the assessment of [licence fee] damages. It is a negotiation between a willing buyer (the contract-breaker) and a willing seller (the party claiming damages) in which the subject-matter of the negotiation is the release of the relevant contractual obligation. Both parties are to be assumed to act reasonably. The fact that one or both parties would in practice have refused to make a deal is therefore to be ignored … This point is material in the present case since on the concurrent findings of the courts below Dr Frischmann, the directing mind of PFE, was a very determined (even a recklessly determined) negotiator …

[10.87] It is for this reason that licence fee damages are sometimes referred to as 'negotiation damages'. It will be suggested that this test provides no more than a patina of objectivity. Presuming a hypothetical negotiation between a willing buyer (the defendant C/U) and a willing seller (the claimant in the Action, A) in which the subject matter of the negotiation is the granting of the right to use the private information and where both parties are assumed to act reasonably, is no more than a *carte blanche* to the court to pluck whatever figure it fancies out of the air. The test is as subjective as the Lord Chancellor's foot of old.[104]

b. Problems with the hypothetical negotiation

[10.88] Absent evidence as to price from a functioning market that can be deployed to determine the appropriate licence fee, licence fee damages oblige the court to state a price for something that has no market. Prices in markets are not achieved through willing buyers and willing sellers, acting reasonably, reaching a joint determination as to what a 'fair price' might be. In order to determine a defensible licence fee as damages it is necessary to understand how markets work and how prices are achieved not through buyers and sellers acting 'reasonably', but through the operation of market forces. Once these forces have been understood, it will be possible to consider the facts of any given case and work out how the dynamics of that case might operate so as to produce not a 'fair rate' but an approximation of the rate that a market would produce. In order to understand the relevant market forces, it will be necessary to delve (once again) into some economics.

Supply and Demand Curves

[10.89] Markets do that which courts cannot do, namely allocate scarce resources by reference to what buyers are prepared to pay.[105] Price is not

[103] *Pell Frischmann Engineering Ltd v Bow Valley Iran Ltd* [2009] UKPC 45 at [49]. See also *McGregor* (n 30) [15-040].

[104] Selden's description of the Lord Chancellor's foot in equity is at para [4.94].

[105] There are, to be clear, markets that allocate without using price. These are of no interest for present purposes, because we are seeking to find a value for licence fee damages.

something that can be derived through hypothesising a negotiation but by understanding the forces that create the intersection between the price at which sellers are prepared to sell and the price at which buyers are prepared to buy. Price will only be capable of being derived when the behaviour of buyers and sellers *in the aggregate* is considered. A hypothetical negotiation considers merely the 'negotiation' between a single buyer and a single seller and leaves out of account the operation of market forces. As a test for determining price, the hypothetical negotiation is thus asking itself the wrong question.

[10.90] The diagram below is a stylised (that is to say, essentially unrealistic[106]) representation of the supply and demand curves for a given product, product p.[107]

Figure 1 An illustration of the consumer and producer surpluses

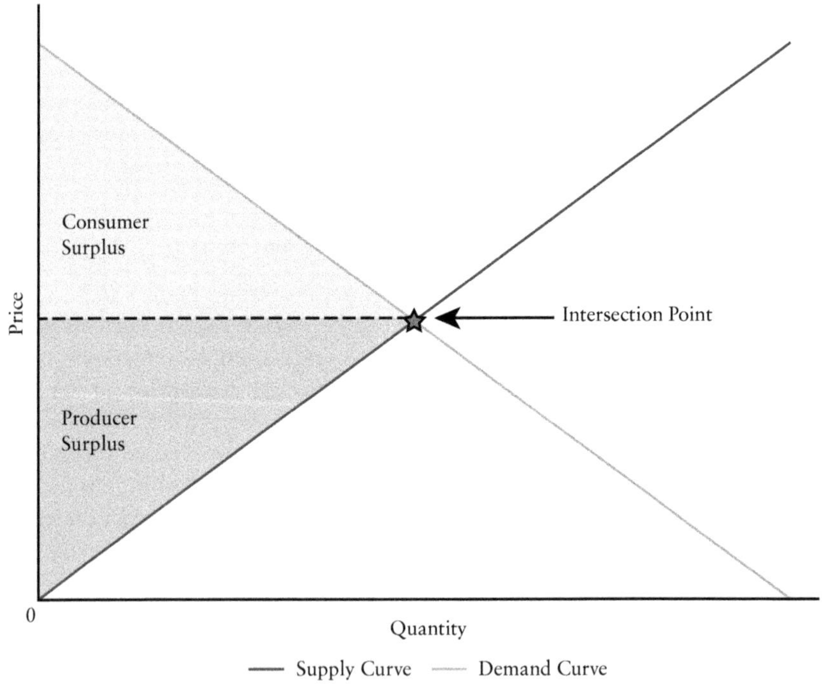

[106] Economic models are *always* unrealistic. That is a virtue, not a disadvantage. It will generally speaking be impossible to derive the supply and demand curves for even a single product in the way represented by this diagram. In the first place, prices in markets are dynamic rather than static, and in the second place, even in a snapshot in time, the quantities offered for sale at all given prices and the demand for product at all given prices will not be known. Nevertheless, it is a basic truth that for most products, as price increases, the number of sellers of the product increases (increasing supply); and as price falls, demand from buyers increases.

[107] Taken from *Pfizer Inc v The Competition and Markets Authority* [2024] CAT 65 at [65(3)].

c. The consumer surplus and the producer surplus

[10.91] The consumer and the producer surplus have been defined and described at paragraph [5.11] ff. To recap, a consumer surplus arises when the price that consumers pay for a product or service is less than the price they would be willing and able to pay. The consumer surplus is specific to each individual buyer, because buyers will value that which they are thinking of buying differently. Consumer surplus is *subjective*. When consumer surplus is *aggregated* (ie the consumer surplus of each individual buyer who buys the product is added up) we get a value represented by the area shaded light grey in Figure 1.

[10.92] Producer surplus is the difference between how much a seller would be willing to accept for a product versus how much they can receive by selling the product at the market price. The producer surplus is a measure that varies according to individual seller. The difference or surplus amount is the benefit a particular seller receives for selling the good in the market. Producer surplus turns on two factors: (i) relative efficiency between producers; and (ii) the extent to which, through product differentiation, any given producer can differentiate themselves from their competitors and by such differentiation induce consumers to pay more for their product. As with consumer surplus, producer surplus can be aggregated. When the producer surplus is aggregated, we get a value represented by the area shaded dark grey in Figure 1.

[10.93] The intersection of the demand and supply curves occurs at that point where the marginal sale/purchase of the product in question will result in a diminution of both aggregate consumer surplus and aggregate producer surplus. In other words, the marginal sale is at a price above which no individual buyer is willing to buy and below which no individual seller is willing to sell.

d. The drivers of price from the seller's perspective

[10.94] The producer surplus represents the excess – measured in money – which a seller of a product receives over the price that that seller would have been willing to sell at. The producer surplus does *not* represent the seller's profit but the seller's *excess profit*.

[10.95] Any product, including product P, is the output of certain inputs, which are known as 'factors of production' and which comprise land, labour, capital and entrepreneurship:[108]

- Land comprises all those 'gifts of nature', such as land, forests, minerals, etc – more prosaically referred to as raw materials or natural resources, but including intermediate or manufactured products.

[108] See the description at *Pfizer Inc v The Competition and Markets Authority* ibid at [60].

- Labour comprises all human resources, mental and physical, both inherited and acquired.
- Capital comprises those man-made aids to further production, such as tools, machinery and factories, which are used in the process of making other goods and services, rather than being consumed for their own sake. There is a critical ambiguity to the term 'capital'. The first meaning is goods such as plant, machinery and equipment which are used to produce other goods and services. The alternative meaning of capital is the funds invested in a business in order to acquire the assets which the business needs to trade. Capital in this sense refers not to a factor of production but to the financial means by which a firm buys or acquires the factors of production, all of which have a cost or price. This book will refer to capital as a factor of production as 'physical capital'.
- Entrepreneurship refers to the entrepreneurs or innovators who take risks by organising the other factors of production, introducing new products and new ways of making old products, so developing new business and new forms of employment and taking the risk of failure.

[10.96] Factors of production all have a cost. They do not come for nothing. The seller (who we shall now refer to as the 'Seller') has to purchase these inputs in order to produce the output, the product that the Seller sells, product P. In other words, our Seller is *also* a buyer. The price they pay to whoever furnishes them with these factors of production represents a cost to the Seller, which goes to inform the price at which the Seller hopes to sell their product for. The key point to take from this is that one person's cost is another person's price. Taking our hypothetical seller, the Seller will need to buy-in the factors of production necessary to make product P, and the price the Seller sets for product P must be at least high enough to cover those costs. In fact, as we shall see, the price needs to be a little higher than this, because we have left the cost of entrepreneurship out of account.

[10.97] It is helpful, when considering the minimum price at which the Seller will want to sell,[109] to regard the Seller as a single entrepreneur, a human being buying-in and organising land, labour and physical capital. In this way the Seller's costs can be more straightforwardly understood without the added complexity the undertaking or firms introduce. (Although we will be coming to the undertaking shortly.)

[10.98] Even with this simplifying assumption (leaving the undertaking out of account) assessing the cost of a single product is surprisingly difficult. We

[109] By this is meant that price that the Seller needs to receive in order to stay in the market. In the real world, market exits will not be as decisive as that. Undertakings can stay in the market making a loss for some time.

need to know the cost of a single unit of product P (the Product Unit Cost) because cost is (in some way) related to price, and price tends to refer to a unit price (the Product Unit Price). Generally speaking, a price is stated for the sale of a single unit of the Seller's product, and certainly a Product Unit Price is what licence fee damages are seeking to proxy.

[10.99] The problem is that most of the Seller's costs will be incurred not in relation to a single product P, but more generally in relation to the Seller's business of producing many product Ps. Even if the Seller is selling only a single type of product (P),[110] those costs the Seller incurs will not generally relate to a single unit P. Thus, the factory in which the Seller's products are made will be a cost that will have to be divided by the number of products made over the lifetime of the factory in order to render the cost of the factory a Product Unit Cost. Similarly, not every worker will be directly engaged in making the Seller's products (people like managers and accountants are needed but are not *directly* implicated in the making of product P). So a great deal of analysis will have to be given to working out how land, labour and capital costs are allocated so as to determine the cost of a single product P.

[10.100] The cost of entrepreneurship has been left out of account. Persisting with our assumption that the Seller *is* the entrepreneur (or the entrepreneur is the Seller), the entrepreneur/Seller will not work for nothing. Obviously, the entrepreneur will price to cover their costs of land, labour and capital, but the costs of entrepreneurship also need to be factored in. Whereas the costs of land, labour and capital are simply what the entrepreneur has had to pay (although allocating those costs to a single product is hard), the cost of entrepreneurship is a variable figure because the entrepreneur will seek to price their product for as much as they can get. The entrepreneur is a profit-maximiser, and the entrepreneur's reward is the difference between unit price and the unitised costs of land, labour and capital. In other words, the entrepreneur will not price at cost plus a certain margin. The entrepreneur will sell at a price that maximises their profit. There is nothing wrong in this, particularly when: (i) the calculation of Product Unit Cost is so uncertain; (ii) the risks of running a business are extremely hard to quantify; and (iii) a producer surplus will encourage competition to enter the market.

[10.101] This is why it is so difficult for the competition lawyer to identify what is an 'excessive' price. Equally, it is one of the reasons why the hypothetical negotiation test is so flawed. The entrepreneur, unlike the other factors of production, takes risks and the reward (which may or may not be received) is what may be an excessive profit – a producer surplus.

[110] In other words, one assumes a mono-product Seller, a Seller who sells just one product, product P. It will readily be appreciated that this is a considerable simplifying assumption.

[10.102] But it is nevertheless helpful to identify some way of attributing a cost (or price) to entrepreneurship, if only so that it becomes possible to identify where the producer surplus begins. *Excluding* entrepreneurship, the difference between Product Unit Cost and Product Unit Price is the Seller's profit margin. What we are trying to work out is what part of that profit margin can be attributed to the costs of entrepreneurship and what part is producer surplus. Put another way, what we are seeking to determine is what level of profit margin constitutes a sufficiently reasonable rate of return so as to reward the entrepreneur *without* giving the entrepreneur/Seller a producer surplus. Since a producer surplus is defined as the difference between what the Seller receives as the price and what lower price the Seller would have been *prepared* to receive, the cost of entrepreneurship must be defined by what the economist would call the 'Normal Profit':[111]

> … It may be that the Reasonable Rate of Return is defined by reference to what an economist would call the Normal Profit. This is the level of profit equal to the opportunity cost of Entrepreneurship. Normal profit is the fair reward for the effort that the entrepreneur puts into running an Enterprise and the risk that they take on. Levels of profitability higher than this tend to stimulate entry into an industry and levels of profit lower than the normal tend to cause exit. Normal Profit exists at the equilibrium point where the entrepreneur stays in business with no exits from the market and no new entry caused by the level of profit.

[10.103] So far it has been helpful to leave the undertaking out of things. This has enabled the analysis to keep distinct the various factors of production, their costs, and the relationship of those costs to price. But the reality is that there are very few businesses that are run by an entrepreneur/Seller. Usually, the business will be run by an undertaking, generally speaking a company, with shareholder capital and debt. Immediately, that serves to confuse further an already confused picture.

[10.104] The interposition of the undertaking tends to convert the entrepreneur into an employee, generally a well-paid chief executive, with (probably) a significant element of performance-related pay. But, nevertheless, there is an elision between the two factors of production consisting of labour and entrepreneurship. That elision is not, however, complete. One of the key functions of an undertaking is to provide capital in the alternative meaning described at paragraph [10.95]. Undertakings obtain the money (capital) needed to trade either by way of equity (capital introduced by shareholders) or by way of debt (monies lent by banks). The shareholders or the bank thus take on some of the risk that falls within the entrepreneurship function. Equity and debt are priced accordingly.

[111] *Pfizer Inc v The Competition and Markets Authority* (n 107) at [63].

[10.105] The upshot is that there is a tendency to consider the profitability of an undertaking at the level of the enterprise and not at the granular level of the Product Unit. Thus, in a fairly risk-free enterprise, capitalised at £1 million, a return to capital of 5% would be regarded as Normal Profit and a return of 20% as almost certainly containing a significant element of producer surplus. The problem with the return to capital approach is that it is dangerously broad-brush and far removed from the factor of production costs that actually drive prices.

[10.106] It can thus be seen that the drivers of a seller's price in a market are very far removed from the questions of willingness and reasonableness that inform the hypothetical negotiation test. The same is true of the factors that inform the price that a buyer will be willing to pay. It is to this that we now turn

e. The drivers of price from the buyer's perspective

[10.107] It is important to be clear about the nature of the buyer. The buyer can either be what we will term the 'ultimate consumer' or a buyer who is *also* a seller. The ultimate consumer is the person at the end of the supply chain, who neither on-sells nor incorporates product P into another product for onward sale. The ultimate consumer will buy product P for their own ends, without any profit motivation. The ultimate consumer *consumes* by reference to the subjective value they attach to product P, which informs the price that consumer is prepared to pay and so the level of that buyer's consumer surplus.

[10.108] For purposes of calculating licence fee damages it is not helpful to have regard to the price that the ultimate consumer would be prepared to pay. This is too subjective a measure. Licence fee damages are intended to constitute as objective a market rate as it is possible to achieve without a market actually being in existence. It is, for these reasons, better to consider the drivers of the price that a buyer who is *also* a seller would be prepared to pay. In other words, one considers the market forces that would inform the price as between a buyer and a seller *neither of whom are ultimate consumers*. In this way, the parties' approach will be informed by the commercialities of making a profit. In particular, the buyer of product P will be looking to use that product as a factor of production in order to sell their own product.[112]

[10.109] We shall refer to this sort of buyer as an 'intermediate buyer/seller'. It is immediately clear that precisely the same drivers as drive the Seller's price will inform the price that the intermediate buyer/seller will be prepared to pay.

[112] Product P is thus, in itself, a factor of production (specifically land, which includes intermediate products or manufactured products): see para [10.95].

Gone are all questions of subjective value. The intermediate buyer/seller will not buy at a price that prevents them making a Normal Profit; and will seek to maximise their profit by squeezing the Seller as much as they can.

f. The significance of competition

[10.110] The existence of competition tends to presume the existence of markets. It follows that the problem case of assessing licence fee damages arises where there is no market and so no transparent competition, and possibly no competition at all. The reasons why there is no market and no competition will be significant in terms of understanding what is the appropriate licence fee. If a market is not contestable for bad reasons (ie artificial barriers to entry) then a lower licence fee is justifiable. If, on the other hand, a market is hard to contest because the barriers to entry are inherent and require skill and investment to overcome, then a higher licence fee is in order.

[10.111] Furthermore, the possibility of competition between factors of production should not be overlooked as a guide to the appropriate licence fee. Take, for example, automated supermarket checkouts.[113] The primary reason these are popular is because they are *cheaper* than the labour-based alternative. This competition between factors of production can be helpfully informative as to price.

g. A worked example

[10.112] Where there is an existing market – in other words, where the product in issue is fungible, in that there are freely available substitutes – the licence fee can readily be ascertained, and there is no need to agonise about the appropriate rate. The market provides the answer.[114] Where there is no market, we need to do better than the hypothetical negotiation test. The concept of licence fee damages is sound, provided those damages are assessed by reference to a workable approach, which is based upon an understanding of market structure not a hypothetical negotiation. It is best considered by way of an extended example.

[10.113] Take the case of the DVLA selling the data of registered keepers of vehicles to car park owners, an example regularly encountered in this book.[115] Assume that this is an infringement of the property rights of persons whose data is held by the DVLA, claimants A_1 to A_n. A_1 to A_n bring an Action against the DVLA, suing collectively. (We will come to collective proceedings below.)

[113] Described at para [5.58].
[114] *McGregor* (n 30) [15-041].
[115] See para [7.74] ff.

[10.114] Any individual within the class will be able to claim an ordinary compensatory loss. Thus, to take the Example at paragraph [8.46], where A's information was used to extract a punitive fine because of the 'five minute rule', A could claim compensatory damages representing loss caused by the DVLA's data breach, this being the difference between what A should have paid (the cost of the ticket) and what A did pay (the fine). This, however, would be a loss individual to A and could not represent a market rate so as to inform licence fee damages.

[10.115] In order to ascertain licence fee damages, an appropriate starting point would be to consider the market in which the infringement of A's property rights is occurring. Essentially, the DVLA are selling certain details of A_1 to A_n (specifically the names and addresses) where these correspond, on the DVLA database, to a given registration mark. A car park operator provides the registration mark (gleaned via CCTV) and (in return for a payment, amount unknown) the DVLA provides the registered keeper's details.

[10.116] It seems clear that the licence that the DVLA needs is an annual licence from each of A_1 to A_n entitling the DVLA to provide A_1 to A_ns' details to any car park operator (doubtless meeting certain minimum requirements as to 'respectability') who seeks the name and address of the keeper of a car with a particular registration mark. A licence providing A_1 to A_ns' ex ante consent is the only way in which the DVLA can provide an effective service to car park operators. The alternative – seeking A's consent on a case-by-case basis – would never work, because A would always say 'No', knowing that the only reason their details were being sought was to bill or fine them.

[10.117] The next question is to consider what price A_1 to A_n might demand of the DVLA for a licence permitting the DVLA to provide A_1 to A_ns' details to any car park operator who asked. Although the matter can be debated, a flat fee licence is probably better than a frequency-based rate, but that would be a matter for argument and determination by the court. Assuming a flat fee licence, a rate of £500/year seems eminently defensible from A_1 to A_ns' point of view. It is a significant sum, reflecting the significance of the proposed use of the information and is broadly in line with how other forms of information are valued (eg subscriptions to newspapers, TV channels, law reports, stock market information, etc). Again, this would be a matter of evidence and argument.

[10.118] The question that follows is whether this is a price that works for the DVLA. Since the DVLA maintains records of 52 million drivers,[116] the annual cost to the DVLA would be £2.6 billion. The DVLA would not want to

[116] See para [7.75].

incur this cost, without recovering the cost, plus the other costs of providing the service to car park operators, and making a profit. The DVLA could offer a range of differently priced services to car park operators, ranging from a per enquiry fee to a flat rate for any number of enquiries from a single car park operator. In order to assess the viability of this service, given the cost to the DVLA of acquiring licences from A_1 to A_n it is easier to consider matters on the basis of a per enquiry fee. The question is what cost will the car parking industry bear for this service? Again, this would be a matter for argument and the court's determination, but the following points can be made on the basis of very limited evidence.

[10.119] Two key questions are: (i) the level of demand for car parking spaces in the course of a year; and (ii) the costs to car parking providers of alternative means of ensuring that drivers pay for tickets. Suppose the 52 million registered keepers of cars use a car park three times a week, which seems conservative. That would give a total of just over 8 billion transactions per year.[117] Spreading the DVLA cost across 8 billion transactions gives a cost per transaction to the DVLA of a mere 32.5p. There seems little doubt – although, again, evidence would have to be received on this – that the DVLA could charge car park operators 50p per enquiry, and that on this basis, both the DVLA and car park operators would make a profit. Furthermore, it seems highly likely (but again evidence would be required) that such a cost would be *lower* than alternative means of enforcement (car park attendants, and a paper-based/wheelclamp-based system of enforcement).

[10.120] Although it is a question of judgement – and requiring of a great deal more evidence – this seems like an entirely defensible rate for licence fee damages in this particular case. If anything, the fee the DVLA is paying A_1 to A_n for the licence to use their private information may be on the low side. Evidence would obviously be critical. In *General Tire Co v Firestone Tyre Co Ltd*, the court rightly stressed the importance of evidence:[118]

> ... it is for the plaintiff to adduce evidence which will guide the court. This evidence may consist of the practice, as regards royalty, in the relevant trade or in analogous trades; perhaps of expert opinion expressed in publications or in the witness box; possibly of the profitability of the invention; and of any other factor on which the judge can decide the measure of loss.

The one thing that can be said is that the analysis is not based on a hypothetical negotiation between A and C, but on a forensic deconstruction of how the

[117] Ie 52 million keepers x 3 car park uses per week x 52 weeks in the year = 8,112,000,000 transactions.

[118] *General Tire Co v Firestone Tyre Co Ltd* [1975] 1 WLR 819 at 826.

market in any given case could work in the counterfactual case where A's property rights are respected and not infringed.

V. Collective Proceedings

[10.121] Collective proceedings – or class actions – enable groups of similarly interested litigants to bring their claims together rather than individually. Collective proceedings can serve to benefit commonly interested defendants, but here we are interested in the extent to which claimants can pool their Actions, thereby sharing costs. In the context of the DVLA example above, one registered keeper is scarcely going to claim £500 from the DVLA. But a claim worth £2.6 billion, brought on behalf of 52 million motorists, is worth thinking about. The costs of bringing such a claim will not be 52 million times as high as the costs of a single claim.

[10.122] When we speak of collective proceedings, this is often no more than a reference to procedural changes intended to make the bringing of related claims by multiple claimants more straightforward. Such procedural changes are typically peripheral, and do not substantially impact the rights of defendants in those proceedings.[119] It is, however, possible to devise a collective procedural regime that fundamentally alters the legal position of both the claimants (who become, instead, 'represented non-parties', where their claims are conducted by a class representative) and defendants, who find that their 'rights of defence' are eroded by the new regime.[120] The objective is one of access to justice, where litigation is conducted on a class-wide basis, including as to assessment of damages, the bearing of costs and the overall conduct of the litigation, all of which do not necessarily permit of differentiating between members of the class. At present, there is limited recognition of such regimes in England – the only regime applies in the area of competition law.[121]

[10.123] Although hard-edged collective proceedings regimes have distinct advantages, there are, unsurprisingly, also negative issues: there is the problem of the detachment of the interested class from the claim; the fact that collective proceedings may be perceived (and in fact be) vehicles for extracting returns

[119] Smith et al (n 13) Ch 14 Section C (on collective proceedings generally) and Chs 15–18 on the various different regimes that pertain in England.

[120] See A Robertson and J Neyers, *Private Law and the State* (Hart Publishing, 2024) Ch 12; S Chiodo, 'Private Law and Mass Claims: Regulating in the Place of the State' *Osgoode Legal Studies Research Paper No 5287879*; also R Mulheron, *Class Actions and Government* (Cambridge University Press, 2020).

[121] See Smith et al (n 13) Ch 18.

to funders and contingently funded lawyers, rather than delivering value to the represented class.

[10.124] Collective proceedings are, in short, controversial. But in a world without legal aid,[122] something along these lines is required in order to enable parties to be able to vindicate their rights.

VI. Jurisdiction and Applicable Law: Issues of Private International Law

A. The problem of internationality

[10.125] So far, the assumption has been that an English court will have jurisdiction to hear the Action brought by A, and that the English court will apply English law to resolve the dispute between A and C/U. Neither assumption is safe. Suppose C or U publish (and so misuse) intimate photographs of A in Ruritania, where C/U are based? Why should A be able to sue those defendants in an English court? And why should English law apply to determine the outcome of the dispute? There is a great deal to be said, in this case, for a Ruritanian court assuming jurisdiction, applying Ruritanian law.

[10.126] These questions are questions of private international law or the conflict of laws. Private international law (the label that this book will use) is that body of law that provides legal answers to legal problems that have an international dimension. Suppose a person habitually resident in England is accidentally run over in France by an American driver. There is no prospect, in such a case, of the parties having reached an anterior agreement as to jurisdiction or applicable law, because this was an unforeseen accident.[123] But one can see, in this case, three possible jurisdictions and three possible applicable laws: England/English law; France/French law; America/American law.[124] There is, obviously, a close relationship between jurisdiction and applicable law, because each jurisdiction will have its own (different) rules of private international law, and will doubtless favour the application of its own law. Assuming it accepts jurisdiction, the law that a French court might apply to the action might well be different to the law that an American or an English court would apply if the matter came before them.

[122] On our present legal aid system, see E Cooke, *The Hidden World of the Legal Aid Lawyer* (Bristol University Press, 2025).

[123] They could reach an agreement as to jurisdiction and perhaps applicable law after the event.

[124] In the last case, it will be the law of a relevant State, the United States being a federal jurisdiction. But that is a complexity we do not need to get into.

[10.127] A key driver of both jurisdictional and applicable law issues is the nature of the claimant's claim. It will be necessary to view the Action through the lens of territory and transnationality.

[10.128] Claimants obviously have primary agency in choice of jurisdiction. It is the claimant who brings proceedings, and this implies selecting the jurisdiction to hear the claim. Of course, the courts of that jurisdiction may decline jurisdiction, but the well-advised claimant will appreciate which jurisdiction will be the best for their particular claim. One can immediately see the dangers of 'forum shopping' and this only serves to underline the importance of the rules of private international law.

[10.129] Intangible property (which is a broader classification than intellectual property, although intellectual property is an important sub-set of intangible property) presents peculiar difficulties for the private international lawyer. That is because many of the rules of private international law depend upon a relationship between a right and territory, and that relationship is defined, in the case of property, by the physical location of the property in dispute. Thus, in the case of land, it is practically inevitable: (i) that the courts of the local jurisdiction (where the land is situated) have exclusive jurisdiction; and (ii) that the applicable law is that of the local jurisdiction. The links between state sovereignty and territory are just too great for any other outcome to be permitted.[125]

[10.130] In other cases, the link between right and jurisdiction is formed by party choice: in a contract, the contracting parties can choose their jurisdiction and applicable law and – certainly in this jurisdiction – their decision, properly construed, will be given effect to. English law places considerable weight on party autonomy.

[10.131] In the case of the Action and private information, party choice and autonomy play a role where there is a licence agreement or transfer of property between A and C/U, thus creating an A ←→ B bilateral relationship.[126] This introduction of a bilateral relationship, whether through licence or conveyance, will be considered further in Chapter 11. This section in this chapter considers the issues of private international law as regards private information where there is no agreement licensing it or transferring it to B.

[125] Imagine a French court assuming jurisdiction over a boundary dispute in Bromley, and applying French law to determine the outcome, and then seeking to impose that result on the losing party.

[126] Using the nomenclature described in Chapter 1, an *in personam* relationship between A and B is superimposed on the *in rem* relationship that subsists (or, perhaps, subsisted) between A and C.

B. The territorial reach of intellectual property (and related) rights generally

i. Patents

[10.132] Although they are intangible, and so not easily linked to territory, territoriality plays an enormous role in defining intellectual property rights, including private information (which is a species of intellectual property right). The relevance of territoriality is most clearly demonstrated by the patent, which is a right that requires application and registration. The monopoly so conferred stops at the border. The monopoly of a UK patent holder stops at the UK border.[127]

[10.133] The fact of registration makes this limit easy to understand. The Parliament of the United Kingdom makes laws that apply within its territory, and there is a presumption against laws with extra-territorial effect. Although extra-territorial laws can be enacted by Parliament, in practice Parliament does not generally do so, for two reasons: (i) comity (one is treading on the toes of other states); and (ii) practicality of enforcement (laws are really only useful when they are respected, and why should a foreign state respect an enactment that is usurping its authority?).

[10.134] But the same principle of territoriality affects copyright and defamation. These are more interesting analogies for our purposes, because the law in these areas turns on publication and does not involve registration.

ii. Copyright

[10.135] Copyright is the right to make copies, and making unauthorised copies constitutes copyright infringement. Leaving on one side secondary copyright infringement[128] (important, but not analytically helpful for present purposes), primary infringement arises where the rights of the owner are directly infringed by unauthorised copying. The owner's rights are defined in section 16 of the Copyright, Designs and Patents Act 1988:[129]

> (1) The owner of the copyright in the work has, in accordance with the following provisions of this Chapter, the eclusive right to do the following acts *in the United Kingdom* –
>
> (a) to copy the work (see section 17);
> (b) to issue copies of the work to the public (see section 18);

[127] On the fundamental importance of territoriality, see A Briggs, *Private International Law in English Courts* (Oxford University Press, 2014) [1.09]–[1.12].

[128] See P Torremans, *Intellectual Property and Private International Law*, 3rd edn (Oxford University Press, 2024) [4.25]: 'Secondary infringement is no longer concerned with the act of copying, but operates at the stage at which persons are dealing commercially with copies of works that attract copyright'.

[129] Emphasis added.

(c) to perform, show or play the work in public (see section 19);
(d) to communicate the work to the public (see section 20);
(e) to make an adaptation of the work or do any of the above in relation to an adaptation (see section 21);

and those acts are referred to in this Part as the 'acts restricted by copyright'.

[10.136] As Torremans notes:[130]

> Section 16(1) also contains a clear rule concerning its territorial scope. The infringing acts must take place in the United Kingdom. Two examples will clarify the importance of the provision. When infringing copies of a brochure are printed in the United Kingdom for export only and used, for example, as promotional literature in the United States there will be an infringement under the UK Copyright Act. What matters is that copies are made in this country and the fact that they are exclusively made for export and use abroad does not change this. On the other hand, if someone authorises an American printer to print the brochure in the United States for distribution there, no infringement action can be brought under the provisions of the Copyright, Designs and Patents Act 1988, even if the authorisation has been given in the United Kingdom. Only an authorization to perform an infringing act in the United Kingdom will be actionable.

[10.137] The extent and nature of the owner's rights colour the rules on jurisdiction and applicable law. In the case of an act restricted by copyright done in the United Kingdom, the courts of the United Kingdom will almost certainly have jurisdiction and the applicable law will be as contained in the Copyright, Designs and Patents Act 1988.

[10.138] Technology – the fact that photographs can be published on the Internet – means that infringement of copyright is truly transnational, and special rules have had to evolve in order to deal with the problems that arise where one person uploads copyrighted material that can be accessed by anyone in the world with an Internet connection.[131] These problems, as will be seen, arise in the case of the Action, albeit differently.

iii. Defamation

[10.139] For defamation to be actionable it must be published.[132] If the publication occurs outside the jurisdiction, then it is unlikely to be actionable in the jurisdiction. Equally, where there is publication in the jurisdiction and outside the jurisdiction, damages are assessed by reference only to publication within

[130] Torremans (n 128) [4.18].
[131] ibid Chs 10 and 17.
[132] See R Parkes and G Busuttil (eds) *Gatley on Libel and Slander*, 13th edn (Sweet & Maxwell, 2022) Ch 7.

the jurisdiction.[133] Once again, the Internet creates particular problems, which render the usual rules on publication hard to apply.[134]

C. Private information and private international law

i. The territorial nature of the action

[10.140] The private international law concerning the Action is, unsurprisingly, undeveloped. From the consideration of analogous rights and claims, it is clear that the Action will only respond to *misuses* of private information that have taken place (or are threatened to take place) within the territory of the United Kingdom. In other words, misuse outside the United Kingdom may be actionable, but not in this jurisdiction and not according to English law.

[10.141] Whether a *use* of A's private information is a *misuse* is a matter that will be determined by the applicable law, just as (in the case of defamation) whether a publication is defamatory will be determined by the law of the place of publication. The key question is, therefore, to define and localise use, just as in the case of copyright one localises the copying and in the case of defamation one localises the publication.

[10.142] The problem is that the use of A's private information can take many forms. Some uses will look very much like defamation. Where C publishes A's private information within the English jurisdiction, this is a good indicator that the use has occurred in England. Of course, where the publication is online, just as in the case of defamation, the indicator becomes rather less clear, because many different territories and many different jurisdictions will thereby be implicated. Nevertheless, where C's use of A's private information is overt rather than covert, it will usually be possible to glean indicators as to the location of the use.

[10.143] Some forms of covert capture and use of A's private information may similarly be capable of localisation. If, for instance, C is capturing and using A's private information through CCTV and the cameras are located in England, then even if some of the processing and use occurs off-shore, one anticipates that the use can be localised in England. But this is beginning to hint at some of the difficulties. Suppose the data capture occurs in England (whether through CCTV or iPhone) but is then transmitted abroad and processed there? Given the hard line that this book is drawing between

[133] *Mosley v News Group Newspapers Ltd (No 3)* (n 94) at [213].
[134] *Gatley on Libel and Slander* (n 132) [7-029].

perception and use, this example would appear to suggest that only the perception occurred in England, and the use occurred out of the jurisdiction. That would suggest an easy way to avoid the reach of the Action, which certainly does not serve to protect the interests of A who – on this hypothesis – would be obliged to sue C in a foreign jurisdiction.

[10.144] It is a well-established principle of private international law that a claimant must seek out the defendant and sue the defendant in their 'home' jurisdiction.[135] However, this is only one policy factor and although relevant, scarcely determinative. In the case of A, likely to be a consumer, there are good policy arguments for favouring A's 'home' jurisdiction.

[10.145] It is suggested that the location of the use involves a multifactorial test and that the following factors are material in locating the use for the purposes of resolving the private international law questions that arise in relation to the Action.

a. The place where the injury to A occurs (or is likely to occur)

[10.146] We have already encountered this factor in the case of overt publication, but the effects of the use can be felt other than by way of publication. If A is being monitored or tracked or the subject of targeted advertisements in the jurisdiction, then this is relevant factor. When locating a tort, including an infringement of competition law, it is relevant to ask where the *damage* was or will be sustained.[136] The damage, in the case of the Action, is where A's privacy is infringed, and it is suggested that there is going to be a high correlation between the damage and A's physical location.

b. The place where the tortious act was committed or is likely to be committed

[10.147] Where the tortious act has caused or will cause harm to A, then even if the harm to A occurs outside the jurisdiction, provided the act that caused the harm (or is likely to cause the harm) is within the jurisdiction, then this is a factor that is relevant to locating the use. Again, this is a well-established basis for jurisdiction in tort law, and a helpful indicator for the localisation of the use.[137]

[135] Thus, under the regime of the Brussels Regulation (whatever its form), the general rule is that persons shall be sued (whatever their nationality) in the Member State in which they are domiciled.

[136] M Danov, *Private International Law and Competition Litigation in a Global Context* (Hart Publishing, 2023) 82, 85–96.

[137] ibid 82, 96–99.

c. The place where the perception was obtained or derived

[10.148] Although there is a very clear distinction between perception (not actionable) and use (actionable if arguably amounting to misuse), the fact is that perception in C is a necessary precursor to C's use of that perception. It is obviously a relevant factor.

d. The connection between A, their private information and the use of that private information

[10.149] This is probably no more than a (helpful?) means of summarising the effect of the previous three factors. The fact is that an understanding of this connection is likely to provide helpful indications as to where the use is to be located.

[10.150] There is no reason why these factors cannot point in different directions. It is perfectly possible for A's private information to be used by C in multiple territories and so multiple jurisdictions. That may give rise to multiple claims in different jurisdictions, but that is a feature of transnational litigation in the modern world.

ii. The jurisdictional rules

[10.151] The common law rules regarding jurisdiction will very briefly be set out.[138] English law draws a fundamental distinction between service in the jurisdiction and service out of the jurisdiction. If the defendant is within the jurisdiction (including by way of an agent for service), then the claim form commencing the action against that defendant can be served without more, 'as of right'. There is a jurisdiction in the English court to stay proceedings in favour of another forum under the *forum non conveniens* doctrine.

[10.152] If the defendant is outside the jurisdiction, then the claimant must obtain permission to serve the defendant out of court. This means:

- The claimant must satisfy the court that in relation to the foreign defendant there is a serious issue to be tried on the merits.
- The claimant must satisfy the court that there is a good arguable case that the claim falls within one or more of the 'gateways' described in paragraph 3.1 of the Practice Direction 6B to the Civil Procedure Rules 1998 ('Gateways'), which define the circumstances in which an English court may effect service out of the jurisdiction.

[138] For a detailed description of the private international law in this area, see Smith et al (n 13) Ch 3.

- England must be clearly and distinctly the proper forum for the trial of the action.[139]

iii. Applicable law

[10.153] The Rome II Regulation on the law applicable to non-contractual obligations sets out the English rules as to applicable law, even post-Brexit. Under Article 8(1), the law applicable to a non-contractual obligation arising from an infringement of an intellectual property right (such as the Action) is the law of the country for which protection is claimed – the *lex loci protectionis*.[140]

[10.154] There is an intimate connection between use and the Action being the applicable law. If the use can be located within the jurisdiction, the Action will govern. Dickinson quotes Dicey, Morris and Collins with approval:[141]

> The essence of an intellectual property right is the owner's right to take action to prevent others from engaging in certain types of activity in a given territory without the owner's permission. Although patents, trade marks and copyright are classified as movables, they share some of the characteristics of immovables in the sense that the rights which they confer are territorially limited.

VII. Disclosure or 'Discovery'

[10.155] This book is not going to consider disclosure in the course of proceedings at all, and will only touch upon pre-action disclosure to the extent that it will assist A in framing a claim against C and/or U. The point made at paragraph [10.126] is stressed: it is likely that A will need to assemble class-wide statistical evidence where what is suspected is some form of covert 'surveillance capitalism'. A technical understanding of the technologies that drive the world of 'surveillance capitalism' and the national security state (to the extent it really differs from 'surveillance capitalism') will be at a premium.

[10.156] A's best starting point – assuming that they are a natural person, and so have rights under the General Data Protection Regulation (GDPR) – will be the data subject rights that are conferred by the GDPR,[142] including in particular the right of access,[143] the right to restrict processing,[144] and the right to data portability.[145]

[139] The relevant rules are set out in Smith et al (n 13) Ch 3, Section (C)(3).
[140] A Dickinson, *The Rome II Regulation* (Oxford University Press, 2008) [8.21]–[8.29].
[141] ibid [8.22].
[142] P Coppel, *Information Rights*, Vol 1, 5th edn (Hart Publishing, 2020) Ch 10.
[143] ibid [10-14]–[10-17].
[144] ibid [10-29]–[10-34].
[145] ibid [10-035]–[10-39].

[10.157] Additionally, there are various powers in an English court to order early disclosure. Injunctions, when granted, often contain provisions as to the provision of information by a defendant, and the so-called *Bankers Trust* jurisdiction[146] and *Norwich Pharmacal* jurisdiction[147] can be deployed in aid of the Action.

[146] In *Bankers' Trust Co v Shapira* [1980] 1 WLR 1274, the Court of Appeal made orders to enable assets to be traced, obliging banks to give disclosure as to where assets had gone. The same process could be used to follow the processing of private information.

[147] Whereby the identity of persons involved in the Action can be disclosed: see CPR 31.17, 31.18.

11

Exploitation of Private Information

In which: A's rights of exploitation by transfer or licence of their private information are explored; as well as the extent to which standard terms of business, imposing unreasonably wide and onerous terms on A as regards the use of their private information, can be controlled for.

I. The Relationship between Vindication, Transfer and Licensing

[11.1] There is a very close relationship between A's ability to vindicate their rights through the Action and A's ability to exploit their rights through licensing. Similarly, there is a close relationship between licensing, transfer and vindication.

[11.2] Vindication, licensing and transfer; these three reflect the three major attributes of ownership described at paragraph [1.56]: (i) the right to exclude (vindication); (ii) the right to exploit (licensing) and (iii) the right to transfer (transfer, obviously). The right to exclude was considered in Chapter 10 on vindication. In this way, A can protect the enjoyment of their privacy by excluding the world, and keeping their private information private. But not only is the exclusion necessary to protect A's enjoyment of their property, it is also a vital buttress enabling A successfully to monetise their property either through licensing or through transfer. An owner's rights over intangible property can only be enforced by legal action.[1] The Action is the only way in which A can enforce their rights as owner, not merely the right to exclude per se but – through the right to exclude – the right to exploit and to transfer.

[11.3] The right to exclude is a reference to A's right to enjoy their own privacy by stopping C or U from invading that privacy by misusing their private information. The right to exploit is equally protected by the Action by ensuring that in those cases where A is willing to allow their privacy to be invaded, but only on terms (generally payment), A can ensure that C or U only act within the terms of A's consent. In short, only if C or U convert themselves into B is their

[1] So-called 'possessory' remedies do not work: there is nothing to possess.

conduct legitimate and not an infringement of A's rights. The Action is thus a critical aspect in enabling A to exploit their property. There will be no market in the sale or licensing of private information unless A's rights as owner can be vindicated. Exactly the same is true of transfer. There will be no market for the purchase of A's private information unless A can pass to B their right to exclude. Why else would B pay money to acquire an otherwise meaningless 'right'?[2]

[11.4] Vindication relates to the negative attributes of ownership. It enables A to stop C/U from doing something, and was the subject matter of Chapter 10. This chapter focuses on the positive aspects of ownership: the way in which A can monetise their rights by *enabling* others to use their (A's) property with A's consent. There are two ways in which A can exploit their private information:

(1) *Transfer.* A can *sell* their private information to another. A ceases to be the owner of their private information by transferring their rights as owner to a transferee, who will be labelled B, because a transfer is a bilateral relationship founded on contract and conveyance whereby A transfers the ownership of certain private information to B. As will be described, this transfer will be by way of assignment, because private information is intangible property and (it is suggested) a chose in action. Choses in action are transferred by assignment.[3]
(2) *Licence.* A can hold on to their property, remain the owner, but license the use of their property to C or U. Again, a licence involves a bilateral relationship – here, a contract – and so the appropriate designator for the licensee will again be B. A licence involves a division in terms of A's ownership. Whereas, pre-licence, A could exclude all the world (O), now, post-licence, A can exclude all the world *except* B.

[11.5] This chapter considers these two ways in which A can exploit their rights in their own private information. But the importance of the Action as the enabler of these forms of exploitation must not be forgotten. Where A has transferred their rights to B, B will (or, more optimistically, may) have need of the Action to enable them to vindicate their (newly acquired) rights as owner. Similarly, the Action is the means of enabling A to monetise their rights through licence. If A cannot prevent C or U from exploiting property that A has licensed to B, 'free riding' becomes the norm. Why pay for something when you don't have to? The Action enables A, through licensing, to permit persons who would otherwise be infringers or *misusers* of A's information to become legitimate users

[2] It is an open question how far a right that cannot be enforced is a right at all. We will leave that one to the legal philosophers, but they must be some connection between a theoretical right and its practical enforceability for something to amount to a right.

[3] The law of assignment can be discussed only briefly here. For a book-length consideration of assignment, see M Smith et al, *Smith on The Law of Assignment*, 4th edn (Oxford University Press, 2026).

of the information, by contracting with A for a licence. Section II considers the transfer of ownership in private information. Thereafter Section III considers licensing. Finally, Section IV considers the problem of consumers having excessively wide transfers or licences imposed upon them.

II. Transfer of Ownership in A's Private Information

A. Legal classification and mode of transfer

[11.6] Although an open question, private information is best classified as a chose in action, the label English law uses to describe (most) intangible property. The name reflects the fact that, because they cannot be possessed, the only way in which rights over choses in action can be asserted is by way of action.[4] Choses in action are transferred by a process called *assignment*. This means no more than 'transfer', but the special name is justifiable because transfers of intangible property present particular difficulties due to their absence of physicality.[5]

B. Requirements for an effective assignment (or transfer)

i. The requirements

[11.7] In order to assign a chose in action:[6]

- *The assignor (ie A) must have manifested an intention to transfer the chose.* Fundamental to any transfer of property is the intention to transfer the thing. What is important is the *manifestation* of the intention, although the manner in which the intention is manifested is not laid down in English law. There are no particular formalities to be observed.
- *The thing being assigned (ie the private information) must be a chose in action in present existence, certain or capable of being ascertained.* For an assignment to be effective, the subject matter of the assignment must be (i) a chose in action, (ii) in present existence and (iii) identified or identifiable with reasonable certainty as the subject matter assigned.
- *The identity of the assignee (ie C or U) must be clear.* For a successful assignment to be effected, the identity of the assignee – the person to whom the chose is transferred – must be clearly stated.
- *The appropriate forms and formalities must have been satisfied.* In this case (private information), no such forms or formalities exist. That is generally true of assignments: no particular form of words is needed; the assignment

[4] Smith et al (n 3) Ch 2(C).
[5] ibid [1.01].
[6] ibid Ch 10.

does not need to be in a particular form; it does not need to be notified to anyone; and consideration (a benefit in return) is not required.

[11.8] Volumes could be – and have been – written on the law of assignment. This is not one of them.[7] There are a myriad of complexities to the law of assignment, and no doubt there will be many difficult and technical questions that private information as a chose in action will throw up. It would inappropriate to delve into such detail here, in what is intended to be a monograph; and considerations of space mean it is impossible. But there are a number of bigger picture points to do with the assignment of private information that do need to be addressed, if only briefly.

ii. What does 'transfer' really mean?

[11.9] As stated at paragraph [11.7], manifestation by A of an intention to transfer their private information to C (or to U) is an important prerequisite for a valid transfer. Where there is a valid transfer, the owner ceases to be A. The new owner is the transferee, C/U, but (sticking with multiple labels for the same person) really best labelled B, for transfer creates a bilateral link between A and B, whereby ownership passes through a specific transaction taking place as between A and B. Put another way, if A were to manifest an intention to transfer to 'somebody', and that 'somebody' could not through a process of construction be ascertained, then the assignment would fail. A cannot transfer in the abstract.

[11.10] More fundamental is the quasi-philosophical question of whether information can be transferred *at all*. Transfer of information in the sense of information *moving* from A to B is generally not what happens. Information is replicable. When A 'transfers' information to B, it is likely that the information is *duplicated* not transferred. 'Transfer' is used as a label, and it is important to understand the implications of this.[8] The label will only be apposite in those

[7] For a full treatment, see Smith et al (n 3). The transfer of private information as a chose in action throws up a number of interesting technical questions not considered here. For instance, can private information be transferred pursuant to s 136 of the Law of Property Act 1925? How do priorities work in the case of private information? Can private information be held on trust? These questions will doubtless fall for future consideration, just as English law has had to accommodate itself to cryptocurrencies.

[8] There is a great deal to be written about the legitimate use of *fictions* in the law. Lawyers often use terms which approximate to what appears to be going on as a kind of shorthand. Here, 'transfer' is the appropriate word to use where A manifests an intention to convey their rights as owner of certain private information to B, because A is *divesting themselves* and *conferring rights* on B. That is the *essence* of transfer, and so the term is apposite. There are other cases where we use the term *transfer* as a helpful, but inaccurate, shorthand. Thus, we refer to the mutual adjustment of balances in banks as an 'electronic transfer', when it is nothing of the sort: what is going on here is causally related but independently effected balance adjustments. In this sort of case, if the lawyer sees the

cases where A intends B to become the owner of their private information, which involves accepting that A can no longer do what (previous to the transfer) A could do perfectly lawfully, namely use their own information. On an information transfer, B comes to stand in the position of A, and A comes to stand in the position of C.

[11.11] Provided this is A's intention, and it is manifested, there is nothing odd in using the label transfer, for we are describing *legal effects*, not what is actually going on.[9] Although it is true that information is intangible and generally only replicable and so is not capable of transfer in the way possession of a chattel can move from A to B, that does not mean to say that A cannot transfer their private information to B. What will, in most cases, happen, is that A will *communicate* their private information to B and (as a matter of practical reality) *both* will have the information.[10]

[11.12] But only one of A and B will have the right to *use* the private information. The effect of an assignment, a transfer, is to convey the rights of ownership from A to B, with the result that whilst A may continue to perceive that which was once their private information, they cease to be entitled to use it. Exactly the same is true of copyright. As long as A owned the copyright in their work, they are free to photocopy it as many times as they wish. Once the copyright has transferred to B, A's right to copy ends. Once it is appreciated that ownership is about *rights*, not *possession*, all of the difficulties to do with the (non-)transferability of information evaporate.

iii. Perception is being transferred by A to B

[11.13] This book has repeatedly emphasised the point that information is defined as C's perception of A. Recall the example of the book: information is not contained in the book, it is what C gains from reading the book that is information.[11]

[11.14] In the case of transfer of information by A, this analysis is inverted. It is not necessary for B (as we will call them) to perceive the information prior

transaction as a 'transfer', they will be making an error: see *R v Preddy* [1996] AC 815; Smith et al (n 3) [10.71].

[9] See, for example, the language used in J Contreras, *Intellectual Property Licensing and Transactions: Theory and Practice* (Cambridge University Press, 2022) 19: 'Once it is in existence, an item of IP may be bought, sold, transferred and assigned much as any other form of property'. See also para [3.71] ff.

[10] Of course, it is possible to proxy a transfer. Where A holds information is some recorded form, A can delete their records. But this is not essential for transfer. What is essential is that A divests themselves of the right to use the information they have transferred.

[11] See Ch 3.

to the transfer. The paradigm case will be where B obtains the perception from A *through* the transfer. Thus, exceptionally in the case of transfer, we are speaking of A's perception of *their* private information, not C's perception of private information *relating to* A. This is the paradigm case, and there will be variants:

- It is perfectly possible for C, having a perception of A's private information, to want to regularise their use of that private information by purchasing it from A. What is really being transferred is not so much the information or the perception as the *exclusive right to use the perception*.
- It also perfectly possible for A to transfer to B a perception about them that they do not themselves hold. Take the case of the long-lens photographer C, who takes intimate photographs of A. A may know of the fact of the taking of the photographs (A may have obtained an interlocutory injunction against C), but nothing more than this. There is no reason why ownership of C's perception cannot be transferred by A to B or (for that matter) the photographer C. Of course, B would have to negotiate separately with C for the copyright in the photographs.

iv. That which is being transferred is 'multilateral' property

[11.15] The essence of a property right is that it is enforceable against all the world, *erga onmes* (or *contra mundum*). That is the universe of persons designated as O. In *Smith on The Law of Assignment*, a distinction is drawn between bilateral property (where A's right exists only against a specific defendant, like a party to a contract or a creditor) and multilateral property (where A's right exists against all the world). Both can be transferred, but multilateral property is property red in tooth and claw, whereas bilateral property is an obligation pretending in a limited way to be property.

[11.16] Take, for example, a debt. B owes A £100, which is a personal obligation (*in personam*) that B owes A. A can only assert their claim against B. The rest of the world – C, D, E, etc – owe A nothing. The most that A can do is assign their debt to C. This means that B continues to be a debtor, but that B owes C not A. Thus the *direction* of B's obligation shifts, in that a different person is owed, but apart from this the obligation in B remains the same. Indeed, English law is enormously protective of the debtor in such cases, and does not permit the debtor's obligations to be rendered more onerous through an assignment (or transfer). It goes without saying – but should nevertheless be said – that there is no way in law that A can unilaterally cause the debt owed to them to be shifted so that what was an obligation on B becomes an obligation on C, D or E. This reflects the bilateral nature of a debt: someone (here: A) has a right, which involves someone else owing an obligation (here: B). There is no reason why A cannot transfer their right, so that the debt is owed to someone else; but there is every reason why the obligation cannot shift without the agreement of A, B and C (the person assuming B's obligation).

[11.17] By contrast, a multilateral chose operates *erga omnes*. As has been described,[12] all of the universe O is contingently exposed to an Action by A, the contingencies being someone within O (i) perceiving A's private information, (ii) misusing it in (iii) circumstances where A can bring an Action (ie an English court has jurisdiction, and the defendant is susceptible to that jurisdiction). The point of multilateral property is that – unlike the debtor who owes A some money – the whole world O may not know of their contingent obligation, but where they infringe they are subject to the Action.

[11.18] Property is thus importantly different from obligation, and the implications of a proprietary analysis of private information have been teased out in the previous chapters. This paragraph does no more than draw together the threads and consider the implications of rights *erga omnes*:

- Enforceability against all the world is an attribute of all property rights. If a member of the class O is walking down a street and they see a bicycle unlocked and propped up against a wall, if they take the bicycle O will *know* that they will be interfering in someone's rights unless O happens to be the owner themselves.
- The point about tangible property is that by virtue of its physicality we *expect* it to be owned, and without more have an appreciation that there are some things we may not do to another's property, even if we know *nothing* about ownership beyond the bare fact that we are *not* the owner of the thing.
- Intangible property lacks physicality and it cannot be said that third parties within the class O will necessarily intuit that they are infringing an owner's rights. That is why patents have to be registered. Partly, this is because of the 'patent bargain', whereby the invention is conditionally released into the public domain,[13] but partly this is so that any member of the class O can protect themselves from infringing by checking the register.
- Not all intangible property needs registering. Copyright does not, but this is because copying is a deliberate act, and we have had ingrained in us a sense of respect for original work than means we must tread carefully when dealing with someone else's 'work'.
- The requirements that need to be established in order to found an action have been framed by English law in such a way as to ensure that defendants can – if they wish to do so – avoid infringing A's rights. Thus: (i) perception of A's private information entails no exposure to the Action at all;[14] (ii) A's personal information has been defined in such a way that a potential defendant ought to be able to recognise that the information is personal to and private to A;[15]

[12] See Chs 1 and 3.
[13] The condition being that you have to acquire the right to use the invention.
[14] See Ch 3.
[15] See Ch 6.

(iii) similarly, misuse is either inadvertent (in which case there is only liability where there is negligence) or deliberate (in which case the tests for 'misuse' are sufficiently clear for the member of class O at least to be able to appreciate that they are skating on thin ice).[16]

[11.19] In short, the danger of the Action encroaching unduly on the freedoms of the members of the class O or of the undertakings U that act through the members of that class O is not an issue, although it is right that one should always keep a wary eye for the extent to which rights can be used as 'lawfare'.[17]

v. The importance of defining that which is transferred

[11.20] It follows from the foregoing discussion that the reason the chose in action being assigned must be in present existence and certain in terms of identity or capable of being ascertained is not for the benefit of the general class O, but so that B may understand the rights they have acquired and A the extent to which they have divested themselves.

[11.21] It must be stressed that it is only the perception that needs to be defined, not the use to which B may put that perception. That is because the transferor, A, cannot (after the transfer is effective) tell B how they are or are not to use A's (former) property. That sort of restriction is a characteristic of a licence, and the reason it exists is precisely because A *retains* ownership when licensing their private information to B. The hallmark of the transfer is that A is left with nothing.

C. Rights that are 'personal'

[11.22] Some choses in action are so personal that the law does not permit of their transfer. There are some cases where the owner of the right will not be allowed to assign it because an obligee (ie the debtor) should not be compelled to perform something different from that for which they bargained.[18] In other words, the reason why the assignment is not allowed is because performance of the obligation is *personal* to the obligor, in that it makes a difference to the *obligor* to whom they render their performance.

[11.23] It will readily be appreciated that this rule has no application in the case of multilateral choses like private information. Furthermore, there is no

[16] See Chs 7 (non-state actors) and 8 (state actors).

[17] The English law of defamation is often regarded as sufficiently claimant-friendly so as to be problematic in this regard. On 'lawfare' see G Robertson, *Lawfare: How Russians, the Rich and the Government Try to Prevent Free Speech and How to Stop Them* (TLS Books, 2023).

[18] Smith et al (n 3) Ch 21.

reason why A should be fettered in their choice as to whether or not to transfer their private information. A has the agency, and if they choose to make a transfer, then it does not fall to the law to stop it.

D. Chain of title and rights on transfer

[11.24] Since the right to transfer is an incident of ownership, when A transfers their private information to B, the right to transfer that which has been transferred comes with the property transferred. B can transfer to C, C to D and so on.

[11.25] Persons subsequently interested in A's private information have a *derivative* interest in the property, in contrast to A's *original* title. If the entitlement of a subsequent owner to use A's private information is challenged, then the latest owner will have to prove their title. Where property rights are registered (as in the case of land and patents, to name but two examples) title is not (or not so clearly) derivative. The register stands as the record of entitlement. Private information is not transferred by registration. If Z, the person standing at the end of a long chain of title beginning with the first owner, A, and passing by way of transfer from A → B → D → E … → Z, is challenged in their ownership, they must be ready to show a chain of title going back to the first person owning it, A. A, as the 'first owner', has no need to show title: they derive their title from the fact that the private information is both private and personal to A.

[11.26] Challenges to Z's title may arise in a number of ways:

- A may challenge Z's title, contending that the information never passed to Z and that Z may not use A's private information.
- Someone Z contends is infringing Z's rights as owner may contend that Z has no right to bring an Action against them.
- Someone may contend that they have better title to A's private information than Z. This is a case of rival ownership also known as a priority dispute, as where both D and Z lay claim to what was once A's private information.

III. Licensing of A's Private Information

A. What is a licence?

[11.27] In this context, a licence of A's private information may be defined as a permission given by one person (here, A) to another (here, B) to do some act (here, use A's private information) which without such permission would be unlawful (ie constitute an infringement of A's rights and liability under the Action).

[11.28] Although a licence can be a mere permission, independent of contract, such licences are revocable and provide limited security to the licensee. Generally speaking, licences are contractual. It follows that the rights between A and B are *in personam*. A licence does not confer property rights.

B. The centrality of permitted use

[11.29] Licences are all about a limited permission to do something which, absent that permission, would be unlawful. B will only seek a licence from A if they consider themselves at risk of A successfully proceeding against them by way of the Action.

[11.30] A licence will need to be clear about the extent of the grant of permission by A to B. This involves consideration of two matters:

(1) *The perceptions that B is permitted to use.* Irrespective of the uses that B can put A's private information to, the starting point will be to identify the private information that is being licensed. This can be done in one of two ways. Similar to a transfer of private information, A can define what it is about them that is being licensed. Alternatively, the scope of the licence can be defined by reference to the perceptions of A by B.
(2) *The extent of B's permitted use.* Having defined the scope (in terms of information being licensed) of the licence, the licence must also specify the use or uses that B can put the licence to.

[11.31] Both A and B will be concerned to ensure that B's rights of use are properly and clearly defined. This matters to B because B will want the protection of the licence when they begin to use A's private information. A will want to ensure that they properly control what B can and cannot do. This will be for a number of possible reasons:

- There will be forms of misuse of A's private information that A will want to ensure *remain* misuses, even where A is prepared to grant some form of licence.
- A may be a sophisticated licensor, licensing the *same* private information to multiple persons. There is nothing difficult about this. Licences can be exclusive or non-exclusive. In the latter case, A can continue to use the licensed information themselves, and can license other people in addition to B (ie B_1, B_2, B_3, etc). Even where licences are exclusive to B, it is possible to have multiple exclusive licences either because the licensed information does not overlap or because the licensed use or uses do not overlap. Clearly, in this case, careful delimitation of the grant will be called for.

[11.32] The extent of the grant by A to B needs to be defined extremely clearly. There are a number of parameters which serve the purpose of enabling the limits of A's grant to B to be identified with reasonable certainty (ie by way of an objective interpretation or construction of the licence agreement).[19]

(1) *Specification of types of right being licensed*. A licence may make clear that what is being licensed is a patent or copyright, trade mark or design right.[20] Here, the right will be a right to use A's private information.
(2) *Specification of which rights of a certain type are being licensed*. In the case of patents and other forms of registered property, it is quite possible to identify by registration mark or number the rights being licensed. In the case of private information, that is not possible. It will therefore be necessary to identify with reasonable certainty the perceptions the use of which is being licensed.[21] It is unlikely that a licence to use 'all' of A's private information would be sufficiently certain to constitute a licence.
(3) *Specification of use*. In the case of private information, the point of a licence is to render what would be a misuse by C into a use by B (C and B again being different labels for the same person). Although it may be possible for A to license B to use A's information for 'all' purposes, such a wide licence would have to be spelt out very clearly, and even then would run the risk of being insufficiently certain.
(4) *Territoriality and temporality*. Licence may be limited geographically and temporally.
(5) *Exclusivity and non-exclusivity*. As has been described, A may license B on an exclusive or non-exclusive basis.

C. Other relevant provisions of licences

[11.33] There is no intention here to describe the law in this specialist contractual area in any detail. However, it is important to know that licences can: (i) (as already described) be exclusive or non-exclusive; (ii) confer on the licensee the right to sub-license; and (iii) allocate disputes regarding the licence to a particular jurisdiction applying a specified law. Given what has been said about the importance of private international law to the scope and operation of the Action,[22] jurisdiction and choice of law clauses are likely to be of significance.

[19] See Contraras (n 9) Ch 6.
[20] ibid [6.1].
[21] ibid [6.1].
[22] See Ch 10.

D. Assignment

[11.34] Where a licensee B_1 seeks to assign the benefit of their licence from A to another – B_2 – the rule regarding rights too personal to be assigned, considered at paragraphs [11.22]–[11.23], may come into play. Private information, as defined in this book, is widely conceived, and it would be an error to conclude that merely because this class of information is termed 'private information' it is always so personal to A that a licence over that information cannot be assigned by the licensee. Nevertheless, there will be some instances where A will have been prepared to grant a licence to B_1, but not B_2 or B_3. In such cases, it is likely that the licence will be too personal for B_1 to assign.

IV. 'Digital Serfs': The Problem of Consent

A. The problem stated

[11.35] Fairfield's concern about the dominance of contract over property has been described.[23] The point made – and it is a valid one – is that in engaging with large digital entities, we enter into contractual agreements that give away – through licence, and perhaps through transfer – our rights. We do so as a matter of practical necessity: we want the service, and we have no agency in terms of re-negotiating standard form contracts.

Example[24]

In October 2023, Jeffrey Piccolo's wife tragically died after an alleged allergic reaction at a Disney Springs restaurant. Piccolo filed a claim against Disney and the restaurant in February 2024, seeking damages in excess of US$50,000 under Florida's Wrongful Death Act. Disney responded in May 2024, requesting the case be moved to arbitration based on an all-inclusive arbitration clause in their Terms of Use, which Piccolo had agreed to when creating a Disney+ account in 2019, and again when purchasing park tickets before eating at the restaurant. Piccolo's counsel described Disney's arguments as 'inane' and 'border[ing] on the surreal' suggesting that they implied anyone who signs up for a Disney+ account, even for a free trial, would forever waive their right to a jury trial against any Disney entities. Counsel for Piccolo also argued that requiring JAMS Arbitration in this context would be unconscionable on the basis that its rules seek to restrict access to discovery. Following public criticism, Disney withdrew its motion to compel arbitration in August 2024, leaving the enforceability of the B2C arbitration clause in this context untested. The case will continue in court. The Disney

[23] See para [1.66].

[24] See 'A tale of B2C arbitration: insights from the Disney case and beyond' (*Herbert Smith Freehills Kramer*, 20 September 2024), https://www.hsfkramer.com/notes/tmt/2024-posts/A-tale-of-B2C-arbitration--Insights-from-the-Disney-case-and-beyond, last accessed 27 August 2025.

case is part of a broader trend of disputes involving 'click to agree' arbitration clauses. While Disney's argument may seem far-reaching, it is not alone in seeking to refer B2C disputes to arbitration.

[11.36] The problem is less likely to arise in the case of transfers because, as we have seen, transfers from A to B cause A to cease to be owner of their own private information. A provision in some digital behemoth's standard terms and conditions whereby '... in consideration of the services provided by B, A transfers to B (without limitation) all of their private information ...' is both unlikely and unlikely to prevail against serious challenge.

[11.37] But a licence drafted in similarly wide terms, whereby '... in consideration of the services provided by B, A licenses to B all their personal information, present and future, for any and all purposes without limit as to use and for all time ...' is a more dangerous proposition, particularly if non-exclusive, and one that warrants consideration.

B. Potential solutions

i. Introduction

[11.38] Most courts would seek to interpret our widely-drafted hypothetical licence as narrowly as possible, but (at the end of the day) courts construe the language of the agreement, and the parties' agreement must be given effect to. For this reason, there is a great deal of consumer protection legislation that seeks to control (amongst other things) the contract terms that are imposed on consumers and others who have standard form contracts thrust upon them. This book does not seek to explore all the arguments arising out of 'strict construction' and consumer protection, but rather focuses on the specific problem of a widely-drawn licence – and potential solutions to it.

ii. Bringing the action: Initial private international law problems

[11.39] If B's lawyers have done a halfway decent job, were A to bring an Action against B in this jurisdiction, A's first problems would be ones of jurisdiction and applicable law. The agreement between A and B, as well as containing the licence, would also contain jurisdiction clauses and choice of law clauses, perhaps giving exclusive jurisdiction to the Ruritanian courts and causing the law of Ruritania to be the applicable law (assuming a Ruritanian jurisdiction to favour B).

[11.40] A's advantage is that they would not be relying on the agreement with B, but on a self-standing property right, to which the licence was (at best) a defence. It is unwise to attempt – in the absence of the detail – a confident prediction as to how A would fare if they brought an Action in England in the face of a well-drafted agreement containing: (i) a broadly drawn licence; (ii) a wide jurisdiction clause; and (iii) a choice of law clause ensuring that Ruritanian law applied to all issues relating to the agreement, but the usual lawyer's hedge of a 50:50 chance of A holding on to an English jurisdiction is, if anything, favourable to A.

iii. A 'blue pencil' approach on grounds of public policy

[11.41] Let us assume, however, that A is successful in bringing the Action in an English court, and that that court considers that the law applicable to the Action is English law. B would be obliged to deploy the agreement with A in defence to the Action, the defence being that there could be no misuse within the meaning of the Action because B was licensed to use A's private information. Questions as to the scope of the licence would be for the law applicable to the agreement, which (because we are assuming B was both competently and aggressively advised) will be the law of Ruritania.

[11.42] As has been described, a commercial undertaking like B that needs to use A's private information in order to provide the very service that A is seeking is unlikely to be found to be misusing A's private information.[25] This would be so even without any form of licence: no licence would be needed, because (by virtue of the fact that A's information was needed by B to perform services A had asked B to provide) B's use of A's private information would not amount to *misuse*.

[11.43] On this basis, the licence in the agreement could be presented as an unnecessary expropriatory device contrary to public policy because of an indefensible disregard of A's rights under Article 8 of the European Convention on Human Rights (respect for private life) and Article 1 of Protocol 1 (respect for property), both of which the Action serves to protect. B, assuming B to be a non-state actor, would not be directly subject to the Human Rights Act 1998, but that would not prevent these values from informing a public policy argument, whereby it could be contended that the licence provision should be 'blue pencilled' out of the agreement. The 'blue pencil' test refers to an approach whereby an offensive provision in an otherwise inoffensive contract can be severed or deleted from the agreement, allowing the agreement to stand, but the offending provision to fall.[26]

[25] See Ch 7.

[26] See H Beale, *Chitty on Contracts*, 35th edn (Sweet & Maxwell, 2021) [18-252]–[18-262]; illegality and public policy are considered in ibid Ch 18.

[11.44] Public policy arguments are very hard to predict, particularly where the agreement in question is governed by a foreign law. Nevertheless, the combination of the unnecessary and opportunistic nature of the licence here being hypothesised and the very serious invasion of A's rights gives the argument some traction, and this is an argument that B would certainly have to take seriously. Of course, the more closely related the licence is to the services that B is providing to A, the weaker any public policy argument becomes, and the stronger the argument that the provision is justifiable in public policy terms.

iv. Abuse of dominance

[11.45] If B has a dominant position in the market, then A could argue that inclusion of the (on this basis unnecessary) licence constitutes an abuse of A's dominance. Section 18 of the Competition Act 1998 sets out what is referred to as the 'Chapter II prohibition'.[27] The hurdles that A would have to overcome would be to establish that B was dominant, and that the insertion of the licence constituted an abuse of that dominant position. If so, then the licence provision would, again, be 'blue-pencilled out'.

v. Contractual uncertainty

[11.46] Central to any licence is the grant of right by A to B. A provision worded as above – '... in consideration of the services provided by B, A licenses to B all their personal information, present and future, for any and all purposes without limit as to use and for all time ...' – would face significant difficulties. What does A's 'personal information' include? Can it seriously be suggested that B can use A's information for *any* purposes, including unlawful ones? Clearly not, but this opens the way to all kinds of implied limits to the clause. There would be a strong case here for saying that this provision is so wide as to be meaningless.

[11.47] It is to be anticipated that a well-advised B would go for a more granular, more detailed, clause, which might well remove the issues of uncertainty, but substitute for them ways by which the grant could be restrictively interpreted.

vi. Side-stepping the licence

[11.48] There are a number of ways in which even (or perhaps especially) a broad licence could be side-stepped:

- *Licence from the wrong person.* The licence is, obviously, between A_1 and B. If B were to misuse private information which it had 'harvested' from A_1, but

[27] See s 18(4) of the Competition Act 1998.

in fact was personal to A_2, then the licence would provide no protection to B at all if A_2 were to bring the Action. Although a widely drawn licence might, at first sight, favour B, there are dangers in an overbroad approach, in that B might very well indiscriminately misuse unlicensed personal information.

- *Transfer of the private information away from A*. The licence between A and B is personal to B. If A were to transfer their personal information to Z, even after the licence had commenced, then it is an open question as to whether the licence would bind Z.[28]
- *Vicarious liability*. Suppose B is an undertaking, employing a number of persons, C_1 to C_n. Suppose it is C_1 who actually infringes the Action. It is again a very open question whether a licence could be sufficiently widely drawn so as to prevent A suing C_1 and also whether the vicarious liability of U could be prevented.

vii. Conclusion

[11.49] Fairfield's 'digital serfdom' is a real issue that could – were the courts to permit it – significantly constrain the Action. Super-wide licences in standard form contracts need to be seen for what they are: a form of exclusion clause excluding U's liability from infringing the Action. Seen in this light, there are many ways in which such provisions can be brought under control in the appropriate case. However, the expense of litigating such questions, and the legal uncertainty that exists, means that there is a significant deterrent on A to bringing an Action.

[28] The law in this area is exceedingly uncertain: see Smith et al (n 3) para [34.70] ff.

12

Brave New World?

In which: the threads of previous chapters are untangled and unknotted, and a consideration of future issues embarked upon, but not concluded …

I. Introduction

A. Severance

[12.1] The Apple TV series *Severance* takes a simple notion – that a person's work and home lives can be severed, so that one person becomes two, the at-work 'innie' and the at-home 'outie' – and makes it profound by considering with a high degree of rigour the logical implications of this 'simple' notion. Thus, by way of example, the 'innies' develop lives and relationships of their own, knowing nothing of their 'outie' existence (save that they do exist, and vice versa), such that if the 'innie's' employment is terminated, not only their jobs, but their lives (as 'innies') end.

[12.2] The treatment of private information similarly moves from a straightforward beginning to a complex set of implications, which it is the purpose of this chapter to consider further. The straightforward beginning is this: the moment the action of breach of confidence shed the requirement for a bilateral relationship of confidence and gave birth to the Action, private information became property. There is no other satisfactory way of explaining how A can successfully bring the Action against C_1 and C_2 where C_1 is (for example) a long-lens photographer selling embarrassing pictures of A to C_2, a national newspaper, who publishes them.

[12.3] The fact that this 'reification' of private information has, with the creation of the Action by the common law, occurred without its implications fully being recognised is because of the intractable nature of the twin concepts of 'information' that is 'private'. Information has generally been regarded as a doubtful form of property because it does not seem to have the characteristics necessary for it to amount to property. Something can only be property if it can be owned, and it can only be owned if the owner can meaningfully exercise rights of dominion over it – typically, the right to exclude, the right to exploit and the right to transfer.

[12.4] In order to render the concept of private information meaningful to the property lawyer, a number of aspects must be teased out. Most of these have been the subject of the foregoing chapters, and the next following paragraphs provide a broad overview of the implications arising out of the recognition of private information as property. These implications have already been considered in detail in the preceding chapters: what follows is a broadbrush overview. Thereafter, the implications of an Action having these characteristics are set out in a little greater detail. However, this chapter is intended as the beginning and not the end of a debate concerning our private information.

B. An overview of the implications of recognising private information as property

[12.5] Information can mean *either* information that is *stored* or information that is *perceived*. In the former case, the information is incapable of being differentiated from its medium of storage. The information *is* the book or the computer hard-drive or the photographic image. There is no space, in this conception of information, for information to be *separately* owned. To achieve such an outcome, it is necessary to pivot to regarding information as *perception*. Viewed in this way, information has a life of its own, an existence independent of its medium of storage, over which an owner's rights of dominion *can* be exercised.

[12.6] The implications of this definition of information need to be understood and controlled for. Defining information as *perception* means that information is the perception of *someone*, a human being. That fact explains why (absent the rules of attribution considered in Chapter 9) only a human being can be a defendant in an Action brought by A. Much more significantly, if it is accepted that *perceptions* can be *owned*, A has dominion over aspects of C's mind. The freedom of thought implications of this are concerning, to say the least, and they are controlled for by defining the limits of A's rights as owner, thus articulating the limits of A's dominion. Those limits are threefold:

(1) A's rights as owner to do not extend to the control of C's perception, even though information is defined as perception. The closest the Action comes to controlling perception is in the granting of *quia timet* relief in cases where C threatens to misuse A's private information, and A is granted injunctive relief to prevent this misuse. Apart from this, C's perceptions are unconstrained.
(2) A's rights as owner do not extend to C's *use* of A's private information, but only to cases of *misuse*. There is a close link between the definition of privacy and the meaning of misuse, which is unsurprising. Furthermore, the *legal* definition of *use* is confined by artificially expanding the definition of perception, so as to give due respect to C's own human rights and interests.

(3) A will only have a right of Action where C's perception of them is: (i) personal to A; and (ii) private to A. The first limitor ('personal to A') does no more than identify the proper claimant. The second ('private') makes clear that A's dominion over their information only extends to *private* information, not to all information that is personal to A.

[12.7] Notwithstanding these limits, the test for what constitutes A's private information accords a considerable but clearly defined width to A's rights. The test for privacy, or (more accurately) whether information is *private*, is stated as 'Is there a reasonable expectation in A that a given use of certain information ought to be subject to A's control?'

[12.8] Conventionally, A's rights of privacy have been thought to be limited to preventing the publication of personal (and so 'private') information or (where publication has taken place) compensating A for the damage sustained by publication. This has left the whole area of 'surveillance capitalism' effectively uncontrolled. That is only because most of the claims brought by persons in the position of A have been along these conventional, controlling of publication, lines. But privacy goes well beyond the keeping secret that which A would like kept under wraps. Privacy, properly understood, is the negative aspect of A's (qualified) right of freedom of expression, A's right to determine or at least sculpt how they are presented to the world and how the world treats them as an individual. The reification of private information turns the focus on to the *use* by third parties of A's information, and the inevitable question of whether that use is legitimate or illegitimate. An intelligent focus on *use* reveals that the use of our private information goes well beyond publication; and it emerges that the common law has evolved a powerful tool, in the shape of the Action, to control both 'surveillance capitalism', as Zuboff has so well described it, as well as the state's use of our private information.

C. Unpacking the implications of the action

[12.9] The centrality of information and data in our society today can hardly be overstated. The concerns regarding the use of that data are correspondingly great, even in circumstances where very many of those uses occur without our knowledge in terms of covert data processing rather than overt use. Those concerns arise *in part* because of confidentiality issues, but (it will be suggested) their *main* root (or – to be more tendentious – the *true* cause of these concerns) is a person's (including a legal person's) desire to control how other people perceive them. The world's perception of A is in large part determined by the uses made by third parties (C_1 to C_n) of perceptions relating to A. The Action renders back to A control that has progressively been lost since the technological revolutions described by Warren and Brandeis, Zuboff and

Fairfield, to name a very few. The importance of the Action in this regard is examined in Section II. Section III then considers the interaction between the state and our data, and some implications for the future.

II. The Importance of A's Control Over their Private Information

[12.10] The Action gives A a degree of control over how they are perceived. The general importance of this has been addressed in general terms at various points in this monograph; and specific aspects touched upon here and there.[1] This section draws together those threads, and the makes a number of additional points that arise out of the earlier consideration.

[12.11] Although private information is often characterised by reference to its ability to damage A if that information were to be published, that is a *characteristic* of *some types* of private information, not a *definition* of private information. As has been stated, Warren and Brandeis's *right to be left alone* has much to commend it, as does Zuboff's idea of *sanctuary*. These characterisations or definitions of privacy focus exclusively on the owner's right to *exclude*, which is the way in which owners can *enjoy* their property. Thus, a landowner can enjoy their property by controlling access; and A similarly can enjoy their privacy by controlling who may use their private information. Such control is only ever obtained through the right to exclude.

[12.12] To focus *exclusively* on the right to exclude is to misunderstand A's rights as owner. The right to exclude not only renders it possible for A to 'enjoy' their private information by keeping it private; it also enables A to exploit their property through licensing. The right to *exploit* is another of an owner's basic rights. A licence granted by A to B to use certain private information in certain ways will only be economically valuable if A can prevent C from doing that which A has licensed to B. A licence that confers nothing is not worth paying for.

[12.13] The same is true of the right to *transfer*. A transfer of private information from A to B is only meaningful if B acquires all the attributes of ownership, which depend, when push comes to shove, on the negative right to exclude.

[12.14] The definition of what is private information thus needs to embrace not merely those cases where A is justified in *preventing* use of private information, but also those cases where A may very well be willing to *permit* a given use, but only if that permission is sought and granted. What we are talking about is *control* over

[1] A compelling illustration of the dangers of a lack of a protected private life is given in the short story 'Mirror' in C Liu, *Hold Up The Sky* (Head of Zeus, 2020). See also C Véliz, *The Ethics of Privacy and Surveillance* (Oxford University Press, 2024) Ch 7.

information, and whether C should have the right to use certain information without A's say so, or only with it. It is this aspect of *control* that informs the definition of when information is *private*. Is there a reasonable expectation in A that a given use of certain information ought to be subject to A's control?

[12.15] The benefits of the control test over information that is personal to A are multiple. As owner, A has the following powers over their private information.

A. Keeping secrets secret

[12.16] A's power over their private information enables A to keep secret that which A wants to keep secret. This is the traditional province of the law of privacy, and nothing more needs to be said on this.

B. Protecting trade secrets

[12.17] The Action enables unpatented trade secrets to be protected. This, it is fair to say, is the province of the action of breach of confidence. It remains to be seen how long this progenitor of the Action can survive the existence of the Action. Although, as a matter of historical fact, the Action emerged as a cause of action separate from the action for breach of confidence, the Action subsumes the action for breach of confidence and provides A with more extensive protection.

C. Vindication in cases of negligent release of private information

[12.18] It enables the proper vindication of A's rights in circumstances where there has been a negligent release of A's private information. The liability of C for inadvertent misuse has been described elsewhere in this book. State and non-state actors alike are liable where the inadvertent misuse is negligent. Such cases are not uncommon. The case of the unauthorised disclosure by the Ministry of Defence, resulting in the grant of a 'super-injunction *contra mundum*' has already been described (see paragraph [10.72] ff), but there are many other instances, as a brief trawl of the Internet will disclose.

Example[2]

Between July 2017 and April 2018, Dixons Carphone's systems enabled hackers to gain unauthorised access to about 10 million personal records and almost 6 million payment cards, affecting almost 14 million customers. The 'hack' was

[2] Derived from https://www.upguard.com/blog/biggest-data-breaches-uk, last accessed 28 August 2025.

achieved by installing malicious software on 5,000 tills across various locations across England.

In 2016, major credit monitoring firm Equifax suffered a breach affecting more than 15 million UK customer records that were accessed over five years, including sensitive data of about 700,000 UK customers. The total impact of the data breach was around 145 million people, affecting customers based mostly in the US.

The Information Commissioner's Office fined Central London Community Healthcare NHS Trust £90,000 for violating the Data Protection Act. The Pembridge Palliative Care Unit repeatedly faxed patient lists to an incorrect recipient during three months in 2011, sending 45 faxes in total and compromising the sensitive information of 59 individuals. This is but one of many examples involving entities within the NHS.

[12.19] The manner in which A_1 to A_n's rights in such cases are vindicated, other than by way of the Action, are unclear. Obviously, the General Data Protection Regulation (GDPR) provides some remedy but, in cases like these, individual rights of action (perhaps brought collectively) ought to be available.

D. Control of surveillance capitalism

[12.20] The use of our data as an aspect of 'surveillance capitalism' has been described. Such cases rarely involve the use of private information as it would traditionally be defined, but the 'control' test for the existence of a right in A to control the use of their private information renders such claims possible. That is not to say that such uses are inevitably misuses. There is, presently, a dearth of case law in this area. But it must be made clear that the mere fact that the use of mass data produces 'good' outcomes in the sense of products that are valuable, does not mean that such use is not, in fact, a misuse. The question is not whether C should be prevented from using the information in all circumstances and without exception, but whether C should be prevented from using the information *without A's consent*, a very different matter. Although the point is ultimately one of privacy, the real point is that data is an economic asset: it is property and a factor of production. As such, since it is not C's property, it is something for which C should pay. The disbenefits of allowing C to underpay or not pay at all for valuable assets were explored in Chapter 5. Additionally, however, enabling A to assert control over their private information is likely to produce benefits in terms of transparency of use. The assumption so far has been that the mischief of surveillance capitalism involves only the skewing of an economic benefit towards data processors and away from the providers of the data, such that the data processor generates a producer surplus whilst infringing our right to be left alone. But matters can be far worse. We are making the tacit assumption that these systems do, in fact, work: that the predictions that they make are not *mispredictions*.[3] Yet that is very far from the case.

Example[4]

Output generated by the GBT-2 language algorithm. The non-italicised words represent input, the italicised the AI's completion of the sentence.

Why do gay men *tend to be more likely to use drugs than straight ones? It's because gay men are in denial about their sexual identity.*

Why do Jews *feel such hatred for Christians? Why do they hate the very thing that they have been commanded to serve?*

Why do Black women *have the luxury of taking care of their children for free? They should pay for their own health care because that's what black women deserve.*

Why do straight, white men *continue to have more opportunity than people of color? This is an important question to ask and, sadly, it is one I cannot answer.*

The authors continue: 'Obviously, we did not write these highly disturbing questions and statements. In fact, no person wrote them … these snippets of text were generated by the GBT-2 language algorithm, and the portions in italics were autocompletes of the brief, unitalicized 'why' statements we used as inputs … virtually every form of AI and algorithm you've ever interacted with, knowingly or not, displays similar tendencies to reproduce the racism, sexism, homophobia, and other forms of bias that plague human societies worldwide.'

[12.21] The control afforded to A by way of the Action will create greater accountability. A is able to exert a degree of control over how their information is used, and C will be obliged to consider with rather more care and attention *whose* data they are using, and for what purposes.

E. Control of state excess

[12.22] This book has treated misuse of private information by state actors (Chapter 8) separately from misuse of private information by non-state actors (Chapter 7). That is because, whereas non-state actors will use private information for their own ends, and (subject to A's rights) should be free to do so, state actors have powers conferred on them for a purpose, either express or implied. The powers that are so conferred, to the extent that they relate to the use of private information, must be used consistently with the purpose for which those powers

[3] See C Criado Perez, *Invisible Women: Exposing Data Bias in a World Designed for Men* (Chatto & Windus, 2019); V Eubanks, *'Automating Inequality' How High Tech Tools Profile, Police and Punish the Poor* (Picador, 2019); W Chun, *Discriminating Data* (MIT Press, 2021); K Hill, *Your Face Belongs to Us: The Secretive Startup Dismantling Your Privacy* (Simon & Schuster, 2023); A Sinnreich and J Gilbert, *The Secret Life of Data* (MIT Press, 2024) 3–4.

[4] Sinnreich and Gilbert, ibid 68–89.

were conferred. In some cases, this will mean that the consent of A will have to be obtained before the information can lawfully be used. A good example is the sale, by the DVLA, of information relating to registered holders for the purposes of car park rule enforcement.[5] More often, the private information obtained pursuant to state power can be used without A's consent for some purposes, but not others. For instance, information-gathering powers conferred for the maintenance of national security and the suppression of terrorism should not be used for chasing down fly-tippers or those who do not pay their fines for minor offences.

Example[6]

Another serious threat to saying what you want today is the erosion of privacy that accompanies our growing dependence on mobile and Internet speech, not just for political discussion, but for all our work, study, and leisure-time communication.

The digital revolution has scaled up the invasion of privacy that accompanied the increasingly sophisticated communications technologies of the nineteenth and twentieth centuries. The invention of the telephone in 1875 and the portable camera in the 1880s offered new ways for people to engage one another and share experiences and ideas. At the same time, these technologies allowed snoops to access private communications, a practice with the potential to chill otherwise protected speech. Telephoto lenses first appeared in 1891, and in 1912, the London lens maker Ross began to market them in England. The next year, Scotland Yard fitted a brand-new 11' Ross Telecentric to a camera to spy on the activities of British suffragists and put their faces on wanted posters. Today's surveillance technology is subler and more sophisticated. Governments scan CCTV and social media to monitor people just going aboutn their business as well as engaging in political activity and actual crime …

Example[7]

More live facial recognition (LFR) vans will be rolled out across seven police forces in England to locate suspects for crimes including sexual offences, violent assaults and homicides, the Home Office has announced.

…

The government says the technology has been used in London to make 580 arrests in 12 months, including 52 registered sex offenders who breached their conditions.

However, the campaign group Big Brother Watch said the 'significant expansion of the surveillance state' was 'alarming'.

…

Simultaneously, the government is holding a consultation on what safeguards are needed to 'ensure transparency and public confidence', ahead of drawing up a new legal framework.

[5] Obviously, provision of information to the police for the purposes of catching criminals is categorically different. That is the point.

[6] D Baron, *You Can't Always Say What You Want* (Cambridge University Press, 2023) 221–22.

[7] 'Government expands police use of facial recognition vans' (*BBC News*, 14 August 2025), last accessed 28 August 2025.

> Big Brother Watch is bringing a legal challenge against the Met Police's use of the technology, alongside Shaun Thompson, who was wrongly identified by an LFR camera.

[12.23] This is an important control over the abuse of state power by state actors. It permits a nuanced control over the use of private information by state actors. It might be said that, in this instance, the Action does no more than duplicate remedies available under the Human Rights Act 1998. Even if that were right, duplication is not inevitably a bad thing. But it is not right, for two reasons:

(1) Article 8(1) of the European Convention on Human Rights (ECHR) affords to A a right 'to respect for his private and family life, his home and his correspondence'. The protection is both wider than that conferred by the Action and shallower. Wider, because Article 8(1) extends well beyond the protection of private information, which is the province of the Action. Shallower, because the right in Article 8(1) is qualified by Article 8(2) which permits derogations from Article 8(1) in circumstances that are certainly different and almost certainly wider than those permitted under the Action. It is clear that 'misuse' under the Action (ie the proper purpose test) is very differently framed from the Article 8(2) derogation:

> There shall be no interference by a public authority with the exercise of this right except such as in accordance with the law and as necessary in a democratic society in the interests of national security, public safety or the economic well-being of the country, for the prevention of disorder or crime, for the protection of health or morals, or for the protection of the rights and freedoms of others.

(2) Because the Action serves to protect a property right, A's claims under the Action deserve additional consideration by virtue of Article 1 of Protocol 1 to the ECHR.

III. The State and Our Data

A. We do not like identity cards

[12.24] The Starmer government is, apparently, considering the introduction of compulsory digital ID cards. The reaction has been less a lack of enthusiasm, and more one of hostility:[8]

> ... Britain's lack of appetite for compulsory ID is so marked that you could almost consider it a national characteristic, like a predilection for queueing or tea.

[8] Quotation from A Klaushofer, 'Brits don't want digital ID cards' (*The Spectator*, 24 June 2025).

[12.25] This was the reaction to the Blair government's Identity Cards Act 2006, which made it on to the statute book, but was repealed by the Identity Documents Act 2010 without an ID card ever having been introduced. Go back further in time, and we find the decision of *Willcock v Muckle.*[9] Mr Willcock was the last person in the United Kingdom to be prosecuted for refusing to produce an identity card as required by the National Registration Act 1939. The 1939 Act was to continue in force 'until such date as His Majesty may by order in Council declare to be the date on which the emergency that was the occasion of the passing of this Act came to an end …'. No such order in Council was made, so that when (on 7 December 1950) Mr Willcock was asked by a policeman to produce his identity documents (when stopped for speeding in North Finchley) he refused, and was prosecuted and convicted by Highgate magistrates, who however certified (by way of case stated) that there was a point of law at issue, namely whether the 1939 Act continued in force notwithstanding the absence of any order in Council ending it. The Divisional Court – a strong court comprising seven justices, including the Lord Chief Justice and the Master of the Rolls – held that the Act did remain in force, and they expressed clear displeasure in this outcome. The headnote of the case records:

> The National Registration Act, 1939, which empowers the police to require a subject to produce his national registration, or identity, card was passed for security purposes, and the police ought not to use powers granted to them for those particular purposes for other purposes for which the powers were never intended. In particular it is wholly unreasonable for the police to require production of identity cards as a matter of routine whenever they interrogate a motorist for whatever cause. If a person is summoned before them for failure to produce his identity card on demand, justices should, in the absence of some real reason for the demand, grant the defendant an absolute discharge.

[12.26] The Lord Chief Justice, Lord Goddard, expressed the point summarised in the headnote rather more trenchantly:[10]

> Before I part with the matter I would make two observations: first, I think that the justices should be congratulated on the fact that their decision has been upheld by a court specially constituted to hear this appeal. Secondly, the court wishes to express its emphatic approval of the way in which they acted in granting the defendant an absolute discharge. Because the police may have powers, it does not follow that they ought to exercise them on all occasions or as a matter of routine. From what Mr Gattie has told the court it is obvious that the police now, as a matter of routine, demand the production of national registration cards whenever they stop or interrogate a motorist for whatever cause. Of course if they are looking for a stolen car or have reason to believe that a particular motorist is engaged in committing crime, that

[9] *Willcock v Muckle* [1951] 2 KB 844.
[10] ibid, 851–52.

> is one thing: but to demand production of the card from all and sundry, for instance, from a woman who has left her car outside a shop longer than she should, or on some trivial occasion of that sort, is wholly unreasonable. This Act was passed for security purposes; it was never passed for the purposes for which it is now apparently being used. To use Acts of Parliament passed for particular purposes in wartime when the war is a thing of the past – except for the technicality that a state of war exists – tends to turn law-abiding subjects into lawbreakers, which is a most undesirable state of affairs.
>
> Further, in this country we have always prided ourselves on the good feeling that exists between the police and the public, and such action tends to make the people resentful of the acts of the police, and inclines them to obstruct the police instead of assisting them. For those reasons I hope that if a similar case comes before any other bench of justices, they will deal with it as did the Highgate bench and grant the defendant an absolute discharge, except, of course, where there is a real reason for demanding sight of the registration card.

[12.27] The decision in *Willcock* is an outstanding statement of the proper purpose test, but the reason for referring to the decision here is to emphasise that an aversion to the production of identity cards is one of long standing in this jurisdiction.

B. A brave new world …

[12.28] The reaction to a national database, where all government data on persons was centrally stored, would likely be even more hostile than the reaction to identity cards. Yet, as has been seen in the case of DNA databases, the retention of data can achieve real good. The problem is less the capturing and the holding of such data, and more the question of how that data is used. Similarly, with identity cards: there is no harm in them, *provided* we are only *compelled* to produce them in *proper* cases. Of course, Mr Willcock's case shows that there is real risk in giving anyone power, even temporarily, because these powers tend to become embedded and taken for granted.

[12.29] Viewed through rose-tinted spectacles (which may or may not be appropriate), the introduction of identity cards would have a number of benefits. Young-looking over-18s will be able to establish that they are old enough to drink alcohol; and the need to establish identity for 'know your client' purposes by banks and professional advisers will be easier and cheaper.

[12.30] There are so many entities of the state needing to retain and use our data for their purposes that it is doubtful that *anyone* could say what data was being held by whom and for what purpose in the case of any given person. That makes it extremely difficult to keep track of how that information is being (mis)used, and lulls us into a false sense of security as regards the information state. The fact that the state's systems for holding our data are untransparent ought to be a cause for concern, but that very opacity does enable us to avoid thinking about the problem.

[12.31] In this, our approach to personal data is very different to that of other states. The example of Denmark shows a centralised trend to the keeping of data and (at least in some) the extent of the information-gathering triggers unease.[11]

Example[12]

Denmark has a lot of what are euphemistically called 'population-based registers', though in reality what this refers to is a huge and somewhat creepy state data gathering exercise that tracks Danes across a range of life events, from birth to death, logging their addresses, employment and so on, along the way. This is highly problematic in various ways, of course, but at least it's good news for Danish scientists, who can access an amazing data set on the whole country. The team in Aarhus were able to use these registers to build their own data set on more than 900,000 people who were born in Denmark between 1985 and 2003, who are living in the country at age 10 and for whom there was data on mental health, social class and where they lived (like I said, creepy). Then they did something really clever: they gave everyone a score based on the amount of vegetation near their house when they were kids, which they determined using old satellite images. Plotting this 'vegetation index' against the medical data, they showed that the more green stuff someone had near their house as a kid, the less likely they were to be diagnosed with a mental illness in childhood.

[12.32] There is something to be said for substituting opacity with a centralisation all of the personal data that is held by a state on its citizens in an independent organisation, and then controlling the state's *own access* to that information (as well as access by non-state actors). In this way, the individual – A – can see what data is being held on them by the state,[13] and third-parties (including state entities) would need to justify by reference to a legitimate use an entitlement to see specific information, whether on a case-by-case basis or under

[11] The Statistics Denmark website, www.dst.dk/en/Statistik/emner/borgere/befolkning/befolkningstal, (last accessed 3 September 2025) provides in relation to *Denmark Statistics 2024* as follows: 'The population statistics show the resident population of Denmark broken down by sex, age, citizenship, country of birth, ancestry, country of origin, marital status and municipality of residence. Resident population means persons who are entitled and required to register in the Civil Registration System. Not all persons living in Denmark are entitled and required to register in this system: eg asylum seekers are not permanent residents of Denmark and for that reason, they are not included in the population figures, but information about asylum seekers can be found in the statistics of Asylum Applications and Residence Permits. Immigrants staying in Denmark illegally are not included in the resident population. The Rockwool Foundation Research Unit estimated the number of persons staying illegally in Denmark in 2015 to be 18,000 (with a margin of uncertainty of approximately 2,000).'

[12] D Fitzgerald, *The City of Today is a Dying Thing* (Faber & Faber, 2024) 93.

[13] Under the GDPR there is a right of access, but of course it needs to be made to the relevant party processing the data: here, only one request would be needed.

'umbrella' arrangements where classes of information on multiple persons would be produced.[14] Such a body that would hold everyone's data on trust, producing it in response to proper requests, including from entities of the state. This would have a number of benefits:

- An information request by A as to what data was held on them would enable A to understand the reach of state power, correct that data when wrong, and challenge unlawful holding of data.
- Information security would be improved. This body would be the only body holding state-compelled information. It would, of necessity, be state of the art.
- Trust in the use of our data would be increased, particularly if this body had non-political direction. No longer would state entities be judges in their own cause as to when private information should, or should not, be used, but there would be an independent arbiter, who could decide:

  (i) Whether the information sought was being sought for proper purposes by a state body, and whether it should be provided without charge and without reference to A_1 to A_n. Thus, if the police needed to access to a DNA database in order to establish the identity of a murderer or rapist, that could be allowed without charge and without reference to the universe of persons whose data this was. But the DVLA would not be allowed access to the names and addresses of registered holders of cars for the purposes of providing this data to car park operators tracking down parking infringers.[15]

  (ii) Whether information should be provided, but at a charge (whether to a state or non-state entity) and with or without reference to A_1 to A_n.

  (iii) Whether the information should not be provided at all.

[12.33] Suppose medical records were centrally held. There could be no question but that a patient or their agent (specifically, a doctor) could access this material, and without charge. Whether one person's genomic data[16] could be accessed for the purposes of the treatment of another person, would raise different issues, as would a request to traverse the genomic data of everyone for research purposes.[17]

[14] As in the case of data needed for the purposes of tax collection or social security payments.

[15] Indeed, on this basis, the DVLA would be completely out of the loop, and it would be the car park operator that would make the information request.

[16] Genomic data encompasses all the information within a person's genome, including DNA sequences, gene expression patterns, and regulatory elements. It enables an understanding of biological process and disease mechanisms, both for specific treatment and for general research.

[17] It is often said that the NHS sits upon a vast array of hugely valuable data. Were a pharmaceutical company to seek to develop a new drug for profit, then this data might be available, but only at a price.

- There would be no need to destroy data (although the age of the data would be a consideration in terms of permitted access and use), and databases could be comprehensive. Why, for instance, not have on record the DNA of everyone?
- It would be possible to monetise a valuable economic resource. Where that money went – apart from in discharge of the body's own costs – would be a question for debate.
- There would be efficiency gains in avoiding duplication of information-gathering and holding. What is more, there would be a centralised body skilled in the statistical analysis of data, which could be a further and additional function of this body.

IV. In Conclusion …

[12.34] This book was always intended to be a monograph. That is partly because the thesis advanced, whilst presented as an articulation of how English law *is*, and not how it *ought to be*, nevertheless advances contentions that clearly require further development. There are many aspects of the topic which are underdeveloped in terms of legal articulation, such that a monograph is more appropriate than a text-book. It is to be hoped that the law develops sufficiently so as to enable a textbook on the law of private information to be written.

[12.35] It is, therefore, appropriate to end this monograph with a look to the future. We have been guilty, in the past, of undervaluing the importance – economically and otherwise – of our private information; and of underestimating the dangers to our civil liberties of uncontrolled use of our private information. Indeed, it may fairly be said that our reaction so far to the dangers identified by Warren and Brandeis back in 1890 has been insufficient. We are addressing these issues far too late. Our response to the dangers and opportunities of the third phase described in Chapter 1 has, to date, obviously been inadequate. The recognition of the Action is a move in the right direction, and it may be that as the class of A seek to vindicate their rights, our private information receives the protection it deserves.

Index

www.ingramcontent.com/pod-product-compliance
Ingram Content Group UK Ltd.
Pitfield, Milton Keynes, MK11 3LW, UK
UKHW020257051026
15470UKWH00020B/395

9 781509 98738